MUSIC TITLES
IN TRANSLATION

MUSIC TITLES
IN TRANSLATION

a checklist of
musical compositions

compiled by
Julian Hodgson

CLIVE BINGLEY
LONDON

LINNET BOOKS
HAMDEN · CONN

FIRST PUBLISHED 1976 BY CLIVE BINGLEY LTD
16 PEMBRIDGE ROAD LONDON W11
SIMULTANEOUSLY PUBLISHED IN THE USA BY LINNET BOOKS
AN IMPRINT OF THE SHOE STRING PRESS INC
995 SHERMAN AVENUE HAMDEN CONNECTICUT 06514
SET IN 10 ON 12 POINT JOURNAL ROMAN
PRINTED AND BOUND IN THE UK BY
REDWOOD BURN LTD TROWBRIDGE & ESHER
COPYRIGHT © JULIAN HODGSON 1976
ALL RIGHTS RESERVED
BINGLEY ISBN: 0-85157-198-0
LINNET ISBN: 0-208-01520-1

Library of Congress Cataloging in Publication Data

Hodgson, Julian.
        Music titles in translation.

        "The list gives in one alphabetical sequence the
original or English language translation followed by the
translation or original as the case may be."
        1. Titles of musical compositions. I. Title.
ML111.H7   784'.0216   75-42015
ISBN 0-85157-198-0 (Bingley)
ISBN 0-208-01520-1 (Linnet)

For Pat
Jo
and Becky

Preface

This book was compiled to provide a ready answer to the questions raised by looking for 'Sleepers, wake' in the Breitkopf catalogue or 'Wachet auf' in the Novello catalogue. Similar questions can of course arise in relation to library catalogues.

The list gives in one alphabetical sequence the original or English language translation followed by the translation or original as the case may be. When the piece is from a larger work, the title of this is given in round brackets following the original title. In a few cases it has been felt necessary to qualify the title with an identification in square brackets— [BWV 58]. Where there is more than one title, either original or translation, they are divided by a slash—/, and of course each title is indexed, but only the original language entry gives all forms of the translation. Composers are identified by surname only, unless there is the possibility of confusion, where initials are given. The best known composer from a family is given in surname only (eg F(anny) Mendelssohn but (Felix) Mendelssohn. By and large, I have preferred modern German spelling to the older usage.

The alphabetical order is word by word rather than letter by letter; thus:

Can y crud
Canción.

The initial article, though given first, is disregarded, but subsequent articles count for alphabetisation. When two or more titles are the same, alphabetical order is determined by the composers' names.

A word about Russian titles will be needed. Although in the past, French or in some cases German translations have been usual in identifying Russian works, it was found that 'accepted' titles were not invariable. In addition transliterations are now becoming accepted as identifying Russian works (*New Oxford history of music, Grove VI*). Transliteration has been used here, but until the practice becomes more common the number of titles listed is very small. A subsequent edition of this book would doubtless list more.

Although an attempt was made to be as comprehensive as possible with this compilation, I am only too well aware of how many omissions there are, mostly opera, especially the choruses and arias. The *British music yearbook 1975* (Bowker, 1975) gives a comprehensive list of available translations of operas.

Only printed sources have been used from which to collect the translations, mostly singing editions, though some non-singing translations have also been given, especially where these are from sources likely to be encountered by the enquirer or concert-goer. Types of work excluded are folk songs and standard Latin works such as requiems.

My thanks are due to all the girls who helped to type from my frequently indecipherable handwriting, to John Buchanan who chivvied me, and to Pat who put up with it all.

J H June 1975

A

A amica meo (motet)—O my love: Morley
A ce joli moys (madrigal)—In this lovely month of May: Jannequin
A che piu debb' io mai l'intensa voglia (Sonnets of Michaelangelo)—Why
    must I go on venting my ardent desire in tears: Britten
A Columbine/Sérénade d'Arlequin—To Columbine: Massenet
A já ti uplynu (Moravské Dvojzpěvy)—The fugitive/The magic chase: Dvořák
A la rivière—To the river: Huybrechts
A la trépassée—To the departed: Massenet
A la voix d'un amant fidèle (La jolie fille de Perth)—The shades of night:
    Bizet
A l'aube dans la montagne—Mountain dawn: Séverac
A les je tichý (ergánské melodie)—Silent and lone: Dvořák
A Louise—Bright object of my adoration: Gounod
A Magyarokhoz—Song of faith: Kodály
A Mignonne—To my fair one: Massenet
A Nerina—To Nerina: Bossi
A notte cupa (Nerone)—When night has fallen: Boito
A Paris, sur le petit pont—On the bridge of Paris: Blanchard
A solis ortus cardine (motet)—From where the rising sun ascends: Binchois
A suoi piedi padre esangue (Tamerlano)—Lost love/She shall see me: Handel
A te o cara (I Puritani)—Love will waken: Bellini
A toutes brides (song: Tel jour telle nuit)—Riding full tilt: Poulenc
A un jeune gentilhomme (song)—To a young gentleman: Roussel
A vucchella—Lips so sweet and tender: Tosbi
The abbé said 'How now'—Sur l'herbe: Ravel
The abduction from the seraglio—Die Entführung aus dem Serail (opera):
    Mozart
L'abeille—The bee: Godard
Der Abend—Evening: R Strauss
Abendbilder—The peace of evening: Wolf
Abenddämmerung (song)—The twilight hour/Twilight: Brahms
Abenddempfindung—Evening thoughts/Thoughts at eventide/Evening
    reverie/Feelings at evening: Mozart
Abendgang im Lenz—Evening walk in spring: Reger
Abendgefuhl—Evening mood: Cornelius
Die Abendglocken—The evening bells: Kalliwoda
Abendlandschaft—Night song: Schoeck
Abendlich strahlt der Sonne (Das Rheingold)—Radiant at eve: Wagner
Abendlied—Evening song: Blech
Abendlied—Dream-flight: Blumenthal
Abendlied (part song)—Even-song: Brahms
Abendlied—Evening song: Mendelssohn

Abendlied—Evensong: Mendelssohn
Abendlied—Evening song: Reger
Abendlied—Evening song/Evensong: Schumann
Abendlied für die Entfernte—Evensong for the distant ones: Schubert
Abendlied unter'm gestirnten Himmel—Even-song: Beethoven
Abendmusik (Bunte Blätter)—Evening strains: Schumann
Abendregen—Evening shower: Brahms
Abends—Evening/At evening: R Franz
Abends—Eventide: R Franz
Des Abends (Fantasiestücke)—At night/Evening: Schumann
Abends am Strande (song)—Evening by the sea: Schumann
Des Abends kann ich nicht schlafen—At eventide I cannot sleep: Brahms
Die Abendschlümmer umarmt die Flur (Der Rose Pilgerfahrt)—The calm
   of evening reigns: Schumann
Abendsegen (Hänsel und Gretel)—Evening prayer: Humperdinck
Abendstänchen (part song)—The serenade: Brahms
Der Abendstern—To the evening star/The evening star: Schumann
Abendstimmung—Evensong: Kjerulf
Abendwolken—Evening clouds: Schoeck
Abgeguckt—Learnt by watching: Reger
Abide in peace—Vivete in pace (Nerone): Boito
Abide with me—Bist du bei mir: Bach
Ablakomba, ablakomba (song)—In my windows shone the moonlight:
   Bartók
Die Ablosung—The relief: Hollaender
Die Abonnenten—The subscribers: E Strauss
About beauty—Von der Schönheit (Das Lied von der Erde): Mahler
About youth—Von der Jugend (Das Lied von der Erde): Mahler
Die Abreise (opera)—The departure: Albert
Abreise—Departure: M Mayer
L'abri—The shelter: Bloch
A-brim with purest milk—Corran di puro latte: Marenzio
Abschied—Parting: Brahms
Abschied—Parting: R Franz
Abschied—Parting: Grieg
Der Abschied (song: Das Lied von der Erde)—The farewell: Mahler
Abschied—Farewell: Pfitzner
Abschied—A leave-taking: Reger
Abschied—Farewell: Schoeck
Abschied (song)—Farewell: Schoenberg
Abschied (song: Schwanengesang)—Departure/Leave-taking/Parting:
   Schubert
Abschied (Waldscenen)—Farewell/Farewell to the forest: Schumann

Abschied (song)—A valediction: Wolf

Abschied vom Walde—Departure: Mendelssohn

Abschied vom Walde (song)—Farewell to the woods: Schumann

Abschied von der Welt (song)—Farewell to the world: Schumann

Abschied von Frankreich—Farewell to France: Schumann

Abschiedslied (part song)—Love, fare thee well: Brahms

Abschiedslied der Zugvögel—Farewell song of the birds/The passage-birds'
farewell: Mendelssohn

Absence—In der Ferne: Brahms

L'absent (song)—The absent one: Gounod

The absent one—Die Entfernten: Cornelius

The absent one—L'absent (song): Gounod

The abyss—Bezdna: Rebikov

Academic Festival Overture—Akademische Festouvertüre (overture):
Brahms

Accompaniment to a film-scene—Begleitungsmusik zu einer Lichtspielszene (orchestral piece): Schoenberg

According to Thy name—Gott, wie dein Name: Bach

The accursed hunter—Le chasseur maudit: Franck

Ach arme Welt (part song)—Thou poor vain world: Brahms

Ach bleib bei uns, Herr Jesu Christ (organ chorale)—Lord Jesus Christ,
with us abide/Ah, Jesus Christ, with us abide: Bach

Ach, dass nicht die letzte Stunde (chorale)—Ah! might but the hour of
dying: Bach

Ach, dass nicht die letzte Stunde—Had I now what most I wish for: Bach

Ach, der Gebirgssohn/Das Heimweh—Home-sickness/Homeland: Schubert

Ach, englische Schäferin—O heavenly shepherdess: Brahms

Ach es schmeckt doch gar zu gut (aria: Mer hahn en neue Oberkeet)—Spring
comes laughing: Bach

Ach, führe mich, O Gott (Herr Christ, der ein'ge Gottes-Sohn)—Ah! lead
me, gracious Lord: Bach

Ach Gott und Herr (organ chorale)—Alas, my God: Bach

Ach Gott vom Himmel sieh'darein (chorale prelude)—Ah God, from
heav'n look down and see/Ah! God in mercy: Bach

Ach Gott, wie manches Herzleid [BWV3]—Ah God, how many pains of
heart: Bach

Ach Gott, wie manches Herzleid [BWV 58]—Ah God, how many a heart-
pang: Bach

Ach Gott, wie weh tut 'Scheiden—Woe's me the parting hour: Brahms

Ach Herr, mein Gott, vergieb mir's doch (chorale)—O Lord my God,
forgive Thou me: Bach

Ach Herr, strafe mich nicht—Ah Lord! chasten me not: Telemann

Ach Herr! was ist ein Menschenkind (Unser Mund sei voll Lachens)—
Ah, Lord, what is a child of man: Bach

Ach, ich fühls (Die Zauberflöte)—Ah, 'tis gone/Ah, I know/Ah, I feel how all hath vanished: Mozart

Ach könnt ich diesen Abend—O could I but this afternoon: Brahms

Ach könnt ich, könnte vergessen—Ah, could I/Could I but once: Brahms

Ach Lieb, ich muss nun scheiden—Sweet love, now I must leave thee: R Strauss

Ach, Liebster, in Gedanken—To thee, in a dream: Reger

Ach není tu—Maiden's lament: Dvořák

Ach nun sind es schon zwei—Ah! 'tis now two days: Henschel

Ach, schläfrige Seele (Mache dich, mein Geist, bereit)—Ah, soul that art drowsy: Bach

Ach, schlage doch bald, sel'ge Stunde (Christus, der ist mein Leben)—Ah, strike then soon, hour most blessed: Bach

Ach! so fromm (aria: Martha)—Ah! so pure: Flotow

Ach, soll nicht dieser grosse Tag (Wachet, betet, seid bereit)—Ah, shall not this great day of wrath/Ah, when on that great day: Bach

Ach, um deine feuchten Schwingen—Ah, how fain thy moisty pinions: Mendelssohn

Ach, und du mein kühles Wasser—At my cool and rippling water: Brahms

Ach, unser Wille bleibt verkehrt (Herr, wie du willst)—Ah, how peverse our will remains: Bach

Ach vojn, vojna—Ah, war!: Janáček

Ach, war'es nie geschehen!—My fate I cannot banish: R Franz

Ach was Kummer—Heigh-ho!: R Strauss

Ach, was soll ich Sünder machen—What shall I, a sinner do?: Bach

Ach weh mir ungluckhaftem Mann—Ah, woe is me unhappy man: R Strauss

Ach, wende diesen Blick (song)—Turn, turn away thy face: Brahms

Ach, wenn ich doch ein Immchen wär—Ah, were I but a little bee: R Franz

Ach, wie flüchtig, ach wie nichtig—Ah how fleeting: Bach

Ach, wie komm' ich—Longing: R Franz

Ach wie nichtig, ach wie flüchtig (Orgelbüchlein)—O how cheating, O how fleeting: Bach

Ach, wie schön ist Nacht—Ah, how fair the night: Schoeck

Ach wie so bald/Herbstlied—Autumn song: Mendelssohn

Achieved is the glorious work—Vollend'et ist das grosse Werk (Die Schöpfung)

Acknowledgement to the brook—Danksagung an den Bach (Die schöne Müllerin): Schubert

The acrobats—Les saltimbanques (operetta): Ganne

Ad dominum cum tribulare (gradvale)—I cried to God in tribulation: M Haydn

Ad te igitur (motet)—Now therefore, O Lord: Byrd

Add no thought—Ah! non giunge (La sonnambula): Bellini

Add reám csókodat, el kell mennem—Kiss me for I have to leave: Bartók

Adieu (song: Poème d'un jour)—Farewell: Fauré
Un adieu—A leave taking: Massenet
Adieu—Last greeting: Schubert-Heller
Adieu, Bessy (Melodies irelandaises)—Farewell, Bessy: Berlioz
L'adieu du matin—Farewell at morn: Pessard
L'adieu en barque (song)—The farewell in a boat: Caplet
Adieu forêts (Joan of Arc)—Farewell ye mountains: Tchaikovsky
Adieux—Farewells: Roussel
Les adieux de l'hôtesse Arabe (song)—The farewell of the Arabian
    hostess/The Arabian girl: Bizet
Les adieux du berger—Shepherd's farewell: Godard
Adonis—Frühlingsfeier: R Franz
Adoramus te (part song)—We adore thee/Sing ye the praises to the
    highest: Brahms
Adoramus te Christe—We adore Thee, O Lord Christ: Viadana
Adoration—Anbetung: Blumenthal
Adoration—Anbetung: R Strauss
Advent hymn—Adventlied: Schumann
The advent of our Saviour—Auf die Zukunft unseres Heilandes: J R Ahle
Adventlied—Advent hymn: Schumann
The adventurer—Der Schrenckenberger: Wolf
The adventures of King Pausole—Les aventures du Roi Pausole: Honegger
Aebleblomst—Apple blossom: Nielsen
Die Aegyptische Helena (opera)—The Egyptian Helen: R Strauss
Das Aehrenfeld—The cornfield/The harvest field: Mendelssohn
An Aeolian harp—An eine Aeolsharfe (song): Brahms
Afar in the wood—Ruhe im Walde: Kjerulf
Afenstemning—Evening mood: Nielsen
Affani del pensier (Ottone)—Ye pangs of anxious thought: Handel
Affection's bliss—Das Glück der Freundschaft: Beethoven
Afflicted sore—Afflicti pro peccatis (motet): Byrd
Afflicti pro peccatis (motet)—Afflicted sore: Byrd
L'Africaine—The African maid: Meyerbeer
The African maid—L'Africaine: Meyerbeer
Aften pa Höjfeldet—Evening in the mountains: Grieg
After a dream—Après un rêve (song): Fauré
After many a pang of sorrow—Dopo tante e tante pene: Marcello
After reading Dante—Après une lecture de Dante (Années de pèlerinage:
    Liszt
After the birth of her son—Nach der Geburt ihres Sohnes (song): Schumann
After the day's work—Am Feierabend (song: Die schöne Müllerin): Schubert
After the summer rain—Sahst du nach dem Gewitterregen: Berg
After work—Am Feierabend (Die schöne Müllerin): Schubert
Afterglow—Nachwirkung (song): Brahms

Aftermath—Nachwirkung (song): Brahms

Las agachadas—The shake-down song: Copland

Again the pallid ghosts are rising—Da sind die bleichen Geister wieder:
R Franz

The age of steel—Stal' noi skok: Prokofiev

The aged—Öregek (part-song): Kodály

The aged minstrel—Das Ständchen: Wolf

Agnes, min deilige sommerfugle—Agnes, my beautiful butterfly: Elling

Agnes, my beautiful butterfly—Agnes, min deilige sommerfugle: Elling

Agnus Dei—Golden light/Heavenly Father: Bizet

Agon—Contest: Stravinsky

Agonies—Schmerzen (song): Wagner

Agreeable landscape—Freundliche Landschaft (Waldscenen): Schumann

Ah, at last a bonny prince—Ah, le joli prince: Blanchard

Ah! che pur troppo è vero (Col partir)—Ah from my dreams I waken:
Handel

Ah! che troppo ineguali—Ah! how poor and unworthy: Handel

Ah che tutta in un momento (Cosi fan tutte)—All my life is sunk in
sorrow: Mozart

Ah! che zucconi (Gianni Schicchi)—Oh! foolish blockheads: Puccini

Ah, could I—Ach könnt ich, könnte vergessen: Brahms

Ah! could I behold—Il balen (Il trovatore): Verdi

Ah could my eyes behold thee—S'io ti vedess' una sol (madrigal): Lassus

Ah! crudel, nel pianto mio—Ah, cruel one, your lovely eyes: Handel

Ah, cruel one, your lovely eyes—Ah! crudel, nel pianto mio: Handel

Ah, do not let us part—Ah non lasciarmi, no: Mozart

Ah dolente partita—Ah, this parting will slay me: Wert

Ah! du wolltest mich nicht (Salome)—Ah! thou wouldst not: R Strauss

Ah! faithless one—Ah! perfido: Beethoven

Ah, fors'è lui (La traviata)—Ah, was it he/Can it be he/Was this the man:
Verdi

Ah from my dreams I waken—Ah! che pur troppo è vero (Col partir):
Handel

Ah! give me back—Ah rendimi: F Rossi

Ah God, from heav'n look down and see—Ach, Gott vom Himmel sieh
darein (chorale prelude): Bach

Ah God, how many a heart-pang—Ach Gott, wie manches Herzleid [BWV
58]: Bach

Ah God, how many pains of heart—Ach Gott, wie manches Herzleid
[BWV 3]: Bach

Ah! God in mercy—Ach Gott vom Himmel sieh' darein: Bach

Ah, how fain thy moisty pinions—Ach, um deine feuchten Schwingen:
Mendelssohn

Ah, how fair the night—Ach, wie schön ist Nacht: Schoeck

Ah how fleeting—Ach, wie flüchtig, ach wie nichtig: Bach

Ah, how perverse our will remains—Ach, unser Wille bleibt verkehrt (Herr, wie du willst): Bach

Ah! how poor and unworthy—Ah! che troppo ineguali: Handel

Ah, I feel how all hath vanished—Ach, ich fühls (Die Zauberflöte): Mozart

Ah, I know—Ach, ich fühls (Die Zauberflöte): Mozart

Ah! if I have to lose—Ah! si la liberté (Armide): Lully

Ah, it is true—Fia dunque vero?: Donizetti

Ah! je veux vivre (Romeo et Juliette)—Ah! lulled by visions/Waltz song: Gounod

Ah, Jesus Christ, with us abide—Ach bleib bei uns, Herr Jesu Christ: Bach

Ah! joy supreme—Glückes genug: Reger

Ah! le joli prince—Ah, at last a bonny prince: Blanchard

Ah, le petit vin blanc—Lingering down the lane: Borel-Clerc

Ah! lead me, gracious Lord—Ach, führe mich, O Gott (Herr Christ, der ein'ge Gottes-Sohn): Bach

Ah! long I tarried—Ah! tardai troppo!: Donizetti

Ah Lord! chasten me not—Ach Herr, strafe mich nicht: Telemann

Ah, Lord, what is a child of man—Ach Herr! was ist ein Menschenkind (Unser Mund sei voll Lachens): Bach

Ah, love is a mime—Ein dunkeler Schacht (part song: Liebeslieder waltzes): Brahms

Ah! lulled by visions—Ah! je veux vivre (Romeo et Juliette): Gounod

Ah, mai non cessate—Continue thy singing: Donandy

Ah, mamma, now you shall know—Ah, vous dirai-je maman (bravura variations): Adam

Ah me, poor maid—Was hab' ich arme dirn' getan?: C Böhm

Ah me! what phantoms—Ah non son io (Ezio): Handel

Ah! might but the hour of dying—Ach, das nicht die letzte Stunde (chorale): Bach

Ah! mio cor! (Alcina)—Canst thou scorn: Handel

Ah, my passion by him ungrateful—Ma la sola ohime! (Beatrice di Tenda): Bellini

Ah! non credea mirarti (La sonnambula)—Yes, for thee time's power/Who thought to see thee languish: Bellini

Ah! non giunge (La Sonnambula)—Do not mingle/Add no thought: Bellini

Ah non lasciarmi, no—Ah, do not let us part: Mozart

Ah non son io (Ezio)—Ah me! what phantoms: Handel

Ah! non son' io che parlo—Yes I must live and suffer: Mozart

Ah! how he has gone—Jetzt ist er hinaus: Henschel

Ah, now I know—Nun seh' ich woll (Kinder-totenlieder): Mahler

Ah, once I had—Ich hatte einst ein schönes Vaterland/Es war ein Traum: Lassen

Ah! perfido—Ah! perjur'd one/Ah! faithless one: Beethoven

7

Ah! perjur'd one—Ah! perfido: Beethoven
Ah, poor heart—Il pensier sta negli oggetti (Orfeo ed Euridice): Haydn
Ah! quel giorno (Semiramide)—Ah! that day: Rossini
Ah rendimi—Ah! give me back/Give me back the heart: F Rossi
Ah se in ciel, benigne stelle—Friendly stars, if yet in heaven: Mozart
Ah! seest thou not—Ne vois-tu pas (Céphale et Procis): Grétry
Ah, shall not this great day of wrath—Ach, soll nicht dieser grosse Tag
   (Wachet, betet, seid bereit): Bach
Ah! si la liberté (Armide)—Ah! if I have to lose: Lully
Ah! so pure—Ach! so fromm (aria: Martha): Flotow
Ah, soul that art drowsy—Ach, schläfrige Seele (Mache dich, mein Geist,
   bereit): Bach
Ah, strike then soon, hour most blessed—Ach, schlage doch bald, sel'ge
   Stunde (Christus, der ist mein Leben): Bach
Ah! suicide—Suicido! (La gioconda): Ponchielli
Ah, sweet as any flower—Du bist wie eine Blume: Liszt
Ah! sweet my love, thou charmest me—Wie bist du, meine Königin (song):
   Brahms
Ah! tardai troppo—Ah! long I tarried: Donizetti
Ah! that day—Ah! quel giorno (Semiramide): Rossini
Ah the thought which torments me—Se'l pensier che mi strugge: Marenzio
Ah, this parting will slay me—Ah dolente partita: Wert
Ah! thou wouldst not—Ah! du wolltest mich nicht (Salome): R Strauss
Ah, 'tis gone—Ach, ich fühls (Die Zauberflöte): Mozart
Ah! 'tis now two days—Ach nun sind es schon zwei: Henschel
Ah, vous dirai-je, maman (bravura variations)—Ah, Mama, now you shall
   know: Adam
Ah, war!—Ach vojn, vojna: Janáček
Ah, was it he—Ah, fors' è lui (La traviata): Verdi
Ah weary am I—Ma per me lasso: Marenzio
Ah, were I but a little bee—Ach, wenn ich doch ein Immchen wär: R Franz
Ah! what awful gloom—Gott! welch Dunkel hier (Fidelio): Beethoven
Ah! what sorrow—No, oh Dio (Calphurnia): Bononcini
Ah, when on that great day—Ach, soll nicht dieser grosse Tag (Wachet,
   betet, seid bereit): Bach
Ah why such distress—Warum betrübst du dich (chorale/aria): Bach
Ah! with joy my heart is pounding—Son vergin vezzosa (I Puritani): Bellini
Ah, woe is me unhappy man—Ach weh mir ungluckhaftem Mann: R Strauss
Ah! wouldst thou I should sing a merry ditty—Las! voulez-vous q'une
   personne chante (madrigal): Lassus
Ai nostri monti (Il trovatore)—Home to our mountains: Verdi
L' aiglou (opera)—The eaglet: Honegger/Ibert
Aimable Aurore (Céphale et Procis): Grétry
Aime moi berger (part-song)—Love me truly: Lefèvre

Air champêtre (song)—Pastoral song/A country song: Poulenc
Air de l'horloge (L'enfant et les sortilèges)—Ding, ding, ding: Ravel
Air grave—Song of grief: Poulenc
The air rings with her laughter—Partout des cris de joie (La jolie fille de
    Perth): Bizet
Air romantique—Romantic song: Poulenc
Air sur trois notes—Long the day and dreary: Rousseau
Air tendre—Tender lay: Engel
Air vif (song)—Lively air/Brisk song: Poulenc
Aiti laulaa (Ungdom)—The mother sings: Palmgren
Aj! kterak trojhranee muji (crgánské melodie)—Hark, hark, how my
    triangle: Dvořák
Ajánlás (from: Tíz könnyü zongoradarab)—Dedication: Bartók
L'ajo nell imbarazzo (opera)—The tutor in trouble: Donizetti
Akademische Festouvertüre (overture)—Academic Festival Overture:
    Brahms
Al desio chi t'adora—Let my longing and supplication: Mozart
Al dolce guidami (Anna Bolena)—Joyous days of childhood: Donizetti
Al lampo dell' armi (Giulio Cesare)—The noise of the battle: Handel
Al senti stringo e parto (Ariodante)—I press thee to my bosom: Handel
Alack-a-day—Haï luli: Coquard
Alas my God—Ach Gott und Herr (organ chorale): Bach
Alas! where shall I Jesus seek—Wo treff' ich meinen Jesum (Mein liebster
    Jesus ist verloren): Bach
L'alba del malato—A sunrise on a sick-bed: Rocca
Alba e tramonto—Sunrise to sunset: Gibilaro
Albumblatt—A simile: Kjerulf
Alegr'as—Festivals: Gerhard
Alegria de la soledad—Joy of solitude: Guastavino
Aleik mindig elkesnek (part-song)—Too late: Kodály
Alexander, at thy triumph—Ne' trionfi d'Alessandro (Alessandro): Handel
Alfedans—Fairy dance: Grieg
Alike at morn and eventide—Ich liebe dich: Beethoven
All alone—Holub na javoře (Moravské Dvojzpěvy): Dvořák
All around is silence and rest—Uber allen Gipfeln ist Ruh: Liszt
All at once—Sous l'effort d'un bras invisible (Semiramis): Catel
All gay!—Tout gai! (song): Ravel
All glory be to God on high—Allein Gott in der Höh sei Ehr /chorale
    fugue/organ chorale/chorale prelude: Bach
All glory to the Father—Deo Patri sit gloria (motet): Byrd
All hail—Honneur, honneur (chorus: La muette de Portici): Auber
All hail thou lovely laughing May—Willkommen, lieber schöner Mai:
    Schubert
All holy Virgin—Allmacht'ge Jungfrau (Tannhäuser): Wagner

All honour, praise and blessing—Sei Lob und Preis mit Ehren (chorale/
motet): Bach
All is prepared now—Tutto è disposto (Le nozze di Figaro): Mozart
All is silent—Alles schweiget (part-song): Mozart
All joy and pleasure—Dalla sua pace (Don Giovanni): Mozart
All' mein Gedanken—My fondest thoughts: Brahms
All' mein Gedanken—All the fond thoughts: R Strauss
All' meine Herzgedanken—Where'er I go/If all my heartfelt thinking:
Brahms
All my heart today rejoices—Warum sollt ich mich denn grämen (chorale:
Bach
All my life from Jesus springeth—Nur mein Jesus ist mein Leben (chorale):
Bach
All my life is sunk in sorrow—Ah che tutta in un momento (Così fan tutti):
Mozart
All of my life—Tanto de meu estado me acho incerto: J Berger
All only according to God's will—Alles nur nach Gottes Willen: Bach
All people at this hour—Kommt, Seelen, diesen Tag: Bach
All people sing Thy praises—All' solch' dein' Güt' wir preisen (chorale:
(Gottlob! Nun geht das Jahr zu Ende): Bach
All praise to Jesus' hallowed name—Gelobet seist du, Jesu Christ (organ
chorale/Chorale prelude/from: Orgelbüchlein): Bach
All praises to the Lord—Gelobet sei der Herr, mein Gott: Bach
All' solch' dein' Güt' wir preisen (chorale: Gottlob! Nun geht das Jahr zu
Ende)—All people sing Thy praises: Bach
All Soul's day—Allerseelen: R Strauss
All the fond thoughts—All' mein Gedanken: R Strauss
All they from Sheba shall come—Sie werden aus Saba alle kommen: Bach
All things are by God ordained—Alles nur nach Gottes Willen: Bach
All things move as God doth will them—Alles nur nach Gottes Willen: Bach
All three—Lieber Alles (song): Wolf
All who seek thee—Alle welche dich suchen (song): Schoenberg
All you lovers—Voi, amanti, che vedete: Giardini
All your shades—Bois épais (Amadis de Gaule): Lully
Alla riva del Tebro (madrigal)—By the banks of the Tiber: Palestrina
Alla vita che t'arride (Un ballo in maschera)—Brightest hope and fairest
treasure: Verdi
Alle Menschen müssen sterben (chorale/from: Orgelbüchlein)—Hark! a voice
saith 'all are mortal': Bach
Alle welche dich suchen (song)—All who seek thee: Schoenberg
Allein—Alone: Reger
Allein Gott in der Höh sei Ehr (organ chorale/chorale fugue/chorale
prelude)—All glory be to God on high/Glory to God in the highest/
Glory be to God on high: Bach

Allein! weh, gang allein (Elektra)—Woe! quite alone!: R Strauss

Allein zur dir, Herr Jesu Christ—Alone in Thee, Lord Jesus Christ: Bach

Alleluia, ascendit deus (motet)—Alleluia, God is ascended: Byrd

Alleluia, cognoverunt piscipuli (motet)—Alleluia, the disciples with
  wondering eyes: Byrd

Alleluia, God is ascended—Alleluia, ascendit deus (motet): Byrd

Alleluia, the disciples with wondering eyes—Alleluia, cognoverunt
  piscipuli (motet): Byrd

Alleluja, laudem dicite—Alleluja, sing praises: Vecchi

Alleluja, sing praises—Alleluja, laudem dicite: Vecchi

Allerseelen—All Souls' day: R Strauss

Alles (song)—Everything: Schoenberg

Alles, alles in den Wind (part song: Neue Liebeslieder)—I will hear no
  more of love: Brahms

Alles nur nach Gottes Willen—All things move as God doth will them/
  All things are by God ordained/All only according to God's will: Bach

Alles schweiget (part-song)—All is silent: Mozart

Alles Vergängliche ist nur ein Gleichnis (Faust Symphony)—Everything
  is transitory: Liszt

Die Allmacht—Great is Jehovah/The Almighty/Hymn to the Almighty/
  Omnipotence: Schubert

Allmacht'ge Jungfrau (Tannhäuser)—Thou blessed Virgin/All holy Virgin:
  Wagner

Die Allmächtige—The all-powerful: R Strauss

Allnächtlich im Träume—When midnight dreams: R Franz

Allnächtlich im Träume—Each night my slumber/In slumber I see thee
  nightly/Vision: Schumann

Allons dans ce petit bois charmant—The little wood: Meister

Allor che sorge (Rodrigo)—When bright and glorious: Handel

Allow but, dear maiden—Erlaube mir, feins Mädchen: Brahms

The all-seeing eye—Vsevydyashcheye oko: Radziyevs'kyi

Allurement—Lockung: Dessauer

Allurement—Det Syng (Haugtussa): Grieg

Allurements the dearest—Lusinghe più care (Alessandro): Handel

Alma del core—Fairest adored: Caldara

Alma grande e nobil core—One whose spirit is true and noble: Mozart

Alma mia, dove ten'vai—Oh, my soul: Gagliano

The Almighty—Die Allmacht: Schubert

(The) almond tree—Der Nussbaum: Schumann

Almost too serious (solemn)—Fast zu ernst (Kinderscenen): Schumann

Alone—Die Trauernde (song): Brahms

Alone—Sonntagslied: Mendelssohn

Alone—Allein: Reger

Alone in the wood—Ich wanderte unter den Bäumen: Dieren

11

Alone at last—Endlich allein (operetta): Lehár
Alone in the forest—Waldseligkeit: R Strauss
Alone in Thee, Lord Jesus Christ—Allein zur dir, Herr Jesu Christ: Bach
Alone she stood by the window—Parole (song): Brahms
Along the banks of the Seine—Sur les bords de la Seine: Blanchard
Der Alpenjäger—The Alpine hunter: Liszt
Der Alpenjäger—The Alpine huntsman/The Alpine ranger: Schubert
Der Alpenjäger—As o'er the Alps: Schubert-Heller
The Alpine herdsman's farewell—Des Sennen Abscheid (song): Schumann
The Alpine hunter—Der Alpenjäger: Liszt
The Alpine huntsman—Der Alpenjäger: Schubert
The Alpine ranger—Der Alpenjäger: Schubert
Already spring is smiling—Schon lacht der holde Frühling: Mozart
Als die Geliebte sich trennen wolte—The separation/At parting from the
    beloved/To the faithless one: Beethoven
Als du in kühnem Sange (Tannhäuser)—When for the palm in song:
    Wagner
Als Eva aus dem Paradies (Die Meistersinger von Nürnberg)—When Eve
    from out of Paradise: Wagner
Als flotter Geist (Der Zigeunerbaron)—An orphan from my early days:
    J Strauss II
Als ich dich kaum geseh'n—When first I saw thee: Lassen
Als ich dich kaum geseh'n—Since first I saw thy face: M Mayer
Als Luis die Briefe/Unglückliche Liebe—Unrequited love/Love-letters:
    Mozart
Als sie nun den König gehört (Weihnachtsoratorium)—And they, when
    they heard the king: Bach
Also auch wir vergeben unsern Schuldigern—As we forgive those who
    trespass against us: Cornelius
Also hat Gott die Welt geliebt (cantata)—God so loved the world/So truly
    God his world did bless: Bach
Also sprach Zarathustra—Thus spake Zarathustra: R Strauss
L'alta naixença del Rei Enjaume—The high birth of King James: Gerhard
Által mennék én a Tiszán ladikon—I would cross the Tisza in a boat: Bartók
Altdeutscher Liebesreim—An old German love song (Minnesong): Meyer-
    Helmund
Altdeutsches Lied—Old German song: Mendelssohn
Die Alte—The old lady: Mozart
Die alte gute Zeit—The dear old days gone by: Schumann
Das alte Jahr vergangen (from: Orgelbüchlein)—The old year now hath
    passed away: Bach
Alte Laute (song)—Old sounds: Schumann
Alte Liebe—The old love: Brahms
Das alte Lied—The old song: Grieg

12

Am Strande—On the shore of the lake: Fielitz
Am Strome—On the stream/To the stream/By the stream: Schubert
Am Ufer—On the shore: R Strauss
Am Wegand (song)—At the wayside: Schoenberg
Am Wildbach die Waiden (part-song)—The meadows at Wildbach/The
   trees by the river: Brahms
Am wilden Klippenstrande—A lovely crag stands yonder: Henschel
Amarilli mia bella—Amaryllis/Amarilli, my fair one: G Caccini
Amarilli, my fair one—Amarilli, mia bella: G Caccini
Amaryllis—Amarilli mia bella: G Caccini
L'âme des iris—The soul of the iris: Rhené-Baton
L'âme évaporée—Soul so subtle: Daia
Amelia all'ballo (opera)—Amelia goes to the ball: Menotti
Amelia goes to the ball—Amelia all'ballo (opera): Menotti
Amen, Amen! come then, lovely joy-crown—Amen, amen, du schöne
   Freudenkrone (Nun komm, der Heiden Heiland): Bach
Amen, amen, du schöne Freudenkrone (Nun komm, der Heiden Heiland)—
   Amen, Amen! come then, lovely joy-crown: Bach
L'amerò (Il rè pastore)—Faithful heart enraptured: Mozart
L'amico Fritz (opera)—Friend Fritz: Mascagni
Amicu ventu—The lone sailor: Gilbaro
Amid the gloomy woods—Ich schleich umher (song): Brahms
Amleto (opera)—Hamlet: Faccio
Among strangers—In der Fremde (song): Brahms
Among the bilberries—Blåberr-li (Haugtussa): Grieg
Among the play of the waves—Im Spiel der Wellen: Reger
El amor brujo (ballet)—Love the magician: Falla
Amor che deggio far (madrigal)—O love regard my plight: Anon
Amor, gioie mi porge—Jealousy: Handel
D'amor sull' ali rosee (Trovatore)—Love fly on rosy pinions: Verdi
Amor ti vieta (Fedora)—Love itself forbids: Giordano
L'amore dei tre re (opera)—The love of three kings: Montemezzi
L'amore medico (opera)—Doctor Love/Doctor Cupid: Wolf-Ferrari
Amore nel mio penar (Flavio)—O love, take pity on my pain!: Handel
Amore traditore—False love: Bach(?)
L'amour—Love: Godard
L'amour au clair de lune—Melody blues: Borel-Clerc
Amour d'automne—As in October: Chaminade
L'amour des trois oranges (opera)—Love for three oranges: Prokofiev
L'Amour est enfant trompeur—That Love's a naughty little god: Meister
Amour et printemps—Love and spring: Waldteufel
L'amour, toujours, l'amour—Love everlasting: Friml
L'amoureuse—A girl in love: P Cannon
L'amoureux (Petites légendes)—The lover: Milhaud

14

Amoureux séparés (song)—Separated lovers/Lovers divided: Roussel
An—To: Wolf
An Babels Wasserflüssen (part-song)—By the waters of Babylon: Cornelius
An Bertha—To Bertha: Cornelius
An Chloe/Wenn die Lieb' aus deinen blauen Augen—To Chloe/With a
    swanlike beauty gliding: Mozart
An den Abendstern—To the evening star: Schumann
An den Frühlingsregen—To the spring rain: Reger
An den Mond—To the moon: Bocquet
An den Mond—To the moon: Brahms
An den Mond (Song: Schwanengesang)—To the moon: Schubert
An den Mond/Füllest wieder Busch und Thal—To the moon: Schubert
An den Mond/ Gruss, lieber Mond—To the moon/The mourning moon:
    Schubert
An den Mond—Sun of the sleepless/To the moon: Schumann
An den Schlaf (song)—To sleep: Wolf
An den Sonnenschein—To the sunshine/O sunny beam/O shining sun/O
    sunshine: Schumann
An den Sturmwind (part-song)—The tempest: Cornelius
An den Tod—To death: Schubert
An den Traum—Dreaming: Cornelius
An den Wind—To the wind: R Franz
An der schönen, blauen Donau (waltz)—Blue Danube/On the beautiful
    blue Danube: J Strauss II
An des lust'gen Brunnens Rand—On the brook's green back:
    F Mendelssohn
An die Apfelbäume—'Neath the apple tree: Schubert
An die Einsamkeit—O solitude/To solitude/Solitude: Mozart
An die ferne Geliebte (song)—To the distant beloved: Beethoven
An die Freude—Ode to joy/Hymn to joy/To my friends: Schubert
An die Geliebte—The tear/To the beloved: Beethoven
An die Geliebte (song)—To the beloved: Wolf
An die Hoffnung—To hope/Hope: Beethoven
An die Hoffnung—Gentle hope/To hope: Mozart
An die Konigin Elisabeth (song)—To Queen Elizabeth: Schumann
An die Künstler (cantata)—To the songs of art: Mendelssohn
An die Laute—The cither/To the lute/The lute-player: Schubert
An die Leier—To the lyre: Schubert
An die Musik (song)—To music: Schubert
An die Nacht—To the night: C Böhm
An die Nachtigall (song)—To the (a) nightingale: Brahms
An die Nachtigall (part-song)—To the nightingale: Henschel
An die Nachtigall/Er liegt und schäft—To the nightingale: Schubert
An die Nachtigall—To the nightingale: Schumann

An die Stolze—To the proud one: Beethoven
An die untergehende Sonne—To the setting sun: Schubert
An ein Veilchen (song)—To a violet: Brahms
An eine Aeolsharfe (song)—To an Aeolian harp/An Aeolian harp: Brahms
An eine Aeolsharfe (song)—To an Aeolian harp: Wolf
An eine Quelle—To a brook/To a brooklet: Schubert
An einen Herbstlied—To an autumn forest: J Marx
An einen Säugling—To an infant: Beethoven
An ihr Bild—To a portrait: Kjerulf
An jeder Hand (part song: Neue Liebeslieder)—Erewhile upon my fingers: Brahms
An leuchtenden Sommermorgen—Summer: Schumann
An Mäzel (canon)—Metronome canon: Beethoven
An mein Clavier—Schubert to his piano: Schubert
An meinem Herzen, an meiner Brust (song: Frauenliebe und -leben)—
    Here on my bosom/On my heart/Here sweetest babe: Schumann
An my love were the lark—Singt mein Schatz: Wolf
An schwager Kronos—Postillion Kronos/Time the charioteer: Schubert
An Sie—To her: R Strauss
An spröde Schönen—To coy beauties: F X Mozart
An Sylvia—Who is Sylvia?: Schubert
An Wasserflüssen Babylon—By the waters of Babylon: Bach
An wollen Büschelzweigen—Upon the tufted branches: R Kahn
Anacreon's grave—Anakreons Grab (song): Wolf
Anakreons Grab (song)—Anacreon's grave/The tomb of Anacreon: Wolf
Anbetung—Adoration: Blumenthal
Anbetung—Adoration: R Strauss
Ancient airs and dances for lute—Antiche danze ed aria per liuto: Respighi
And all for half-a-crown—Für fünfzehn Pfennige: R Strauss
And I must wander far—E me ne voglio andar: Bimboni
And in a dream—Und unser lieben Frauen: Bauernfeind
And Jesus, the all-blessed—Et Jesum benedictum (motet): Byrd
And may I believe it?—So willst du (song): Brahms
And say—Und sprich: Liszt
And that same day, when evening had fallen—Am Abend aber derselbigen
    Sabbats: Bach
And the roses, they flourish—Und die Rosen, die prangen: R Franz
And they when they heard the king—Als sie nun den König gehöret
    (Weihnachtsoratorium): Bach
And through portals of gold he departed—Et exivit per auream portam
    (motet): Byrd
And when the moon—Soll sich der Mond nicht heller scheinen: Brahms
And ye this horror—E il soffrirete (Tamerlano): Handel
Andenken—I think of thee/Remembrance: Beethoven

Andenken (part-song)—Remembrance: Mendelssohn
Andenken—My thoughts: Wolf
And're Maienlied/Hexenlied—Witches' song of May/Another May
    song: Mendelssohn
Andre's woman friend—La dame d'André (song: Fiancailles pour rire):
    Poulenc
Anemone—Blaaveis: A Backer-Grøndahl
Anfangs wollt'ich fast verzagen—Vainly first I sought to bear it: Liszt
Angedenken—Remembrance/An ivy leaf: Cornelius
The angel—Die Sterne schau'n in stiller Nacht: Mendelssohn
The angel—Der Engel (Wesendonck Lieder): Wagner
Angel divine—Angiolo, delicato: Wolf-Ferrari
Angel fair with golden hair—Angiolin dal biondo crin: Liszt
Angel of beauty—Sei mir gegrüsst: Schubert
The angel of my life—Mein guter Engel: Blumenthal
The angels and the shepherds—Angyalok és Pásztorok (part-song): Kodály
The angel's greeting—Der englische Gruss (part-song: Marienlieder): Brahms
Angels guard thee—Oh, ne t'éveille (Jocelyn): Godard
The angel's love-message—Himmelsboten zu Liebchens Himmelbett:
    R Strauss
Angel's serenade—La serenata: Braga
Angelus ad pastores ait—Shepherds quaked when the angels told them—
    H L Hassler
Angelus autem Domini (motet)—Lo the bright angel: Anerio
Angiolin dal biondo crin—Angel fair with golden hair: Liszt
Angiolo, delicato—Angel divine: Wolf-Ferrari
The angler—Der Fischer: Schubert
The angry bard—Der zürende Barde: Schubert
The angry Diana—Der zurende(n) Diana: Schubert
The angry wife—La mal mariée: P Cannon
Angyolok és Pásztorok (part-song)—The angels and the shepherds: Kodály
Ángyomasszony kertje—In my sister-in-law's garden: Bartók
Anklänge (song)—Fragment/Anticipation/A memory: Brahms
Anmutiger Vertag (Lieder der Liebe)—Sweet bargain: Kilpinen
L'anneau d'argent—The silver ring: Chaminade
L'année en vain chasse l'année (L'enfant prodigue)—The years roll by:
    Debussy
Années de pèlerinage—Years of travel: Liszt
Annie Miller—Molnár Anna (part-song): Kodály
Anoche te besé—A kiss in the night: Caroliș
Another May song—Andres Maienlied: Mendelssohn
Anselmo's grave—Am Grabe Anselmos: Schubert
Answer to a maid's question—Antwort auf die Frage eines Mädchens:
    Haydn

Antiche danze ed aria per liuto—Ancient airs and dances for lute: Respighi
Anticipation—Anklänge (song): Brahms
Anticipation—Erwartung (opera): Schoenberg
Antique garden—Jardin antiguo: Guastavino
Antonius of Padua's Fish Sermon—Des Antonius von Padua Fischpredigt
     (Des Knaben Wunderhorn): Mahler
Des Antonius von Padua Fischpredigt (Des Knaben Wunderhorn)—St
     Anthony's sermon to the fishes/St Anthony of Padua preaches to the
     fish/Antonius of Padua's fish sermon/St Anthony and the fishes:
     Mahler
Antwort auf die Frage eines Mädchens—Answer to a maid's question: Haydn
Anvil chorus—Vedi! le fosche (Trovatore): Verdi
Anxiety—Sklíčenost: Smetana
El aparecido (El amor brujo)—The homecomer: Falla
Apegado a mi—Close to my heart: Guastavino
Aperite mihi portas justitiae (cantata)—Open to me gates of justice:
     Buxtehude
Apollo as master of the muses—Apollo Musagètes: Stravinsky
Apollo Musagètes—Apollo as master of the muses: Stravinsky
Apparebit in finem—He will come at the last day: Byrd
An appeal—Auftrag: Wolf
The appeasement of Aeolus—Der zufrieden gestellte Äolus: Bach
Apporte les cristaux dorés—The gilded crystals: Rhené-Baton
L'apprenti sorcier (orchestral piece)—The sorcerer's apprentice: Dukas
The apprentice's song—Gesellenlied (song): Wolf
The approach of night—Um Mitternacht: R Franz
Après un rêve—After a dream: Fauré
Après une lecture de Dante (Années de pèlerinage)—After reading Dante/
     Dante sonata: Liszt
Aprite un pò queql' occhi (Le Nozze di Figaro)—Those eyes at least now
     open: Mozart
The Arabian girl—Adieux de l'hôtesse arabe: Bizet
Arabian song—Chanson arabe: Godard
Der Arbeitsmann—The workman: R Strauss
Ardent longing—Brünstiges vorlangen: J G Ahle
Ardenti mei sospiri (madrigal)—My ardent sighs: Dering
Ardon gl'incensi (Lucia di Lammermoor)—Incense is burning/The incense
     rises (Mad scene): Donizetti
Ardor felic'e caro (canzonet)—Passion so dear and blessed: Dering
Are they pains?—Sind es Schmerzen, sind es Freuden (song): Brahms
Are they sorrows, are they pleasures—Sind es schmerzen, sind es Freuden
     (song): Brahms
Are ye coming soon, ye small holders?—Kommer I snart, I husmaend?
     (Ulvenssøn): Nielsen

Ariadne—Arianna (opera): Monteverdi
Ariadne and Bluebeard—Ariane et Barbe-Bleue (opera): Dukas
Ariadne auf Naxos (opera)—Ariadne on Naxos: R Strauss
Ariadne on Naxos—Ariadne auf Naxos: R Strauss
Ariane et Barbe-Bleue—Ariadne and Bluebeard: Dukas
Arianna (opera)—Ariadne: Monteverdi
Ariettes oubliées (songs)—Forgotten airs: Debussy
Arise, beloved spirit—Steig auf, Geliebter: Brahms
Arise, beloved vision—Steig auf, Geliebter: Brahms
Arise, Lord, why sleepest Thou?—Exurge, Domine: (motet): Byrd
Arise, O Lord, why sleepest Thou?—Exurge, Domine (motet): Byrd
Arise, shine forth in splendour—Surge illuminare (motet): Byrd
Arise, ye Russian people—Vstavaite lyndi russkiye! (Aleksandr Nevsky):
    Prokofiev
L'Arlesiana—The girl from Arles: Cilèa
L'Arlesienne—The girl from Arles: Bizet
The arm of the Lord—Insanae et vanae curae (motet): Haydn
Der arme Heinrich (opera)—Poor Henry: Rheinberger
Arme Peter (1)—Young Hans and Margot/Smart John and his Marg'ret:
    Schumann
Arme Peter (2)—My breast doth ache/Within my breast: Schumann
Arme Peter (3)—Whene'er poor Peter/Now poor young Peter/Poor Peter:
    Schumann
Der arme Thomas—Poor Hans: Zelter
L'armellin vita non aura (Flavio)—As the ermine: Handel
Armer Sunder, du (Drei Volkstexte)—Wretched sinner you: Webern
Armida abandoned—Armida abbandonata: Handel
Armida abbandonata—Armida abandoned: Handel
The armourer—Der Waffenschmied von Worms (opera): Lortzing
Around my beloved idol—Intorno all'idol mio: Cesti
Arouse thyself to anger—Svegliatevi nel core (Giulio Cesare): Handel
A-roving—Das Wandern: Schubert
Arpège (song)—Arpeggio: Fauré
Arpeggio—Arpège (song): Fauré
L'art de toucher le clavecin—The art of playing the harpsichord: Couperin
Art lässt nicht von Art—The devil a monk would be: Hindemith
Are not Thine eyes, Lord?—Herr, deine Augen sehen nach dem Glauben:
    Bach
The art of playing the harpsichord—L'art de toucher le clavecin: Couperin
Art Thou, Lord Jesus, from heaven to earth now descending?—Kommst
    du nun, Jesu, von Himmel herunter? (organchorale): Bach
Art thou troubled?—Dove sei amato bene (Rodelinda): Handel
Arthur's chase—Le chasseur maudit: Liszt
Artist's life—Künstler-Leben (waltz): J Strauss II

Artsan Alimi (Shire' Chalutzim)—Come to the land: Binder
As a sunbeam at morn—Come raggio di sol: Caldara
As before, one after the other—Nach wie vor der Reihe nach: Kreneck
As butterfly that blindly—Qual farfalletta amante: D Scarlatti
As Cupid once enjoyed his ease—Einstmals das Kind Kupido (madrigal):
  Friderici
As fame and power fast fade away—Wie schnell verschwindet (song):
  Brahms
As flowers that waken—Wie schnell verschwindet (song): Brahms
As hearts that languish—Dem Herzen ähnlich: R Strauss
As I leave you—Mentre ti lascio, o figlia: Mozart
As I saw Clora walk—Leggiadretto Clorino: Vecchi
As I walked in green forest—Mi sfidate, guerriera (madrigal): Giovanelli
As in October—Amour d'automne: Chaminade
As o'er the alps—Der Alpenjäger: Schubert-Heller
As on the swelling wave—Come raggio di sol: Caldara
As rays of setting sun—Come raggio di sol: Caldara
As the dragonfly quivers—Die Libelle schweft zitternd (Chinesische
  Liebeslieder): Liebermann
As the ermine—L'armellin vita non aura (Flavio): Handel
As the hour drew nigh—Da die Stunde kam: R Franz
As the moon's reflections—Wie des Mondes Abbild: R Franz
As through the street—Quando men vo (La bohème): Puccini
As waves in endless motion—Com' onda incalza altr' onda (Scipione):
  Handel
As we forgive those who trespass against us—Also auch wir vergeben
  unsern Schuldigern: Cornelius
As when a sunny beam rests—Come raggio di sol: Caldara
As you like it—Was ihr wollt (incidental music): Humperdinck
Ascendit deus—God goes up on high: Gallus
Ascendo ad patrem meum (motet)—I ascend unto my father: Handl
The ascension—Na nebe vstoupenf Páně (part-song): Martinů
The ascent to the pastures—Montée aux Alpes: Liszt
Aschenbrödel (cantata)—Cinderella: Abt/Reinecke
Ascolti . . . Io moriró (Germania)—Oh! hear me!: Franchetti
Asia—Asie (song: Shéhérazade): Ravel
Aside dark sorrow laying—Serena i vaghi rai (Semiramide): Rossini
Asie (song: Shéhérazade)—Asia: Ravel
Ask me not—Frage nicht: Wolf
Ask thy heart—Tu lo sai: Torelli
Asleep one day—Das Traumbild: Mozart
Aspice Domine (motet)—Look upon us, O Lord: Byrd
Aspice Domine de sede (motet)—Look down, O Lord: Byrd
Aspri rimorsi atroci—Bitter terrible remorse: Mozart

L'assassinio nel cattedrale—Murder in the cathedral: Pizzeti

Assisa a piè d'un salice (Otello)—Willow song/Beside a weeping willow tree: Rossini

Astray—Vilse: Sibelius

At a wedding—Bei einer Tranung (song): Wolf

At Anselmo's tomb—Am Grabe Anselmos: Schubert

At evening—Abends: R Franz

At eventide I cannot sleep—Des Abends kann ich nicht schlafen: Brahms

At forty—Mit vierzig Jahren: Brahms

At heaven's gate—Seliger Eingang: Henschel

At home—U maměnky: Martinů

At last—So willst du: Brahms

At midnight—Um Mitternacht: Bruch

At midnight—Um Mitternacht (song): Mahler

At midnight—Um Mitternacht (song): Wolf

At midnight hour—Um Mitternacht: Mahler

At midnight the blushing roses—Um Mitternacht: Reger

At morning—Le matin: Berlioz

At morning in the dew—Ging heut Morgen ubers Feld (Lieder eines fahrenden Gesellen): Mahler

At mother's grave—Ved moders Grav: Grieg

At my cool and rippling water—Ach, und du mein kühles Wasser: Brahms

At night—Nachts: Cornelius

At night—Des Abends (Fantasiestücke): Schumann

At night—Nachtgang: R Strauss

At night at their spinning—Auf die Nacht in den Spinnstubn: Brahms

At night-time—Nächtens (part-song): Brahms

At parting—Scheiden und meiden (song): Brahms

At parting from the beloved—Als die Geliebte sich trennen wolte: Beethoven

At sea—Meerfahrt: Brahms

At sea—Auf dem Meere: R Franz

At sea—Till havs: Sibelius

At Seville—Sevillanas: Laparra

At sunset—Le coucher du soleil (Melodies Irlandaises): Berlioz

At sunset—Im Abendrot: Schubert

At the bier of a young artist—Ved en ung kunstners båre: Nielsen

At the bier of a young woman—Ved en ung hustrus båre: Grieg

At the brook—U potoka: Dvořák

At the brookside—Langs en å: Grieg

At the cradle—Badnlet: Grieg

At the crossroads—Am Scheideweg (part-song): Schoenberg

At the door—Vor der Tür (vocal duet): Brahms

At the fireside—Am Kamin (Kinderscenen): Schumann

21

At the foot of the cross—Stabat mater: Dvořák
At the fountain—Am Brunnele: Reger
At the gates of Sevilla—Aux portes de Séville: Fourdrain
At the inn—Herberge (Waldscenen): Schumann
At the last day—Am jüngsten Tag ich aufersteh: Brahms
At the martyr's grave—Vértanuk Sirjánál (part song): Kodály
At the old bleaching house—Na starém bělide (opera): Kovarovic
At the quiet night-time—Auf die ruhige Nochzeit: Huber
At the smithy—Au bruit des lourds (Philémon et Baucis): Gounod
At the spinning wheel—Die Spinnerin (song): Schumann
At the stream—Auf dem Flüsse (Die Winterreise): Schubert
At the wayside—Am Wegand (song): Schoenberg
At the window—Vor dem Fenster (song): Brahms
At your feet—For dine Födder: Grieg
The attack on the mill—Der Sturm auf der Mühle: Weis
L'attente (song)—The waiting one: Saint-Saëns
Attollite portas (motet)—Lift up your heads: Byrd
Au bord de l'eau (song)—On the banks of the river: Fauré
Au bord d'une fontaine—Beside a lonely fountain: Bertaud
Au bord d'une source (Années de pèlerinage)—Beside a spring: Liszt
Au bruit des lourds (Philémon et Baucis)—At the smithy/Vulcan's song:
    Gounod
Au caprice du vent—Moon fancies: Pesse
Au cimetière (Les nuits d'été)—The tomb/Moonlight: Berlioz
Au cimetière (song)—In the cemetery: Fauré
Au joli bois—To lovely groves: Tessier
Au marche (chorus: La muette de Portici)—Come hither: Auber
Au paradis! —To one in paradise: Luzzatti
Au pays où se fait la guerre (song)—To the country where they are at
    war: Duparc
Au printemps—Love in spring/Spring/To spring: Gounod
Au rossignol (song)—To the nightingale: Gounod
Aubade/Puis qu'on ne peut fléchir (Le roi d'Ys)—In olden Spain: Lalo
Auch kleine Dinge (Italianisches Liederbuch)—Even little things: Wolf
Auch mit gedämpfen, schwachen Stimmen (Schwingt freudig euch
    empor)—Even with subdued and weak voices: Bach
Audivi vocem de coelo—I heard a voice from heaven: Tallis
Auf, auf! mein Herz, mit Freuden (chorale)—Up, up my heart with
    gladness: Bach
Auf, auf, mit hellem Schall (Auf Christi Himmelfahrt allein)—Up, up,
    with trumpet tone: Bach
Auf Christi Himmelfahrt allein—On Christ's ascension alone: Bach
Auf das Trinklas eines verstorbenen Freundes (song)—A dead friend's
    drinking glass/To the wine glass of a dead friend/The last toast: Schuman

Auf das Wohl (part-song)—Here's good health: Mozart

Auf dem Flüsse (Die Winterreise)—On the river/At the stream/The ice: Schubert

Auf dem grünen Balkon (song)—From her green balcony: Wolf

Auf dem Hügel sitz ich (An die ferne Geliebte)—From a mountain's high projection: Beethoven

Auf dem Kirchhofe (song)—In the churchyard: Brahms

Auf dem Meere (chorus: Rinaldo)—On the sea: Brahms

Auf dem Meere—At sea: R Franz

Auf dem Meere/Aus den Himmelsangen—On the ocean: R Franz

Auf dem Meere/Das Meere hat seine Perlen—On the ocean/The sea hath pearls: R Franz

Auf dem Rhein—On the Rhine: Schoeck

Auf dem Schiffe—A birdling flew over the Rhine/A bird flies over: Brahms

Auf dem See—On the lake: Brahms

Auf dem See (part-song)—On the sea: Mendelssohn

Auf dem See—On the lake: Schubert

Auf dem Strom—On the stream: Schubert

Auf dem Teich, dem regungslosen—On the lake, so calm, so placid: R Franz

Auf dem Wasser zu singen—On the water/Evening boat-song/To be sung on the waters: Schubert

Auf der Brück—On the bridge: Schubert

Auf der Wanderung—Oh, what a day—Wolf

Auf die Nacht in den Spinnstubn/Mädchenlied—At night at their spinning/Song of a maid: Brahms

Auf die ruhige Nachzeit—At the quiet night-time: Huber

Auf die Zukunft unseres Heilandes—The advent of our Saviour: J R Ahle

Auf ein altes Bild (song)—Lines on an old picture/An old painting: Wolf

Auf ein Kind—To a child: Schoeck

Auf ein Kind—On a child: R Strauss

Auf ein schlummerndes Kind—O'er a sleeping child: Cornelius

Auf eine Christblume (song)—To a Christmas rose: Wolf

Auf eine Unbekannte—To one unknown: Cornelius

Auf einem verfallenen Kirchhof (Lieder um den Tod)—In a ruined churchyard: Kilpinen

Auf einer Burg (song)—In a castle/An old castle/On a castle's height: Schumann

Auf einer Wanderung (song)—On a journey: Wolf

Auf Flügeln des Gesanges—On wings of song/I'll spread my music's pinions: Mendelssohn

Auf geheimem Waldespfade—Through the woods as oft I wander: R Franz

Auf geheimem Waldespfade—By a lonely forest path: Griffes

Auf ihrem Grab (part-song)—Over their grave: Mendelssohn

Auf meinen lieben Gott (organ chorale)—In God, my faithful God: Bach

Auf meines Kindes Tod—On the death of my child: Schoeck
Auf Nimmerwiedersehen—A good-bye: Blumenthal
Aufwolkigen Höh'n (Siegfried)—On cloud-cover'd heights: Wagner
Aufblick—Looking upwards: Wolf
Aufbruch—The skies are getting brighter: R Franz
Aufenthalt (Schwanengesang)—Resting place/My abode: Schubert
Aufforderung zum Tanze (piano piece)—Invitation to the dance: Weber
Die Aufgeregten (song)—The excited ones: Schoenberg
Aufschwung (Fantasiestücke)—Soaring: Schumann
Aufsperren sie den Rachen weit (chorale: Wo Gott, der Herr, nicht bei
    uns halt)—Our foes press on us far and wide: Bach
Aufsteig und Fall der Stadt Mahagonny—The rise and fall of the city
    (town) of Mahagonny: Weill
Auftrag (song)—An appeal: Wolf
Auftrage—The charge: Cornelius
Aufträge (song)—Messages: Schumann
Der Augen schein—O eyes the fairest: Krieger
Der Augenblick—The moment: Haydn
Das Augenlicht—The light of the eye: Webern
Aunt Caroline's will—La testament de la tante Caroline: Roussel
Auprès de cette grotte sombre (song: Le promenoir des deux amants)—
    Close to this dark grotto: Debussy
Auprès de ma vie—Near my beloved: Chaminade
Aura, che intorno spiri—Hear, o ye winds of heaven: Mozart
Aure soari e liete ombre—Welcome! ye soft whisp'ring zephyrs: Handel
Aurora tell me—Aimable Aurore (Céphale et Procis): Grétry
Aus aller Herren Länder—From foreign parts: Moszkowski
Aus alten Märchen (Dichterliebe)—Old stories: Schumann
Aus banger Brust—O, wert thou here: Sibelius
Aus Christi Himmelfahrt allein—Now Christ is risen to God: Bach
Aus dem Dankliede zu Gott (part-song)—'Tis thou to whom: Haydn
Aus dem hohen Lied (Brautlieder)—From the song of songs: Cornelius
Aus dem Walde—Forest voices: Blech
Aus den "Hebraischen Gesängen" (from: Myrten)—From "Hebrew
    melodies": Schumann
Aus den östichen Rosen (Myrthen)—Sweet greeting/From "Eastern
    Roses": Schumann
Aus der Erde quellen—True lover's heart: Brahms
Aus der Heimat/In der Fremde—In foreign parts/Far from home:
    Schumann
Aus der Tiefe (Achilleus)—From the depths of my sorrow: Bruch
Aus der Tiefe rufe ich (chorale partita)—From the depths to Thee I call:
    Bach (?)

Aus einem Totenhaus—From the (a) house of the dead: Janáček
Aus meinem Tagebuch—From my diary: Reger
Aus meinen grossen Schmerzen—From grief, I cannot measure/Where
  sorrows touch me nearest/Out of my dark despairing: R Franz
Aus meinen grossen Schmerzen—From out my heart's great sorrow: Wolf
Aus meinen Tränen (Dichterliebe)—Love's tears/Tears and sighs/Where fall
  my burning teardrops: Schumann
Aus meiner sünden Tiefe (madrigal)—Though deep has been my falling:
  Lassus
Aus tiefer Not schrei ich zu dir (chorale/cantata)—Yea, though our sin be
  ne'er so great/From the depths of woe I call on Thee: Bach
Aus tiefer Not schrei' ich zu dir (chorale prelude)—Out of the depths I cry
  to Thee: Bach
Ausdrucksweise (part-song)—Means of expression: Schoenberg
Die Auswanderer: Flucht—The emigrants: flight: Bruch
Die Auswanderer: Heimatbild—The emigrants: a home-scene: Bruch
Author of all my joys—O del mio dolce ardor (Paride ed Elena): Gluck
Autograph—Manuscripte: E Strauss
Automne—Autumn: d'Arba
Automne—September serenade: Chaminade
Automne (song)—Autumn: Fauré
Autumn—Automne: d'Arba
Autumn—Automne (song): Fauré
Autumn—Im Herbst: Pfitzner
Autumn—Herbstgefühl: Schoeck
Autumn—Herbstlied: Schumann
Autumn brooding—Herbstgefühl (song): Brahms
Autumn fogs—Spätherbstnebel: Wolf
Autumn leaves—Les feuilles mortes: Kosma
Autumn loneliness—Der Einsame im Herbst (Das Lied von der Erde):
  Mahler
Autumn manoeuvres—Tártájárás (operetta): Kálmán
Autumn moods—O senneye: Prokofiev
Autumn night—Nuit d'automne: Roussel
Autumn serenade—Sérénade d'automne: Massenet
Autumn song—Herbstlied/Ach wie so bald: Mendelssohn
Autumn song—Herbstlied/Im Walde rauschen: Mendelssohn
Autumn song—Im Herbst: Mendelssohn
Autumn song—Herbstlied: Schumann
An autumn thought—Pensée d'automne: Massenet
Autumn thoughts—På Skogstien: Grieg
Autumnal cradle song—Wegenlied im Herbst: Blech
Autumnal gloom—Herbstgefühl (song): Brahms
Aux cyprès de la villa d'Este (Années de pèlerinage)—By the cypresses at
  the Villa d'Este: Liszt

Aux portes de Séville—At the gates of Sevilla: Fourdrain

Avant que tu ne t'en ailles . . . (song: La bonne chanson)—Before you vanish: Fauré

Ave Maria—Father eternal/Evening meditation/Lord of mercy: Bach-Gounod

Ave Maria—Ellen's hymn: Schubert-Heller

Ave Maria, blest among women—Ave Maria, piena di grazie (Otello): Verdi

Ave Maria, piena di grazie (Otello)—Ave Maria, blest among women: Verdi

Ave, Regina—Hail, queen of heaven: Webern

Ave Regina coelorum—Thou art the queen of all heaven: Lasso

Ave vera Virginitas—Sun of my soul: Josquin

Ave verum corpus (motet)—Hail, O hail, true body: Byrd

Les aventures du Roi Pansole—The adventures of King Pansole: Honegger

Avril—In April: Godard

Awake, awake, ye sheep that wander—Wacht auf, wacht auf, verlorne Schafe (O Ewigkeit du Donnerwort): Bach

Awake, my love, my sweeting—Wach auf mein Herzensschöne: Brahms

Awake, my pretty maiden—Wach auf mein Herzensschöne: Brahms

Awake, sweet joy—Wach auf, mein Hort: Brahms

Awake, thou wintry earth—Dem wir das Heilig itzt (chorale: Gelobet sei der Herr, mein Gott): Bach

Awake us Lord and hasten—Ertöt' uns durch dein' Güte (chorale: Jesus nahm zu sich die Zwölfe): Bach

The awakening of the bride—Reveil de la mariée (song): Ravel

The awaking child's dream—Hymne de l'enfant à son reveil: Liszt

Away from home—Der Jüngling in der Fremde: Beethoven

Away in a manger—Erstanden ist der heilige Christ (chorale): Bach

Away now with lessons—Ricetti gramezza e pavento (aria: Non sa che sia dolore): Bach

Away then, ye cares that so vainly beset me—Doch weichet, ihr tollen vergeblichen Sorgen (Liebster Gott, wann werd' ich sterben):

Away to the meadows—Das Lied im Grünen: Schubert

Awkward for the man—Schlimm für die Männer (part-song): Henschel

Ay! cross-bow and dart—Traum! Bogen und Pfeil sind gut für den Feind (song): Brahms

Ayzeh Peleh (Shire' Chalutzim)—Oh, what wonder: Binder

Az ágyam hírogat—My bed calls me: Bartók

Az egri ménes mind szürke (song)—The horses of Eger are all grey: Bartók

Az én szerelmem—My love: Bartók

Az öszi lárma—Sounds of autumn: Bartók

B

Babushkiny skazki—Tales of a grandmother: Prokofiev
Baby at the well—Das Kind am Brunnen: Wolf
Baby's family—A prole do bêbê: Villa-Lobos
Bachanal—Hulanka: Chopin
Bäche von gesalz'nen Zähren (Ich hatte viel Bekümmerniss)—From my
    eyes salt tears are streaming: Bach
Le bachelier de Salamanque—The bachelor of Salamanca: Roussel
The bachelor—Kit kéne elvenni? (part-song): Kodály
The bachelor of Salamanca—Le bachelier de Salamanque (song): Roussel
Des Baches Wiegenlied (song: Die schöne Müllerin)—The mill stream's
    lullaby/The lullaby of the brook: Schubert
Baci amorosi e cari—My lady is so charming: Mozart (?)
Baci soave e cari (madrigal)—O sweet and dear caresses: Gesualdo
Il bacio—Love's messenger/The dream of home/The kiss: Arditi
Un bacio di mano—A hand kiss: Mozart
A backward glance—Rückblick (song: Die Winterreise): Schubert
Bad weather—Schlecht' Wetter: Reger
Bad weather—Schlectes Wetter: R Strauss
Badnlat—At the cradle: Grieg
Baekken—Brooklet: Grieg
Le baiser de la Fée—The fairy's kiss: Stravinsky
Les baisers sont des fleurs—Kisses are like flowers: Fontenailles
Bakhchisaraysky fontan—The fountain of Bakhchisaray: Asafyer
Balatoni rege—The tale of Balaton: E Ábrányi
Le balcon—The balcony: Debussy
The balcony—Le balcon: Debussy
Les baleines—The whales: Pierné
Il balen (It trovatore)—Ah! could I behold/The tempest of my heart: Verdi
Ballad made at the request of his mother, for a prayer to Our Lady—
    Ballade que Villon fait à la requête de sa mère pour prier Notre-Dame
    (song): Debussy
The ballad of Herrn von Falkenstein—Das Lied von Herrn von Falkenstein
    (song): Brahms
Ballad of the big fat turkeys—Ballade des gros dindons (song): Chabrier
The ballad of the Lord of Falkenstein—Das Lied von Herrn von Falken-
    stein: Brahms
Ballad of the three tailors—Romanze von den drei Schneidern: Himmel
Ballad of the women of Paris—Ballade des femmes de Paris (song): Debussy
Ballad of Villon to his love—Ballade de Villon à s'amie (song): Debussy
The ballad singer—La gioconda: Ponchielli
Ballade de Villon à s'amie (song)—Ballad of Villon to his love: Debussy
Ballade des femmes de Paris (song)—Ballad of the women of Paris/Dames
    of Paris: Debussy

Ballade des gros dindons (song)—Ballad of the big fat turkeys: Chabrier
Ballade des Harfners (song)—The harper's ballad: Schumann
Ballade que Villon fait à la requête de sa mère pour prier Notre-Dame
   (song)—Ballad made at the request of his mother, for a prayer to Our
   Lady/Made by Villon at his mother's request: Debussy
Ballgeflüster—In the ballroom: Meyer-Helmund
Un ballo in maschera (opera)—A masked ball: Verdi
The band of roses—Das Rosenband: Schubert
Bänkelsänger Willie—Rattlin', roarin' Willie: Schumann
A baratinha de papel (A prolé do bêbê)—Little paper bug: Villa-Lobos
Barbe-bleu (operetta)—Bluebeard: Offenbach
The barber of Bagdad—Der Barbier von Bagdad (opera): Cornelius
The barber of Seville—Il barbiere di Siviglia (opera): Rossini
Der Barbier von Bagdad (opera)—The barber of Bagdad: Cornelius
Il barbiere di Siviglia (opera)—The barber of Seville: Rossini
The bard—Der Sänger: Schubert
Der Bardengeist—The spirit bard/The phantom bard: Beethoven
The barefoot lass—Feinsliebchen, du sollst mir nicht barfuss geh'n: Brahms
Der Bärenhäuter—The bearskin: S Wagner
Barmherziges Herze der ewigen Liebe—Fond heart, full of mercy: Bach
Barnets Vaardag—Child's spring day: A Backer-Grøndahl
Barnlige Sanger—Children's songs: Grieg
Baron Magnus—Hertig Magnus: Sibelius
The bartered bride—Prodaná Nevěsta (opera): Smetana
Base and worthless—Tutta rea la vita umana (Scipione): Handel
La basoche (operetta)—King of the students: Messager
The bat—Die Fledermaus (opera): J Strauss II
Batti, batti, O bel Masetto (Don Giovanni)—Strike, O strike/Dearest boy,
   oh do but chide me/Chide me, if you will: Mozart
Battle on the ice—Lyodovoye poboishche (Aleksandr Nevsky): Prokofiev
Battle song—Schlachtgesang: R Strauss
The battleship Potemkin—Bronenosets Potemkin: Chishko
Bauerne Kantate/Mer hahn en neue Oberkeet—Peasant cantata/Village
   gossip: Bach
Bavard et Bavarde (operetta)—The magpies: Offenbach
Be gay—Tout gai!: Ravel
Be glad—Getrost! (Ich freue mich in dir): Bach
Be greeted, ye ladies—Vaer hilset, i Damer: Grieg
Be kind, be kind, I beg you—Pietà, pietà ti chiedo: F Ricci
Be mine—Sei mein! (An Bertha): Cornelius
Be neither grieved nor glad—Non pianger, non gioir: Quaranto
Be not afraid—Fürchte dich nicht, ich bin bei dir (motet): Bach
Be not troubled—Nicht so traurig: Bach
Be silent, host of Hell—Verstumme Höllenheer (Wo soll ich fliehen hin): Ba

Be still—Sei still: Liszt
Be still—Stehe still (Wesendonck Lieder): Wagner
Be still my heart—Sei still mein Herz: Spohr
Be thou contented—Gib dich zufrieden und sei stille: Bach
Be thou welcome, dear friend—Ti riveggo, Fanny (Il castello di Kenilworth):
    Donizetti
Be Thou with me—Bist du bei mir: Bach
Be ye watchful—Vigilate (motet): Byrd
The bear—L'ours [symphony]: Haydn
The bear—Medvěd: Smetana
Bear dance—Medvetánc (Tíz könnyü zongoradarab): Bartók
The bearskin—Der Bärenhäuter: S Wagner
Beata es Virgo—Blessed art thou o Virgin Mary: Handl
Beata viscera (motet)—Happy art thou: Byrd
Beati Estis (motet)—O blessed are ye: Handl
Beati Mortui (motet)—For ever blessed: Mendelssohn
The beating of my own heart—Hirtenmädchens Lied: Kjerulf
The Beatitudes—Die Seligpreisungen:Schein
Beato in ver chi puo—Thrice happy is he who stands: Handel
Béatrice et Bénédict (opera)—Much ado about nothing: Berlioz
Beau le cristal—Fair is the crystal: Lassus
Le beau navire (Petites legendes)—The ship: Milhaud
Beau soir (song)—Beautiful evening: Debussy
Beauteous cradle—Schöne Wiege: Schumann
Beautiful evening—Beau soir (song): Debussy
The beautiful Galatea—Die schöne Galatea (operetta): Suppé
Beautiful Helen—La belle Hélène (operetta): Offenbach
Beauty—Von der Schönheit (Das Lied von der Erde): Mahler
Beauty and the beast—Les entretiens de la belle et de la bête (Ma mère
    l'oye): Ravel
Beauty lately—Questo è il cielo (Alcino): Handel
Because Plaisance is dead—Pour ce que Plaisance est morte (song: Deux
    rondels . . .): Debussy
Because the nightingale's sweet lay—Das Macht, es hat die Nachtigall:
    Meyer-Helmund
Běda, běda, Ubohá, rusalko bledá (Rusalka)—Woe is you, Rusalka: Dvořák
Bedeckt mich mit Blumen (Spanische Liebeslieder)—O deck me with
    flowers/The flower shroud: Schumann
The bee—L'abeille: Godard
Bee's wedding—Spinnerlied: Mendelssohn
Befiehl dem Engel (cantata)—Command thine angel: Buxtehude
Before my fair one's window—Von alten Liebesliedern (part-song): Brahms
Before Thy throne, my God, I stand—Vor deinem Thron tret' ich hermit
    (organ chorale): Bach

Before you vanish—Avant que tu ne t'en ailles . . . (song: La bonne chanson): Fauré

Befreit—Death the releaser/Release: R Strauss

The beggar-maid's song—Lied des Harfenmädchens: M Mayer

The beggar student—Der Bettlerstudent (operetta): Millocker

Beggar's opera—Opernburlesken (opera): Calmus

Beggar's opera—Carneval de Londres/L'opera du Gueux: Milhaud

The beggar's opera—Die Dreigroschenoper: Weill

Begleitungsmusik zu einer Lichtspielszene (orchestral piece)—Accompaniment to a film-scene: Schoenberg

Beglück darf nun dich (Tannhäuser)—Once more with joy/Pilgrims' chorus: Wagner

Beglückte Heerde (Du Hirte Israel, höre)—Ye happy flock/Oh, blessed flock: Bach

Beglückter Stand getreuer Seelen (chorale)—How blest are they whose faith unshaken: Bach

Begräbnissgesang (chorus)—Funeral hymn/Lord we leave thy servant sleeping: Brahms

Beh! szomoru—Know ye not: Ábrányi

Beharrliche Liebe—Lasting love: Henschel

Der beherrschen der Geister—The ruler of the spirits: Weber

Beherzigung (part-song)—Stout hearted: Brahms

Beherzigung (song)—A lesson learned: Wolf

Behind the garden of Gyula—A gyulai kert alatt: Bartók

Behind the garden of Kertmeg—A kertmegi kert alatt: Bartók

Behold and see—Schauet doch und sehet: Bach

Behold dear God—Schau, lieber Gott: Bach

Behold, O Lord—Respice Domine (motet): Byrd

Behold, O Lord God—Vide Domine afflictionem (motet): Byrd

Behold, the godess—Ecco, la dea si china (Nerone): Boito

Behold the marshes—Laggiù, tra i giunchi di Genesareth: Boito

Behold! the roses are blooming—Nun steh'n die Rosen in Blütte (part-song): Brahms

Behold there—O guarda, guarda: Wolf-Ferrari

Behold thou shalt conceive—Ecce concipies (motet): Handl

Behold Titania—Je suis Titania (Thomas): Thomas

Bei der Linde—Under the lime-tree: R Franz

Bei der Wiege—Cradle song/Slumber song/By the cradle: Mendelssohn

Bei dir sind meine Gedanken—My every thought/With thee: Brahms

Bei einer Tranung (song)—At a wedding: Wolf

Bei Männern (Die Zauberflöte)—The manly heart: Mozart

Bei mir bist du schön—Means that you're grand: Secunda

Bei nächtlicher Weil (part-song)—The Naides: Brahms

Die beiden Grenadiere (song)—The two grenadiers: Schumann

Die beiden Schützen (opera)—The two marksmen: Lortzing
Beim Abscheid—Parting: Brahms
Beim Abscheid zu singen—Parting and meeting: Schubert
Beim Ritt auf dem Knie—The ride on the knee: Brahms
Beim Schlafengehen (song: Vier letzte Lieder)—Going to sleep: R Strauss
Beim Schneewetter—In snowy weather: Reger
Die Bekehrte (song)—Converted/The sad shepherdess/Damon with his flute: Wolf
Bel raggio lusinghier (Semiramide)—Here's hope's consoling ray: Rossini
Belief—Je crois en vous: Berlioz
The bell—La cloche (song): Saint-Saëns
Bell of dawn—Cloche d'aube: Caplet
Bell ringing—Klokkeklang: Grieg
The bell ringer's daughter—Das Glockentürmers Töchterlein: Loewe
Bell song—Où va la jeune Indore (Lakmé): Delibes
The bell that walked—Die wandelnde Glocke: Schumann
Bella mia fiamma—Farewell my beloved: Mozart
Bella vittoria—Lovely kind, and kindly loving: G M Bononcini
La belle fougère—My pretty ferns: Blanchard
La belle Hélène (operetta)—Beautiful Helen/Helen: Offenbach
Les belles vacances (cantata)—Summer holidays: Jacques-Dalcroze
The bells—Les cloches (song)—Debussy
The bells—I bubboli: Masetti
The bells—Kolokola: Rachmaninov
The bells at Speyer—S'leut zu Speyer: Senft
The bells of Geneva—Les cloches de Genève: Liszt
Bells of Marling—Ihr Glocken von Marling (song): Liszt
The bells of morning—Las campanas del almanecer (El amor brujo): Falla
The bells of Strasburg Cathedral—Die Glocken des Strassburger Münsters (cantata): Liszt
The bells of Zlonice—Zlonické Zvony (symphony): Dvořák
Bells through the leaves—Cloches à travers les feuilles: Debussy
The beloved colour—Die liebe Farbe (song: Die schöne Müllerin): Schubert
Beloved Emmanuel, Lord of the righteous—Liebster Immanuel, Herzog der Frommen: Bach
Beloved have no fear—E tanto c'è pericol: Wolf-Ferrari
Beloved Jesus, my desire—Liebster Jesu, mein Verlangen: Bach
Beloved love, our parting—Herzlieblich Lieb, durch Scheiden (part-song): Schoenberg
Beloved soul, thy thoughts withdraw now—O liebe Seele, zieh' die Sinnen: Bach
Beloved swan—Mein lieber Schwan (Lohengrin): Wagner
The beloved voice—Milovany Hlas: Weinberger

Below yonder valley—Da unten im Tale: Brahms
Belsatzar (song)—Belshazzar: Schumann
Belshazzar—Belsatzar (song): Schumann
Ben che mi sprezzi (Tamerlano)—Though now she slight me: Handel
Ben' io sento l'ingrata (Atalanta)—In my bosom a fell fury: Handel
Beneath her window—Zu meiner Laute: Zelter
Beneath the almond tree—Unter dem Mandelbaum (part-song): Henschel
Beneath the branches reclining—Da lieg' ich unter den Bäumen:
     Mendelssohn
Beneath the curtain of the night—Ninfa de ojos brujos: Brito
Beneath the window—Unter'm Fenster: Schumann
Beneath thy leafy shade—Care selve (Atalanta): Handel
Beneath thy window—O sole mio: E Capua
Benedictio et claritas (motet)—Blessing and glory: Byrd
Bénédiction de Dieu dans la solitude—The blessing of God in solitude:
     Liszt
Benumbed—Erstarrung (Die Winterreise): Schubert
Les berceaux (song)—The cradles: Fauré
Berceuse—Oh, ne t'eveille (Jocelyn): Godard
Berceuse—Cradle-song: Rhené-Baton
The bereaved mother—La madre foll: Malipiero
Bereavement—Verlust: F Mendelssohn
Bereitet die Wege—Prepare the way: Bach
Die Berge sind spitz (part-song)—The mountains are cold/The mountains
     are steep: Brahms
Bergerotte Savoysienne (madrigal)—Bonnie lassie, merry maiden: Josquin
Den Bergtekne—The mountain thrall: Grieg
Berherzigung—Reflections: Wolf
The Berlin Requiem—Das Berliner Requiem: Weill
Das Berliner Requiem—The Berlin Requiem: Weill
The berry—Tyteberet: Grieg
Beruhigung—Soothing: Goetz
Bescheidene Liebe—Modest heart: Wolf
Der bescheidene Schäfer—The shy lover: J Marx
Das bescheidene Wünschlein—The modest little wish: Schoeck
Beside a lonely fountain—Au bord d'une fontaine: Bertaud
Beside a spring—Au bord d'une source (Années de pèlerinage): Liszt
Beside a weeping willow tree—Assisa a piè d'un salice (Otello): Rossini
Beside the lake of Nemi—Am grünen See von Nemi: Henschel
Beside the streams of Babylon—An Wasserflüssen Babylon (organ chorale/
     chorale prelude): Bach
Beside thy cradle here I stand—Schant hin! dort liegt im finstern Stall
     (chorale: Weihnachts-Oratorium): Bach

Besos en mis sueños—Kisses in my dreams: A Brandt
The best love letter—Der beste Liebesbrief: Cornelius
The best of all—Ja die schönst: Wolf
Bestanden! (Das Examen)—Passeo!: P Burkhard
Der beste Liebesbrief—The best love letter: Cornelius
Le bestiaire (song cycle)—The book of beasts: Poulenc
Bethlehem—Dans cette étable: Gounod
Betrachte, meine Seel' (Johannes-passion)—Consider, O my soul: Bach
The betrayal—Verrath: Meyer-Helmund
The betrayed secret—Ein verrathenes Geheimniss: Blumenthal
Die betrogene Welt—The cheated world: Mozart
The betrothal—Piosnka litewska: Chopin
Betrothal dance—Der Brauttanz: R Strauss
Betrothal in a priory (monastery)—Obruchenie v monastïre: Prokofiev
Bethothed—Brautung: Reger
Der Bettlerstudent (operetta)—The beggar student: Millöcker
Between two litigants, a third succeeds—Fra i due litiganti il terzo gode:
    Sarti
Bevelise und Lysidor—The phoenix: C P E Bach
Beware—Gebt acht! (part-song): Brahms
Beware—Hüt du dich: Brahms
Beware—Se dig for: Grieg
Beware of the Rhine—Warnung vor dem Rhein: Mendelssohn
The bewitched child—L'enfant et les sortilèges (opera): Ravel
Bewundert, O Menschen, dies grosse Geheimnis (Nun komm, der Heiden
    Heiland)—Marvel, O men, at this great mystery: Bach
Der bezaubernte Knabe (part-song)—The youth enchanted: Henschel
Bezdna—The abyss: Rebikov
La bianca rosa—The white rose: Handel
Il biano e dolce cigno—The gentle swan: Arcadelt
Biblical songs—Biblické písně: Dvořák
Biblické písně—Biblical songs: Dvořák
La biche—The doe: Hindemith
Bid me not utter—Heiss' mich nicht reden: Schubert
Bide with us, for now night is approaching—Bleib' bei uns, denn es will
    Abend werden: Bach
La bien aimée—A girl whose love shines fair: P Cannon
La bien mariée—The merry wife: P Cannon
Bienensegen—Blessing of the bees: J N David
Bild der Nacht—Vision of the night: Curschmann
Bilder des Tods—Portrait of death: Bresgen
Dies Bildnis ist bezaubernd schön (Die Zauberflöte)—O loveliness beyond
    compare: Mozart
Birch—Björken: Sibelius

The birch tree—Ungbirken: Grieg
A bird flies over—Auf dem Schiffe: Brahms
Bird in the air—Vöglein durchrauscht (Liebeslieder waltzes): Brahms
A bird is softly calling—Ich hör' ein Vöglein locken: Mendelssohn
A bird is sweetly singing—Ich hör' ein Vöglein locken: Mendelssohn
A bird sat on an alder bough—Zweigesang: Spohr
Bird, say whither thy flight?—Vöglein, wohin so schnell?: Lassen
The bird that came in spring—La capinera: Benedict
Birdie in the wood—Die Vöglein im Walde: Kreutzer
A birdling flew over the Rhine—Auf dem Schiffe: Brahms
Birdling, whither away?—Vöglein, wohin so schnell?: Lassen
The birds—Gli ucelli: Respighi
The birds—Die Vögel: Schubert
Birds and springs—Les oiseaux et les sources (Messe de la Pentecôte):
  Messiaen
A bird's cry—Der Skreg en fugl: Sinding
Birds swift to change the air—Oiseaux, si tous les ans: Mozart
The bird-seller—Der Vogelhändler: Zeller
A bird-song—En Fugelvise: Grieg
The birth of our Lord—Narozeni páné: Martinů
The birth of sound—Die erste Ton: Weber
Birthday cantata—Was mir behagt: Bach
A birthday greeting—Köszöntö: Kodály
Birthday march—Geburtstagmarsch: Schumann
La bisbetica domata—The taming of the shrew: Castuelnuovo-Tedesco
La bise (Petites légendes)—The north wind: Milhaud
Bisher habt ihr nichts gebeten in meinem Namen—Hitherto have you
  nothing asked in my name: Bach
The bishop of autumn—L'évêque d'autun: Françaix
Bist du! —Soft as the zephyr/Thou art: Liszt
Bist du bei mir—Abide with me/Be thou with me/Come, come my voice/
  If thou art near/Stay, my beloved/If you are there: Bach
A bit tipsy—Kicsit ázottan: Bartók
Biterolf—Weary, with sword in hand: Wolf
Bitte—Request/Invocation/Rest on me thou eye of darkness/Night: R Fran.
Bitte—Petition: J Marx
Bitten—Prayer: Beethoven
Bittendes Kind (Kinderscenen)—Entreating child: Schumann
Bitter terrible remorse—Aspri rimorsi atroci: Mozart
Bitter words—Bitteres zu sagen denkst du: Brahms
Bitteres zu sagen denkst du—Smiles about thy lips are straying/You may
  try to vex or flout me/Bitter words/Fain art thou: Brahms
Die bittre Leidens Zeit—Now is the mournful time: Bach
Bizánc—Byzantium: E Ábrányi

34

Björken—Birch: Sibelius
Blaaveis—Blue flowers/Anemone: A Backer-Grøndahl
Blabaer-li (Haugtussa)—Among the bilberries: Grieg
The Black Cliff—Chorny yar: Pashchenko
The Black Crag—Chorny yar: Pashchenko
Black keys—Touches noires: Milhaud
Black roses—Svarta rosor: Sibelius
The black spider—Die schwartze Spinne: Burkhard
The blackbird—Der schwartze Amsel: Meyer-Helmund
The blacksmith—Der Schmied: Brahms
The blacksmith—Der Hufschmied: Schoeck
The blacksmith of Lesetin—Lešétínský Kovář: Weis
Blacksmith's song—Lied eines Schmiedes: Schumann
Das Blatt in Buche—Memories: Blumenthal
Blätter lässt die Blume fallen—Strews the ground with leaves each flower:
    R Franz
Blätter und Blüten: Leaves and blossoms: Reger
Blaue Augen hat das Mädchen (Spanische Liebeslieder)—Eyes of azure
    hath the maiden: Schumann
Die blaue Mazur—The blue mazurka: Lehár   1971399
Die blauen Frühlingsaugen—The eyes of spring: R Franz
Die blauen Frühlingsaugen/Frühlingslied—The bright blue eyes of spring/
    Spring song/The blue starred eyes of springtime/The sweet blue eyes
    of spring: A Rubinstein
Blauer Sommer—Summer: R Strauss
Bleib' bei uns, denn es will Abend werden—Bide with us, for now night
    is approaching/Stay with us: Bach
Blessed—Gesegnet: Cornelius
Blessed are they—Selig alle: Mozart
Blessed art thou, O virgin Mary—Beata es Virgo: Handl
Blessed be he—Gesegnet sei (Italienisches Liederbuch): Wolf
Blessed be Thy name—Mihi autem nimis: Tallis
The blessed Christ is ris'n today—Erstanden ist der heil'ge Christ (Orgel-
    büchlein): Bach
The blessed damozel—La damoiselle élue: Debussy
Blessed is the man—Selig ist der Mann: Bach
Blessed Jesu, at Thy word—Liebster Jesu, wir sind hier (Orgelbüchlein):
    Bach
Blessed morn, when Jesus was born—Süsser Trost, mein Jesus kommt: Bach
Blessed resurrection day—Seligster Erquickungs-Tag (Wachet, betet, seid
    bereit): Bach
Blessed spirit—Spirito amato (Poro): Handel
Blessing and glory—Benedictio et claritas: Byrd
Blessing, glory, wisdom and thanks—Lob und Ehre und Weisheit und
    Dank: Bach

The blessing of God in solitude—Bénédiction de Dieu dans la solitude: Liszt

Blessing of the bees—Bienensegen: J N David

Blest are they who are persecuted—Selig sind, die Verfolgung leiden (Der Evangelimann): Kienzl

Blest are they who feel compassion—Selig sind, die aus Erbarmen (Brich dem Hungrigen dein Brot): Bach

Blest is he who thinks on Him—Selig, **wer** an Jesum denkt: Bach

Blick' ich umher (Tannhäuser)—When I behold: Wagner

Blicke mir nicht in die Lieder—Do not look at my songs/Look not, love, on my work unended: Mahler

The blind beggars—Les deux aveugles: Offenbach

The blind boy—Der blinde Knabe: Schubert

Blind man's buff—Blinde Kuh: Brahms

Blind man's buff—Hasche-Mann (Kinderscenen): Schumann

Der blinde Knabe—The blind boy: Schubert

Blinde Kuh—Blind man's buff: Brahms

Blindenklage—Lament of the blind: R Strauss

Bliss—Seligkeit: Schubert

The bliss of love—Liebesglück: Wolf

Blissful night—Selige Nacht: J Marx

En blomma stod vid vägen—The wildflower: Sibelius

Blomstersanking—Flower gathering: A Backer-Grøndahl

Blondels Lied—Blondel's song: Schumann

Blondel's song—Blondels Lied: Schumann

The blood of the people—Krov naroda: Dzershinsky

The blood wedding—Die Bluthochzeit: Fortner

Blossom time—Das Dreimäderlhaus: Schubert-Berté

Blue Danube—An der schönen, blauen Donau: J Strauss (II)

The blue eyes of my dear—Die zwei blauen Augen von meinem Schatz (Lieder eines fahrenden Gesellen): Mahler

Blue flowers—Blaaeveis: A Backer-Grøndahl

The blue forest—La forêt bleue: Aubert

The blue mazurka—Die blaue Mazur: Lehár

The blue starred eyes of spring-time—Die blauen Frühlingsaugen: A Rubinstein

Bluebeard—Barbe-bleu: Offenbach

Bluebeard's castle—A Kékszakállu herceg vára: Bartók

The bluebird—L'oiseau bleu: Wolff

Blüh auf, gefrorner Christ—Unfold thou frozen Christ: Wellesz

Die Blume der Ergebung—The flower of resignation: Schumann

Blume und Duft—Flower and fragrance/Flower and scent: Liszt

Eine Blume weiss ich— The healing flower: Goetz

Der Blumenbrief—The flower letter/The flower message/The message of flowers: Schubert

Blumengruss—Flower greeting: Wolf
Der Blumenkranz—The garland/By Celia's arbour: Mendelssohn
Blumenlied—The flower song: Schubert
Der Blumenstrauss—The nosegay: Mendelssohn
Blushing rose buds—Rothe Rosenknospen (Zigeunerlieder): Brahms
The blust'ring winds loud raging—Del minaccia del vento (Ottone): Handel
Die Bluthochzeit—The blood wedding: Fortner
Boat journey—Venematka: Sibelius
A boat on the waves—Der Gynger en baad paa Bølge: Grieg
Bogeyman's coming—Furchtenmachen (Kinderscenen): Schumann
Bohatá milá—The rich sweetheart: Martinů
La Bohème—The Bohemians: Puccini; Leoncavallo
The Bohemians—La Bohème: Puccini; Leoncavallo
Bois épais (Amadis de Gaule)—Sombre grove/Sombre woods/All your
    shades/Forest glade/Gloomy woods: Lully
O boisinho de chumbo (A prolé do bêbê)—The little tin ox: Villa Lobos
Bölcsödal (Dedinské Scény)—Lullaby: Bartók
The bold hunter—Der Kühe: Pfitzner
Boldly and blithely to death—Forte e lieto a morte (Tamerlano): Handel
Bon voyage—Glückliche Reise: Künneke
Bona nox—Hear our call: Mozart
Bondens sang: Peasant's song: Grieg
Bone pastor—Very bread: Palestrina
Bonjour, mon coeur—Good-day, sweetheart: Lassus
La bonne chanson—The good song: Fauré
Bonne humeur—In happy mood: Chaminade
Bonne journée (Tel jour telle nuit)—A good day: Poulenc
The bonnie lad—Sliczny chlópiee: Chopin
The bonnie lad that's far away—Weit, weit (Myrthen): Schumann
Bonnie lassie, merry maiden—Bergerotte Savoysienne: Josquin
A bonny black-eyed maiden—Mir ist ein schönes braun Maidelein: Brahms
The bonny Earl of Murray—Murray's Ermordung: Brahms
The book of beasts—Le bestiaire: Poulenc
The book of the hanging garden—Das Buch der hängenden Garten:
    Schoenberg
Bootgesang—Hail to the chief: Schubert
Le boquet navi (Sancho Pança)—I am but a shepherd maiden: Monsigny
Bordal—Drinking song/Tavern song: Kodály
Born amid the rugged wildwood—Nasce al bosco: Handel
Born today—Hodie Christus natus est: Sweelinck
Børnene leger/Børnene spiller (Moderen)—The children at play: Nielsen
Børnene spiller/Børnene leger (Moderen)—The children at play: Nielsen
Borte! —Departed/Gone: Grieg
Die böse Farbe (Die schöne Müllerin)—The hateful colour: Schubert
Das böse Jahr—The luckless year: Henschel

Die bösen Beinchen—The naughty legs: Blech
Ber Bote—The messenger: R Franz
Die Boten der Liebe—Envoys of love: Brahms
Die Botschaft—King Duncan's daughters: Allitsen
Botschaft—The message: Brahms
Botschaft (Rheinische Lieder)—A message: Cornelius
Botschaft (Albumblätter)—The message: Schumann
Bouře—The tempest: Fibich
La boutique fantasque—The fantastic toyshop: Rossini-Respighi
Bow thine ear—Civitas sancti tui: Byrd
The boy and the bee—Der Knabe und das Immlein: Wolf
The boy who said yes—Der Jasager: Weill
The boy with the magic horn—Der Knabe mit dem Wunderhorn: Schumann
The boy's hunting song—Des Buden Schutzenlied: Schumann
Boy's love—Junggesellenschwur: R Strauss
Bože! Bože! (Biblické Písně)—I will sing new songs: Dvořák
Boží Mulka—The wayside cross: Martinů
The branded—Der Gezeichneten: Schreker
Die Braut—The bride: Brahms
Die Braut—Sad bride: Hanschel
Der Bräutigam—The bridegroom: Brahms
Der Bräutigam und die Birke—The bridegroom and the birch tree:
    Schumann
Brautlieder—Songs of a bride: Cornelius
Brautring—Betrothed: Reger
Ber Brauttanz—Betrothal dance: R Strauss
Bread of the world—O sacrum convivium: Palestrina
Bread, pure angelical—Panis angelicus: Franck
Breadbaking—Cipósütés: Bartók
Break, fairest dawn—Danksei dir, Herr: Handel
Break forth O beauteous heavenly light—Brich an, O schönes Morgenlicht:
    Bach
Break in twain—Brich entzwei, mein armes Herze: Bach
Break the coconut—Quebra o coco, meniuo: Guarnieri
The break-through—Prorïv: Pototsky
The breasts of Tirésias—Les mamelles de Tirésias: Poulenc
Breath of God life giving—Brunquell aller Güter: Bach
Breathe lightly, my lay—Klung' liese, mein Lied: Liszt
Breathless—Soñando: Cobian
Breeze of the night—D'amor sull'alo rosee (Il trovatore): Verdi
Breezes—Brises: F Schmitt
Breit über mein Haupt—Droop o'er my head: R Strauss
Brennessel steht an Weges Rand (Zigeunerlieder): Sparkleth the forge
    near roadside pound: Brahms

Briar-rose—Dornröschen: Abt
The briar rose—Dornröschen (Volkskinderlieder): Brahms
Brich an, O schönes Morgenlicht—Break forth O beauteous heavenly
    light: Bach
Brich dem Hungrigen dein Brot—Give the hungry man thy bread: Bach
Brich entzwei, mein armes Herze—Break in twain: Bach
Bridal chorus—Treulich geführt ziehet dahin (Lohengrin): Wagner
Bridal party on the Hardanger Fjord—Brudefaerdeb I Hardanger: Kjerulf
The bride: Die Braut: Brahms
The bride of Lammermoor—Lucia di Lammermoor: Donizetti
The bride of Messina—Nevêsta Messinská: Fibich
The bridegroom—Der Bräutigam: Brahms
The bridegroom—Narzecsony: Chopin
The bridegroom and the birch tree—Der Bräutigam und die Birke:
    Schumann
Bride's song—Mutter, mutter: Schumann
The bridge—Le pont: Poulenc
The brigands—I masnadieri: Verdi
The brigand's castle—Roverborgen: Kuhlau
Bright and buxom lasses—Mädchen brav un treu (Martha): Flotow
Bright as the moontide—Come raggio di sol: Caldara
The bright blue eyes of spring—Die blauen Frühlingsaugen: A Rubinstein
Bright May now returns—Es kehret der Maien (An die ferne Geliebte):
    Beethoven
Bright object of my adoration—A Louise: Gounod
Bright shines the silver moon—Wie glänzt der helle Mond: Wolf
Bright star of eve—O du mein holder Abendstern (Tannhäuser): Wagner
Bright they sheen—Sieh' wie ist die Welle (Liebeslieder waltzes): Brahms
Brightest and best—O bien-aimé: Massenet
Brightest hope and fairest treasure—Alla vita che t'arride (Un ballo in
    maschera): Verdi
Brillez dans ces beaux lieux (Les éléments)—Shine out in this fair place:
    Destouches
Brilliant butterfly—Charmant papillon (Festes Vénitiennes): Campra
Bring ye to God the honour due Him—Bringet dem Herrn Ehre seines
    Namens: Bach
Bringet dem Herrn Ehre seines Namens—Bring ye to God the honour due
    Him: Bach
Brinquedo de roda—The toy wheel: Villa-Lobos
Brises—Breezes: F Schmitt
Brisk song—Air vif: Poulenc
The broken heart—Verlust: F Mendelssohn
The broken heart—Und wüssten's die Blumen: Schumann
The broken spirit—Il lacerato spirito (Simon Boccanegra): Verdi

The broken voice—Sortunut: Sibelius
Bronenosets Potemkin—The battleship Potemkin: Chishko
The bronze horse—Le cheval de bronze: Auber
The bronze statue—La statue de bronze: Satie
Brooklet—Baekken: Grieg
The brooklet—Quel ruscelletto: Paradisi
Brother devil—Fra diavolo: Auber
Brother good for nothing—Bruder Liederlich: R Strauss
The brother in love—Lo Frate'nnamorato: Pergolesi
Brother Straubinger—Bruder Straubinger: Eysler
Brotherhood—Veljeni vierailla mailla: Sibelius
The brothers' feud—Die feindlichen Brüder: Schumann
The brow like a lost flag—Le front comme un drapeau perdu (Tel jour
    telle nuit): Poulenc
Brudefaerdeb I Hardanger—Bridal party on the Hardanger Fjord: Kjerulf
Bruder liederlich—Brother good for nothing: R Strauss
Bruder Straubinger—Brother Straubinger: Eysler
Brüderlein Fein—Darby and Joan: Fael
Brüderlein und Schwesterlein (Die Fledermaus)—Let's be friends:
    J Strauss (II)
Un bruit de rames—A sound of oars: Rhené-Baton
Brunnensang—The fountain's song: Reger
Brunnquell aller Güter—Breath of God life giving: Bach
Brünstiges verlangen—Ardent longing: J G Ahle
Bryllupsdag pa Troldhaugen—Wedding day at Troldhaugen: Grieg
I bubboli—The bells: Masetti
Das Buch der hängenden Garten—The book of the hanging garden:
    Schoenberg
Der bucklichte Fiedler—The hump-backed fiddler: Brahms
Des Buden Schutzenlied—The boy's hunting song: Schumann
The buffoon—Shut: Prokofiev
Buona figliuola –The good girl: Piccinni
Die Bürgschaft—The pledge/The security: Weill
Burial—Funérailles: Liszt
A burial place—Ein Friedhof: R Franz
The buried past—Die alten, bösen Lieder (Dichterliebe): Schumann
Busslied—Song of repentance: Cornelius
Busslied—Contrition: Beethoven
Busy as a thrush—Min vastas vaataa: Sibelius
But I am poor—Ich aber bin elend: Brahms
But my bird is long in homing—Men min fågel märks dock icke: Sibelius
But one dear face—Nur ein Gesicht auf Erden lebt: Brahms
But the Lord is mindful of His own—Doch der Herr vergisst (Paulus):
    Mendelssohn

But thou didst not leave his soul in hell! —Doch du liessest ihn im Grabe nicht! : Reger

But thou, O my God—Sed tu, Domine: Byrd

Butterflies—Les papillons: Chaminade

The butterflies—Les papillons: Chausson

Butterflies—Der Schmetterling: Schulz

Butterflies—Papillons: Schumann

The butterfly—Schmetterling: Cornelius

Butterfly—Sommerfugl: Grieg

The butterfly—Der Schmetterling: Schubert

Butterfly—Schmetterling: Schumann

The butterfly on a forget-me-not—Der Schmetterling auf einem Vergiss-meinnicht: F X Mozart

Butterfly's entrance—Entrata di Butterfly (Madama Butterfly): Puccini

The butterfly's fallen in love—Der Schmetterling ist in die Rose verliebt: R Franz

By a lonely forest path—Auf geheimem Waldespfade: Griffes

By Celia's arbour—Der Blumenkranz: Mendelssohn

By moonlight—Mondnacht: Schumann

By summer sea—Am Strande: Brahms

By the banks of the Tiber—Alla riva del Tebro: Palestrina

By the brook—Langs en å: Grieg

By the brook in spring—Am Bach im Frühling: Schubert

By the cradle—Bei der Wiege: Mendelssohn

By the cypresses at the Villa d'Este—Aux cyprès de la villa d'Este (Années de pèlerinage): Liszt

By the fireside—Am Kamin (Kinderscenen): Schumann

By the fountain—Am Springbrunnen: Schumann·

By the lake—Am See: Cornelius

By the riverside—Langs en å: Grieg

By the sea—Das Meer: Blumenthal

By the sea—Am Meer (Schwanengesang): Schubert

By the stream—Am Strome: Schubert

By the waters of Babylon—An Wasserflüssen Babylon: Bach

By the waters of Babylon—An Babels Wasserflüssen: Cornelius

By the waters of Babylon—Při řekách Babylonských (Biblické Písné): Dvořák

By the window—Vor dem Fenster: Brahms

By this falchion lightning-garnished—Dal fulgor di questa spada (Guilio Cesare): Handel

By waters mighty—Nad woda wielka: Paderewski

By way of warning—Zur Warnung: Wolf

By your lovely hand—Per questa bella mano: Mozart

Bygone days—Entschwundene Tage: Kjerulf

Byzantium—Bizánc: E Ábrányi

41

C

El caballito (Canciones de niños)—The little horse: Revueltas

La cabane sur des pattes de poule (Tableaux d'une exposition)—The hut on fowl's legs: Mussorgsky

O cachorrinho de borracha (A prolé do bêbê)—Little rubber dog: Villa Lobos

Cäcilie—Cecily: R Strauss

Cäcilien-Walzer—Cecily waltz: J Strauss (I)

The caged nightingale—Trostlos schluchzet Philomele (Zaïde): Mozart

La calandria—The lark: Gerhard

Call and implore the heavens—Ruft und fleht den Himmel an (Christen, ätzet diesen Tag): Bach

Call from the mountain—Ruf vom Berge: Beethoven

Call of the woods—Schlummerlied: Schubert

Call to remembrance, O Lord—Memento Domine: Byrd

Call to the dance—Tanzlied: Schumann

Call to Thy remembrance, Lord—Recordare Domini: Byrd

El callejón—The narrow street: J Berger

Calm and silent—En sourdine (Fêtes galantes): Debussy

Calm and tranquil lie the sheepfolds—Schafe könen sicher weiden: Bach

Calm at sea—Meeresstille: R Franz

Calm at sea—Meeres stille: Schubert

Calm, friendly shade—Ombra mai fù (Serse): Handel

Calm in slumber—Come è bello (Lucrezia Borgia): Donizetti

Calm is the glassy ocean—Placido è il mar (Idomeneo): Mozart

The calm of evening reigns—Die Abendschlümmer umarmt die Flur (Der Rose Pilgerfahrt): Schumann

Calm repose, contentment smiling—Nel riposo e nel contento (Deidemia): Handel

A calm sea and a prosperous voyage—Meeresstille und glückliche Fahrt: Beethoven

La campana sommersa—The sunken bell: Respighi

Las campanas del almanecer (El amor brujo)—The bells of morning: Falla

Il campanello di notte—The night bell: Donizetti

Il campiello—The piazza: Wolf-Ferrari

O camundongo de massa (A prolé do bêbê)—Little toy mouse: Villa Lobos

Can it be he—Ah, fors' è lui (La traviata): Verdi

Can y crud—Cradle song: W S G Williams

Canción de cuna (Canciones de niños)—Cradle song: Revueltas

Canción de la gitana habilidosa—Song of the clever gypsy girl: Castel

Canción del fuego fatuo (El amor brujo)—Song of the will-o'-the-wisp: Falla

Canción picaresca—Roguish song: Palomino

Canción tonto (Canciones de niños)—Nonsense song: Revueltas

Canciones amatorias—Seven last songs: Granados
Canciones de niños—Songs of childhood: Revueltas
Cangio d'aspetto (Admeto)—How changed the vision/My heart is beating/
My soul awakens: Handel
Canso de Nadál—The Christmas rose: Alió
Canst thou scorn—Ah! mio cor! (Alcina): Handel
Cantando un día—Laurinda sang one day: Clari
Cantar sin ilusión—Make love with a guitar: Grever
Cantata about the fatherland—Kantata o rodine: Arutyunyan
Cantata misericordium—Cantata of mercy: Britten
Cantata of mercy—Cantata misericordium: Britten
Cantata profana—A kilenc csodaszarvas: Bartók
Cantata secularis—The four seasons: Seiber
Une cantate de Noël—A Christmas cantata: Honegger
Cantate Domine—O sing unto the Lord/With voice of melody: Byrd
Cantate Domino canticum novum—O sing ye unto the Lord: Schütz
Cante, cante, fiette—O sing, fair maid: Bimboni
Cántec de ploaie oriental—Japanese rain song: Daia
La canterina—The songstress: Haydn
Canti di prigionia—Prison songs: Dallapiccola
The canticle of creation—Le cantique des créatures de Saint François:
Inghebrecht
Cantiga ingenua—When you peer into my heart: Coelho
Cantique à l'épouse—Song of praise to a wife: Chausson
Cantique d'amour—Hymn of love: Liszt
Le cantique des créatures de Saint François—The canticle of creation:
Inghelbrecht
Il canto sospeso—The interrupted song: Nono
The cantor of St Thomas Church—A Tamás templon karnagya: E Ábrányi
Canzone del salice (Otello)—The willow song: Verdi
Canzone di Natale—Christmas lullaby: Bimboni
La campinera—The wren/Tom-tit/The bird that came in spring: Benedict
Captain Dreadnaught—Der Schreckenberger: Wolf
The captain's wife—Hauptmanns Weib: Schumann
La captive—The captive maid: Berlioz
The captive maid—La captive: Berlioz
Captive tho' my soul is pining—Prigioniera ho l'alma in pena (Rodelinda):
Handel
The capture of Troy—La prise de Troie: Berlioz
Capulets and Montagues—I Capuletti ed I Montecchi: Bellini
I Capuletti ed I Montecchi—Capulets and Montagues/Romeo and Juliet:
Bellini
Cara e lieta giovantù (Il ritorno d'Ulisse)—Well-beloved and happy time:
Monteverdi

43

Cara sposa (Radamisto)—Cease from grieving: Handel
Cara sposa (Rinaldo)—Dearest consort/Dear companion/Dearest love: Handel
Cara ti lascio il core—Darling I leave my heart: L Leo
Card game—Jeu de cartes: Stravinsky
Care selve (Alalanta)—Come beloved/Beneath thy leafy shade/Lovely woodland/Charming woodlands: Handel
Il carillon magico—The magic chime: Pick-Mangiagalli
Carnaval de Londres/L'opera du gueux—Beggar's opera: Milhaud
Le carnaval des animaux—Carnival of the animals: Saint-Saëns
Carnaval romain—Roman carnival: Berlioz
Carnival fairy—Die Faschingsfee: Kálmán
Carnival in Rome—Der Karneval in Rom: J Strauss (II)
Carnival jest from Vienna—Fanschingsschwank aus Wien: Schumann
Carnival of the animals—Le carnaval des animaux: Saint-Saëns
Carnaval romain—Roman carnival: Berlioz
Caro mio ben—Fair is my love/Deep in my heart/Rose, lovely flower/Dearest from thee/Turn once again/Heart of my heart/Come happy spring/Come once again/Queen of my heart/Star of my soul/Thou all my bliss/Parted from thee: Giordani
Caro nome (Rigoletto)—Dearest name: Verdi
Caro voi siete all'alma (Serse)—Dearest of all men chosen: Handel
The carp—La carpe (Le bestiaire): Poulenc
La carpe (Le bestiaire)—The carp: Poulenc
The Carpathians—Karpaty: Kostenko
The carrier dove—Die Taubenpost (Schwanengesang): Schubert
The carrier pigeon—Die Taubenpost (Schwanengesang): Schubert
The Carthusian monastery—La chartreuse de Parme: Sauget
Casta diva, che inargenti (Norma)—Goddess fairest: Bellini
The castle by the sea—Das Schloss am Meere: R Strauss
Castles in the air—Frau Luna: Lincke
Cat and dog—Hund und Katz: Meyer-Helmund
Catch-as-catch-can—Hasche-mann (Kinderscenen): Schumann
Catch me (if you can)—Hasche-mann (Kinderscenen): Schumann
La cathédrale engloutie—The engulfed cathedral: Debussy
The Caucasus—Kaukaz: Lejudkevych
Le cauchemar—The nightmare: Françaix
The cavalier of the rose—Der Rosenkavalier: R Strauss
Cavaliers of Artois—Gentils galants de France: Meister
O cavalinho de páu (A prolé do bêbê)—The little wooden horse: Villa Lobos
Cavalleria rusticana—Rustic chivalry: Mascagni
Ce moys de mai, ma verte cotte—When May displays her flowers: Jannequin
Ce qu'a vu le vent d'ouest—What the west wind saw: Debussy

Ce que j'aime—What I love: Rhené-Baton
Ce que je suis sans toi—Without thee!: Gounod
Cease, oh cease—O cessate di piargarmi: A Scarlatti
Cease, oh maiden—O cessate di piargarmi: A Scarlatti
Cease then to give me sorrow—Resta di darmi moia: Gesualdo
Cease your bitter weeping—Semmit ne bánkodjal: Kodály
La cecchina—The good girl: Piccinni
Cecily—Cäcilie: R Strauss
Cecily waltz—Cäcilien-walzer: J Strauss (I)
Cedan l'antiche—Thou queen of all the world: Marenzio
The celebration of spring—Frühlingsfeier: Mendelssohn
Celeste Aida (Aida)—Heavenly Aida: Verdi
Celo tropical—Jealous moon: Grever
Celý svět nedá ti (Rusalka)—Ne'er the world will give you peace/Song of
    the water-gnome: Dvořák
Le cena delle beffe—The feast of the jest: Giordano
Cendrillon—Cinderella: Delannoy
Cendrillon—Cinderella: Massenet
La cenerentola—Cinderella: Rossini; Wolf-Ferrari
Un cenno leggiadretto (Serse)—A gesture with discretion: Handel
Cent esclaves ornaient (Gulistan)—A hundred lovely slaves: Dalayrac
Les cents vierges—The hundred virgins: Lecocq
Čert a Káča—Kate and the devil/The devil and Kate: Dvořák
Certain coucou (Le judgement de Midas)—The cuckoo-bird: Grétry
Certain Frenchmen—De quelques français: Françaix
Ces airs joyeux (L'enfant prodigue)—What joyous airs: Debussy
C'est ainsi que tu es—It is thus that you are: Poulenc
C'est bien l'air (L'étoile du nord)—That's the tune: Meyerbeer
C'est grande fête (Fra Diavolo)—Hail festal morning: Auber
C'est l'Espagne (Les bavards)—In the south: Offenbach
C'est l'extase (Ariettes oubliées)—It is ecstasy: Debussy
C'est l'extase—It is ecstasy: Fauré
C'est l'histoire amoureuse (Manon Lescaut)—Laughing song: Auber
C'est une fleur sauvage/Sérénade—Wildflower: Pierné
Cesta k milé—Journey to the beloved: Martinů
Cesta k ráji—The way to paradise: Martinů
Chain, circle and mirror—Kette, Kreis und Spiegel: Křenek
Chalamti chalom—I've dreamed a dream: Lavry
Le chaland qui passe—Love's last word is spoken: Bixio
Chalet girl's Sunday—Saeterjentens Söntag: Bull
Ch'ami la vita mia—In thy sweet name: Bertani
Chamber symphony—Kammersymphonie: Schoenberg
Les champs—To the fields: Berlioz
La chance (Petites légendes)—Luck: Milhaud

Le chanoin Recupëro—The confession: Françaix
Chanson—A song: Poulenc
Chanson à boire (Don Quichotte à Dulcinée)—Drinking song: Ravel
Chanson arabe—Arabian song: Gobard
Chanson au pêcheur—Song of the fisherman: Fauré
Chanson d'avril: Song of April: Bizet
Chanson de la mariée/Le reveille de la mariée—Wake up, my dear: Ravel
Chanson de la nuit durable—Song of the endless night: Séverac
Chanson de la sorcière (Mireille)—Now's the time to love: Gounod
Chanson de mer—E'en as the sea: Aubert
Chanson des cueilleuses de lentisques—Song of the lentisk-gatherers: Ravel
La chanson des près—The song o' green fields: Godard
Chanson d'Orkenise—Song of Orkenise: Poulenc
Chanson du berger—Shepherd's song: Godard
Chanson du printemps—Song of springtime: Gounod
Chanson épique (Don Quichotte à Dulcinée)—Epic song: Ravel
Chanson espagnole—Spanish love-song: Chaminade
Chanson perpétuelle—Song without end: Chausson
Chanson pour Jeanne—Song for Jeanne: Chabrier
Chanson pour le petit cheval—Song of the little bay horse: Séverac
Chanson romanesque (Don Quichotte à Dulcinée)—Romanesque song:
    Ravel
Chanson slave—Slav song: Chaminade
Chanson triste—Sorrowful song/Song of solace: Duparc
Chansons de Bilitis—Songs of Bilitis: Debussy
Chant hindou—Hindoo song: Bemberg
Chant of the priestess of Apollo—Gesang der Apollopriesterin: R Strauss
Chant provençal—Provençal song: Massenet
Chant vénitien—A song of Venice: Bemberg
Le chapelier—The mad hatter: Satie
The charcoal-wife is drunken—Köhlerweib ist trunken: Wolf
The charge—Auftrage: Cornelius
The charm—Le charme: Chausson
Charmant oiseau (La perle du Brésil)—Thou charming bird: F David
Charmant papillon (Festes vénitiennes)—Brillant butterfly: Campra
Le charme—The charm: Chausson
Le charme (Petites légendes)—The spell: Milhaud
Charming airs and loveliness—Etre jolie, être belle: Meister
The charming flower—Schön Blümelein: Schumann
Charming woodlands—Care selve (Atalanta): Handel
La chartreuse de Parme—The Carthusian monastery: Sauguet
La chasse [symphony]—The hunt: Haydn
Chasse-neige—Snow-drift: Liszt
Le chasseur maudit—The accursed hunter: Franck
Le chasseur maudit—Arthur's chase: Liszt

Che dissi? (Otello)—What said I?: Rossini

Che faro senza Euridice? (Orfeo ed Euridice)—What is life to me without thee?/What shall I do without Eurydice?: Gluck

Che fiero costume—Oh! love thou art cruel/With cunning conniving/How void of passion: Legrenzi

Che poi ch'a mortal rischio—Now past, the deadly peril: Erlebach

Che puro ciel (Orfeo ed Euridice)—What pure sky: Gluck

Che sento o dio (Giulio Cesare)—Thy sentence: Handel

Che splendor de'luminosi rai—O radiant glory: Palestrina

Che tua madre (Madama Butterfly)—That your mother should take you: Puccini

The cheated world—Die betrogene Welt: Mozart

The cheerful sunbeams glisten—Die helle Sonne leuchtet: R Franz

Cheerfulness—Heiterkeit: Mozart

Ch'ella mi creda (La fanciulla del West)—Let her believe: Puccini

Cher objet de ma pensée (Aucassin et Nicolette)—Heart of hearts: Grétry

Cherv-Pobeditel—The conqueror worm: Gniessin

The chestnut—Der Nussbaum: Schumann

Le cheval de bronze—The bronze horse: Auber

Chevaux de bois (Ariettes oubliées)—Merry-go-round: Debussy

La chevelure (Chansons de Bilitis)—The tresses of hair: Debussy

La chèvre de Thibet (Le bestiaire)—The goat from Tibet: Poulenc

Chi in amore (Amore traditore)—He who still loveth: Bach (?)

Chi sà, chi sà, qual sia—Who knows my swain's affliction: Mozart

Chi scherza colle rose (Imeneo)—Who plays among the roses: Handel

Chi vuol la zingarella (I zingari in Fiera)—Who wants the gipsy-maiden: Paisiello

Chiamo il mio ben così (Orfeo ed Euridice)—Thus I call my beloved: Gluck

Chide me, if you will—Batti, batti, O bel Masetto (Don Giovanni): Mozart

The child—Das Kind: Cornelius

The child and the sorceries—L'enfant et les sortilèges: Ravel

The child and witchcraft—L'enfant et les sortilèges: Ravel

Child falling asleep—Kind im einschlummern (Kinderscenen): Schumann

A child is born in Bethlehem—Puer natus in Bethlehem: Bach

Child voices—Kinderstimmen: Fielitz

Childhood of Christ—L'enfance du Christ: Berlioz

The children at play—Børnene leger (Moderen): Nielsen

Children of the king—Königskinder: Humperdinck

The children's crusade—La croisade des enfants: Pierné

Children's desire for spring—Sehnsucht nach dem Frühling: Mozart

Children's folk-songs—Volkskinderlieder: Brahms

Children's games—Jeux d'enfants: Bizet

Children's party—Kindergesellschaft: Schumann

Children's play—Das Kinderspiel: Mozart

Children's pleasures—Das Kinderspiel: Mozart
The children's prayer—Des Kindes Gebet: Reger
Children's rhymes—Rikadla: Janáček
A child's dream—Traum eines Kinds: Schumann
A child's prayer—Kindergebet: Blech
A child's smile—Kinderslächen: Reger
Child's spring day—Barnets Vaardag: A Backer-Grøndahl
The chimes of Normandy—Les cloches de Corneville: Planquette
Chimes ring out the moment longed for—Schlage doch, gewünschte
    Stunde: Bach
The Chinese—Le Cinesi: Gluck
Chinese love songs—Chinesische Liebeslieder: Liebermann
Chinese suite—Kitaiskiye syuity: Vasilenko
Chinesische Liebeslieder—Chinese love songs: Liebermann
Ch'io mai vi possa (Siroe)—How could I ever: Handel
The chocolate soldier—Der tapfere Soldat: Straus
Chodníček—The footpath: Martinů
Les choéphores—The libation bearers: Milhaud
Choeur des matelots—Far o'er the bay: Franck
The choice—Nò, nò, nò, non voglio: Steffani
Chorny yar—The black crag/The black cliff: Pershchenko
Chorus of the dead—Choro di morti: Petrassi
Les choses visibles et invisibles (Messe de la Pentecôte)—Things visible
    and invisible: Messiaen
The Christ Child shall be still my hope—Das Jesulein soll doch mein
    Trost: Bach
Christ, der du bist der helle Tag—O Christ, Thou art our lamp and light:
    Bach
Christ der du bist der helle Tag [chorale partita]—O Christ, Thou art the
    light of day: Bach
Christ is my life—Christus, der ist mein Leben: Bach
Christ is risen—Christ ist erstanden (Orgelbüchlein): Bach
Christ ist erstanden (Orgelbüchlein)—Christ is risen: Bach
Christ lag in Todesbanden [cantata]—Christ lay in death's dark prison:
    Bach
Christ lag in Todesbanden (Orgelbüchlein)—In death's strong grasp the
    Saviour lay: Bach
Christ lay in death's dark prison—Christ lag in Todesbanden [cantata]:
    Bach
Christ on the Mount of Olives—Christus am Oelberge: Beethoven
Christ our helper and life giver—Jesus unser Trost und Leben: Bach
Christ our hope and comfort! —Christe, aller Welt Trost: Bach
Christ the friend of children—Christus der Kinderfreund (Weihnachts-
    lieder): Cornelius

Christ, unser Herr, zum Jordan kam—To Jordan's stream came Christ our
　　Lord: Bach
Christ who art the light and day—Christe qui lux es et dies: Byrd
Christbaum (Weihnachtslieder)—Christmas tree: Cornelius
The Christ-child—Christkind (Weihnachtslieder): Cornelius
The Christchild asleep—Schlafendes Jesuskind: Wolf
Christe, aller Welt Trost—Christ our hope and comfort!: Bach
Christe, du Lamm Gottes (Orgelbüchlein)—Lamb of God, our Saviour:
　　Bach
Christe Jesu pastor bone—O Christ Jesus, loving shepherd: Taverner
Christe qui lux es et dies—Christ who art the light and day: Byrd
Christen, ätzet diesen Tag—Christians [en]grave ye this glad day: Bach
Christi Glieder, ach bedenket (Bereitet die Wege)—Members of Christ, ah,
　　consider: Bach
Christian, never let sin o'erpower thee—Widerstehe doch, der Sünde: Bach
Christians be joyful—Jauchzet, froh locket (Weihnachts-Oratorium): Bach
Christians, [en]grave ye this glad day—Christen, ätzet diesen Tag: Bach
Christkind (Weihnachtslieder)—The Christ-child: Cornelius
A Christmas cantata—Une cantate de Noël: Honegger
Christmas carol—Weihnachtslied: Schumann
Christmas carol for homeless children—Noël des enfants qui n'ont plus de
　　maisons: Debussy
Christmas carol of the children who have no homes—Noël des enfants qui
　　n'ont plus de maisons: Debussy
Christmas dance of the shepherds—Karácsoyi pásztortánc: Kodály
Christmas eve—Noeh pered Rozhdestvom: Rimsky-Korsakov
Christmas lullaby—Canzone di Natale: Bimboni
Christmas night—Christnacht: Wolf
Christmas oratorio—Weihnachtsoratorium: Bach
The Christmas rose—Canso de Nadál: Alió
Christmas snow—Julesne: Grieg
Christmas song—Sang til Julestraeet: Grieg
A Christmas song—Shchedryk: Leontovych
Christmas song—Joululaulu: Sibelius
Christmas songs—Weihnachtslieder: Cornelius
The Christmas story—Historia von der Geburt Jesu Christi: Schütz
Christmas tree—Christbaum (Weihnachtslieder): Cornelius
Christmas tree: Weihnachtsbaum: Liszt
Christnacht: Christmas night: Wolf
Christum wir sollen loben schon—Now must we Jesus laud and sing/Lord
　　Christ we now Thy praises sing: Bach
Christus am Oelberge [cantata]—Christ on the Mount of Olives/Mount of
　　Olives/Engedi: Beethoven
Christus, der ist mein Leben—My life is hid in Jesus/O Christ, my all in
　　living/Christ is my life: Bach

Christus der Kinderfreund (Weihnachtslieder)—Christ the friend of children: Cornelius
Christus, der uns selig macht—He, whose life was as the light: Bach
Christus, der uns selig macht (Orgelbüchlein)—See the Lord of life and light: Bach
Christus e miserere—Go not far from me, O God: Zingarelli
Christus resurgens ex mortius—Christ being raised from the dead: Byrd
Chudoba (Moravské dvojzpěvy)—The silken band: Dvořák
Church windows—Vetrate di chiesa: Respighi
La chute de la maison Usher—The fall of the house of Usher: Debussy
Chvalozpěv—The hymn of praise: Vycpalek
Ciascun lo dice (La fille du régiment)—None can gainsay it: Donizetti
Cibulička—The little onion: Smetana
The cicada—La cigale: Chausson
The cicadas—Les cigales: Chabrier
Le ciel est, par-dessus le toit—In prison: Séverac
Ciel pietoso, ciel clemente (Zelmira)—Powers eternal: Rossini
Cielo azul—Skies are blue: Longás
Cielo e mar! (La gioconda)—Heaven and ocean: Ponchielli
La cigale—The cicada: Chausson
La cigale et la fourmi—The grasshopper and the ant: Audran
Les cigales—The cicadas: Chabrier
Cigánské melodie—Gypsy songs: Dvořák
Il cimento dell'armonia e dell'inventione—The trial of harmony and invention: Vivaldi
Las cinco horas (Canciones de niños)—The five hours: Revueltas
Cinderella—Aschenbrödel: Abt/Reinecke
Cinderella—Cendrillon: Delannoy
Cinderella—Cendrillon: Massenet
Cinderella—Zolushka: Prokofiev
Cinderella—La cenerentola: Rossini/Wolf-Ferrari
The cinema-star—Die Kino-Königen: Gilbert
Le Cinesi—The Chinese: Gluck
Les cinq doigts—The five fingers: Françaix
Cipósütés—Breadbaking: Bartók
Cirandas—Rounds: Villa-Lobos
El círculo mágico (El amor brujo)—The magic circle: Falla
Circumdederunt me—The snares of death: Byrd
The circus princess—Die Zirkusprinzessin: Kálmán
The citadel—Die Zwingburg: Křenek
The cither—An die Laute: Schubert
Civet à toute vitesse (La bonne cuisine)—Rabbit at top speed: Bernstein
Civitas sancti tui—Bow thine ear: Byrd
Claire de lune (Fêtes galantes)—Light of the moon/Moonlight: Debussy

Claire de lune—Moonlight: Fauré
The clandestine marriage—Il matrimonio segreto: Cimarosa
Clara's song—Freudvoll und Leidvoll: Liszt
Classical symphony—Klassicheskaya simfoniya: Prokofiev
Clavierübung—Keyboard practice: Bach
Clear streams—Svetly ruchey: Shostakovich
The clemency of Titus—La clemenza di Tito: Mozart
La clemenza di Tito—The clemency of Titus: Mozart
Cleopatra's night—Une nuit de Cleopatra: H Hadley
The climax—Ende vom Lied (Fantasiestücke): Schumann
The cloak—Il tabarro: Puccini
La cloche—The bell: Saint-Saëns
Cloche d'aube—Bell of dawn: Caplet
Les cloches—The bells: Debussy
Cloches à travers les feuilles—Bells through the leaves: Debussy
Les cloches de Corneville—The chimes of Normandy: Planquette
Les cloches de Genève—The bells of Geneva: Liszt
The clock—Die Uhr: Loewe
Cloclo—The song of Provence: Lehár
Cloister—Cloître: F Schmitt
Cloître—Cloister: F Schmitt
Close both my eyes: Schleisse mir die Augen beide: Berg
Close, o close my eyes at parting—Schliess mir die Augen beide: Berg
Close, tired eyes—Schlummer ein, ihr matten Augen (Ich habe genug): Bach
Close to my heart—Apegado a mí: Guastavino
Close to this dark grotto—Auprès de cette grotte sombre (Le promenoir
    des deux amants): Debussy
Closely wrapped in murky vapours—Eingehüllt in graue Wolken: Grieg
Cloud cuckoo land—Vom Schlaraffenland: Schubert
The cloudlet—Das Wölklein: Reger
Clouds and darkness—Oblak a mrákota (Biblické Písně): Dvořák
Clouds may rise—Sorge infausta (Orlando): Handel
Clouds that o'er the mountain—Diese Wolken (An die ferne Geliebte):
    Beethoven
Cloudy heights of Tatra—Dejte klec jestřábu (Cigánské melodie): Dvořák
Clover—Kleeblätter: d'Arba
Clowns—Pagliacci: Leoncavallo
Clown's song—Schusslied des Narren: Schumann
The coachman of Longjumeau—Le postillion de Longjumeau: Adam
The coat-of-arms—Das Wappenschild: Schoenberg
A coaxing kitten—Schmeichelkätzchen: Reger
Cock up your beaver—Der Rekrut: Schumann
The cocquette—Se tu m'ami: Pergolesi
Coeli enarrant—The heavens declare: Saint-Saëns

Coeur en péril—Heart in danger: Roussel
Le coeur et la main—With heart and hand/Incognito: Lecocq
Coffee cantata—Schweight, stille, plauderte nicht: Bach
Col partir—Since we parted: Handel
Colas Breugnon—Master iz Klamsi: Kabalevsky
Cold winter, villain that thou art—Yver, vous n'estes qu'un villain
    (Chansons de Charles d'Orléans): Debussy
Le colibri—The humming bird: Chausson
Colla bocca e non cole nore (La finta semplice): Love likes courting:
    Mozart
Collier's wife is drunk—Köhlerweib ist trunken: Wolf
Les collines d'Anacapri—The hills of Anacapri: Debussy
Colloque sentimentale (Fêtes galantes)—Colloquy/Sentimental colloquy:
    Debussy
Colloquy—Colloque sentimentale (Fêtes galantes): Debussy
La colombe—The pet dove: Gounod
Colombine—Kolombine: J Marx
Come—Viens: Godard
Come—Viens!: Saint-Saëns
Come alla tortorella (Atalanta)—Like as the love-lorn turtle: Handel
Come away, come away, death!—Komm herbei, komm herbei, Tod!:
    Brahms
Come away, death—Kom nu hit Död: Sibelius
Come back again, my dear—Ritorna, o cara e dolce (Rodelinda): Handel
Come back to Sorrento—Torna a Surriento: E de Curtis
Come beloved—Care selve (Atalanta): Handel
Come, child, beside me—Komm, lass uns spielen: Bleichmann
Come, come my voice—Bist du bei mir: Bach
Come è bello (Lucrezia Borgia)—Calm in slumber/Rest in peace: Donizetti
Come fuggir per selv' ombrosae—How may I fly: Marenzio
Come gentle death—Komm süsser Tod: Bach
Come gentle night—O fraîche nuit: Franck
Come, gentle sleep—Du bist die Ruh': Schubert
Come gladsome spring—Ombra mai fù (Serse): Handel
Come, God, Creator, Holy Ghost—Komm, Gott, Schöpfer, Heiliger Geist:
    Bach
Come happy spring—Caro mio ben: Giordani
Come here, birdie dear—Fecském édes fecském: Erkel
Come hither—Au marche (La muette de Portici): Auber
Come, Holy Ghost, Creator come—Komm, Gott, Schöpfer, heiliger Geist:
    Bach
Come, Holy Spirit, come apace—Komm, heiliger Geist, Herre Gott: Bach
Come in my dreams—Oh, quand je dors: Liszt
Come innocente Giovane (Anna Bolena)—O, for one hour: Donizetti

Come, Jesu, come—Komm, Jesu, komm: Bach
Come, Jesus, come to Thy church—Komm, Jesu, komm zu deine Kirche
    (Nun komm, der Heiden Heiland): Bach
Come kindly death—Komm, süsser Tod, komm, sel'ge Ruh': Bach
Come let me prove thee—Vedrai carimo, se sei buonino (Don Giovanni):
    Mozart
Come let us all this day—Komm, Seelen! dieser Tag: Bach
Come let us go up to Jerusalem—Sehet, wir geh'n hinauf gen Jerusalem:
    Bach
Come let us lift up our hearts—Levemus corda: Byrd
Come let us sing—Sus, egayons nous an Seigneur: Le Jeune
Come let us to the bagpipe's sound—Wir gehn nun wo der Tudelsack (Mer
    hahn en neue Oberkeet): Bach
Come Lord, direct my feeble will—Nun Herr, regiere meinen Sinn (Der
    Friede sei mit dir): Bach
Come love, be mine—Lasciati amar: Leoncavallo
Come mai creder deggio (Don Giovanni)—I can scarce comprehend it:
    Mozart
Come, make my heart Thy home—Komm in mein Herzenhaus (Ein feste
    Burg ist unser Gott): Bach
Come, my love to me—Viens, mon bienaimé: Chaminade
Come, my spirit, come exalt—Meine Seele rühmt und preist: Bach
Come now, turn now—Vieni, torna, idolo mio (Teseo): Handel
Come, O sweet companion—Kume, kum, Geselle min: Haselböck
Come once again—Caro mio ben: Giordani
Come open your window—Deh vieni all finestra (Don Giovanni): Mozart
Come out, my dearest—Le retour des promis: Dessauer
Come per me sereno (La sonnambula)—Ne'er did the day seem fairer/Oh!
    love, this soul beguiling: Bellini
Come raggio di sol—Like as a silver stream/As a sunbeam at morn/As rays
    of setting sun/As when a sunny beam rests/Bright as the noontide/Like
    to a ray of sun/As on the swelling wave: Caldara
Come redeemer of our race—Nun komm, der Heiden Heiland (Schwingt
    freudig euch empor) [cantata]: Bach
Come rejoice ye faithful—Freue dich, erlöste Schar: Bach
Come sereno è il di (Bianca e Falliero)—Welcome, thou longed for day:
    Rossini
Come sons of the free! —Freiwillige her!: Brahms
Come soon—Komm bald: Brahms
Come soothing death—Komm, süsser Tod, komm, sel'ge Ruh': Bach
Come summer night—O komme, holde Sommernacht: Brahms
Come sweet death—Komm süsser Tod: Bach
Come sweet morning—Viens aurore: A L(ehmann)
Come sweetest death—Komm, süsser Tod, komm, sel'ge Ruh': Bach

Come, the lawns are green—Viens, les gazons sont verts: Gounod
Come then, O holy breath of God—Dunque divin sporacolo: Palestrina
Come thou, blessed hour—Komm, du süsse Todesstunde: Bach
Come, thou lovely hour of dying—Komm, du süsse Todesstunde: Bach
Come, throw your mantilla around you with grace—Hüll in die Mantilla
    dich fester ein: D'Albert
Come to me, soothing sleep—Vieni o figlio (Ottone): Handel
Come to the land—Artsah Alinu (Shire' Chalutzim): Binder
Come with flowers—Hyménée, ta journée (Guillaume Tell): Rossini
Come with me—Vieni, deh, vien, la notte è placida: Catalani
Come with me, fairest—Wechsellied zum Tanze: Brahms
Come, ye playmates—Kommt ihr gespielen: M Franck
Come ye with psalmody—Psallite Domino: Byrd
Comedy overture—Lustspielouverture: Busoni
Comes death apace with footfall eager—Ich stehe mit einem Fuss in Grabe: Ba
Comfort—Noveta (Moravské Dvojzpévy): Dvořák
Comfort in song—Trost im Gesang: Schumann
Comfort in sorrow—Trost im Unglück (Des Knaben Wunderhorn): Mahler
Comfort in tears—Trost in Tränen: Brahms/Schubert
Comfort me, Jesu, in my sadness—Tröste mir, Jesu, mein Gemüte (Ach
    Herr, mich armen Sünder): Bach
Comfort sweet, my (Lord) Jesus comes—Süsser Trost, mein Jesus kommt:
    Bach
Coming sorrow—Leides Ahnung (Albumblätter): Schumann
Coming woe—Leides Ahnung (Albumblätter): Schumann
Comment, disaient-ils—O, how now escape?/O how, fairest ones?/
    Questions and answers: Liszt
Como castaño en flor—Flow'ring chestnut tree: N Fraser
Com'onda incalza altr'onda (Scipione)—As waves in endless motion: Hande
Complainte de la reine Marie Stuart—Mary Stuart's lament: Martini
Complainte des arches de Noé—The Noah's ark: Pierné
Comrades, fill your glasses—En bons militaires (Fra Diavolo): Auber
Le comṭe Ory—Count Ory: Rossini
Con rauco mormorio (Rodelinda)—With murmer hoarsely swelling/With
    mournful sounds of weeping: Handel
Conclusion—Zum Schluss (Neue Liebeslieder): Brahms
Condotta ell' era in ceppi (Il trovatore)—In galling fetters: Verdi
The confession—Le chanoin Recupéro: Françaix
Confession—Geständnis: Mendelssohn/Schumann
Confirm in us, O God—Confirma hoc deus: Byrd
Confirma hoc deus—Confirm in us, O God: Byrd
Confitemini Domino—God is merciful: M Haydn
Confounded and trembling—Confusa si miri (Rodelinda): Handel
Confusa si miri (Rodelinda)—Confounded and trembling: Handel

Connais-tu le pays (Mignon)—Far away lies a land/Knowest thou that
  dear land: Thomas
The conqueror worm—Cherv-Pobedital: Gniessin
The conjurer—Die Zauberer: Mozart
Consecration of the house—Die Weihe des Hauses: Beethoven
Consider, O man—Memento homo: Byrd
Consider, O my soul—Betrachte, mein Seel' (Johannes-passion): Bach
Consolati e spera—Forget thy grief: D Scarlatti
Consolation—Trost: Cornelius
Consolation in sorrow—Trost im Unglück (Des Knaben Wunderhorn):
  Mahler
Consolation of Mary with the risen Christ—Stillung Mariä mit dem Auf-
  erstandenen (Das Marienleben): Hindemith
The conspirators—Die Verschworenen: Schubert
Constancy—Liebestreu: Brahms
Consuming love—Liebesglut: Brahms
Contemplation—Recueillement: Debussy
Content—Genügsamkeit: Haydn
Content—Die Einsame: Schubert
Content my God—Einun, mein Gott, so fall' ich dir (chorale: Ich hab in
  Gottes Herz und Sinn): Bach
Contentment—Die Zufriedenheit: Mozart
Contentment—Glückes genug (Kinderscenen): Schumann
Les contes d'Hoffmann—The tales of Hoffmann: Offenbach
Contest: Agon: Stravinsky
Continue thy singing—Ah, mai non cessate: Donaudy
A contrast—Contraste: Blumenthal
Contraste—A contrast: Blumenthal
Contratador dos diamantes—The diamond merchant: Mignone
Contrition—Busslied: Beethoven
Contumelias et terrores—Many are the insults: Byrd
The convent walls—Klosterfräulein: Brahms
Converted—Die Bekehrte: Wolf
The converted drunkard—L'ivrogne corrigé: Gluck
Convien partir! (La fille du régiment)—Dear friends, farewell: Donizetti
Le convoi—The convoy: Bleichmann
The convoy—Le convoi: Bleichmann
The coolness and the fire—La fraicheur et le feu: Poulenc
Cophtisches Lied—Coptic song: Wolf
The coquette and her lover—Vor der Tür: Brahms
Corderito—Little lambkin: Guastavino
The cornfield—Das Aehrenfeld: Mendelssohn
Cornflower—Kornblumen: R Strauss

Coro di morti—Chorus of the dead: Petrassi
Coronation march—Le marche du Sacre (Le prophète): Meyerbeer
The coronation of Poppea—L'incoronazione di Poppea: Monteverdi
Corran di puro latte—A-brim with purest milk: Marenzio
Der Corregidor—The magistrate: Wolf
Cortigiani, vil razza dannata (Rigoletto)—Hated courtiers: Verdi
Una cosa rara—A rare thing: Soler
Così fan tutte—So do they all/The school for lovers: Mozart
Così piange pierrot—While the world is dreaming: Bixio
The cossack song—Kazach'ya pesuya (Podnyataya tselina): Dzerzhinski
El cotiló—Old cotiló: Gerhard
The cottage—Die Hütte: Schumann
Le coucher du soleil (Melodies irlandaises)—At sunset: Berlioz
Le coucou au fond des bois (Carnaval des animaux)—The cuckoo:
  Saint-Saëns
Could I—Vorrei: Tosti
Could I but once—Ach könnt ich, könnte vergessen: Brahms
Could I once again caress thee—Wieder möcht' ich dir begegnen: Liszt
Couldst thou only see me now—Rote Äugelein: R Franz
Counsels—Guter Rat: Brahms
Count Ory—Le comte Ory: Rossini
The countess—Hrabina: Moniuszko
Countess Dubarry—Gräfin Dubarry: Millöcker
The countess Mariza—Die Gräfin Mariza: Kálmán
A country song—Air champêtre: Poulenc
A country walk—Fussreise: Wolf
Country-life—Von dem Landleben: Keiser
Les coups des pieds—The kick: Françaix
Courage—Mut (Die Winterreise): Schubert
Courted by all—Enfant chéri: Thomas
The cousin from nowhere—Der Vetter aus Dingsda: Künneke
Covered with roses—Mit Rosen betreut: Reger
The cow girl—Die Sennin: Schumann
The coy shepherdess—Die Spröde: Wolf
Což ta voda s výše stráni (Tajemství)—From the mountains: Smetana
The crab—L'écrevisse (Le bestiaire): Poulenc
The cradle—Vor meiner Wiege: Schubert
Cradle song—Wiegenlied: Blech
Cradle song—Weihnachten: Brahms
Cradle song—Wiegenlied: Brahms
Cradle song—Wiegenlied: Flies (attrib Mozart)
Cradle song—Vuggesang: Grieg
Cradle song—Wiegenlied: Humperdinck
Cradle song—Bei der Wiege: Mendelssohn

Cradle song—Wiegenlied: Reger
Cradle song—Canción de cuna (Canciones de niños): Revueltas
Cradle song—Berceuse: Rhené-Baton
Cradle song—Wiegenlied: Schumann
Cradle song—Wiegenliedchen (Albumblätter): Schumann
Cradle song—Wiegenliedchen: R Strauss
Cradle song—Can y crud: W S G Williams
Cradle song in the northern winter—Vuggesang i mørketiden: F Backer-Grøndahl
Cradle song of the Virgin—Giestliches Wiegenlied: Brahms
The cradles—Les berceaux: Fauré
The creation—Die Schöpfung: Fortner
The creation—Die Schöpfung: Haydn
La création du monde—The creation of the world: Milhaud
Creation mass—Schöpfungsmesse: Haydn
The creation of the world—La création du monde: Milhaud
Creation's hymn—Die Ehre Gottes aus der Natur: Beethoven
Creative activity—Genialisch Treiben: Wolf
Creou a natureza damas bellas—Although the ancient poets: J Berger
Crépuscule—Twilight: Gounod/Massenet/Rhené-Baton
The cricket—Le grillon (Histoires naturelles): Ravel
The cricket on the hearth—Das Heimchen am Herd: Goldmark
Crimean suite—Krymskaya Syuita: Vitachek
The critic—Le critique: Françaix
Le critique—The critic: Françaix
Crois mon conseil, chère Climène (Le promenoir des deux amants)—Take my counsel, dear Climène: Debussy
La croisade des enfants—The children's crusade: Pierné
La croix douloureuse—The cross of affliction: Caplet
Cross most faithful—Crux fidelis: King John IV
The cross of affliction—La croix douloureuse: Caplet
Cross purposes—Ein Jungling liebt ein Mädchen (Dichterliebe): Schumann
Cross that held Thee—Crux fidelis: King John IV
The crow—Die Krähe (Die Winterreise): Schubert
The crown diamonds—Les diamants de la couronne: Auber
The crown of all my heart—Du meines Herzens Krönelein: Reger
A crown of dreams—Traumgekrönt: Berg
A crown of grace for man is wrought—Es ist das Heil uns kommen her: Brahms
Crown of my heart—Du meines Herzens Krönelein: Reger
Crucem tuam adoramus—We venerate Thy cross: Goodman
Crudel tirano amor—O cruel tyrant love: Handel
Crudele? (Don Giovanni)—I cruel?: Mozart

Cruel archer—Sù, ferisci: Steffani
The crusaders—Korsfarerne: Gade
Crushed by fate—Non lasciar (Floridante): Handel
Crux fidelis—Cross most faithful/Cross that held Thee: King John IV
The cry of the wind—La plainte du vent: Rhené-Baton
A cry to Mary—Ruf zu Maria (Marienlieder): Brahms
Csalfa legény—False man: Erkel
[Csar . . . see: Czar]
A csodálatos mandarin—The miraculous mandarin: Bartók
Ctverice muzskych sboru—National choruses: Janáček
Los cuatro soles—The four ages: Chavez
The cuckoo—Le coucou au fond des bois (Carnaval des animaux):
    Saint-Saëns
The cuckoo—Im Krappenwald: J Strauss II
Cuckoo in hiding—Guguk im Versteck (Album für die Jugend): Schumann
The cuckoo-bird—Certain coucou (Le judgement de Midas): Grétry
Cuentos de España—Spanish tales: Turina
Coeurs desolez—Hearts in despair: Josquin
Cunctis diebus—Throughout the long days: Byrd
The cunning little vixen—Prihody lisky hystrovsky: Janáček
The cunning man—Le devin du village: Rousseau
The cunning peasant—Šelma sedlák: Dvořák
Cuore vagabondo—Happy gigolo: Bixio
The cup of oblivion—Die Schale der Vergessenheit: Brahms
Cupid asleep—Dans un bois solitaire: Mozart
Cupid, wanton infant—Cupido, loser Knabe: R Franz
Cupido, loser Knabe—Cupid, wanton infant: R Franz
Cupid's intrusion—D'amor la face (Le astuzie femminili): Cimarosa
Curiose Begebenneit—A strange event: Meyer-Helmund
Curiose Geschichte (Kinderscenen)—A curious story/A funny story/
    A strange story: Schumann
Curiosity—Der Neugierige (Die schöne Müllerin): Schubert
A curious story—Curiose Geschichte (Kinderscenen): Schumann
Cycle of Heine songs—Liederkreiss von Heine: Schumann
Un cygne—A swan: Hindemith
Le cygne (Histoires naturelles)—The swan: Ravel
Le cygne (Le carnaval des animaux)—The swan: Saint-Saëns
The cushat dove—Das Waldvöglein: Anon
Czar and carpenter—Zar und Zimmermann: Lortzing
Czardas of my homeland—Klänge der Heimat (Die Fledermaus): J Strauss II
Die Czardasfürstin—The gipsy princess: Kálmán
The czarevich—Der Zarewitsch: Lehár

D

Da die Stunde kam—As the hour drew nigh: R Franz

Da draussen in der Wachau—My heart has learned to sing: E Arnold

Da fahr ich still im Wagen—I journey slowly onward: Wolf

Da Jesus an dem Kreuze stund (Orgelbüchlein)—When on the cross the
saviour hung: Bach

Da lieg' ich unter den Bäumen—Beneath the branches reclining: Mendelssohn

Da mihi auxilium—O help me against the enemy: Byrd

Da sind die bleichen Geister wieder—Again the pallid ghosts are rising: R Franz

Da tempeste (Giulio Cesare)—When by storms: Handel

Da unten im Tale—Below yonder valley: Brahms

Dai campi, dai prati (Mephistofele)—From the fields, from the groves: Boito

Daily I will love Thee—Herzlich Lieb hab ich dich, O Herr: Schütz

The daily question—Du fragst mich täglich: Meyer-Helmund

Dainty damsels—Réjouissez vous bourgeoises: Anon

Dal fulgor di questa spada (Giulio Cesare)—By this falchion lightning-
garnished: Handel

Dalekaya yunost—Far-off youth: Shaporin

Daleko ot Moskvï—Far off Moscow: Dzerzhinsky

Dalla sua pace (Don Giovanni)—All joy and pleasure/On her contentment:
Mozart

La dame blanche—The white lady: Boildieu

La dame d'Andre (Fiancailles pour rire)—André's woman friend: Poulenc

Dame fortune's knight—Der Glücksritter: Wolf

Une dame noble et sage (Les Huguenots)—'Tis a lady wise and noble:
Meyerbeer

Dame swallow—Die Schwalbe: Humperdinck

Dame's violets—Nachtviolen: Schubert

Dämmerempfindung—Moods: Cornelius

Dämmerung senkt—Twilight falls to earth/Twilight dropping down: Brahms

Dämm'rung senkte sich von oben—Twilight from above: Schoeck

La damoiselle élue—The blessed damozel: Debussy

Damon and Chloe—Sobald Damoetas Chloen sieht: Mozart

Damon with his flute—Die Bekehrte: Wolf

D'amor la face (Le astuzie femminili)—Cupid's intrusion: Cimarosa

D'amor sull'ali rosee (Il trovatore)—Breeze of the night: Verdi

Danae's love—Der Liebe der Danae: R Strauss

A dance—Ein Tanzchen: Reger

Dance, O dance, maiden gay—Danza, danza, fanciulla gentile: Durante

Dance of death—Totentanz: Bresgen

The dance of death—La danse des morts: Honegger

Dance of Saint-Loup—La sabotée de Saint-Loup: Blanchard

Dance of the cockerel—Hanendans (Maskarade): Nielsen

Dance of the cocks—Hanendans (Maskarade): Nielsen

Dance of the game of love—Danza del fuego de amor (El amor brujo): Falla

Dance of the gnomes—Gnomenreigen: Liszt

Dance of the hours—Danza delle ore (La Gioconda): Ponchielli

Dance of the morning mists—Morgentågernes dans: Nielsen

Dance of the sprites—Menuet des follets (Faust): Berlioz

Dance on, dance on—Danza, danza, fancuilla gentile: Durante

Dance suite—Tánc suite: Bartók

The dances of Lormont—Les danses de Lormont: Franck

Dance-song in May—Tanzlied im Mai: R Franz

The dancing fawn—Le faune (Fêtes galantes): Debussy

Dancing in a sack—Els Ballaires dins un sac: Gerhard

The dancing ring—La ronde: Caplet

Dancing round the world—La ronde autour du monde: Pierné

The dancing Viennese—Eine vom Ballet: Straus

The Danish song is like a young, fair girl—Den danske sang er en ung blond pige: Nielsen

Dank—Thanks: Schoenberg

Dank des Paria—The prayer of the outcast: Wolf

Danksagung an dem Bach (Die schöne Müllerin)—A grateful address to the millstream/Gratitude to the brook/Acknowledgement to the brook/Thanks to the brook/Recognition: Schubert

Danksei dir, Herr—Laud we our God/Break, fairest dawn: Handel

D'Anne jouant de l'espinette—To Anne, at the spinet: Ravel

Dans cette étable—Bethlehem: Gounod

Dans le chemin (Tristesses)—Down by the rain-soaked woodland path: Milhaud

Dans le printemps de mes années—In the fair spring-time: Garat

Dans le sentier—Down by the path: Massenet

Dans l'herbe (Fiancailles pour rire)—In the grass: Poulenc

Dans un bois solitaire—Cupid asleep/Scarce a gleam of sun/Lonely through the grove: Mozart

Dans un piège fatal (Amadis de Gaule)—He is drawn to the snare: Lully

La danse des morts—The dance of death: Honegger

Les danses de Lormont—The dances of Lormont: Franck

Den danske sang er en ung blond pige—The Danish song is like a young, fair girl: Nielsen

Dante Sonata—Après une lecture de Dante: Liszt

Danton's death—Dantons Tod: Einem

Danza, danza, fancuilla gentile—Dance on, dance on/Dance, O dance, maiden gay: Durante

Danza del fuego de amor (El amor brujo)—Dance of the game of love: Falla

Danza delle Ore (La Gioconda)—Dance of the hours: Ponchielli

Danza ritual del Fuego (El amor brujo)—Ritual fire dance: Falla

Darby and Joan—Brüderlein fein: Fall

Darf ich die Antwort sagen (Tristan und Isolde)—May I an answer make:
  Wagner
Dark clouds o'er heaven are sweeping—Das ist ein Brausen und Heulen:
  Wolf
The dark kingdom—Das dunkle Reich: Pfitzner
Dark night of the soul—Noche oscura: Petrassi
Dark the sky, the clouds are flying—Trobe wird's, die Wolken jagen: R Franz
Dark-eyed maiden—O die Frauen (Liebeslieder waltz): Brahms
Darkness made dim the world—Tenebrae factae sunt: M Haydn
Dark'ning brightness—Dunkler Lichtglanz (Spanische Liebeslieder):
  Schumann
Darksome wood—Schwartzer Wald (Neue Liebeslieder): Brahms
Darling I leave my heart--Cara ti lascio il core: L Leo
Darling where are you?—Liebchen, wo bist du?: Wolf
Darthula's Grabgesang—The dirge of Darthula/Daughter of Colla: Brahms
Darum sollt ihr nicht sorgen (Es warter alles auf dich)—Therefore be ye
  not anxious: Bach
Das ist ein Brausen—Hark, how the tempest: R Franz
Das ist ein Brausen und Heulen—Dark clouds o'er heaven are sweeping:
  Wolf
Das ist ein Flöten und Geigen (Dichterliebe)—Lost love: Schumann
Das ist im Leben—'Tis life's unkindest lesson: Meyer-Helmund
Das Mach das unkelgrüne Laub—Those dark green leaves: Meyer-Helmund
Das Macht, es hat die Nachtigall—Because the nightingale's sweet lay:
  Meyer-Helmund
Dass sie hier gewesen—Would she were here/Presence of the lov'd one/
  That she has been here: Schubert
The daughter of Colchis—La hija de Cólquide: Chavez
Daughter of Colla—Darthula's Grabgesang: Brahms
The daughter of Jairus—Talitha Kumi: Wolf-Ferrari
The daughter of Jephtha—Die Tochter Jeptha's: Schumann
The daughter of the regiment—La fille du régiment: Donizetti
The daughters of Cádiz—Les filles de Cadix: Delibes
Daughters of the Virgin Mary—Filhas de Maria: Villa-Lobos
Le dauphin (Le bestiaire)—The dolphin: Poulenc
David chantant devant Saül—David singing before Saul: Bordèse
David singing before Saul—David chantant devant Saül: Bordèse
Davidde penitente—The penitent David: Mozart
The dawn—Zarya: Molchanov
The dawn—Morgenrot: R Strauss
Dawn may be early breaking—Oh mattutini albori! (La donna del lago):
  Rossini
Day dreams—Mit deinen blauen Augen: Lassen
The day hath dawned—the day of days—Erschienen ist der herrliche Tag
  (Orgelbüchlein): Bach

Day is past—Der Tag ist vergangen: Weber
The day of peace—Der Friedenstag: R Strauss
The day this jewel upon my finger—Quando la gemma di questo anello: Braga
Day-break—Und schäfst du, mein Mädchen: Schumann
The days of youth—O Jugend, O schöne Rosenzeit: Mendelssohn
The days that were—Ruckblick (Die Winterreise): Schubert
Daz iuwer min Engel Walte—My angel shall guard thee: Reger
Dazu ist erschienen der Sohn Gottes—To this end appeared the Son of God/Wherefore has appeared the Son of God: Bach
De fleurs (Proses lyriques)—Of flowers: Debussy
De grève (Proses lyriques)—Of the shore: Debussy
De Norske Fjelde (Barnlige Sanger)—Song of the mountains: Grieg
De quelques français—Certain Frenchmen: Françaix
De rêve (Proses lyriques)—Of dreams: Debussy
De soir (Proses lyriques)—Of evening: Debussy
De son coeur (Mignon)—See, my song: Thomas
Dead—Tot: Schoenberg
The dead bodies of Thy faithful and true servants—Posuerunt morticinia: Byrd
The dead city—Die tote Stadt: Korngold
The dead drummer—Revelge: Mahler
A dead friend's drinking glass—Auf das Trinkglas eines verstorbenen Freundes: Schumann
Dead leaves—Feuilles mortes: Debussy
Dead is my lord—Ho perduto (Rodelinda): Handel
The dead nightingale—Die tote Nachtigall: Liszt
Deadly sickness—Todliche Krankheit: Henschel
Deal with me Father—Schaff's mit mir, Gott, nach dienem Willen: Bach
Dear Christians, one and all rejoice—Nun freut euch, liebe Christen g'mein: Bach
Dear companion—Cara sposa (Rinaldo): Handel
Dear friend—Süsser Freund (Frauenliebe und -leben): Schumann
Dear friends, farewell—Convien partir! (La fille du régiment): Donizetti
Dear hall of song—Dich, teure Halle (Tannhäuser): Wagner
Dear little hand—Manella mia: Giannini
Dear love—Lieb' Liebchen: Medtner
Dear love—Lieb' Liebchen: Schumann
Dear love, believe me: Mio caro bene (Rodelinda): Handel
Dear love, thou'rt like a blossom—Du bist wie eine Blume: Liszt
Dear loving sisters—Helf mir, ihr Schwestern (Frauenliebe und -leben): Schumann
Dear lute—Wir mussen uns trennen: Brahms
Dear Minna—Lieb Minna: Schubert

Dear mother, how you toil—Gamle Mor: Grieg
Dear night—Notte Cara (Floridante): Handel
The dear old days gone by—Die alte gute Zeit: Schumann
Dear placid vale—Mich locket nicht: Mozart
Dearest boy, Oh do but chide me—Batti, batti, O bel Masetto (Don
  Giovanni): Mozart
Dearest consort—Cara sposa (Rinaldo): Handel
Dearest daughter—Figlia mia, non pianger, nò (Tamerlano): Handel
Dearest Fernando—O mio Fernando (La favorita): Donizetti
Dearest friend, look kindly on me—Lieber Schatz, sei wieder gut mir:
  R Franz
Dearest from thee—Caro mio ben: Giorani
Dearest heart, my angel—Schönster Schatz, mein Engel: Brahms
Dearest Lord Jesu—Liebster Herr Jesu: Bach
Dearest Lord, when wilt thou summon? —Liebster Gott, wann werd' ich
  sterben?: Bach
Dearest lover—Cara sposa (Rinaldo): Handel
Dearest maid, O list to me—Liebes Mädchen, hör mir zu: Haydn
Dearest maiden, come to me—Liebes Mädchen, hör mir zu: Haydn
Dearest name—Caro nome (Rigoletto): Verdi
Dearest of all men chosen—Caro voi siete all' alma (Serse): Handel
Dearest saviour, priceless treasure—Liebster Jesu, mein Verlangen: Bach
Dearest sister, lovely bride—Meine Schwester, liebe Braut: M Franck
Dearest Virgin we pray to thee—Liebste Jungfrau, wir sind dein (Drei
  Volkstexte): Webern
Dearest we part now—Resta, oh cara! : Mozart
Dearest, where'er I view thee—Quando col mio s'incontra: Clari
Death: Vom Tode: Beethoven
Death and life—Mors et vita: Gounod
Death and the girl (maiden)—Der Tod und das Mädchen: Schubert
Death and the lonely drinker—Der Tod und der einsame Trinker (Leider
  um den Tod): Kilpinen
Death and the maiden—La mort i la donzella: Gerhard
Death and transfiguration—Tod und Verklarung: R Strauss
Death is the cool night—Der Tod, das ist die kühle Nacht: Brahms
Death is the cooling night—Der Tod, das ist die kühle Nacht: Brahms
Death of Danton—Dantons Tod: Einem
Death of the lovers—La mort des amants: Debussy
Death of the nightingale—Sie ist dahin: Mozart
The death of Trenar—Gesang aus Fingal: Brahms
Death reigns in many a human breast—Vtak mnohém srdci mrtvo jest
  (Pisné milostné): Dvořák
Death stricken was I—Seliger Tod: Liszt
Death, the reaper—Schnitter Tod: Brahms

Death the releaser—Befreit: R Strauss
Death-song of the Boyard—Todeslied des Bojaren: Mendelssohn
The Decembrists—Dekabristï: Shaporin
The Decembrists—Dekabristï: Zolotarev
Deception—Täuschung (Die Winterreise): Schubert
Deck thyself, my soul, with gladness—Schmücke dich, O liebe Seele:
  Bach
Deck thyself out, o my soul—Schmücke dich, O liebe Seele: Brahms
Declaraçao—I love you: Guarnieri
A declaration—Ich liebe dich: Blumenthal
Le déclin—The waning: Bloch
Dedication—Ajánlás (Tís könnyü zongoradarab): Bartók
Dedication—Widmung: R Franz
Dedication—Widmung (Myrthen): Schumann
Dedinské Scény: Village scenes: Bartók
Deep enambushed—Hinter Büschen, hintern Laub (Die Bürgschaft):
  Schubert
Deep in my heart—Caro mio ben: Giordani
Deep in my nightly longing—In meiner nächte Sehnen: Brahms
Deep in the woodland—Honkain Keskellä: Ennola
Defecit in delore—Have mercy, Lord upon me: Byrd
The defenders of Sevastopol—Sevastopolstï: Koval
Deh calma, o ciel (Otello)—Descend thou sleep: Rossini
Deh come trista—Mourn now with me: Arcadelt
Deh vieni all finestra (Don Giovanni)—Come open your windows/Oh,
  come now to the casement: Mozart
Deh vieni non tardar (Le nozze di Figaro)—O come do not delay: Mozart
Dein!—Thine only: C Bohm
Dein Auge—Thine eyes: Reger
Dein Bildnis—Thine image: Cornelius
Dein Bildnis wunderselig—Thine image pure: Schumann
Dein blaues Auge—Thy blue eyes/So clear thine eyes: Brahms
Dein Herzlein mild—Thou gentle girl: Brahms
Dein ist mein ganzes Herz! (Die gelbe Jacke/Das Land des Lächelns)—
  You are my heart's delight: Lehár
Dein Wachstum sei feste (Mer hahn en neue Oberkeet): Bach
Dein Wille geschehe—Thy will be done: Cornelius
Deine Rosen an der Brust (Lieder der Liebe)—The roses on my breast/
  With thy roses on my breast: Kilpinen
Deine weissen Lilienfinger—Thy dear fingers: R Franz
Dejte klec jestřábu (Cigánské melodie)—Cloudy heights of Tatra: Dvořák
Dekabristï—The Decembrists: Shaporin
Dekabristï—The Decembrists: Zolotarev
Del bell' idolo mio—My beautiful face: Handel

Del minaccia del vento (Ottone)—When winds are fiercely raving/When furious winds/The blust'ring winds loud raging: Handel
Del mio caro Bacco (Serse)—Smiling Bacchus: Handel
Delight in melancholy—Wonne der Wehmuth: Beethoven
Delight of melancholy—Wonne der Wehmuth: R Franz
The delights of youth—Jugendglücke: Liszt
Deliver me, O Lord, from eternal death—Libera me Domine de morte aeterna: Byrd
Deliver us from all evil—Ut eruas nos a malis: Byrd
Deliver us from evil—Erlöse uns vom Übel: Cornelius
Dell' antro magico—Gates of gloom: Cavalli
Della rosa il bel vermiglio (Bianca e Falliero)—This fair rose may tell: Rossini
The deluded spouse—Lo sposa deluso: Mozart
Delusion—Täuschung (Die Winterreise): Schubert
Dem also hat uns der Herr geboten (Paulus)—For so hath the Lord commanded: Mendelssohn
Dem Helden—The hero: Schumann
Dem Herzen ähnlich—As hearts that languish: R Strauss
Dem Himmel will ich klagen—To Heaven pain and sorrow: Brahms
Dem roten Röslein gleicht mein Lieb—O, my luve's like a red, red rose/My love is like a red, red rose: Schumann
Dem Unendlichen—To the eternal: Schubert
Dem wir das Heilig itzt (Gelobet sei der Herr, mein Gott)—Awake, thou wintry earth: Bach
Demain fera un an qu'à audaux (Tristesse)—A year ago tomorrow: Milhaud
Demande et réponse—Question and answer: Coleridge-Taylor
Denk es, o Seele!—O soul, remember this!/Think on this my soul: Wolf
Denk' ich dein!—Thoughts of thee: R Franz
Denkst du an mich—Think'st thou of me: Cornelius
Denn es gehet dem Menschen—One thing befalleth: Brahms
Denn in seiner Hand—Far in His own hand/In His hand are all the corners: Mendelssohn
Deo Patri sit gloria—All glory to the Father: Byrd
Le départ—The departure: Roussel
Departed—Borte!: Grieg
The departure—Die Abreise: Albert
Departure—Abreise: M Mayer
Departure—Abschied vom Wald: Mendelssohn
The departure—Le départ: Roussel
Departure—Abschied (Schwanengesang): Schubert
Depuis le jour (Louise)—E'er since the day: Charpentier
Der du bist dem Vater gleich (Schwingt freudig euch empor)—Thou that art equal to the Father: Bach

Der du von Himmel bist—Thou who down from Heaven: Wolf
Les dernières pensées—Last thoughts: Pierné
Des pas sur la neige—Footsteps in the snow: Debussy
Descend thou sleep—Deh calma, o ciel (Otello): Rossini
Descendit de coelis—He came down from on high: Byrd
Deseo—The wish: Guastavino
The deserted maiden—Der verlassene Mägdlein: Schumann
Desire for spring—Sehnsucht nach dem Frühling: Mozart
Desolation—V Zoufalství: Smetana
Despair—Schwermuth: Brahms
Despair—Verzweiflung: Brahms
Despair—Die Verzweiflung: Haydn
Despair—Otchayaniye: Prokofiev
The despairing lover—Der verzweifelte Liebhaber: Wolf
El despechado—The enraged one: J Berger
La despedida—Farewell: Pouce
Despise me not—Verachtet mir die Meister nich (Die Meistersinger von
    Nürnberg: Wagner
Despised be all worldly wealth—Mauldicte soit la mondaine richesse:
    Sermisy
Despisest thou the riches of His goodness—Verachtest du den Reichtum
    seiner Gnade? (Herr, deine Augen sehen nacht dem Glauben): Bach
Desponding and responsive love—Seufzer eines Ungeliebten und
    Gegenliebe: Beethoven
Dessen Fahne donnerstürme wallte—He whose flag: Schubert
Destined—Proměny (Moravské dvojzpěvy): Dvořák
Destinée (Petites légendes)—Fate: Milhaud
Deus, misereatur nostri—O Lord have mercy: Schütz
Deus venerunt gentes—O God, the heathen are coming: Byrd
Deutsches Kantate/Die ihr des unermesslichen Weltalls—Ye who the
    great creator: Mozart
Ein deutsches Kriegslied/Meine Wünsche—My wishes: Mozart
Ein deutsches Requiem—A German requiem: Brahms
Deutschland—The victor's return: Mendelssohn
Les deux aveugles—The blind beggars: Offenbach
Deux ancolies se balançaient (Tristesses)—Two columbines together:
    Milhaud
Les deux enfants du roi—Of yore there dwelt two kingly ones: d'Arba
Les deux journées—The water carrier/The two days: Cherubini
Deux rondels de Charles d'Orléans—Two rondels of Charles d'Orléans:
    Debussy
Děvče z Maravy—Moravian girl: Martinů
The devil a monk would be—Art lässt nicht von Art: Hindemith
The devil and Kate—Čert a Káča: Dvořák

The devil in the belfry—Le diable dans le beffroi: Debussy
The devil in the belfry—Le diable dans le beffroi: Inghelbrecht
The devil's Christmas Eve—La noche buena del diablo: Esplà
The devil's share—La part du diable: Auber
Le devin du village—The village soothsayer/The cunning man: Rousseau
Devotion—Recueillement: Liszt
Devotion—Widmung: Schumann
Devotion—Zueignung: R Strauss
Dew—Rosička: Martinů
Dewdrops—Duggdraaper: A Backer-Grøndahl
Dewdrops—Rocio: Guastavino
Dewy violets—Le violette: A Scarlatti
Dì ad Irene (Atalanta)—Tell fair Irene/Say to Irene/Go! call Irene: Handel
Di Cupido impiego i vanni (Rodelina)—On love's wings/I avail me of
  Cupid's pinion: Handel
Di marmo siete voi—Of marble you are fashioned: Gagliano
Di notte il pellegrino (Riccardo Primo)—When midnight fears assail him:
  Handel
Di piacer mi balza il cor (La gazza ladra)—To my native home I'm near:
  Rossini
Di Provenza il mar (La traviata)—To our fair Provence/Who has banished
  from your heart: Verdi
Le diable dans le beffroi—The devil in the belfry: Debussy
Le diable dans le beffroi—The devil in the belfry: Inghelbrecht
A dialogue—Zweisprach: Reger
Dialogue in the woods—Waldesgespräch: Schumann
Les diamantes de la couronne—The crown diamonds: Auber
The diamond merchant—Contratador dos diamantes: Mignone
Diario polacca 1958—Polish diary 1958: Nono
Diary of a young man—Zapisník zmizelého: Janáček
Diary of one who disappeared (vanished)—Zapisník zmizelého: Janáček
Diary of the man who vanished—Zapisník zmizelého: Janáček
Dich bet' ich an, mein höchster Gott—I worship Thee: Bach
Dich, teure Halle (Tannhäuser)—Dear hall of song/Ye halls beloved:
  Wagner
Dichter und Bauer—Poet and peasant: Suppé
Dichterliebe—A poet's love: Schumann
Dichters Abendgang—The poet's eventide walk: R Strauss
Dichters Genesung—The poet's recovery: Schumann
Didst thou but know—O wüsstest du (Italianisches Liederbuch): Wolf
Die, love and joy—Stirb, Lieb' und Freud': Schumann
Dies sanctificatus—Now there lightens upon us: Byrd
Dies sind die heil'gen zehn Gebot (Orgelbüchlein)—These are the holy
  ten commandments: Bach

Diese Wolken (An die ferne Geliebte)—Clouds that o'er the mountain:
  Beethoven
Dieu, qu'il la fait bon regarder (Chansons de Charles d'Orléans)—Lord,
  Thou has made my dear/Lord, lovely has Thou made my dear: Debussy
Le dieu le fort—The God of gods: Le Jeune
Difference—Die Unterscheidung: Schubert
Digterhjertet/Du fatter ej Bølgernes evige bryst—The poet's heart/You know
  not the waves' eternal motion: Grieg
En Digters sidste Sang—The poet's last lay: Grieg
Digtervise—Poet's mind: Grieg
Diliges Dominum—Thou shalt love the Lord thy God: Byrd
Dimmi, crudele amore (Muzio Scevola)—Tell me, thou cruel love: Handel
D'inaspettali eventi (Poro)—Of unexpected happ'nings: Handel
Dios en la Edad Media—God in the Middle Ages: Engelbrecht
Dir, dir, Jehovah, will ich singen—To Thee, Jehovah/Jehovah: Bach
Dir Jehovah will ich singen—For Thee, Jehovah are our praises: Bach
Dire non voglio—No, let me not reproach you: D Scarlatti
Dirge—Pohrební písen: Bartók
The dirge of Darthula—Darthula's Grabgesang: Brahms
Dirges for children—Kindertotenlieder: Mahler
Dirges for girls—Mädchentotenlieder: Nilsson
The disappointed serenader—Vergebliches Ständchen: Brahms
Discord—Nesvár: Smetana
Discovery—Hallazgo: Guastavino
Dissi a l'amata mia lucida stella—Hearken thou, my fond heart's queen/
  Hear me now beloved: Marenzio
Distance—Sehnsucht: F Mendelssohn
Distant bells—Entfernte Glocken: Blumenthal
The distant sound—Der ferne Klang: Schreker
Distress—La peine (Petites légendes): Milhaud
Diverte a malo—Eschew evil: Byrd
Divided love—Mondes ailber Rinnt: Kjerulf
Divinités du Styx (Alceste)—Ye powers that dwell below/Ye powers that
  rule below/Ye gods of endless night: Gluck
Divorce court scene—Tamperretsscene (Maskarade): Nielsen
The Dnieper Cossack on the Danube—Zaporozhets za Dunayem: Hulak-
  Artemovs'kyi
Do not doubt my true affection—Spera si, mio caro bene (Admeto):
  Handel
Do not gaze—Nein, Geliebter (Neue Liebeslieder): Brahms
Do not look at my songs—Blicke mir nicht in die Lieder: Mahler
Do not mingle—Ah! non giunge (La sonnambula): Bellini
Do thine alms—Wohlzutum und mitzuteilen (Brich dem Hungrigen
  dein Brot): Bach

Do you know the land—Kennst du das Land (Lieder der Mignon): Wolf

Do you often call to mind—Kommt dir manchmal in den Sinn (Zigeuner-lieder): Brahms

Do you remember?—Te souviens-tu?: Godard

Do you remember if 'twas fine—Faisait-il beau (Tristesses): Milhaud

Dobbin's goodnight song—Kveldsang for Blakken (Barnlige Sanger): Grieg

Dobrú noc—Good night: Dvořák

Doch der Herr, er leitet die/Geistliche Lied—For the Lord shall guide them/Sacred song: Mendelssohn

Doch der Herr vergisst (Paulus)—But the Lord is mindful of his own: Mendelssohn

Doch du liessest ihn im Grabe nicht!—But thou didst not leave his soul in hell!: Reger

Doch weichet, ihr tollen vergeblichen Sorgen (Liebster Gott, wann werd' ich sterben)—Away then, ye cares that so vainly beset me: Bach

Doctor and apothecary—Der Doktor und der Apotheker: Dittersdorf

Doctor Cupid—L'amore medico: Wolf-Ferrari

Doctor love—L'amore medico: Wolf-Ferrari

The doe—La biche: Hindemith

Der Doktor und der Apotheker—Doctor and apothecary: Dittersdorf

Dolce pensiero (Semiramide)—Vision entrancing: Rossini

Dolçe recort—Remembrance of a lullaby: Longás

Il dolce suono (Lucia di Lammermoor)—His voice enthralled me/It was his accents: Donizetti

Die dollar Princessin—The dollar princess: Fall

Doll's march—Dukkemarch (Humoreske): Nielsen

Doll's slumber song—Puppenwiegenlied: Schumann

Dolly's doctor—Die kranke Puppe: Meyer-Helmund

The dolphin—Le dauphin (Le bestiaire): Poulenc

Domestic warfare—Der häusliche Krieg: Schubert

Domine exaudi—Lord do I beseech Thee: Byrd

Domine, non sum dignus—O my Lord, I am not worthy: Byrd

Domine, non sum dignus—Holy Lord, though not worthy: Victoria

Domine praestolamur—Lord, we look for Thy coming: Byrd

Domine salve nos—O Lord succour us: Byrd

Domine secundum actum meum—O my God, according to my doings: Byrd

Domine secundum multitudinem—O Lord God, according to the multitude: Byrd

Domine tu iurasti—O Lord God, thou hast sworn: Byrd

Le don de sagesse (Messe de la Pentecôte)—The gift of wisdom: Messiaen

Don Quichotte—Don Quixote: Massenet

Don Quichotte à Dulcinée—Don Quixote to Dulcinée: Ravel

Don Quijote velando las armas—Quixote keeping vigil by his arms: Esplà
Don Quixote—Don Quichotte: Massenet
Don Quixote to Dulcinée—Don Quichotte à Dulcinée: Ravel
Donauwellen—Night on the Danube: Ivanovici
Donc, ce sera par un clair jour d'été (La bonne chanson)—So, it will be
    on a clear summer day: Fauré
Donde lieta (La bohème)—To the home that she left: Puccini
La donna del lago—The lady of the lake: Rossini
La donna è mobile (Rigoletto)—Woman's a fickle jade: Verdi
Donna non vidi mai (Manon Lescaut)—Never did I behold so fair a
    maiden: Puccini
La donna serpente—The serpent woman: Casella
Le donne curiose—(The) inquisitive women: Wolf-Ferrari
Le donne di buon umore—The good-humoured ladies: Scarlatti-
    Tommasini
Don't be too sure—Non ti fidar (Muzio Scevola): Handel
Don't leave me—Ne menj el!: Bartók
Don't our children—Hat man nicht mit seinen Kindern (Schweigt stille,
    plaudert nicht): Bach
Dopo tante e tante pene—After many a pang of sorrow: Marcello
Der Doppelgänger (Schwanengesang)—The double/The ghostly double/
    My phantom double/The spectral self: Schubert
Doppelt beflugeltes Band—Tape and double: Křenek
Das Dorf—The village: Reger
Das Dorf ohne Glocke—The village without a bell: Künneke
Die Dorfmusik—The village band: Fryberg
Die Dorfsängerinnen—The village songstress: Fioravanti
La dormeuse (Petites légendes)—The sleeper: Milhaud
Dormi, dormi, bel bambino—Sweetest infant all endearing: F Ricci
Dornröschen—Briar-rose: Abt
Dornröschen—Little rose-bud: Brahms
Dornröschen—Little rosebud of the sleeping beauty: Reinecke
Dornröschen (Volkskinderlieder)—The briar rose/The sleeping beauty in
    the wood: Brahms
Dors, enfant, dors—Sleep, dearest, sleep: Randegger
Dort in den Weiden—There 'mong the willows/The house in the willows/
    'Neath the willow trees: Brahms
Dost thou know?—Weisst du noch?: R Franz
Dost thou yet seek—Wehe, so willst du: Brahms
The double—Der Doppelgänger (Schwanengesang): Schubert
The double loss—Leichter verlust: Meyer-Helmund
Douce dame jolie—Sweetheart, gentle and pretty: Machaut
The dove—La paloma: Yradier
Dove, dove, scintillano—My heart's true home: Bossi

Dove mi spingi, amor—Where will you lead me, love: L Rossi
Dove sei amato bene (Rodelinda)—Where art thou?/Where now art thou?/
   Art thou troubled?: Handel
Dove sono (Le nozze di Figaro)—Gone forever: Mozart
Dove voli ò mio pensiero—Where, my thoughts, where do you flutter?:
   A Scarlatti
Down by the path—Dans le sentier: Massenet
Down by the rain-soaked woodland path—Dans le chemin (Tristesses):
   Milhaud
Down from a trembling aspen tree—Lehullot a rezgó nyárfa: Erkel
Down her pale cheek—Una furtiva lagrima (L'elisir d'amore): Donizetti
Drang in die Ferne—Longing to roam/Flight into distance: Schubert
Draw near beloved—Lehn deine Wang an meine Wang: Jensen
Dreadful Cerberus—Il tricherbero (Rinaldo): Handel
The dream—Der Traum: Blech
The dream—Le rêve: Bruneau
Dream—Songe: Caplet
A dream—Ein Traum: Grieg
The dream—Le rêve (Manon): Massenet
A dream—Le rêve: Rollinat
A dream—Un rêve: Séverac
A dream—Son: Stetsenko
Dream in the twilight—Traum durch die Dämmerung: Reger
Dream in the twilight—Traum durch die Dämmerung: R Strauss
Dream of an hour—Rêve d'un soir: Chaminade
The dream of love—Il bacio: Arditi
Dream of love—Liebestraum: Liszt
The dream of Saga—Saga-Drøm: Nielsen
A dream of spring—Ein Frühlingstraum: Goetz
(A) dream of spring(time)—Frühlingstraum (Die Winterreise): Schubert
The dream of the Virgin Mary—Sen panny Marie: Martinů
Dream vision—Im Traum: Dohnányi
Dream-flight—Abendlied: Blumenthal
Dreaming—An dem Traum: Cornelius
Dreaming—Ich hab' im Traum geweinet (Dichterliebe): Schumann
Dreaming—Träumerei (Kinderscenen): Schumann
Dreaming, dreaming—Mon rêve: Waldeufel
Dreaming in the twilight—Traum durch die Dämmerung: R Strauss
Dreamland—Rêverie: Rhené-Baton
Dream-life—Traumleben (song): Schoenberg
Dreams—Wanderträume: Fielitz
Dreams—Träume: R Franz
Dreams—Drömme: Grieg
Dreams—Träumes Wirren (Fantasiestücke): Schumann

Dreams—Träume (Wesendonck Lieder): Wagner
Dreams of home—Lindes rauschen: Brahms
Dreams on the ocean—Traume auf dem Ozean: Gung'l
Drei Volkstexte—Three traditional rhymes: Webern
Drei Walzer—Three waltzes: Straus
Drei Wanderer—The three comrades: Hermann
Die drei Zigeuner—The three gipsies: Liszt
Die drei Zigeuner—The three gipsies: Schoeck
Die Dreigroschenoper—The threepenny opera/The beggar's opera: Weill
Das Dreimäderlhaus—Lilac time/Blossom time: Schubert-Berté
Dreimal tausend jahre—Thrice a thousand years: Schoenberg
Drifting—Mens jeg venter: Grieg
Drifting of the sea—Meerfahrt: R Franz
Driftwood—Lastu Lainehílla: Sibelius
Drinking song—Hulanka: Chopin
Drinking song—Bordal: Kodály
Drinking song—Chanson à boire (Don Quichotte à Dulcinée): Ravel
Drinking song of the earth's misery (sorrow)—Das Trinklied vom Jammer
    der Erde (Das Lied von der Erde): Mahler
Le dromadaire (Le bestiaire)—The dromedary: Poulenc
The dromedary—Le dromadaire (Le bestiaire): Poulenc
Drömme—Dreams: Grieg
Droop o'er my head—Breit über mein Haupt: R Strauss
Drop dew ye heavens—Rorate coeli: Tye
Drüben geht die Sonne scheiden—Yonder now the sun is sinking: R Franz
Drum serenade—Trommel-Ständchen: Loewe
Drum sing' ich mit meinem Liede (Lobgesang)—My song therefore shall
    be: Mendelssohn
The drum-major's daughter—La fille du tambour-major: Offenbach
The drummer boy—Der Tambourgg'sell: Mahler
The drummer-boy—Der Tambour: Wolf
The drums are beating—Die Trommel gerühret (Egmont): Beethoven
The drums they are beating—Die Trommel geruhret (Egmont): Beethoven
The drunkard—L'ubriaco: Malipiero
The drunkard in spring—Der Trunkene im Frühling (Das Lied von der
    Erde): Mahler
The drunken man in spring—Der Trunkene im Frühling (Das Lied von
    der Erde): Mahler
Dry flowers—Trockne Blumen (Die schöne Müllerin): Schubert
Du!—Love: Meyer-Helmund
Du bist aller Dinge schön—Thou art all fair: M Franck
Du bist die Ruh'—You are rest and peace/Rest, thou art my peace/Rest/
    Thou art my rest/The inner light/Love's peace/Peace/My sweet repose/
    Thou art repose/Come gentle sleep/My peace thou art: Schubert

Du bist die Ruh'—Sweet image thou: Schubert-Heller
Du bist meine Sonne (Giuditta)—Stay with me for ever: Lehár
Du bist wie eine Blume—The white pig: Berners
Du bist wie eine Blume—Like a flower in beauty blushing/Dear love,
    thou'rt like a blossom/Ah, sweet as any flower/Thou art like a flower/
    Thou art like a tender flow'ret/So like a flower/A flower thou re-
    semblest: Liszt
Du bist wie eine Blume—A pure and tender blossom/O fair, and sweet
    and holy/A flower art thou/A flower thou resemblest/Thou standest
    like a flower: A Rubinstein
Du bist wie eine Blume (Myrthen)—Thou art like a lovely flower/You
    are like a flower: Schumann
Du bist wie eine Blume—A flower you stand before me: Wolf
Du Falscher, suche nur den Herrn zu fällen (Weihnachtsoratorium)—Thou
    traitor, who dost seek the Lord to kill: Bach
Du fatter ej Bølgernes evige bryst/Digterhjertet—You know not the
    waves' eternal motion/The poet's heart: Grieg
Du fragst mich, du mein blondes Lieb—Silent love/My golden love:
    Kjerulf
Du fragst mich täglich—The daily question: Meyer-Helmund
Du Friedefürst, Herr Jesu Christ—O Jesu Christ, Thou prince of peace/Now
    let Thy gracious spirit shine: Bach
Du grüne Rast—Thou forest green: R Franz
Du hast Diamanten und Perlen—Diamonds hast thou and pearls: Allitsen
Du Herr, du krönst allein (Es warter alles auf dich)—Thou Lord alone,
    dost crown: Bach
Du Hirte Israel, höre—Thou guide of Israel/Thou shepherd of Israel, hear:
    Bach
Du kleine Biene—Thou bee so tiny: Cornelius
Du liebes Auge—Thou gentle gazer: R Franz
Du liebst mich nicht—Thou lov'st me not: Schubert
Du machst, O Tod, wir nun nicht ferne bange (Ach, lieben Christen, seid
    getrost)—Thou canst, O Death, no further now affright me: Bach
Du mein einzig Licht—Thou my only light: Brahms
Du meines Herzens Krönelein—Crown of my heart/The crown of all my
    heart: Reger
Du meines Herzens Krönelein—Pride of my heart: R Strauss
Du milchjunger Knabe—Why gaze upon me: Pfitzner
Du Ring an meinem Finger (Frauenlieben und -leben)—The ring/Thou
    ring upon my finger/Ring on my finger: Schumann
Du schönes Fischermädchen—My pretty fishermaiden: Coleridge-Taylor
Du silbernes Mondenlicht—Haste, silvery moonbeams: Dohnányi
Du sollst nicht, du musst—Thou shall not, thou must: Schoenberg

Du sprichst, das ich mich täuschte—You say my heart deceived me/You say you did not love me/You say I was deceived: Brahms

Du var mig kjaer—I loved thee well: F Backer-Grøndahl

Der du von dem Himmel bist—Thou who from Heaven art sent/Peace: Liszt

Der du von dem Himmel bist/Wanderers Nachtlied—Thou who from Thy heavenly home/Song of the night: Loewe

Der du von dem Himmel bist/Wanderers Nachtlied—Thou that born of Heaven art/Wanderers night song: J Marx

Du wahrer Gott und Davids Sohn—Thou very God and David's son: Bach

Du wollest dem Feinde (Gott ist mein König)—The Lord will not suffer thy foot to be moved: Bach

The duchess of Chicago—Die Herzogin von Chicago: Kálmán

Dudaryk—The fife player: Leontovych

Due bell'alme (Deidamia)—When two fond hearts: Handel

I due Foscari—The two Foscari: Verdi

I due timidi—The two shy people: Rossini

Duggdraaper—Dewdrops: A Backer-Grøndahl

Duke Bluebeard's castle—A Kékszakállú herceg vára: Bartók

Dukkemarch (Humoreske)—Doll's march: Nielsen

Der dukker af disen—Out of the mist: Nielsen

Dulgt Kjaerlighed—Hidden love: Grieg

Duma Chornomorska—Thoughts of the Black Sea: Yamovskyi

The dumb girl—La muette de Portici: Auber

D'un amant inconstant (Les troqueurs)—For a lover's caprice: Dauvergne

D'un vanneur de blé aux vents—The thresher: Berkeley

Das dunkele Reich—The dark kingdom: Pfitzner

Ein dunkeler Schacht (Liebeslieder waltzes)—Ah, love is a mine: Brahms

Dunkler Lichtglanz (Spanische Liebeslieder)—Dark'ning brightness: Schumann

Dunque divin spiracolo—Come then, O holy breath of God: Palestrina

Durch Adams Fall ist ganz verderbt—When Adam fell, the human race: Bach

Durch den Wald—Through the woods: R Franz

Durch den Wald/Frühlingslied—A spring morning: Mendelssohn

Duri e penosi (Il ritorno d'Ulisse)—Grievous and cruel: Monteverdi

The dustman—Der Sandman: M Mayer

Dvenadtsat—The twelve: Salmanov

Dwell not upon the morrow—Es wartet, Alles auf dich: Bach

The dwelling place of Rosamonde—La manoire de Rosemonde: Duparc

Dwojaki koniec—Twofold end: Chopin

Dyby byla kosa nabróšená (Moravské Dvojzpěvy)—The slighted heart: Dvoŗ

The dying child—Das kleinste Lied: Reger

The dying sound—Sehnsucht: F Mendelssohn

Dyvnyi flot—The wonderful fleet: Kozyts'kyi

E

È il soffrirete (Tamerlano)—And ye this horror: Handel
È l'uccellino—A little birdie: Puccini
È me ne voglio andar—And I must wander far: Bimboni
È pena troppo barbara—Too cruel is the bitter pain: Galuppi
È prezzo leggiero (Poro)—The life of a vassal: Handel
È pur bello dal verdi d'un clivo—It is good to lie under green hedges:
    Cagnoni
È pur cosi in un giorno (Giulio Cesare)—Thus by one sole disaster/So
    shall one day's disaster: Handel
È pur io—Lovely maiden: Amadori
È Susanna non vien (Le nozze di Figaro)—Oh! Susanna is late: Mozart
È tanto c'e pericol—Beloved have no fear: Wolf-Ferrari
È vera quella voce (Queen of Sheba)—It was a true report: Castelnuovo-
    Tedesco
Each in other's arms—Hier umarmen sich getreue Gatten: Schubert
Each night in my slumber—Allnächtlich im Traume: Schumann
Each silken thread—Ein jedes Band: Hindemith
The eagle mutiny—Orliny bunt: Pashchenko
The eagles' revolt—Orliny bunt: Pashchenko
The eaglet—L'aiglon: Honegger/Ibert
Earliest green—Erstes Grün: Schumann
Early death—Knabentod: Wolf
Early green—Erstes Grün: Schumann
Early loss—Erste Verlust: R Franz
Early spring—Frühzeitiger Frühling: Mendelssohn
Earth and sky—Feldeinsamkeit: Brahms
Earth, of the rain drinks to her mind—La terre les eaux va beauvant:
    Lassus
Earthly life—Das irdische Leben (Des Knaben Wunderhorn): Mahler
Earthly paradise—Seligkeit: Schubert
Earth's voices—Die Gebüsche: Schubert
Easter oratorio—Oster-Oratorium: Bach
Easter song—Osterlied: Grieg
Ebben? Ne andrò lontana (La Wally)—Farewell to my horse: Catalani
Ecce concipies—Behold thou shalt conceive: Handel
Ecce sacerdos—Great is the Lord: M Haydn
Ecco d'oro l'eta—Hail, age of pure gold: Arcadelt
Ecco, la dea si china (Nerone)—Behold, the godess: Boito
Ecco l'Aurora con l'Aurata fronte—Lo, how Aurora: A Gabrieli
Ecco ridente in cielo (Il barbiere di Siviglia)—Smiling the dawn
    approacheth: Rossini
Eccomi alfine in Babilonia (Semiramide)—Once more behold me in
    Babylon: Rossini

Echo—Similitudine: Bossi
Echo song—Er liebt nur mich allein: Eckert
Echoes of home—Klänge der Heimat (Die Fledermaus): J Strauss II
Echoes of the woods—Geschichten aus dem Wienerwald: J Strauss II
L'écrevisse (Le bestiaire)—The crab: Poulenc
Ecstasy of woe—Wonne der Wehmuth: Beethoven
Ecstasy—Extase: Duparc
E'en as the sea—Chanson de la mer: Aubert
E'en like a ship—Qual nave smarrita (Radamisto): Handel
E'en the shepherd—Pastorello d'un poverto armento (Rodelinda): Handel
E'er since the day—Depuis le jour (Louise): Charpentier
E'er since thine eye—Seitdem dein Aug': R Strauss
E'er when I hear them singing—Hor' ich das Liedchen (Dichterliebe):
    Schumann
Effunderunt sanguinem—Yea, their blood most wantonly did they shed:
    Byrd
Efteraarsstormen—Autumn storms: Grieg
Efterklang—Remembrances: Grieg
Egy ideális (Két portré)—One ideal: Bartók
Egy torz (Két portré)—One grotesque: Bartók
Egydül a tengerrel—I cannot come to you: Bartók
The Egyptian Helen—Die Aegyptische Helena (opera): R Strauss
Die Ehre Gottes aus der Natur—The praise of God/Creation's hymn/The
    glory of God in nature/The heavens declare Him/God's glory divined:
    Beethoven
Ei Mühle, liebe Mühle (Der Rose Pilgerfahrt)—Old mill, beloved so
    dearly: Schumann
Eia mea anima—Now my soul to Bethlehem: Praetorius
Der eidgenossen Nachtwache—The night watch: Schumann
Eifersucht und Stolz (Die schöne Müllerin)—Jealousy and pride: Schubert
Einen Brief soll ich schreiben—The letter/I a note must be writing: Reger
Eingehüllt in granve Wolken—Closely wrapped in murky vapours: Grieg
Einkehr—My hostel: R Strauss
Einklang—Harmony: Wolf
Einsam bin ich, nich alleine (Preciosa)—Lonely am I now no longer: Weber
Einsam in trüben Tagen (Lohengrin)—Lonely and sad and lowly: Wagner
Die Einsame—The soul of solitude: Pfitzner
Der Einsame—Lonesome/The solitary/The recluse/Content: Schubert
Der Einsame—The solitary one: R Strauss
Die Einsame—Lonely girl: Webern
Einsame Blumen (Waldscenen)—Solitary flowers: Schumann
Der Einsame im Herbst (Das Lied von der Erde)—The lonely man in
    autumn/Autumn loneliness/The solitary in autumn: Mahler
Einsamkeit—Solitude: R Khan

Einsamkeit—Solitude: Medtner
Einsamkeit (Die Winterreise)—Loneliness: Schubert
Einsamkeit—Solitude: Schumann
Der Einsiedler—The hermit: Schumann
Einst wollt' ich einen Kranz—Once a wreath for thee/Once and now: Liszt
Einstmals das Kind Kupido—As Cupid once enjoyed his ease: Friderici
Eintritt (Waldscenen)—Entering the forest/Entrance: Schumann
Einun, mein Gott, so fall' ich dir (Sie werden aus Saba alle kommen)—
   My God I give myself to Thee: Bach
Einun, mein Gott, so fall' ich dir (Ich hab in Gottes Herz und Sinn)—
   Content my God: Bach
Einzug der Gladiatoren—Entry of the gladiators: Fučik
Ej, mam já koňa faku—Loved and lost: Dvořák
Die Elfen—The elfin fairies: Beethoven
Elfenlied—Fairy song/Elf-song: Wolf
Elfenliedchen—Song of the elves: Medtner
The elfin fairies—Die Elfen: Beethoven
The Elfking—Näcken: Sibelius
The elf's trip—Où voulez-vous aller?: Gounod
Elf-song—Elfenlied: Wolf
Eliland—Song of Chiemsee: Fielitz
Elindulatam szép hazámbul—I left my fair homeland: Bartók
L'elisir d'amore (opera)—The elixir of love: Donizetti
The elixir of love—L'elisir d'amore (opera): Donizetti
Ella giamma m'amò (Don Carlos)—No! she has never lov'd: Verdi
Elle a fui, la tourterelle (Les contes d'Hoffman)—My pretty dove:
   Offenbach
Elle avait emporté (Tristesses)—She was carrying bunches of lilac: Milhaud
Elle est gravement gaie (Tristesses)—She is gravely gay: Milhaud
Elle était descendue (Tristesses)—She had gone to the edge: Milhaud
Ellen's Gesang/Raste Krieger—Rest thee soldier/Soldier, rest: Schubert
Ellen's hymn—Ave Maria: Schubert-Heller
The elm of Hirsau—Die Ulme zu Hirsau: R Strauss
Els Ballaires dins un sac—Dancing in a sack: Gerhard
Elsk (Haugtussa)—Love: Grieg
Elverskud—The Erl-king's daughter: Gade
Emendemus in melius—Now amend we our sinful lives: Byrd
The emigrants: a home-scene—Die Auswanderer: Heimatbild: Bruch
The emigrants: flight—Die Auswanderer: Flucht: Bruch
Emperor waltz—Kaiser-walzer: J Strauss II
The emperor's new clothes—Des Kaisers neue Kleider: Lofer
Empfindungen bei—see: Als die Geliebte sich trennen wolte
L'empio rigor del fato (Rodelinda)—Fortune, the cruel-hearted: Handel
Empio per farti (Tamerlano)—Monster from hell: Handel

Empty pageant of mourning—Pompe vane di morte (Rodelinda): Handel
En bons militaires (Fra Diavolo)—Comrades, fill your glasses: Auber
En Crimée—On the southern shores of the Crimea: Mussorgsky
En fermant les yeux/Le rêve (Manon)—The dream: Massenet
En la cueva (El amor brujo)—The gipsies: Falla
En hiver—In winter: Hindemith
En natus est Emanuel—This day is born Emmanuel/To us is born Emanuel
     Praetorius
En septembre—In September: A L(ehmann)
En sourdine (Fêtes galantes)—Muted/Calm and silent: Debussy
En sourdine—Muted: Fauré
Encantamiento—Enchantment: Guastavino
The enchanted castle—Das Waldschloss: Mendelssohn
The enchanted flute—La flûte enchantée (Shéhérazade): Ravel
The enchanted forest—La selva incantada: Righini
The enchanted hour—L'heure exquise: Hahn
The enchanted lake—Le lac enchanté: Liadov
The enchanted swans—Die wilden Schwane: Reinecke
Enchanting song—Jószág-igézö: Bartók
Enchantment—Wie die Wolke nach der Sonne: Brahms
Enchantment—Encantamiento: Guastavino
Encounters—Incontri: Nono
The end—Zum Schluss: Schumann
The end is come, the pain is over—Es ist vollbracht, das Leid ist alle
     (Sehet, wir geh'n hinauf gen Jerusalem): Bach
Ende vom Lied (Fantasiestücke)—The climax/The finish: Schumann
Endless sorrow—Lied ohne Ende (Albumblätter): Schumann
Endlich allein—Alone at last: Lehár
Ének Szeut István királyhoz—Hymn to King Stephen: Kodály
Éneklö Dervisek—Singing dervishes: E Ábrányi
Enemic de les dones—The women-hater: Gerhard
L'enfance du Christ—Childhood of Christ: Berlioz
Enfant chéri—Courted by all: Thomas
L'enfant et les sortilèges—The child and the sorceries/The bewitched
     child/The child and witchcraft: Ravel
Enfant, si j'étais roi—Sweet child, if I were king: Liszt
Engedi—Christus am Oelberge: Beethoven
Der Engel (Wesendonck Lieder)—The angel: Wagner
Der englische Gruss (Marienlieder)—The angel's greeting: Brahms
Engravings—Estampes: Debussy
Engulfed—Versunken: Brahms
The engulfed cathedral—La cathédrale engloutie: Debussy
Engulfed in ocean's deepest wave—Wie oft in Meeres tiefsten Schlund
     (Der fliegende Holländer): Wagner

The enigma—Räthsel: Schumann
The enraged one—El despechado: J Berger
Enraptured—Versunken: Schubert
Ensom Vandrer—Solitary traveller: Grieg
Enter in, lordly warrior—Tretet ein, höher Krieger: Pfitzner
Enter not then into judgement—Et non intres in judicium: Byrd
Entering the forest—Eintritt (Waldscenen): Schumann
Entfernte Glocken—Distant bells: Blumenthal
Der Entfernten—The absent one: Cornelius
Entflieh' mit mir—O fly with me: Mendelssohn
Entfliehet, verschwindet, entweichet, ihr Sorgen—Shepherd's cantata: Bach
Entführung—O lady Judith: Brahms
Die Entführung aus dem Serail—The abduction from the seraglio/The
    seraglio: Mozart
Entrance—Eintritt (Waldscenen): Schumann
Entrata di Butterfly (Madama Butterfly)—Butterfly's entrance: Puccini
Entreating child—Bittendes Kind (Kinderscenen): Schumann
Les entretiens de la belle et de la bête (Ma mère l'oye)—Beauty and the
    beast: Ravel
Entry of the gladiators—Einzug der Gladiatoren: Fučik
Entsagung—Resignation: Mendelssohn
Entschwundene Tage—Bygone days: Kjerulf
Envoys of love—Die Boten der Liebe: Brahms
Epheu—Ivy: R Strauss
Das Epheublatt—The ivy leaf: Lassen
Epic song—Chanson épique (Don Quichotte à Dulcinée): Ravel
Epiphanias—The three wise kings: Wolf
Epiphany—Vizkereszt: Kodály
Eprise se d'un (Anacreon chez Polycrate)—A prey to my passion: Grétry
Er, der herrlichste von Allen (Frauenliebe und -leben)—He, the best of all/
    He is the finest of all men/He, the greatest and the noblest/He is noble/
    Humility: Schumann
Er ist gekommen—Lo! he has come: R Franz
Er ist's—Spring is here!/'Tis spring: Schumann
Er ist's—Spring is here: Wolf
Er liebt nur mich allein—Echo song: Eckert
Er liegt und schäft/An die Nachtigall—To the nightingale: Schubert
Er rufet seinen Schafen mit Namen—He calls his sheep by name: Bach
Er und Sie—He and she: Schumann
Era la notte (Otello)—I lay with Cassio: Verdi
Erasi al sole il mio bel sole assiso—My queenly sun before the sun was
    seated: Porta
Erbarme dich, mein Gott (Matthäus-Passion)—Have mercy upon me,
    O Lord: Bach

Erbarme dich, mein, O Herre Gott—Have mercy Lord, my sin forgive: Bach

Erbarmen—The pity of it: Blumenthal

Ercole amanti—Hercules in love: Cavalli

Erdélyi táncok—Transylvanian dances: Bartók

Erewhile upon my fingers—An jeder Hand (Neue Liebeslieder): Brahms

Erfreut euch, ihr Herzen—Rejoice ye hearts: Bach

Erfreute Zeit im Bunde—Joyful time in the new dispensation: Bach

Ergebung—Resignation: Fielitz

Ergebung—Resignation: Schoeck

Ergebung—Submission: Wolf

Erhalt uns, Herr, bei deinem Wort—Uphold us, Lord, with Thy word: Bach

Erhebung—Exaltation: Schoenberg

Erhöhtes Fleisch und Blut—Exalted flesh and blood: Bach

Eri to che macchiavi (Un ballo in maschera)—It was thou the destroyer/ It is thou who hast blighted: Verdi

Erinnerung—Still is the night: Abt

Erinnerung—Remembrance: Brahms

Erinnerung—When all was love: J Marx

Erinnerung (Album für die Jugend)—Recollections/Souvenir: Schumann

Erinnerung an's Schätzle—Old love and new: Erk

Erlaube mir, feins Mädchen—Allow but, dear maiden: Brahms

Erleucht' auch unsern Sinn und Herz (Du Friedefürst, Herr Jesu Christ)— Now at Thy feet creation lies: Bach

Erliebung—Exaltation: Wolf

The Erl-king—Der Erlkönig: Loewe

The Erl-king—Erlkönig: Schubert

The Erl-king's daughter—Elverskud: Gade

Der Erlkönig—The wood-demon/The Erl-king: Loewe

Erlkönig—The Erl-king: Schubert

Erlkönig—O who rides by the night: Schubert-Heller

Erlöse uns vom Übel—Deliver us from evil: Cornelius

Erlösung—A release: Blumenthal

Erlösung—Salvation: Webern

Ermuntre dich, mein schwacher Geist—Look up, faint heart: Bach

Ernani! come to me—Ernani, Ernani, involami (Ernani): Verdi

Ernani, Ernani, involami (Ernani)—Hernani! oh haste to me/Ernani! come to me: Verdi

Erndtlied—The reaper: Mendelssohn

Erndtlied—Harvest song: F X Mozart

Erndtliedchen (Album für die Jugend)—Harvest song/A little harvest song: Schumann

Ernst ist der Frühling—Spring-time is solemn: Wolf

Ero e Leandro—Hero and Leander: Mancinello
An error—Verwechslung: Meyer-Helmund
Erschaffen und Beleben—Genesis and Exodus: Wolf
Erschallet, ihr Lieder—Sing praises: Bach
Erschienen ist der herrliche Tag (Orgelbüchlein)—The day hath dawned—
  the day of days: Bach
Erstanden ist der heil'ge Christ—Luther's cradle hymn/Away in a
  manger: Bach
Erstanden ist der heil'ge Christ (Orgelbüchlein)—The blessed Christ is
  ris'n today: Bach
Erstarrung (Die Winterreise)—Frozen rigidity/Numbness/Benumbed/The
  frozen heart: Schubert
Erste Begegnung—First meeting: Schumann
Der erste Kuss—The first kiss: Haydn
Die erste Ton—The birth of sound: Weber
Das erste Veilchen—The first violet: Mendelssohn
Die erste Walpurgisnacht—The first Walpurgis night: Mendelssohn
Erster Schnee—First snow: Blumenthal
Erster Verlust—Early loss: R Franz
Erster Verlust—First loss: Medtner
Erster Verlust—First sorrow: Mendelssohn
Erster Verlust—First loss: Schubert
Erster Verlust (Album für die Jugend)—First loss/First grief: Schumann
Erstes grün—Early green/Earliest green/First green: Schumann
Erstes Liebeslied eines Mädchens—A girl's first love-song: Wolf
Ertödt uns durch dein' Güte (Bereitet die Wege)—Mortify us by Thy grace:
  Bach
Ertöt' uns durch dein' Güte (Jesus nahm zu sich die Zwölfe/Herr Christ,
  der ein'ge Gottessohn)—Awake us Lord and hasten/O'erwhelm us with
  Thy mercy: Bach
Erwachen—Love's awakening: Blumenthal
Erwartung [opera]—Anticipation/Expectation: Schoenberg
Erwartung [song]—Expectation: Schoenberg
Erwartung—Waiting: Wolf
Erwunschtes Freudenlicht—Longed for joy-light: Bach
Erwürgtes Lamm—O spotless Lamb: Bach
Es bebet das Gestrauche (Liebeslieder waltzes)—Tremor in the branches:
  Brahms
Es bleibt wohl dabei—The joys of constant love: Gounod
Es blüht ein Blümlein—A flow'ret bloomed: Reger
Es brechen im schallenden Reigen/Frühlingslied—Spring song: Mendelssohn
Es fiel ein Reif—One night there came: Mendelssohn
Es geht ein Wehen—I hear a sighing/A sigh goes stirring: Brahms
Es gibt ein Reich (Ariadne auf Naxos)—There is a land: R Strauss

Es ging ein Maidlein zarte—There walked a pretty maiden: Brahms
Es ging sich uns're Frau—Our lady fair reposes: Brahms
Es gingen zwei Gespielen gut [song/part song]—Two comely maidens:
   Schoenberg
Es glänzet der Christen in wediges Leben—God kindles his fire: Bach
Es hat die Rose sich beklagt—Oh! why so soon, the rose complained/
   I heard the rose make sad complaint: R Franz
Es hing der Reif—The frost was white: Brahms
Es ist bestimmt/Volkslied—Mourn not: Mendelssohn
Es ist das Heil uns kommen her (Orgelbüchlein)—Salvation now is come
   to earth: Bach
Es ist das Heil uns kommen her—A crown of grace for man is wrought:
   Brahms
Es ist ein Ros' entsprungen—A rose breaks into bloom/Lo how a rose
   e'er blooming: Brahms
Es ist ein Ros' entsprungen—I know a flower: Praetorius
Es ist ein Trotzig und verzagt Ding—Man's heart's rebellious: Bach
Es ist euch gut, dass ich hingehe—It is for your good that I now leave
   you: Bach
Es ist kein Berg so hoch—There is no mount so high: Hildach
Es ist nichts Gesundes an meinem Liebe—There is naught of soundness
   in all my body: Bach
Es ist nun aus mit meinem Leben—My days of sorrow: Bach
Es ist vollbracht!—It is finished/It is fulfilled: Bach
Es ist vollbracht, das Leid ist alle (Sehet, wir geh'n hinauf gen Jerusalem)—
   The end is come, the pain is over/It is fulfilled: Bach
Es ist vorbei—When love has gone: C Franz
Es kehret der Maien (An die ferne Geliebte)—Bright May now returns:
   Beethoven
Es klingt in der Luft—There sounds in the air: R Franz
Es kummt ein Schiff geladen—There comes a ship full laden: Beck
Es muss ein Wunderbares sein—Oh, who can feel the bliss/O wondrous
   mystery of love/It must be wonderful, withal/Love/Love's marvel/
   It is a wondrous mystery/It must a wondrous rapture be: Liszt
Es ragt in's Meer—The runic rock: R Franz
Es rausche die Winde—The storm winds are roaring: Liszt
Es rauschet das Wasser—Love and the stars/The streamlet flows onwards:
   Brahms
Es reit ein Herr und auch sein Knecht—A master and his man: Brahms
Es ritt ein Ritter—A knight was riding: Brahms
Es ritten drei Reiter zum Tore hinaus—Three riders rode out of the city
   gate: Kämpf
Es sass ein schneeweiss Vögelein—There sat a snow-white birdie: Brahms
Es schauen die Blumen alle—The flow'rs are ever looking: Brahms

Es steht ein Lind—A limetree stands: Brahms
Es stunden drei Rosen—Three roses were growing: Brahms
Es sungen drei Engel (3rd Symphony)—Three angels were singing: Mahler
Es tönt ein voller Harfenklang—I hear a harp/Whene'er the sounding harp
   is heard: Brahms
Es träumte mir, ich sei dir teuer—I dreamed at night that I was dear to
   thee: Brahms
Es treibt mich hin—I pace along here: R Franz
Es war ein alter König—There was an ancient king: Henschel
Es war ein alter König—There was an aged monarch: Meyer-Helmund
Es war ein alter König—There was an aged monarch/There lived an aged
   king: A Rubinstein
Es war ein König in Thule/Der König von Thule—There reigned a
   monarch in Thule/There was a king in Thule/The king of Thule: Liszt
Es war ein Markgraf überm Rhein—There was a margrave: Brahms
Es war ein Traum/Ich hatte einst ein schönes Vaterland—It was a dream/
   The exile's dream/Ah, once I had/Only a dream: Lassen
Es war eine schöne Jüdin—There lived once a handsome Jewess: Brahms
Es war einmal ein König—Song of the flea: Beethoven
Es war einmal ein Zimmergesell—There lived once a carpenter/No man
   knows where love will light: Brahms
Es wartet, alles auf dich—Dwell not upon the morrow: Bach
Es weiss und rät es doch Keiner—No man can guess: Henschel
Es weiss und rät es doch Keiner—Maiden thoughts: Mendelssohn
Es wohnet ein Fiedler—There lived an old fiddler: Brahms
Es woll' uns Gott genädig sein (Die Himmel erzählen die Ehre Gottes)—
   Lord in Thy love: Bach
Escales—Ports of call: Ibert
Eschew evil—Diverte a malo: Byrd
Estampes—Engravings: Debussy
Este—Evening: Kodály
Este a székelyeknél (Tíz könnyü zongoradarab)—An evening at the
   village: Bartók
Esto mihi in deum protectorum—God, in Thee I seek my salvation:
   M Haydn
Estrellita—Little star/Star of love: Ponce
L'estro harmonico—Harmonic inspiration: Vivaldi
Et exivit per auream portam—And through portals of gold he departed:
   Byrd
Et exultavit (Magnificat)—My heart rejoiceth/My soul rejoices: Bach
Et Jesum benedictum—And Jesus, the all-blessed: Byrd
Et non intres in dudicium—Enter not then into judgement: Byrd
Et Vennestykke—Friendship/False friendship: Grieg
Eternal love—Von ewiger Liebe: Brahms

Eternal spring—Ver aeternum: Goltermann
L'étoile du nord—The star of the north: Meyerbeer
Etre jolie, être belle—Charming airs and loveliness: Meister
Etude pour le palais hanté—The haunted palace: F Schmitt
Eva boszorkány—Sorceress ere: E Ábrányi
Der Evangelimann—The evangelist: Kienzl
The evangelist—Der Evangelimann: Kienzl
Eve of battle—Kriegers Ahnung: Schubert
The eve of St Nepomuk—St Nepomuks Vorabend: Wolf
Even as the rain and snow—Gleich wie der Regen und Schnee von
    Himmel fällt: Bach
Even little things—Auch kleine Dinge (Italienisches Liederbuch): Wolf
Even with subdued and weak voices—Auch mit gedampfen, schwachen
    Stimmen (Schwingt freudig euch empor): Bach
Evening—Vorabend (Brautlieder): Cornelius
Evening—Soir: Fauré
Evening—Abends: R Franz
Evening—Este: Kodály
Evening—Des Abends (Fantasiestücke): Schumann
Evening—Kvoelden: Sinding
Evening—Der Abend: R Strauss
Evening at sea—Soirée en mer: Saint-Saëns
An evening at the village—Este a székelyeknél (Tíz könnyü zongoradarab):
    Bartók
The evening bells—Die Abendglocken: Kalliwoda
Evening boat-song—Auf dem Wasser zu singen: Schubert
Evening breezes, softly sighing—Ständchen (Schwannengesang): Schubert
Evening breezes—Ständchen: Schubert-Heller
Evening by the sea—Abends am Strande: Schumann
Evening clouds—Abendwolken: Schoeck
Evening glow—Im Abendrot: Schubert
Evening harmonies—Harmonies du soir: Debussy
Evening harmonies—Harmonies du soir: Liszt
Evening in the mountains—Aften pa Höjfeldet: Grieg
An evening in the mountains—Un soir dans les montagnes: Liszt
Evening meditation—Ave Maria: Bach-Gounod
Evening mood—Abendgefühl: Cornelius
Evening mood—Afenstemning: Nielsen
Evening prayer—Abendsegen (Hänsel und Gretel): Humperdinck
Evening rest—Am Feierabend: Schubert
Evening reverie—Abendempfindung: Mozart
Evening shower—Abendregen: Brahms
Evening song—Abendlied: Blech
Evening song—Abendlied: Mendelssohn

Evening song—Abendlied: Reger
Evening song—Abendlied: Schumann
Evening songs—Večerní písně: Smetana
The evening star—Der Abendstern: Schumann
Evening strains—Abendmusik (Bunte Blätter): Schumann
Evening thoughts—Abendempfindung: Mozart
The evening twilight—Hamaariv Arouim: Gould
Evening walk in spring—Abendgang im Lenz: Reger
Evening winds are sleeping—Die Meere: Brahms
Even-song—Abendlied: Brahms
Evensong—Le soir: Gounod
Evensong—Abendstimmung: Kjerulf
Evensong—Abendlied: Mendelssohn
Evensong—Abendlied: Schumann
Evensong for the distant ones—Abendlied für die Entfernte: Schubert
Eventide—Mot kveld: A Backer-Grøndahl
Eventide—Abends: R Franz
L'évêque d'Autun—The bishop of Autun: Françaix
Ever and anon—Strahlt zuweilen auch ein mildes Licht: Brahms
Ever lighter—Immer leiser wird mein Schlummer: Brahms
Ever near thee—Immer bei dir: Raff
Every Sabbath thine altar—Ogni Sabato: Gordigiani
Everything—Alles: Schoenberg
Everything is transitory—Alles Vergangliche ist nur ein Gleichnis (Faust
    Symphony): Liszt
Everywhere the moorland is still—Uber allen Gipfeln ist ruh': Loewe
An evil day—Vond Dag (Haugtussa): Grieg
Ev'ry kiss is a song—La mélodie des baisers: Massenet
Exaltation—Erhebung: Schoenberg
Exaltation—Erhebung: Wolf
Exalted flesh and blood—Erhöhtes Fleisch und Blut: Bach
Das Examen—The examination: P Burkhard
The examination—Das Examen: P Burkhard
Except the Lord build the house—Nisi Dominus: Handel
The excited ones—Die Aufgeregten: Schoenberg
Exil—Exile: Chaminade
Exile—Exil: Chaminade
Exile—Siralmas nékem: Kodály
The exile—In der Ferne: Schubert
Exiled from thee—Lungi da te, ben mio: Mercadante
The exile's dream—Es war ein Traum/Ich hatte einst ein schönes
    Vaterland: Lassen
Expectation—Die Harrende: R Franz
Expectation—Erwartung [opera]: Schoenberg

Expectation—Erwartung [song]: Schoenberg

The experienced heart—Geubtes Herz: Schoenberg

Explosion—Vybukh: Yanovskyi

The expulsion of Adam and Eve from Paradise—Maledictus evis inter omnia: Tomasi

Exspectans exspectavi—I waited expectantly: Lassus

Exultate Deo—Sing with joy and gladness: Palestrina

Exsurge, Domine—Arise, Lord, why sleepest Thou: Byrd

Extase—Ecstasy: Duparc

Exultate Deo—Sing aloud with gladness: S Wesley

Eyes, cease from weeping—Vaghe pupille, no non piangete (Orlando): Handel

Eyes of azure hath the maiden—Blaue Augen hat das Mädchen (Spanische Liebeslieder): Schumann

Eyes of beauty, blue as azure—Schwebe, schwebe, blaues Augen: Liszt

Eyes of lightning—Flammenauge dunkles Haar (Neue Liebeslieder): Brahms

The eyes of my beloved—Le luci del mio bene (Teseo): Handel

The eyes of spring—Die blauen Frühlingsaugen: R Franz

Ezerével terem—In summer the meadow: Erkel

F

The fable of the changeling—La favola del figlio cambiato: Malipiero
A fából faragott Királyfi—The wooden prince: Bartók
Fac cum servo—O deal with Thy servant: Byrd
Facti sumus opprobrium—We became thus an open shame: Byrd
Factum est silentium—Silence prevailed in heaven: Dering
Faded flowers—Trockne Blumen (Die schöne Müllerin): Schubert
Faedrelands-Salme—Fatherland's psalm: Grieg
Fagnes de Wallonie—Walloon uplands: Poulenc
Fahrt zum Hades—Voyage to Hades/Passing to Hades: Schubert
Fahr' wohl—Farewell: Brahms
Faiblesse de la race humaine! (La reine de Saba)—How frail and weak a
    thing is man: Gounod
Fain art thou—Bitteres zu sagen denkst du: Brahms
Fain would I bow—Voglio chinar la fronte: Magaldi
Faint and fainter—Immer leiser wird mein Schlummer: Brahms
Fair are roses—Schön sind Rosen: Kirnberger
Fair as the morn—Wie bist du, meine Königin: Brahms
The fair begins—Der Markt beginnt (Martha): Flotow
Fair cheeks ye ensnare me—O liebliche Wangen: Brahms
Fair Hedwig—Schön Hedwig: Schumann
Fair hours of youth and pleasure—Oh! de'verd' anni miei (Ernani): Verdi
Fair is my love—Caro mio ben: Giordani
Fair is the crystal—Beau le cristal: Lassus
The fair Magelone—Die schöne Magelone: Brahms
The fair maid of Perth—La jolie fille de Perth: Bizet
The fair maid of the mill—Die schöne Müllerin: Schubert
Fair maiden—Ma mie: A L(ehmann)
Fair maidens—Les filles de Cadix: Delibes
Fair May is past—Rosen aus dem Süden: J Strauss II
Fair red-rose—Treu Röschen: Loewe
Fair Tirsi—No, Tirsi, to non hai: Veracini
A fair vision—Eit Syn: Grieg
Fairest adored—Alma del core: Caldara
Fairest flower—Schön Blümelein: Schumann
The fairest mead—Un verde practicello: Wolf-Ferrari
The fairest one—La plus belle: Godard
The fairies—Die Feen: Wagner
Fairies are beautiful dancers—Fées sont d'exquises danseuses: Debussy
Fairy dance—Alfedans: Grieg
Fairy household—Kleiner Haushalt: Loewe
The fairy Reedfoot—Nixe Binsefuss: Wolf
Fairy revel—Neue Liebe: Mendelssohn

Fairy song—Elfenlied: Wolf
The fairy tale—Märchenwunder (Brautlieder): Cornelius
Fairy tale—Satu (Ungdom): Palgrem
Fairy tale—Skazka: Prokofiev
Fairy tale—Pohádka: Smetana
The fairy's kiss—Le baiser de la fée: Stravinsky
Faisait-il beau (Tristesses)—Do you remember if 'twas fine: Milhaud
Faites lui mes aveux (Faust)—Flower song: Gounod
Faith—Trudom: Grieg
Faith and hope play—Tro og håb spiller (Moderen): Nielsen
Faith, hope and love—Glaube, Hoffnung und Liebe: Schubert
Faith in spring—Frühlingsglaube: Schubert
Faithful and true—Treulich geführt ziehet dahin (Lohengrin): Wagner
Faithful heart enraptured—L'amerò (Il re pastore): Mozart
Faithful love—Liebestreu: Brahms
Faithful love—Treue Liebe: Brahms
Faithful love this heart inspiring—Non temer, amato bene [K 490]:
    Mozart
Faithfulness—Treue: Cornelius
Faithless—Untreu: Cornelius
Faithless as fair—Tu lo sai: A Scarlatti
The falcon—Der Falke: Brahms
The falcon—Waldvögelein's Bitte: Gerle
Der Falke—The falcon: Brahms
Fall asleep, ye cares and troubles—Schläfert aller Sorgen Kummer (Gott
    ist uns're Zuversicht): Bach
Fall asleep ye weary eyes—Schlummert ein, ihr matten Augen (Ich habe
    genug): Bach
The fall of Arkun—Päd Arkuna: Fibich
The fall of the house of Usher—La chute de la maison Usher: Debussy
Falsa immagine (Ottone)—Fond illusion: Handel
Falsche Welt, dir trau' ich nicht—Treacherous world, I trust thee not:
    Bach
The false dream—Tränenregen (Die schöne Müllerin): Schubert
The false dream—Täuschung (Die Winterreise): Schubert
False friends—Et Vennestykke: Grieg
False love—Amore traditore: Bach (?)
False man—Csalfa legény: Erkel
A falsehood love has told me—Die Liebe hat gelogen: Schubert
A falu tánca (Két Kép)—Village dance: Bartók
Falun—Village scenes: Bartók
Familien gemalde—Love's morn and eve: Schumann
Fancies—Gedenken: Cornelius
Fanciful dance—Phantasientanz (Fantasiestücke): Schumann

La fanciulla del West—The girl of the golden West: Puccini
Fancy dance—Phantasientanz (Fantasiestücke): Schumann
Fancy piece—Phantasiestück (Albumblätter): Schumann
Fangernes dans (Aladdin)—Prisoners' dance: Nielsen
Fanschingsschwank aus Wien—Carnival jest from Vienna: Schumann
Fantasia—Phantasiestücke (Albumblätter): Schumann
En fantasirejse til Ferøerne—A phantasy/Journey to the Faroe Islands:
    Nielsen
Fantastic dance—Phantasientanz (Fantasiestücke): Schumann
Fantastic symphony—Symphonie fantastique: Berlioz
The fantastic toyshop—La boutique fantasque: Rossini-Respighi
Fantastie—Fantouches (Fêtes galantes): Debussy
Fantasy—Phantasiestück (Albumblätter): Schumann
Fantouches (Fêtes galantes)—Marionettes/Fantastic: Debussy
Far away—In der Ferne: Brahms
Far away—In der Ferne: Kalliwoda
Far away—In der Ferne: Kreutzer
Far away lies a land—Connais-tu le pays (Mignon): Thomas
Far from home—In der Fremde: Schumann
Far from Moscow—Daleko ot Moskvï: Dzerzhinsky
Far from my dear one—Lungi dal caro bene (Giulio Sabino): Sarti
Far from my love—Lungi dal caro bene (Giulio Sabrio): Sarti
Far from the scene—Queste ad un lido fatal (Nerone): Boito
Far greater in his lowly state (La reine de Saba)—Plus grand dans
    son obscurité: Gounod
Far o'er the bay—Choeur des matelots: Franck
Far o'er the moorland reaches—Über den dunklen Heide: Henschel
Far over the hill—Wer hat dies Liedlein erdacht? (Des Knaben Wunderhorn):
    Mahler
Die Farben Helgolands—Helgoland's colours: R Franz
Fare thee well—Parto si (Flavio): Handel
Fare thee well!—Isten veled!: Liszt
Fare thee well, thou worldly tumult—Gute Nacht, die Weltgetümmel
    (Wer weiss, wie nahe mir mein Ende): Bach
The farewell—Non temer, non son più amante: Anfossi
The farewell—La partenza: Beethoven
A farewell—Lebewohl: Blumenthal
Farewell—Fahr' wohl: Brahms
Farewell—Adieu (Poème d'un jour): Fauré
Farewell—Gute Nacht: R Franz
Farewell—Vou-me embora: Guarnieri
The farewell—Der Abschied (Das Lied von der Erde): Mahler
Farewell—Abschied: Pfitzner
Farewell—La despedida: Ponce

Farewell—Abschied: Schoeck
Farewell—Abschied: Schoenberg
Farewell—Abschied (Waldscenen): Schumann
The farewell—Wanderlied: Schumann
A farewell—Ich schwebe: R Strauss
Farewell—Lebe wohl: Wolf
Farewell at morn—L'adieu du matin: Pessard
Farewell, Bessy—Adieu, Bessy (Melodies irlandaises): Berlioz
Farewell I gladly bid Thee—Valet will ich dir geben: Bach
Farewell my beloved—Bella mia fiamma: Mozart
Farewell, my native town—Farvel, min velsignede fødeby: Nielsen
Farewell, my noble, valorous child—Leb' wohl, du kühnes (Die
    Walküre): Wagner
The farewell of the Arabian hostess—Les adieux de l'hôtesse arabe: Bizet
Farewell song of the birds—Abschiedslied der Zugvögel: Mendelssohn
Farewell sweet shepherdess—O pastorelle addio (Andrea Chénier): Giorda▶
Farewell to France—Abschied von Frankreich: Schumann
Farewell to my house—Ebben? Ne andrò lontano (La Wally): Catalani
Farewell to the forest—Abschied (Waldscenen): Schumann
Farewell to the woods—Abschied vom Walde: Schumann
Farewell to the world—Abschied von der Welt: Schumann
Farewell ye mountains—Adieu forêts (Joan of Arc): Tchaikovsky
Farewell! your country calls you—Lascia amor (Orlando): Handel
Farewells—Adieux: Roussel
Farmboy, load the cart well—Béreslegény, jol megratcd a szekeret: Bartók
Farmyard song—Lok (Barnlige Sanger): Grieg
Far-off land—Schöne Fremde: Schumann
Far-off youth—Dalekaya yunost: Shaporin
Farsangi ladoalom—Wedding in carnival: Poldini
Farvel, min velsignede fødeby—Farewell, my native town: Nielsen
Die Faschingsfee—Carnival fairy: Kálmán
Fast zu ernst (Kinderscenen)—Almost too serious (solemn): Schumann
The fatal Loreley—Lorelei: Silcher
Fate—Destinée (Petites légendes): Milhaud
Fated love—Liebeserwachen: Blumenthal
Father eternal—Ave Maria: Bach-Gounod
Father eternal—O bone Jesu: Brahms
The Father hath appointed him—Der Vater hat ihm ja ein ewig (Gott
    fähret auf mit jauchzen): Bach
Father in heaven—Ombra mai fù (Serse): Handel
Fatherland's psalm—Faederlands Salme: Grieg
Father's cradle-song—Vuggesang: Grieg
Fatto inferno è il mio petto (Roselinda)—Hell is raging in my bosom:
    Handel

The faun—Le faune (Fêtes galantes): Debussy
Le faune (Fêtes galantes)—The faun/The dancing faun: Debussy
La fauvette avec ses petits (Zemire et Azor)—The pretty warbler: Grétry
De favitska jungfrurna—The wise and foolish virgins: Atterberg
La favola del figlio cambiato—The fable of the changeling: Malipiero
The favourite spot—Lieblingsplätzchen: Mendelssohn
Fear thou not—Non temer, amato bene [K 505]: Mozart
The feast of the jest—La cena delle beffe: Giordano
Feast of the Pentecost—Das Liebesmahl der Apostel: Wagner
Fecském, fecském édes fecském—Come here, birdie dear: Erkel
Feelings at evening—Abendempfindung: Mozart
Die Feen—The fairies: Wagner
Fées sont d'exquises danseuses—Fairies are beautiful dancers: Debussy
Fehér László lovat lopott—Fehér László stole a horse: Bartók
Fehér László stole a horse—Fehér László lovat lopott: Bartók
Die feindlichen Brüder—The brothers' feud: Schumann
Feinsliebchen, du sollst mir nicht—My darling shall never/Why go
    barefoot/The barefoot lass: Brahms
Fekete szem éjczakája—Thine eyes are black: Erkel
Feldeinsamkeit—In the summerfields/Spell of the fields/Solitude in the
    fields/Earth and sky/Solitude in summer fields/Lone dreamer: Brahms
Les femmes de Magdala—Women of Magdala: Massenet
Die Fensterschiebe—The window pane: Schumann
Ferito, prigionier (Germania)—I'm a prisoner and wounded: Franchetti
Fermez vous pour jamais (Amadis de Gaule)—Ye must close to the day:
    Lully
Ferne—To far-off chimes: Mendelssohn
Der ferne Klang—The distant sound: Schreker
Die fernen, fernen Berge/Mädchenlied—The love-lorn lassie: Reger
Fernes Klingen—Forebodings: Dohnányi
The ferry-boat—Das Schifflein: Mendelssohn
The ferryman's brides—Koskenlaskijan morsiamet: Sibelius
Fervent passion, fiercely burning—Quella fiamma che m'accende:
    Marcello
Ein' feste Burg ist unser Gott—A mighty fortress is our God/A stronghold
    is our God/A stronghold sure: Bach
Feste Romane—Roman festivals: Respighi
Feste's closing song from Twelfth night—Schlusslied des Narren: Schumann
Le festin d'araignée—The spider's feast: Roussel
The festival—Sontagslied: Mendelssohn
Festival of Love and of Bacchus—Les fêtes de l'Amour et de Bacchus: Lully
Festival of spring—Frühlingsfeier: R Strauss
Festival overture—Fest-ouverture: Schumann
Festivals—Alegr'as: Gerhard

Fest-ouverture—Festival overture: Schumann
Les fêtes de l'Amour et de Bacchus—Festival of Love and Bacchus: Lully
Le feu qu'en ce temple on adore (Les éléments)—The flame we adore
     in this temple: Destouches
Das Feuerkreuz—The fiery cross: Bruch
Der Feuerreiter—The fire-rider: Wolf
Feuersnot—Fire famine: R Strauss
Feuerzauber (Die Walküre)—Magic fire music: Wagner
Les feuilles (Petites légendes)—The leaves: Milhaud
Feuilles mortes—Dead leaves: Debussy
Les feuilles mortes—Autumn leaves: Kosma
Feux d'artifices—Fireworks: Debussy
Feux-follets—Will-o-the-wisp: Liszt
Fia dunque vero?—Ah! it is true: Donizetti
Fiancailles pour rire—Whimsical betrothal: Poulenc
Der Fichtenbaum—The fir-tree: R Franz
Ein Fichtenbaum steht einsam—A pine-tree stands forsaken: Liszt
Fickle-hearted Mimi—O Mimi tu più non torni (La bohème): Puccini
Fiddle songs—Fiedellieder: Křenek
Der fiddle Bauer—The merry peasant: Fall
Fidelity—Treue: Haydn
Fidelity—So wahr die Sonne scheint: Schumann
Fiedellieder—Fiddle songs: Křenek
The fiery cross—Das Feuerkreuz: Bruch
Fièvre jaune—Yellow fever: Honegger
The fife player—Dudaryk: Leontovych
Figlia mia, non pianger, nò (Tamerlano)—Oh! my daughter/Dearest
     daughter: Handel
Il figliuol prodigo—The prodigal son: Ponchielli
Figure de force brulant et farouche (Tel jour telle nuit)—Image of fiery
     wild forcefulness: Poulenc
Filhas de Maria—Daughters of the Virgin Mary: Villa-Lobos
Fill high—Libiamo ne' lieti calici (La traviata): Verdi
Fille à la blonde chevelure—Maiden with the golden hair: Godard
La fille aux cheveux de lin—The girl with the flaxen hair: Debussy
La fille de Madame Angot—Madame Angot's daughter: Lecoq
La fille du regiment—The daughter of the regiment: Donizetti
La fille du tambour-major—The drum-major's daughter: Offenbach
Filled with flowers—Fyldt med blomster: Nielsen
Filled with that sweetness—Voll jener Süsse: Schoenberg
Les filles de Cadix—Fair maidens/The maids of Cadiz/The daughters of
     Cadiz: Delibes
Il filosofo di campagna—The peasant philosopher: Galuppi
Fils de la Vièrge—The Virgin's threads: Schmitt

The finch—Das Zeisig: Schumann
Finch' han dal vino (Don Giovanni)—While from the wine cup: Mozart
Finchè lo strale (Floridante)—'Tis worth observing: Handel
Finger exercise—Ujigyakorlat (Tíz könnyü zongoradarab): Bartók
The finish—Ende vom Lied (Fantasiestücke): Schumann
Finstere Schatten (Neue Liebeslieder)—Shadowy gloom: Brahms
La finta giardiniera—The pretended gardener: Mozart
La finta semplice—The pretended simpleton: Mozart
Fire famine—Feuersnot: R Strauss
Fire on the island—Saarella palaa: Sibelius
De fire temperamenter [symphony]—The four temperaments: Nielsen
Firebird—Zhar-ptitsa: Stravinsky
The fire-rider—Der Feuerreiter: Wolf
Fireside bliss—Hardglück: Bocquet
Fireworks—Feux d'artifices: Debussy
The first—Première: Aubert
The first cavalry—Pervaya Konnaya: Davidenko
The first commandment—Die Schuldigkeit des ersten und fürnehmsten
    Gebotes: Mozart
The first day of spring—Frühlingsahnung: Mendelssohn
First green—Erstes grün: Schumann
First grief—Erster Verlust (Album für die Jugend): Schumann
The first kiss—Der erste Kuss: Haydn
The first kiss—Den första kyssen: Sibelius
First loss—Erster Verlust: Medtner
First loss—Erster Verlust: Schubert
First loss—Erster Verlust (Album für die Jugend): Schumann
The first meeting—Det første Møde: Grieg
First meeting—Erste Begegnung: Schumann
The first primrose—Med en Primula veris: Grieg
First snow—Erster Schnee: Blumenthal
First sorrow—Erster Verlust: Mendelssohn
The first thing—Det Förste: Grieg
The first violet—Das erste Veilchen: Mendelssohn
The first Walpurgis night—Die erste Walpurgisnachte: Mendelssohn
The fir-tree—Der Fichtenbaum: R Franz
Der Fischer—The fisherman: Hauptman
Der Fischer—The fisherman/The angler: Schubert
Der Fischerknabe—The fisher-boy: Liszt
Das Fischermädchen (Schwanengesang)—The fisher girl: Schubert
Fischers Liebesglück—The fisher's love delight/Fisherman's bliss/The
    fisherman's wooing: Schubert
Die Fischerstochter—The fisherman's daughter: Liszt

Fischerweise—Fisher-ways/Fisher's song/Fisher-rhyme/Fisher-song:
  Schubert
The fisher—Le pêcheur: Berlioz
The fisher-boy—Der Fischerknabe: Liszt
The fisher girl—Das Fischermädchen (Schwanengesang): Schubert
Fisher-rhyme—Fischerweise: Schubert
Fisher-song—Fischerweise: Schubert
Fisher-ways—Fischerweise: Schubert
The fisherman—Hullámzo balaton tetején: Erkel
The fisherman—Der Fischer: Hauptman
The fisherman—Der Fischer: Schubert
The fisherman and his wife—Vom Fischer und seiner Frau: Schoeck
A fisherman sat thoughtfully—Der sad en fisker så tankefuld: Nielsen
Fisherman thy bait now lower—Pescator, affonda l'esca (La gioconda): Ponch
Fisherman's bliss—Fischers Liebesglück: Schubert
The fisherman's daughter—Die Fischerstochter: Liszt
The fisherman's wooing—Fischers Liebesglück: Schubert
The fisher's love delight—Fischers Liebesglück: Schubert
Fisher's song—Fiskervise (Barnlige Sanger): Grieg
Fisher's song—Fischerweise: Schubert
Fiskervise (Barnlige Sanger)—Fisher's song: Grieg
The five fingers—Les cinq doigts: Françaix
The five hours—Las cinco horas (Canciones de niños): Revueltas
The flame of Paris—Plamya Parizha: Asaf'yev
The flame of passion—Il mio bel foco: Marcello
The flame we adore in this temple—Le feu qu'en ce temple on adore
  (Les éléments): Destouches
The flames of Paris—Plamya Parizha: Asaf'yev
The flaming angel—Ognennïy Angel: Prokofiev
Flammenauge dunkles Haar (Neue Liebeslieder)—Eyes of lightning:
  Brahms
Die Fledermaus—The bat/Pink champagne: J Strauss II
Fleecy cloud—Leichte Segler (An die ferne Geliebte): Beethoven
Fleeting love—Plaisir d'amour: Martini
Fleur du vallon—Flower of the valley: Godard
La fleur que tu m'avais jetée (Carmen)—Flower song: Bizet
Fleurs (Fiancailles pour rire)—Flowers: Poulenc
Flieder—Under the lilacs: Reger
Der fliegende Holländer—The flying Dutchman: Wagner
Flight into distance—Drang in die Ferne: Schubert
Flight of time—Der Flug der Zeit: Schubert
Flocks in green pastures abiding—Schafe können sicher weiden (Was mir
  behagt): Bach
Flood—Wasserflut (Die Winterreise): Schubert

The flood that spent in torrent roaring—Der Strom, der neben mir verrauschte: Brahms
Florentine serenade—Sérénade florentine: Duparc
Flower and fragrance—Blume und Duft: Liszt
Flower and scent—Blume und Duft: Liszt
A flower art thou—Du bist wie eine Blume: A Rubinstein
Flower greeting—Blumengruss: Wolf
The flower letter—Der Blumenbrief: Schubert
The flower message—Der Blumenbrief: Schubert
The flower of resignation—Die Blume der Ergebung: Schumann
Flower of the valley—Fleur du vallon: Godard
The flower shroud—Bedeckt mich mit Blumen: Schumann
Flower song—La fleur que tu m'avais jetée (Carmen): Bizet
Flower song—Faites-lui mes aveux (Faust): Gounod
The flower song—Blumenlied: Schubert
A flower thou resemblest—Du bist wie eine Blume: Liszt
A flower thou resemblest—Du bist wie eine Blume: A Rubinstein
A flower you stand before me—Du bist wie eine Blume: Wolf
A flow'ret bloomed—Es blüht ein Blümlein: Reger
Flow'ring chestnut tree—Como castaño en flor: N Fraser
Flowers—Fleurs (Fiancailles pour rire): Poulenc
The flow'rs are ever looking—Es schauen die Blumen alle: Brahms
Flowers are gay when they open—Quando uma flôr desabroche: Mignone
The flowers' secret—Die Verschweigen: R Strauss
Flowers that bloomed (for me)—Ich sah als Knabe Blumen blühen: Brahms
Flucht—Soaring: Schubert
Die Fluchlinge—The fugitives: Schumann
Der Flug der Zeit—Flight of time: Schubert
Die Flut—The tide: Blacher
La flûte de Pan (Chansons de Bilitis)—The flute of Pan: Debussy
La flûte enchantée (Shéhérazade)—The enchanted flute: Ravel
The flute of Pan—La flûte de Pan (Chansons de Bilitis): Debussy
Fly forth, fly forth, my pretty dove—Waldvöglein: Ditforth
Fly my soul this doleful mood—Nicht so traurig, nicht so sehr: Bach
Fly then to my beloved—Il mio tesoro (Don Giovanni): Mozart
The flying Dutchman—Der fliegende Holländer: Wagner
Fog-land—Nebel: R Franz
Fold within fold—Pli selon pli: Boulez
Folding time—Der Sandmännchen: Brahms
Foliage of the heart—Herzgewächse: Schoenberg
Folk song from Langeland—Langelandsk Folkemelodi: Grieg
Folk-song—Volksliedchen: Schumann
Folk-song suite—Suite dos cânticos sertanejos: Villa-Lobos

Folle è colui (Ezio)—Senseless the man: Handel
Föllszallot a páva—The peacocks: Kodály
Fond heart, full of mercy—Barmherziges Herze der ewigen Liebe: Bach
Fond illusion—False immagine (Ottone): Handel
Fondly complaining—Spiagge amate (Paride ed Elena): Gluck
Fontane di Roma—The fountains of Rome: Respighi
Fool's paradise—Das Schlaraffenland: Brahms
The footpath—Chodníček: Martinů
Footsteps in the snow—Des pas sur la neige: Debussy
For a lover's caprice—D'un amant inconstant: Dauvergne
For an album—Page d'album: Berlioz
For as a loving Father—Wie sich ein Vat'r erbarmet (Wer Dank opfert,
    der preiset mich): Bach
For children—Gyermekeknek: Bartók
For dine Fodder—At your feet: Grieg
For ever blessed—Beati Mortui: Mendelssohn
For ever dear—Oh! divina Agnese (Beatrice di Tenda): Bellini
For everything there is a season—Heinieden alles hat seine Stunde: Rozsa
For God's angels ne'er depart—Gottes Engel weichen nie (Man singet mit
    Freuden von Sieg): Bach
For in his own hand—Denn in seiner Hand: Mendelssohn
For in those days justice shall arise—Orientur: Byrd .
For music—Für musik: R Franz
For in my heart's place—Per non penar: Astorga
For Red Petrograd—Za Krasny Petrograd: Triodin
For so hath the Lord commanded—Den also hat uns der Herr geboten
    (Paulus): Mendelssohn
For somebody—Für Einen: R Franz
For the beauty of the earth—Hilf, Herr Jesu, lass gelingen: Bach
For the new year—Neujahrslied: Mendelssohn
For the glory of adoring—Per la gloria d'adorarvi (Griselda):
    G B Bononcini
For the Lord shall guide them—Doch der Herr, er leitet die: Mendelssohn
For the love my heart doth prize—Per la gloria d'adorarvi (Grisela):
    G B Bononcini
For the sake of somebody—Jemand (Myrthen): Schumann
For Thee, Jehovah, are our praises—Dir Jehovah will ich singen: Bach
For these things justly have we suffered—Nos enim pro peccatio: Byrd
For three long days—Tre giorno son che Nina: Pergolesi
For what, for what may prove—Volkslied: R Franz
Forårsregn—Spring showers: Grieg
Forbi—Gone: Grieg
Forbidden melody—Musica proibita: Gastaldon
The force of destiny—La forza del destino: Verdi

Forebodings—Fernes Klingen: Dohnányi
Forebodings—Vergessen: R Franz
Die Forelle—The trout: Schubert
Forest—Forêt: Caplet
The forest—Der Wald: Smyth
The forest calls—Schlaflied: Schubert-Heller
The forest castle—Das Waldschloss: Mendelssohn
The forest fairy—Waldmädchen: Wolf
Forest glade—Bois épais (Amadis de Gaule): Lully
Forest legend—Waldesgespräch: Schumann
Forest murmers—Waldesrauschen: Liszt
Forest murmers—Waldweben (Siegfried): Wagner
The forest of the Samodivas—La foresta delle Samodive: Rocca
Forest scenes—Waldszenen: Schumann
Forest voices—Aus dem Walde: Blech
La foresta delle Samodive—The forest of the Samodivas: Rocca
Forest-nymph—Waldmärchen: Wolf
The forest's greeting—Waldesgruss: Reinecke
Forêt—Forest: Caplet
La forêt bleue—The blue forest: Aubert
Forever—Toujours (Poème d'un jour): Fauré
The forge—Der Schmied: Brahms
Forget me not—Vergissmeinnicht: Bach
Forget me not—Vergissmeinnicht: R Franz
Forget me not—Vergissmeinnicht: Mozart
Forget thy grief—Consolati e spera: D Scarlatti
Forget us not, O Lord—Vergiss es fernes nicht (Wir danken dir, Gott,
    wir danken dir): Bach
Forgetfulness—Das Kraut Vergessenheit: Hildach
Forget-me-not—Vergissmeinnicht: E de Curtis
Forgive us our trespasses—Vergib uns uns're Schuld: Cornelius
Forgotten airs—Ariettes oubliées: Debussy
Forgotten, forgotten—Vorüber die stuhnende Klage: Schubert
Forlorn—Ich schleich umher: Brahms
The forlorn—Die Trauernde: Brahms
The former life—La vie antérieure: Duparc
Formosos olhos—O lovely eyes: J Berger
Forsake me not—Vergiss mein nicht, mein allerliebster Gott: Bach
Forsake me not—Verlass' mich nicht: R Franz
Forsaken—Nachwirkung: Brahms
Forsaken—Holub na javoře (Moravské Dvojzpévy): Dvořák
Forsaken—Verlassen: Liszt
Forsaken—Verlust: F Mendelssohn
Forsaken—Unbegehrt: Reger

Forsaken—Verlassen: Schoenberg
Forsaken love—Opuštěný milý: Martinů
The forsaken maiden—Das verlassene Mägdlein: Goetz
Den första Kyssen—The first kiss: Sibelius
Det Förste—The first thing/The only thing: Grieg
Det fórste Mode—The first meeting: Grieg
Forte e lieto a morte (Tamerlano)—Boldly and blithely to death: Handel
Forunderligt at sige—How strange it is to say: Nielsen
Fortune once made us happy—Fummo felici un tempo: Vecchi
The fortune teller—Die Kartenlegerin: Schumann
Fortune, the cruel-hearted—L'empio rigor del fato (Rodelinda): Handel
La forza del destino—The force of destiny/The power of destiny: Verdi
Found—Gefunden: R Strauss
The foundry—Zavod: Mosolov
Fount of tears—Das Weinen: Schubert
The fountain—Le jet d'eau: Debussy
The fountain of Bakhchisaray—Bakhchisarysky fontan: Asafyev
The fountains at the villa d'Este—Les jeux d'eaux à la villa d'Este
    (Années de pèlerinage): Liszt
The fountains of Rome—Fontane di Roma: Respighi
The fountain's song—Brunnensang: Reger
The four ages—Los cuatro soles: Chavez
Four dirges—Négy Siratoének: Bartók
Four hussar songs—Vier Husarenlieder: Schumann
Four last songs—Vier letzte Lieder: R Strauss
Four pieces—Négy zenekari darab [op 12]: Bartók
The four ruffians—I quattro rusteghi: Wolf-Ferrari
The four seasons—Cantata secularis: Seiber
Four serious songs—Vier ernste Gesänge: Brahms
The four temperaments—De fire temperamenter [symphony]: Nielsen
The four years' sentry—Der Vierjährige Posten: Schubert
Fourteen bagatelles—Tizennégy zongoradarab: Bartók
The fox—Renard: Stravinsky
Fra Diavolo—Brother devil: Auber
Fra Fjeld og Fjord—Reminiscences of mountain and fiord: Grieg
Fra i due litiganti il terzo gode—Between two litigants, a third succeeds:
    Sarti
Fra monte Pincio—From Mount Pincio: Grieg
Fra Ungdomsdagene—From early years: Grieg
Frage—Is it so?/Question/Is it true?: Mendelssohn
Frage—A Question: Schumann
Frage nicht—Ask me not: Wolf
Frage und Antwort—Question and answer: J Marx
Frage und Antwort—Question and answer: Wolf

Fragen—Questionings/Questions: Brahms
Fragment—Anklänge: Brahms
La fraicheur et le feu—The coolness and the fire: Poulenc
The frail one—La traviata: Verdi
Les francs juges—The judges of the secret court: Berlioz
Lo frate'nnamorato—The brother in love: Pergolesi
Frau Luna—Castles in the air: Lincke
Frau Musica—In praise of music: Hindemith
Die Frau ohne Kuss—The woman without a kiss: Kollo
Die Frau ohne Schatten—The woman without a shadow: R Strauss
Die Frauen sind oft fromm—Sweet woman oft in silence prays: R Strauss
Frauenklage—Lady's lament: Hindemith
Frauenliebe und- leben—(A) woman's love and (woman's) life: Schumann
Frauenschöne—Maiden-beauty: Spervogel
Frauenwörter—It was a day: Fielitz
Frech und froh—Uninhibited: Wolf
Free as air—Sempre libera (La traviata): Verdi
Free is he—Keinem hat es noch gereut: Brahms
The free man—Der freie Mann: Beethoven
Freedom is the brightest of gold—Frihed er det bedste guld: Nielsen
Freehold—Freihold: Schoenberg
The freeshooter—Der Freischütz: Weber
Freide auf Erden—Peace on earth: Schoenberg
Der freie Mann—The free man: Beethoven
Freihold—Freehold: Schoenberg
Der Freischütz—The free-shooter: Weber
Freisinn—Independence: Schubert
Freisinn (Myrthen)—Independence: Schumann
Freiwillige her!—United are we/Come, sons of the free!/Sing, sons of
   the free: Brahms
Frêle comme un harmonica—Softly as sweet harmonica: Rhené-Baton
Fremde Erde—Strange land/Strange world: Rathaus
Fremder Mann (Album für die Jügend)—The stranger: Schumann
Frenzy—Schwung: R Strauss
Freudig begrüssen (Tannhäuser)—Hail bright abode/Tournament of song:
   Wagner
Freudvoll und leidvoll (Egmont)—Joyful and mournful: Beethoven
Freudvoll und leidvoll—Joyful and woeful/Joyful and griefful/Clara's
   song: Liszt
Freue dich, erlöste schon—Come rejoice ye faithful: Bach
Der Freund—The friend: Wolf
Freundliche Landschaft (Waldscenen)—Agreeable landscape/Pleasant
   scenery/Pleasing landscape: Schumann
Freundliche Vision—A welcome vision: R Strauss

Freut euch des Lebens—Joys of life: J Strauss II
Fridolins darskap—Fridolin's folly: Sibelius
Fridolin's folly—Fridolins darskap: Sibelius
Friede—Peace: Reger
Der Friede sei mit dir—My peace I give to you: Bach
Frieden—The magic touch: Blumenthal
Der Friedenstag—The day of peace/Peace day: R Strauss
Ein Friedhof—A burial place/God's acre: R Franz
The friend—Der Freund: Wolf
Friend Fritz—L'amico Fritz: Mascagni
Friend, thou art staunch—Tak for dit Rad: Grieg
Friendly forest—Selve amiche: Caldara
Friendly stars, if yet in heaven—Ah se in ciel, benigne stelle: Mozart
Friendship—Et vennestykke: Grieg
Friendship—Vanskapens blomma: Sibelius
Friendship and love—Quella che tutta fé (Serse): Handel
Frightening—Furchtenmachen (Kinderscenen): Schumann
Frihed er det bedste guld—Freedom is the brightest of gold: Nielsen
The froggery—La grenouillère: Poulenc
Frohe Botschaft—Good news: Wolf
Der frohe Wandersmann—The merry wanderer: Schumann
Frölicher Landmann (Album für die Jügend)—The merry peasant/The
    joyful peasant/The merry farmer/Happy farmer: Schumann
From a mountain's high projection—Auf dem Hügel sitz ich (An die
    ferne Geliebte): Beethoven
From afar—Liebe kamm aus fernen Landen: Brahms
From Bohemia's woods and fields—Z Českých luhů a hájů: Smetana
From early years—Fra Ungdomsdagene: Grieg
From 'Eastern Roses'—Aus den 'Ostlichen Rosein' (Myrthen): Schumann
From end to end—Ot kraya i do kraya (Tirhii Don): Dzerzhinski
From foreign lands and people—Von fremden Ländern (Kinderscenen):
    Schumann
From foreign parts—Aus aller Herren Lander: Moszkowski
From foreign parts—Von fremden Ländern (Kinderscenen): Schumann
From God shall nought divide me—Von Gott will ich nicht lassen: Bach
From grief, I cannot measure—Aus meinen grossen Schmerzen: R Franz
From heaven above—Der Himmel hat eine Thräne geweint: Schumann
From heaven above to earth I come—Von Himmel hoch, da komm ich her
    (Orgelbüchlein): Bach
From Heaven above to earth I come—Von Himmelhoch: Schein
From Heaven sank—Von Himmel sank: R Kahn
From 'Hebrew melodies'—Aus den 'Hebraischen Gesängen': Schumann
From her green balcony—Auf dem grünen Balkon: Wolf
From kissing—Vom Küssen: Reger

From Mount Pincio—Fra monte Pincio: Grieg
From my diary—Aus meinem Tagebuch: Reger
From my eyes salt tears are streaming—Bache vom gesalz'nen Zähren
(Ich hatte viel Bekümmernis): Bach
From out my heart's great sorrow—Aus meinen grossen Schmerzen: Wolf
From secret caves and bowers—Sul fil d'un soffio et esio: Verdi
From the Bohemian Forest—Ze šumary: Dvořák
From the church at Geneva—Psaulme de l'église à Genève: Liszt
From the depth of the ocean—Vineta: Brahms
From the depth of my sorrow—Aus der Tiefe (Achilleus): Bruch
From the depths of woe I call on Thee—Aus tiefer Not schrei ich zu dir:
Bach
From the depths to Thee I call—Aus der Tiefe rufe ich: Bach
From the eye to the heart—Vom Auge zum Herzen: R Franz
From the fields, from the groves—Dai campi, dai prati (Mephistofele):
Boito
From the (a) house of the dead—Aus einem Totenhaus: Janáček
From the mountains—Což ta voda s výše stvrání (Tajemství): Smetana
From the song of songs—Aus dem hohen Lied (Brautlieder): Cornelius
From the withered branch no rose blooms—Száraz ágtól messze virít a
rozsa: Bartók
From today till tomorrow—Von Heute auf Morgen: Schoenberg
From Villon to his love—Ballade de Villon à s'amye: Debussy
From where the rising sun ascends—A solis ortus cardine: Binchois
From where the upland towers—Von Waldberkränzter höhe: Brahms
From yon hills—Vom Gebirge (Neue Liebeslieder): Brahms
Fromm—A prayer: Reger
Le front comme un drapeau perdu (Tel jour telle nuit)—The brow like
a lost flag: Poulenc
The frost was white—Es hing der Reif: Brahms
The frozen heart—Erstarrung (Die Winterreise): Schubert
Frozen rigidity—Erstarrung (Die Winterreise): Schubert
Frozen tears—Gefrorene Tränen (Die Winterreise): Schubert
Der Frühling—Spring/Springtime: Brahms
Frühling—Spring: R Franz
Frühling—Spring time: Lehár
Frühling (Vier letzte Lieder)—Spring: R Strauss
Der Frühling kommt! —The return of spring: Goetz
Frühling im Moselthal (Siechentrost)—Spring in the Mosel valley: Bruch
Frühling im Sommer—Spring in summer: Cornelius
Der Frühling macht mit Brausen/Frühlingslied—Spring song: Mendelssohn
Frühling übers Jahr—Spring all the year: Wolf
Frühling und Liebe—Spring and love: R Franz
Frühlings Ankunft—Spring's approach: R Franz

Frühlings Ankunft—Spring's arrival: Schumann
Frühlings Lied—Spring song: Kjerulf
Frühlings Wiederkehr—Spring is come again: Goetz
Frühlingsahnung—The first day of spring: Mendelssohn
Frühlingsblumen—Spring flowers: Reinecke
Frühlingsboten—Messengers of spring: Raff
Frühlingsbotschaft—Spring's harbinger: Schumann
Frühlings-Chor (Manuel Venegas)—Spring chorus: Wolf
Frühlingsfahrt—Spring journey: Schubert
Frühlingsfahrt—Springtide wandering/The two comrades/A spring
     journey: Schumann
Frühlingsfeier—Adonis: R Franz
Frühlingsfeier—The celebration of spring: Mendelssohn
Frühlingsfeier—Festival of spring: R Strauss
Frühlingsgedränge—Spring's profusion: R Franz
Frühlingsgedränge—Voices of spring: R Strauss
Frühlingsgesang (Album für die Jügend)—Song of spring/Spring song:
     Schumann
Frühlingsglaube—Trust in spring: Mendelssohn
Frühlingsglaube—Faith in spring/The heart of spring: Schubert
Frühlingsglocken—Spring bells: Blech
Frühlingsglocken—Spring-chimes: Wolf
Frühlingsgruss—A greeting to spring: Schumann
Frühlingsliebe—Love in spring: R Franz
Frühlingsliebe—In the sweet spring-time: Schulz
Frühlingslied—Spring song: Mendelssohn
Frühlingslied—A song of spring: Mendelssohn
Frühlingslied/Durch den Wald—A spring morning: Mendelssohn
Frühlingslied/Es brechen im schallenden Reigen—Spring song:
     Mendelssohn
Frühlingslied/Der Frühling naht mit Brausen—Spring song: Mendelssohn
Frühlingslied/In dem Walde—Spring song: Mendelssohn
Frühlingslied—Spring: Meyer-Helmund
Frühlingslied/Die blauen Frühlingsaugen—The bright blue eyes of spring/
     Spring song/The blue starred eyes of springtime/The sweet blue eyes
     of spring: A Rubinstein
Frühlingslied/In dem Walde—In the forest/In the wood: A Rubinstein
Frühlingslied/Leise zieht—Spring song/Lightly play/A message/Music on
     my spirit plays: A Rubinstein
Frühlingslied—Spring song: Schumann
Frühlingslust—The joy of spring: Schumann
Frühlingsnacht—She is thine/Spring night/Night in spring: Schumann
Frühlingsrauschen—Rustle of spring: Sinding
Frühlingsruhe—My resting place: Schoeck

Frühlingssehnsucht (Schwanengesang)—Spring longings/The lover in
   spring: Schubert
Frühlingsspiel—Spring delights: Blech
Frühlingstimmen—Voices of spring: J Strauss II
Ein Frühlingstraum—A dream of spring: Goetz
Frühlingstraum (Die Winterreise)—(A) Dream of spring (time): Schubert
Frühlingswonne—Spring's delights: R Franz
Frühzeitiger Frühling—Early spring: Mendelssohn
En Fugelvise—A bird-song: Grieg
The fugitive—A já ti uplyno (Moravské Dvojzpévy): Dvořák
Fugitive love—Plaisir d'amour: Martini
The fugitives—Die Fluchtlinge: Schumann
Führe uns nicht in Versuchung—Lead us not into temptation: Cornelius
Fülle der Liebe—Love's fullness: Schubert
Füllest wieder Busch und Thal/An den Mond—To the moon: Schubert
Fummo felici un tempo—Fortune once made us happy: Vecchi
Funérailles—Burial: Liszt
Funeral hymn—Begräbnissgesang: Brahms
Funeral march of a marionette—March funèbre d'une marionette: Gounod
Funeral ode—Lass, Fürstin: Bach
Funeral ode—Traurnaya oda: Krein
The funny little man—Le petit rentier: Pierné
A funny story—Curiose Geschichte (Kinderscenen): Schumann
Für Einen—For somebody: R Franz
Für funfzehn Pfennige—And all for half-a-crown: R Strauss
Für Musik—For music: R Franz
Fürcht der Geliebten—Love's affright: Schubert
Fürchte dich nicht, ich bin bei dir—Be not afraid: Bach
Fürchenmachen (Kinderscenen)—Bogeyman's coming/Frightening:
   Schumann
Furibondo spira il vento (Partenope)—Hark, the tempest wildly raging:
   Handel
Una furtiva lagrima (L'elisir d'amore)—Down her pale cheek: Donizetti
Fussreise—A country walk: Wolf
Fyldt med blomster—Filled with flowers: Nielsen
Fynsk forår—Spring-time in Funen: Nielsen
Fyremål—My goal/The goal: Grieg

G

Gaily singing—Jubel töne: Weber

Gallans qui par terre et par mer—Gallants who hail from land and sea: Lass

Gallants who hail from land and sea—Gallans qui par terre et par mer: Lass

The gambler—Igrok: Prokofiev

The game of love and chance—Le jeu d'amour et du hasard: Rabaud

Gamle Anders Røgters sang (Ulvens søn)—Old Anders the Tender's song:
  Nielsen

Gamle Mor—The old mother/Dear mother, how you toil: Grieg

Gandegili—The hermit: Kiladze

Der Gang zum Liebchen—The trysting place/The watchful lover: Brahms

Gang zur Liebsten—The road to my love/Wooing/So secretly: Brahms

Gar lieblich hat sich gesellet—So soon were our hearts united: Brahms

The garden by the sea—Im Garten am Seegestade: Brahms

Garden in the rain—Le jardin mouillé: Roussel

The gardener—Der Gärtner: Brahms

The gardener—Der Gärtner: Pfitzner

The gardener—Der Gärtner: Schumann

The gardener—Der Gärtner: Wolf

Gardens in the rain—Jardins sous la pluie (Estampes): Debussy

The garland—Der Blumenkranz: Mendelssohn

The garlands—Die Kränze: Brahms

Der Gärtner—Greetings/The open air/The gardener: Brahms

Der Gärtner—The gardener: Pfitzner

Der Gärtner—The gardener: Schumann

Der Gärtner—The gardener: Wolf

Gates of gloom—Dell' antro magico: Cavalli

O gatinho de papelao (A prolé do bêbê)—Little cardboard cat: Villa Lobos

Gaudent in Coelis—Glorious in heaven: Victoria

Gaudete omnes—O shout with gladness: Sweelinck

The gay girl—Veselá dievča: Martinů

Gay madcap—Schön Rothraut: Schumann

Gazing upon my goodness—Mirando la mia dea: Dering

Gazetnie obyavleniya—Newspaper advertisements: Deshevov

La gazza ladra—The thieving magpie/The thievish magpie: Rossini

Gdzie lubi—What she likes: Chopin

Das Gebet (Das Examen)—The prayer: P Burkhard

Gebet—Prayer: Henschel

Gebet—A prayer/Lord, on Thy tender love relying: Hiller

Gebet—Prayer: Liszt

Gebet—Prayer: J Marx

Gebet—Prayer: Schumann

Gebet—Prayer: Wolf

Gebet während der Schlacht—Prayer during the battle: Schubert

Gebt acht! —On guard/Beware/Keep watch: Brahms

Geburtstagmarsch—Birthday march: Schumann

Die Gebüsche—Earth's voices: Schubert

Gedenk' an uns mit deiner Liebe (Wir danken dir, Gott, wir danken dir)—
    Remember us with loving kindness/O think on us with Thy compassion:
    Bach

Gedenke doch, mein Geist zurück—O think my soul: Bach

Gedenken—Fancies: Cornelius

Gedichte der Königin Maria Stuarda—Poems of Mary, Queen of Scots:
    Schumann

Geduld—O wait: R Strauss

Der gefangene Admiral—The imprisoned admiral: Loewe

Die gefangene Nachtigall—The (im)prisoned nightingale: Henschel

Die Gefangenen—Two captives: Blumenthal

Die gefangenen Sänger—The imprisoned singers: Schubert

Gefrorne Träuen (Die Winterreise)—Frozen tears: Schubert

Gefunden—Found: R Strauss

Gegenwart—Presence: R Franz

Geheiliget werde dein Name—Hallowed be Thy name: Cornelius

Das geheime Königreich—The secret kingdom: Křenek

Geheimes (Schwanengesang)—Secret/Love's answer: Schubert

Das Geheimnis—The secret: Beethoven

Geheimnis—The secret: Brahms

Geheimnis—The secret: Goetz

Geheimnis/Ich trag—Love's secret: Reger

Das Geheimnis—The secret: R Strauss

Die geheimnisvolle Flöte—The mysterious flute: Webern

Gehn wir im prater—Let's go to Hampstead/Who'll buy my roses: Mozart

Der geigende Eremit—The hermit with the violin: Reger

Der Geist des Wojewoden—The ghost of Voyvode: Grossmann

Der Geist hilft unserer Schwachheit auf—The spirit also helpeth us: Bach

Die Geister am Mummelsee—The ghosts of the lake: Wolf

Geistergruss—The hero's voice: Zelter

Geisternähe—Near in spirit: Schumann

Der Geistertanz—The ghost dance/Spectre-dance/Ghostly dance/Ghost-
    dance/The spectre's dance: Schubert

Geistliche Lied/Doch der Herr, er leitet die—Sacred song/For the Lord
    shall guide them: Mendelssohn

Geistliches Lied—O heart subdued with grieving: Brahms

Geistliches Wiegenlied—Cradle song of the Virgin: Brahms

Gekommen ist der Maie—He comes with vernal flowers: R Franz

Die gelbe Jacke—The yellow jacket: Lehár

Geleit—The soldier's death/The last hour: Brahms

Geliebter, wo zaudert dein irrender fuss?—Sweet love, what can hinder thy coming so long?/Thy love rapture: Brahms

Gelobet sei der Herr, mein Gott—All praises to the Lord: Bach

Gelobet seist du, Jesu Christ—Praised be Thou, (O) Jesus Christ/All praise to Jesus' hallowed name: Bach

Der Genesene an die Hoffnung—To Hope, on recovering from illness: Wolf

Genesis and Exodus—Erschaffen und Beleben: Wolf

Genesung—Renewal: R Franz

Genialische Treiben—Creative activity: Wolf

Genre picture—Genrebillede: Nielsen

Genrebillede—Genre picture: Nielsen

Gentils galants de France—Cavaliers of Artois: Meister

Gentle hope—An die Hoffnung: Mozart

Gentle maid in life's sweet morning—Männer suchen stets zu Naschen: Mozart

Gentle shepherd—Se tu m'ami: Pergolesi

Gentle swallow—Liebe Schwalbe, kleine Schwalbe (Zigeunerlieder): Brahms

The gentle swan—Il bianco e dolce cigno: Arcadelt

Gentle the night winds—Ständchen: Schubert

The gentle touch—Schliesse mir die Augen beide: Goetz

Gentle zephyrs—Murmelndes Lüftchen, blutenwind: Jensen

Gentle zephyrs—Zeffiretti lusinghieri (Idomeneo): Mozart

Gently play, o zephyrs—Leise, leise: Reger

Gelido, in ogni vena (Siroe)—Thro' my frame: Handel

Genügsamkeit—Content: Haydn

Genügsamkeit ist ein Schatz in diesem Leben (Nimm was dein ist, und gehe hin)—O sweet content: Bach

A German requiem—Ein deutsches Requiem: Brahms

A German requiem—Musikalische Exequiem: Schütz

Gertrude's song—Lied der Gertrud: Goetz

Gesang aus Fingal—Song from Ossian's 'Fingal'/The death of Trenar: Brahms

Gesang der Apollopriesterin—Chant of the priestess of Apollo: R Strauss

Gesang der Geister über den Wassern—Song of the spirits over the waters: Schubert

Gesang der Jünglinge—Song of the youths: Stockhausen

Gesang der Parzen—Song of the fates: Brahms

Gesang über das Rheinweinlied—Song of the Rhine wine: Schumann

Gesang von der Schlacht am Nil—Lines from the battle of the Nile: Haydn

Gesang Weylas—Weyla's song: Wolf

Geschichten aus dem Wienerwald—Echoes of the woods/Tales from the Vienna Woods/Stories from the Vienna Woods/Whisp'rings of the Vienna Woods: J Strauss II

Die geschiedene Frau—The girl in the train: Fall
Geschwinde, geschwinde, ihr wirbelnden Winde—Phoebus and Pan: Bach
Geschwindmarsch (Bünte Blätter)—Quick march: Schumann
Gesegnet—Blessed: Cornelius
Gesegnet sei (Italienisches Liederbuch)—Blessed be he/Give praise to
    him: Wolf
Gesellenlied—The apprentice's song: Wolf
Gesellenreise/Wenn den langen Weg—The journey of life: Mozart
Das Gesetz—The law: Schoenberg
Das Gesicht Jesajas—The vision of Isaiah: Burkhard
Geständnis—Confession: Mendelssohn
Geständnis—Confession: Schumann
Gestern war ich Atlas—Like the valiant Atlas: R Strauss
Gestillte Sehnsucht—Longing at rest: Brahms
Die Gestirne—The constellations: Schubert
Gestorben war ich vor Liebeswonne/Seliger Tod—Resurrection/Death
    stricken was I: Liszt
A gesture with discretion—Un cenno leggiadretto (Serse): Handel
Gesungen!—Singing: Schumann
Geszte Jóska bársony lovát nyergeli/Béreslegény, jol megrakd a szekeret—
    Jóska Geszte saddles his velvety horse/Farmboy, load the cart well:
    Bartók
Get your hat, get your coat—G'rechtelt's enk: Mozart
Getrost! (Ich freue dich in mir)—Be glad: Bach
Geübtes Herz—The experienced heart: Schoenberg
Gruss, lieber Mond/An den Mond—The mourning moon/To the moon:
    Schubert
Die Gewalt des Blickes—The night of a glance: Himmel
Gewitternacht—The stormy night: R Franz
Die Gezeichneten—The stigmatized ones/The branded: Schreker
The ghost dance—Der Geistertanz: Schubert
The ghost of Voyvode—Der Geist des Wojewoden: Grossmann
Ghost-dance—Der Geistertanz: Schubert
Ghostly dance—Der Geistertanz: Schubert
The ghostly double—Der Doppelganger (Schwanengesang): Schubert
The ghosts of the lake—Die Geister am Mummelsee: Wolf
Già che morir non posso (Radamisto)—Hither to me, ye furies: Handel
Già il sole dal Gange—O'er the Ganges now launched/The sun on the
    Ganges: A Scarlatti
Già mi sembra (Lotario)—Now behold! the car advances: Handel
Giammai provai (La donna vana)—Love's flame: Piccinni
The giant stag—A kilenc csodaszarvas: Bartók
La giara—The jug: Casella
Gib dich zufrieden und sei stille—Be thou contented: Bach
The gibbet—Le gibet: Ravel
Le gibet—The gibbet: Ravel

Gibt es auf Erden?—Is there a measure on earth?: Henze

The gift of wisdom—Le don de sagesse (Messe de la Pentecôte): Messiaen

The gilded crystals—Apporte les cristaux dorés: Rhené-Baton

Ging Heut' Morgen über's Feld (Lieder eines fahrenden Gesellen)—At morning in the dew/Through the field: Mahler

La gioconda—The ballad singer: Ponchielli

I gioiella della Madonna—The jewels of the Madonna: Wolf-Ferrari

Gioje, venite in sen (Amadigi di Gaula)—Joys, make my breast your home/Joy, come into my breast: Handel

Giovanna d'Arco—Joan of Arc: Verdi

Giovinette, che fate all'amore (Don Giovanni)—Let's enjoy: Mozart

The gipsies—En la cueva (El amor brujo): Falla

Gipsies—Zigeuner: J Marx

The gipsy baron—Die Zigeunerbaron: J Strauss II

Gipsy chorus—Vedi! le fosche (Il trovatore): Verdi

Gipsy ditties—Zigeunerliedchen: Schumann

The gipsy girl—Die Zigeunerin: Wolf

Gipsy love—Zigeunerliebe: Lehár

Gipsy maid—La zingari: Donizetti

The gipsy maid—Die Zigeunerin: Wolf

The gipsy primate—Der Zigeunerprimas: Kálmán

The gipsy princess—Die Czardasfürstin: Kálmán

Gipsy songs—Zigeunerlieder: Brahms

Gipsy songs—Cigánské melodié: Dvořák

A gipsy wagon roofed with tiles—Une roulotte couverte en tuiles (Tel jour telle nuit): Poulenc

The girl from Arles—L'Arlesiana: Cilea

The girl from Arles—L'Arlesienne: Bizet

The girl from Navarre—La Navarraise: Massenet

The girl from the Black Forest—Das Schwartzwaldmädel: Jessel

A girl in love—L'amoureuse: P Cannon

The girl in the taxi—Die keutsche Suzanne: Gilbert (ie Winterfeld)

The girl in the train—Die geschiedene Frau: Fall

The girl left lonely—Das verlassene Mägdlein: Schumann

The girl left lonely—Das verlassene Mägdlein: Wolf

The girl of the golden west—La fanciulla del West: Puccini

A girl whose love shines fair—La bien aimée: P Cannon

The girl with the flaxen hair—La fille aux cheveux de lin: Debussy

A girl's first love-song—Erstes Liebeslied eines Mädchens: Wolf

A girl's melancholy—Mädchen-Schwermut: Schumann

The girls of Vienna—Wiener Frauen: Lehár

Giulio Cesare—Julius Caesar: Malipiero/Handel

Giunse al fin il momento (Le nozze di Figaro)—Now at last comes the moment: Mozart

Giunto sul passo estremo (Mephistofele)—Nearing the extreme: Boito
Give back to my eyes—Rendete a gli occhi miei (Sonnets of Michelangelo):
  Britten
Give me back the heart—Ah rendimi: F Rossi
Give me that heart of thine—Willst du dein Herz mir schenken: Bach (?)
Give me thy golden comb—Schenk mir deinen goldenen Kamm:
  Schoenberg
Give me thy heart—Willst du dein Herz mir schenken: Bach (?)
Give praise to him—Gesegnet sei (Italienisches Liederbuch): Wolf
Give the hungry man thy bread—Brich dem Hungrigen dein Brot: Bach
Give us joy for this new year—Gott, gib Gluck zum neuen Jahr: Erlebach
Give us this day our daily bread—Unser täglich Brot gib uns heute:
  Cornelius
Gjaetergut—Shepherd boy: Grieg
Glad days of youth—O schöne Jugendtage (Der Evangelimann): Kienzl
Glad days of youth—Die Jugendzeit: Meyer-Helmund
Glagolitic mass—Msa Glagolskaja: Janáček
Glas—Knell: F Schmitt
Glaube, Hoffnung und Liebe—Love, trust and hoping/Faith, hope and
  love: Schubert
Gleich und Gleich—Like to like: Webern
Gleich und Gleich—Like with like: Wolf
Gleich wie der Regen und Schnee—Like as the showers and snow/Even
  as the rain and snow: Bach
G'leut zu Speyer—The bells at Speyer: Senfl
Glittering, fluttering butterfly—Schimmernder, flimmernder Schmetter-
  ling: Manén
Die Glocken des Strassburger Münsters—The bells of Strasburg cathedral:
  Liszt
Das Glockentürmers Töchterlein—The bellringer's daughter: Loewe
Gloom of woods—Waldesnacht: Brahms
Gloomy clouds—Nuages gris: Liszt
Gloomy woods—Bois épais (Amadis de Gaule): Lully
Gloria Patri—Praise to the Father: Byrd
Gloria Patri—Praise be unto the Father: Tallis
Glorious in Heaven—Gaudet in Coelis: Victoria
The glorious hour—Der glorreiche Augenblick: Beethoven
Der glorreiche Augenblick/The glorious hour/The praise of music:
  Beethoven
Glory be to God on high—Allein Gott in der Höh sei Ehr: Bach
Glory now to Thee be given—Wachet auf, ruft uns die Stimme: Bach
The glory of God in nature—Die Ehre Gottes aus der Natur: Beethoven
Glory to God in the highest—Allein Gott in der Höh sei Ehr: Bach
Glory to the Lord—Kol Slaven: Bortniansky

The glove—Der Handschuh: Schumann
Glowing with ecstasy—Der Glühende: Berg
Glück—Happiness: Reger
Glück—Happiness: Schoenberg
Das Glück—Joy: Schumann
Das Glück der Freundschaft—Affection's bliss/The joy of friendship/
  The happiness of friendship: Beethoven
Glückes genug—Ah! joy supreme: Reger
Glückes genug (Kinderscenen)—Contentment/Perfect happiness/Quite
  happy: Schumann
Glückes genug—True love's bliss: R Strauss
Der Glückliche—In bliss: Liszt
Der Glückliche—The happy lover: Mendelssohn
Die glückliche Hand—The hand of fate: Schoenberg
Glückliche Reise—Bon voyage: Künneke
Der Glücksritter—Dame fortune's knight/The soldier of fortune: Wolf
Der Glühende—Glowing with ecstasy: Berg
Gnome dance—Gnomenreigen: Liszt
Gnomenreigen—Dance of the gnomes/Gnome dance: Liszt
Go! call Irene—Dì ad Irene (Atalanta): Handel
Go, fetch a flask of sparkling wine—Non holt mir eine Kanne Wein:
  R Franz
Go, leave my sight—Precz z moich iczu!: Chopin
Go not far from me, O God—Christus e miserere: Zingarelli
Go thou false and fickle hope—Va, speme infida, pur: Handel
Go wandering on a summer's day—Se dig en sommerdag: Nielsen
Go where glory waits thee—Willst du glanz gewinnen: Kjerulf
The goal—Fyremål: Grieg
The goal—Das Ziel: Schoeck
The goat from Tibet—La chèvre du Thibet (Le bestiaire): Poulenc
God be praised! now goes the year to its end—Gottlob! nun geht das
  Jahr zu Ende: Bach
God goes up on high—Ascendit deus: Gallus
God goeth up with shouting—Gott fähret auf mit Jauchzen: Bach
God in the middle ages—Dios en la Edad Media: Engelbrecht
God in the thunderstorm—Gott im Ungewitter: Schubert
God, in Thee I seek my salvation—Esto mihi in deum protectorum:
  M Haydn
God, in Thy great goodness—Gott, durch deine Güte (Orgelbüchlein):
  Bach
God is aye our sun and shield—Gott ist unser Sonn' und Schild! (Gott
  der Herr ist Sonn' und Schild!): Bach
God is merciful—Confitemine Domino: M Haydn
God is my shepherd—Hospodin jest muj pastýř (Biblické Písně): Dvořák

110

God is thy keeper—Gott ist mein König: Bach
God kindles His fire—Es glänzet der Christen in wediges Leben: Bach
God leads, God helps—Justum deduxit Dominus: Mozart
God liveth aye—Gott lebet noch: Bach
God liveth still—Gott lebet noch: Bach
The God of gods—Le Dieu le fort: Le Jeune
God of love—Porgi amor (Le nozze di Figaro): Mozart
God the creator—Gott, der Weltschöpfer: Schubert
God the Lord is sun and shield—Gott, der Herr, ist Sonn' und Schild:
    Bach
God, Thou art great—Gott, du bist gross: Spohr
God Thou hast it well ordained—Gott, du hast es wohlgefüget (Christen,
    ätzet, diesen Tag): Bach
Goddag, Goddag—How do you do?: Nielsen
Goddess fairest—Casta diva, che inargenti: Bellini
The goddess in the garden—Mañanica era (Canciones amatorias): Granados
God's acre—Ein Friedhof: R Franz
God's angels together—Guds engle i flok: Nielsen
God's blessing—Gottes Segen: Reger
God's glory divined in nature—Die Ehre Gottes aus der Natur: Beethoven
Gods of Greece—Die Götter Griechenlands: Schubert
God's self alone my heart possesses—Gott soll allein mein Herz haben:
    Bach
God's time is the best—Gottes Zeit ist die allerbeste Zeit: Bach
Goest Thou now, Jesu, from heaven to earth?—Kommst du nun, Jesu,
    von Himmel herunter?: Bach
Going to sleep—Beim Schlafengehen (Vier letzte Lieder): R Strauss
Gold and silver waltz—Gold und Silber Walzer: Lehár
The gold and white celestial light—Det gyldenhvide himmellys: Nielsen
Gold outweighs love—Gold überwiegt die Liebe: Brahms
Gold überwiegt die Liebe—Love betrayed for riches/Gold outweighs love:
    Brahms
Gold und Silber Walzer—Gold and silver waltz: Lehár
The golden apple—Il pomo d'oro: Cesti
The golden bird—Zum Schlafen: Reger
The golden canon—Non nobis domine: Byrd (?)
The golden cockerel—Zolotoy Petushok: Rimsky-Korsakov
The golden cross—Das goldene Kreuz: Brüll
The golden hoop—Zolotyi obruch: Lyatoshyns'kyi
Golden light—Agnus dei: Bizet
The golden morning light—Die Sonne scheint nicht mehr: Brahms
The golden spinning wheel—Zlatý kolovrat: Dvořák
Golden stars—Güldne Sternlein: R Franz
Das goldene Kreuz—The golden cross: Brüll

Die goldene Meisterin—The lady goldsmith: Eysler
Die goldene Sonne, voll Freud' und Wonne—Sunbeams down streaming: Bach
Goldfish—Poissons d'or: Debussy
Goldschmieds Tochterlein—The goldsmith's daughter: Loewe
The goldsmith's daughter—Goldschmieds Tochterlein: Loewe
Gólya, gólya, gilice—The swallow's wooing: Kodály
Der Gondelfahrer—Gondolier's serenade: Schubert
Gondoliera—A gondolier's love song: Meyer-Helmund
A gondolier's love song—Gondoliera: Meyer-Helmund
Gondolier's serenade—Der Gondelfahrer: Schubert
Gone—Borte!: Grieg
Gone—Forbi: Grieg
Gone for ever—Dove sono (Le nozze di Figaro): Mozart
Gone is the day—Der Tag ist hin: Bach
A good advice—Der gute Rath: Reger
Good Christian men rejoice—Ihr lieben Christen, freut euch nun: Buxtehude
Good counsel—Gute Lehre: Henschel
A good day—Bonne journée (Tel jour telle nuit): Poulenc
Good fellows be merry—Dein Wachstum sei feste (Mer hahn en neue Oberkeet): Bach
Good Friday music—Karfreitagszauber (Parsifal): Wagner
The good girl—La cecchina/La buona figliuola: Piccinni
The good humoured ladies—Le donne di buon umore: Scarlatti-Tommasini
Good morning—Gud morgen: Grieg
Good news—Frohe Botschaft: Wolf
Good night—Dobrú noc: Dvořák
Good night—Gute Nacht: R Franz
Good night—Nos da: M Jones
Good night—Gute Nacht (Die Winterreise): Schubert
Good night—Gute Nacht: Schumann
Good old times—Régi jó idök: K Ábrányi
The good song—La bonne chanson: Fauré
A good-bye—Auf Nimmerwiedersehen: Blumenthal
Good-day, sweetheart—Bonjour, mon coeur: Lassus
Goodman and Goodwife—Gutmann und Gutweib: Wolf
Goodnight—Nachtgruss: Wolf
The goose(girl) of Cairo—L'oca del Cairo: Mozart
Gott der Herr ist Sonn' und Schild—The Lord is a sun and shield/God the Lord is sun and shield: Bach
Gott, der Weltschöpfer—God the creator: Schubert
Gott, du bist gross—God, Thou art great: Spohr

112

Gott, du hast es wohlgefüget (Christen, ätzet diesen Tag)–God, Thou
   hast it well ordained: Bach
Gott, durch deine Güte (Orgelbüchlein)–God, in Thy great goodness:
   Bach
Gott fähret auf mit Jauchzen–God goeth up with shouting: Bach
Gott, gib Glück zum neuen Jahr–Give us joy for this new year: Erlebach
Gott im Ungewitter–God in the thunderstorm: Schubert
Gott ist mein Hirt–The Lord is my shepherd: Schubert
Gott ist mein König–God is thy keeper: Bach
Gott ist unser Sonn' und Schild! (Gott der Herr ist Sonn' und Schild!)–
   God is aye our sun and shield: Bach
Gott lebet noch–God liveth still/God liveth aye: Bach
Gott soll allein mein Herze haben–God's self alone my heart possesses:
   Bach
Gott! welch Dunkel hier (Fidelio)–Ah! what awful gloom: Beethoven
Gott, wie dein Name–Lord, as Thy name is/According to Thy name:
   Bach
Gott, wie gross ist deine Güte–Lord, how wondrous: Bach
Gott, woll' dass ich daheime war (Siechentrost)–Would God that I at
   home: Bruch
Die Götter Griechenlands–Gods of Greece: Schubert
Die Götterdämmerung–The twilight of the gods: Wagner
Gottes Engel weichen nie (Man singet mit Freuden von Sieg)–For God's
   angels ne'er depart: Bach
Gottes Segen–God's blessing: Reger
Gottes Sohn ist kommen (Orgelbüchlein)–Once he came in blessing:
   Bach
Gottes Zeit ist die allerbeste Zeit–God's time is the best: Bach
Gottlob, es geht uns wohl (Wir danken dir, Gott, wir danken dir)–Thank
   God! now all is well! : Bach
Gottlob! nun geht das Jahr zu Ende–Praise God! the year is nearly
   ended/O praise the Lord for all his mercies/Rejoice! The old year now
   is ended/God be praised, now the year goes to its end: Bach
The government inspector–Der Revisor: Orff
Ein Grab–A grave: Wolf
Gracious and kind–Wie bist du, meine Königin: Brahms
Gracious Lord of all our being–Herz und Mund und Tat und Leben:
   Bach
Gräfin Dubarry–Countess Dubarry: Millöcker
Die Gräfin Mariza–The countess Mariza: Kalmán
Un grand sommeil noir–Sleep and black shadow: Stravinsky
La grande pâque russe–Russian Easter (Festival) overture: Rimsky-
   Korsakov

La grande porte de Kiev (Tableaux d'une exposition)—The great gate of
Kiev: Mussorgsky
Les grands jasmins—The jasmin blooms: Rhené-Baton
Les grands vents—The north wind: Ravel
Grant, I beseech thee—Tribue Domine: Byrd
Grant me but one single smile—Wenn du nur zuweilen Lächelst: Brahms
Grant us Thy peace—Pax dei: Troman
The grasshopper—La sauterelle (Le bestiaire): Poulenc
The grasshopper and the ant—La cigale et la fourmi: Audran
A grateful address to the mill-stream—Danksagung an den Bach (Die
schöne Müllerin): Schubert
Gratitude to the brook—Danksagung an den Bach (Die schöne
Müllerin): Schubert
A grave—Ein Grab: Wolf
The gravedigger—Totengräbers Heimweh: Schubert
Gravedigger's song—Totengräberslied: Schubert
Great event—Wichtige Begebenheit (Kinderscenen): Schumann
Great Fatherland—Rodina velikaya: Kabalevsky
The great friendship—Velikaya druzhba: Muradeli
The great gate of Kiev—La grande porte de Kiev (Tableaux d'une
exposition): Mussorgsky
The great holy war—Narodnaya svya shchennaya voina: Koral'
Great is Jehovah—Die Allmacht: Schubert
Great is our Lord Jesus' name—Magnum nomen Domini: Praetorius
Great is the Lord—Ecce sacerdos: M Haydn
Great is our Lord—Der Herr ist gross: Schütz
Great is the Lord—Surr' olet, Herra: Sibelius
Great Isis, great Osiris—O Isis und Osiris (Die Zauberflöte): Mozart
Great Lord have mercy—Pièta, Signore: Stradella
The great Motherland—Rodina Velikaya: Kabalevsky
Great Thy love, Lord—Starkes lieben (Himmelskönig, sei willkommen):
Bach
The great unknown—Die grosse Unbekannte: Suppé
G'rechtelt's enk—Get your hat, get your coat: Mozart
Green and peaceful are the pastures—Schafe können sicher weiden: Bach
Green hat—Volksliedchen: Schumann
Green leaved walnut tree—Zold leveles diófa: Erkel
The green parrot—Vert-vert: Offenbach
The greenwood calls—Schlummerlied: Schubert
Greet, oh skylark—Hlásej, ptácku: Smetana
Greeting—Gruss: Mendelssohn
Greeting—Gruss/Wohin ich geh': Mendelssohn
Greeting—Die tausend Grüsse: Schumann
A greeting to spring—Frühlingsgruss: Schumann

Greetings—Der Gärtner: Brahms
Der Greis—The old man: Haydn
Der greise Kopf (Die Winterreise)—The hoary head: Schubert
Greisengesang—Grey-beard's song/The old man/Old man's song: Schubert
La grenouillère—The froggery: Poulenc
Grenzen der Menschheit—Man's limitations: Schubert
Grenzen der Menscheit—The limits of mankind: Wolf
Gretchem am Spinnrade—Margaret at the spinning wheel: Schubert
Gretchen to the Mater Dolorosa—Gretchens Bitte: Schubert
Gretchens Bitte—Gretchen to the Mater Dolorosa/Gretchen's prayer/
    Margaret's prayer: Schubert
Gretchen's prayer—Gretchens Bitte: Schubert
Grey-beard's song—Greisengesang: Schubert
Grief—Trauer: Cornelius
Grief—Und wussten's die Blumen (Dichterliebe): Schumann
Grief—Schmerzen (Wesendonck Lieder): Wagner
Grief is mine—Piangerò la sorte mia (Giulio Cesare): Handel
Grief of love—Schmerz der Liebe: Nicolai
Grief within my heart—Tief im Herzen (Spanische Liebeslieder): Schumann
Grief without end—Leid ohne Ende (Albumsblätter): Schumann
Grief's forebodings—Leides Ahnung (Albumblätter): Schumann
Grief's lowest depth he sounded—Non sa che sia dolore: Bach
The grief's of Orpheus—Les malheurs d'Orphée: Milhaud
Grieve ye no more—Plus nulz regretz: Josquin
Grievous and cruel—Duri e penosi (Il ritorno d'Ulisse): Monteverdi
Grillen (Fantasiestücke)—Whims: Schumann
Le grillon (Histoires naturelles)—The cricket: Ravel
Grøn er vårens haek—The hedges are green in springtime: Nielsen
Die grosse Unbekannte—The great unknown: Suppé
Grosser Herr und starker König (Weihnachtsoratorium)—Mighty Lord,
    and king all glorious: Bach
La grotte—The grotto: Debussy
The grotto—La grotte: Debussy
A group in Tartarus—Gruppe aus dem Tartarus: Schubert
Groups—Gruppen: Stockhausen
Groza—The storm: Trambitsky
Die grüne Hopfenkranke (Liebeslieder Waltz)—Thou tender trailing ivy:
    Brahms
Gruppe aus dem Tartarus—A group in Tartarus/Hark, like surges:
    Schubert
Gruppen—Groups: Stockhausen
Gruss/Leise Zieht durch mein Gemuth—Greeting/Summer days are
    coming: Mendelssohn
Gruss/Wohin ich geh'—Greeting: Mendelssohn

Grüsse zur Nacht—Nocturne: Dohnányi
Guard thy son—Wahre, wahre deinen Sohn (Neue Liebeslieder): Brahms
The guardian angel—Dem Schutzengel: Brahms
Un guardo vogli a me—One glance, love: Marcello
Gud Morgen—Good morning: Grieg
Guds engle i flok—God's angels together: Nielsen
Gugliemo Ratcliff—William Ratcliff: Mascagni
Guguk im Versteck (Album für die Jugend)—Cuckoo in hiding:
    Schumann
The guiding light—Vado ben spesso: Rosa
Guillaume Tell—William Tell: Rossini
The guinea-fowl: La pintade (Histoires naturelles): Ravel
Güldne Sternlein—Golden stars: R Franz
Gunnar's dream—Saga-Drøm: Nielsen
Gute Lehre—Good counsel: Henschel
Gute Nacht—Farewell/Good night: R Franz
Gute Nacht (Die Winterreise)—Good night: Schubert
Gute Nacht—Good night: Schumann
Gute Nacht, die Weltgetümmel (Wer weiss, wie nahe mir mein Ende)—
    Fare thee well, thou worldly tumult: Bach
Der gute Rath—A good advice: Reger
Guten—The youth: Grieg
Guten Abend, guten Abend—Good evening: Brahms
Guter Rat—Counsels: Brahms
Gutmann und Gutweib—Goodman and Goodwife: Wolf
Gweddi—A prayer: A Hughes
Gyermekeknek—For children: Bartók
Det gyldenhvide himmellys—The gold and white celestial light: Nielsen
Der Gynger en baad paa Bølge—A boat on the waves: Grieg
Gypsy. . . see: Gipsy. . .
A gyulai kert alatt—Behind the garden of Gyula: Bartók

H

Ha! my pretty brace of fellows—Ha! wie will ich triumphiren (Die
  Entführung aus dem Serail): Mozart
Ha, what splendour—Ma, che insolita (La Resurrezione): Handel
Ha! wie will ich triumphieren (Die Entfürhung aus dem Serail)—Ha! my
  pretty brace of fellows: Mozart
Et Hab—A hope: Grieg
Habanera (Carmen)—Love the vagrant: Bizet
Hab' mir's Gelobt (Der Rosenkavalier)—I made a vow: R Strauss
Habt Dank, ihr Lieben von Brabant (Lohengrin)—Have thanks good
  lieges: Wagner
Habt ihr sie schon geseh'n—Swayed by the pride of youth: R Franz
Had I now what most I wish for—Ach, dass nicht die letzte Stunde: Bach
Had not the Lord been on our side—Wo Gott der Herr nicht bei uns
  hält: Bach
Haec dicit dominus—Thus saith the Lord: Byrd
Haec dies—This is the day/This glad day: Byrd
Haec dies—This is the day: Palestrina
Haï luli—Alack-a-day: Coquard
The Haidamaks—Haidamaky: Stetsenko
Haidamaky—The Haidamaks: Stetsenko
Heideröslein—Heath rose: Schumann
Hail, age of pure gold—Ecco d'oro l'eta: Arcadelt
Hail bright abode—Freudig begrüssen (Tannhäuser): Wagner
Hail festal morning—C'est grande fête (Fra Diavolo): Auber
Hail, glad day—Heil dem Tag: Mozart
Hail moon—Terve kuu: Sibelius
Hail, o hail, true body—Ave verum corpus: Byrd
Hail! O light immortal—Lumen ad revelationem: Byrd
Hail, queen of heaven—Ave, Regina: Webern
Hail to the chief—Botgesang: Schubert
Hail, Thou most holy—Salve Regina: Byrd
Hajej, muj andilku (Hubička)—Slumber, my pretty one: Smetana
Hallazgo—Discovery: Guastavino
Hallowed be Thy name—Geheiliget werde dein Name: Cornelius
Halt' im Gedächtniss Jesum Christ—Hold in affection (remembrance)
  Jesus Christ: Bach
Hamaariv Arovim—The evening twilight: Gould
Hamlet—Amleto: Faccio; Thomas
The hammer without a master—Le marteau sans maître: Boulez
A hand kiss—Un bacio di mano: Mozart
The hand of fate—Die glückliche Hand: Schoenberg
Der Handschuh—The glove: Schumann
The handsome Joseph—Yosif prekrasnyi: Vasilenko
Hanendans (Maskarade)—Dance of the cockerels/Dance of the cocks: Nielsen

Hans Beutler der wollt reiten aus—Hans Beutler must ride out one day: Senfl
Hans Beutler must ride out one day—Hans Beutler der wollt reiten aus: Senfl
Happiness—Glück: Reger
Happiness—Schastye: Khachaturian
Happiness—Glück: Schoenberg
The happiness of friendship—Das Glück der Freundschaft: Beethoven
Happy art thou—Beata viscera: Byrd
Happy farmer—Fröhlicher Landmann (Album für die Jugend): Schumann
Happy flock—Schafe können sicher wieden (Was mir behagt): Bach
Happy gigolo—Cuore vagabondo: Bixio
Happy is the lowly maiden—Quanto mai felice siete (Ezio): Handel
The happy island—L'îsle joyeuse: Debussy
The happy isle—L'île heureuse: Chabrier
Happy love—Liebesglück: Wolf
The happy lover—Der Glückliche: Mendelssohn
Happy world—Selige Welt: Schubert
Har du mod?—Hast thou courage: Sibelius
The hare and the corn—Le lièvre et le blé (Petites légendes): Milhaud
Harfenspieler/Wer nie sein Brod—Who never ate with tears/Who ne'er
    his bread: Schubert
Harfenspieler/Wer sich der Einsamkeit ergibt—Who gives to loneliness/
    To solitude himself who gives/Whoe'er for loneliness: Schubert
Harfenspieler Lieder—Songs of the harper/The harpers: Wolf
Hark! a voice said (saith) "all are mortal"—Alle Menschen müssen
    sterben (Orgelbüchlein): Bach
Hark, hark, how my triangle—Aj! kterak trohranec muji (Cigánské
    melodie): Dvořák
Hark, hark, the echo falling—O la, O che buon eco: Lassus
Hark, hear ye not a heavenly choir—Horch, horst du nicht: Schoeck
Hark, how light the wings—Hør, hvor let dens vinger: Nielsen
Hark, how the drums are rolling—Sprona il tamburo e incora (La fille
    du regiment): Donizetti
Hark, how the tempest—Das ist ein Brausen: R Franz
Hark, like surges—Gruppe aus dem Tartarus: Schubert
Hark, the tempest wildly raging—Furibondo spira il vento (Partenope):
    Handel
Hark to me, oh ye fair maidens—Usez mieux, o beautés fières: Lully
The harm of love—Voyez le tort d'amour: Sandrin
Harmonic inspiration—L'estro harmonico: Vivaldi
Die Harmonie der Welt—The harmony of the world: Hindemith
Die Harmonie in der Ehe—Harmonius wedlock: Haydn
Harmonie du soir—Evening harmonies: Debussy
Harmonies du soir—Evening harmonies: Liszt
Harmonies poétiques et religieuses—Poetic and religious harmonies:
    Liszt

Harmonius wedlock—Die Harmonie in der Ehe: Haydn
Harmony—Einklang: Wolf
Harmony of the world—Die Harmonie der Welt: Hindemith
Három öszi könnycsepp—Three autumn tears: Bartók
The harp—Harpen: Grieg
Harpen—The harp: Grieg
The harper's ballad—Ballade des Harfners: Schumann
Die Harrende—Expectation: R Franz
The harvest field—Das Aehrenfeld: Mendelssohn
Harvest song—Erntelied: F X Mozart
Harvest song—Erndtliedchen (Album für die Jugend): Schumann
Has a father with his children—Hat man nicht mit seinen Kindern
    (Schweigt stille, plaudert nicht): Bach
Hasche-mann (Kinderscenen)—Blindman's buff/Catch-as-catch-can/
    Catch me (if you can): Schumann
Hast thou courage—Har du mod?: Sibelius
Haste, silvery moonbeams—Du silbernes Mondenlicht: Dohnányi
Hat dich die Liebe berührt—If love hath entered my heart: J Marx
Hat gesagt—bleibt's nicht dabei—Saying is not doing/Promises made and
    broken: R Strauss
Hat man nicht mit seinen Kindern (Schweight stille, plaudert nicht)—
    Don't our children/Have not people with their children/Has a father
    with his children: Bach
Hated courtiers—Cortigiani, vil razza dannata (Rigoletto): Verdi
The hateful colour—Die böse Farbe (Die schöne Müllerin): Schubert
Hatikvah (Shire' Chalututzim)—Song of hope: Binder
Haughty and proud art thou—Hoffärtig seid Ihr (Italienisches Liederbuch):
    Wolf
Haugtussa—The mountain maid: Grieg
Haunted—Was zögerst du?: Blumenthal
Haunted—Ein Ton: Cornelius
Haunted—Quando emblada: Guarnieri
The haunted mansion—Straszny Dwór: Moniuszko
The haunted palace—Etude pour le palais hanté: F Schmitt
Haunted place—Verrufene Stelle (Waldscenen): Schumann
Haunted spot—Verrufene Stelle (Waldscenen): Schumann
Hauptmanns Weib (Myrthen): The captain's lady (wife): Schumann
Der häusliche Krieg: Domestic war(fare): Schubert
Have faith in God—So glaube nun! (Alles nur nach Gottes Willen): Bach
Have I lost thee?—Sposa Euridice (Orfeo ed Euridice): Gluck
Have mercy Lord, my sin forgive—Erbarme dich, mein, O Herre Gott:
    Bach
Have mercy, Lord, upon me—Defecit in dolore: Byrd
Have mercy upon me, O Lord—Erbarme dich, mein Gott (Matthäus-
    passion): Bach

Have not people with their children—Hat man nicht mit seinen Kindern (Schweigt stille, plaudert nicht): Bach

Have thanks good lieges—Habt Dank, ihr Lieben von Brabant (Lohengrin) Wagner

Have you seen the brave peasant lad—Saa du Knøssen, som strøg forbi: Grieg

Havet (Barnlige Sanger)—Sea-song: Grieg

Havets sang (Willemoes)—The ocean's song: Nielsen

Havets visa—The sea's music: Nyström

The Haze-king—A Ködkirály: E Ábrányi

He and She—Er und Sie: Schumann

He calls his sheep by name—Er rufet seinen Schafen mit Namen: Bach

He came down from on high—Descendit de coelis: Byrd

He comes with vernal flowers—Gekommen ist der Maie: R Franz

He flies—Il vole (Fiancailles pour rire): Poulenc

He is drawn to the snare—Dans un piège fatal (Amadis de Gaule): Lully

He is noble—Er, der Herrlichste (Frauenliebe und -leben): Schumann

He is the finest of all men—Er, der Herrlichste von Allen (Frauenliebe und -leben): Schumann

He loves me—loves me not—M'ama—non n'ama: Mascagni

He loves me no more—Non m'ama più: Tosti

He, the best of all—Er, der Herrlichste von Allen (Frauenliebe und -leben): Schumann

He, the greatest and the noblest—Er, der Herrlichste (Frauenliebe und -leben): Schumann

He who loves me—Wer mich liebet: Bach

He who rides—Keinem hat es noch gereut: Brahms

He who still loveth—Chi in amore (Amore traditore): Bach (?)

He who trusts in God to guide him—Wer nur den lieben Gott lässt walten: Bach

He whose flag—Dessen Fahne Donnerstürme wallte: Schubert

He, whose life was as the light—Christus, der uns selig macht: Bach

He will come at the last day—Apparebit in finem: Byrd

The healing flower—Eine Blume weiss ich: Goetz

Hear me now, beloved—Dissi a l'amata mia lucida stella: Marenzio

Hear my prayer, O God—Slyš ó Bože (Biblické Písně): Dvořák

Hear my prayer, O Lord—Veni, Domine: Mendelssohn

Hear, O love my bitter sighing—Porgi amor (Nozze di Figaro): Mozart

Hear, o ye winds of heaven—Aura, che intorno spiri: Mozart

Hear our call—Bona nox: Mozart

Hear the cry of a lover's yearning—Partout des cris de joie (La jolie fille de Perth): Bizet

Hear thou my weeping—Laschia ch'io pianga (Rinaldo): Handel

Hear us Isis and Osiris—O Isis and Osiris (Die Zauberflöte): Mozart

Hear ye, Israel—Shema, Yisroel: Milhaud

Hear ye the voice of Jesus—Jelenti magát Jézus: Kodály

Hearken thou, my fond heart's queen—Dissi a l'amata mia lucida stella: Marenzio

Heart and mouth to Thee are open—Mund und Herze steht dir offen
    (Bringet dem Herrn Ehre): Bach

Heart and voice and all our being—Herz und Mund und Tat und Leben: Bach

Heart for heart—Herzenstauch: Reger

The heart here wells over—Unendliche Freude: Schubert

The heart I ask from thee—Willst du dein Herz mir schenken: Bach (?)

Heart in danger—Coeur en péril: Roussel

Heart of hearts—Cher objet de ma pensée (Aucassin et Nicolette): Grétry

Heart of my heart—Caro mio ben: Giordani

The heart of spring—Frühlingsglaube: Schubert

The heart of the mountains—Serdtse gor: Balanchivadze

Heart on fire—Imhol nyitva én kebelem: Kodály

Heart, repent thee not—Lass dich nicht gereu'n: Henschel

A heart that knows his Jesus lives—Ein Herz, das seinen Jesum lebend weiss: Bach

The heart that thou hast given—Willst du dein Herz mir schenken: Bach (?)

Heartache—Herzleid: Schumann

A heartfelt sigh—Seufzer: Wolf

Heart's desire—Widmung: Schumann

Hearts in despair—Coeurs desolez: Josquin

The heart's morning—Hjärtats morgon: Sibelius

The heart's purple eagle—Des Herzens Purpurvögel: Webern

Heath rose—Heideröslein: Schumann

A heathen sonnet—Sonnet payen: Massenet

The heather boy—Vom Heideknaben: Schumann

Heaven and earth—Himmel und Erde: Schumann

Heaven and ocean—Cielo e mar! (La gioconda): Ponchielli

Heaven beams so clearly—Himmel strahlt so helle und klar (Zigeuner-
    lieder): Brahms

Heaven to me my love restoring—Or che il cielo a me ti rende: Mozart

Heavenly Aida—Celeste Aida (Aida): Verdi

Heavenly bread—Panis angelicus: Franck

Heavenly love—Hohe Liebe: Liszt

Heavenly Father—Angus Dei: Bizet

A heavenly light falls from the sky—Von Gott kommt mir ein Freuden-
    schein (Erschallet, ihr Lieder): Bach

Heavenly star-eyes—Luci care (Admeto): Handel

The heavens are telling—Die Himmel erzählen (Die Schopfung): Haydn

The heavens are telling—Der Himmel erzählen die ehre Gottes: Schütz

The heavens declare—Coeli enarrant: Saint-Saëns

The heavens declare him—Die Ehre Gottes aus der Natur: Beethoven

The heavens laugh—Der Himmel lacht, die Erde jubilieret: Bach

The heavens proclaim the glory of God—Die Himmel erzählen die Ehre
    Gottes: Bach

The heavens rejoice, the earth exults—Der Himmel lacht, die Erde jubilieret: Bach

The heavens shout—Der Himmel lacht, die Erde jubilieret: Bach

Hebt euer Haupt empor (Wachet, betet, seid bereit)—Lift up your heads on high: Bach

The hedge rose—Heidenröslein: Schubert

Hedge-roses—Heidenröslein: Schubert

The hedges are green in spring time—Grøn er vårens haek: Nielsen

Hee balou—Hochländisches Wiegenlied (Myrthen): Schumann

The heedless one—L'indifférent (Shéhérazade): Ravel

Hegyi éjszakák—Mountain nights: Kodály

Heidenröslein—Wild rose: Brahms

Heidenröslein—Rose-bud/The wild rose/Wild rosebud/Red rose/Hedge-roses/The hedge rose/Rose among the heather/Meadow rose/Little heath-rose: Schubert

Heigh-ho!—Ach was Kummer: R Strauss

Heil dem Tag—Hail, glad day: Mozart

Heiland, uns're Missetaten (Drei Volkstexte)—Saviour, with our sins we've paid Thee: Webern

Heilig—Holy is God: C P E Bach

Der heilige Josef singt—St Joseph's song: Wolf

Die heiligen drei Könige—The three holy kings: R Strauss

Heiligste Dreieinigkeit (Erschallet, ihr Lieder)—O most holy Three in One: Bach

Die Heilung—Love's healing: Himmel

Heimat (Lieder der Liebe)—Home: Kilpinen

Heimat—Home: Reger

Das Heimchen am Herd—The cricket on the hearth: Goldmark

Heimkehr—Return (home)/Home-coming: Brahms

Die Heimkehr—The homeward journey: Cornelius

Heimkehr—Homeward: R Strauss

Die Heimkehr aus der Fremde—Son and stranger: Mendelssohn

Heimkehr vom Feste—Return from the banquet: Blech

Heimliche Aufforderung—The lover's pledge: R Strauss

Heimliche Grüsse—Secret greetings: Fielitz

Heimliches Verschwinden—Secret departure: Schumann

Die Heimschung—The visitation: Schuller

Heimsyn—Homeward bound: Sinding

Das Heimweh—The home-sigh/Homesickness/Thoughts of home/The home thought: F Mendelssohn

Das Heimweh/Ach, der Gebirgssohn—Homeland/Home-sickness: Schubert

Heimweh—Longing for home: Wolf

Heinieden alles hat seine Stunde—For everything there is a season: Rozsa

Heinrich der Vögler—Henry the fowler: Loewe

Heiss' mich nicht reden—Bid me not utter/Naught mays't thou ask me: Schubert
Heitere Lieder—Merry songs: R Trunk
Heiterkeit—Cheerfulness: Mozart
Dem Helden—To the hero: Schumann
Ein Heldenleben—A hero's life: R Strauss
Helen—La belle Hélène: Offenbach
Helft mir Gott's Güte preisen (Orgelbüchlein)—Ye Christians in this nation!: Bach
Helft mir, ihr Schwestern (Frauenliebe und -leben)—Help me, my (oh) sisters/Dear loving sisters: Schumann
Hell is raging in my bosom—Fatto inferno è il mio petto (Rodelinda): Handel
Die helle Sonne leuchtet—The cheerful sunbeams glisten: R Franz
Help me, my (oh) sisters—Helft mir, ihr Schwestern (Frauenliebe und -leben): Schumann
Help us, O Lord, deliver us—Propituis esto domine: M Haydn
Hémiones (Carnaval des animaux)—Wild horses: Saint-Saëns
Hemmelighed—Secret: Grieg
Hemmung—Restraint: Schoenberg
The hen—La poule [symphony]: Haydn
Hen and rooster—Herr Hahn und Fraulein Huhn: Blech
Hen wlad fy nhadan—Land of my fathers: J James
Hence, all ye evil-doers—Weicht all', ihr Übelthäter (Ach Herr, mich armen Sünder): Bach
Hence with earthly treasure—Weg mit allen Schätzen (Jesu meine Freude): Bach
Die Henne—The lost chicken/The pet chicken/My black hen: Brahms
Henry the fowler—Heinrich der Vögler: Loewe
Her eyes—Ihr Auge: R Franz
Her highness waltzes—Hoheit tanzt Walzer: Ascher
Her love-letter—Die Liebende schreibt: Mendelssohn
Her picture—Ihr Bild (Schwanengesang): Schubert
Her portrait—Ihr Bild (Schwanengesang): Schubert
Her step-daughter—Její pastorkyňa: Janáček
Her tomb—Ihr Grab: Blumenthal
Her voice—Ihre Stimme: Schubert
Her voice—Ihre Stimme: Schumann
Her window—Vor dem Fenster: Brahms
Une herbe pauvre (Tel jour telle nuit)—Scanty grass: Poulenc
Herberge (Waldscenen)—At the inn/The inn/Wayside inn: Schumann
Herbst—Autumn: Wolf
Herbstgefühl—Autumnal gloom/Autumn brooding: Brahms
Herbstgefühl—Autumn: Schoeck
Herbstlied/Ach wie so bald—Autumn song: Mendelssohn

Herbstlied/Im Walde rauschen—Autumn song: Mendelssohn
Herbstlied—Autumn/Autumn song: Schumann
Hercules in love—Ercole amanti: Cavalli
Herdglück—Fireside bliss: Bocquet
Here at thy feet—Zu deinen Füssen: Meyer-Helmund
Here, in the silence—In questo muto: Dering
Here, in the valley—Itt lent a völgyben: Bartók
Here is Lethe—Hier is Friede: Berg
Here lies he now—Hier lieg' ich nun: Bach
Here on my bosom—An meinem Herzen, an meiner Brust (Frauenliebe
    und -leben): Schumann
Here sweetest babe—An meinem Herzen (Frauenliebe und -leben):
    Schumann
Here the pretty birds—Ici les tendres oiseaux (Isse): Destouches
Here, within my Father's mansions—Hier, in meines Vaters Stätte
    (Liebster Jesu, mein verlangen): Bach
Here's good health—Auf das wohl: Mozart
Here's hope's consoling ray—Bel raggio lusinghier (Semiramide):
    Rossini
L'heréu Riera—Noble Riera: Alió
The hermit—Gandegili: Kiladze
The hermit—Der Einsiedler: Schumann
The hermit with the violin—Der geigende Eremit: Reger
Hernani! oh haste to me—Ernani, Ernani, involami (Ernani): Verdi
The hero—Dem Helden: Schumann
Hero and Leander—Ero e Leandro: Mancinelli
Herod, why dreadest thou a foe?—Was fürchtst du, Feind Herodes, sehr?:
    Bach
Heroic overture—Heroïchna Uvertyura: Kosenko
Heroïchna Uvertyura—Heroic overture: Kosenko
A hero's life—Ein Heldenleben: R Strauss
Hero's song—Píseň Bohatýrská: Dvořák
The hero's voice—Geistergruss: Zelter
Hero's song—Píseň Bohatýrská: Dvořák
Herr Christ, der einig Gottes Sohn (Orgelbüchlein)—O Thou, of God the
    Father: Bach
Herr, deine Augen sehen nach dem Glauben—Lord, are Thine eyes not
    searching for the righteous/Are not Thine eyes, Lord?: Bach
Herr! Deine Hand (Jesu, nun sei gepreiset)—Lord, may Thy hand: Bach
Der Herr denket an uns—The Lord cares for us: Bach
Der Herr erhör—The Lord shall hear: Schütz
Herr, gehe nicht ins Gericht—Lord, enter not into wrath (judgement):
    Bach
Herr, gib, dass ich dein' Ehre (Was willst du dich betrüben)—So let me
    sing God's praises: Bach

Herr Gott, Beherrscher aller Dinge—Lord God, great master of creation: Bach

Herr Gott, dich loben wir! (Singet dem Herrn ein neues Lied)—Lord, we give to Thee: Bach

Herr Gott, dich loben wir! —Lord God! our praise we give: Bach

Herr Gott, nun schleuss den Himmel auf (Orgelbüchlein)—Lord God, now open wide Thy heav'n: Bach

Her Gott, nun sei gepreiset (Orgelbüchlein)—Lord God, our praise we render: Bach

Herr Hahn und Fraulein Huhn—Hen and rooster: Blech

Herr, ich hoffe darauf—Lord, my trust is in Thee: Schütz

Der Herr ist gross—Great is our Lord: Schütz

Der Herr ist König—The Lord is king: Schütz

Der Herr ist mein getreuer Hirt—The Lord is my shepherd: Bach

Herr Jesu Christ, dich zu uns wend (Orgelbüchlein)—Lord Jesus Christ, be present now: Bach

Herr Jesu Christ, du höchstes Gut—Lord Jesus, pure source of all: Bach

Herr Jesu Christ, mein's Lebens Licht—Lord Jesus Christ, light of my life: Bach

Herr Jesu Christ, wahr'r Mensch und Gott—Lord Jesus Christ, true man and God: Bach

Herr Lenz—Sir spring: R Strauss

Herr, nicht schicke deine Rache—Lord, pour not Thy vengeance on me: Bach

Herr Oluf—Sir Olaf: Loewe

Herr, so du willst (Herr, wie du willst)—Lord, as thou wilt: Bach

Herr, was du willst soll mir gefallen (Ich steh' mit einem Fuss im Grabe)—Lord, what Thou wilst shall be my pleasure: Bach

Herr, wie du willt, so schicks mit mir—Lord as Thou wilt, so deal with me: Bach

Herr wie lange—Lord how long: Brahms

Hertig Magnus—Baron Magnus: Sibelius

Ein Herz, das seinen Jesum lebend weiss—A heart that knows his Jesus lives: Bach

Herz und Mund und Tat und Leben—Heart and voice and all our being/Jesu source of bliss eternal/Gracious Lord of all our being: Bach

Des Herzens Purpurvogel—The heart's purple eagle: Webern

Herzenstauch—Heart for heart: Reger

Herzgewächse—Foliage of the heart: Schoenberg

Herziges Schätzle du! —Sweetheart dearest: R Franz

Herzlich lieb hab ich dich, O Herr—Daily I will love Thee: Schütz

Herzlich tut mich erfreuen—My inmost heart rejoiceth: Brahms

Herzlich tut mit verlangen—My inmost heart doth yearn: Brahms

Herzlich tut mich verlangen—My heart is filled with longing: Bach

Herzliebster Jesu—Saviour of my heart: Brahms

Herzleid—Heartache: Schumann
Herzlieblich Lieb, durch Scheiden—Beloved love, our parting: Schoenberg
Herzliebster Jesu, was hast du verbrochen—O wondrous love: Bach
Die Herzogin von Chicago—The duchess of Chicago: Kálmán
He's a pretty cuckoo—Il est bel et bon: Passereau
He's wrong who imagines—S'inganna chi crede (Medoro): Sarti
L'heure espagnole—The Spanish hour: Ravel
L'heure exquise—The hour of dreaming/The perfect hour/The enchanted hour: Hahn
Les heures—The hours: Chausson
Heut' triumphieret Gottes Sohn—Jesus today rose triumphing: Bach
Heut' triumphieret Gottes Sohn (Orgelbüchlein)—Today God's only-gotten son: Bach
Hexenlied/And'res Maienlied—Witches' song of May/Another May song: Mendelssohn
Hey balloo! —Hochländisches Wiegenlied (Myrthen): Schumann
Hey for the town's factotum—Largo al factotum (Il barbiere di Siviglia): Rossini
Heyday, the liquor flows—Juhe der Wein ist da (Jahreszeiten): Haydn
Les hiboux—The owls: Séverac
Hidden love—Dulgt Kjaerlighed: Grieg
Hidden tears—Stille Tränen: Schumann
Die heiligen zehn Gebote—The holy ten commandments: Haydn
Hier—The past: Poulenc
Hier, au fond des bois—In the woods: Blanchard
Hier, in meines Vaters Stätte (Liebster Jesu, mein Verlangen)—Here, within my Father's mansions: Bach
Hier ist das rechte Osterlamm (Christ lag in Todesbanden)—The Paschal victim here: Bach
Hier ist Friede—Here is Lethe: Berg
Hier lieg' ich nun—Here lies he now: Bach
Hier sitz' ich zur Wacht (Götterdämmerung)—I sit here on guard: Wagner
Hier umarmen sich getreue Gatten—Each in other's arms: Schubert
The high birth of King James—L'alta naixença del Rei En Jaume: Gerhard
High, high are the mountains—Hoch, hoch sind die Berge (Spanische Liebeslieder): Schumann
High over the wold—Lied aus dem Gedichte 'Ivan': Brahms
The high steeple—Vysoká veža: Martinů
Highest contemplate in mercy—Höchster, schau in Gnaden an (Christen, ätzet diesen Tag): Bach
Highland cradle song—Hochländisches Wiegenlied: Schumann
The highland lad—Hochlandbursch: Schumann
The highland watch—Die Hochlands Wache: Beethoven
The highland widow—Die Hochländer-Witwe (Myrthen): Schumann

La hija de Cólquide—The daughter of Colchis: Chavez
Hilf, Gott, dass mirs gelings (Orgelbüchlein)—O help me, Lord, to praise
  Thee: Bach
Hilf, Herr Jesu, lass gelingen—For the beauty of the earth: Bach
The hills of Anacapri—Les collines d'Anacapri: Debussy
Die Himmel erzählen die Ehre Gottes—The heavens proclaim the glory
  of God: Bach
Die Himmel erzählen (Die Schöpfung)—The heavens are telling: Haydn
Die Himmel erzählen die Ehre Gottes—The heavens are telling: Schütz
Der Himmel hat eine Träne geweint—Tears of price: Reger
Der Himmel hat eine Träne geweint—From heaven above: Schumann
Der Himmel lacht, die Erde jubilieret—The heavens rejoice, the earth
  exults/The heavens shout/The heavens laugh: Bach
Himmel strahlt so helle und klar (Zigeunerlieder)—Heaven beams so
  clearly: Brahms
Himmel und Erde—Heaven and earth: Schumann
Himmelsboten zu Liebchens Himmelbett—The angel's love-message:
  R Strauss
Himmelskönig, sei willkommen—King of heaven, Thou art welcome/
  King of heaven, be Thou welcome: Bach
Die himmlische Vorsicht der ewigen Güte (Schleicht, spielende
  Wellen)—They peep in each nest: Bach
Himno pan americano—Pan-American hymn: A Brandt
Himnusz az Urhoz—Hymn to the Lord: E Ábrányi
Hin und zurück—There and back: Hindemith
Hinaus ins Freie—Out in the open air: Schumann
Hindoo song—Chant hindou: Bemberg
Hinter Büschen, hintern Laub (Die Bürgschaft)—Deep enambushed:
  Schubert
Hippodamia's death—Smirt Hippodamie: Fibich
Hirschlein ging im Wald—Once a little fawn: Cornelius
Der Hirt—The shepherd: Liszt
Der Hirt auf dem Felsen—Shepherd on the rock: Schubert
Die Hirten (Weihnachtslieder)—The shepherds: Cornelius
Hirtenchor (Rosamunde)—Shepherd's chorus: Schubert
Hirtengesang an der Krippe (Christus)—Shepherd's song at the manger:
  Liszt
Hirtenlied—The shepherd's song: Mendelssohn
Hirtenmädchens Lied—The beating of my own heart: Kjerulf
His father's nose—Die Mutter bei der Wiege: Schulz
His love writes—Die Liebende schreibt: Schubert
His voice enthralled me/Mad scene—Il dolce suono (Lucia di Lammermoor):
  Donizetti
L'histoire de Babar—The story of Babar: Poulenc
Histoire du soldat—A (The) soldier's tale: Stravinsky

Histoires naturelles—Natural histories: Ravel
Historia von der Geburt Jesu Christi—Story of the birth of Christ/The
 Christmas story: Schütz
Hither to me, ye furies—Già che morir non posso (Radamisto): Handel
Hither to thee once spoke—Vieni, mi disse un giorno: Magaldi
Hitherto have you nothing asked in my name—Bisher habt ihr nichts
 gebeten in meinem Namen: Bach
L'hiver a cessé (La bonne chanson)—Winter is ended: Fauré
Hjärtats morgon—The heart's morning: Sibelius
Hjemad—Homewards: Grieg
Hjemve—Home-sickness: Grieg
Hjertets melodier—Melodies of the heart: Grieg
Hlásej, ptáku (Hubička)—Greet, oh skylark/Skylark's song: Smetana
Hlásný—The night watchman: Martinů
Ho! broadsword and spear—Traun! Bogen und Pfeil sind gut für den
 Feind: Brahms
Hó hull a sárba—White snowflakes: Antalffy
Ho perduto (Rodelinda)—Dead my lord is: Handel
The hoary head—Der greise Kopf (Die Winterreise): Schubert
Hoch, hoch sind die Berge (Spanische Liebeslieder)—High, high are the
 mountains: Schumann
Hochgelobter Gottessohn (Bleib' bei uns, denn es will Abend werden)—
 Thou whose praises never end: Bach
Hochlandbursch—The highland lad: Schumann
Hochländers Abschied (Myrthen)—My heart's in the highlands: Schumann
Die Hochländer-Witwe (Myrthen)—The highland widow: Schumann
Hochländisches Wiegenlied (Myrthen)—Hee balou/Hey baloo!/Highland
 cradle song: Schumann
Das Hochlandmädchen—Nae gentle dames tho': Schumann
Die Hochlands Wache—The highland watch: Beethoven
Höchster, schau in Gnaden an (Christen, ätzet diesen Tag)—Highest
 contemplate in mercy: Bach
Hochzeitlich Lied—Nuptial song: R Strauss
Hochzeitlied—Wedding song: Schoenberg
Hochzeitlieder—Wedding songs: E Strauss
Hochzeitmarsch (Ein Sommernachtstraum)—Wedding march: Mendelssohn
Hodie beata Virgo Maria—On this day, the blessed Virgin Mary: Palestrina
Hodie Christus natus est—'Tis the day of Christ our Lord: Byrd
Hodie Christus natus est—Born today: Sweelinck
Hoesternae rosae—Roses of yesterday: Rummel
Hoffärtig seid ihr (Italienisches Liederbuch)—You are arrogant/Haughty
 and proud art thou: Wolf
Hoffen und wieder verzagen—Hoping, yet ever despairing: R Strauss
Hoffnung—When roses bloom/Hope: J Reichardt
Hoffnungslos—Sad heart: Reger

Hohe Liebe—Love's heaven/Heavenly love: Liszt
Hoheit tanzt Walzer—Her highness waltzes: Ascher
Hold in affection (remembrance) Jesus Christ—Halt' im Gedächtnis
   Jesum Christ: Bach
Hold thou me up, O Lord—O Domine adiuva me: Byrd
A holiday evening—Am Feierabend (Die schöne Müllerin): Schubert
Holiday on the Rhine—Sonntags am Rhein: Schumann
Das Hollandweibchen—The little Dutch girl: Kálmán
Holoubek—The wild dove: Dvořák
Holub na javoře (Moravské Dvojzpěvy)—Forsaken/All alone: Dvořák
Holy body of the Saviour—Pange lingua: Victoria
Holy Ghost, dispel our sadness—Liebster Gott, wann werd' ich sterben?:
   Bach
Holy is God—Heilig: C P E Bach
Holy Lord, though not worthy—Domine, non sum dignus: Victoria
The holy ten Commandments—Die heiligen zehn Gebote: Haydn
Holy week—Karwoche: Wolf
Homage—Huldigung: R Strauss
Homage march—Huldigungsmarsch: Wagner
Home—Heimat (Lieder der Liebe): Kilpinen
Home—Heimat: Reger
Home—Jung Hexenlied: R Strauss
Home of my fathers—Terra adorata (Don Sebastiano): Donizetti
Home to our mountains—Ai nostri monti (Il trovatore): Verdi
The home thought—Das Heimweh: F Mendelssohn
The homecomer—El aparecido (El amor brujo): Falla
Home-coming—Heimkehr: Brahms
A home-coming—Ruckkehr: Wolf
Homeland—Ach, der Gebirgssohn: Schubert
Homeland—Klänge der Heimat (Die Fledermaus): J Strauss II
Home-sickness—Hjemve: Grieg
Homesickness—Das Heimweh: F Mendelssohn
Home-sickness—Ach, der Gebirgssohn: Schubert
The home-sigh—Das Heimweh: F Mendelssohn
Homeward—Heimkehr: R Strauss
Homeward bound—Heimsyn: Sinding
The homeward journey—Die Heimkehr: Cornelius
Homewards—Hjemad: Grieg
Homlefar—The humble·bee: A Backer-Grøndahl
Honkain keskellä—Deep in the woodland: Ennola
Honneur, honneur (La muette de Portici)—All hail: Auber
Hope—An die Hoffnung: Beethoven
A hope—Et Hab: Grieg
Hope—Naděje: Martinů
Hope—Hoffnung: J Reichardt

Hope and light of man's endeavour—Jesus bleibet meine Freude: Bach
Hope no more—Piangerò la sorte mia (Giulio Cesare): Handel
Hope on—Nur Mut: R Strauss
Hope, smile upon me—Ridente speme vola nell'alma: Rispoli
The hope would hear me—Vorresti si vorresti: D Scarlatti
Hoping, yet ever despairing—Hoffen und wieder verzagen: R Strauss
Hør, hvor let dens vinger—Hark, how light the wings: Nielsen
Hor' ich das Liedchen (Dichterliebe)—Old songs/E'er when I hear them
    singing: Schumann
Hora grave—Tragic hour: Engelbrecht
Horch, horst du nicht—Hark, hear ye not a heavenly choir: Schoeck
Hörer jeg Sangen klinge—When to that song I listen: Grieg
L'horizon chimérique—The illusory horizon: Fauré
The horseman—Reiterstück (Album für die Jugend): Schumann
The horses of Eger are all grey—Az Egri ménes mind szürke: Bartók
Hört doch! der sanfen Flöten (Schleicht, spielende Wellen)—Spring
    is the year's pleasant king: Bach
Hospodin jest muj pastýř (Biblické Písne)—God is my shepherd: Dvořák
The hostess at the inn—Khozyayka gostinitsi: Spadavecchia
Hostile force—Vrazh' ya sila: Serov
The hour of dawn—Morgengrüss: Mendelssohn
The hour of dreaming—L'heure exquise: Hahn
The hour of our parting—Wir mussen uns trennen: Brahms
The hours—Les heures: Chausson
The house in the willows—Dort in den Weiden steht ein Haus: Brahms
The house of the dead—Z Mrtveno domu: Janáček
The house of dreams—Traumnacht: Weingartner
The household war—Die Verschworenen: Schubert
How appalling a sight—Quel funesti appareil (Jepthé): Montéclair
How art thou, O my queen—Wie bist du, meine Königin: Brahms
How blest are they whose faith unshaken—Beglückten stand getreuer
    Seelen: Bach
How brightly beams the morning star—Wie schön leuchtet der
    Morgenstern: Bach
How brightly shines the morning star—Wie schön leuchtet der
    Morgenstern: Bach
How brightly shines yon star of morn—Wie schön leuchter der
    Morgenstern: Bach
How calm is my spirit—Ridente la calma: Mozart
How can I be blithe—Weit, weit: Schumann
How can I be happy—Wie soll ich freudig sein (Italienisches Liederbuch):
    Wolf
How can I e'er rejoice—Wie soll ich fröhlich sein (Italienisches Liederbuch):
    Wolf

How can I blithe and cheerful be?—Wie kann ich froh und lustig sein?:
    Mendelssohn
How can I sustain?—Wo soll ich die Freude: Brahms
How can life be life without thee?—Muss es eine Trennung geben: Brahms
How can love?—Voi che sapete (Le nozze di Figaro): Mozart
How can this be?—Non so come l'alma mia: Agostini
How canst thou sleep—Wie kannst du ruhig schlafen?: Blumenthal
How changed the vision—Cangio d'aspetto (Admeto): Handel
How coldly shines the moon—Wie glänzt der helle Mond: Pfitzner
How could I ever—Ch'io mai ri possa (Siroe): Handel
How could I greater bliss—Wie mochte je mir wohler sein (Siechentrost):
    Bruch
How crushing are such words—Quel language accablant (Iphigénie en
    Tauride): Gluck
How do you do?—Goddag, Goddag: Nielsen
How fair are thy tents—Ma tovu: Tansman
How fair is the earth—Juch he!: Brahms
How flies the time—In dulce jubilo: Hofmann
How fondly I love—Wie lieb ich dich hab' (An Bertha): Cornelius
How frail and weak a thing is man—Faiblesse de la race humaine! (La reine
    de Saba): Gounod
How free and fresh—Wie froh und frisch: Brahms
How Georg von Frundsberg sang about himself—Wie Georg von Frundsberg
    von sich selber sang: Schoenberg
How hast Thou then, my God—Wie hast du dich, mein Gott (Ich hatte
    viel Bekümmernis): Bach
How jovial is my laughter—Wie will ich lustig lachen (Zerreist, zersprenget,
    Zertrümmer der Gruft): Bach
How light and gay—Wie froh und frisch: Brahms
How lovely is the earth—Wie ist doch die Erde so schön: Blech
How lovely is Thy dwelling place—Wie lieblich sind deine Wohnungen
    (Ein deutsches Requiem): Brahms
How may I fly—Come fuggir per sehr' ombrosae: Marenzio
How often our happiness flows—Souvent de nos biens: Aubert
How proud and stately—Wie stolz und stattlich: Henschel
How short does the hour seem—Que l'heure est donc brève: Massenet
How strange it is to say—Forunderligt at sige: Nielsen
How sweet—Wohl schön bewandt (Liebeslieder Walzer): Brahms
How sweet the elder smells—Was duft doch der Flieder (Die Meistersinger
    von Nürnberg): Wagner
How sweet the skylark's song—Wie singt die Lerche schön: Liszt
How sweetly echo in my hearing—Wie lieblich klingt es in den Ohren:
    Bach
How sweetly sings the lark—Wie singt die Lerche schön: Liszt

How to make naughty children good—Um schlimme Kinder artig zu machen: Mahler

How void of passion—Che fiero costume: Legrenzi

How wondrous sweet, O Lord—O quam suavis est: Byrd

How wretched am I—Infelix ego: Byrd

Hrabina—The countess: Moniuszko

Hubicka—The kiss: Smetana

Der Hufschmied—The blacksmith: Schoeck

Hugdietrich in search of a wife—Hugdietrichs Brautfahrt: Straus

Hugdietrichs Brautfahrt—Hugdietrich in search of a wife: Straus

Hulán—Lancers: Smetana

Hulanka—Drinking song/Bachanal: Chopin

Huldigung—Homage: R Strauss

Huldigungsmarsch—Homage march: Wagner

Hüll in der Mantille dich fester ein (Tiefland)—Come, throw your mantilla around you with grace: d'Albert

Hullámzo balaton tetején—The fisherman: Erkel

The humble bee—Homlefar: A Backer-Grøndahl

Humility—Er, der herrlichste von Allen (Frauenliebe und -leben): Schumann

The humming bird—Le colibri: Chausson

Humming song—Trällerliedchen (Album für die Jugend): Schumann

The hump-backed fiddler—Der bucklichte Fiedler: Brahms

The humpbacked horse—Konek-Gorbunok: Shchedrin

Hun danser—She dances: Grieg

Hun er saa huid—She was so fair/So white is she: Grieg

Hunc arguta—Praise him, sharp-toned strings: Byrd

Hund und Katze—Cat and dog: Meyer-Helmund

A hundred lovely slaves—Cent esclaves ornaient (Gulistan): Dalayrac

The hundred virgins—Les cent vierges: Lecocq

Hungarian dances—Ungarische Tänze: Brahms

Hungarian folk-songs—Magyar nepclolock: Bartók

Hungarian folk-songs—Két zoborvidéki népdal: Kodály

Hungarian sketches—Magyar képek: Bartók

The hunt—La chasse [symphony]: Haydn

The hunter—Der Jäger (Marienlieder): Brahms

Hunter on the lookout—Jäger auf der Lauer (Waldscenen): Schumann

A hunter went a-riding—Mit Lust tät ich ausreiten: Brahms

The hunter's farewell—Der Jäger Abschied: Mendelssohn

The hunter's lament—Ich schell' mein Horn: Brahms

Hunter's song—Jaegersang (Tove): Nielsen

Hunting cantata—Jagdkantate: Bach

Hunting chorus—Jägerchor (Rosamunde): Schubert

Hunting song—Jagdlied: R Franz

Hunting song—Jägerlied: Grieg

Hunting song—Jagdlied: Mendelssohn
Hunting song—Jagdlied (Waldscenen): Schumann
Hunting song—Jägerliedchen (Album für die Jugend): Schumann
The huntsman—Der Jäger im Walde: Brahms
The huntsman—Jägerlied: Brahms
The huntsman—Der Jäger (Die schöne Müllerin): Schubert
The huntsman—Parole: Brahms
The huntsman—Der Jäger: Wolf
The huntsman and his lass—Der Jäger und sein Liebchen: Brahms
Huntsman's even-song—Jägers Abendlied: Schubert
Huntsman's farewell—Jäger und sein Liebchen: Brahms
Huntsman's song—Jägerslied: Wolf
The hurdy-gurdy man—Der Leiermann (Die Winterreise): Schubert
The hurricane—L'uragano: Rocca
A husband on the mat—Un mari à la porte: Offenbach
Hush, in silence fulfil we our errand—Zitti, zitti, moviarmo a vendetta:
    Verdi
Hush of the sea—Meeresstille: Schubert
Hussar—Huszárnŏta: Bartók
The hussars march off—Huzarenabzug: Schumann
Huszárnŏta—Hussar: Bartók
Huszt—The ruins: Kodály
The hut—Hytten: Grieg
Hüt du dich—Beware: Brahms
The hut on fowls' legs—La cabane sur des pattes de poule (Tableaux
    d'une exposition): Mussorgsky
Hüte dich! O, beware: Meyer-Helmund
Die Hütte—The cottage: Schumann
Huzarenabzug—The hussars march off: Schumann
Hyménée, ta journée (Guillaume Tell)—Come with flowers: Rossini
A hymn for the new year—Zum neuen Jahr-Kirchengesang: Wolf
Hymn of love—Cantique d'amour: Liszt
Hymn of praise—Lobgesang: Mendelssohn
The hymn of praise—Chvalozpèv: Vycpalek
Hymn of Zrinyi—Zrinyi szózata: Kodály
Hymn to joy—An die Freude: Schubert
Hymn to King Stephen—Ének Szent István királyhoz: Kodály
Hymn to the Almighty—Die Allmacht: Schubert
Hymn to the eternal—Hymne an den Unendlichen: Schubert
Hymn to the Lord—Himnusz az Urhoz: E Ábrányi
Hymn to the nations—Inno delle nazioni: Verdi
Hymne an den Unendlichen—Hymn to the eternal: Schubert
Hymne de l'enfant à son reveil—The awakening child's dream: Liszt
Hytten—The hut/Love in a cottage: Grieg

I

I a note must be writing—Einen Brief soll ich schreiben: Reger
I adore you arrows of love—V'adoro, pupille (Giulio Cesare): Handel
I am alone at last—Me voilà seule enfin! (La reine de Saba): Gounod
I am but a child—Je suis presqu' enfant (Don César de Bazan): Massenet
I am but a shepherd maiden—Le boquet navi (Sancho Pança): Monsigny
I am happy in my good fortune—Ich bin vergnügt mit meinem Glücke: Bac
I am much honoured—Mir ist die Ehre (Der Rosenkavalier): R Strauss
I am spent with crying—Laboravi clamans: Rameau
I am the good shepherd—Ich bin einer guter Hirt: Bach
I am the mother—Io sono la madre: Respighi
I am the phoenix—Io sono fenice: Vecchi
I ascend unto my Father—Ascendo ad patrem meum: Handl
I avail me of Cupid's pinion—Di Cupido impiego i vanni (Rodelinda): Hand
I bear a knife within my breast—Ich hab' ein glühend Messer (Lieder eines
    fahrenden Gesellen): Mahler
I behold thee, I enfold thee—Pur ti miro, pur ti stringo (L'incoronazione di
    Poppea): Monteverdi
I believed that—J'avais cru que (Semiramis): Catel
I blow my horn adown the vale—Ich schell' mein Horn: Brahms
I breathed a gentle scent of lime—Ich atmet' einen linden Duft: Mahler
I breathed the breath—Ich atmet' einen linden Duft: Mahler
I can but love thee—Ich will dich lieben, meine Krone (Liebe): Cornelius
I can not, dare not believe it—Ich kann's nicht fassen, nicht glauben
    (Frauenliebe und -leben): Schumann
I can scarce comprehend it—Come mai creder deggio (Don Giovanni): Moz.
I cannot come to you—Egyedül a tengerrel: Bartók
I cannot fathom it—Ich kann's nicht fassen, nicht glauben (Frauenliebe
    und -leben): Schumann
I cannot sing any more—Nicht länger kann ich singen (Italianisches Liederb
    Wolf
I carry my burden with joy—Jeg baerer med smil min byrde: Nielsen
I chant my lay—Má písen zas (Cigánské melodie): Dvořák
I cherish thee—Ich liebe dich: Liszt
I chide thee not—Ich grolle nicht (Dichterliebe): Schumann
I creep away in mute despair—Ich schleich umher: Brahms
I cried to God in tribulation—Ad Dominum cum tribulare: M Haydn
I cruel?—Crudele? (Don Giovanni): Mozart
I do not dare despond—Non posso disperar: Luca
I do not wish—Je ne désire point ces ardeurs (Tristesses): Milhaud
I don't eat my bread dry—Ich esse nun (Italianisches Liederbuch): Wolf
I dreamed at night that I was dear to thee—Es träumte mir, ich sei dir teuer:
    Brahms

I ever have withstood a woman's charms—Vždy odolal jsem čarozraku (Dalibor):
   Smetana
I fain would know—So wunsch' ich mir zu guter letzt: Bach
I fain would rest—Lehn deine Wang an meine Wang: Jensen
I fold thee in my loving arms—In meinen Armen wieg' ich dich: R Franz
I followed treacherous paths—J'allais par des chemins perfides (La bonne
   chanson): Fauré
I forget what I am—Non sò più cosa son (Le nozze di Figaro): Mozart
I go to death—Vado a morir (Arminio): Handel
I go to the rest in peace—Jeg laegger mig så trygt til ro: Nielsen
I had conceived a little song—Ich hab' ein kleines Lied erdacht: Bungert
I hardly know—Mein Lieb ich bin gebunden: Kjerulf
I have a burro—Yo tinc un burro: J Rodrigo
I have a little cake—J'ai encore un tel pâté: La Halle
I have embarked—Je me suis embarqué (L'horizon chimérique): Fauré
I have enough—Ich habe genug: Bach
I have into God's heart and being—Ich hab in Gottes Herz und Sinn: Bach
I have lost my Euridice—Sposa Euridice (Orfeo ed Euridice): Gluck
I have won—Ripportai gloriosa (Atalanta): Handel
I hear a harp—Es tönt ein voller Harfenklang: Brahms
I hear a sighing—Es geht ein Wehen: Brahms
I hear a songster—Ich hör ein Vöglein: Mendelssohn
I hear the mill—J'entends le moulin taqueter: Blanchard
I heard a voice from heaven—Audivi vocem de coelo: Tallis
I heard the rose make sad complaint—Es hat die Rose sich beklagt:
   R Franz
I Hjemmet—In my native country: Grieg
I in Rome like Jove am reigning—Io di Roma il Giove sono (Agrippina):
   Handel
I journey slowly onward—Da fahr ich still im Wagen: Wolf
I keep a little medal—Je garde une médaille (Tristesses): Milhaud
I know—Ja vím (Pisné milostné): Dvořák
I know a flower—Es ist ein Ros' entsprungen: Praetorius
I know a lark's nest—Jeg ved en laerkerede: Nielsen
I know a maiden—Ich weiss mir'n Maidlein: Brahms
I know how to tie the ribbons—Je sais attacher des rubans: Dourlen
I do not know from whither—Non so d'onde viene: Mozart
I know not who my father was—Ich weiss nicht, wer mein Vater war
   (Tiefland): d'Albert
I know that my redeemer lives—Ich weiss, dass mein Erlöser lebt: Bach
I know that my redeemer liveth—Ich weiss, dass mein Erlöser lebt: J M Bach
I lay with Cassio—Era la notte (Otello): Verdi
I lean against the mast—Ich stand gelehnt an den Mast: Mendelssohn
I leave thee, love—Ich scheid von dir: Hassler

I leave thee not—Ich lasse dich nicht: Bach
I left my fair homeland—Elindulatam szép hazámbul: Bartók
I lift mine eyes—Ich hebe mein Augen: Schütz
I linger restless all along—Ich schleiche bang' (Die Verschworenen):
    Schubert
I live a life of longing—Jeg lever mit Liv i Laengse: Grieg
I long only to love you—Je n'ai envie que de t'aimer (Tel jour telle nuit):
    Poulenc
I love a fair floweret—Ich lieb' eine Blume: R Franz
I love but thee—Ich liebe dich: Liszt
I love but thee—Ich liebe dich: R Strauss
I love the highest—Ich liebe den Höchsten: Bach
I love thee—Ich liebe dich: Beethoven
I love thee—Jeg elsker dich: Grieg
I love you—Ich liebe dich: Beethoven
I love you—Declaraçao: Guarnieri
I loved thee well—Du var mig kjaer: F Backer-Grøndahl
I made a vow—Hab' mir's Gelobt (Der Rosenkavalier): R Strauss
I may not thank thee—Ich darf nicht dankend: Schoenberg
I ne'er will roam—Ich wand're nicht: Schumann
I no longer recall—Je ne me souviens plus: Rhené-Baton
I pace along here—Es treibt mich hin: R Franz
I, Pereda, for honour am fated—Son Pereda, son ricco d'onore (La forza
    del destino): Verdi
I press thee to my bosom—Al senti stringo e parto (Ariodante): Handel
I promised thee—Nicht mehr zu dir zu gehen: Brahms
I promised to see thee no more—Nicht mehr zu dir zu gehen: Brahms
I rejoice in my death—Ich freue mich auf meinen Tod (Ich habe genug):
    Bach
I remember—Penso!: Tosti
I remember a girl—Kann mich auch an ein Mädel (Der Rosenkavalier):
    R Strauss
I roused me from sleep—Wie rafft ich mich auf in der Nacht: Brahms
I said 'I will forget thee'—Nicht mehr zu dir zu gehen: Brahms
I see my soul—Ich sehe wie in einem Spiegel: R Strauss
I seek not glory—Mich locket nicht: Mozart
I seek Thee daily, yearning ever—Ich geh' und suche mit Verlangen: Bach
I send thee—Jo dei saluti: Wolf-Ferrari
I shall mourn my cruel fortune—Piangerò la sorte mia (Giulio Cesare):
    Handel
I shall not wander—Ich wand're nicht: Schumann
I should have wished for death—Ich wünschte mir den Tod (Selig ist der
    Mann): Bach
I sit here on guard—Hier sitz' ich zur Wacht: Wagner

I sought at night—Ich sucht des Nachts: M Franck
I stand beside thy crib—Ich steh' an deiner Krippen: Bach
I stand with one foot in the grave—Ich steh' mit einem Fuss im Grabe:
    Bach
I stilla Timmar—In quiet hours: Alfvén
I stood and gazed on her image—Ich stand in dunkeln Träumen: Wolf
I stood in gloomy musing—Ich stand in dunkeln Träumen: Grieg
I stood upon the mountain—Ich stand auf hohem Berge: Brahms
I suffered with great heaviness—Ich hatte viel Bekümmernis: Bach
I swear no more to woo thee—Nicht mehr zu dir zu gehen: Brahms
I think of thee—Andenken: Beethoven
I think of thee—Ich denke dein: Schumann
I think oft—Oft denk' ich (Kinder-totenlieder): Mahler
I to my love—O ma tante douce Colombelle: Monsigny
I tremble when I see your face—Je tremble en voyant ton visage (Le
    promenoir des deux amants): Debussy
I triumph! I triumph!—Vittoria! Vittoria!: Carissimi
I trust in God's good will—Steh' ich bei meinem Gott: Bach
I trust in thee—Je crois en vous: Berlioz
I waited expectantly—Exspectans exspectavi: Lassus
I waited for the Lord—Ich harrete des Herrn (Lobgesang): Mendelssohn
I walk in the sun—I solen går jeg bag min plov: Nielsen
I walked to the end of the great street in Tárkány—Végigmentem a
    Tárkányi: Bartók
I wander along—Mir fehlt das Beste: R Franz
I wander 'mid the flow'rets—Ich wandle unter Blumen: Lassen
I wander 'mongst the blossoms—Ich wandle unter Blumen: Lassen
I wander oft—Kol domu se teď potácím (Pisně milostné): Dvořák
I wander this summer morning—Am leuchtenden Sommermorgen:
    R Franz
I wander thro' the gateway—Nun schreit' ich aus dem Tore: Henschel
I wander through the still night—Ich wand're durch die stille Nacht:
    R Franz
I wandered in the fields tending the sheep—Jeg gik i marken og vogtede får:
    Nielsen
I want to see—Je la désire (Tristesses): Milhaud
I was by hope of grace—Ich habe mich dem Heil: Schoeck
I will hear no more of love—Alles, alles in den Wind (Neue Liebeslieder):
    Brahms
I will lift mine eyes—Pozdvihuji oví svých (Biblické Pisné): Dvořák
I will lift up mine eyes unto the hills—Wer da glaubet und getauft wird:
    Bach
I will not grieve—Ich grolle nicht (Dichterliebe): Schumann

I will not let Thee go—Ich lasse dich nicht: J C Bach

I will sing new songs—Bože! Bože! (Biblické Pisné): Dvořák

I will suffer yet with meekness—Ich will leiden, ich will schweigen (Bisher habt ihr nichts gebeten in meinem Namen): Bach

I will the cross with gladness carry—Ich will den Kreuzstab gerne tragen: Bach

I wish—Je veux: Rhené-Baton

I wished her thus—So wünsch ich ihr ein gute Nacht: Brahms

I woke and arose in the night—Wie rafft ich mich auf in der Nacht: Brahms

I wonder what thou 'rt doing—Möcht' wissen, was sie schlagen: R Franz

I worship Thee—Dich bet' ich an, mein höchster Gott: Bach

I would believe—Tu me dirais: Chaminade

I would cross the Tisza in a boat—Által mennék én a Taszán Ladikon: Bartók

I would that my love—Ich wollt' meine Lieb: Mendelssohn

I wound my horn—Ich schwing' mein Horn: Brahms

I wrestle and pray—Ich lasse dich nicht: J C Bach

The ice—Auf dem Flusse (Die Winterreise): Schubert

Ice and steel—Lyed i stal': Deshevov

Ich aber bin elend—But I am poor: Brahms

Ich armer Mensch, ich Sudenknecht—Poor wretched man, a slave of sin: Bach

Ich atmet' einen linden Duft—I breathed the breath/I breathed a gentle scent of lime: Mahler

Ich bin dein Baum, O Gartner—The tree and the gardener: Schumann

Ich bin der Welt abhanden gekommen—Lost to the world/O garish world: Mahler

Ich bin einer guter Hirt—I am the good shepherd: Bach

Ich bin vergnügt mit meinem Glucke—My life is sweet with gracious blessing/I am happy in my good fortune: Bach

Ich bitt' dich—The scale of D flat: Beethoven

Ich bitte dich, Herr Jesu Christ (Wo gehest du hin?)—Lord Christ above: Bach

Ich darf nicht dankend—I may not thank thee: Schoenberg

Ich denke dein—I think of thee: Schumann

Ich esse nun (Italienisches Liederbuch)—I don't eat my bread dry/No more unmoistened: Wolf

Ich flüstre deinen Namen—Thy name I whisper: Kücken

Ich folge Christo nach (Weinen, Klagen, Sorgen, Zagen)—With Jesus will I go: Bach

Ich freue mich auf meinem Tod (Ich habe genug)—I rejoice in my death: Bach

Ich fuhr über Meer—The search: Kjerulf

Ich furcht' mit Gespenster: Pfitzner

Ich geh' durch—Through alley and lane: Wolf
Ich geh' und suche mit Verlangen—I seek Thee daily, yearning ever: Bach
Ich glaub', lieber Schatz—Once in the woods: Reger
Ich grolle nicht (Dichterliebe)—I will not grieve/I chide thee not/Why
    blame thee now: Schumann
Ich hab ein glühend Messer (Lieder eines fahrenden Gesellen)—I bear a
    knife within my breast/There is a glowing dagger: Mahler
Ich hab' ein kleines Lied erdacht—I had conceived a little song: Bungert
Ich hab' im Traum—A tearful dream: Hue
Ich hab' im Traum geweinet (Dichterliebe)—Dreaming/In dreams my tears
    were flowing/In dreams I fell a-weeping: Schumann
Ich hab' im Traume geweinet—In dreams I've wept: R Franz
Ich hab' in deinem Auge—Once in thine eyes: R Franz
Ich hab' in Gottes Herz und Sinn—I have into God's heart and being: Bach
Ich hab' mein Sach Gott heim gestellt—My cause is God's, and I am still:
    Bach
Ich habe genug—O Lord, tis enough/I have enough/It is enough: Bach
Ich habe mich dem Heil—I was by hope of grace: Schoeck
Ich halte treulich still—In faith I quiet wait: Bach
Ich harrete des Herrn (Lobgesang)—I waited for the Lord: Mendelssohn
Ich hatte einst ein schönes Vaterland/Es war ein Traum—Ah, once I had/
    Only a dream/It was a dream/The exile's dream: Lassen
Ich hatte viel Bekümmernis—My spirit was in heaviness/I suffered with
    great heaviness: Bach
Ich hebe mein Augen—I lift my eyes: Schütz
Ich hör' die Bachlein/In der Fremde—Memories: Schumann
Ich hör ein Vöglein—I hear a songster/A bird is sweetly singing/A bird is
    softly calling: Mendelssohn
Ich kann's nicht fassen, nicht glauben—I can not, dare not believe it/
    I cannot fathom it/It cannot be: Schumann
Ich kose süss (Neue Liebeslieder)—To many a maid: Brahms
Ich lasse dich nicht [cantata]—I leave Thee not: Bach
Ich lasse dich nicht [motet]—I wrestle and pray/I will not let Thee go:
    J C Bach
Ich lieb' eine Blume—I love a fair floweret: R Franz
Ich liebe den Höchsten—I love the Highest: Bach
Ich liebe dich—I love you/I love thee/Alike at morn and eventide:
    Beethoven
Ich liebe dich—A declaration: Blumenthal
Ich liebe dich—I love but thee/I cherish thee: Liszt
Ich liebe dich—I love but thee: R Strauss
Ich lobe mir die Vöglein—O happy, happy little birds: R Franz
Ich möchte hingeh'n—Would I could pass hence: Liszt

Ich nehme mein Leiden mit Freuden auf mich (Die Elenden sollen essen)—
My earthly afflictions with gladness: Bach

Ich ruf zu dir, Herr Jesu Christ (Orgelbüchlein)—Lord, hear the voice of
my complaint: Bach

Ich sah als Knabe Blumen blüh'n (Heimweh)—The flow'rs that bloomed/
Flowers that bloomed for me: Brahms

Ich scheid von dir—I leave thee, love: Hassler

Ich scheide—I'm going: Liszt

Ich schell' mein Horn—I blow my horn adown the vale/The hunter's
lament: Brahms

Ich schleich' umher—Amid the gloomy woods/I creep away in mute despair/
When mute and sad/Forlorn: Brahms

Ich schleiche bang' (Die Verschworenen)—I linger restless all along: Schubert

Ich schwebe—A farewell: R Strauss

Ich schwing' mein Horn—The old hunter/I wound my horn: Brahms

Ich sehe dich—In thousand forms I see: Reger

Ich sehe schon im Geist (Gott fähret auf mit Jauchzen)—My spirit Him
descries: Bach

Ich sehe wie in einem Spiegel—I see my soul: R Strauss

Ich stand auf höhem Berge—I stood upon the mountain: Brahms

Ich stand gelehnt an den Mast—I lean against the mast: Mendelssohn

Ich stand in dunkeln Träumen—I stood in gloomy musing: Grieg

Ich stand in dunkeln Träumen—I stood and gazed on her image: Wolf

Ich steh' an deine Krippen—I stand beside thy crib: Bach

Ich steh' mit einem Fuss im Grabe—Comes death apace with footfall
eager/I stand with one foot in the grave: Bach

Ich sucht' des Nachts—I sought at night: M Franck

Ich trag/Geheimnis—Love's secret: Reger

Ich trage meine Minne—To none will I my love: R Strauss

Ich vergönn' es ihn—Not a tear: Henschel

Ich wanderte unter den Bäumen—Alone in the wood: Dieren

Ich wandle unter Blumen—I wander 'mongst the blossoms/I wander
'mid the flowrets: Lassen

Ich wand're durch die stille Nacht—I wander through the stilly night: R Franz

Ich wand're nicht—I ne'er will roam/Pleasures of home/I shall not wander:
Schumann

Ich wandte mich und sahe an—So I returned: Brahms

Ich weiss, dass mein Erlöser lebt—I know that my Redeemer lives: Bach

Ich weiss, dass mein Erlöser lebt—I know that my Redeemer liveth:
J M Bach

Ich weiss mir 'n Maidlein—I know a maiden: Brahms

Ich weiss nicht, wer mein Vater war (Tiefland)—I know not who my father
was: d'Albert

Ich will den Kreuzstab gerne tragen—I will the cross with gladness carry/
My cross with gladness I carry: Bach

Ich will dich lieben, meine Krone—I can but love thee: Cornelius
Ich will dir mein Herz schenken (Matthäuspassion)—Saviour make me all
 Thine own: Bach
Ich will leiden, ich will schweigen (Bisher habt ihr nichts gebeten in
 meinem Namen)—I will suffer yet with meekness: Bach
Ich will meine Seele tauchen (Dichterliebe)—Love's whisper: Schumann
Ich wollt' meine Lieb'—I would that my love: Mendelssohn
Ich wünschte mir den Tod (Selig ist der Mann)—I should have wished for
 death: Bach
Ici les tendres oiseaux (Isse)—Here the pretty birds: Destouches
I'd carve it on the bark—Ungeduld: Schubert-Heller
I'd fain to thee express—Porterti dir vorrei (Partenope): Handel
I'd rather—Lieber alles: Wolf
Ideal hope—Sehnsucht [D 636]: Schubert
Ideo deprecor—Wherefore do I beseech: Byrd
Idolo del cor mio (L'incoronazione di Poppea)—Thou art my heart's own
 idol: Monteverdi
If all my heartfelt thinking—All' meine Herzgedanken: Brahms
If all the world—Wenn alle Welt: Reger
If all this is but a fleeting dream—Si tout ceci (Tristesses): Milhaud
If but my death may ease thee—S'è tuo piacer ch'io mora (Atalanta): Handel
If even the flow'rets—Und wüssten's die Blumen: Schumann
If Florindo be faithful—Se Florindo è fedele (La donna ancora è fedele):
 A Scarlatti
If God has willed it so—Wenn Gott es hatt' gewollt: Reger
If heaven doth divide me—Se il ciel mi divide (Alessandro nell'Indie):
 Piccinni
If I, oh heaven, could tell you—Vorrei spiegarvi, oh Dio: Mozart
If indeed I've lost my lover—Si j'ai perdu mon amant: Delusse
If love be chaste—S'un casto amor (Sonnets of Michelangelo): Britten
If love hath entered my heart—Hat dich die Liebe berührt: J Marx
If manly valor—Se un bell' ardire (Ezio): Handel
If my songs were only winged—Si mes vers avaient des ailes: Hahn
If only by deserving—Se meritar potessi: Bruni
If she see—Se vedrà l'amena sponda (Partenza): Handel
If someone looks into the mirror—Wenn einer in den Spiegel siehet
 (Chamber music): Henze
If there be a charming lawn—S'il est un charmant gazon: Liszt
If Thou art near—Bist du bei mir: Bach
If thou but smile—Si le bonheur (Faust): Gounod
If thou but suffer God to guide thee—Wer nur den lieben Gott lässt
 walten: Bach
If thou lov'st me—Se tu m'ami: Pergolesi
If thou shalt confess with thy mouth—So du mit deinem Munde: Bach
If thou thy heart will give me—Willst du dem Herz mir schenken: Bach

If thou wert my love—Wenn: R Strauss

If thou wilt suffer God to guide thee—Wer nur den lieben Gott lässt walten: Bach

If through the church yard—Und gehst du über den Kirchhof: Brahms

If you are asking—Saper vorreste (Un ballo in maschera): Verdi

If you are there—Bist du bei mir: Bach

If you do not take pity on me—Se pieta di me non senti (Giulio Cesare): Handel

If you have ever borne me—Se mi portate affetto: V Ciampi

If you love for beauty—Liebst du um Schönheit: Mahler

If you, sighing—Se tu m'ami: Rousseau

If you will beloved—Si tu veux, Mignon: Massenet

If you will promise me—Vedrai carino, se sei buonino (Don Giovanni): Mozart

If you wish for true happiness—Il segreto per esser felici (Lucrezia Borgia): Donizetti

If you would dance—Se vuol ballare (Le nozze di Figaro): Mozart

If you would of love assure me—Se feder vuoi ch'io ti creda (Orlando): Handel

Ifiheniya v Tauridi—Iphigenia in Tauris: Stetsenko

Igrok—The gambler: Prokofiev

Ihr Auge—Her eyes: R Franz

Ihr Bild (Schwanengesang)—Her portrait/Her picture/The portrait: Schubert

Die ihr des unermesslichen Weltalls/Deutsche Kantate—Ye who the great creator/Ye who acknowledge a universal creator: Mozart

Ihr, dir ihr euch von Christo nennet—Ye who the sons of God dare call ye: Bach

Ihr Gedanken—Thoughts of darkness: Erlanger

Ihr Glocken von Marling—Bells of Marling/Ye bells of old Marling: Liszt

Ihr Grab—Her tomb: Blumenthal

Ihr lieben Christen, freut euch nun—Good Christian men rejoice: Buxtehude

Ihr Mächtigen (Zaide)—You who are powerful: Mozart

Ihr schwarzen Augen (Neue Liebeslieder)—Ye eyes of darkness: Brahms

Ihr werdet weinen und heulen—Ye shall weep and lament: Bach

Ihre Augen—Thine eyes: R Strauss

Ihre Stimme—Her voice: Schubert

Ihre Stimme—Your voice/Her voice: Schumann

Il est bel et bon—He's a pretty cuckoo: Passereau

Il mio tesoro—Fly then to my beloved (Don Giovanni): Mozart

Il pleure dans mon coeur (Ariettes oubliées)—Tears fall in my heart: Debussy

Il s'en va tard—A storm has brewed: Jannequin

Il vole (Fiancailles pour rire)—He flies: Poulenc

L'île heureuse—The happy isle: Chabrier
L'île inconnue (Les nuits d'été)—The unknown land/The undiscovered
    country: Berlioz
I'll ever gay and merry be—So will ich frisch und fröhlich sein: Brahms
I'll spread my music's pinions—Auf Flugeln des Gesanges: Mendelssohn
I'll wage war—Vò far guerra (Rinaldo): Handel
Illalle—To evening: Sibelius
Ill-omen'd coffer—Urna fatale del mio destino (La forza del destino): Verdi
Illusion—Täuschung (Die Winterreise): Schubert
Illusion's magic spell—So lasst mich scheinen [D 727]: Schubert
Illusions perdues—Lost illusions: Blumenthal
The illusory horizon—L'horizon chimérique: Fauré
Ilsea's heart—Ilseino srdce: Karel
Ilseino srdce—Ilsea's heart: Karel
Im Abendrot—In the red of evening/Sunset glow/The orb of day departs/
    In the sunset/Evening glow/At sunset: Schubert
Im Abendrot (Vier letzte Lieder)—In the sunset glow: R Strauss
Im April—In April: Lassen
Im Arm der Liebe—O come, sweet slumber: Beethoven
Im Dorfe (Die Winterreise)—In the village: Schubert
I'm dreaming of the day—Je songe à ce jour (Tristesses): Milhaud
Im Feld ein Mädchen singt—A maiden yonder sings: Sibelius
Im Freien—Love in starlight: Schubert
Im Frühling—In spring: R Franz
Im Frühling—Joys of spring: Mendelssohn
Im Frühling—In the spring/Love in April: Schubert
Im Frühling—In spring: Wolf
Im Frühlingsanfang—The opening spring: Mozart
Im Garten—In the garden: Blumenthal
Im Garten am Seegestade—The garden by the sea: Brahms
Im Gebirge—On the hillside: Kjerulf
I'm going—Ich scheide: Liszt
Im Grünen—The woods: Mendelssohn
Im Grünen—Welcome to spring: Mendelssohn
Im Haine—In the wood/Thro' the pinewood: Schubert
Im Herbst—In autumn: Brahms
Im Herbst—In the Autumn/In autumn: R Franz
Im Herbst—In autumn/Autumn song: Mendelssohn
Im Herbst—Autumn: Pfitzner
Im Himmelreich ein Haus steht—In heaven doth a house rise: Reger
Im Krappenwald—The cuckoo: J Strauss II
Im Kreuxgang von St Stefano—In the cloister of San Stefano: Schoeck
Im Lenz—In spring: Cornelius
Im Mai—In May: R Franz

I'm prisoner and wounded—Ferito, prigionier (Germania): Franchetti
Im Regen und im Sonnenschein—In shower and sunshine: Koss
Im Rhein—On the Rhine: R Franz
Im Rhein (Dichterliebe)—Noble Rhine: Schumann
Im Rhein im schönen Strome—The Rhine's green waters: Liszt
Im Sommer—In summer/Summertime: R Franz
Im Spätboot—Last boat across/In the late boat: R Strauss
Im Spiel der Wellen—Among the play of the waves: Reger
Im Süden—Land of beauty: Mendelssohn
I'm the slave of love's devotion—Preda son d'un fido amore: S Palma
Im tiefen Keller—In cellar cool: Fischer
Im tiefsten Herzen—Within my heart: Cornelius
Im Traum—Dream vision: Dohnányi
Im Treibhaus (Wesendonck Lieder)—In the hothouse/In the greenhouse:
    Wagner
Im Volkston—The shepherd's reproach: Meyer-Helmund
Im Wald—In the forest: Mendelssohn
Im Wald—In the wood: Schumann
Im Wald bei der Amsel—The nightingale: Erk
Im Walde—In the woods: Mendelssohn
Im Walde—In the wood(s): Schumann
Im Walde rauschen/Herbstlied—Autumn song: Mendelssohn
Im Weissen Rössl—White Horse Inn: Benatzky (et al)
Im Westen (Myrthen)—In the west: Schumann
Im wunderschönen Monat Mai—'Twas in the beauteous month of May:
    R Franz
Im wunderschönen Monat Mai (Dichterliebe)—May-Song/'Twas in the
    lovely month of May/In May/The month of May: Schumann
Im Zimmer—Indoors: Berg
Image of fiery wild forcefulness—Figure de force brulante et farouche
    (Tel jour telle nuit): Poulenc
Imeninï—The name day: Zhelobinsky
Imhol nyitva én kebelem—Heart on fire: Kodály
Immer bei dir—Ever near thee/In thy dear eyes: Raff
Immer leiser wird mein Schlummer—Faint and fainter/Ever lighter/
    Lighter far is now my slumber/My slumber grows ever softer: Brahms
Impara ingrata (Atalanta)—Then learn, haughty beauty: Handel
Impatience—Ungeduld (Die schöne Müllerin): Schubert
Imperial mass—Missa in angustiis: Haydn
Imperial waltz—Kaiser-walzer: J Strauss II
The imperishable perfume—Le parfum impérissable: Fauré
An important event—Wichtige Begebenheit (Kinderscenen): Schumann
The impresario—Der Schauspieldirektor: Mozart
The imprisoned admiral—Der gefangene Admiral: Loewe

The imprisoned nightingale—Die gefangene Nachtigall: Henschel
The imprisoned singers—Die gefangenen Sänger: Schubert
L'improvisateur—Look down that lane: Massenet
In a castle—Auf einer Burg: Schumann
In a far country—In der Ferne (Schwanengesang): Schubert
In a peaceful valley—Zwischen grünen Bäumen (Der Rose Pilgerfahrt):
    Schumann
In a ruined churchyard—Auf einem verfallenen Kirchhof (Lieder um
    den Tod): Kilpinen
In a strange land—In der Fremde: Brahms
In a strange land—In der Fremde: Webern
In allen meinen Taten—The moon's pale beams are shining: Bach
In April—Avril: Godard
In April—Im April: Lassen
In autumn—Im Herbst: Brahms
In autumn—Im Herbst: R Franz
In autumn—Im Herbst: Mendelssohn
In blessed contentment—Ridente la calma: Mozart
In bliss—Der Glücklicke: Liszt
In braccio al mio rival (Il trovatore)—In the arms of my foe: Verdi
In cellar cool—Im tiefen Keller: Fischer
In conclusion—Zum Schluss (Myrthen): Schumann
In death's strong grasp the Saviour lay—Christ lag in Todesbanden
    (Orgelbüchlein): Bach
In deepest forest glade—Zde vlese v potoka (Pisné milostné): Dvořák
In deine Hände (Gottes Zeit ist die allerbeste Zeit)—Into Thine hands:
    Bach
In dem Schatten meiner Locken—In the shadow óf my tresses: Wolf
In dem Walde/Frühlingslied—Spring song: Mendelssohn
In dem Walde/Frühlingslied—In the forest/In the wood: A Rubinstein
In der Ferne—Parted/Far away/Absence: Brahms
In der Ferne—In the distance: Cornelius
In der Ferne (Rheinische Lieder)—In the distance: Cornelius
In der Ferne—Far away: Kreutzer
In der Ferne—Far away/Secret sorrow: Kalliwoda
In der Ferne—In foreign lands: Patáky
In der Ferne (Schwanengesang)—In a far country/The exile: Schubert
In der Fremde—Among strangers/In a strange land: Brahms
In der Fremde—The wanderer: R Franz
In der Fremde/Aus der Heimat—In foreign parts/Far from home: Schumann
In der Fremde/Ich hör' die Bächlein—Memories: Schumann
In der Fremde—In a strange land: Webern
In der Frühe—Near dawn: Wolf
In der Gasse—In the street: Brahms

In der Johannisnacht—On St John's Eve: Meyer-Helmund
In der Mondnacht—In the moonlight: Cornelius
In der Nacht—Night-song: Schumann
In der Nacht (Fantasiestücke)—Night: Schumann
In des Lebens Frühlingstagen (Fidelio)—When by earthly joys surrounded:
    Beethoven
In des Sees Wogenspiele/Am See—Summer waves: Schubert
In dich hab' ich gehoffet, Herr (Orgelbüchlein)—In Thee, Lord, have I put
    my trust: Bach
In diesem Wetter (Kinder-totenlieder)—In such a tempest: Mahler
In diesen heil'gen Hallen (Die Zauberflöte)—Within these sacred bowers
    (portals)/Who treads the path of duty/Within these temple walls:
    Mozart
In diesen Wintertagen—In these winter days: Schoenberg
In Dir ist Freude (Orgelbüchlein)—In Thee is gladness: Bach
In dreams I fell a-weeping—Ich hab' im Traum geweint (Dichterliebe):
    Schumann
In dreams I've wept—Ich hab' in Träume geweinet: R Franz
In dreams my tears were flowing—Ich hab' im Traum geweint (Dichterliebe)
    Schumann
In dulci jubilo—How flies the time: Hofmann
In einem Rosengärtlein—Within a garden-rosery: Hildach
In einem Rosengärtlein—Within a garden: Reger
In exita Israel—When Israel came out of Egypt: S Wesley
In faith I quiet wait—Ich hatte treulich still: Bach
In far-off land—In fernem Land (Lohengrin): Wagner
In fernem Land (Lohengrin)—In far-off land: Wagner
In foreign lands—In der Ferne: Patáky
In foreign parts—In der Fremde: Schumann
In full flower—Virágzás (Két kép): Bartók
In galling fetters—Condotta ell'era in ceppi (Il trovatore): Verdi
In gay mood strolled a maiden—Lustwandelnd schritt ein Mädchen:
    d'Albert
In God, my faithful God—Auf meinen lieben Gott: Bach
In goldener Fülle—A vision of glory: R Strauss
In happy mood—Bonne humeur: Chaminade
In his hand are all the corners—Denn in seiner Hand: Mendelssohn
In his wide and ample, airy linen vesture—Široké rukávy a široké gatě
    (Cigánské melodié): Dvořák
In how kind a fashion—So willst du: Brahms
In Jesu Demut kann ich Trost (Süsser Trost, mein Jesus kommt)—
    In Jesu's meekness I find hope: Bach
In Jesu's meekness I find hope—In Jesu Demut kann ich Trost
    (Süsser Trost, mein Jesus kommt): Bach

In joy and sorrow—In Lust und Schmerzen: Cornelius
In Liebeslust—In love's delight: Liszt
In lieblicher Blaue (chamber music)—In lovely blueness: Henze
In lonely wood—In Waldeseinsamkeit: Brahms
In lovely blueness—In lieblicher Blaue (chamber music): Henze
In love's delight—In Liebeslust: Liszt
In love's service—Minnedienst: Meyer-Helmund
In Lust und Schmerzen—In joy and sorrow: Cornelius
In May—Im Mai: R Franz
In May—Im wunderschönen Monat Mai (Dichterliebe): Schumann
In Meeres Mitten—In ocean's midst: Schumann
In meinem Garten die Nelken—My treasured flowers are dying: R Franz
In meinem Armen wieg' ich dich—I fold thee in my loving arms: R Franz
In meiner nächte Sehnen—Deep in my nightly longing: Brahms
In memory—Nachruf: Schoeck
In memory of Esenin—Pamyati Sergeya Esenina: Sviridov
In mem'ry of the dead—Pensée des morts: Liszt
In men and women no true harmony—Die rechte Stimmung: Telemann
In my bosom a fell fury—Ben' io sento l'ingrate (Atalanta): Handel
In my heart I feel no more—Nel cor più non mi sento (La molinara):
    Paisiello
In my heart the flames—Quella fiamma che m'accende: Marcello
In my native country—I Hjemmet: Grieg
In my sister-in-law's garden—Ángyomasszony kertje: Bartók
In my windows shone the moonlight—Ablakomba, ablakomba: Bartók
In nature's realm—V přirodé: Dvořák
In ocean's midst—In Meeres Mitten: Schumann
In olden Spain—Aubade/Puis qu'on ne peut fléchir (Le roi d'Ys): Lalo
In paradise—Die Zufriedenen: Blumenthal
In peace thy sheep may graze—Schäfe können sicher weiden (Was mir
    behagt): Bach
In pity then—So willst du: Brahms
In praise of high intellect—Lob des hohen Verstand (Des Knaben Wunder-
    horn): Mahler
In praise of Mary—Maria's Lob (Marienlieder): Brahms
In praise of music—Frau Musica: Hindemith
In praise of sorrow—Lob des Leidens: R Strauss
In praise of spring—Lob des Frühlings: Mendelssohn
In praise of the lofty intellect—Lob des hohen Verstand (Des Knaben
    Wunderhorn): Mahler
In prison—Le ciel est, par-dessus le toit: Séverac
In quali eccessi (Don Giovanni)—In what excesses: Mozart
In quelle trine morbide (Manon Lescaut)—In those soft silken curtains:
    Puccini

In questa reggia (Turandot)—Within this palace: Puccini
In questa tomba oscura—In this sepulchral darkness/Within the tomb
    forgotten/In this dark tomb/Mark yonder tomb/This lowly tomb/
    In yonder tomb: Beethoven
In questo muto—Here, in the silence: Dering
In quiet hours—I stilla Timmer: Alfvén
In resurrectione tua—On this Thy resurrection morning: Byrd
In seclusion—Stille Sicherheit: R Franz
In secret hidden from care—Non la sospiri (Tosca): Puccini
In seiner Blüte bleichen (Rienzi)—Scarce in full blossom: Wagner
In September—En Septembre: A L(ehmann)
In shower and in sunshine—Im Regen und im Sonnenschein: Koss
In sickness and health—Quand je te vois souffrir: I Albéniz
In silent night—In stiller Nacht: Brahms
In sleep's sweet oblivion—Nel dolce dell' oblio: Handel
In slumber I see thee nightly—Allnächtlich im Traume: Schumann
In snow-bound hall—Am stillen Herd (Die Meistersinger von Nürnberg):
    Wagner
In snowy weather—Bein Schneewetter: Reger
In spring—Im Lenz: Cornelius
In spring—Im Frühling: R Franz
In spring—Im Frühling: Wolf
In spring-time—Das Lied im Grünen: Schubert
In spring time—Vesnon'ko, vesno: Stetsenko
In stiller Nacht—In silent night/Night lay so still: Brahms
In stilly night—Um Mitternacht: R Franz
In such a tempest—In diesem Wetter (Kinder-totenlieder): Mahler
In summer fields—Feldeinsamkeit: Brahms
In summer—Im Sommer: R Franz
In summer the meadow—Ezerevel terem: Erkel
In the arms of my foe—In braccio al mio rival (Il trovatore): Verdi
In the autumn—Im Herbst: R Franz
In the ballroom—Ballgeflüster: Meyer-Helmund
In the cemetery—Au cimetière: Fauré
In the churchyard—Auf dem Kirchhofe: Brahms
In the cloister of San Stefano—Im Kreuzgang von St Stefano: Schoeck
In the cool and dewy morning—La vezzosa pastorella: Bruni
In the distance—In der Ferne (An Bertha): Cornelius
In the distance—In der Ferne (Rheinische Lieder): Cornelius
In the fair spring-time—Dans le printemps de mes années: Garat
In the fire—V ogne: Kabalevsky
In the forest—Im Wald: Mendelssohn
In the forest—In dem Walde: A Rubinstein
In the forest—Im Walde: Schumann

In the forge—Srši jiskry: Dvořák
In the garden—Im Garten: Blumenthal
In the grass—Dans l'herbe (Fiancailles pour rire): Poulenc
In the greenhouse—Im Treibhaus (Wesendonck Lieder): Wagner
In the hay—Vieux chant à danser: Borjan
In the hothouse—Im Treibhaus (Wesendonck Lieder): Wagner
In the late boat—Im Spätboot: R Strauss
In the moonlight—In der Mondnacht: Cornelius
In the night—Wie rafft ich mich auf in der Nacht: Brahms
In the pleasure of heaven we're joyous—Wir geniessen die Himmlischen
    (4th symphony): Mahler
In the red of evening—Im Abendrot: Schubert
In the shadow—Schatten: Blumenthal
In the shadow of my tresses—In dem Schatten meiner Locken: Wolf
In the south—C'est l'Espagne: Offenbach
In the spring—Im Frühling: Schubert
In the storm—V buryn: Khrennikov
In the street—In der Gasse: Brahms
In the sunset—Im Abendrot: Schubert
In the sunset glow—Im Abendrot (Vier letzte Lieder): R Strauss
In the sweet spring time—Frühlingsliebe: Schulz
In the temple do the priests—Sacerdotes Domini: Byrd
In the village—Im Dorfe (Die Winterreise): Schubert
In the west—Im Westen (Myrthen): Schumann
In the wood—In dem Walde: A Rubinstein
In the wood—Im Haine: Schubert
In the wood—Im Wald: Schumann
In the woods—Hier, au fond des bois: Blanchard
In the woods—Waldesrauschen: Liszt
In the woods—Im Walde: Mendelssohn
In the woods—Im Walde: Schumann
In the woods—V lese: Smetana
In Thee do I rejoice—Ich freue mich in dir: Bach
In Thee, Lord, have I put my trust—In dich hab' ich gehoffet, Herr
    (Orgelbüchlein): Bach
In these winter days—In diesen Wintertagen: Schoenberg
In Thine arm I rest me—Unter deinen Schirmen (Jesu meine Freude):
    Bach
In this dark tomb—In questa tomba oscura: Beethoven
In this grace believe O mortals—Menschen, glaubt doch dieser Gnade
    (Christ unser Herr zum Jordan kam): Bach
In this last caress—Per questo dolce amplesso (Artaserse): Hasse
In this lovely month of May—A ce joli mays: Jannequin
In this sepulchral darkness—In questa tomba oscura: Beethoven

In this solemn hour—Solenne in quest'ora (La forza del destino): Verdi
In those soft silken curtains—In quelle trine morbide (Manon Lescaut):
    Puccini
In thousand forms I see—Ich sehe dich: Reger
In thy dear eyes—Immer bei dir: Raff
In thy sweet name—Ch'ami la vita mia: Bertani
In truth, I am almost afraid—J'ai presque peur, en vérité (La bonne chanson)
    Fauré
In vain—Umsonst: R Franz
In vain I strive to fly thee—Nich mehr zu dir zu gehen: Brahms
In vivid dreams—Szines álomban: Bartók
In Waldeseinsamkeit—In lonely wood/In woodland solitude: Brahms
In what excesses—In quali eccessi (Don Giovanni): Mozart
In winter—En hiver: Hindemith
In wood embower'd—Am Donaustrande (Liebeslieder Walzer): Brahms
In woodland solitude—In Waldeseinsamkeit: Brahms
In yonder tomb—In questa tomba oscura: Beethoven
In your eyes—Vous m'avez regardé (Tristesses): Milhaud
Incense is burning (mad scene)—Ardon gl'incensi (Lucia di Lammermoor):
    Donizetti
The incense rises (mad scene)—Ardon gl'incensi (Lucia di Lammermoor):
    Donizetti
The incessant—Das Unaufhörliche: Hindemith
Inclina ad te—Incline Thine ear to me: Himmel
Incline Thine ear to me—Inclina ad te: Himmel
Incognito—Le coeur et la main: Lecocq
Incontri—Encounter: Nono
L'incoronazione di Poppea—The coronation of Poppea: Monteverdi
Independence—Freisinn: Schubert
Independence—Freisinn (Myrthen): Schumann
Les Indes galantes—The indigo suitors: Rameau
L'indifférent (Shéhérazade)—The indifferent one/The heedless one: Ravel
The indifferent one—L'indifférent (Shéhérazade): Ravel
Indigo and the forty thieves—Indigo und die vierzig Räuber: J Strauss II
The indigo suitors—Les Indes galantes: Rameau
Indigo und die vierzig Räuber—Indigo and the forty thieves: J Strauss II
Indoors—Im Zimmer: Berg
Inescapable—Unentrinnbar: Schoenberg
The inextinguishable—Det uudslukkelige [symphony]: Nielsen
Infelice—Lone and joyless: Mendelssohn
Infelice, e tuo crederi (Ernani)—Oh illusion: Verdi
Infelix ego—How wretched am I: Byrd
The ingenuous ones—Les ingénus (Fêtes galantes): Debussy
Les ingénus (Fêtes galantes)—Youthful loves/The ingenuous ones: Debussy
Ingrid's Lied—On the Ling ho!/Ingrid's song: Kjerulf

Ingrid's song—Ingrid's Lied: Kjerulf
Inky Jimmy and dripping Polly—Tintenheinz und Platscherlottchen: Blech
The inn—Das Wirthaus (Die Winterreise): Schubert
The inn—Herberge (Waldscenen): Schumann
Innen aus verschiedenem entsteht (Chamber music)—Within, out of
    diversity, a serious mind is formed: Henze
The inner light—Du bist die Ruh': Schubert
Inno delle nazioni—Hymn to the nations: Verdi
Innocence—Nevinnost: Smetana
The inquirer—Der Neugierige (Die schöne Müllerin): Schubert
The inquisitive girl—Zvědava dievča: Martinů
The inquisitive women—Le donne curiose: Wolf-Ferrari
Ins Freie—Into the open: Schumann
Insanae et vanae curae—The arm of the Lord: Haydn
L'insana parola (Aida)—Ye gods watching over me: Verdi
Insatiable love—Nimmersatte Liebe: Wolf
Inspirez moi! (La reine de Saba)—Lend me your aid: Gounod
The Interrupted song—Il canto sospeso: Nono
Into the open—Ins Freie: Schumann
Into Thine hands—In deine Hände (Gottes Zeit ist die allerbeste Zeit):
    Bach
Into your hands—Mon coeur se recommande à vous: Lassus
Intorno all' idol mio—Around my beloved idol: Cesti
The invalid—Der Kranke: Schoeck
Invan mi danni! (Nerone)—Thy sentence is useless: Boito
L'invitation au voyage—The invitation to a journey/The voyage: Duparc
The invitation to a journey—L'invitation au voyage: Duparc
Invitation to the dance—Aufforderung zum Tanze: Weber
Invocation—Bitte: R Franz
Io d'altro regno (Muzio Scevola)—Now of another kingdom: Handel
Io di Roma il Giove sono (Agrippina)—I in Rome like Jove am reigning:
    Handel
Io non so come vivo—O tell me weary heart: A Stabile
Io son Fenice e voi sete la fiamma—The Phoenix and the flames/I am the
    Phoenix: Vecchi
Io sono la madre—I am the mother: Respighi
Io ti levo l'impero dell' armi (Partenope)—Though I raised you to the
    rank of commander: Handel
Iphigenia in Aulis—Iphigénie en Aulide: Gluck
Iphigenia in Tauris—Iphigénie en Tauride: Gluck
Iphigenia in Tauris—Ifiheniya v Tavridi: Statsenko
Iphigénie en Aulide—Iphigenia in Aulis: Gluck
Iphigénie en Tauride—Iphigenia in Tauris: Gluck
Das irdische Leben—Life on earth/Earthly life (Des Knaben Wunderhorn):
    Mahler

Irene—La reine de Saba: Gounod
Ein irrender Sohn—A straying son: Nilsson
Irrlicht (Die Winterreise)—Will-o'-the-wisp: Schubert
Is it bliss or is it sorrow—Sind es Schmerzen, sind es Freuden: Brahms
Is it joy?—Sind es Schmerzen, sind es Freuden: Brahms
Is it not so?—N'est-ce pas? (La bonne chanson): Fauré
Is it pain?—Sind es Schmerzen, sind es Freuden: Brahms
Is it so?—Frage: Mendelssohn
Is it then Holy Heaven's will—So ist es denn des Himmels Will: H Albert
Is there a measure on earth?—Gibt es auf Erden? (Chamber music): Henze
Island of shadows—Varjojen saari: Palmgren
L'île joyeuse—The happy island: Debussy
Isle of the dead—Toteninsel: Rachmaninov
The isle of the dead—Die Toteninsel: Reger
Die Israeliten in der Wüste—The Israelites in the desert: C P E Bach
The Israelites in the desert—Die Israeliten in der Wüste: C P E Bach
Ist ein Traum (Der Rosenkavalier)—'Tis a dream: R Strauss
Isten veled!—Fare thee well!: Liszt
It cannot be—Ich kann's nicht fassen (Frauenliebe und -leben): Schumann
It is a wondrous mystery—Es muss ein Wunderbares sein: Liszt
It is all my heart's delight—Jesu meines Herzens Freud: Bach
It is ecstasy—C'est l'extase (Ariettes oubliées): Debussy
It is ecstasy—C'est l'extase: Fauré
It is enough—Ich habe genug: Bach
It is finished—Es ist vollbracht!: Bach
It is for your good that I now leave you—Es ist euch gut, dass ich hingehe:
    Bach
It is fulfilled—Es ist vollbracht!: Bach
It is fulfilled—Es ist vollbracht, das Leid ist alle (Sehet, wir geh'n hinauf
    gen Jerusalem): Bach
It is good to lie under green hedges—E pur bello dal verdi d'un clivo:
    Cagnoni
It is my heart—So wird denn Herz und Mund (Es ist dir gesagt, Mensch, wa
    gut ist): Bach
It is not wealth or grandeur—Se pensi amor tu solo (Deidamia): Handel
It is thou who hast blighted—Eri tu che macchiavi (Un ballo in maschera):
    Verdi
It is thus that you are—C'est ainsi que tu es: Poulenc
It must a wondrous rapture be—Es muss ein Wunderbares sein: Liszt
It must be wonderful, withal—Es muss ein Wunderbares sein: Liszt
It seems as though—Mir ist als Zögen: Cornelius
It was a day—Frauenwörter: Fielitz
It was a dream—Es war ein Traum/Ich hatte einst ein schönes Vaterland:
    Lassen

It was a true report—È vera quella voce (Queen of Sheba): Castelnuovo-
Tedesco
It was his accents (mad scene)—Il dolce suono (Lucia di Lammermoor):
Donizetti
It was thou the destroyer—Eri tu che macchiavi (Un ballo in maschera):
Verdi
The Italian girl in Algiers—L'Italiana in Algeri: Rossini
Italian serenade—Sérénade italienne: Chausson
Italian songbook—Italianisches Liederbuch: Wolf
L'Italiana in Algeri: The Italian girl in Algiers: Rossini
Italien—Italy: F Mendelssohn
Italianisches Liederbuch—Italian songbook: Wolf
Italy—Italien: F Mendelssohn
The itinerant scholar—Der Scholar: Wolf
It's our wedding day—Je sais que vous êtes gentil (The better 'ole): Christiné
Itt lent a völgyben—Here, in the valley: Bartók
Ivan the terrible—Pskovityanka: Rimsky-Korsakov
I've a garden—Yesh Le Gan (Shire' Chalutzin): Binder
I've dreamed a dream—Chalamti Chalom: Larry
L'ivrogne corrigé—The reformed drunkard/The converted drunkard:
Gluck
Ivy—Epheu: R Strauss
An ivy leaf—Angedenken: Cornelius
The ivy leaf—Das Epheublatt: Lassen

J

Ja die Schönste—The best of all: Wolf

Ja, dieses Wort ist meiner Seelen Speise (Du Hirte Israel, höre)—O how that word gives comfort: Bach

Ja, du bist elend—Yes, thou art wretched: R Franz

Ja, ja, ich kann die Feinde schlagen (Selig ist der Mann)—Yes, yes, Thy foes I soon will conquer: Bach

Ja vím (Písně milostné)—I know: Dvořák

Jääkärimarssi—March of the Finnish infantry: Sibelius

The Jacobin—Jakobín: Dvořák

Jaegersang (Tove)—Hunter's song: Nielsen

Jag är ett träd—The tree: Sibelius

Jagdkantate/Was mir behagt—Hunting cantata/My one delight: Bach

Jagdlied—Hunting-song: R Franz

Jagdlied: Hunting song/Waken lords and ladies gay: Mendelssohn

Jagdlied—Hunting song: Schumann

Der Jäger (Marienlieder)—The hunter: Brahms

Der Jäger (Die schöne Müllerin)—The huntsman/The rival: Schubert

Der Jäger—The huntsman: Wolf

Der Jäger Abschied—The hunter's farewell: Mendelssohn

Jäger auf der Lauer (Waldscenen)—Hunter on the lookout: Schumann

Der Jäger im Walde—The huntsman: Brahms

Der Jäger und sein Liebchen—The huntsman and his lass/The huntsman's farewell: Brahms

Jägerchor (Rosamunde)—Hunting chorus: Schubert

Jägerlied—The huntsman: Brahms

Jägerlied—Hunting song: Grieg

Jägerlied—Swiftly fly the birds: Schumann

Jägerlied—Huntsman's song: Wolf

Jägerliedchen (Album für die Jugend)—Hunting song/The little hunter's song: Schumann

Jägers Abendlied—Huntsman's evening song/Huntsman's even-song: Schube

Die Jahreszeiten—The seasons: Haydn

Die Jahreszeiten—The seasons: Křenek

J'ai encore un tel pâté—I have a little cake: La Halle

J'ai presque peur, en vérité (La bonne chanson)—In truth, I am almost afraid: Fauré

J'ai quelqu'un dans le coeur (Tristesses)—There is someone I love: Milhaud

Jaj istenem, kire várok—Oh God, for whom am I waiting: Bartók

Jakobín—The Jacobin: Dvořák

J'allais par des chemins perfides (La bonne chanson)—I followed treacherous paths: Fauré

Jámbor Gál János háza—The straw guy/Johnny Martin owns this house: Kodály

154

János vitéz—John the brave: Kacsóh
Japanese lyric poems—Tri stikhotvoreniya iz yaponsky: Stravinsky
Japanese rain song—Cántee de ploaie orienke: Daia
Japanese rain song—Japanisches Regenlied: J Marx
Japanisches Regenlied—Japanese rain song: J Marx
Jardin antiguo—Antique garden: Guastavino
Le jardin mouillé—Garden in the rain: Roussel
Jardins sous la pluie (Estampes)—Gardens in the rain: Debussy
Jarní Romance—The romance of spring: Fibich
Jaro—Spring-tide: Dvořák
Der Jasager—The boy who said yes: Weill
The jasmine blooms—Les grands jasmins: Rhené-Baton
The jasmine bush—Jasminenstrauch: Schumann
Jasminenstrauch—The jasmine bush: Schumann
Jauchzet, froh locket (Weihnachts Oratorium)—Christians be joyful: Bach
Jauchzet Gott in allen Landen—Praise to God in every land: Bach
J'avais cru que (Semiramis)—I believed that: Catel
Jazz at night—Jazz dans la nuit: Roussel
Jazz dans la nuit—Jazz at night: Roussel
Je crois en vous—Belief/I trust in thee: Berlioz
Je garde une medaille (Tristesses)—I keep a little medal: Milhaud
Je la désire (Tristesses)—I want to see: Milhaud
Je me suis embarqué (L'horizon chimérique)—I have embarked: Fauré
Je n'ai envie que de t'aimer (Tel jour telle nuit)—I long only to love you: Poulenc
Je ne désire point ces ardeurs (Tristesses)—I do not wish: Milhaud
Je ne me souviens plus—I no longer recall: Rhené-Baton
Je sais attacher des rubans—I know how to tie the ribbons: Dourlen
Je sais que vous êtes gentil (The better 'ole)—It's our wedding day:
    Christiné
Je songe à ce jour (Tristesses)—I'm dreaming of the day: Milhaud
Je suis presqu' enfant (Don César de Bazan)—Page's song/I am but a
    child: Massenet
Je suis Titania (Mignon)—Behold Titania/Titania am I: Thomas
Je tir' ma reverence—Pardon my intrusion: Bastia
Je tremble en voyant ton visage (Le promenoir des deux amants)—I
    tremble when I see your face: Debussy
Je vais revoir ma charmante maîtresse (Le devin du village)—To her I go:
    Rousseau
Je veux—I wish: Rhené-Baton
Jealous moon—Celo tropical: Grever
Jealousy—Amor, gioie mi porge: Handel
Jealousy and pride—Eifersucht und Stolz (Die schöne Müllerin): Schubert
Jean, p'tit Jean—Reaper John, come take thy sickle: Bax
Jeanne d'Arc au bûcher—Joan of Arc at the stake: Honegger

Ein jedes Band—Each silken thread: Hindemith

Jeg baerer med smil min byrde—I carry my burden with joy: Nielsen

Jeg elsker dich—I love thee: Grieg

Jeg gik i marken og vogtede får—I wandered in the fields tending the sheep: Nielsen

Jeg giver mit digt til Våren—To springtime my song I utter/To thee will I sing, fair spring time: Grieg

Jeg laegger mig så trygt til ro—I go to rest in peace: Nielsen

Jeg lever mit Liv i Laengsel—I live a life of longing: Grieg

Jeg reiste en deilig Sommerkvaeld—A lovely evening in summer 'twas: Grieg

Jeg ved en laerkerede—I know a lark's nest: Nielsen

Jehovah—Dir, dir, Jehovah: Bach

Její Pastorkyná—Jenufa/Her step-daughter: Janáček

Jelenti magát Jézus—The voice of Jesus/Hear ye the voice of Jesus: Kodály

Jemand (Myrthen)—Somebody/For the sake of somebody: Schumann

Jens vejmand—The stonecutter: Nielsen

J'entends le moulin taqueter—I hear the mill: Blanchard

Jenufa—Její Pastorkyná: Janáček

Jeptha's daughter—Die Tochter Jeptha's: Schumann

Jerusalem, Heil und Freude—Jerusalem, joy and healing: Cornelius

Jerusalem, joy and healing—Jerusalem, Heil und Freude: Cornelius

Jesu, bleibet meine Freude (Herz und Mund und Tat und Leben)—Jesu joy of man's desiring: Bach

Jesu, der aus grosser Liebe (O heil'ges Geist und Wasserbad)—Jesu in Thy love enduring: Bach

Jesu, der du meine Seele—Jesus, my beloved Saviour/Jesu, who my soul eternal: Bach

Jesu, dulcis memoria—Jesu, the very thought is sweet: Dering

Jesu dulcis memoria—Jesu! the very thought is sweet: Victoria

Jesu, hope of men—Jesus unser Trost und Leben: Bach

Jesu, in Thy love enduring—Jesu, der aus grosser Liebe (O heil'ges Geist und Wasserbad): Bach

Jesu, Jesu, du bist mein—Jesu, Jesu, Thou art mine: Bach

Jesu, Jesu, Thou art mine—Jesu, Jesu, du bist mein: Bach

Jesu, joy and treasure—Jesu meine Freude: Buxtehude

Jesu, joy of man's desiring—Wohl mir, dass ich Jesum habe (Herz und Mund und Tat und Leben): Bach

Jesu, joy of man's desiring—Jesu, bleibet meine Freude (Herz und Mund und Tat und Leben): Bach

Jesu, lass dich finden (Mein liebster Jesus ist verloren)—Jesus, let me find Thee: Bach

Jesu, lass durch Wohl und Weh (Himmelskönig, sei willkommen)—Jesu, through weal and woe: Bach

156

Jesu, longed-for consolation—O du Liebe meiner Liebe: Bach
Jesu, meine Freude—Jesu, priceless treasure/Jesus, joy and treasure/Jesus,
    King of glory/Jesu my friend: Bach
Jesu meine Freude—Jesu, joy and treasure: Buxtehude
Jesu, meines Glaubens Zier—Jesu, treasure passing price: Bach
Jesu meines Herzens Freud—It is all my heart's delight/King of glory,
    king of peace: Bach
Jesu my friend—Jesu meine Freude: Bach
Jesu, nun sei gepreiset—Jesus now will we praise Thee: Bach
Jesu, priceless treasure—Jesu, meine Freude: Bach
Jesu sacred name—Seelen bräutigam, Jesu, Gottes Lamm!: Bach
Jesu source of bliss eternal—Herz und Mund und Tat und Leben: Bach
Jesu, the very thought is sweet—Jesu, dulcis memoria: Dering
Jesu! the very thought is sweet—Jesu dulcis memoria: Victoria
Jesu, through weal and woe—Jesu, lass durch Wohl und Weh (Himmels-
    könig sei willkommen): Bach
Jesu, treasure passing price—Jesu, meines Glaubens Zier: Bach
Jesu, who my soul eternal—Jesu, der du meine Seele: Bach
Das Jesulein soll doch mein Trost—The Christ child shall be still my hope:
    Bach
Jesus and the traders—Jézus és a kufárok: Kodály
Jesus bleibet meine Freude—Hope and light of man's endeavour: Bach
Jesus called to Him the twelve—Jesu nahm zu sich die Zwölfe: Bach
Jesus Christ, my sure defence—Jesus, meine Zuversicht: Bach
Jesus Christ, our Lord and Saviour—Jesus Christus, unser Heiland
    (Orgelbüchlein): Bach
Jesus Christ the son of God—Jesus Christus, Gottes Sohn (Christ lag in
    Todesbanden): Bach
Jesus Christus, Gottes Sohn (Christ lag in Todesbanden)—Jesus Christ
    the son of God: Bach
Jesus Christus, unser Heiland (Orgelbüchlein)—Jesus Christ, our Lord
    and saviour: Bach
Jesus is this dark world's light—Jesus ist das schönste Licht: Bach
Jesus ist das schönste Licht—Jesus is this dark world's light: Bach
Jesus, joy and treasure—Jesu, meine Freude: Bach
Jesus, king of glory—Jesu, meine Freude: Bach
Jesus, let me find Thee—Jesu, lass dich finden (Mein liebster Jesus ist
    verloren): Bach
Jesus, meine Zuversicht—Jesus Christ, my sure defence: Bach
Jesus, my beloved Saviour—Jesu, der du meine Seele: Bach
Jesus nahm zu sich die Zwölfe—Jesus took unto Him the twelve/Jesus
    called to Him the twelve: Bach
Jesus now will we praise Thee—Jesu, nun sei gepreiset: Bach

Jesus schläft, was soll ich hoffen?—Jesus sleeps, what shall I hope for?/
Jesus sleeps, what hope remaineth?/Jesus sleepeth, what hope have I?:
Bach

Jesus sleepeth, what hope have I?—Jesus schläft, was soll ich hoffen?: Bach

Jesus sleeps, what hope remaineth?—Jesus schläft, was soll ich hoffen?:
Bach

Jesus sleeps, what shall I hope for?—Jesus schläft, was soll ich hoffen?:
Bach

Jesus soll mein erstes Wort (Gott, wie dein Name, so ist auch dein
Ruhm)—Jesus, the first word shall be: Bach

Jesus, the first word shall be—Jesus, soll mein erstes Wort (Gott, wie dein
Name, so ist auch dein Ruhm): Bach

Jesus today rose triumphing—Heut' triumphiret Gottes Sohn: Bach

Jesus took unto Him the twelve—Jesus nahm zu sich die Zwölfe: Bach

Jesus, unser Trost und Leben—Jesu, fount of consolation/Christ our
helper and life-giver/Jesu, hope of men/Wake, the welcome day: Bach

Le jet d'eau—The fountain: Debussy

Jetzt ist er hinaus—Ah! now he has gone: Henschel

Jeu de cartes—Card game: Stravinsky

Le jeu de l'amour et du hazard—The game of love and chance: Rabaud

Le jeu de Robin et Marion—Robin and Marion: La Halle

Un jeune coeur (Les aveux indiscrets)—A youthful heart: Monsigny

La jeunesse n'a qu'un temps—The only time to love: A L(ehmann)

Les jeux d'eau à la villa d'Este (Années de pèlerinage)—The fountains at
the villa d'Este: Liszt

Jeux d'enfants—Children's games: Bizet

The jewels of the Madonna—I gioielli della Madonna: Wolf-Ferrari

The Jewess—La Juive: Halévy

Jésus és a kufárok—Jesus and the traders: Kodály

Jo dei saluti—I send thee: Wolf-Ferrari

Joan of Arc—Giovanna d'Arco: Verdi

Joan of Arc at the stake—Jeanne d'Arc au bûcher: Honegger

Johannespassion—St John passion: Bach

John the brave—János vitéz: Kacsóh

Johnny Martin owns this house—Jámbor Gál János háza: Kodály

Johnny strikes up—Jonny spielt auf: Křenek

Join we our souls—Soyons unis: Rhené-Baton

La jolie fille de Perth—The fair maid of Perth: Bizet

Le jongleur de Notre Dame—The juggler of Our Lady: Massenet

Jonny spielt auf—Johnny strikes up: Křenek

Jóska Geszte saddles his velvety horse—Geszte Jóska bársony lovát
nyergeli: Bartók

Jószág-igézö—Enchanting song: Bartók

Joululaulu—Christmas song: Sibelius

Jour d'été à la montagne—Summer day on the mountain: D'Indy
Journey in winter—Die Winterreise: Schubert
The journey of life—Wenn den langen Weg: Mozart
The journey to Emmaus—Peregrinus: Anon
Journey to the beloved—Cesta k milé: Martinů
Joutsen (Ungdom)—The swan: Palmgren
Joy—Juch he!: Brahms
Joy—Das Glück: Schumann
Joy—Radost: Smetana
Joy bells are pealing—Sciolgo le labbra a un cantico: Magaldi
Joy, come into my breast—Gioje, venite in sen (Amadigi di Gaula):
    Handel
Joy and love—Per la gloria d'adorarvi (Griselda): G B Bononcini
Joy in a stormy night—Lust der Sturmnacht: Schumann
The joy of friendship—Das Glück der Freundschaft: Beethoven
Joy of love—Plaisir d'amour: Martini
Joy of solitude—Alegria de la soledad: Guastavino
The joy of spring—Frühlingslust: Schumann
Joy that dwells in two hearts that love—Lykke mellem to Mennesker:
    Alnaes
Joyful and griefful—Freudvoll und leidvoll: Liszt
Joyful and mournful—Freudvoll und leidvoll (Egmont): Beethoven
Joyful and woeful—Freudvoll und leidvoll: Liszt
Joyful hearts to heaven raise—Resonet in laudibus: Handel
Joyful time in the new dispensation—Erfreute Zeit in Bunde: Bach
The joyful peasant—Fröhlicher Landmann (Album für die Jugend):
    Schumann
Joyous days of childhood—Al dolce guidami (Anna Bolena): Donizetti
Joys, make my breast your home—Gioje, venite in sen (Amadigi di
    Gaula): Handel
The joys of constant love—Es bleibt wohl dabei: Gounod
Joys of life—Freut euch des Lebens: J Strauss II
The joys of love—Plaisir d'amour: Martini
Joysong of spring—Wein, Weib und Gesang: J Strauss II
Jubel töne (Euryanthe)—Gaily singing: Weber
Jubilee cantata—Yubileinaya kantata: Vasilenko
Juch he!—How fair is the earth/Joy/The reason why: Brahms
The judges of the secret court—Les francs juges: Berlioz
The jug—La giara: Casella
Jugend, Rausch und Liebe—Love and youth: Cornelius
Jugend Glück—The delights of youth: Liszt
Die Jugendzeit—Glad days of youth: Meyer-Helmund
The juggler of Our Lady—Le jongleur de Notre Dame: Massenet
Juhe, der Wein ist da (Jahreszeiten)—Heyday, the liquor flows: Haydn

Le Juif polonais—The Polish Jew: Erlanger
La Juive—The Jewess: Halévy
Julens vuggesang—Yuletide cradle song: Grieg
Julesne—Christmas snow: Grieg
Julius Cesar—Giulio Cesare: Malipiero; Handel
The jumping jack—Spraellmanden: Nielsen
Jung Hexenlied—Home: R Strauss
Jung Volkers Lied—Jung Volker's song: Schumann
Jung Volker's song—Jung Volkers Lied: Schumann
Die junge Magd—The young farm servant: Hindemith
Die junge Nonne—The young nun/The novice: Schubert
Der junge Tag erwacht—The youthful day awakens: R Franz
Ein junger Dichter—A young poet: J Marx
Die Jungfrau von Orléans—The maid of Orleans: Rezniček
Jungfräulein, soll ich mit euch geh'n—O maiden, may I see awhile: Brahms
Junggesellenschwur—Boy's love: R Strauss
Der Jüngling—Tell me: Kjerulf
Der Jüngling am Bache—Youth by the brook: Schubert
Der Jüngling an der Quelle—Lad and the stream/Softly murmuring stream:
    Schubert
Der Jüngling auf dem Hügel—(The) youth upon the hill: Schubert
Der Jüngling in der Fremde—Away from home/The young exile:
    Beethoven
Ein Jüngling liebt ein Mädchen (Dichterliebe)—Cross purposes: Schumann
Der Jüngste Tag—The last judgement: O Jochum
Júrame—Promise, love: Grever
Just as there is a high, a low—Si come nelle penna e nell' inchiostro
    (Sonnets of Michelangelo): Britten
Just before dawn—Ein Stündlein wohl vor Tag: Wolf
Just before daybreak—Ein Stündlein wohl vor Tag: Franz
Just you be quiet—Schweig einmal still (Italianisches Liederbuch): Wolf
Justorum animae—The souls of the righteous: Byrd
Justum deduxit Dominus—God leads, God helps: Mozart

K

Kaffe Kantate—Coffee cantata: Bach
Kaiserin Josephine—The empress Josephine: Kálmán
Des Kaisers neue Kleider—The emperor's new clothes: Lofer
Kaiserwalzer—Imperial waltz/Emperor waltz: J Strauss II
Kamennyi gost—The stone guest: Dargomyzhsky
Kamennyi tsvetok—The stone flower: Molchanov
Kamenyari—Stonemasons: Lyudkevych
Kammersymphonie—Chamber symphony: Schoenberg
Kann mich auch an ein Mädel (Der Rosenkavalier)—I remember a girl:
   R Strauss
Kantata o rodine—Cantata about the fatherland: Arutyunyan
Karácsoyi pásztortánc—Christmas dance of the shepherds: Kodály
Karádi Nóták—Songs from Karod: Kodály
Karfreitagszauber (Parsifal)—Good Friday music: Wagner
Der Karneval in Rom—Carnival in Rome: J Strauss II
Karpathy—The Carpathians—Kostenko
Die Kartenlegerin—The fortune teller: Schumann
Karwoche—Holy week: Wolf
Kashchey bessmertny—Kashchey the immortal: Rimsky-Korsakov
Kashchey the immortal—Kashchey bessmertny: Rimsky-Korsakov
Kate and the devil—Čert a Káča: Dvořák
Kate Kabanova—Katja Kabanowá: Janáček
Der Kater—The tom cat: J N David
Katja, die Tänzerin—Katja the dancer: Gilbert (ie Winterfeld)
Katja Kabanowá—Kate Kabanova: Janáček
Katja, the dancer—Katja, die Tänzerin: Gilbert (ie Winterfeld)
Katonadal—Soldier's song: Kodály
Der Kaufmann von Vendig—The merchant of Venice: Humperdinck
Das Käuzchen—Owlet: J N David
Käuzlein—Little owl: Schumann
Kavkaz—The Caucasus: Lyudkevych
Kazach'ya pesnya (Podnyataya tselina)—The Cossack song: Dzerhinski
Když mne stará malka (Ciganské melodié)—Songs my mother taught me:
   Dvořák
Keep watch—Gebt acht!: Brahms
Kein Feuer, keine Kohle—No fire ever burns: Henschel
Kein Graben so breit—No river so broad: Henschel
Kein Hälmlein wachst auf Erden—Soft dews from heaven falling:
   W F Bach (attrib)
Kein Haus, keine Heimat—No home, no country: Brahms
Kein Stündlein geht dahin—No hour goes ever by: Bach
Kein Wort—Resignation: Blumenthal

Keine gleicht von allen schönen—Number beauty's fairest: Wolf
Keine Rast—No rest: Schoeck
Keine Sorg' um den Weg—Love finds out the way: Raff
Keine von der Erde schönen—There be none of beauty's daughters:
  Mendelssohn
Keinem hat es noch gereut—None has ever mourned/Merry as a marriage
  morn/Free is he/He who rides: Brahms
A Kékszakállú herceg vára—Bluebeard's castle/Duke Bluebeard's castle:
  Bartók
Kennst du das Land—Knowst thou the land/Mignon's song: Beethoven
Kennst du das Land/Mignons Lied—Mignon's song/Song of Mignon/
  Thou knowst the land/Knowest thou the land: Liszt
Kennst du das Land/Mignon—Knowst thou the land: Schumann
Kennst du das Land (Lieder der Mignon)—Do you know the land/
  Knowest thou the land: Wolf
A Kertmegi kert alatt—Behind the garden of Kertmeg: Bartók
Két arckép—Two portraits: Bartók
Két elégia—Two elegies: Bartók
Két kép—Two pictures: Bartók
Két portré—Two portraits: Bartók
Két Román tánc—Two Romanian dances: Bartók
Két Zoborvidéki népdal—Hungarian folk songs: Kodály
Kette, Kreis und Spiegel—Chain, circle and mirror/Lace, circle and
  mirror: Křenek
Die keusche Suzanne—The girl in the taxi: Gilbert (ie Winterfeld)
Keyboard practice—Clavierübung: Bach
Kéž duch můj sám—Leave me alone: Dvořák
Khozyayka gostinitsï—The hostess at the inn: Spadavecchia
The kick—Les coups de pieds: Françaix
Kicsi a lány—She is too small: Erkel
Kicsit ázottan—A bit tipsy: Bartók
Kid-dance—Killingdans (Haugtussa): Grieg
A kilenc csodaszarvas—Cantata profana/The giant stag: Bartók
Killingdans (Haugtussa)—Kid-dance: Grieg
Das Kind—The child: Cornelius
Das Kind am Brunnen—Baby at the well: Wolf
Kind im einschlummern—Child falling asleep: Schumann
Kindergebet—A child's prayer: Blech
Kindergesellschaft—Children's party: Schumann
Kinderscenen—Scenes of childhood: Schumann
Das Kinderspiel—Children's pleasures/Children's play: Mozart
Kinderstimmen—Child voices: Fielitz
Kindertotenlieder—Songs on the death of children (infants)/Dirges for
  children: Mahler

Kinderwacht—Vigil: Schumann
Des Kindes Gebet—The children's prayer: Reger
Kindeslächen—A child's smile: Reger
King and charcoal burner—Král a uhlíř: Dvořák
The king at the coronation—Der König bei der Krönung: Wolf
King Carotte—Le roi Carotte: Offenbach
King Duncan's daughters—Die Botschaft: Allitsen
King in spite of himself—Le roi malgré lui: Chabrier
King of glory, king of peace—Jesu meines Herzens Freud: Bach
King of heaven be Thou welcome—Himmelskönig, sei willkommen: Bach
King of heaven, Thou art welcome, Himmelskönig, sei willkommen: Bach
The king of Lahore—Le roi de Lahore: Massenet
King of the students—La basoche: Messager
The king of Thule—Le roi de Thule (La damnation de Faust): Berlioz
The king of Thule—Der König von Thule: Liszt
A king of Thule—Der König in Thule: Schubert
The king of Ys—Le roi d'Ys: Lalo
The king of Yvetot—Le roi d'Yvetot: Adam
The king of Yvetot—Le roi d'Yvetot: Ibert
The king said so—Le roi l'a dit: Lalo
The kingfisher—Le martin-pêcheur (Histoires naturelles): Ravel
King Roger—Król Roger: Symanowski
King Stag—König Hirsch: Henze
The kings—Die Könige (Weihnachtslieder): Cornelius
The king's children—Die Königskinder: Humperdinck
A king's prayer—Königlich Gebet: Wolf
The king's son—Der Königssohn: Schumann
Die Kino-Königin—The cinema star: Gilbert
Kirov is with us—Kirov s nami: Myaskovsky
Kirov s nami—Kirov is with us: Myaskovsky
A kis léany kertjébe—The maiden in her garden: Erkel
Kis Menyeckse—Little bride: Antalffy
The kiss—Il bacio: Arditi
The kiss—Der Kuss: Beethoven
The kiss—Der Kuss: Brahms
The kiss—Der Kuss: Meyer-Helmund
The kiss—Hubicka: Smetana
A kiss in the night—Anoche te besé: Carolis
Kiss me for I have to leave—Add reám csokodat, el kell mennem: Bartók
Kiss waltz—Küss-walzer: J Strauss II
Kisses are like flowers—Les baisers sont des fleurs: Fontenailles
Kisses in my dreams—Besos en mis sueños: A Brandt
Kissing-time—Schelmenliedchen: Reger
Kit kéne elvenni?—The bachelor: Kodály

Kitaiskiye syuity—Chinese suite: Vasilenko
Kjaerlighed—Love: Grieg
Klage—Plaint: Brahms
Klage an dem Mond—Lament to the moon: F X Mozart
Klänge der Heimat (Die Fledermaus)—Echoes of home/Homeland/Czardas of my homeland: J Strauss II
Klassicheskaya simfoniya—Classical symphony: Prokofiev
Kleeblätter—Clover: d'Arba
Klein Venevil—Young Venevil: Kjerulf
Die Kleine—Little innocence: Wolf
Eine kleine Nachtmusik—A little night music: Mozart
Kleine Orgelmesse—Little organ mass: Haydn
Die kleine Spinnerin—The little spinner/The spinning girl/Spinning Jenny: Mozart
Die kleinen Wellen von Breffny—Little waves of Breffney: M Mayer
Kleiner Haushalt—Fairy household: Loewe
Ein kleiner hübscher Vogel (Liebeslieder Walzer)—Was once a pretty tiny birdie flew: Brahms
Ein kleines Lied—A little song: Blech
Kleines Lied (Lieder der Liebe)—Little song: Kilpinen
Ein kleines versehen—A slight mistake: Meyer-Helmund
Das kleinste Lied—The dying child: Reger
Klein-Zschocher müsse so zart und süsse (Mer hahn en neue Oberkeet)—Of flowers the fairest: Bach
Kling—Thanksgiving: R Strauss
Kling' leise, mein Lied—Breathe lightly my lay/Plead softly my song: Liszt
Klokkelelang—Bell ringing: Grieg
Klosterfräulein—The convent walls: Brahms
Die Kluge—The wise one: Orff
Der Knabe an die Mutter—The youth to his mother: Henschel
Der Knabe mit dem Wunderhorn—The boy with the magic horn: Schumann
Der Knabe und das Immlein—The boy and the bee: Wolf
Knabe und Rose—Rose and huntsman: Henschel
Des Knaben Berglied—Song of the mountain lad: Schumann
Des Knaben Wunderhorn—Youth's magic horn: Mahler
Knabentod—Early death: Wolf
Knecht Ruprecht (Album für die Jugend)—Knight Rupert/Old bogie/Old goblin: Schumann
Knell—Glas: F Schmitt
The knight and the jewess—Der Templer und die Judin: Marschner
Knight Bluebeard—Ritter Blaubart: Reznicek
Knight of the hobby-horse—Ritter vom Steckenpferd (Kinderscenen): Schumann

Knight of the rocking horse—Ritter vom Steckenpferd (Kinderscenen):
  Schumann
The knight of the rose—Der Rosenkavalier: R Strauss
Knight Rupert—Knecht Ruprecht (Album für die Jugend): Schumann
A knight was riding—Es ritt ein Ritter: Brahms
The knight's wedding-ride—Ritter Kurts Brautfahrt: Wolf
Know what pangs—Soffri in pace (Atalanta): Handel
Know ye not—Beh! szomoru: K Ábrányi
Knowest thou that dear land—Connais-tu le pays (Mignon): Thomas
Knowest thou the land—Kennst du das Land: Liszt
Knowest thou the land—Kennst du das Land: Wolf
Know'st thou the land—Kennst du das Land: Beethoven
Know'st thou the land—Kennst du das Land: Schumann
Knyaz' Igor—Prince Igor: Borodin
A Ködkirály—The haze-king: E Ábrányi
Köhlerweib est trunken—Collier's wife is drunk/The charcoal-wife is
  drunken: Wolf
Kol domu se teď potácím (Písně milostné)—I wander oft: Dvořák
Kol Slaven—Glory to the Lord: Bortniansky
Kolokola—The bells: Rachmaninov
Kolombine—Colombine: J Marx
Komm bald—Come soon/Nay but why tarry! : Brahms
Komm du süsse Todesstunde—Come thou blessed hour/Come thou
  lovely hour of dying: Bach
Komm, Gott, Schöpfer, heiliger Geist—Come God, Creator, Holy Ghost:
  Bach
Komm, Gott, Schöpfer, heiliger Geist (Orgelbüchlein)—Come, Holy
  Ghost, Creator, come: Bach
Komm, heiliger Geist, Herre Gott—Come, Holy Spirit, come apace: Bach
Komm herbei, komm herbei, Tod! —Come away, come away, death:
  Brahms
Komm in mein Herzenshaus (Ein' feste Burg ist unser Gott)—Come, make
  my heart Thy home: Bach
Komm, Jesu, komm—Come, Jesu, come/When called by Thee: Bach
Komm, Jesu, komm zu deiner Kirche (Nun komm, der Heiden Heiland)—
  Come, Jesus, come to Thy church: Bach
Komm, komm! Held meiner Träume (Der tapfere Soldat)—My hero:
  O Strauss
Komm lass uns spielen—Come, child, beside me: Bleichmann
Komm nu hit Död—Come away, death: Sibelius
Komm, Seelen! dieser Tag—Come let us all this day: Bach
Komm, süsser Tod, komm, sel'ge Ruh' (Todessehnsucht)—Come gentle
  death/Come soothing death/Come sweetest death/Come kindly
  death: Bach

Komm süsser Tod—Come gentle death/Come sweet death: Bach
Komm, wir wandeln zusammen—Come, we'll wander: Cornelius
Kommen und scheiden—Meeting and parting: Schumann
Kommer I snart, I husmaend? (Ulvens søn)—Are ye coming soon, ye
smallholders?: Nielsen
Kommet her, ihr frechten Sünder—Sinners come: Mozart
Kommst du nun, Jesu, von Himmel herunter?—Art Thou, Lord Jesus,
from heaven to earth now descending?/Goest Thou now, Jesu,
from heaven to earth: Bach
Kommt dir manchmal in den Sinn (Zigeunerlieder)—Do you often call
to mind: Brahms
Kommt ein schlanker Bursch gegangen (Der Freischütz)—When a
gallant youth: Weber
Kommt feins Liebchen heut'?—Will he come today?: R Franz
Kommt ihr gespielen—Come, ye playmates: M Franck
Kommt, Seelen, diesen Tag—All people at this hour/Now thank we all
our God: Bach
Kommt wieder aus der finstern Gruft—The third day he rose again: Bach
Konek-Gorbunok—The little humpbacked horse/The humpbacked horse:
Shchedrin
Die Kön'ge aus Saba kamen dar (Sie werden aus Saba alle kommen)—
To us a child is born: Bach
Der König bei der Krönung—King at the coronation: Wolf
König Hirsch—King stag: Henze
Der König in Thule—The king of Thule: Schubert
König Thamos—Thamos, king of Egypt: Mozart
Der König von Thule/Es war ein König in Thule—There reigned a monarch
in Thule/There was a king in Thule/The king of Thule: Liszt
Die Könige (Weihnachtslieder)—The kings/Three kings: Cornelius
Königlich Gebet—A king's prayer: Wolf
Königskinder—Children of the king/The royal children/The king's children:
Humperdinck
Der Königssohn—The king's son: Schumann
Der Kontrabandiste—The smuggler: Schumann
Kophtisches Lied—Koptic song: Bruch
Koptic song—Kophtisches Lied: Bruch
Kornblumen—Cornflower: R Strauss
Korsfarerne—The crusaders: Gade
Koskenlaskijan morisamet—The ferryman's brides: Sibelius
Köszöntö—A birthday greeting: Kodály
Die Kraft versagt (Der widerspanstigen Zähmung)—My strength is spent: Goet
Die Krähe (Die Winterreise)—The crow: Schubert
Král a uhlíř—King and charcoal burner: Dvořák
Der Kranke—The invalid: Schoeck

Die kranke Puppe—Dolly's doctor: Meyer-Helmund
Der Kranz—The wreath: Brahms
Die Kränze—The garlands: Brahms
Krásne oc! Tve—Thy lovely eyes: Janáček
Krasny mak—The red poppy: Glière
Das Kraut Vergessenheit—Forgetfulness: Hildach
Kreml' noch' yu—The Kremlin at night: Miaskovsky
The Kremlin at night—Kreml' noch' yu: Miaskovsky
Krepostnaya balerina—The serf ballerina: Korchmarev
Des Kriegers Abschied—The warrior's farewell/The soldier's farewell:
    Beethoven
Kriegers Ahnung (Schwanengesang)—Eve of battle/The warrior's fore-
    boding: Schubert
Kriegslied—Warrior's song: Berlioz
Kriegslied (Album für die Jugend)—War song/Warrior's song: Schumann
Kriegmarsch der Priester (Athalia)—War march of the priests: Mendelssohn
Król Roger—King Roger: Symanowski
Krov naroda—The blood of the people: Dzerzhinsky
Krymskaya syinta—Crimean suite: Vitachek
Der Kühe—The bold hunter: Pfitzner
Kuin hiipuva hiillos tummentuu—Like the glow on the hearth: Merikanto
Kume, kum, Geselle min—Come, O sweet companion: Haselböck
Kunsterleben—Artist's life: J Strauss II
Der Kuss—The kiss: Beethoven
Der Kuss—The kiss: Brahms
Der Kuss—The kiss: Meyer-Helmund
Kuss-walzer—Kiss waltz/Merry war: J Strauss II
Kvarnhjulet—The mill wheel: Sibelius
Kveldsang for Blakken (Barnlige Sanger)—Dobbin's good night song:
    Grieg
En kviddrende Laerke—The warbling lark: A Backer-Grøndahl
Kvoelden—Evening: Sinding
Kyrie, Gott, heiliger Geist—Kyrie, O God, Holy Ghost!: Bach
Kyrie! God our Father evermore!—Kyrie, Gott Vater in Ewigkeit: Bach
Kyrie, Gott Vater in Ewigkeit—Kyrie! God our Father evermore!: Bach
Kyrie, O God, Holy Ghost!—Kyrie, Gott heiliger Geist: Bach

L

Là-bas, vers l'église—Yonder, near the church/Out there where the church tower: Ravel

Laboravi clamans—I am spent with crying: Rameau

Labour lost—Verlorne Müh (Des Knaben Wunderhorn): Mahler

Le lac de Wallenstadt—Lake Wallenstadt: Liszt

Le lac enchanté—The enchanted lake: Liadov

Il lacerato spirito (Simon Boccanegra)—Tortured and torn/Thy father's heart/The broken spirit: Verdi

Lace, circle and mirror—Kette, Kreis und Spiegel: Křenek

Lachen und weinen—Laughing and weeping/Smiles and tears: Schubert

Der lachende Ehemann—The laughing husband: Eysler

Lacrimoso son io—Willow, willow: Mozart

Lad and the stream—Der Jüngling an der Quelle: Schubert

Ladies pray tell me—Voi che sapete (Le nozze di Figaro): Mozart

Lad's dance—Legéntytánc (Devinské Scény): Bartók

The lads of Zvolyn—Zvolenovcí chlapci: Martinů

The lady dandies—Les merveilleuses: Félix

The lady goldsmith—Die goldene Meisterin: Eysler

Lady Macbeth of Mtsensk—Ledi Markbet Mtsenskovo uyezda: Shostakovic

The lady of the lake—La donna del lago: Rossini

The ladybird—Marienwürmchen (Volkskinderlieder): Brahms

Ladybird—Marienwürmchen: Schumann

Lady's lament—Frauenklage: Hindemith

Laet ons nu al verblijden in desen Soeten Tijt—Now let there be rejoicing: Beethoven

Laetentur coeli—Rejoice, ye heavens: Byrd

El lagarto (Canciones de niños)—Mr and Mrs Lizard: Revueltas

Laggiù, tra i giunchi di Genesareth (Nerone)—Behold the marshes: Boito

Lagoon waltz—Lagunen-walzer: J Strauss II

Lagrime—O ye tears: Dering

Lagunen-walzer—Lagoon waltz: J Strauss II

Lake Wallenstadt—Le lac de Wallenstadt: Liszt

Lake Rits—Ozera Ritsa: Balanchivadze

Lakodalom (Dedinské Scény)—Wedding: Bartók

Lament—Verzagen: Brahms

The lament of Mary—Planctus Mariae: Anon

Lament of the blind—Blindenklage: R Strauss

Lament on the death of Lorenzo de Medici—Quis dabit capiti meo aquam: Isaac

Lament to the moon—Klage an dem Mond: F X Mozart

Lamento d'Arianna/Lasciatemi morire—No longer let me languish: Monteverdi

Lampaan polska—The sheep's polka: Kuula
Lampoon from 'Wilhelm Meister'—Spottlied aus 'Wilhelm Meister': Wolf
Das Land des Lächelns—The land of smiles: Lehár
Land ever calm and peaceful—Luoghi sereni e cari: Donaudy
Land of beauty—Im Süden: Mendelssohn
The land of dreams—Se non mi vuolamar (Tamerlano): Handel
Land of my fathers—Hen wlad fy nhadan: J James
The land of smiles—Das Land des Lächelns: Lehár
Landkjending—Landsighting: Grieg
Die ländliche Hochzeit [symphony]—The rustic wedding: Goldmark
Landliches Lied—The May-time/Villanelle: Schumann
Landliches Lied (Album für die Jugend)—Rustic village/Villager's song:
    Schumann
Landsighting—Landkjending: Grieg
Landsknechte—Yeomen: Schoenberg
Landsknechtstrinklied—Troopers' drinking song: Hindemith
Langelandsk Folkemelodi—Folk song from Langeland: Grieg
Langs en å—By the riverside/By the brook/At the brookside: Grieg
Längtan heter min arvedel—Longings vain are my heritage: Sibelius
Language of love—Sprache der Liebe: Schubert
Les langues de feu (Messe de la Pentecôte)—The tongues of fire: Messiaen
Largo—Ombra mai fù (Serse): Handel
Largo al factotum (Il barbiere di Siviglia)—Hey for the town's factotum:
    Rossini
The lark—La calàndria: Gerhard
The Lark's song—Lerchengesang: Mendelssohn
Lark's sweet cloud-approaching music—Die Lerche wolkennahe Lieder:
    Schubert
Une larme—A tear: Mussorgsky
Las! Voulez-vous qu'une personne chante—Ah! Wouldst thou I should
    sing a merry ditty: Lassus
Laschia ch'io pianga (Rinaldo)—Weeping for ever/Hear thou my weeping/
    Leave me, deceiver/Let me still languish/Leave me my anguish/Sadly I
    languish/So shall my weeping/Look down and hearken/Rest of the
    weary: Handel
Lascia amor (Orlando)—Farewell! Your country calls you: Handel
Lascia ch'io parta solo (Atalanta)—Let me have leave: Handel
Lasciatemi morire/Lamento d'Arianna—No longer let me languish:
    Monteverdi
Lasciati amar—Come love, be mine: Leoncavallo
Láska—Love: Smetana
Lass dich nicht gereu'n—Heart, repent thee not: Henschel
Lass dich nur nichts nich dauern—O heart subdued with grieving: Brahms
Lass, Fürstin—Lord rebuke me not/Funeral ode: Bach

Lass mich ihm am Busen hangen/Lied der Braut—Strange the joy that overwhelms me: Schumann

Lass uns, O höchster Gott (Jesu, nun sei gepreiset)—May we complete this year: Bach

Lasset uns mit Jesu ziehen—Let us walk as Jesus willeth: Bach

Lasst froh uns sein—Melancholy: Mozart

Lasst mich ruhen—Let me rest: Liszt

Lasst uns das Angesicht (Es erub sich ein Streit)—When angels visit us: Bach

Last boat across—Im Spätboot: R Strauss

Lassú vergődés (Tíz könnyű zongoradarab)—Painful wrestling: Bartók

Last eve he brought me—Und gestern hat er mir Rosen gebracht: J Marx

Last greeting—Adieu: Schubert-Heller

Last happiness—Letztes Glück: Brahms

Last hope—Letzte Hoffnung (Die Winterreise): Schubert

The last hour—Geleit: Brahms

The last judgement—Der Jüngste Tag: O Jochum

The last judgement—Die letzten Dinge: Spohr

Last night—Sehnsucht: Kjerulf

Last night in the deep sea—L'altra notte in fono al mare (Mephistofele): Boito

The last of his clan—Die Vätergruft: Liszt

Last prayer—Letzte Bitte: Wolf

The last request—Nur einmal noch: Blumenthal

The last rose—Die letzte Rose: R Franz

The last rose of summer—Letzte Rose (Martha): Flotow

Last Sunday morn(ing)—Am Sonntag-morgen: Brahms

Last thoughts—Les dernières pensées: Pierné

The last toast—Auf das Trinkglas: Schumann

The last waltz—Der letzte Walzer: Straus

The last wish—Vuré šuhaj, vuře (Moravské dvojzpevy): Dvořák

Lasting happiness—Sichers Glück: Bocquet

Lasting love—Beharrliche Liebe: Henschel

Lastu Lainehilla—Driftwood: Sibelius

Late Autumn—Spätherbst: Brahms

The latter-day Amadis—Der neue Amadis: Wolf

Laud we our God—Dank sei dir, Herr: Handel

Laudate Dominum—Praise Jehovah all ye heathen: Mozart

Laudate eum, elementa, Christus natus est—Down a narrow silver way: d'Arba

Laudate nomen Domini—O come ye servants of the Lord: Tye

Laudate pueri Dominum—Praise the Lord, ye servants: Byrd

Laudate pueri Dominum—O praise the Lord: Mendelssohn

Laudibus in sanctis—Praise the Lord among his holy ones: Byrd

Lauf der Welt—The way of the world: Grieg

Laughing and weeping—Lachen und Weinen: Schubert
The laughing husband—Der lachende Ehemann: Eysler
Laughing song—C'est l'histoire amoureuse (Manon Lescaut): Auber
Laughing song—Mein Herr Marquis (Die Fledermaus): J Strauss II
Laurinda sang one day—Cantando un dí: Clari
Die laute Klage—The loud complaint/The loud lament: Beethoven
The law—Das Gesetz: Schoenberg
Lawn in the park—Weise im Park: Webern
The lay of the bell—Das Lied von der Glocke: Bruch
The lay of the Norseman—Normannenzug: Bruch
Lead us not into temptation—Führe uns nicht in Versuchung: Cornelius
Leánykérö—The wooing of a girl: Bartók
The leap over the shadow—Der Sprung über den Schatten: Křenek
Learnt by watching—Abgeguckt: Reger
Leave me alone—Kéž duch můj sám: Dvořák
Leave me, deceiver—Laschia ch'io pianga (Rinaldo): Handel
A leave taking—Un adieu: Massenet
The leaves—Les feuilles (Petites légendes): Milhaud
Leaves and blossoms—Blätter und Blüten: Reger
A leave-taking—Abschied: Reger
Leave-taking—Abschied: Schubert
Leb' woh, du kühnes (Die Walküre)—Farewell, my noble, valorous child:
   Wagner
Lebe wohl—Farewell: Wolf
Das Leben des Orest—The life of Orestes: Křenek
Das Leben ist ein Traum—Life is a dream: Haydn
Lebenlust—Life's joy: Schubert
Lebewohl—A farewell: Blumenthal
Ledi Makbet Mtsenskovo uyezda—Lady Macbeth of Mtsensk: Shostakovich
The legend of the invisible city of Kitezh and the maiden Fevronia—Skazanie
   o nevidimom grave Kitezhe i deve Fevronii: Rimsky Korsakov
Legend of the Rhine—Rheinlegendchen (Des Knaben Wunderhorn): Mahler
Legénycsúfoló—Mocking of youth/Teasing song: Bartók
Legénytánc (Dedinské Scény)—Lad's dance: Bartók
Leggiadretto Clorino—As I saw Clora walk: Vecchi
Lehn deine Wang an meine Wang—Together/Draw near beloved/I fain would
   rest: Jensen
Lehre—Lesson: R Franz
Lehrstücke—The lesson: Hindemith
Lehullott a rezgó nyárfa—Down from a trembling aspen tree: Erkel
Leichte Segler (An die ferne Geliebte)—Fleecy cloud: Beethoven
Leichter Verlust—The double loss: Meyer-Helmund
Leichtes Blut—Quick silver: J Strauss II
Leichtgesinnte Flattergeister—Scatterbrained and shallow people: Bach

Leid ohne Ende (Albumblätter)—Endless sorrow/Grief without end/ Sorrow never ending: Schumann

Der Leidende—The mourner/Sad heart: Schubert

Leides Ahnung (Albumblätter)—Coming woe/Coming sorrow/Grief's forebodings: Schumann

Der Leiermann (Die Winterreise)—The hurdy-gurdy man/The organ grinder: Schubert

Leis' rudern hier—Row gently here/Row gently row: Schumann

Leise, leise/Wiegenlied—Gently play, oh zephyrs: Reger

Leise, leise, fromme Weise (Die Freischütz)—Softly sighs the voice of evening: Weber

Leises Lied—Silent longing: R Strauss

Leise Lieder—Whisp'ring songs: R Strauss

Leise, um dich nicht zu wecken—Soft amid the bed of roses/Serenade: Brahms

Leise zieht/Frühlingslied—Lightly play/Spring song/A message/Music on my spirit plays: A Rubinstein

Leise zieht durch—Softly through my heart: R Franz

Leise zieht durch mein Gemuth/Grüss—Summer days are coming/ Greeting: Mendelssohn

Lekaszálták már a rétet—They mowed the pasture already: Bartók

Lekaszálták már—The mead is bare: Erkel

The Lemko wedding—Lemkyvs'ke vesylla: Kolessa

Lemkyvs'ke vesylla—The Lemko wedding: Kolessa

Lemon butterfly in April—Zitronenfalter im April: Wolf

Lend me your aid—Inspirez moi! (La reine de Saba): Gounod

Lenda do caboclo—Tale of a peasant: Villa-Lobos

Lenz—Spring: Hildach

Lenzgesang—A song of spring: Sibelius

Lenz-Tageweis—Springtime-ditty: Manén

Die Lerche wolkennahe Lieder/Sehnsucht—Lark's sweet cloud-approaching music/Longing/Yearning: Schubert

Lerchengesang—The skylark's song/Song of the skylark: Brahms

Lerchengesang—The lark's song: Mendelssohn

Lešétínský Kovář—The blacksmith of Lesetin: Weis

Lesson—Lehre: R Franz

The lesson—Lehrstücke: Hindemith

A lesson learned—Beherzigung: Wolf

Let all with gladsome voices—Was frag ich nach der Welt (Sehet, welch eine Liebe hat uns der Vater erzeiget): Bach

Let all together praise our God—Lobt Gott, ihr Christen allzugleich (Orgelbüchlein): Bach

Let an abyss—Verschling der Abgrund (Italienisches Liederbuch): Wolf

Let anguish have its due—Dem Schmerz sein Recht: Berg

Let ev'ry heart be merry—So ben mi ch'a bon tempo: Vecchi

Let her believe—Ch'ella mi creda (La fanciulla der West): Puccini

Let me ever as I wander—Sempre libera (La traviata): Verdi
Let me have leave—Lascia ch'io parta solo (Atalanta): Handel
Let me rest—Lasst mich ruhen: Liszt
Let me still languish— Lascia ch'io pianga (Rinaldo): Handel
Let my entreaties—Pièta, Signore: Stradella
Let my longing and supplication—Al desio chi t'adora: Mozart
Let my prayers—Quando mai spietata (Radamisto): Handel
Let our hearts e'er be joyful—Unser Mund sei voll Lachens: Bach
Let our mouth be full of laughter—Unser Mund sei voll Lachens: Bach
Let songs of rejoicing be raised—Man singet mit freuden: Bach
Let them find out—Takálják ki: Erkel
Let us but rest awhile in quiet—Man halte nur ein wenig stille
    (Wer nur den lieben Gott lässt walten): Bach
Let us lift up our hearts—Sursum corda (Années de pèlerinage): Liszt
Let us walk as Jesus willeth—Lasset uns mit Jesu ziehen: Bach
Let's be friends—Brüderlein und Schwesterlein (Die Fledermaus):
    J Strauss II
Let's enjoy—Giovinette, che fate all' amore (Don Giovanni): Mozart
Let's go to Hampstead—Gehn wir im Prater: Mozart
The letter—Einen Brief soll ich schreiben: Reger
Letzte Bitte—Last prayer: Wolf
Letzte Hoffnung (Die Winterreise)—Last hope: Schubert
Letzte Rose (Martha)—The last rose of summer: Flotow
Die letzte Rose—The last rose: R Franz
Der letzte Walzer—The last waltz: Straus
Letztes Glück—Last happiness: Brahms
Die letzten Dinge—The last judgement: Spohr
Leucht't heller als die Sonne—An old love song: Mendelssohn
Levemus corda—Come let us lift up our hearts: Byrd
The leveret—Myúlacska: Kodály
The libation bearers—Les choéphores: Milhaud
Die Libelle schwebt zitternd (Chinesische Liebeslieder)—As the dragonfly
    quivers: Liebermann
Libellentanz—The three graces: Lehár
Libera me Domine—Set me free, O Lord my God: Byrd
Libera me Domine de morte aeterna—Deliver me, O Lord, from eternal
    death: Byrd
Libiamo ne'lieti calici (La traviata)—Fill high/To joy let us drain/Where
    beauty and mirth: Verdi
Liden Fugl—Little bird: Grieg
Liden Kirsten—Little Kirsten: Grieg
Lieb' Liebchen—My darling: R Franz
Lieb' Liebchen—Dear love: Medtner
Lieb' Liebchen—My love, lay thy hand/Dear love: Schumann
Lieb' Minna—Dear Minna: Schubert

Liebchen ist da!—Sweetheart is there: R Franz
Liebchen, wo bist du—Darling where are you?: Wolf
Liebe—Love: Cornelius
Die Liebe—Love: Meyer-Helmund
Der liebe Augustin—Princess Caprice: Fall
Der Liebe der Danae—Danae's love/The love of Danae: R Strauss
Liebe, dir ergeb ich mich (Liebe)—Love, I give myself to thee: Cornelius
Die liebe Farbe (Die schöne Müllerin)—The beloved colour/The pleasing
  colour: Schubert
Die Liebe hat gelogen!—Love has promised falsely: R Franz
Die Liebe hat gelogen—Love has falsely spoken/Oh, love hath falsely
  spoken/A falsehood love has told me/Love was false: Schubert
Liebe kam aus fernen Landen—Love came forth from far-off places/
  Love from distant lands/Love came wandering/From afar: Brahms
Der liebe Lohn (Brautlieder)—The reward of love: Cornelius
Liebe im Schnee—Love adrift: Benatzky
Liebe ohne Heimat—Love without a home: Cornelius
Liebe Schwalbe, kleine Schwalbe (Zigeunerlieder)—Gentle swallow/Pretty
  swallow: Brahms
Liebe schwärmt auf allen wegen—Love comes gaily forth to meet you:
  Schubert
Liebe und Frühling—Love and spring: Brahms
Die Liebe zieht mit sanften Schritten (Schwingt freudig euch empor)—
  Love guides with gentle steps: Bach
Der Liebende—The lover: Beethoven
Das liebende Mädchen—The lovesick maiden: F X Mozart
Die Liebende schreibt—To the beloved one/To her beloved: Brahms
Die Liebende schreibt—Her love-letter: Mendelssohn
Die Liebende schreibt—His love writes: Schubert
Lieber alles—I'd rather/All three: Wolf
Lieber Schatz, sei wieder gut mir—Dearest friend, look kindly on me:
  R Franz
Liebes Mädchen, hör mir zu—Dearest maid, O list to me/Dearest maiden,
  come to me: Haydn
Liebesbotschaft (Schwanengesang)—Love's messenger/The lover's
  messenger: Schubert
Liebesbotschaft—A message of love: Schumann
Liebeserwachen—Fated love: Blumenthal
Liebesfeier—Thanksgiving: R Franz
Liebesfrühling—The spring of love/The wood is green and gay/Love's
  spring: R Franz
Liebesgarten—O love, it is a rose-tree fair: Schumann
Liebesgeschenke—Love gifts: R Strauss
Liebesglück—The bliss of love/Happy love: Wolf

Liebesglut—Consuming love/Love's fever: Brahms
Liebesgram—Love's rest: Schumann
Liebeshymnus—Love's pleading: R Strauss
Liebesklage des Mädchens—The maid forlorn/The maiden's lament: Brahms
Liebeslauschen—Love's listening: Schubert
Liebeslied—Lovesong: Schumann
Liebeslieder-walzer [See also Neue Liebeslieder]—Love-song waltzes/Love
  songs: Brahms
Das Liebesmahl der Apostel—Feast of the Pentecost: Wagner
Liebesode—Lovers' ode: Berg
Liebespredigt—Love voices: Kjerulf
Liebesprobe—The love test: Cornelius
Liebestraum/O Lieb' so lang du lieben kannst—O love, as long as love is
  young/Dream of love/Love's dream: Liszt
Liebestreu—True love/Love's faith/Faithful love/Constancy: Brahms
Liebestrunken—Love's intoxication: Patáky
Das Liebesverbot—Love's prohibition: Wagner
Liebeszauber—Love's enchantment: Schulz
Liebliches Kind, kannst du mir sagen—Question: Brahms
Lieblingsplätzchen—The favourite spot: Mendelssohn
Liebst du um Schönheit—If you love for beauty/Lov'st thou but beauty:
  Mahler
Liebste Jungfrau, wir sind dein (Drei Volkstexte)—Dearest Virgin we pray
  to Thee: Webern
Des Liebsten Schwur—The lover's vow: Brahms
Liebster Gott, wann werd' ich sterben?—When will God recall my spirit?/
  Holy Ghost, dispel our sadness/Dearest Lord, when wilt Thou summon:
  Bach
Liebster Herr Jesu—Dearest Lord Jesu/Wherefore Lord Jesu: Bach
Liebster Herr Jesu! Wo bleibst du so lange—Wherefore, O Saviour:
  Bach
Liebster Immanuel, Herzog der Frommen—Beloved Emmanuel, Lord
  of the righteous/O sweet Emmanuel: Bach
Liebster Jesu, mein verlangen—Dearest Saviour, priceless treasure/
  Beloved Jesus, my desire: Bach
Liebster Jesu, wir sind hier (Orgelbüchlein)—Blessed Jesu, at Thy word:
  Bach
Lied—Song: Chabrier
Lied an die Nacht—Song of the night: Reichardt
Lied an meinen Sohn—To my son: R Strauss
Lied aus dem Gedichte 'Ivan'—Song from 'Ivan'/High over the world:
  Brahms
Lied aus der Ferne—(A) song from afar: Beethoven
Lied der Braut/Lass mich ihm am Busen hangen—Strange the joy that
  overwhelms me: Schumann

Lied der Braut/Mutter, Mutter—Mother, mother, do not grieve/Bride's song: Schumann

Lied der Freiheit—Song of freedom: Mozart

Lied der Freundschaft—A song of friendship: R Strauss

Lied der Gertrud—Gertrude's song: Goetz

Lied der Suleika (Myrthen)—Suleika's song: Schumann

Das Lied der Trennung—Separation and reunion: Mozart

Lied des Harfenmädchens—The beggar-maid's song: M Mayer

Lied des Steinklopfers—The stone breaker: R Strauss

Lied des Verfolgten im Turm (Des Knaben Wunderhorn)—Song of the prisoner in the tower: Mahler

Lied eines Mädchens—A maiden's longing: J Marx

Lied eines Mädchens—Love-lorn maiden's song: Reger

Lied eines Schmiedes—Blacksmith's song: Schumann

Lied eines Verliebten—A lover's song: Wolf

Das Lied im Grünen—Away to the meadows/In spring-time: Schubert

Lied maritime—A song of the sea: Indy

Lied vom Winde—Song of the wind: Wolf

Das Lied von der Erde—The song of the earth: Mahler

Das Lied von der Glocke—The lay of the bell: Bruch

Das Lied von Herrn von Falkenstein—The ballad of Herr von Falkenstein/The ballad of the Lord of Falkenstein: Brahms

Lieder der Braut—Songs of a bride-to-be: Schumann

Lieder der Liebe—Songs of love: Kilpinen

Lieder der Mignon—Mignon's songs: Wolf

Lieder eines fahrenden Gesellen—Songs of a wayfarer/Songs of a young wayfarer: Mahler

Lieder ohne Worte—Songs without words: Mendelssohn

Lieder um den Tod—Songs of death: Kilpinen

Liederalbum für die Jugend—Song album for the young: Schumann

Liederkreis von Heine—Cycle of Heine songs: Schumann

Lieutenant Kije—Poruchik Kizhe: Prokofiev

Le lièvre et le blé (Petites légendes)—The hare and the corn: Milhaud

Life—La vie: Pierné

Life is a dream—Das Leben ist ein Traum: Haydn

Life is short—La vida breve: Falla

The life of a vassal—È prezzo leggiero (Poro): Handel

The life of Orestes—Das Leben des Orest: Křenek

The life of the Virgin Mary—Das Marienleben: Hindemith

Life on earth—Das irdische Leben (Des Knaben Wunderhorn): Mahler

Life's joy—Lebenslust: Schubert

Lift up your heads—Attollite portas: Byrd

Light and shade—Ljus och skugga: Palmgren

Lift up your heads on high—Hebt euer Haupt empor (Wachet, betet, seid bereit): Bach

Light is my heart—Qual farfalletta (Partenope): Handel

The light of Asia—La luce dell' Asia: De Lara

The light of the eye—Das Augenlicht: Webern

Light of the moon—Clair de lune (Fêtes galantes): Debussy

Lighter far is now my slumber—Immer leiser wird mein Schlummer: Brahms

Lightly play—Leise zieht: A Rubinstein

Like a blossoming—Meine Liebe ist grün (Junge Lieder): Brahms

Lied Lynceus des Türmers—Song of Lynceus the lynx-eyed, keeper of the watch-tower: Schumann

Like a fleet eager to set sail—Som en rejselysten flåde/Moderen: Nielsen

Like a flower in beauty blushing—Du bist wie eine Blume: Liszt

Like a lordly star—Mein Herr Marquis: J Strauss II

Like a shepherd—Schafe können sicher weiden (Was mir behagt): Bach

Like a violet—Skromna (Moravské Dvojzpěvy): Dvořák

Like any foolish moth—Qual farfalletta amante: D Scarlatti

Like as a silver stream—Come raggio di sol: Caldara

Like as the hart—Sicut cervus desiderat: Palestrina

Like as the love-lorn turtle—Come alla tortorella (Atalanta): Handel

Like as the showers and snow—Gleich wie der Regen und Schnee: Bach

Like as we oft have heard—Sicut audivimus: Byrd

Like brooks the end of something sweeps one away—Wie Bäche reisst das Ende von etwas mich dahin: Henze

Like melodies it floweth—Wie Melodien zieht es mir: Brahms

Like strains of sweetest music—Wie Melodien zieht es mir: Brahms

Like the driven cloud—Wie die Wolke nach der Sonne: Brahms

Like the glow on the hearth—Kuin hiipuva hiillos tummentuu: Merikanto

Like the sunset's crimson splendour—Wie des Abends (Liebeslieder Walzer): Brahms

Like the valiant Atlas—Gestern war ich Atlas: R Strauss

Like to a ray of sun—Come raggio di sol: Caldara

Like to like—Gleich und gleich: Webern

Like with like—Gleich und gleich: Webern

Der lila Domino—The lilac Domino: Cuvillier

The lilac Domino—Der lila Domino: Cuvillier

Lilac time—Das Dreimäderlhaus: Schubert-Berté

The lilac trees—Les lilas qui avaient fleuri (Tristesses): Milhaud

Les lilas qui avaient fleuri (Tristesses)—The lilac trees: Milhaud

Liliomos herceg—The prince with the lilies: E Ábrányi

En lille langsom Vals—A little slow waltz: Nielsen

The lime tree—Der Lindenbaum (Die Winterreise): Schubert

A lime tree stands—Es steht ein Lind: Brahms
The limits of mankind—Grenzen der Menschheit: Wolf
Der Lindenbaum (Die Winterreise)—The lime tree/The old elm: Schubert
Lindes rauschen—Trees that sway/Rustling tree top/Dreams of home:
  Brahms
Lines from the battle of the Nile—Gesang von der Schlacht am Nil: Haydn
Lines on an old picture—Auf ein altes Bild: Wolf
Lines with the lute's green ribbon—Mit dem grünen Lautenbande (Die
  schöne Müllerin): Schubert
Lingering down the lane—Ah, le petit vin blanc: Borel-Clerc
Lingering, lonely rose—Ultima rosa: Sibella
The lion's betrothed—Die Löwenbraut: Schumann
The lion's bride—Die Löwenbraut: Schumann
Lips of roses—Pur dicesti o bocca bella: Lotti
Lips so sweet and tender—A vucchella: Tosti
Litanie auf das Fest aller Seelen—Litany for All Souls' Day: Schubert
Litany for All Souls' Day—Litanie auf das Fest aller Seelen: Schubert
Lithuanian song—Piosnka litewska: Chopin
Little bird—Liden Fugl: Grieg
The little bird—Das Vöglein: Wolf
The little bird despair—Vöglein Schwermut (Lieder um den Tod):
  Kilpinen
Little bird if you sing sweetly—Passarinho está cantando: Mignone
A little birdie—È l'uccellino: Puccini
Little birdie—Kis Menyeckse: Antalffy
Little cardboard cat—O gatinho de papelao (A prolé do bêbê): Villa-Lobos
The little cloth bird—O passarinho de panno (A prolé do bêbê):
  Villa-Lobos
The little cotton bear—O ursozinho de algodâo (A prolé do bêbê):
  Villa-Lobos
The little duke—Le petit duc: Lecocq
The little dustman—Sandmännchen (Volkskinderlieder): Brahms
The little Dutch girl—Das Hollandweibchen: Kálmán
Little folk song—Volksliedchen: Schumann
Little forehead, no more aching—Preziosas Sprüchlein gegen Kopfweh:
  Cornelius
The little glass wolf—O lobosinho de vidro (A prolé do bêbê): Villa-Lobos
A little harvest song—Erndliedchen (Album für die Jugend): Schumann
Little heath-rose— Heidenröslein: Schubert
The little hen—Slepička: Smetana
The little horse—El caballito (Canciones de niños): Revueltas
The little hump-backed horse—Konek-Gorbunok: Shchedrin
The little hunter's song—Jägerliedchen (Album für die Jugend):
  Schumann

Little innocence—Die Kleine: Wolf
Little Kirsten—Liden Kirsten: Grieg
Little lady—Madamina! Il catalogo (Don Giovanni): Mozart
Little lambkin—Corderito: Guastavino
Little legends—Petites légendes: Milhaud
The little Michus—Les p'tites Michu: Messager
The little mother—La madrecita: J Berger
A little night music—Eine kleine Nachtmusik: Mozart
The little onion—Cibulička: Smetana
Little organ book—Orgelbüchlein: Bach
Little organ mass—Kleine Orgelmesse: Haydn
Little owl—Kauzlein: Schumann
Little paper bug—A baratinha de papel (A prolé do bêbê): Villa-Lobos
Little princess—Prinzesschen: Manén
Little Red Ridinghood—Rotkappchen: Abt
The little rifle—Vintovochka: Davidenko
Little rose—Röslein, röslein: Schumann
Little rose-bud—Dornröschen: Brahms
Little rosebud of the sleeping beauty—Dornröschen: Reinecke
The little rough rider—Wilder Reiter (Album für die Jugend): Schumann
Little rubber dog—O cachorrinho de borracha (A prolé do bêbê):
    Villa-Lobos
The little sandman—Der Sandmännchen: Brahms
The little shepherdess—La pastorella delle Alpi: Rossini
The little shoes—Tcherevichky: Tchaikovsky
The little sick boy—Le petit garçon malade: Poulenc
A little slow waltz—En lille langsom Vals: Nielsen
Little snowdrop—Schneewittchen: Reinecke
A little song—Ein kleines Lied: Blech
Little song—Kleines Lied (Lieder der Liebe): Kilpinen
The little spinner—Die kleine Spinnerin: Mozart
Little star—Estrellita: Ponce
Little sweetheart—Schatzerl klein: Webern
The little tin ox—O boisinho de chumbo (A prolé do bêbê): Villa Lobos
Little toy mouse—O camundongo de massa: Villa-Lobos
The little waves of Beffny—Die kleinen Wellen von Beffny: M Mayer
The little white donkey—Le petit âne blanc: Ibert
The little wood—Allons dans ce petit bois charmant: Meister
The little wooden horse—O cavalinho de páu (A prolé do bêbê):
    Villa Lobos
Little zephyr—Zeffiretto: Handel
Lively air—Air vif: Poulenc
Ljus och skugga—Light and shade: Palmgren
Llanfair—Yonder see the dawn appear: W S G Williams
Lo, from his tomb—Tulerunt Dominum meum: Mendelssohn

Lo! he has come—Er ist gekommen: R Franz
Lo, how a rose e'er blooming—Es ist ein Ros' entsprungen: Brahms
Lo, how Aurora—Ecco l'Aurora con l'Aurata fronte: A Gabrieli
Lo, I come—Siehe, ich komme (Himmelskönig, sei willkommen): Bach
Lo, I entreat thee, Sire!—Signore, ascolta (Turandot): Puccini
Lo the bright angel—Angelus autem Domini: Anerio
Lo, the earth did quake—Terra tremuit: Byrd
Lo, 'tis evening light and long—Nu er Aftnen lys og lang: Grieg
Loafer—Resteknek nótája: Bartók
Lob der Faulheit—Praise of indolence: Haydn
Lob der Frühlings—Praise of spring/In praise of spring: Mendelssohn
Lob des hohen Verstand (Des Knaben Wunderhorn)—In praise of high
    intellect/In praise of the lofty intellect: Mahler
Lob des Leidens—In praise of sorrow: R Strauss
Lob sei dem allmächtigen Gott (Orgelbüchlein)—To God we render
    thanks and praise: Bach
Lob sei Gott, dem Vater, g'tan (Nun komm, der Heiden Heiland)
    (Schwingt freudig euch empor)—Praise to God the Father be
    given: Bach
Lob und Ehre und Weisheit und Dank—Blessing, glory, wisdom
    and thanks: Bach
Lobe den Herrn, meine Seele—Praise the Lord, O my soul: Bach
Lobe den Herren, den mächtigen König der Ehren—Praise the Lord!
    the Almighty, the King of creation/Praise Him the highest/Praise Him,
    the Lord, the Almighty: Bach
Lobet den Herren—Oh praise the Lord: Staden
Lobet den Herrn alle Heiden (Herden)—Oh praise the Lord all ye heathens
    (nations): Bach
Lobet Gott in seinen Reichen—Praise our God who reigns in heaven/
    Praise God in all his splendour: Bach
Lobgesang—Hymn of praise: Mendelssohn
O lobosinho de vidro (A prolé do bêbê)—The little glass wolf: Villa Lobos
Lobt Gott, ihr Christen allzugleich (Orgelbüchlein)—Let all together
    praise our God: Bach
The lock—Otevřeni Slovečkem: Martinů
Locke nur—Tempt me not: Telemann
Locksmith, ho—Schlosser auf (Liebeslieder Walzer): Brahms
Lockung—Allurement: Dessauer
Lockung—Temptation: Schoenberg
Loin de moi ta lèvre qui ment—Take away thy lip: Massenet
Lok (Barnlige Sanger)—Farmyard song: Grieg
I Lombardi—The Lombards: Verdi
The Lombards—I Lombardi: Verdi
Lone and joyless—Infelice: Mendelssohn

Lone dreamer—Feldeinsamkeit: Brahms
The lone sailor—Amicu ventu: Gilbaro
Loneliness—Einsamkeit (Die Winterreise): Schubert
Lonely am I now no longer—Einsam bin ich, nicht alleine: Weber
Lonely and sad and lowly—Einsam in trüben Tagen (Lohengrin): Wagner
A lonely crag stands yonder—Am wilden Klippenstrande: Henschel
Lonely girl—Die Einsame: Webern
The lonely man in autumn—Der Einsame im Herbst (Das Lied von der
    Erde): Mahler
The lonely man's wine—Der Wein des Einsamen (Der Wein): Berg
Lonely tear—Was will die einsame Träne: Schumann
Lonesome—Der Einsame: Schubert
Long ago—Vorüber: Brahms
Long ago—Wie einst: J Marx
Long ago I told you—Rég megmondtam bús gerlice: Bartók
Long the day and dreary—Air sur trois notes: Rousseau
Longed for joy-light—Erwunschtes Freudenlicht: Bach
Longing—Sehnsucht: Beethoven
Longing—Sehnsucht: Brahms
Longing—Ach, wie komm' ich: R Franz
Longing—Sehnsucht: Kjerulf
Longing—Touha: Martinů
Longing—Sehnsucht: Schoenberg
Longing—Sehnsucht: Schubert
Longing—Sehnsucht/Die Lerche wolkennahe Lieder: Schubert
Longing—Sehnsucht: Schumann
Longing—Sehnsucht: Sibelius
Longing—Touha: Smetana
Longing—Sehnsucht: R Strauss
Longing at rest—Gestille Sehnsucht: Brahms
Longing for death—Todessehnsucht: Bach
Longing for home—Heimweh: Wolf
Longing for spring—Sehnsucht nach dem Frühling: Mozart
Longing for the forest lands—Sehnsucht nach der Waldgegend:
    Schumann
Longing hearts—Schlagende Herzen: R Strauss
Longing to roam—Drang in die Ferne: Schubert
Longings—Wie die Wolke nach der Sonne: Brahms
Longings vain are my heritage—Längtan heter min arvedel: Sibelius
Look down and hearken—Laschia ch'io pianga (Rinaldo): Handel
Look down, O Lord—Aspice Domine de sede: Byrd
Look down that lane—L'improvisateur: Massenet
Look, fair lady—Pensa, oh bella (Scipione): Handel
Look here, this is a dollar—Schau her, das ist ein Taler (Tiefland): d'Albert

Look not, love, on my work unended—Blicke mir nicht in die Lieder: Mahler

Look on me with mercy—Miserere mei: Byrd

Look up, faint heart—Ermuntre dich, mein schwacher Geist: Bach

Look upon us, O Lord—Aspice Domine: Byrd

Looking backward—Rückblick (Die Winterreise): Schubert

Looking upwards—Aufblick: Wolf

Loquebantur variis—With other tongues: Palestrina

Lord, are Thine eyes not searching for the righteous—Herr, deine Augen sehen nach dem Glauben: Bach

Lord as Thou wilt—Herr, so du willst (Herr, wie du willt): Bach

Lord as Thou wilt, so deal with me—Herr, wie du willt, so schicks mit mir: Bach

Lord, as Thy name is—Gott, wie dein Name: Bach

The Lord cares for us—Der Herr denket an uns: Bach

Lord Christ above—Ich bitte dich, Herr Jesu Christ (Wo gehest du hin?): Bach

Lord Christ we now Thy praises sing—Christum wir sollen loben schon: Bach

Lord do I beseech Thee—Domine exaudi: Byrd

Lord enter not into wrath (judgement)—Herr, gehe nicht ins Gericht: Bach

Lord, for Thee my spirit longs—Nach dir, Herr, verlanget mich: Bach

Lord God almighty—Siderum rector: Byrd

Lord God, great master of creation—Herr Gott, Beherrscher aller Dinge: Bach

Lord God! our praise we give (render)—Herr Gott, dich loben wir (Orgelbüchlein): Bach

Lord, hear the voice of my complaint—Ich ruf zu dir, Herr Jesu Christ: Bach

Lord how long—Herr wie lange: Brahms

Lord, how wondrous—Gott, wie gross ist deine Güte: Bach

Lord in Thy love—Es woll' uns Gott genädig sein (Die Himmel erzählen die Ehre Gottes): Bach

The Lord is a sun and shield—Gott der Herr ist Sonn' und Schild: Bach

The Lord is king—Der Herr ist König: Schütz

The Lord is my shepherd—Der Herr ist mein getreuer Hirt: Bach

The Lord is my shepherd—Gott ist mein Hirt: Schubert

Lord Jesus Christ, be present now!—Herr Jesus Christ, dich zu uns wend (Orgelbüchlein): Bach

Lord Jesus Christ, light of my life—Herr Jesu Christ, mein's Lebens Licht: Bach

Lord Jesus Christ, true man and God—Herr Jesu Christ, wahr'r Mensch und Gott: Bach

Lord Jesus Christ, with us abide—Ach bleib bei uns, Herr Jesu Christ: Bach

Lord Jesus, pure source of all—Herr Jesu Christ, du höchtstes Gut: Bach

Lord, lovely has Thou made my dear—Dieu! qu'il la fait bon regarder:
Debussy
Lord, may Thy hand—Herr! Deine Hand (Jesu, nun sei gepreiset): Bach
Lord, my soul doth thirst for Thee—Nach dir, Herr, verlanget mich: Bach
Lord, my trust is in Thee—Herr, ich hoffe darauf: Schütz
Lord of mercy—Ave Maria: Bach-Gounod
Lord of the depths—Re del abisso (Un ballo in maschera): Verdi
Lord on Thy tender love relying—Gebet: Hiller
Lord, pour not Thy vengeance on me—Herr, nicht schicke deine
Rache: Bach
Lord, rebuke me not—Lass, Furstin: Bach
The Lord shall hear—Der Herr erhör: Schütz
The Lord shall preserve thee from evil—Das neue Regiment (Gott ist
mein König): Bach
Lord, Thou art my refuge—Skrýše má a pavéza (Biblické Písně): Dvořák
Lord, Thou has made my dear—Dieu, qu'il la fait bon regarder (Chansons
de Charles d'Orléans): Debussy
Lord turn Thy wrath away—Ne irascaris Domine: Byrd
Lord, we give to Thee—Herr Gott, dich loben wir! (Singet dem Herrn
ein neues Lied): Bach
Lord we leave Thy servant sleeping—Begräbnissgesang: Brahms
Lord, we look for Thy coming—Domine praestolamur: Byrd
Lord, what Thou wilst shall be my pleasure—Herr, was du willst soll mir
gefallen (Ich stehe mit einem Fuss im Grabe): Bach
The Lord will not suffer thy foot to be moved—Du wollest dem
Feinde (Gott ist mein König): Bach
The Lorelei—Loreley: Schumann
Lorelei—That fatal Loreley: Silcher
Loreley—The Lorelei: Schumann
Loreley—Waldesgespräch: Schumann
Lose not the hours—Il vostro maggio (Rinaldo): Handel
Das Lösegold—The price: Reichardt
Loss—Verlust: Cornelius
The lost battalion—Der verlorene Haufen: Schoenberg
The lost chicken—Die Henne: Brahms
The lost daughter—Die verlorene Tochter: Loewe
Lost happiness—Nun hast du mir (Frauenliebe und -leben): Schumann
Lost illusions—Illusions perdues: Blumenthal
The lost lamb—Die Mutter sucht ihr liebes Kind (Die Bürgschaft): Schubert
Lost love—A suoi piedi padre esangue (Tamerlano): Handel
Lost love—Das ist ein Flöten und Geigen (Dichterliebe): Schumann
The lost one—La traviata: Verdi
The lost path—Le sentier perdu: Massenet
Lost to the world—Ich bin der Welt abhanden gekommen: Mahler

Lost youth—Verlorene Jugend: Brahms
Die Lotosblume/Die stille Wasserrose—Lotus flower/The quiet waterlily:
   R Franz
Die Lotosblume (Myrthen)—The lotus flower: Schumann
Die Lotosblume ängstigt sich—The lotus flower repines: R Franz
Die Lotosblumen—Lotus flowers: Patáky
Lotus flower—Die Lotosblume: R Franz
Lotus flowers—Die Lotosblumen: Patáky
The lotus flower—Die Lotosblume (Myrthen): Schumann
The lotus flower repines—Die Lotosblume ängstigt sich: R Franz
The loud complaint—Die laute Klage: Beethoven
The loud lament—Die laute Klage: Beethoven
Love—Liebe: Cornelius
Love—L'amour: Godard
Love—Elsk (Haugtussa): Grieg
Love—Kjaerlighed: Grieg
Love—Lubov: G Karnovitch
Love—Es muss ein Wunderbares sein: Liszt
Love—Du!: Meyer-Helmund
Love—Die Liebe: Meyer-Helmund
Love—Von der Liebe: Reger
Love—Láska: Smetana
Love adrift—Liebe im Schnee: Benatzky
Love and music—Vissi d'arte, vissi d'amore: Puccini
Love and sorrow—Wer lieben will, muss leiden: R Strauss
Love and spring—Liebe und Frühling: Brahms
Love and spring—Amour et printemps: Waldteufel
Love and the lilac flower—Meine Liebe ist grün (Junge Lieder): Brahms
Love and the stars—Es rauschet das Wasser: Brahms
Love and youth—Jugend, Rausch und Liebe: Cornelius
Love betrayed—Verratene Liebe: Schumann
Love betrayed for riches—Gold überwiegt die Liebe: Brahms
Love came forth from far-off places—Liebe kam aus fernen Landen: Brahms
Love came wandering—Liebe kam aus fernen Landen: Brahms
Love eternal—Von ewiger Liebe: Brahms
Love everlasting—L'amour, toujours, l'amour: Friml
Love, fare thee well—Abschiedslied: Brahms
Love finds out the way—Keine Sorg' um den Weg: Raff
Love fly on rosy pinions—D'amor sull'ali rosee (Il trovatore): Verdi
Love for the first time—La verginella come la rosa: Bertoni
Love for three oranges—Lyubov k trem apelsinam: Prokofiev
Love from distant lands—Liebe kam aus fernen Landen: Brahms
Love gifts—Liebesgeschenke: R Strauss

Love guides with gentle steps—Die Liebe zieht mit sanften Schritten (Schwingt freudig euch empor): Bach

Love has falsely spoken—Die Liebe hat gelogen: Schubert

Love has promised falsely—Die Liebe hat gelogen!: R Franz

Love hath not departed—Phänomen: Brahms

Love, I give myself to thee—Liebe, dir ergeb ich mich (Liebe): Cornelius

Love, if true, must last for ever—Treue Liebe dauert lange: Brahms

Love in a cottage—Hytten: Grieg

Love in April—Im Frühling: Schubert

Love in May—Villanelle (Les nuits d'été): Berlioz

Love in spring—Frühlingsliebe: R Franz

Love in spring—Au printemps: Gounod

Love in starlight—Im Freien: Schubert

Love is for ever—Von ewiger Liebe: Brahms

Love itself forbids—Amor ti vieta (Fedora): Giordano

Love leads to battle—Pupille nere: G B Bononcini

Love likes courting—Colla bocca e non cole nore (La finta semplice): Mozart

Love long tried hath long endured—Treue Liebe dauert lange: Brahms

The love-lorn lassie—Die fernen, fernen Berge/Mädchenlied: Reger

Love me truly—Aime moi berger: Lefèvre

The love of Danae—Die Liebe der Danae: R Strauss

The love of three kings—L'amore dei tre re: Montemezzi

Love song—Minnelied: Brahms

Love song—Wie der Quelle so lieblich/Minnelied: Mendelssohn

Love songs—Rimes tendres: Aubert

Love songs—Liebeslieder Walzer: Brahms

Love songs—Pisně milostné: Dvořák

Love songs—Minnespiel: Schumann

The love test—Liebesprobe: Cornelius

Love that keeps its council—Verschwiegene Liebe: Wolf

Love that's true—Si tra i ceppi (Berenice): Handel

Love the magician—El amor brujo: Falla

Love the vagrant—Habanera (Carmen): Bizet

Love triumphant—Von ewiger Liebe: Brahms

Love, trust and hoping—Glaube, Hoffnung und Liebe: Schubert

Love voices—Liebespredigt: Kjerulf

Love was false—Die Liebe hat gelogen: Schubert

Love will find out a way—Weg der Liebe: Brahms

Love will waken—A te o cara: Bellini

Love without a home—Liebe ohne Heimat: Cornelius

Loved and lost—Ej, mam já kŏna faku: Dvořák

Loved one, Euridice—Sposa Euridice (Orfeo ed Euridice): Gluck

Love-letters—Unglückliche Liebe: Mozart
Love-longings—Und hab' so grosse: Reger
Love-lorn maiden's song—Lied eines Mädchens: Reger
Love castle of my grieving—Schöne Wiege: Schumann
Lovely castle of my sorrow—Schöne Wiege: Schumann
A lovely evening in summer 'twas—Jeg reiste en deilig Sommerkraeld:
   Grieg
Lovely eyes—Les yeux: Aubert
Lovely eyes with loving power—Schöner Augen, schöne Strahlen: Brahms
A lovely foreign land—Schöne Fremde: Schumann
Lovely kind, and kindly loving—Bella vittoria: G M Bononcini
A lovely land far away—Schöne Fremde: Schumann
Lovely maiden—E pur io: Amadori
Lovely meadows—Spiagge amato (Paride ed Elena): Gluck
The lovely waterlily—Die schankle Wasserlilie: R Franz
Lovely woodland—Care selve (Atalanta): Handel
The lover—Der Liebende: Beethoven
The lover—L'amoureux (Petites légendes): Milhaud
The lover—Rakastava: Sibelius
The lover in spring—Frühlingssehnsucht: Schubert
Lovers divided—Amoureux séparés: Roussel
Lovers' ode—Liebesode: Berg
The lover's pledge—Heimliche Aufforderung: R Strauss
A love's song—Lied eines Verliebten: Wolf
The lover's wine—Der Wein der Liebenden (Der Wein): Berg
The lover's wish—Der Wunsch des Liebhabers: Schoenberg
Love's affright—Furcht der Geliebten: Schubert
Love's answer—Geheimes (Schwanengesang): Schubert
Love's awakening—Erwachen: Blumenthal
Love's awakening—Wenn Liebe erwacht: Künneke
Love's burning passion—Quand je, vous ayme ardentement: Arcadelt
Love's dream—Liebestraum: Liszt
Love's enchantment—Liebeszauber: Schulz
Love's faith—Liebestreu: Brahms
Love's fever—Liebesglut: Brahms
Love's flame—Giammai provai (La donna vana): Piccinni
Love's fond fever—Quel d'amore è un certo male (Amalasunta): Chelleri
Love's fullness—Fülle der Liebe: Schubert
Love's garden—Si j'étais jardinier: Chaminade
Love's greeting—Salitana: Favra
Love's healing—Die Heilung: Himmel
Love's heaven—Hohe Liebe: Liszt
Love's intoxication—Liebestrunken: Patáky
Love's last words spoken—Liebeslauschen: Schubert

Love's listening—Liebeslauchen: Schubert
Love's marvel—Es muss ein Wunderbares sein: Liszt
Love's message—Il bacio: Arditi
Love's messanger—Liebesbotschaft (Schwanengesang): Schubert
Love's morn and eve—Familien—Gemalde: Schumann
Love's peace—Du bist die Ruh': Schubert
Love's pleading—Liebeshymnus: R Strauss
Love's presence—Nähe des Geliebten: Schubert
Love's prohibition—Das Liebesverbot: Wagner
Love's raptured song—Plaisir d'amour: Martini
Love's rest— Liebesgram: Schumann
Love's richest dower—Ombra mai fù (Serse): Handel
Love's sanctuary—Stille Sicherheit: R Franz
Love's secret—Ich trag: Reger
Love's spring—Liebesfrühling: Franz
Love's tears—Aus meinen Tränen (Dichterliebe): Schumann
Love's wavering joy—Plaisir d'amour: Martini
Love's way—Weg der Liebe: Brahms
Love's whisper—Ich will meine Seele tauchen (Dichterliebe):
    Schumann
The lovesick hunter—Der verliebte Jäger: Reger
The lovesick maiden—Das liebende Mädchen: F X Mozart
Love-song—Minnelied: Reger
Lovesong—Liebeslied: Schumann
Love-song waltzes—Liebeslieder Walzer: Brahms
Lov'st thou but beauty—Liebst du um Schönheit: Mahler
Love-thoughts—Volksliedchen: Schumann
Die Löwenbraut—The lion's betrothed/The lion's bride: Schumann
Lower thy head—Saenk kun dit hoved: Nielsen
The lowland—Tiefland: Albert
Lubov—Love: G Karnovitch
La luce dell' Asia—The light of Asia: De Lara
Luci care (Admeto)—Heavenly star-eyes: Handel
Le luci del mio bene (Teseo)—The eyes of my beloved: Handel
Lucia di Lammermoor—The bride of Lammermoor: Donizetti
Luck—La chance (Petites légendes): Milhaud
The luckless year—Das böse Jahr: Henschel
Lukaspassion—St Luke Passion: Bach
Lullaby—Bölcsödal (Dedinské Scény): Bartók
Lullaby—Wiegenlied: Blech
Lullaby—Wiegenlied: Brahms
Lullaby—Wiegenlied: Flies (attrib Mozart)
Lullaby—Pai, pai, paitaressu: Merikanto

Lullaby—Schlummerlied (Albumblätter): Schumann
Lullaby—Wiegenlied: R Strauss
Lullaby of the brook—Des Baches und der Bach (Die schöne Müllerin): Schubert
Lulu's song—Wenn sich die Menschen (Lulu): Berg
Lumen ad revelationem—Hail! O light immortal: Byrd
La lune blanche (La bonne chanson)—The white moon: Fauré
La lune blanche—A moonlight pallid: Stravinsky
Lune de cuivre—Moon copper-coloured: Rhené-Baton
Lungi da te, ben mio—Exiled for thee: Mercadante
Lungo dal caro bene (Giulio Sabino)—Parted/Far from my dear one/Far from my love: Sarti
Luoghi sereni e cari—Land ever calm and peaceful: Donaudy
Lusinghe più care (Alessandro)—With loving caresses/Allurements the dearest: Handel
Lust der Sturmnacht—Joy in a stormy night: Schumann
Der lustige Krieg—The merry war: J Strauss II
Die lustige Witwe—The merry widow: Lehár
Die lustigen Weiber von Windsor—The merry wives of Windsor: Nicolai
Lustspielouverture—Comedy overture: Busoni
Lustwandelnd schritt ein Mädchen/Das Mädchen und der Schmetterling—In gay mood strolled a maiden: d'Albert
The lute-player—An die Laute: Schubert
Luther's cradle hymn—Erstanden ist der heilige Christ: Bach
Lykken mellem to Mennesker—Joy that dwells in two hearts that love: Alnaes
Lyod i stal'—Ice and steel: Deshevov
Lyodovoye poboishche (Aleksandr Nevsky)—Battle on the ice: Prokofiev
Lyrical prose—Proses lyriques: Debussy
Lys Nat—Summer night: Grieg
Lyubov k trem apelsinam—Love for three oranges: Prokofiev

M

Ma, che insolita (La resurrezione)—Ha, what splendour: Handel

Ma la sola ohime! (Beatrice di Tenda)—Ah, my passion by him ungrateful:
Bellini

Ma mère l'oye—Mother goose: Ravel

Ma mie—Fair maiden: A L(ehmann)

Ma per me lasso—Ah weary am I: Marenzio

Má písen zas (Cigánské melodie)—I chant my lay: Dvořák

Ma poupée chérie—My dolly dear: Séverac

Ma tovu—How fair are Thy tents: Tansman

Má vlast—My country: Smetana

Mach mich zum Wächter deiner Weiten—Make me the watcher of thy
distances: Schoenberg

Mache dich, mein Geist bereit—Ready be, my soul, alway: Bach

Das macht das dunkelgrüne Laub—'Tis this that gives the silv'ry shade:
R Franz

Die Macht des Gesanges—The power of song: Bruch

Macht hoch die Tür—Raise high the door: Bauernfeind

Mack the knife—Moritat von Mackie Messer (Die Dreigroschenoper): Weill

The mad hatter—Le chapelier: Satie

Mad! mad!—Wahn! wahn! (Die Meistersinger von Nürnberg): Wagner

Madame Angot's daughter—La fille de Madame Angot: Lecoq

Madamina! Il catalogo (Don Giovanni)—Little lady: Mozart

Das Mädchen—The maiden/Stood a maiden: Brahms

Mädchen brav und treu (Martha)—Bright and buxom lasses: Flotow

Mädchen mit dem roten Mündchen—With thy rosy lips, my maiden/
Maiden with the lips like roses: R Franz

Mädchen mit dem roten Mündchen—Maiden, with those lips: Wolf

Das Mädchen spricht—The maiden speaks/Swallow from over the seas:
Brahms

Das Mädchen und die Hasel—Maiden and the hazel: Brahms

Das Mädchen und der Schmetterling/Lustwandelnd schritt ein Mädchen—
In gay mood strolled a maiden: d'Albert

Mädchenfluch—Maiden's curse: Brahms

Mädchenlied/Am jüngsten Tag ich aufersteh—Maiden song/At the last day:
Brahms

Mädchenlied/Auf die Nacht in den Spinnstubn—Song of a maid/At night
at their spinning: Brahms

Mädchenlied—A new-blown rose: Dieren

Mädchenlied—Mother darling: Meyer-Helmund

Mädchenlied—To the evening star: Raff

Mädchenlied/Die fernen, fernen Berge—The love-lorn lassie: Reger

Mädchenlied—Maiden's song: Schoenberg

Mädchen-Schwermut—A girl's melancholy: Schumann

Des Mädchens Klage—The maiden's lament: Mendelssohn
Mädchens Klage—The voice of the tempest: Schubert-Heller
Mädchentotenlieder—Dirges for girls: Nilsson
Made by Villon at his mother's request—Ballade que Villon feit à la reques
de sa mère: Debussy
Madonna's image—Das Marienbild: Schubert
La madre foll—The bereaved mother: Malipiero
La madrecita—The little mother: J Berger
Madrigali guerrieri ed amorosi—Madrigals of war and peace: Monteverdi
Madrigals of war and peace—Madrigali guerrieri ed amorosi: Monteverdi
Magdalena (Marienlieder)—Mary Magdalene: Brahms
Das Mägdlein und der Spatz—The maiden and the sparrow: Reger
Magic—Sortilège (Petites légendes): Milhaud
The magic chase—A já ti uplynu (Moravské Dvojzpěvy): Dvořák
The magic chime—Il carillon magico: Pick-Mangiagalli
The magic circle—El círculo mágico (El amor brujo): Falla
Magic fire music—Feuerzauber (Die Walküre): Wagner
The magic flute—Die Zauberflöte: Mozart
The magic of thy voice—Das Zauberlied: Meyer-Helmund
The magic potion—Le vin herbé: Martin
The magic touch—Frieden: Blumenthal
Magical midnights—Magické pulnoci: Vycpalek
Magické pulnoci—Magical midnights: Vycpalek
Le magistrat suisse—The Swiss magistrate: Françaix
The magistrate—Der Corregidor: Wolf
Magnificum Domine—The majesty of His name: Byrd
Magnum nomen Domini—Great is our Lord Jesus name: Praetorius
The magpies—Bavard et bavarde: Offenbach
Magyar képek—Hungarian sketches: Bartók
Magyar love-song—Magyarisch: Brahms
Magyar népclolok—Hungarian folk-song: Bartók
Magyarisch—Magyar love-song: Brahms
Magyarország határánál—On Hungary's frontier: K Ábrányi
Mai, lieber Mai (Album für die Jugend)—May, charming May/May, dearest
May/May, lovely May/Welcome to May: Schumann
Mai, Mai, Mai (Siechentrost)—May, May, May: Bruch
Der Mai tritt ein mit Freuden—Now May has come with gladness:
Schoenberg
The maid as mistress—La serva padrona: Pergolesi
The maid forlorn—Liebesklage des Mädchens: Brahms
The maid imprisoned—Zajata (Moravské Dvojzpěvy): Dvořák
The maid mistress—La serva padrona: Pergolesi
The maid of Orleans—Die Jungfrau von Orleans: Rezniček
The maid of the inn—Der Wirtin Töchterlein: Loewe
The maid of the mill—Die Müllerin: Grieg

The maid of the mill—La molinara: Paisiello
The maiden—Das Mädchen: Brahms
Maiden and nightingale—Sie wissen's nicht: R Strauss
Maiden and the hazel—Das Mädchen und die Hasel: Brahms
The maiden and the nightingale—Quejas ó la maja y el ruiseñor:
    Granados
The maiden and the sparrow—Das Mägdlein und der Spatz: Reger
The maiden in her garden—A kis léany kertjébe: Erkel
A maiden rose—Vom verwunderung Knaben: Brahms
Maiden song—Mädchenlied: Brahms
The maiden speaks—Das Mädchen spricht: Brahms
Maiden thoughts—Es weiss und räth es doch keiner: Mendelssohn
Maiden with the golden hair—Fille à la blonde chevelure: Godard
Maiden with the lips like roses—Mädchen mit dem roten Mündchen:
    R Franz
Maiden with those lips—Mädchen mit dem roten Mündchen: Wolf
A maiden yonder sings—Im Feld ein Mädchen singt: Sibelius
Maiden-beauty—Frauenschöne: Spervogel
Maiden's curse—Mädchenfluch: Brahms
The maiden's lament—Liebesklage des Mädchens: Brahms
Maiden's lament—Ach není tu: Dvořák
The maiden's lament—Des Mädchens Klage: Mendelssohn
A maiden's longing—Lied eines Mädchens: J Marx
A maiden's portraiture—Schilderung eines Mädchens: Beethoven
Maiden's song—Mädchenlied: Schoenberg
A maiden's wish—Życzenie: Chopin
Maids may boast—Si les filles d'Arles: Gounod
The maids of Cadiz—Les filles de Cadix: Delibes
Maienkätzchen—Pussy willows: Brahms
Die Maienkönigin—The May queen: Fuchs (attrib Gluck)
Maienlied—A song of May: Mendelssohn
Maiennacht—A night in May: Reger
Maiglockchen und die Blumelein—May-bells and flowers: Mendelssohn
Mailied—A song of May/Maysong: Beethoven
Mailied—May song: R Franz
Mailied—May song: Medtner
Mailied—May song: Mendelssohn
Mailied—May song: Schubert
Mailied—May-song: Schumann
Die Mainacht—The May night/Night in May/That night in May: Brahms
Mairegen—May rain: Blech
Maj—May: Sibelius
Maja and the nightingale—La maja y el ruiseñor (Goyescas): Granados
La maja y el ruiseñor (Goyescas)—Maja and the nightingale: Granados

The majesty of His name—Magnificum Domine: Byrd
Make love with a guitar—Cantar sin ilusion: Grever
Make me, O Lord God, pure in heart—Schaffe in mir Gott ein rein Herz:
  Brahms
Make me the watcher of thy distances—Mach mich zum Wächter deiner
  Weiten: Schoenberg
Make yee a joyfull sounding noyse—Vous tous qui la terre: Le Jeune
The Makropulos affair—Věc Makropulos: Janáček
Maktah—The white seal: Delage
Le mal du pays (Années de pèlerinage)—Nostalgia: Liszt
La mal mariée—The angry wife: P Cannon
Maledictus eris inter omnia—The expulsion of Adam and Eve from Paradis:
  Tomasi
Les malheurs d'Orphée—The misfortunes of Orpheus/The griefs of
  Orpheus: Milhaud
M'allontano sdegnose pupille (Atalanta)—Veil your lightnings: Handel
M'ama—non m'ama—He loves me—loves me not: Mascagni
Les mamelles de Tirésias—The breasts of Tirésias: Poulenc
La mamma è come il pane caldo—My mother's like bread that's new
  baked: Respighi
Man, be from God reborn—Mensch, werd aus Gott geborn: Wellesz
Man halte nur ein wenig stille (Wer nur den lieben Gott lässt walten)—
  Let us but rest a while in quiet/Only be still: Bach
Man lebt nur einmal—Man lives but once: J Strauss II
A man like you—Mein Herr Marquis (Die Fledermaus): J Strauss II
Man lives but once—Man lebt nur einmal: J Strauss II
A man of his word—Der Mann von Word: Beethoven
Man singet mit freuden—Let songs of rejoicing be raised/The sound of
  rejoicing is heard: Bach
Man weiss oft—We know then often times: Hindemith
The man who thought he was Socrates—Socrate immaginario: Paisiello
The man with three wives—Der Mann mit den drei Frauen: Lehár
Mañana de primavera—On a fair morn in spring: P Morales
Mañanica era (Canciones amatorias)—The goddess in the garden: Granados
Manella mia—Dear little hand: Giannini
The manly heart—Bei Männern (Die Zauberflöte): Mozart
Der Mann—The old man: Brahms
Der Mann mit den drei Frauen—The man with three wives: Lehár
Der Mann von Wort—My word's my bond/A man of his word: Beethoven
Männer suchen stets zu Naschen/Warnung—Gentle maid in life's sweet
  morning/Warning: Mozart
Le manoir de Rosamonde—The manor of Rosamund/The dwelling-place
  of Rosamonde: Duparc
The manor of Rosamund—Le manoir de Rosamonde: Duparc

Mans Adam war ein Erdenkloss—Man's creation: R Strauss
Man's creation—Mans Adam war ein Erdenkloss: R Strauss
Man's heart's rebellious—Es ist ein Trotzig und verzagt Ding: Bach
Man's limitations—Grenzen der Menschheit: Schubert
Mansken—Moonlight: Palmgren
Manuscripte—Autograph: E Strauss
Many are the insults—Contumelias et terrores: Byrd
A March night—Märznacht: Brahms
March of the dwarfs—Troldtog: Grieg
March of the Finnish infantry—Jääkärimarssi: Sibelius
March of the joyful lads—Marsh vesyolykh rebyal: Dunayevski
March of the little lead soldiers—Marche des petits soldats de plomb:
    Pierné
March of the territorials—Marschiven: Brahms
Le marchand de sable qui passe—The sandman: Roussel
Marche des petits soldats de plomb—March of the little lead soldiers:
    Pierné
Le marche du sacré (march: Le prophète)—Coronation march: Meyerbeer
Marche funèbre d'une marionnette—Funeral march of a marionette:
    Gounod
Märchenwunder (Brautlieder)—The fairly tale: Cornelius
Marching—Marschiren: Brahms
Margaret at the spinning-wheel—Gretchen am Spinnrade: Schubert
Margaret's cradle song—Margretes Vuggesang: Grieg
Margaret's prayer—Gretchens Bitte: Schubert
Margretes Vuggesang—Margaret's cradle song: Grieg
Un mari à la porte—A husband on the mat: Offenbach
Maria durch ein Dornwald ging—Once through a woodland Mary walked:
    Bauernfeind
Maria Egiziaca—Mary in Egypt: Respighi
Maria ging aus wandern—Saint Mary once did wander: Brahms
Maria Gnadenmutter—Mother of mercies: Sinding
Maria Wiegenlied—The Virgin's slumber-song: Reger
Mariage des roses—The wooing of the rose: Franck
Maria's Kirchgang (Marienlieder)—Mary and the boatman/Mary's way to
    church: Brahms
Maria's Lob (Marienlieder)—In praise of Mary/Praise of the Virgin: Brahms
Maria's Wallfahrt (Marienlieder)—Mary's wandering/Mary's quest: Brahms
Das Marienbild—Madonna's image: Schubert
Das Marienleben—The life of the Virgin Mary: Hindemith
Marienlied—Song of St Mary/Ode to the Virgin Mary: J Marx
Marienwürmchen (Volkskinderlieder)—The ladybird: Brahms
Marienwürmchen—Ladybird/Come, pretty little ladybird: Schumann
Mariettas Lied zur Laute (Die tote Stadt)—Marietta's song: Korngold

Marietta's song—Mariettas Lied zur Laute (Die tote Stadt): Korngold
Marionettes—Fantoches (Fêtes galantes): Debussy
Mark, O my heart, evermore only this—Merkes, mein Herz, beständig nur
   dies (Auf, mein Herze, des herren Tag): Bach
Mark yonder tomb—In questa tomba oscura: Beethoven
Market place at Ispahan—Tarvet i Ispahan (Aladdin): Nielsen
Der Markt beginnt (Martha)—The fair begins: Flotow
The marriage—Sposalizio (Années de pèlerinage): Liszt
The marriage—Zhenitba: Mussorgsky
The marriage of Figaro—Le nozze di Figaro: Mozart
Marschiren—Marching/On the march/March of the territorials: Brahms
Marsh vesyolykh rebyat—March of the joyful lads: Dunayevski
Le marteau sans maître—The hammer without a master: Boulez
Martin, the hare—Matten Has: Blech
Le martin-pecheur (Histoires naturelles)—The kingfisher: Ravel
Marvel, O men, at this great mystery—Bewundert, O Menschen, dies grosse
   Geheimnis (Nun komm, der Heiden Heiland): Bach
Marvel, O men, at this great mystery—Streite, siege, starker Held (Nun
   komm, der Heiden Heiland): Bach
Mary and the boatmen—Maria's Kirchgang (Marienlieder): Brahms
Mary at the cradle—La Vièrge a la crèche: Franck
Mary in Egypt—Maria Egiziaca: Respighi
Mary Magdalene—Magdalena (Marienlieder): Brahms
Mary Stuart's lament—Complainte de la reine Marie Stuart: Martini
Mary's quest—Maria's Wallfahrt (Marienlieder): Brahms
Mary's wandering—Maria's Wallfahrt (Marienlieder): Brahms
Mary's way to church—Maria's Kirchgang (Marienlieder): Brahms
Märznacht—A March night: Brahms
Märzveilchen—Sweet violets: Schumann
A masked ball—Un ballo in maschera: Verdi
I masnadieri—The brigands: Verdi
Masonic funeral music—Mauerische Trauermusik: Mozart
Le masque de la mort rouge—The masque of the red death: Caplet
Le masque de la mort rouge—The masque of the red death: Tcherepnin
The masque of the red death—Le masque de la mort rouge: Caplet
The masque of the red death—Der rote Tod: F Schreker
The masque of the red death—Le masque de la mort rouge: Tcherepnin
Mass in the time of war—Missa in tempore belli: Haydn
A master and his man—Es reit ein Herr und auch sein Knecht: Brahms
Master iz Klamsi—The master of Clamecy/Colas Breugnon: Kabalevsky
The master of Clamecy—Master iz Klamsi: Kabalevsky
Master Peter's puppet show—El retablo de Maese Pedro: Falla
The mastersingers of Nuremburg—Die Meistersinger von Nürnberg: Wagner
Mat—Mother: Davidenko

Mat—The mother: Zhelobinsky
Mathis der Maler—Mathis the painter: Hindemith
Mathis the painter—Mathis der Maler: Hindemith
Le matin—At morning: Berlioz
Matka—The mother: Hába
Matona lovely maiden—Matona mia cara: Lassus
Matona mia cara—Matona lovely maiden: Lassus
Il matrimonio segreto—The secret marriage: Cimarosa
Matrosernes Opsang—Sailor's song: Grieg
Matten Has—Martin, the hare: Blech
Matthäuspassion—St Matthew passion: Bach
Mattinata—'Tis the day: Leoncavallo
Mattino di luce—O morning of glory: Respighi
Il matrimonio segreto—The clandestine marriage: Cimarosa
Mauerische Trauermusik—Masonic funeral music: Mozart
Mauldicte soit la mondaine richesse—Despised be all worldly wealth:
    Sermisy
Mausfallen-Sprüchlein—Mousetrap magic: Wolf
May—Maj: Sibelius
May, charming May—Mai, lieber Mai (Album für die Jugend): Schumann
May, dearest May—Mai, lieber Mai (Album für die Jugend): Schumann
May gentle sleep attend thee—Schlafe wohl (Martha): Flotow
May God bless you—Pan Buh vam zaplat!: Janáček
May I an answer make—Darf ich die Antwort sagen (Tristan und Isolde):
    Wagner
May laurels crown thy brow—Ritorna vincitor (Aida): Verdi
May love song—Minnelied im Mai: Mendelssohn
May, lovely May—Mai, lieber Mai (Album für die Jugend): Schumann
May, May, May—Mai, Mai, Mai (Siechentrost): Bruch
The May night—Die Mainacht: Brahms
The May queen—Die Maienkönigin: Fuchs (attrib Gluck)
May rain—Mairegen: Blech
May song—Mailied: R Franz
May song—Mailied: Medtner
May song—Mailied: Schubert
May song—Im wunderschönen Monat Mai (Dichterliebe): Schumann
May we complete this year—Lass uns, o höchster Gott (Jesu, nun sei
    gepreiset): Bach
May-bells and flowers—Maiglockchen und die Blumelein: Mendelssohn
Maysong—Mailied: Beethoven
May-song—Mailied: Mendelssohn
May-song—Mailied: Schumann
The May-time—Landliches Lied: Schumann
Me voila seule enfin! (La reine de Saba)—I am alone at last: Gounod

The mead is bare—Lekaszálták már: Erkel
Meadow rose—Heidenröslein: Schubert
The meadows at Wildbach—Am Wildbach die Waiden: Brahms
Means of expression—Ausdruckweisse: Schoenberg
Means that you're grand—Bei mir bist du schön: Secunda
Measures of time—Zeitmasse: Stockhausen
Meciendo—Rock-a-by: Guastavino
Med en Vandlilje—With a water-lily: Grieg
Med en primula veris—The first primrose/With a primrose: Grieg
Le médecin malgré lui—The mock doctor: Gounod
A media noche (El amor brujo)—Midnight: Falla
Meditation—Recueillement: Debussy
Madvěd—The bear: Smetana
Medvetáne (Tiz könnyu zongoradarab)—Bear dance: Bartók
Das Meer—By the sea: Blumenthal
Das Meer erstrahlt—The sea: R Franz
Die Meere—The two deeps/The sea/Slumbering deep/Evening winds are
   sleeping: Brahms
Das Meere hat seine Perlen/Auf dem Meere—The sea hath pearls/On the
   ocean: R Franz
Meeres stille—Hush of the sea/Sea calm/Calm at sea: Schubert
Meeresstille—Calm at sea: R Franz
Meeresstille und glückliche Fahrt—A calm sea and a prosperous voyage:
   Beethoven
Meerfahrt—At sea: Brahms
Meerfahrt—Drifting of the sea: R Franz
Meerfahrt—Sea voyage: Hauptman
Meerfey—The mermaid: Schumann
Die Meerfee—The sea-fairy: Schumann
Meeting—Rencontre (Poème d'un jour): Fauré
The meeting—Mio caro bene (Rodelinda): Handel
A meeting—Begegnung: Wolf
Meeting and parting—Kommen und Scheiden: Schumann
Meghalok, meghalok—Woe is me: Kodály
Mei Bua—My lad: Reger
Le meilleur moment—The moment eternal: Blumenthal
Mein (Die schöne Müllerin)—Mine: Schubert
Mein Alles—My all: Blumenthal
Mein altes Ross—My old steed: Schumann
Mein Auge—My vision: R Strauss
Mein Freund—My friend: Blumenthal
Mein Garten—My garden: Schumann
Mein glaubiges Herze (Also hat Gott die Welt geliebt)—My heart that
   believest/My pious heart be full of glee/My heart ever faithful/
   O trusting heart: Bach

196

Mein G'müt ist mir verwirret—My lusty cheer is waning: Hassler
Mein Gott, öffne mir die Pforten (Liebster Jesu, mein verlangen)—Open
    wide the gates of mercy: Bach
Mein Gott, verwirf mich nicht (Herr, gehe nicht in's Gericht)—My God!
    forsake me not: Bach
Mein Gott, wie lang', ach lange?—My God, how long, how long?: Bach
Mein guter Engel—The angel of my life: Blumenthal
Mein Herr Marquis (Die Fledermaus)—Laughing song/O noble sir/My dear
    marquis/Like a lordly star/A man like you: J Strauss II
Mein Herr und Gott (Lohengrin)—O Lord of Lords: Wagner
Mein Herz—My heart: Reger
Mein Herz in steten Treuen—To her I shall be faithful: Schoenberg
Mein Herz ist mit gemenget—My heart is in confusion: Schoenberg
Mein Herz ist schwer—My soul is dark: Schumann
Mein Herz ist stumm—My heart so sad: R Strauss
Mein Herz ist wie die dunkle Nacht—My heart is as the darksome night/My
    heart is like a dreary night—Lassen
Mein Herz und meine Leyer—My heart and lute: Kjerulf
Mein Herze schwimmit im blut—My heart with grief doth swoon: Bach
Mein Jesu, der du mich—My Jesus, Thou who didst: Brahms
Mein Jesu! was für Seelenweh—O Saviour mine, what agony/My Jesu
    what affliction: Bach
Mein Jesu ist erstanden (Halt' im Gedächtniss Jesum Christ)—My Jesus is
    risen: Bach
Mein Lieb ich bin gebunden—I hardly know: Kjerulf
Mein Liebchen—My bride: Meyer-Helmund
Mein lieber Schwan (Lohengrin)—Beloved swan: Wagner
Mein Liebster ist ein Weber—The weaver: Hildach
Mein liebster Jesus ist verloren—My dearest Jesu, I have lost Thee: Bach
Mein Mädel hat einen Rosenmund—My girl has rosy lips/My maiden's lip/
    Rose-lipt maid: Brahms
Mein Odem ist schwach—My breath is corrupt: Reger
Mein Schatz ist auf der Wanderschaft—My sweetheart now so long ago:
    R Franz
Mein Schatz(e)lein—My little sweetheart/My sweetheart: Reger
Meine Schwester, liebe Braut—Dearest sister, lovely bride: M Franck
Mein Seelenschatz ist Gottes wort (Gleich wie der Regen und Schnee)—
    The word of God my treasure is/My soul's delight: Bach
Meine Liebe ist grün (Junge Lieder)—Love and the lilac flower/Like
    a blossoming lilac: Brahms
Meine Rose—My rose: Schumann
Meine Seele ist still—My soul waiteth on God: Reger
Meine Seele erhebt den Herren—My soul doth magnify the Lord/My soul
    exalts the Lord: Bach
197

Meine Seele rühmt und preist—Come, my spirit, come exalt: Bach
Meine Seufzer, meine Tränen—My sighs, my tears: Bach
Meine Wünsche/Ein deutsches Kreigslied—My wishes: Mozart
Meinem Hirten blieb' ich treu (Ich hab in Gottes Herz und Sinn)—On my
    shepherd I rely: Bach
Meinem Kinde—To my baby: R Strauss
Meinen Jesum lass' ich nicht—Never Jesus will I leave/My Jesus leave I
    not: Bach
Die Meistersinger von Nürnberg—The mastersingers of Nuremburg:
    Wagner
Melancholie—Melancholy: Schumann
Melancholy—Tungsind: Grieg
Melancholy—Lasst froh uns sein: Mozart
Melancholy—Melancholie: Schumann
La mélodie des baisers—Ev'ry kiss is a song: Massenet
Melodies of the heart—Hjertets Melodier: Grieg
Melodieux automne—A song of autumn: Ladmirault
Melodious strains—Wie Melodien zieht es mir: Brahms
Melody—Melodya: Chopin
Melody blues—L'amour au clair de lune: Borel-Clerc
Melodya—Melody: Chopin
Members of Christ, ah, consider—Christi Glieder, ach bedenket (Bereitet
    die Wege): Bach
Memento Domine—Call to remembrance, O Lord: Byrd
Memento homo—Consider, O man: Byrd
Memories—Das Blatt im Buch: Blumenthal
Memories—Ich hör' die Bächlein: Schumann
Memories of childhood—Ved Rudarne: Grieg
A memory—Tant que mes yeux: Berkeley
A memory—Anklänge: Brahms
A memory—Unvergessen: Reger
Men min fågel märks dock icke—But my bird is long in homing: Sibelius
La menace—The threat: Roussel
Mens jeg venter—Drifting: Grieg
Mensch, werd aus Gott geborn—Man be from God reborn: Wellesz
Menschen, glaubt doch dieser Gnade (Christ unser Herr zum Jordan kam)—
    In this grace believe O mortals: Bach
Mentre ti lascio, o figlia—Once in these arms I'll fold thee/As I leave you:
    Mozart
Menuet des follets (Faust)—Dance of the sprites/Minuet of the will-o'-the-
    wisps: Berlioz
La mer—The sea: Debussy
Mer hahn en neue Oberkeet—Peasant cantata/Village gossip: Bach
La mer est infinie (L'horizon chimérique)—The sea is infinite: Fauré

The merchant of Venice—Der Kaufmann von Vendig: Humperdinck
Mercy for me—Robert, toi que j'aime (Robert le diable): Meyerbeer
Merke, mein Herze, beständig nur dies (Auf, mein Herz, des herren Tag)—
   Mark, O my heart, evermore only this: Bach
The mermaid—Meerfey: Schumann
A mermaid's holiday—Na rusalchyn velykden': Leontovych
The mermaid's song—Die Seejungfer: Haydn
Merry as a marriage morn—Keinem hat es noch gerent: Brahms
The merry farmer—Fröhlicher Landmann (Album für die Jugend):
   Schumann
The merry peasant—Der fidele Bauer: Fall
The merry peasant—Fröhlicher Landmann (Album für die Jugend): Schumann
A merry soldier—Der Reiter: Brahms
Merry songs—Heitere Lieder: R Trunk
The merry time of Maying—Die Wollust in den Maien: Brahms
Merry vintage time—Weinlesezeit (Album für die Jugend): Schumann
The merry wanderer—Der fröhe Wandersmann: Schumann
Merry war—Küss-Walzer: J Strauss II
The merry war—Der lustige Krieg: J Strauss II
The merry widow—Die lustige Witwe: Lehár
The merry wife—La bien mariée: P Cannon
The merry wives of Windsor—Die lustigen Weiber von Windsor: Nicolai
Merry-go-round—Chevaux de bois (Ariettes oubliées): Debussy
Merry-go-round—Ringeltanz: Gade
Merrymaking—Mulató gajd: Kodály
Les merveilleuses—The lady dandies: Félix
The message—Priletel pták: Bartók
The message—Botschaft: Brahms
A message—Botschaft (Rheinische Lieder): Cornelius
The message—Die Sendung: Himmel
A message—Leise zieht: A Rubinstein
The message—Botschaft (Album Blätter): Schumann
The message of flowers—Der Blumenbrief: Schubert
The message of love—O légère hirondelle (Mireille): Gounod
A message of love—Liebesbotschaft: Schumann
Messages—Aufträge: Schumann
Messe de la Pentecôte—Whitsun mass: Messiaen
The messenger—Posél: Chopin
The messenger—Der Bote: R Franz
Messengers of spring—Frühlingsboten: Raff
Lo mestre—Where hast thou gone my master: Alió
Metronome canon—An Mäzel: Beethoven
Metsämiehen—Woodman's song: Sibelius
M'hai salvato (La Wally)—You that saved me: Catalani

Mi lagnero tacendò (Siroe)—My cruel fate lamenting: Handel
Mi restano le lagrime (Alcina)—My tears alone: Handel
Mi sfidate, guerriera—As I walked in green forest: Giovanelli
Mi tradi (Don Giovanni)—Thus betrayed: Mozart
Mia piccirella (Salvator Rosa)—Sweet pretty maiden: Gomes
Mich locket nicht/Verdankt sei es dem Glanz—Dear placid vale/I seek not
    glory: Mozart
Mich zieht es nach dem Dörfchen hin—There is a charm that bids me hie:
    Schumann
Mickey mouse—Topolini: Castelnuovo-Tedesco
Midnight—A media noche (El amor brujo): Falla
Midnight—Mitternacht: Manén
Midsommarvaka—Midsummer vigil: Alfvén
A midsummer night's dream—Ein Sommernachtstraum: Mendelssohn
Midsummer vigil—Midsommarvaka: Alfvén
Might I linger near thee—Star vicino: Rosa
The might of a glance—Die Gewalt des Blickes: Himmel
A mighty fortress is our God—Ein feste Burg ist unser Gott: Bach
Mighty Lord, and king all glorious—Grosser Herr und starker König
    (Weihnachtsoratorium): Bach
Mignon/Kennst du das Land—Knows't thou the land: Schumann
Mignon/So lasst mich scheinen [D 727]—O let me seem now/Illusion's
    magic spell: Schubert
Mignon/So lasst mich scheinen [S 877]—O, let me dream/So whilst I am
    not/So let me dream: Schubert
Mignons Lied/Kennst du das Land—Mignon's song/Song of Mignon/Thou
    know'st the land/Knowest thou the land: Liszt
Mignon's song—Kennst du das Land: Beethoven
Mignon's song—Mignons Lied: Liszt
Mignon's songs—Lieder der Mignon: Wolf
Mihi autem nimis—Blessed be Thy name: Tallis
The mild day is bright and long—Den milde dag er lys og land: Nielsen
Den milde dag er lys og land—The mild day is bright and long: Nielsen
The mill wheel—Das Mühlrad: Erk
The miller and mill stream—Der Müller und der Bach (Die schöne Müllerin)
    Schubert
The miller and the brook—Der Müller und der Bach (Die schöne Müllerin):
    Schubert
The miller's daughter—Die Müllerin: Brahms
The miller's flowers—Des Müllers Blumen (Die schöne Müllerin): Schubert
The miller's maid—Die Müllerin: Brahms
Millom Rosor—'Neath the roses: Grieg
The mill-stream's lullaby—Des Baches Wiegenlied (Die schöne Müllerin):
    Schubert

The millwheel—Kvarnhjulet: Sibelius
Milovany Hlas—The beloved voice: Weinberger
Min Jesus lad mit hjerte få—Oh Jesus, may my heart: Nielsen
Min pige er så lys som rav (Moderen)—My girl is as fair as amber: Nielsen
Min raslas raataa—Busy as a thrush: Sibelius
Min Tanke er et maegtigt Fjeld—My mind is like the mountain steep/My thoughts are like the mighty hills: Grieg
Mine—Mein (Die schöne Müllerin): Schubert
Mine art thou—Wie bist du, meine Königin: Brahms
Minnedienst—In love's service: Meyer-Helmund
Minnelied—Love song: Brahms
Minnelied/Leucht't heller als die Sonne—An old love song: Mendelssohn
Minnelied/Wie der Quell so lieblich—Love song: Mendelssohn
Minnelied—Love-song: Reger
Minnelied im Mai—May love song: Mendelssohn
Minnespiel—Love songs: Schumann
The minstrel—Der Spielman: Hildach
The minstrel—Der Musensohn: Schubert
The minstrel—Der Musikant: Wolf
The minstrel—Der Sänger: Wolf
Minstrel awaken—Sônner af Norge: Blom
The minstrel's song—Spillemaend: Grieg
Minstrel's treasure—Des Sängers Habe: Schubert
Minuet of the will-o-the-wisps—Menuet des follets (Faust): Berlioz
Il mio bel foco—My glowing heart/The flame of passion/My joyful ardour: Marcello
Mio caro bene (Rodelinda)—The meeting/Dear love, believe me: Handel
Mir fehlt das Beste—I wander alone: R Franz
Mir Glänzen die Augen—My eyes glow as brightly: Pfitzner
Mir ist, als Zögen—It seems as though: Cornelius
Mir ist die Ehre (Der Rosenkavalier)—I am much honoured: R Strauss
Mir ist ein schöns braun Maidelein—A bonny black-eyed maiden: Brahms
Mir ist's zu wohl ergangen—Too fair shone hope: Henschel
Mir tat die Helligkeit der Lampe weh (Chinesische Liebeslieder)—The pure light of the lamp: Liebermann
The miracle—Das Wunder: Humperdinck
The miraculous mandarin—A csodálatos mandarin: Bartók
Mirando la mia dea—Gazing upon my goodness: Dering
Miriam's song—Mirjams Siegesgesang: Schubert
Mirjams Siegesgesang—Miriam's song: Schubert
Mirror song—Scintille diamant: Offenbach
Misera dove son (Ezio)—Misery, where am I now: Handel
Miserere mei—Show Thy mercy on me/Look on me with mercy: Byrd
Miserere mihi Domine—O have mercy on me: Byrd

The miserly knight—Skupoy Ritsar: Rachmaninov
Misery, where am I now—Misera dove son (Ezio): Handel
The misfortunes of Orpheus—Les malheurs d'Orphée: Milhaud
Mishap—Unfall: Wolf
Misplaced affection—Verfelte Liebe: R Franz
Miss Decima—Miss Hellyett: Audran
Miss Hellyett—Miss Decima: Audran
Missa in angustiis—Nelson mass/Imperial mass/Coronation mass: Haydn
Missa in tempore belli—Mass in the time of war: Haydn
Missa St Cecelia—St Cecelia mass: Haydn
Missverstanden—Misunderstood: Blumenthal
Mr and Mrs Lizard—El lagarto (Canciones de niños): Revueltas
Mr Broucek's excursion to the moon—Výlety páně Broǔckovy: Janáček
Mists—Nebbie: Respighi
Misunderstood—Missverstanden: Blumenthal
Mit deinen blauen Augen—When thy blue eyes/Thy blue eyes/Day dreams/
    Thy deep blue eyes: Lassen
Mit deinen blauen Augen—When with thine eyes of azure: R Strauss
Mit dem grünen Lautenbande (Die schöne Müllerin)—Lines with the lute's
    green ribbon/With the green ribbon: Schubert
Mit einem gemalten Band—With a painted ribbon: Beethoven
Mit einem gemalten Band—With a painted ribbon: Schoeck
Mit Fried und Freud ich fahr dahin—In peace and joy I now depart/
    Simeon's song of praise/With peace and joy I journey hither: Bach
Mit Gewitter und Sturm (Der fliegende Holländer)—On the wings of the
    storm/Steerman's song: Wagner
Mit lust tät ich ausreiten—A hunter went a-riding: Brahms
Mit Madeln sich vertragen—To get along with girls: Beethoven
Mit Myrthen und Rosen—With myrtle and roses: Schumann
Mit Rosen bestreut—Covered with roses: Reger
Mit schwarzen Segeln—With dusky sails: R Franz
Mit schwarzen Segeln—With black sails: Wolf
Mit Verlangen (Geschwinde, geschwinde, ihr wirbelnden Winde)—With
    desiring: Bach
Mit vierzig Jahren—At forty: Brahms
Mittag—Noon: Reger
Mitternacht—Midnight: Manén
Mládí—Youth: Janáček
Möcht ich ein Kornet sein?—Would I like to be a cornet?: Henze
Möcht' im Walde—In the wood I'd go: Cornelius
Möcht' wissen, was sie schlagen—I wonder what thou'rt doing: R Franz
The mock doctor—Le médecin malgré lui: Gounod
Mocking of youth—Legénycsúfoló: Bartók
Moderen—The mother: Nielsen

Modersorg—A mother's sorrow/A mother's grief: Grieg
Modest heart—Bescheidene Liebe: Wolf
The modest little wish—Das bescheidene Wünschlein: Schoeck
The modest maid—Skromna (Moravské Dvojzpěvy): Dvořák
Mögst du, mein Kind (Der fliegende Holländer)—Wilt thou my child: Wagner
Mohnblumen—Poppies: R Strauss
Moja piésczotka—My sweetheart: Chopin
Molchanie—Silence: Miaskowsky
The Moldau—Vltava: Smetana
La molinara—The maid of the mill: Paisiello
Molnár Anna—Annie Miller: Kodály
The moment—Der Augenblick: Haydn
The moment eternal—Le meilleur moment: Blumenthal
Mon cadavre est doux comme un gant (Fiancailles pour rire)—My corpse is
   as limp as a glove: Poulenc
Mon cher troupeau—My tender flock: Anon
Mon coeur chante—My heart sings: Chaminade
Mon coeur se recommande à vous—Into your hands/My heart is offered still
   to you: Lassus
Mon coeur s'ouvre à ta voix (Samson et Dalila)—Softly awakes my heart:
   Saint-Saens
Mon rêve—Dreaming, dreaming: Waldteufel
Der Mönch von Pisa—The monk of Pisa: Loewe
Der Mond—The moon: Orff
Mond und Menschen—Moon and mankind: Schoenberg
Der Mondabend—Moonlight evening: Schubert
Mondes silber Rinnt—Divided love: Kjerulf
Mondnacht—Moonlight: Fielitz
Mondnacht—Moonlit night/Moonlight/(A) Summer's night: Schumann
Il mondo della lune—The world on (of) the moon: Haydn
The monk of Pisa—Der Mönch von Pisa: Loewe
Monster from hell—Empio per farti (Tamerlano): Handel
Montée aux Alpes—The ascent to the pastures: Liszt
The month of May—Im wunderschönen Monat Mai: Schumann
Moods—Dämmerempfindung: Cornelius
Moods and fancies—Stimmungsbilder: R Strauss
The moon—Tiranni miei pensieri (Tolomeo): Handel
The moon—Der Mond: Orff
Moon and mankind—Mond und Menschen: Schoenberg
Moon copper coloured—Lune de cuivre: Rhené-Baton
Moon fancies—Au caprice du vent: Pesse
The moonbeam—Le soir: Gounod
Moonlight—Au cimetière (Les nuits d'été): Berlioz
Moonlight—Claire de lune (Fêtes galantes): Debussy

Moonlight—Claire de lune: Fauré
Moonlight—Mondnacht: Fielitz
Moonlight—Mansken: Palmgren
Moonlight—Mondnacht: Schumann
Moonlight evening—Der Mondabend: Schubert
A moonlight idyll—Sensazione lunare: Sibella
A moonlight pallid—La lune blanche: Stravinsky
Moonlight's magic hour—Nuit d'Espagne: Massenet
Moonlit night—Mondnacht: Schumann
The moon's pale beams are shining—In allen meinen Taten: Bach
Moonstruck Pierrot—Pierrot lunaire: Schoenberg
Moravian duets—Moravské dvojzpěvy: Dvořák
Moravian girl—Děvče z Maravy: Martinů
Moravské dvojzpěvy—Moravian duets: Dvořák
Morceaux en forme de poire—Pieces in the shape of a pear: Satie
Mörder, Hoffnung der Frauen—Murderer, hope of women: Hindemith
More yarostno stonalo—The sea was moaning furiously: Davidenko
Morgen—Tomorrow: R Strauss
Morgen steh' ich auf und frage—When I rise each morn I wonder: Liszt
Morgenblätter—Morning journals/Morning papers: J Strauss II
Morgengang—A morning walk: Bocquet
Morgengebet—Morning prayer: Mendelssohn
Morgengesang—Morning song: Brahms
Morgengesang am Schöpfungsfeste—Morning song and creation feast: C P E B
Morgengrüss—The hour of dawn/Morning greeting: Mendelssohn
Morgengrüss (Die schöne Müllerin)—Morning greeting: Schubert
Morgenrot—The dawn: R Strauss
Morgensonne—Morning sunlight: Meyer-Helmund
Morgenstimmung—Morning mood: Wolf
Morgentågernes dans—Dance of the morning mists: Nielsen
Morgentau—Morning dew: Grieg
Morgentau—Morning dew: Wolf
Morgenwind—Morning wind: Cornelius
Morgonsong—Morning song: Sinding
Mori quasi il mio core—My heart it seemed was dying: Palestrina
Morir vogl'io—That I might die: Astorga
Moritat von Mackie Messer (Die Dreigroschenoper)—Mack the knife:
    Weill
Morning—Am Morgen (Brautlieder): Cornelius
Morning dew—Morgentau: Grieg
Morning dew—Morgentau: Wolf
Morning greeting—Morgengrüss: Mendelssohn
Morning greeting—Morgengrüss (Die schöne Müllerin): Schubert
Morning journals—Morgenblätter: J Strauss II

Morning mood—Morgenstimmung: Wolf
Morning papers—Morgenblätter: J Strauss II
Morning prayer—Morgengebet: Mendelssohn
Morning song—Morgengesang: Brahms
Morning song—Morgonsong: Sinding
Morning song and creation feast—Morgengesang am Schöpfungsfeste:
    C P E Bach
Morning sunlight—Morgensonne: Meyer-Helmund
A morning walk—Morgengang: Bocquet
Morning wind—Morgenwind: Cornelius
Morrai si (Rodelinda)—Thou shalt die: Handel
Mors et vita—Death and life: Gounod
La mort des amants—Death of the lovers: Debussy
La mort i la donzella—Death and the maiden: Gerhard
A mortal being am I—Mortal cosa son io: Monteverdi
Mortal cosa son io—A mortal being am I: Monteverdi
Mortify us by Thy grace—Ertödt uns durch dein Güte (Bereitet die Wege):
    Bach
Mosè in Egitto—Moses in Egypt: Rossini
Moses in Egypt—Mosè in Egitto: Rossini
Most loving Saviour—Salvator mundi: Tallis
Mot kveld—Eventide: A Backer-Grøndahl
Møte (Haugtussa)—The tryst: Grieg
Mother—Mat: Davidenko
The mother—Matka: Hába
The mother—Moderen: Nielsen
The mother—Mat: Zhelobinsky
The mother at the cradle—Die Mutter bei der Wiege: Blech
Mother darling—Mädchenlied: Meyer-Helmund
Mother goose—Ma mère l'oye: Ravel
Mother, I want something—Och Mod'r, ich well en Ding han: Brahms
Mother, mother do not grieve—Mutter, Mutter: Schumann
Mother, O hide me—Rend' il sereno al ciglio (Sosarme): Handel
Mother of mercies—Maria Gnadenmutter: Sinding
Mother, Oh sing me to rest!—Mutter, O sing' mich zur Ruh'!: R Franz
Mother says—Die Mutter spricht: Reger
The mother sings—Äiti laulaa (Ungdom): Palmgren
A mother's dallying—Muttertandelei: R Strauss
A mother's dream—Muttertraum: Schumann
Mother's grave—Der Totenkranz: Manén
A mother's grief—Modersorg: Grieg
A mother's sorrow—Modersorg: Grieg
Un moto di gioja—My heart in my bosom is bounding/A throbbing of glad-
    ness/Now flutters my true loving bosom: Mozart

Mount of olives—Christus am Oelberge: Beethoven
Mountain brook—Ved Gjaetle-bekken (Haugtussa): Grieg
Mountain dawn—A l'aube dans la montagne: Séverac
The mountain maid—Haugtussa: Grieg
The mountain maid—Veslemøy (Haugtussa): Grieg
Mountain nights—Heghi éjszakák: Kodály
The mountain thrall—Den Bergtakne: Grieg
The mountains are cold—Die Berge sind spitz: Brahms
The mountains are steep: Die Berge sind spitz: Brahms
The mountains of Norway: Norges Fjelde: Kjerulf
Mourn not—Es ist bestimmt: Mendelssohn
Mourn now with me—Deh come trista: Arcadelt
The mourner—Die Trauernde: Brahms
The mourner—Die Trauernde: R Franz
The mourner—Der Leidende: Schubert
The mourning moon—Gruss, lieber Mond: Schubert
Mousetrap magic—Mausefallen-Sprüchlein: Wolf
Les mousquetaires au couvent—Musketeers in a convent: Ferrier (et al)
Mouth so charmful—Pur dicesti o bocca bella: Lotti
The mower—Zalo dievča, zalo travu: Dvořák
Msa Glagolskaja—Glagolitic mass: Janáček
Much ado about nothing—Béatrice et Bénédict: Berlioz
Des Müden Abendlied—The weary one's evensong: R Franz
La muette de Portici—The dumb girl: Auber
Das Mühlrad—The mill wheel: Erk
Mulató gajd—Merrymaking: Kodály
Der Müller und der Bach (Die schöne Müllerin)—The miller and mill-stream/
    The miller and the brook: Schubert
Die Müllerin—The miller's daughter/The miller's maid: Brahms
Die Müllerin—The maid of the mill: Grieg
Des Müllers Blumen (Die schöne Müllerin)—The miller's flowers: Schubert
Mund und Herze steht dir offen (Bringet dem Herrn Ehre)—Heart and
    mouth to Thee are open: Bach
Murder in the cathedral—L'assassinio nel cathedrale: Pizzeti
The murder of Murray—Murray's Ermordung: Brahms
Murderer, hope of women—Mörder, Hoffnung der Frauen: Hindemith
Murmelndes Lüftchen, blutenwind—O murm'ring breezes/Gentle zephyrs/
    Murm'ring breezes: Jensen
Murmer not, Christian soul—Murre nicht, lieber Christ (Nimm was dein
    ist, und gehe hin): Bach
Murm'ring breezes—Murmelndes Lüftchen, blutenwind: Jensen
Murray's Ermordung—The bonny Earl of Murray/The murder of Murray/
    Murray's lament: Brahms
Murray's lament—Murray's Ermordung: Brahms

Murre nicht, lieber Christ (Nimm was dein ist, und gehe hin)—Murmer not, Christian soul/Pardon us, gracious Lord: Bach

Der Musensohn—Wandering minstrel/The muse's son/A son of the muses/The minstrel/The muse's son/My flute and I: Schubert

The muse's son—Der Musensohn: Schubert

Music from heaven—Sphärenklange: Josef Strauss

Music on my spirit plays—Leise zieht: A Rubinstein

Music softly streaming—Sia pur sonno di morte: A Scarlatti

Musica proibita—Unspoken words/Forbidden melody: Gastaldon

The musical box—Spillevaerket (Humoreske): Nielsen

A musical joke—Ein musikalischer Spass: Mozart

The musician—Der Spielmann: Schumann

Il musico ignorante—The would-be musician: Clari

Musikalische Exequiem—A German requiem: Schütz

Ein musikalischer Spass—A musical joke: Mozart

Der Musikant—The wandering minstrel/The minstrel: Wolf

Musje Morgenrots Lied/Wie trag ich doch im Sinne—Why is my mood so happy?: Cornelius

Musketeers in a convent—Les mousquetaires au couvent: Ferrier (et al)

Muss es eine trennung geben—Must we then once more be parted/How can life be life without thee?: Brahms

Must he die, for whom I languish—Se peri l'amato bene (Riccardo Primo): Handel

Must we then once more be parted—Muss es eine Trennung geben: Brahms

Mut (Die Winterreise)—Courage: Schubert

Muted—En sourdine (Fêtes galantes): Debussy

Muted—En sourdine: Fauré

Mutiges Lied—Valiant song: Blech

Die Mutter bei der Wiege—The mother at the cradle: Blech

Die Mutter bei der Wiege—His father's nose: Schulz

Mutter, mutter/Lied der Braut—Bride's song/Mother, mother do not grieve: Schumann

Mutter, O sing' mich zur Ruh'!—Mother, Oh sing me to rest!: R Franz

Die Mutter spricht—Mother says: Reger

Die Mutter sucht ihr Liebes Kind (Die Bürgschaft)—The lost lamb: Schubert

Der Mutter vorzusingen—To be sung to mother: Blech

Muttertändelei—A mother's dallying: R Strauss

Muttertraum—A mother's dream: Schumann

My abode—Aufenthalt (Schwanengesang): Schubert

My all—Mein Alles: Blumenthal

My angel shall guard thee—Daz iuwer min Engel Walte: Reger

My ardent sighs—Ardenti mei sospiri: Dering

My beautiful face—Del bell' idolo mio: Handel

My bed calls me—Az ágyam hírogat: Bartók

My black hen—Die Henne: Brahms
My bluebird—Vai, azuläo: Guarnieri
My breast doth ache—Arme Peter (2): Schumann
My breath is corrupt—Mein Odem ist schwach: Reger
My bride—Mein Liebchen: Meyer-Helmund
My cause is God's, and I am still—Ich hab mein Sach Gott heim gestellt: Bach
My cizinou jsme bloudili (Jakobin)—We wandered far through foreign lands: Dvořák
My corpse is as limp as a glove—Mon cadavre est doux comme un gant (Fiancailles pour rire): Poulenc
My country—Má vlast: Smetana
My cross with gladness I carry—Ich will den Kreuzstab gerne tragen: Bach
My cruel fate lamenting—Mi lagnero tacendo (Siroe): Handel
My darling—Lieb' Liebchen: R Franz
My darling shall never—Feinsliebchen, du sollst mir nicht: Brahms
My days of sorrow—Es ist nun aus mit meinem Leben: Bach
My dearest Jesu, I have lost Thee—Mein liebster Jesus ist verloren: Bach
My dearest life—Nun lass uns Frieden schliessen (Italienisches Liederbuch) Wolf
My dolly dear—Ma poupée chérie: Séverac
My dreams since our first meeting—Si de mon premier rêve: Aubert
My earthly afflictions with gladness—Ich nehme mein Leiden mit Freuden auf mich (Die Elenden sollen essen): Bach
My every thought—Bei dir sind meine Gedanken: Brahms
My eyes glow as brightly—Mir glänzen die Augen: Pfitzner
My fate I cannot banish—Ach, war'es nie geschehen!: R Franz
My flute and I—Der Musensohn: Schubert
My fondest thoughts—All mein Gedanken: Brahms
My friend—Mein Freund: Blumenthal
My garden—Mein Garten: Schumann
My gentle ladye young and fair—Tresbelle, bonne jeune et gente: Meister
My girl has rosy lips—Mein Mädel hat einen Rosenmund: Brahms
My girl is as fair as amber—Min pige er så lys som rav (Moderen): Nielsen
My glowing heart—Il mio bel foco: Marcello
My goal—Fyremål: Grieg
My God! forsake me not—Mein Gott, verwirf mich nicht (Herr, gehe nicht in's Gericht): Bach
My God, how long, how long?—Mein Gott, wie lang', ach lange?: Bach
My God I give myself to Thee—Ei nun, mein Gott, so fall' ich dir (Sie werden aus Saba alle kommen): Bach
My golden love—Du fragst mich, du mein blondes Lieb: Kjerulf
My heart—Mein Herz: Reger
My heart and lute—Mein Herz und meine Leyer: Kjerulf

My heart ever faithful—Mein glaubiges Herze (Also hat Gott die Welt geliebt): Bach

My heart has learned to sing—Da draussen in der Wachau: E Arnold

My heart in my bosom is bounding—Un moto di gioja: Mozart

My heart is as the darksome night—Mein Herz ist wie die dunkle Nacht: Lassen

My heart is beating—Cangio d'aspetto (Admeto): Handel

My heart is filled with longing—Herzlich tut mich verlangen: Bach

My heart is in confusion—Mein Herz ist mit gemenget: Schoenberg

My heart is like a dreary night—Mein Herz ist wie die dunkle Nacht: Lassen

My heart is offered still to you—Mon coeur se recommande à vous: Lassus

My heart it seemed was dying—Mori quasi il mio core: Palestrina

My heart only sighs—Si può rimirar: Gaffi

My heart rejoiceth—Et exultavit (Magnificat): Bach

My heart sings—Mon coeur chante: Chaminade

My heart so sad—Mein Herz ist stumm: R Strauss

My heart that believest—Mein glaubiges Herze (Also hatt Gott die Welt geliebt): Bach

My heart with grief doth swoon—Mein Herze schwimmit im Blut: Bach

My heart's in the highlands—Hochländers Abschied (Myrthen): Schumann

My heart's true home—Dove, dove, scintillano: Bossi

My hero—Komm, Komm! Held meiner Träume (Der tapfere Soldat): O Straus

My hope-star royal!—Tua mi speranza (Amadigi di Gaula): Handel

My hostel—Einkehr: R Strauss

My inmost heart doth yearn—Herzlich tut mit verlangen: Brahms

My inmost heart rejoiceth—Herzlich tut mich erfreuen: Brahms

My Jesu what affliction—Mein Jesu, was für Seelenweh: Bach

My Jesus is risen—Mein Jesus ist erstanden (Halt' im Gedächtniss Jesum Christ): Bach

My Jesus leave I not—Meinen Jesum lass ich nicht: Bach

My Jesus, Thou who didst—Mein Jesu, der Du mich: Brahms

My joyful ardour—Il mio bel foco: Marcello

My lad—Mei Bua: Reger

My lady is so charming—Baci amorosi e cari: Mozart (?)

My life is hid in Jesus—Christus, der ist mein Leben: Bach

My life is sweet with gracious blessing—Ich bin vergrügt mit meinem Glucke: Bach

My little sweetheart—Mein Schatzelein: Reger

My Lord, it's all the wind—Patron, das Macht der Wind (Geschwinde, geschwinde, ihr wirbelnden Winde): Bach

My lord, only believe—Signor, lo credi a me (Admeto): Handel

My lost one—Nostalgias: Cobian
My love—Az én szerelmem: Bartók
My love and I agree—So stehen wir: Brahms
My love is like a red, red rose—Dem roten Röslein: Schumann
My love, lay thy hand—Lieb' Liebchen: Schumann
My loved one has left me—Nachwirkung: Brahms
My lusty cheer is waning—Mein G'mut ist mir verwirret: Hassler
My maiden's lip—Mein Mädel hat einen Rosenmund: Brahms
My mind is like the mountain steep—Min Tanke er et maegtigt Fjeld:
  Grieg
My mother loves me not—Die Trauernde: Brahms
My mother's like bread that's new-baked—La mamma è como il pane caldo
  Respighi
My Nina still lies dreaming—Tre giorno son che Nina: Pergolesi
My noble lords—Nobles seigneurs (Les Huguenots): Meyerbeer
My old steed—Mein altes Ross: Schumann
My one delight—Was mir behagt: Bach
My peace I give to you—Der Friede sei mit dir: Bach
My peace thou art—Du bist die Ruh': Schubert
My phantom double—Der Doppelgänger (Schwanengesang): Schubert
My pious heart be full of glee—Mein glaubiges Herze (Also hat Gott der
  Welt geliebt): Bach
My pretty and my kitty—Schätzlein und Kätzlein: Meyer-Helmund
My pretty bird—Wüsstest du den Weg: Kjerulf
My pretty dove—Elle a fui, la tourterelle (Les contes d'Hoffman): Offenbach
My pretty ferns—La belle fougère: Blanchard
My pretty fishermaiden—Du schönes Fischermädchen: Coleridge-Taylor
My queen—Wie bist du, meine Königin: Brahms
My queenly sun before the sun was seated—Erasi al sole il mio bel sole
  assiso: Porta
My resting place—Frühlingsruhe: Schoeck
My rose—Mein Rose: Schumann
My sad heart—Wehmut: Schubert
My sentence—Che sento o dio (Giulio Cesare): Handel
My sighs, my tears—Meine Seufzer, meine Tränen: Bach
My sins are with me every day—Paccantem me quotidie: Palestrina
My slumber grows ever softer—Immer leiser wird mein Schlummer: Brahms
My song therefore shall be—Drum sing' ich mit meinem Lieder (Lobgesang)
  Mendelssohn
My soul awakens—Cangio d'aspetto (Admeto): Handel
My soul doth magnify the Lord—Meine Seele erhebt den Herren: Bach
My soul exalts the Lord—Meine Seele erhebt den Herren: Bach
My soul is dark—Mein Herz ist schwer: Schumann
My soul, now praise thy Lord God—Nun komm, der Heiden Heiland: Bach

My soul rejoices—Et exultavit (Magnificat): Bach
My soul waiteth still on God—Meine Seele ist still: Reger
My soul's delight—Mein Seelenschatz ist Gottes Wort (Gleich wie der Regen und Schnee): Bach
My soul's delight and treasure—O luce di quest' anima (Linda di Chamounix): Donizetti
My spirit Him descries—Ich sehe schon im Geist (Gott fähret auf mit Jauchzen): Bach
My spirit was in heaviness—Ich hatte viel Bekümmernisse: Bach
My strength is spent—Die Kraft versagt (Der widerspanstigen Zähmung): Goetz
My sun—O sole mio: E Capua
My sunshine—O sole mio: E Capua
My sweet repose—Du bist die Ruh': Schubert
My sweetheart—Moja piésczotka: Chopin
My sweetheart—Mein Schatz(e)lein: Reger
My sweetheart is ploughing—Szant a babím: Bartók
My sweetheart now so long ago—Mein Schatz ist auf der Wanderschaft: R Franz
My tears alone—Mi restano le lagrime (Alcina): Handel
My tender flock—Mon cher troupeau: Anon
My thoughts—Andenken: Wolf
My thoughts are like the mighty hills—Min Tanke er et maegtigt Fjeld: Grieg
My treasured flowers are dying—In meinem Garten die Nelken: R Franz
My vision—Mein Auge: R Strauss
My William—Volksliedchen: Schumann
My wishes—Meine Wünsche: Mozart
My word's my bond—Der Mann von Word: Beethoven
Myatezh—The revolt: Khodzha-Eynatov
Myrthenblüten—Myrtle blossoms: J Strauss II
Ein Myrtenreis (Brautlieder)—A myrtle spray: Cornelius
Myrthen—Myrtles: Schumann
Myrtle blossoms—Myrthenblüten: J Strauss II
A myrtle spray—Ein Myrthenreis (Brautlieder): Cornelius
Myrtles—Myrthen: Schumann
The mysterious flute—Die geheimnisvolle Flöte: Webern

N

Na nebe vstoupenf Páně—The Ascension: Martinů
Na pole Kulikovom—On the field of Kulikovo: Shaporin
Na polye smerti (Aleksandr Nevsky)—On the field of death: Prokofiev
Na rusalchyn velykden'—A mermaid's holiday: Leontovych
Na starém bělidle—At the old bleaching house: Kovarovic
Na tych fojtovych lukaeh—On the meadows: Janáček
Nabucco—Nebuchadnezzar: Verdi
Nach dem Abscheide—Separation: Wolf
Nach der Geburt ihres Sohnes—After the birth of her son: Schumann
Nach Dir, Herr, verlanget mich—Lord, for Thee my spirit longs/Lord, my
    soul doth thirst for Thee: Bach
Nach wie vor der Reihe nach—As before, one after the other: Křenek
Nachklang—Remembrance: Schoeck
Nachklänge aus dem Theater (Album für die Jugend)—Recollections of
    the theatre/Reminiscences of the pantomine: Schumann
Nachruf—In memory: Schoeck
Nachruf—Posthumous fame: Wolf
Nacht—Night: Berg
Die Nacht—Night: Schubert
Die Nacht—Night: R Strauss
Die Nacht—Night: Wolf
Ein Nacht in Vendig—A night in Venice: J Strauss II
Nacht und Träume—Night and dreams/Quiet night: Schubert
Nächtens—At night-time: Brahms
Nachtgang—At night: R Strauss
Nachtgeflüster—Voices of the summer night: Reger
Nachtgesang—Night song: Hauptman
Nachtgesang im Walde—Night in the forest: Schubert
Nachtgruss—Goodnight: Wolf
Die Nachtigall—The nightingale: Berg
Nachtigall—(The) Nightingale: Brahms
Die Nachtigall—The nightingale: Mendelssohn
Nachtigall, sag, was für Grüss—Nightingale, for whom's thy song: Brahms
Nachtigall, sie singt so schön (Liebeslieder waltzes)—Nightingale, thy sweet
    song: Brahms
Nachtigallen schwingen—Nightingales are winging/The nightingale's call/
    Nightingales: Brahms
Nachtlang—Tears: Brahms
Nachtlied—Song of the night/Night song: R Franz
Nachtlied—Night song: Schoeck
Nachtlied—Song of the night: Schumann
Nachts—At night: Cornelius

212

Nachtviolen—Dame's violets: Schubert
Nachtwache—Nightwatch: Brahms
Nachtwandler—The sleeper/The sleep walker: Brahms
Nachwirkung—Forsaken/Aftermath/Afterglow/My loved one has left me: Brahms
Nachtzauber—Night's glory/Night's magic spell: Wolf
Näcken—The elfking: Sibelius
Nad krajan véno-dí lehký spánek (Pisně milostné)—Nature lies peaceful in slumber: Dvořák
Nad woda wielka—By waters mighty: Paderewski
Naděje—Hope: Martinů
Nae gentle dames tho'—Das Hochlandmädchen: Schumann
Naebody—Niemand (Myrthen): Schumann
Nagen am Herzen (Neue Liebeslieder)—Sharp poisoned arrow: Brahms
Nähe des Geliebten—Near the beloved/To the beloved one/The beloved presence/Love's presence: Schubert
The Naides—Bei nächtlicher Weil: Brahms
The name day—Imenini: Zhelobinsky
Name-day—Namensfeier: Beethoven
Namensfeier—Name-day: Beethoven
Nar jag drömmer—When I dream: Sibelius
Narcisse à la fontaine—Narcissus at the fountain: Massenet
Narcissus at the fountain—Narcisse à la fontaine: Massenet
Namluvy Pelopvy—The wooing of Pelops/Pelop's wooing: Fibich
Narodnaya svyashchennaya voina—The people's holy war/The great holy war: Koval'
Narozeni Páné—The birth of our Lord: Martinů
The narrow street—El callejóu: J Berger
Nasce al bosco (Ezio)—Born amid the rugged wildwood: Handel
Naše jaro—Our spring: Vycpalek
Našim děvám—To our girls: Smetana
National choruses—Ctverice muzskych sboru: Janáček
National song—Volkslied: Brahms
Natur—Nature: Schoenberg
Natural histories—Histoires naturelles: Ravel
Nature—Natur: Schoenberg
Nature, amour (Castor et Pollux)—Not love alone: Rameau
Nature lies peaceful in slumber—Nad krajan vévo-dí lehký spánek (Pisné milostné): Dvořák
Natus est nobis—Unto us is born this day: Vittoria
Naught is left me—Non mi resta (L'amico Fritz): Mascagni
Naught may'st thou ask me—Heiss' mich nicht reden: Schubert
The naughty legs—Die bösen Beinchen: Blech
La Navarraise—The girl from Navarre: Massenet

La nave—The ship: Montemezzi

Le navire est à l'eau—Saved: Blumenthal

Navozhdeniyl—Temptation: Prokofiev

Nay but why tarry—Komm bald: Brahms

Nay tarry sweetheart—Nicht wandle (Liebeslieder waltzes): Brahms

Ne hagyj itt!—Only tell me: Bartók

Ne irascaris Domine—Lord turn Thy wrath away/O Lord turn Thy wrath
   away: Byrd

Ne menj el!—Don't leave me: Bartók

Ne' trionfi d'Alessandro (Alessandro)—Alexander, at thy triumph: Handel

Ne vois-tu pas (Céphale et Procis)—Ah! seest thou not: Grétry

Near dawn—In der Frühe: Wolf

Near in spirit—Geisternähe: Schumann

Near Moscow—Pod Moskvoy: Kabalevsky

Near my beloved—Auprès de ma mie: Chaminade

Near the beloved—Nähe des Geliebten: Schubert

Near the fireside—Am Kamin (Kinderscenen): Schumann

Nearing the extreme—Giunto sul passo estremo (Mephistofele): Boito

'Neath the apple tree—An die Apfelbaume: Schubert

'Neath the branches—Sous les branches: Massenet

'Neath the roses—Millom Rosor: Grieg

'Neath willow trees—Dort in den Weiden: Brahms

Nebbie—Mists: Respighi

Nebel—Fog-land: R Franz

Die Nebensonnen (Die Winterreise)—Phantom suns: Schubert

Nebuchadnezzar—Nabucco: Verdi

Neckerein—Oh maiden dearest, my heart is true: Brahms

Ne'er did the day seem fairer—Come per me sereno (La sonnambula): Bellini

Ne'er, mistress, did I weary—Nie ward' ich Herrin müd: Schoenberg

Ne'er the world will give you peace—Celý svět nedá ti (Rusalka): Dvořák

Ne'er were such leaves—Ombra mai fù (Serse): Handel

Negerdans (Aladdin)—Negroes' dance: Nielsen

Negroes' dance—Negerdans (Aladdin): Nielsen

Négy Siratóének—Four dirges: Bartók

Négy zenekar i darab [op 12]—Four pieces: Bartók

Nehmt meinen Dank—Thank you, my friends: Mozart

Il neige—'Tis snowing: Bemberg

The neighbours—Sousedká: Smetana

The neighbour's stable—Súsedove stajňa: Martinů

Nein!—No!: F X Mozart

Nein, es ist nicht (Liebeslieder waltzes)—No, there is no bearing: Brahms

Nein, Geliebter (Neue Liebeslieder)—Seat thyself/Do not gaze: Brahms

Nel cor piu non mi sento (La molinara)—Why feels my heart so dormant/
   In my heart I feel no more: Paisiello

Nel dolce dell' oblio—In sleep's sweet oblivion/Sweet forgetting: Handel
Nel mondo e nell' abisso (Riccardo Primo)—There's naught upon this earth:
   Handel
Nel riposo e nel contento (Deidamia)—Calm repose, contentment
   smiling: Handel
Nel sogno (Adriana Lecouvreur)—O radiant vision: Cilèa
Nel verde Maggio (Loreley)—Once in the May-time: Catalani
Nelson mass—Missa in angustiis: Haydn
Nem messze van ide Kis Margitta—Not far from here is Kis Margitta:
   Bartók
Nero—Nerone: Boito
Nerone—Nero: Boito
Nessun dorma! (Turandot)—None shall sleep tonight: Puccini
N'est-ce pas? (La bonne chanson)—Is it not so?: Fauré
Nesvár—Discord: Smetana
Nettuno s'onori (Idomeneo)—To thee, mighty Neptune: Mozart
Der neue Amadis—The latter-day Amadis: Wolf
Neue Liebe—New love/Fairy revel: Mendelssohn
Neue Liebe—New love: Wolf
Neue Liebe, neues Leben—New love, new life: Beethoven
Neue Liebeslieder—New love songs: Brahms
Das neue Regiment (Gott ist mein König)—The Lord shall preserve thee
   from evil: Bach
Neues vom Tage—News of the day: Hindemith
Das neugebor'ne Kindelein—Sing we the birth/The newborn child: Bach
Der Neugierige (Die schöne Müllerin)—Curiosity/The question/The
   inquirer: Schubert
Neujahrslied—For the new year: Mendelssohn
Neujahrslied—New year's song/Song for the new year: Schumann
Never did I behold so fair a maiden—Donna non vidi mai (Manon
   Lescaut): Puccini
Never Jesus will I leave—Meinen Jesum lass' ich nicht: Bach
Never tell—Sag' es nicht: Reger
Never will love lead us—Ó naší lásce nekvěte (Pisně milostné): Dvořák
Nevesta Messinska—The bride of Messina: Fibich
Nevinnost—Innocence: Smetana
New love—Neue Liebe: Mendelssohn
New love—Neue Liebe: Wolf
New love, new life—Neue Leibe, neues Leben: Beethoven
New love songs—Neue Liebeslieder: Brahms
New year's eve—Sylvester-lied (Album für die Jugend): Schumann
New year's song—Neujahrslied: Schumann
New year's song—Sylvester-lied (Album für die Jugend): Schumann
A new-blown rose—Mädchenlied: Dieren

The newborn child—Das neugebor'ne Kindelein: Bach
News of the day—Neues vom Tage: Hindemith
Newspaper advertisements—Gazetnia obyarleniya: Deshevov
Ni jamais, ni toujours—Yea and nay: A L(ehmann)
The Nibelungen hoard—Der Nibelungenhort: Finke
Der Nibelungenhort—The Nibelungen hoard: Finke
Nicht die Träne kann es sagen—Sorrow's tears: Cornelius
Nicht länger kann ich singen (Italienisches Liederbuch)—I cannot sing any
    more/No longer can I sing: Wolf
Nicht mehr zu dir zu gehen—I promised thee/That I no more would see
    thee/I swear no more to woo thee/In vain I strive to fly thee/
    I promised to see thee no more/No longer to entreat thee/I said
    'I will forget thee': Brahms
Nicht send' ich dich (Die Walküre)—No more shall I: Wagner
Nicht so traurig, nicht so sehr—Fly my soul this doleful mood/Be not
    troubled: Bach
Nicht wandle (Liebeslieder waltzes)—Nay tarry sweetheart: Brahms
Nichts—Nought: R Strauss
Nichts ist gekommen—Nothing is come: Berg
Nichts labt mich mehr als Wein—Up with the glossy holly/Sorrow with
    song come drown: Mozart
Nichts Schöneres—Nothing more beautiful: Schumann
Nie ward' ich Herrin müd—Ne'er, Mistress, did I weary: Schoenberg
Niemand (Myrthen)—Naebody: Schumann
Night—Nacht: Berg
Night—Bitte: R Franz
Night—Die Nacht: Schubert
Night—In der Nacht (Fantasiestücke): Schumann
Night—Die Nacht: R Strauss
Night—Die Nacht: Wolf
Night and dream—Nacht und träume: Schubert
The night bell—Il campanello di notte: Donizetti
Night breezes—La pesca: Rossini
Night descends in peace—Über allen Gipfeln ist Ruh': Schubert
Night flight—Volo di notte: Dallapiccola
Night gloom and shadows—Von dunklem Schleier: R Strauss
Night has cast her shadow—Über allen Gipfeln ist Ruh': Schubert
The night has known my tears—No lloro más: Carolis
Night in May—Die Mainacht: Brahms
A night in May—Maiennacht: Reger
Night in spring—Frühlingsnacht: Schumann
Night in the forest—Nachtgesang im Walde: Schubert
A night in Venice—Ein Nacht in Vendig: J Strauss II
Night lay so still—In stiller Nacht: Brahms

Night of desire—A vágyak éjjele: Bartók
Night on the Danube—Donauwellen: Ivanovici
Night on the sea—Yö meren rannalla: Kaski
Night song—Nachtlied: R Franz
Night song—Nachtgesang: Hauptman
Night song—Abendlandschaft: Schoeck
Night song—Nachtlied: Schoeck
The night was calm and peaceful—Tacea la notte (Il trovatore): Verdi
The night watch—Der eidgenossen Nachtwache: Schumann
The night watchman—Hlásný: Martinů
Night-fall—Stiller Gang: R Strauss
The nightingale—Die Nachtigall: Berg
(The) nightingale—Nachtigall: Brahms
The nightingale—Le rossignol: Delibes
The nightingale—Im Wald bei der Amsel: Erk
The nightingale—Die verschwiegene Nachtigall: Grieg
The nightingale—Die Nachtigall: Mendelssohn
The nightingale—Solovey: Stravinsky
Nightingale for whom's thy song—Nachtigall, sag, was für Grüss:
    Brahms
Nightingale, sing—Syng, syng: Kjerulf
Nightingale, thy sweetest song—Nachtigall, sie singt so schön (Liebeslieder
    waltzes): Brahms
Nightingales—Nachtigallen schwingen: Brahms
Nightingales are winging—Nachtigallen schwingen: Brahms
The nightingale's call—Nachtigallen schwingen: Brahms
Nightingales in the wood—Rossignols amoureux (Hippolyte et Aricie):
    Rameau
The nightmare—Le cauchemar: Françaix
Night's glory—Nachtzauber: Wolf
Nights in the gardens of Spain—Noches en los jardines de España: Falla
Night's magic spell—Nachtzauber: Wolf
Night-song—In der Nacht: Schumann
Nightwatch—Nachtwache: Brahms
Nimm einen Strahl der Sonne—Take one bright ray of sunlight: Liszt
Nimm mich dir zu eigen hin (Sie werden aus Saba alle kommen)—Take me
    to Thee for Thine own: Bach
Nimm sie hin den (An die ferne Geliebte)—Take the tribute: Beethoven
Nimm, was dein ist, und gehe hin—Take what is thine and go thy way:
    Bach
Nimmersatte Liebe—Insatiable love: Wolf
Nincsen annyi tenger csillag—There is no star: Erkel
Ninfa de ojos brujos—Beneath the curtain of the night: Brito
Nisi Dominus—Except the Lord shall build the house: Handel
Nixe Binsefuss—The fairy Reedfoot: Wolf

No!—Nein!: F X Mozart
No dalar—Sunset: Sinding
No doubt—Ein safek: Miron
No fairies and witches—Ich fürcht' mit Gespenster: Pfitzner
No fire ever burns—Kein Feuer, keine Kohle: Henschel
No fragrant garland—Non piu di fiori (La clemenza di Tito): Mozart
No home, no country—Kein Haus, keine Heimat: Brahms
No hour goes ever by—Kein Stündlein geht dahin: Bach
No, if my plighted fealty—Se la giurata fede (Tosca): Puccini
No joy could be more thrilling—Page d'album: Berlioz
No, let me not reproach you—Dire non voglio: D Scarlatti
No lloro más—The night has known my tears: Carolis
No longer can I sing—Nicht länger kann ich singen (Italienisches
    Liederbuch): Wolf
No longer let me languish—Lasciatemi morire: Monteverdi
No longer to entreat thee—Nicht mehr zu dir zu gehen: Brahms
No man can guess—Es weiss und rath es doch Keiner: Henschel
No man knows where love will light—Es war einmal ein Zimmergesell: Bra
No matter which—So oder so: Beethoven
No more can earthly joy be mine—Vergangen ist mir Glück und Heil:
    Brahms
No more in sorrow languish—Rend' il sereno al ciglio (Sosarme): Handel
No more shall I—Nicht send' ich dich (Die Walküre): Wagner
No more unmoistened—Ich esse nun (Italienisches Liederbuch): Wolf
No more we twain go forth a-Maying—So stehen wir: Brahms
No, no, che non sei capace—No, no, no, truly you know nothing: Mozart
Nò nò il tuo sdegno placè (Tamerlano)—No, no, now thy noble heart:
    Handel
Nò, nò, nò, mai nol dirò—No, no, no, ne'er shalt thou know: Steffani
No, no, no, ne'er shalt thou know—Nò, nò, nò, mai nol dirò: Steffani
Nò, nò, nò, non voglio—The choice: Steffani
No, no, no, truly you know nothing—No, no, che non sei capace: Mozart
No, no, now thy noble heart—Nò nò il tuo sdegno placè (Tamerlano):
    Handel
No non chiuder (Germania)—Tell thy lover: Franchetti
No, non è morto il figlio tuo—No, your child is not dead: Respighi
No, oh Dio (Calphurnia)—Ah! what sorrow: Bononcini
No one! all is silent!—Nulla! silenzio! (Manon Lescaut): Puccini
No rest—Keine Rast: Schoeck
No river so broad—Kein Graben so breit: Henschel
No! she has never loved—Ella giamma m'amò (Don Carlos): Verdi
No sylvan shade—Ombra mai fù (Serse): Handel
No there is no bearing—Nein, es ist nicht (Liebeslieder Walzer): Brahms
No, Tirsi, tu non hai—Fair Tirsi: Veracini

No, your child is not dead—No, non è morto il figlio tuo: Respighi
The Noah's ark—Complainte des arches de Noé: Pierné
Nobis est natus—This happy morn: Praetorius
Noble Rhine—Im Rhein (Dichterliebe): Schumann
Noble Riera—L'Heréu Riera: Alió
Nobles seigneurs (Les Huguenots)—My noble lords: Meyerbeer
Les noces—The wedding: Stravinsky
Noch pered Rozhdestvom—Christmas eve: Rimsky-Korsakov
La noche buena del diablo—The devil's Christmas eve: Esplà
Noche oscura—Dark night of the soul: Petrassi
Noches en los jardines de España—Nights in the gardens of Spain: Falla
Der Nöck—The water-sprite: Loewe
Nocturne—Grüsse zur Nacht: Dohnányi
Nocturne of the roses—Nocturno de las rosas: Ponce
Nocturno de las rosas—Nocturne of the roses: Ponce
Noël—O Christmas night: Adam
Noël des enfants qui n'ont plus de maisons—Christmas carol of the children
    who have no homes/Christmas carol for homeless children: Debussy
The noise of the battle—Al lampo dell' armi (Giulio Cesare): Handel
Non la sospiri (Tosca)—In secret hidden from care: Puccini
Non lasciar (Floridante)—Crushed by fate: Handel
Non lo diro col labbro (Tolomeo)—Silent worship: Handel
Non m'ama più—He loves me no more: Tosti
Non mi dir (Don Giovanni)—Tell me not: Mozart
Non mi resta (L'amico Fritz)—Naught is left me: Mascagni
Non nobis Domine—The golden canon: Byrd (?)
Non pianger, non gioir—Be neither grieved nor glad: Quaranta
Non più andrai (Le nozze di Figaro)—Now no more/So, sir page/So your
    gay life of pleasure is over: Mozart
Non più di fiori (La clemenza di Tito)—No fragrant garland: Mozart
Non posso disperar—I do not dare despond: Luca
Non sa che sia dolore—Grief's lowest depth he soundeth: Bach
Non so come l'alma mia—How can this be?: Agostini
Non so d'onde viene—I know not from whither: Mozart
Non sò più cosa son (Le nozze di Figaro)—I forget what I am/What I am,
    what I do: Mozart
Non sò se sia la speme (Serse)—'Tis hope that sustains us/O hope, within
    my bosom: Handel
Non sospirar—These broken sighs: Handel
Non temer, amato bene [K 490]—Faithful love this heart inspiring: Mozart
Non temer, amato bene [K 505]—Fear thou not: Mozart
Non temer, non son più amante—The farewell: Anfossi
Non ti fidar (Muzio Scevola)—Don't be too sure!: Handel

Non vi piacque (Siroe)—Wherefore was I not intended: Handel
None but the weary heart—Nur wer die Sehnsucht kennt: Schubert
None can gainsay it—Giascun lo dice (La fille du régiment): Donizetti
None has ever mourned—Keinem hat es noch gerent: Brahms
None shall sleep tonight—Nessun dorma! (Turandot): Puccini
Die Nonne—The nun: Brahms
Die Nonne—The nun: F Mendelssohn
Die Nonne—The nun: Schumann
Die Nonne und der Ritter—The nun and the knight: Brahms
Nonsense song—Canción tonto (Canciones de niños): Revueltas
Noon—Mittag: Reger
The noon witch—Polednice: Dvořák
Nord oder Süd—North or south: Schumann
Norges Fjelde—The mountains of Norway: Kjerulf
Normannerzug—The lay of the Norseman: Bruch
Den Norske Sjømand—The Norwegian sailor: Grieg
North or south—Nord oder Süd: Schumann
North wind—Severny veter: Knipper
The north wind—La bise (Petites légendes): Milhaud
The north wind—Les grands vents: Ravel
Norvég leányok—Norwegian girls: Kodály
Norwegian girls—Norvég leányok: Kodály
The Norwegian sailor—Den Norske Sjømand: Grieg
Norwegian spring night—Norwegische Frühlingsnacht: R Franz
Norwegische Frühlingsnacht—Norwegian spring night: R Franz
Nos—The nose: Shostakovich
Nos da—Good night: M Jones
Nos enim pro peccatis—For these things justly have we suffered: Byrd
The nose—Nos: Shostakovich
The nosegay—Der Blumenstrauss: Mendelssohn
Nostalgia—La mal du pays (Années de pèlerinage): Liszt
Nostalgias—My lost one: Cobian
Not a breath in heaven stirs—Unbewegte laue Luft: Brahms
Not a tear—Ich vergönn' es ihm: Henschel
Not far from here is Kis Margitta—Nem messze van ide Kis Margitta: Bartók
Not love alone—Nature, amour (Castor et Pollux): Rameau
Nothing is come—Nichts ist gekommen: Berg
Nothing more beautiful—Nichts Schöneres: Schumann
Notre amour—Our love: Fauré
Notte cara (Floridante)—Dear night: Handel
Nought—Nichts: R Strauss
Nous avons fait la nuit (Tel jour telle nuit)--We have made night: Poulenc
Nous nous aimerons (Tristesses)—We shall be so in love: Milhaud

Nova Atlantida—The new Atlantis: Kozyts'kyi
Noveta (Moravské Dvojzpěvy)—Comfort: Dvořák
Now a poet once said—Un poète disait que (Tristesses): Milhaud
Now advance, haughty warrior—Trete ein, hoher Kreiger: Wolf
Now all the roses are blooming—Nun steh'n die Rosen in Blüte: Brahms
Now all the woods are sleeping—Nun ruhen alle Wälder: Bach
Now amend we our sinful lives—Emendemus in melius: Byrd
Now at last comes the moment—Giunse al fin il momento (Le nozze di
    Figaro): Mozart
Now at Thy feet creation lies—Erleucht' auch unsern Sinn und Herz
    (Du Friedefürst, Herr Jesu Christ): Bach
Now behold the car advances—Già mi sembra (Lotario): Handel
Now cheer our hearts this eventide—Uns ist ein Kindlein heut' gebor'n:
    Bach
Now Christ is risen to God—Aus Christi Himmelfahrt allein: Bach
Now come redeemer of our race—Nun komm, der Heiden Heiland [BWV 61]:
    Bach
Now come, the heathens' saviour—Nun komm, der Heiden Heiland
    [BWV 62]: Bach
Now come, the world's salvation—Nun komm, der Heiden Heiland
    (Schwingt freudig euch empor): Bach
Now daylight's youthful glory—Der Tag mit seinem Lichte: Bach
Now flutters my true loving bosom—Un moto di gioja: Mozart
Now for the first time thou hast given me pain—Nun hast du mir den
    ersten Schmerz getan (Frauenliebe und -leben): Schumann
Now for the first time you have hurt me—Nun hast du mir den ersten
    Schmerz getan (Frauenliebe und -leben): Schumann
Now hath the grace—Nun ist das Heil: Bach
Now hear and attend—Nun hört, und versteht (Die Meistersinger von
    Nürenberg): Wagner
Now hear and mistake not—Nun hört, und versteht (Die Meistersinger
    von Nürenberg): Wagner
Now hope—Ein schöne Stern: Blumenthal
Now in the meadows—Pur dicesti o bocca bella: Lotti
Now is the mournful time—Die bittre Leidens Zeit: Bach
Now it's finished—Nun ist alles aus! (Das Examen): P Burkherd
Now let every tongue adore Thee—Wachet auf, ruft uns die Stimme: Bach
Now let there be rejoicing—Laet ons nu al verblijden in desen soeten Tijt:
    Beethoven
Now let Thy gracious spirit shine—Du Friedefürst, Herr Jesu Christ: Bach
Now let us make our peace—Nun lass uns Frieden schliessen (Italienisches
    Liederbuch): Wolf
Now May has come with gladness—Der Mai tritt ein mit Freuden:
    Schoenberg
221

Now melts the snow—Der Schnee zerrinnt: Schubert
Now must we Jesus laud and sing—Christum wir sollen loben (Orgel-büchlein): Bach
Now my good staff in peace may rest—Nun hat mein Stecken gute Rast: R Franz
Now my soul to Bethlehem—Eia mea anima: Praetorius
Now no more—Non più andrai (Le nozze di Figaro): Mozart
Now of another kingdom—Io d'altro regno (Muzio Scevola): Handel
Now past, the deadly peril—Che poi ch'a mortal rischio: Erlebach
Now poor young Peter—Arme Peter (3): Schumann
Now shall the grace—Nun ist das Heil: Bach
Now shalt be known—Voglio provar (Amore traditore): Bach (?)
Now shines the silver moon—Wie glanzt der helle Mond: Wolf
Now sorrow has an ending—Nun hat das Leid ein Ende: R Franz
Now spring is come at last—Nu er da våren kommen: Nielsen
Now thank we all our God—Kommt, Seelen, diesen Tag: Bach
Now thank we all our God—Nun danket alle Gott: Bach
Now the dancing sunbeams—Die Seejungfer: Haydn
Now the day is full of song—Nu er dagen fuld af song: Nielsen
Now the groves come into leaf—Nu lyser løv i lunde: Nielsen
Now there lightens upon us—Dies sanctificatus: Byrd
Now therefore, O Lord—Ad te igitur: Byrd
Now we are ambassadors—So sind wir nun Botschafter (Paulus): Mendelssohn
Now, welcome my wood—Willkommen, mein Wald!: R Franz
Now when I am strong and well—Ores que je suis dispos: Lassus
Now, will not he sometimes in thinking?—Wird er wohl noch meiner gedenken?: R Franz
Now you start out on the road of life—Ud går du nu på livets vej: Nielsen
Now's the time to love—Chanson de la sorcière (Mireille): Gounod
Le nozze di Teti e Peleo—The wedding of Thetis and Peleus: Cavalli
Le nozze di Figaro—The marriage of Figaro: Mozart
Nu er Aftnen lys og lang—Lo, 'tis evening light and long: Grieg
Nu er da våren kommen—Now spring is come at last: Nielsen
Nu er dagen fulf af sang—Now the day is full of song: Nielsen
Nu lyser løv i lunde—Now the groves come into leaf: Nielsen
Nuages gris—Gloomy clouds: Liszt
Nuit d'automne—Autumn night: Roussel
Une nuit de Cléopâtre—Cleopatra's night: H Hadley
Nuit d'Espagne—Moonlight's magic hour: Massenet
Nuit d'étoiles—Starry summer night: Debussy
Les nuits d'été—Summer nights: Berlioz
Nulla! silenzio! (Manon Lescaut)—No one! all is silent!: Puccini
Number beauty's fairest—Keine gleicht von allen schönen: Wolf

Numbness—Erstarrung (Die Winterreise): Schubert
The nun—Die Nonne: Brahms
The nun—Die Nonne: F Mendelssohn
The nun—Die Nonne: Schumann
The nun and the knight—Die Nonne und der Ritter: Brahms
Nun danket alle Gott—Now thank we all our God: Bach
Nun freut euch, liebe Christen g'mein—Dear Christians, one and all
    rejoice: Bach
Nun hast du mir den ersten Schmerz getan (Frauenliebe und -leben)—
    Now for the first time you have hurt me/Now for the first time thou
    hast giv'n me pain/Lost happiness: Schumann
Nun hat das Leid ein Ende—Now sorrow has an ending: R Franz
Nun hat mein Stecken gute Rast—Now my good staff in peace may rest:
    R Franz
Nun Herr, regiere meinen Sinn (Der Friede sei mit dir)—Come Lord,
    direct my feeble will: Bach
Nun holt mir eine Kanne Wein—Go, fetch a flask of sparkling wine:
    R Franz
Nun hört, und versteht (Die Meistersinger von Nürenberg)—Now hear
    and attend/Now hear and mistake not: Wagner
Nun ist alles aus! (Das Examen)—Now it's finished: P Burkhard
Nun ist das Heil—Now shall the grace/Now hath the grace: Bach
Nun komm, der Heiden Heiland [BWV 61]—Come redeemer (of our
    race)/Now come redeemer of our race: Bach
Nun komm, der Heiden Heiland [BWV 62]—Now come, the heathen's
    saviour: Bach
Nun komm, der Heiden Heiland (Schwingt freudig euch empor)—Now
    come, the world's salvation: Bach
Nun komm, der Heiden Heiland (Orgelbüchlein)—Saviour of the
    nations, come: Bach
Nun lass uns Frieden schliessen (Italienisches Liederbuch)—Now let
    us make our peace/My dearest life: Wolf
Nun liegt die Welt—The world lies dark: Henschel
Nun lob, mein Seel, den Herren—My soul, now praise thy Lord God: Bach
Nun ruhen alle Wälder—Now all the woods are sleeping: Bach
Nun schrei' ich aus dem Tore—I wander thro' the gateway: Henschel
Nun seh' ich wohl (Kinder-totenlieder)—Ah, now I know: Mahler
Nun steh'n die Rosen in Blüte—Now all the roses are blooming/Behold!
    The roses are blooming: Brahms
Nun will die Sonn' (Kinder-totenlieder)—Once more the sun: Mahler
Nuptial song—Hochzeitlich Lied: R Strauss
Nur ein Gesicht auf Erden lebt—But one dear face: Brahms
Nur einmal noch—The last request: Blumenthal
Nur mein Jesus ist mein Leben—All my life from Jesus springeth: Bach
Nur Mut—Hope on: R Strauss

Nur wer die Sehnsucht kennt—None but the weary heart/Ye who have yearned alone: Schubert

Der Nussbaum—The nut tree/Almond tree/The walnut-tree/The chestnut: Schumann

The nut tree—Der Nussbaum: Schumann

Nyár—Summer: Bartók

Nýari este—Summer evening: Kodály

Nymphes et sylvains—Nymphs and fawns: Bemberg

Nymphs and fawns—Nymphes et sylvains: Bemberg

Nyúlacska—The leveret: Kodály

O

O all ye that pass by—O vos omnes: Dering
O amoureusich mondeken Root—Thy cheery red lips: Beethoven
O Armut, der kein Reichtum gleicht (Die Elenden sollen essen)—
 'Tis poverty: Bach
O at my lady's feet—O del mio dolce ardor (Paride ed Elena): Gluck
O beautiful May—O schöner Mai: J Strauss II
O bella O bianca—O fair lady so bright: Vecchi
O, beware—Hüte dich!: Meyer-Helmund
O beware—O habet Acht (Zigeunerbaron): J Strauss II
O bien-aimé—Brightest and best: Massenet
O Bimba, Bimbetta—O fleet little fairy: Sibella
O blessed are ye—Beati estis: Handel
O blessed rest—Vernügte Ruh': Bach
O bocca dolorosa—O mournful lips: Sibella
O bone Jesu—O gracious Jesus/Father eternal: Brahms
O bone Jesu—O holy Jesus: Palestrina
O born of light—O nata lux de lumine: Tallis
O cessate di piargarmi—Cease, oh cease/O forbear/Cease, oh maiden/
 O, no longer seek: A Scarlatti
O charming night—O schöne Nacht: Brahms
O Christ Jesus, loving shepherd—Christe Jesu pastor bone: Taverner
O Christ my all in living—Christus, der ist mein Leben: Bach
O Christ, Thou art our lamp and light—Christ, der du bist der helle
 Tag: Bach
O Christ, Thou art the light of day—Christ, der du bist der helle Tag:
 Bach
O Christmas night—Noël: Adam
O cieli azzuri (Aida)—O skies cerulean: Verdi
O come, dear loved one—Venez, ma bien aimée (Tristesses): Milhaud
O come do not delay—Deh vieni non tardar (Le nozze di Figaro): Mozart
O come into the arbour—Venez sous la tonelle (Tristesses): Milhaud
O come quickly Lord—Veni Domine: Byrd
O come sweet night—O komme, holde Sommernacht: Brahms
O come, sweet slumber—Im Arm der Liebe: Beethoven
O! come to me in dreams—Oh, quand je dors: Liszt
O come ye—Venite comedite: Byrd
O come ye servants of the Lord—Laudate nomen Domini: Tye
O could I but find the way—O wüsst ich doch den Weg zurück: Brahms
O could I but this afternoon—Ach könnt ich diesen Abend: Brahms
O cruel tyrant love—Crudel tirano amor: Handel
O crux—O Jesu Christ: Palestrina
O cupid, baby bowman—O pargoletto arciero: Pasquini

O days that may ne'er come again—O temps à jamais effacé (L'enfant prodigue): Liszt

O deal with Thy servant—Fac cum servo: Byrd

O death, it is the cold—Der Tod, das ist die kühle Nacht: Allitsen

O death, O death—O Tod, O Tod: Brahms

O death thou art the tranquil night—Der Tod, das ist die kühle Nacht: Cornelius

O deck me with flowers—Bedeckt mich mit Blumen (Spanische Liebeslieder): Schumann

O del mio dolce ardor (Paride ed Elena)—O my fond heart's desire/Author of all my joys/O, at my lady's feet/O thou belov'd/O my beloved/O zephyr soft and kind: Gluck

O di che lode—O say what glory: Marcello

O die Frauen (Liebeslieder Walzer)—Dark-eyed maiden: Brahms

O Dieu, mon honneur—O Lord, God of my praise: Le Jeune

O doblestyakh, o podvigakh, o slave—Of heroism, great deeds and fame: Nechaev

O Domine adiuva me—Hold Thou me up, O Lord: Byrd

O don fatale (Don Carlos)—O fatal gift: Verdi

O, douce joie—Welcome to spring: Gounod

O du Liebe meiner Liebe—Jesu, longed-for consolation: Bach

O, du mein holder Abendstern (Tannhäuser)—O thou beloved evening star/O pure and tender star of eve/O star divine/Bright star of eve: Wagner

O duše draha (Pisné milostné)—Thou only dear one: Dvořák

O ever-faithful God—O Gott, du frommer Gott (Ein ungefärbt Gemüte): Bach

O ewiges Feuer—O light everlasting/O fire everlasting: Bach

O eyes the fairest—Der Augen schein: Kreiger

O fair and sweet and holy—Du bist wie eine Blume: A Rubinstein

O fair as a flower—Recordati, oh bella (Teseo): Handel

O fair cheeks of roses—O liebliche Wangen: Brahms

O fair lady so bright—O bella O bianca: Vecchi

O faithless little maiden—O piccola Maria: Bossi

O fatal gift—O don fatale (Don Carlos): Verdi

O finistre Nacht—O gloomy night when com'st Thou to: Bach

O fiorellin di siepe—O little flower: P Morales

O fire everlasting—O ewiges Feuer: Bach

O fleet little fairy—O Bimba, Bimbetta: Sibella

O fly with me—Entflieh' mit mir: Mendelssohn

O, for one hour—Come innocente Giovane (Anna Bolena): Donizetti

O forbear—O cessate di piargarmi: A Scarlatti

O forest cool—O kühler Wald: Brahms

O fraîche nuit—Come gentle night: Franck

O friend of souls what joy to waken—Wie wohl ist mir: Bach
O garish world—Ich bin der Welt: Mahler
O give back to me my beloved—O rendetemi il mio bene (Amadigi di
    Gaula): Handel
O gloomy night when coms't Thou to: O finistre Nacht: Bach
O God, the heathen are coming—Deus venerunt gentes: Byrd
O God, Thou faithful God—O Gott, du frommer Gott [chorale partita]: Bach
O God, Thou holiest—O Gott, du frommer Gott: Brahms
O God when Thou appearest—Splendente te Deus: Mozart
O golden age—O wüsst ich doch den Weg zurück: Brahms
O Gott, du frommer Gott (Ein ungefärbt Gemüte)—O ever-faithful God:
    Bach
O Gott, du frommer Gott [chorale partita]—O God, Thou faithful God:
    Bach
O Gott, du frommer Gott—O God Thou holiest: Brahms
O gracious Jesus—O bone Jesu: Brahms
O guarda, guarda—Behold there: Wolf-Ferrari
O habet Acht (Zigeunerbaron)—O beware: J Strauss II
O hail this brightest day of days—Der Tag der ist so freudenreich: Bach
O happy eve!—Selige Nacht!: R Franz
O happy, happy little birds—Ich lobe mir die Vöglein: R Franz
O Haupt voll Blut und Wunden (Matthäuspassion)—O sacred head sore
    wounded/O sacred head surrounded: Bach
O have mercy on me—Miserere mihi Domine: Byrd
O hear when I cry to Thee—O sacrum convivium: Tallis
O heart subdued with grieving—Lass dich nur nichts nich dauern: Brahms
O heaven let me here implore thee—O Himmel! Lass' ich jetzt erflehen
    (Tannhäuser): Wagner
O heavenly shepherdess—Ach, englische Schäferin: Brahms
O Heiland, reiss die Himmel auf—O sorrow, rend the heavens wide/O
    Saviour rend the heavens wide: Bauernfeind
O Heiland reiss die Himmel auf—O rend the heavens/O Saviour, ope
    the heavenly gates: Brahms
O heiliges Geist—O holy spirit: Bach
O help me against the enemy—Da mihi auxilium: Byrd
O help me, Lord, to praise Thee—Hilf, Gott, dass mir's gelinge: Bach
O help me, Lord, to promise Thee—Hilf Gott, dass mir's gelinge
    (Orgelbüchlein): Bach
O Herr, gib jedem seinem—O Lord give every man: Hindemith
O Himmel! Lass' dich jetzt erflehen (Tannhäuser)—O heaven, let me here
    implore thee: Wagner
O holy and heavenly feast—O sacrum convivium: Byrd
O holy Jesus—O bone Jesu: Palestrina
O holy spirit—O heiliges Geist: Bach

O hope, within my bosom—Non sò se sia la speme (Serse): Handel
O how blessed, faithful spirits, are ye—O wie selig seid ihr doch,
  ihr Frommen: Brahms
O how cheating, O how fleeting—Ach wie nichtig, ach wie flüchtig: Bach
O how cruel—Weh, wie zornig ist das Mädchen (Spanische Liebeslieder):
  Schumann
O how fair—O wie lieblich ist das Mädchen (Spanische Liebeslieder):
  Schumann
O how, fairest ones?—Comment, disaient-ils: Liszt
O how glorious is the kingdom—O quam gloriosum: Byrd
O, how happy I am today—O, hvor er jeg glad i dag: Nielsen
O how lovely is my darling—O wie lieblich ist das Mädchen: Schumann
O how now escape?—Comment, disaient-ils: Liszt
O how that word gives comfort—Ja, dieses Wort ist meine Seelen Speise
  (Du Hirte Israel, höre): Bach
O how throbs my heart—Wo soll ich die Freude: Brahms
O, hvor er jeg glad i dag—O, how happy I am today: Nielsen
O, if you knew—O wüsstest du (Italienisches Liederbuch): Wolf
O Ihr Herren—Tell me: Schumann
O Isis, und Osiris (Die Zauberflöte)—Great Isis, great Osiris/Hear us Isis
  and Osiris: Mozart
O Jesu Christ, Thou prince of peace—Du Friedefürst, Herr Jesu Christ:
  Bach
O Jesu Christ—O crux: Palestrina
O Jesu so meek, O Jesu so kind—O Jesulein süss, O Jesulein mild: Bach
O Jesulein süss, O Jesulein mild—O Jesu so meek, O Jesu so kind: Bach
O Jesus glad I am—Ich freue mich in dir: Bach
O joy out of measure—Wo soll ich die Freude: Brahms
O Jugend, O schöne Rosenzeit—O youth/The days of youth: Mendelssohn
O King of glory—O Rex gloriae: Marenzio
O komme, holde Sommernacht—O come sweet night/Come, summer
  night: Brahms
O kühler Wald—O forest cool/The quiet wood: Brahms
O la, O che buon eco—Hark, hark, the echo falling: Lassus
O lady Judith—Entführung: Brahms
O Lamb of God, most stainless—O Lamm Gottes, unschuldig (Orgel-
  büchlein): Bach
O Lamm Gottes, unschuldig (Orgelbüchlein)—O Lamb of God,
  most stainless: Bach
O lásko—Of love: Janáček
O légère hirondelle (Mireille)—The message of love: Gounod
O let me seem now—So lasst mich scheinen [D 727]: Schubert
O let thine anger cease from us—Quiescat Domine: Byrd
O Lieb', O Lieb', du Wonnemeer—O love, O love, thou blissful sea: Goetz

O Lieb' so lang du lieben kannst/Liebestraum—O, love as long as love
  is young/Dream of love/Love's dream: Liszt
O liebe Seele, zieh' die Sinnen—Beloved soul, thy thoughts withdraw
  now: Bach
O lieber Herre Gott—O mighty Lord our God: Schütz
O liebliche Wangen—O fair cheeks of roses/Fair cheeks ye ensnare me/
  O lovely her cheeks: Brahms
O light everlasting—O ewiges Feuer: Bach
O light, O blessed Trinity—O lux beata Trinitas: Byrd
O light of light—O nata lux de lumine: Tallis
O little flower—O fiorellin di siepe: P Morales
O Lord give every man—O Herr, gib jedem seinem: Hindemith
O Lord God, according to the multitude—Domine secundum multitudinem:
  Byrd
O Lord, God of my praise—O Dieu, mon honneur: Le Jeune
O Lord God succour us—Domine salve nos: Byrd
O Lord God, Thou hast sworn—Domine tu iurasti: Byrd
O Lord have mercy—Deus, misereatur nostri: Schütz
O Lord, have mercy—Pieta, Signore: Stradella
O Lord my God, forgive Thou me—Ach Herr, mein Gott, vergib mir's
  doch: Bach
O Lord of glory—Panis Angelicus: Franck
O Lord of Lords—Mein Herr und Gott (Lohengrin): Wagner
O Lord, Thou hast searched me out—Surrexit Pastor bonus: Mendelssohn
O Lord, 'tis enough—Ich habe genug: Bach
O Lord turn Thy wrath away—Ne irascaris domine: Byrd
O, love as long as love is young—O Lieb' so lang du lieben kannst: Liszt
O love, it is a rose-tree fair—Liebesgarten: Schumann
O love, O love, thou blissful sea— O Lieb', O Lieb', du Wonnemeer: Goetz
O love regard my plight—Amor che deggio far: Anon
O love, take pity on my pain!—Amore nel mio penar (Flavio): Handel
O loveliness beyond compare—Dies Bildnis ist bezaubernd schön (Die
  Zauberflöte): Mozart
O lovely eyes—Formosos olhos: J Berger
O lovely her cheeks—O liebliche Wangen: Brahms
O lovely May—O süsser Mai: Brahms
O lovely tree—Ombra mai fù (Serse): Handel
O luce di quest' anima (Linda di Chamounix)—Oh! light and joy of all my
  heart/My soul's delight and treasure: Donizetti
O lüge nicht!—O star deceive me not: R Franz
O lux beata Trinitas—O light, O blessed Trinity: Byrd
O ma lyre immortelle (Sapho)—O thou friend of my sorrow: Gounod
O ma tant douce Colombelle—I to my love: Monsigny
O magnum mysterium—O wonderful mystery: Byrd

O maiden, may I see awhile—Jungfräulein, soll ich mit: Brahms

O man!—O Mensch! (3rd symphony): Mahler

O man bewail thy grievous (mortal) fall—O Mensch, bewein dein'
Sünde gross (Orgelbüchlein): Bach

O Mensch! (3rd symphony)—O man!: Mahler

O Mensch, bewein dein' Sünde gross (Orgelbüchlein)—O man, bewail thy
grievous (mortal) fall: Bach

O mes soeurs (Mary Magdelaine)—'Tis in vain that I seek: Massenet

O mighty Lord our God—O lieber Herre Gott: Schütz

O mighty ocean—O monumenta! (La gioconda): Ponchielli

O Mimi tu piè non torni (La bohème)—Fickle-hearted Mimi: Puccini

O mio babbino caro (Gianni Schicchi)—Oh! my beloved daddy: Puccini

O mio Fernando (La favorita)—O my Fernando/Dearest Fernando:
Donizetti

O mon coeur (Tristesses)—O my heart: Milhaud

O Mond, O lösch dein gold'nes Licht—O moon, conceal thy golden light:
R Franz

O monumento! (La gioconda)—O mighty ocean: Ponchielli

O moon, conceal thy golden light—O Mond, lösch dein gold'nes Licht:
R Franz

O morning of glory—Mattino di luce: Respighi

O morning star! how fair and bright—Wie schön leuchtet der Morgenstern: Bach (?)

O most holy Three in One—Heiligste Dreieinigkeit (Erschallet, ihr
Lieder): Bach

O mother, I want something—Och Moder, ich well en Ding han: Brahms

O mournful lips—O bocca dolorosa: Sibella

O murm'ring breezes—Murmelndes Lüftchen, blutenwind: Jensen

O my beloved—O del mio dolce ardor (Paride ed Elena): Gluck

O my Fernando—O mio Fernando: Donizetti

O my fond heart's desire—O del mio dolce ardor (Paride ed Elena):
Gluck

O my God, according to my doings—Domine secundum actum meum:
Byrd

O my heart—O mon coeur (Tristesses): Milhaud

O my Lord, I am not worthy—Domine, non sum dignus: Byrd

O my love—War es dir: Brahms

O my love—A amica meo: Morley

O, my luve's like a red, red rose—Dem roten Röslein: Schumann

O, my luvels like a red, red rose—Dem roten Röslein: Schumann

O, my people—Popule meo: Victoria

O my soul, prepare to meet Him—Schmücke dich, o liebe Seele: Bach

O naší láscenekvěte (Pisně milostné)—Never will love lead us: Dvořák

O nata lux de lumine—O light of light/O born of light: Tallis

O, no longer seek—O cessate di piargarmi: A Scarlatti

O noble sir—Mein Herr Marquis (Die Fledermaus): J Strauss II
O paradise of souls—O Seelen-Paradies (Erschallet, ihr Lieder): Bach
O pargoletto arciero—O Cupid, baby bowman: Pasquini
O pastorelle addio (Andrea Chénier)—Farewell sweet shepherdess:
  Giordano
O piccola Maria—O faithless little maiden: Bossi
O praise the Lord—Laudete pueri Dominum: Mendelssohn
O praise the Lord all ye heathens (nations)—Lobet den Herrn alle
  Herden: Bach
O praise the Lord for all his mercies—Gottlob! nun geht das Jahr zu
  Ende: Bach
O pure and tender star of eve—O du mein holder Abendstern (Tannhäuser):
  Wagner
O quam gloriosum—O how glorious is the kingdom: Byrd
O quam suavis est—How wondrous sweet, O Lord: Byrd
O radiant glory—Che splendor de' luminosi rai: Palestrina
O radiant vision—Nel sogno (Adriana Lecouvreur): Cilèa
O rend the heavens—O Heiland reiss die Himmel auf: Brahms
O rendetemi il mio bene (Amadigi di Gaula)—O give back to me my
  beloved: Handel
O Rex gloriae—O King of glory: Marenzio
O riante nature (Philémon et Baucis)—O, the smile of the spring-time!:
  Gounod
O Roman maid—O Römerin: Henschel
O Römerin—O Roman maid: Henschel
O royal tree—Ombra mai fù (Serse): Handel
O sacred head sore wounded—O Haupt voll Blut und Wunden (Matthäus-
  passion): Bach
O sacred head surrounded—O Haupt voll Blut und Wunden (Matthäus-
  passion): Bach
O sacrum convivium—O holy and heavenly feast: Byrd
O sacrum convivium—Bread of the world: Palestrina
O sacrum convivium—O hear when I cry to Thee: Tallis
O sah ich auf der Heide dort—O wert thou in the angry storm: R Franz
O sah ich auf der Heide—O wert thou in the cauld blast: Mendelssohn
O Saviour friend, O loving guide—Ombra mai fù (Serse): Handel
O Saviour mine, what agony—Mein Jesu! was für Seelenweh: Bach
O Saviour, ope the heavenly gates—O Heiland reiss die Himmel auf:
  Brahms
O Saviour rend the heavens wide—O Heiland, reiss die Himmel auf:
  Bauernfeind
O Saviour sweet, O Saviour kind—O Jesulein süss, O Jesulein mild: Bach
O say what glory—O di che lode: Marcello
O say you believe me—So willst du: Brahms

O schöne Jugendtage (Der Evangelimann)—Glad days of youth: Kienzl
O schöne Nacht—O charming night: Brahms
O schöner Mai—O beautiful May: J Strauss II
O see a vision greets my sight—Sieh' da ein herrlich Frauenbild (Der
    Zigeunerbaron): J Strauss II
O Seelen—Paradies (Erschallet, ihr Lieder)—O paradise of souls: Bach
O sel'ge Frühlingszeit (Der Rose Pilgerfahrt)—Oh! happy spring!:
    Schumann
O shining sun—An den Sonnenschein: Schumann
O should'st thou pass—Und gehst du über den Kirchhof: Brahms
O shout with gladness—Gaudete omnes: Sweelinck
O sing, fair maid—Cante, cante, fiette: Bimboni
O sing unto the Lord—Cantate Domino: Byrd
O sing ye unto the Lord—Cantate Domino canticum novum: Schütz
O skies cerulean—O cieli azzuri (Aida): Verdi
O sole mio—My sunshine/Beneath thy window/My sun: E Capua
O solitude—An die Einsamkeit: Mozart
O Sonn', o Meer, o Rose—Oh sun, oh sea, oh rose!: Schumann
O sorrow, rend the heavens wide—O Heiland, reiss die Himmel auf:
    Bauernfeind
O soul, remember this!—Denk es, o Seele!: Wolf
O spotless lamb—Erwürgtes Lamm: Bach
O star deceive me not—O lüge nicht!: R Franz
O star divine—O du mein holder Abendstern (Tannhäuser): Wagner
O stars, treacherous stars—Stelle, perfida stelle (Partenza): Handel
O sunny beam—An den Sonnenschein: Schumann
O sunshine—An den Sonnenschein: Schumann
O süsser Mai—O lovely May: Brahms
O süsser Mai—Sweet lovely May: R Strauss
O süsser Tod—O sweet death: J Marx
O sweet and dear caresses—Baci soave e cari: Gesualdo
O sweet content—Genügsamkeit ist ein Schatz in diesem Leben (Nimm
    was dein ist, und gehe hin): Bach
O sweet death—O süsser Tod: J Marx
O sweet Emmanuel—Liebster Immanuel, Herzog der Frommen: Bach
O taste and see—Wohl euch, ihr auserwählten Seelen (O ewiges Feuer): Bach
O teach me Lord my days to number—Wer weiss, wie nahe mir meine Ende?: B
O tell me weary heart—Io non so come vivo: A Stabile
O temps à jamais effacé (L'enfant prodigue)—O days that may ne'er come
    again: Debussy
O tender shadow—Ombre légère (Dinorah): Meyerbeer
O that I might retrace—O wüsst ich doch den Weg züruck: Brahma
O the smile of the spring-time!—O riante nature (Philémon et Baucis):
    Gounod

O think my soul—Gedenke doch, mein Geist zurück: Bach
O think on us with Thy compassion—Gedenk' an uns mit deiner Liebe
    (Wir danken Dir, Gott, wir danken Dir): Bach
O thou belov'd—O del mio dolce ardor (Paride ed Elena): Gluck
O thou beloved evening star—O du mein holder Abendstern (Tannhäuser):
    Wagner
O thou friend of my sorrow—O ma lyre immortelle (Sapho): Gounod
O Thou, of God the Father—Herr Christ, der einig Gottes Sohn (Orgel-
    büchlein): Bach
O Tod, O Tod—O death, O death: Brahms
O toi l'objet (Iphigénie en Aulide)—To thee I kneel: Gluck
O trusting heart—Mein glaubiges Herze (Also hat Gott die Welt geliebt):
    Bach
O voi del mio (Orlando)—O ye, my spirits true: Handel
O voi dell' Erebo (La Resurrezione)—Up! Lords of Erebus: Handel
O vos omnes—O all ye that pass by: Dering
O wait—Geduld: R Strauss
O wärst du mein—O wert thou mine: R Strauss
O well for you, ye souls elected—Wohl euch, ihr auserwählten Seelen
    (O ewiges Feuer): Bach
O Welt, ich muss dich lassen—O world, I e'en must leave thee: Brahms
O Welt ich muss dich lassen—O world, I must be parting: Isaac
O, wert thou here—Aus banger Brust: Sibelius
O wert thou in the cauld blast—O säh ich auf der Heide: Mendelssohn
O wert thou mine—O wärst du mein: R Strauss
O, what pleasure—Vanne, segn' il mio desio (Floridante): Handel
O where?—Der Strom, der neben mir verrauschte: Brahms
O where is there a sward so green—S'il est un charmant gazon: Liszt
O, while I sleep—Oh, quand je dors: Liszt
O whither shall I flee—Wo soll ich fliehen hin: Bach
O who rides by the night—Erklönig: Schubert-Heller
O why are all the roses so pale—Warum sind denn die Rosen: Cornelius
O wie lieblich ist das Mädchen—O how lovely is my darling: Schumann
O wie lieblich ist das Mädchen (Spanische Liebeslieder)—O how fair:
    Schumann
O wie sanft (Liebeslieder Walzer)—Oh, how soft: Brahms
O wie selig seid Ihr doch, ihr Frommen—O how blessed, faithful spirits,
    are ye: Brahms
O wilt thou—So willst du: Brahms
O wonderful mystery—O magnum mysterium: Byrd
O wondrous heavenly bread—Panis angelicus: Franck
O wondrous love—Herzliebster Jesu, was hast Du verbrochen: Bach
O wondrous mystery of love—Es muss ein Wunderbares sein: Liszt
O world, I e'en must leave thee—O Welt, ich muss dich lassen: Brahms

O world, I must be parting—O Welt ich muss dich lassen: Isaac
O wüsst ich doch den Weg zurück—O golden age/O that I might retrace/
O could I but find the way: Brahms
O wüsstest du (Italianisches Liederbuch)—O, if you knew/Didst thou
but know: Wolf
O ye, my spirits true—O roi del mio (Orlando): Handel
O ye tears—Lagrime: Dering
O yes, just so—Patron, das macht der Wind! (Geschwinde, geschwinde,
ihr wirbelnden Winde): Bach
O youth—O Jugend, O schöne Rosenzeit: Mendelssohn
O zephyr, soft and kind—O del mio dolce ardor (Paride ed Elena): Gluck
The oath—Der Schwur: Meyer-Helmund
Oats—Oves: Smetana
Ein Obdach gegen Sturm—Wand'rer by the tempest: R Strauss
Oblak a mrákota (Biblické Písně)—Clouds and darkness: Dvořák
Obligation—Verbundenheit: Schoenberg
The obligation of the first and greatest commandment—Die Schuldigkeit
des ersten und fürnehmsten Gebotes: Mozart
Obruchenie v monastire—Betrothal in a priory (monastery): Prokofiev
L'oca del Cairo—The goose of Cairo/The goosegirl of Cairo: Mozart
The ocean's song—Havets sang (Willemoes): Nielsen
Och Mod'r, ich well en Ding han—Mother, I want something/O mother,
I want something: Brahms
Oculi omnium—Waiting on thee: Byrd
Ode to joy—An die Freude: Schubert
Ode to the tooth-ache—Zahnweh: Schumann
Ode to the Virgin Mary—Marienlied: J Marx
Odins Meeres-ritt—Odin's ride over the sea: Loewe
Odin's ride over the sea—Odins Meeres-ritt: Loewe
L'odolom—The thaw: Leontovych
O'er a sleeping child—Auf ein schlummerndes Kind: Cornelius
O'er mountain and valley—Zu Tanze, zu Sprunge (Geschwinde, geschwinde,
ihr wirbelnden Winde): Bach
O'er the billows—Über den Wellen: Frankenstein
O'er the forest branches—Über allen Gipfeln is Ruh': Schubert
O'er the Ganges now launches—Già il sole dal Gange: A Scarlatti
O'er the rocks—Am Gesteine (Liebeslieder Walzer): Brahms
O'erwhelm us with Thy mercy—Ertöt' uns durch dein' Gute (Herr
Christ, der ein'ge Gottes Sohn): Bach
Of dreams—De rêve (Proses lyriques): Debussy
Of evening—De soir (Proses lyriques): Debussy
Of ev'ry joy I am bereft—Vergangen ist mir Glück und Heil: Brahms
Of flowers—De fleurs (Proses lyriques): Debussy
Of flowers the fairest—Klein-Zschocher müsse so zart und süsser (Mer
hahn en neue Oberkeet): Bach

Of heroism, great deeds, and fame—O doblestyakh, O podvigakh, oslave: Nechaev

Of household rule—Vom Hausregiment: Hindemith

Of love—O lasko: Janáček

Of marble you are fashioned—Di marmo siete voi: Gagliano

Of strange countries—Von fremden Ländern (Kinderscenen): Schumann

Of the shore—De grève (Proses lyriques): Debussy

Of unexpected happ'nings—D'inaspettati eventi (Poro): Handel

Of yore there dwelt two kingly ones—Les deux enfants du roi: d'Arba

The offering—Le présent: Poulenc

Offne dich, mein ganzes Herze (Nun komm, der Heiden Heiland)—Open thyself, my whole breast: Bach

Oft denk ich (Kinder-totenlieder)—I think oft: Mahler

Oft I am happy—Tit er jeg glad: Nielsen

Ognenniy Angel—The flaming angel: Prokofiev

Ogni momento dicon le donne (L'oca del Cairo)—Women may swear they'll never desert you: Mozart

Ogni pena più spietata—Though my day be dark: Pergolesi

Ogni Sabato—Every Sabbath thine altar: Gordigiani

Ogni vento (Agrippina)—When in danger: Handel

Oh, blessed flock—Beglückte Heerde (Du Hirte Israel, höre): Bach

Oh can there be given?—Wo soll ich die Freude: Brahms

Oh, come now to the casement—Deh vieni all finestra (Don Giovanni): Mozart

Oh, cruel thoughts have pity—Pensieri, voi mi tormentate (Agrippina): Handel

Oh! de' verd' anni miei (Ernani)—Fair hours of youth and pleasure: Verdi

Oh, dear companions—Oh, mie fedeli (Beatrice di Tenda): Bellini

Oh, death is like the cooling night—Der Tod, das ist die kuhle Nacht: Brahms

Oh! divina Agnese (Beatrice di Tenda)—For ever dear: Bellini

Oh! foolish blockheads—Ah! che zucconi (Gianni Schicchi): Puccini

Oh, give an answer—Rede, Mädchen (Liebeslieder Walzer): Brahms

Oh God, for whom I am waiting—Jag istenem, kire várok: Bartók

Oh! happy spring—O selge Frühlingszeit (Der Rose Pilgerfahrt): Schumann

Oh! hear me!—Ascolti . . . Io moriró (Germania): Franchetti

Oh, heart of mine—Più non penser: Astorga

Oh, how soft—O wie sanft (Liebeslieder Walzer): Brahms

Oh, illusion—Infelice, e tuo crederi (Ernani): Verdi

Oh Jesus, may my heart—Min Jesus lad mit hjerte få: Nielsen

Oh! let me die—Vorrei morire!: Tosti

Oh, let me dream—So lasst mich scheinen [D 877]: Schubert

Oh! light and joy of all my heart—O luce di quest' anima (Linda di Chamounix): Donizetti

Oh, love hath falsely spoken—Die Liebe hat gelogen: Schubert

Oh! love long lost—Sei mir gegrüsst: Schubert

Oh! love, this soul beguiling—Come per me sereno (La sonnambula):
Bellini

Oh! love thou art cruel—Che fiero costume: Legrenzi

Oh maiden dearest, my heart is true—Neckerein: Brahms

Oh mattutini albori! (La donna del lago)—Dawn may be early breaking:
Rossini

Oh! mie fedeli (Beatrice di Tenda)—Oh, dear companions: Bellini

Oh! my beloved daddy—O mio babbino caro (Gianni Schicchi): Puccini

Oh, my daughter—Figlia mia, non pianger, nò (Tamerlano): Handel

Oh, my soul—Alma mia, dove ten'rai: Gagliano

Oh, ne t'éveille (Jocelyn)—Angels guard thee/Berceuse: Godard

Oh praise the Lord—Lobet den Herren: Staden

Oh! quand je dors—O! come to me in dreams/O, while I sleep/Come in
my dreams: Liszt

Oh! return—Revenez, amours, revenez: Lully

Oh, Robert, oh my beloved—Robert, toi que j'aime (Robert le diable):
Meyerbeer

Oh, se sapeste (La fanciulla del West)—Oh, you've no notion: Puccini

Oh, summer night—Die Sommernacht: Henschel

Oh sun, oh sea, oh rose! —O sonn', o Meer, o Rose: Schumann

Oh, Susanna is late—E Susanna non vien (Le nozze di Figaro): Mozart

Oh! sweet eyes so ardently—Vezzosette e care: Falconieri

Oh! tell me love—Sagt's ihr: Kotchubei

Oh tranquil night—Paisible nuits (Les amours déguisés): Bourgeois

Oh, wert thou in the angry storm—O säh' ich auf der Heide dort: R Franz

Oh, what a day—Auf der Wanderung: Wolf

Oh, what is love?—Was Liebe sei?: Liszt

Oh, what wonder—Ayzeh Peleh (Shire' Chalutzim): Binder

Oh, who can feel the bliss—Es muss ein Wunderbares sein: Liszt

Oh! why so soon, the rose complained—Es hat die Rose sich beklagt:
R Franz

Oh! ye sweet nightingales—Rossignols amoureux (Hippolyte et Aricie):
Rameau

Oh, you've no notion—Oh, se sapeste (La fanciulla del West): Puccini

L'oiseau bleu—The bluebird: Wolff

Les oiseaux et les sources (Messe de la Pentecôte)—Birds and springs:
Messiaen

Oiseaux, si tous les ans—The year of spring/Birds swift to change the air:
Mozart

Les oiselets—The little birds: Massenet

Old Anders the tender's song—Gamle Anders Røgters sang (Vivens søn):
Nielsen

Old bogie—Knecht Ruprecht (Album für die Jugend): Schumann

An old castle—Auf einer Burg: Schumann
Old Cotiló—El Cotiló: Gerhard
The old elm—Der Lindenbaum (Die Winterreise): Schubert
An old German love-song (Minnesong)—Altdeutscher Liebesreim: Meyer-
 Helmund
Old German song—Altdeutsches Lied: Mendelssohn
Old goblin—Knecht Ruprecht (Album für die Jugend): Schumann
The old house—Am Fenster: Schubert
The old hunter—Ich schwing' mein Horn: Brahms
The old lady—Die Alte: Mozart
The old love—Alte Liebe: Brahms
Old love and new—Erinnerung an's schätzle: Erk
An old love song—Minnelied: Mendelssohn
The old man—Der Mann: Brahms
The old man—Der Greis: Haydn
The old man—Greisengesang: Schubert
Old man's song—Greisengesang: Schubert
Old mill, beloved so dearly—Ei Mühle, liebe Mühle (Der Rose Pilgerfahrt):
 Schumann
The old mother—Gamle Mor: Grieg
Old song—Altes Lied: R Franz
The old song—Das alte Lied: Grieg
Old songs—Hor' ich das Liedchen (Dichterliebe): Schumann
Old sounds—Alte Laute: Schumann
Old stories—Aus alten Märchen (Dichterliebe): Schumann
The old woman's advice—Rat einer Alten: Wolf
The old year now hath passed away—Das alte Jahr vergangen (Orgelbüchlein):
 Bach
An old-world serenade—Rococo Ständchen: Meyer-Helmund
Ombra cara (Radamisto)—Though divided/Shade departed: Handel
L'ombra di Don Giovanni—The shade of Don Juan: Alfano
Un ombra di pace (Calphurnia)—The trumpet is calling: Bononcini
Ombra mai fù (Serse)—Largo/No sylvan shade/Slumber dear maid/Shade
 like unto thine/Calm, friendly shade/Ne'er were such leaves/O lovely
 tree/The plane tree/Shadows so sweet/Come gladsome spring/Father
 in heaven/Rest/Love's richest dower/O royal three/O Saviour friend,
 O loving guide: Handel
L'ombre des arbres (Ariettes oubliées)—The shadow of the trees: Debussy
Ombre légère (Dinorah)—Shadow song/O tender shadow: Meyerbeer
Ombre, piante, urne funeste (Rodelinda)—Shadows, cypress, urns
 funereal: Handel
Omens—Zelenaj se, zelenaj (Moravské Dvojzpévy): Dvořák
Ominous a storm upsurging—Sorge infausta (Orlando): Handel
Omnipotence—Die Allmacht: Schubert

Omphale's spinning wheel—Le rouet d'Omphale: Saint-Saëns
On a balcony—På verandan vid havet: Sibelius
On a castle's height—Auf einer Burg: Schumann
On a child—Auf ein Kind: R Strauss
On a fair morn in spring—Mañana de primavera: P Morales
On a journey—Auf einer Wanderung: Wolf
On Christ's ascension alone—Auf Christi Himmelfahrt allein: Bach
On cloud-cover'd heights—Auf wölkigen Höh'n (Siegfried): Wagner
On guard—Gebt acht!: Brahms
On her contentment—Dalla sua pace (Don Giovanni): Mozart
On love's wings—Di Cupido impiego i vanni (Rodelinda): Handel
On my heart—An meinem Herzen, an meiner Brust (Frauenliebe und
    -leben): Schumann
On my love's wedding day—Wenn mein Schatz fröhliche Hochzeit macht
    (Lieder eines fahrenden Gesellen): Mahler
On my shepherd I rely—Meinem Hirten bleib' ich treu (Ich hab in Gottes
    Herz und Sinn): Bach
On St John's eve—In der Johannisnacht: Meyer-Helmund
On the banks of the river—Au bord de l'eau: Fauré
On the beautiful blue Danube—An der Schönen, blauen Donau: J Strauss I
On the bridge—Auf der Bruck: Schubert
On the bridge of Paris—A Paris, sur le petit pont: Blanchard
On the brook's green back—An des lust'gen Brunnens Rand: F Mendelssoh
On the death of my child—Auf meines Kindes Tod: Schoeck
On the field of death—Na polye smerti (Aleksandr Nevsky): Prokofiev
On the field of Knlikovo—Na pole Knlikovom: Shaporin
On the hillside—Im Gebirge: Kjerulf
On the lagoons—Sur les lagunes (Nuits d'été): Berlioz
On the lake—Auf dem See: Brahms
On the lake—Wasserfahrt: R Franz
On the lake—Auf dem See: Schubert
On the lake—Der Schiffer: Schubert
On the lake, so calm, so placid—Auf dem Teich, dem regungslosen: R Franz
On the Ling, ho!—Ingrids Lied: Kjerulf
On the march—Marschiren: Brahms
On the meadows—Na tych fojtovych lukach: Janáček
On the mountain—Vom Berge: R Franz
On the ocean—Auf dem Meere: R Franz
On the Rhine—Am Rhein (Rheinische Lieder): Cornelius
On the Rhine—Im Rhein: R Franz
On the Rhine—Auf dem Rhein: Schoeck
On the Rhine—Auf dem Rhein: Schumann
On the river—Auf dem Flüsse (Die Winterreise): Schubert
On the rocking horse—Ritter vom Steckenpferd (Kinderscenen): Schumann

On the sea—Auf dem Meere (Rinaldo): Brahms
On the sea—Auf dem Meere: R Franz
On the sea—Auf dem See: Mendelssohn
On the shore—Am Ufer: R Strauss
On the shore of the lake—Am Strande: Fielitz
On the southern shores of the Crimea—En Crimée: Mussorgsky
On the stream—Am Strome: Schubert
On the stream—Auf dem Strom: Schubert
On the water—Auf dem Wasser zu singen: Schubert
On the way home—Ved Rundarne: Grieg
On the wings of the storm—Mit Gewitter und Sturm (Der fliegende
    Holländer): Wagner
On this day, the blessed Virgin Mary—Hodie beata Virgo Maria:
    Palestrina
On this Thy resurrection morning—In resurrectione Tua: Byrd
On waters the silver moon was spilling—Der Strom Floss, der Mond
    vergass (Chinesische Liebeslieder): Liebermann
On wings of song—Auf Flügeln des Gesanges: Mendelssohn
On with the motley—Vesti la giubba (Pagliacci): Leoncavallo
Once a little fawn—Hirschlein ging im Wald: Cornelius
Once a wreath for thee—Einst wollt' ich einen Kranz: Liszt
Once again I fain would meet thee—Wieder möcht' ich dir begegnen:
    Liszt
Once and now—Einst wollt' ich einen Kranz: Liszt
Once he came in blessing—Gottes Sohn ist kommen (Orgelbüchlein):
    Bach
Once in my childhood—Un di, ero piccina (Iris): Mascagni
Once in the May-time—Nel verde Maggio (Loreley): Catalani
Once in the woods—Ich glaub', lieber Schatz: Reger
Once in these arms I'll fold thee—Mentre ti lascio, o figlia: Mozart
Once in thine eyes—Ich hab' in deinem Auge: R Franz
Once more behold me in Babylon—Eccomi alfine in Babilonia
    (Semiramide): Rossini
Once more the sun—Nun will die Sonn' (Kindertotenlieder): Mahler
Once more with joy—Beglück darf nun dich (Tannhäuser): Wagner
Once through a woodland Mary walked—Maria durch ein Dornwald
    ging: Bauernfeind
Onda—Wave: Ponce
Onde porei meus olhos—Where can eyes like mine: J Berger
One day with Cupid playing—Un di la bella Clori: Cesarini
One fine autumn day—Par un frais sentier (Don César de Bazan): Massenet
One fine day—Un bel dì (Madama Butterfly): Puccini
One glance love—Un guardo vogli a me: Marcello
One grotesque—Egy torz (Két portré): Bartók

One hour before the day—Ein Stundlein wohl vor Tag: R Franz

One I love—Sono amate: D Scarlatti

One ideal—Egy idealis (Két portré): Bartók

One night there came—Es fiel ein Reif: Mendelssohn

One power—Yks' voima: Sibelius

One shaft from thy bow—Traun! Bogen und Pfeil sind gut für den Feind:
   Brahms

One thing befalleth—Denn es gehet dem Menschen: Brahms

One whose spirit is true and noble—Alma grande e nobil core: Mozart

Only a dream—Ich hatte einst ein schönes Vaterland/Es war ein Traum:
   Lassen

Only be still—Man halte nur ein wenig stille (Wer nur den lieben
   Gott lässt walten): Bach

The only thing—Det Förste: Grieg

Only tell me—Ne hagyi itt!: Bartók

The only time to love—La jeunesse n'a qu'un temps: A L(ehmann)

Only wait—Warte nur: Reger

The open air—Der Gärtner: Brahms

Open thy blue eyes—Ouvre tes yeux bleus: Massenet

Open thyself, my whole breast—Öffne dich, mein ganzes Herze (Nun
   komm, der Heiden Heiland): Bach

Open wide the gates of mercy—Mein Gott, öffne mir die Pforten (Liebster
   Jesu, mein Verlangen): Bach

The opening spring—Im Frühlingsanfang: Mozart

The opera ball—Der Opernball: Heuberger

An operatic squabble—Der Schauspieldirektor: Mozart

Der Opernball—The operaball: Heuberger

Opernburlesken—Beggar's opera: Calmus

Opferlied—Sacrificial chant/Sacrificial hymn: Beethoven

Opuštěný milý—Forsaken love: Martinů

Or che il cielo a me ti rende—Heaven to me my love restoring: Mozart

Or Djupet—Out of the depth: Sinding

Or sus, serviteurs du Seigneur—Ye servants of the Lord of might: Le Jeune

L'ora, o Tirse (Manon Lescaut)—These are hours of joy's creating:
   Puccini

La oración del torero—The prayer of the bullfighter: Turina

L'oracolo—The sage: Leoni

Orage (Années de pèlerinage)—Storm: Liszt

The orb of day departs—Im Abendrot: Schubert

Orchard—Verger: Hindemith

Öregek—The aged: Kodály

Ores que je suis dispos—Now when I am strong and well: Lassus

Orfeo—Orpheus: Monteverdi

Orfeo ed Euridice—Orpheus and Eurydice: Gluck, Haydn

The organ grinder—Der Schwanderer: Hindemith
The organ grinder—Der Leiermann (Die Winterreise): Schubert
Un organetto suona per la ria—The street-organ: Sibella
Orgelbüchlein—Little organ book: Bach
Orietur—For in those days justice shall arise: Byrd
Orliny bunt—The eagles' revolt/The eagle mutiny: Pashchenko
The orphan—Sirotek: Dvořák
The orphan—Die Waise; Grieg
An orphan from my early days—Als flotter geist (Der Zigeunerbaron):
    J Strauss II
The orphan girl—Die Waise: Schumann
Orphée aux enfers—Orpheus in the underworld: Offenbach
Orpheus—Orfeo: Monteverdi
Orpheus and Eurydice—Orfeo ed Euridice: Gluck, Haydn
Orpheus in the underworld: Orphée aux enfers: Offenbach
Osenneye—Autumn moods: Prokofiev
Oster-Oratorium—Easter oratorio: Bach
Osterlied—Easter song: Grieg
Ot kraya i do kraya (Tirhii Don)—From end to end: Dzerzhinski
Ot vsevo serdtsa—With all one's heart: Zhukovskyi
Otchayaniye—Despair: Prokofiev
Otello—Othello: Verdi; Rossini
Otevřeni Slovečkem—The lock: Martinů
Othello—Otello: Verdi; Rossini
Otho—Ottone: Handel
Ottone—Otho: Handel
Où suis-je? (Sapho)—Where am I?: Gounod
Où va la jeune Indove (Lakmé)—Bell-song: Delibes
Où voulez-vous aller?—Whither wouldst thou repair/The elf's trip:
    Gounod
Our days are as a shadow—Unser Leben ist ein Schatten: J Bach
Our Father in heaven—Vater unser im Himmelreich: Bach
Our Father, Thou in heav'n above—Vater unser im Himmelreich (Orgel-
    büchlein): Bach
Our Father, who art in heaven—Vater unser, der du bist im Himmel:
    Cornelius
Our foes press on us far and wide—Aufsperren sie den Rachen weit (Wo
    Gott, der Herr, nicht bei uns halt): Bach
Our flock will dance—R'kod Hat'laim (Shire' Chalutzim): Binder
Our lady fair reposes—Es ging sich uns're Fraue: Brahms
Our love—Notre amour: Fauré
Our spring—Naše jaro: Vycpalek
L'ours—The bear: Haydn
Ours are like gifts—Pari siamo (Rigoletto): Verdi
241

Out in the open air—Hinaus ins Freie: Schumann
Out of doors—Szabadban: Bartók
Out of my dark despairing—Aus meinem grossen Schmerzen: R Franz
Out of the depth—Or Djupet: Sinding
Out of the depths I cry to Thee—Aus tiefer Not schrei' ich zu Dir: Bach
Out of the mist—Der dukker af disen: Nielsen
Out there where the church tower—Là-bas vers l'église: Ravel
Out over the Forth—Wohl schau' ich nach Nord: M Mayer
The outermost isles—Ute i Skären: Myström
Outward bound—Udfarten: Grieg
Ouvre tes yeux bleus—Open thy blue eyes: Massenet
Ove celare (Don Sebastiano)—Would I could hide: Donizetti
Over de höje Fjelde—Over the lofty mountains: Kjerulf
Over her embroidery—Pri vyšíváni: Dvořák
Over hill and vale—Über allen Gipfeln ist Ruh': Liszt
Over the brink of beyond—Über die Grenzen des All . . . : Berg
Over the lofty mountains—Over de höje Fjelde: Kjerulf
Over the moor—Über die Heide: Brahms
Over the thousand mountains—Über die tausend Berge (Lieder der Liebe):
    Kilpinen
Over the waves—Sobre las olas: Rosas
Over their grave—Auf ihrem Grab: Mendelssohn
Overheard in the woods—Waldesgespräch: Schumann
Overture of welcome—Privetstvennaya uvertyura: Miaskovsky
Oves—Oats: Smetana
Owlet—Das Kaüzchen: J N David
The owls—Les hiboux: Séverac
Ox tails—Queues de boeuf (La bonne cuisine): Bernstein
Oxana's caprices—Tcherevichky: Tchaikovsky
Ozero Ritsa—Lake Rits: Balanchivadze

P

På det jaevne—The plain and simple ways of life: Nielsen

På Hamars Ruinen—On the ruins of Hamar: Grieg

På Skogstien—Autumn thoughts: Grieg

På verandan vid havet—On a balcony: Sibelius

Paccantem me quotidie—My sins are with me every day: Palestrina

Päd Arkuna—The fall of Arkun: Fibich

Paesaggi toscani—Tuscan landscapes: Tommasini

Page d'album—For an album/No joy could be more thrilling: Berlioz

Pagenlied—Song of the Savoyard/Page's song: Mendelssohn

Page's song—Je suis presqu' enfant (Don César de Bazan): Massenet

Page's song—Pagenlied: Mendelssohn

Pagliacci—Clowns/The players: Leoncavallo

Pai, pai, paitaressu—Lullaby: Merikanto

Painful wrestling—Lassú vergödés (Tiz könnyü zongoradarab): Bartók

Paisible nuit (Les amours déguisés)—Oh tranquil night: Bourgeois

La paloma—The dove: Yradier

Pamyati sergeya Esenina—In memory of Esenin: Sviridov

Pan Buh vam zaplat!—May God bless you: Janáček

Pan is master—Pan ist Meister (Geschwinde, geschwinde, ihr wirbelnden
   Winde): Bach

Pan ist Meister (Geschwinde, geschwinde, ihr wirbelnden Winde)—
   Pan is master: Bach

Pan-American hymn—Himno Pan-americano: A Brandt

Pange lingua—Holy body of the Saviour: Victoria

Pange lingua—Speak, my tongue: W S G Williams

Panis Angelicus—Heavenly bread/Bread, pure angelical/O wond'rous
   heavenly bread/O Lord of glory: Franck

Le paon (Histoires naturelles)—The peacock: Ravel

Les papillons—Butterflies: Chaminade

Les papillons—The butterflies: Chausson

Papillons—Butterfly: Schumann

Par ce que j'ai souffert (Tristesses)—Since I have suffered much: Milhaud

Par che me dica ancora (Il castello di Kenilworth)—When me fair
   dreams awaken: Donizetti

Par un frais sentier (Don César de Bazan)—One fine autumn day: Massenet

Le paradis retrouvé—Paradise regained: I Albeniz

Paradise regained—Le paradis retrouvé: I Albeniz

Pardon my intrusion—Je tir' ma révérence: Bastia

Pardon us, gracious Lord—Murre nicht, lieber Christ (Nimm was dein ist,
   und gehe hin): Bach

Parfois, je suis triste (Tristesses)—Sometimes I am sad: Milhaud

Parfons regretz—Woe, grief, despair: Josquin

Le parfum impérissable—The imperishable perfume: Fauré
Pari siamo! (Rigoletto)—Ours are like gifts!: Verdi
Paride ed Elena—Paris and Helen: Gluck
Paris and Helen—Paride ed Elena: Gluck
Parisian life—La vie parisienne: Offenbach
Parla!—Speak: Arditi
Parle-moi d'autre chose—There's no more you can say: Delage
Parlez-moi d'amour—Speak to me of love: Lenoir
Parole—The huntsman/Truth/Alone she stood by the window: Brahms
La part du diable—The devil's share: Auber
Partant pour la Syrie—Proclaim to every son of France: Queen Hortense
Parted—In der Ferne: Brahms
Parted—Sehnsucht: Brahms
Parted—Lungi dal caro bene (Giulio Sabino): Sarti
Parted from thee—Caro mio ben: Giordani
La partenza—Separation/The farewell: Beethoven
Partenza—Parting: Handel
Parting—Abschied: Brahms
Parting—Beim Abschied: Brahms
Parting—Scheiden und Meiden: Brahms
Parting—Trennung: Brahms
The parting—Rozlovčění (Moravské dvojzpěvy): Dvořák
Parting—Abschied: R Franz
Parting—Abschied: Grieg
Parting—Trennung: Henschel
Parting—Scheidenlied: Mendelssohn
Parting—Abschied (Schwanengesang): Schubert
Parting and meeting—Beim Abschied zu singen: Schumann
Parting without sorrow—V dobrým sme se sešil (Moravské Dvojzpěvy):
    Dvořák
Parto, parto, ma tu ben mio (La clemenza di Tito)—Vengeance, vengeance:
    Mozart
Parto si (Flavio)—Fare thee well: Handel
Partout des cris de joie (La jolie fille de Perth)—The air rings with her
    laughter/Hear the cry of a lover's yearning/'Tis a faithful lover's
    greeting: Bizet
Parvalus nobis nascitur—To us a little child is born: Praetorius
Pas des echarpes—Scarf dance: Chaminade
The Paschal victim here—Hier ist das rechte Osterlamm (Christ lag in
    Todesbanden): Bach
The passage-bird—Wandervöglein: Goetz
The passage-bird's farewell—Abschiedslied der Zuvögel: Mendelssohn
O passarinho de panno (A prolé do bêbê)—The little cloth bird: Villa Lobos
Passarinho esta cantando—Little bird if you sing sweetly: Mignone

Passed!—Bestamdem! (Das Examen): P Burkhard
The passing bell—Das Zügenglocklein: Schubert
Passing to Hades—Fahrt zum Hades: Schubert
Passion hymn—Passionlied: Reger
Passion so dear and blessed—Ardor felice caro: Dering
Passionlied—Passion hymn: Reger
The past—Hier: Poulenc
Pastoral song—Air champêtre: Poulenc
Il pastore canta—The shepherd sings: Recli
La pastorella delle Alpi—The little shepherdess: Rossini
Pastorello d'un povero armento (Rodelinda)—E'en the shepherd: Handel
La pastoreta—Shepherdess I love: Alió
Pastýřka—Shepherdess: Smetana
Pateticheskaya oratoriya—Pathetic oratorio: Sviridov
The path of faith now run—Tritt auf die Glaubensbahn: Bach
The path of love—Weg der Liebe: Brahms
Pathetic oratorio—Pateticheskaya oratoriya: Sviridov
Les patineurs—The skaters: Waldteufel
Patron, das macht der Wind! (Geschwinde, geschwinde, ihr wibelnden
    Winde)—My Lord, it's all the wind/Oh yes, just so: Bach
Paulus—St Paul: Mendelssohn
Le pauvre matelot—The poor sailor: Milhaud
Pavane de la belle au bois dormant (Ma mère l'oye)—Sleeping beauty:
    Ravel
Pavane for a dead Infanta—Pavane pour une Infante défunte: Ravel
Pavane pour une Infante défunte—Pavane for a dead Infanta: Ravel
Pavaszti nóta (Tiz könnyü zongoradarab)—Peasant's song: Bartók
Pavements of Paris—Sur le pavé: Auric
Pax Dei—A song of rest: E W Naylor
Pax Dei—Grant us Thy peace: Troman
Paysage—Landscape: Liszt
Peace—Der du von dem Himmel bist: Liszt
Peace—Friede: Reger
Peace—Du bist die Ruh': Schubert
Peace and content—Ridente la calma: Mozart
Peace day—Friedenstag: R Strauss
The peace of evening—Abendbilder: Wolf
Peace of the woods—Skovstilhed: Grieg
Peace on earth—Friede auf Erden: Schoenberg
Peace thou unruly sea—Schweig', aufgetürmtes Meer! (Jesus schläft, was
    soll ich hoffen?: Bach
The peaceful lake—Der traumende See: Schumann
Peaceful shall be my departure—Sanfte soll mein Todeskummer (Öster-
    oratorium): Bach

The peacock—Le paon (Histoires naturelles): Ravel
The peacocks—Föllszallot a páva: Kodály
The pearl—Die Perle: R Franz
The pearl fishers—Les pêcheurs de perles: Bizet
The pearl of Brazil—La perle du Brésil: F David
The pearly shining necklace—Die Schnur die Perl' an Perle: Brahms
Peasant cantata—Mer hahn en neue Oberkeet: Bach
The peasant philosopher—Il filosofo di campagna: Galuppi
Peasant's song—Pavaszti nóta (Tiz könnyü zongoradarab): Bartók
Peasant's song—Bondens Sang: Grieg
Le pêcheur—The fisher: Berlioz
Les pêcheurs de perles—The pearl fishers: Bizet
Peccantem me quotidie—When daily living sinfully: Byrd
La peine (Petites légendes)—Distress: Milhaud
Les pelerins de la Mecque/La rencontre imprévue—The pilgrims of (to)
    Mecca: Gluck
Pelop's wooing—Námluvy Pelopovy: Fibich
The penitent David—Davidde penitente: Mozart
Pensa, oh bella (Supione)—Look fair lady: Handel
Pensée d'automne—An autumn thought: Massenet
Pensée des morts—In mem'ry of the dead: Liszt
Il penseroso (Années de pèlerinage)—The pensive one: Liszt
Il pensier sta negli oggetti (Orfeo ed Euridice)—Ah, poor heart: Haydn
Pensieri, voi mi tormentate (Agrippina)—Oh, cruel thoughts have pity:
    Handel
Pensiero—Thoughts: Leoncavallo
The pensive one—Il penseroso (Années de pèlerinage): Liszt
Penso!—I remember: Tosti
People on a terrace in moonlight—La terace des audiences au clair de
    lune: Debussy
The people's holy war—Narodnaya svyashchennaya voina: Koval'
Per la gloria d'adorarvi (Griselda)—For the love my heart doth prize/
    For the glory of adoring/Joy and love/Proud and peerless:
    G B Bononcini
Per me giunto è il dì supremo (Don Carlos)—'Tis that day I so long
    awaited: Verdi
Per non penar—For my heart's peace: Astorga
Per pietà, non ricercate—Smile o'er my grieving: Mozart
Per questa bella mano—By your lovely hand: Mozart
Per questo dolce amplesso (Artaserse)—In this last caress: Hasse
Per rapir quel tesoro (Serse)—To despoil this your treasure: Handel
Per salvarti idolo mio (Lotario)—To save thy life: Handel
Per valli, per boschi—Thro' valley, thro' woodland: Blangini
Peregrinus—The journey to Emmaus: Anon

Perfect happiness—Glückes genug (Kinderscenen): Schumann
The perfect hour—L'heure exquise: Hahn
Periti autem—The righteous living for ever: Mendelssohn
Die Perle—The pearl: R Franz
La perle du Brésil—The pearl of Brasil: F David
Perpatuar—Quarrel: Bartók
The perpetual—Das Unaufhörliche: Hindemith
A personal confession—Selbstgeständnis: Wolf
Pervaya Konnaya—The first cavalry: Davidenko
La pesca—Night breezes: Rossini
Pescator, affonda l'esca (La gioconda)—Fisherman thy bait now lower:
    Ponchielli
Pesn o'lesakh—Song of the forests: Shostakovich
Pesna bor'by—The poem of struggle: Kabalevski
Pesnya likovaniya—Song of triumph: Veprik
Pesnya o rodine—The song of my country: Dunayevski
The pet chicken—Die Henne: Brahms
The pet dove—La colombe: Gounod
The petals drop noiselessly down—Il pleut des pétales de fleurs: Rhené-
    Baton
Peter the shipwright—Zar und Zimmerman: Lortzing
Le petit âne blanc—The little white donkey: Ibert
Le petit duc—The little duke: Lecoq
Le petit garçon malade—The little sick boy: Poulenc
Petit Poucet (Ma mère l'oye)—Tom Thumb: Ravel
Le petit rentier—The funny little man: Pierné
El petit vailet—The ploughboy: Gerhard
Une petite fille—While her parents were a-praying: Bax
La petite mariée—The scarlet feather: Lecoq-Monckton
Petites légendes—Little legends: Milhaud
Petition—Bitte: J Marx
Phänomen—Love hath not departed: Brahms
Phänomen—Phenomenon: Wolf
Phantasientanz (Fantasiestücke)—Fancy/Dance/Fanciful dance/Fantastic
    dance: Schumann
Phantasiestücke (Albumblätter)—Fancy piece/Fantasia/Fantasy: Schumann
A phantasy-journey to the Faroe Islands—En fantasirejse til Færøerne:
    Nielsen
The phantom bard—Der Bardengeist: Beethoven
Phantom suns—Die Nebensonnen (Die Winterreise): Schubert
Phenomenon—Phänomen: Wolf
Phoebus and Pan—Geschwinde, geschwinde, ihr wirbelnden Winde: Bach
The phoenix—Bevelise und Lysidor: C P E Bach
The phoenix and the flames—Io son fenice e voi sete la fiamma: Vecchi

Phyllis and her mother—Phyllis und die Mutter: Erk
Phyllis und die Mutter—Phyllis and her mother: Erk
Piangero la sorte mia (Giulio Cesare)—Hope no more/Grief is mine/I shall
   mourn my cruel fortune: Handel
The piazza—Il campiello: Wolf-Ferrari
Pictures at an exhibition—Tableaux d'une exposition: Mussorgsky
Pieces in the shape of a pear—Morceaux en forme de poire: Satie
The pied-piper—Der Rattenfänger: Wolf
Pierrot et Pierrette—The stranger: Holbrooke
Pierrot lunaire—Moonstruck Pierrot: Schoenberg
Pierrot's dance song—Tanzlied des Pierrot (Die tote Stadt): Korngold
Pierścien—The ring: Chopin
Pietà, pietà ti chiedo—Be kind, be kind, I beg you: F Ricci
Pietà, Signore—Let my entreaties/O Lord, have mercy/Righteous art
   Thou/Great Lord have mercy: Stradella
Piiritanssi (Ungdom)—Round dance: Palmgren
Pikovaya dama—The queen of spades: Tchaikovsky
Pilgers Morgenlied—Pilgrim's morning song: R Strauss
Pilgerspruch—Pilgrim's song: Mendelssohn
The pilgrimage of the rose—Der Rose Pilgerfahrt: Schumann
Pilgrim's chorus—Beglück darf nun dich (Tannhäuser): Wagner
Pilgrim's morning song—Pilgers Morgenlied: R Strauss
The pilgrims of (to) Mecca—Les pèlerins de la Mecque: Gluck
Pilgrim's song—Pilgerspruch: Mendelssohn
A pine-tree stands forsaken—Ein Fichtenbaum steht einsam: Liszt
The pines of Rome—Pini di Roma: Respighi
Pink champagne—Die Fledermaus: J Strauss II
Pini di Roma—The pines of Rome: Respighi
La pintade (Histoires naturelles)—The guinea-fowl: Ravel
Pioneer songs of Palestine—Shire' Chalutzim: Binder
Piosnka litewska—Lithuanian song/The betrothal: Chopin
Il pirata—The pirate: Bellini
The pirate—Il pirata: Bellini
Els Pirineus—The Pyrenees: Pedrell
Piros, piros, piros—Red, red, red: Erkel
Píseň bohatýrská—Hero's song: Dvořák
Píseň Rusalky oměsičku (Rusalka)—Rusalka's song to the moon: Dvořák
Písně milostné—Love songs: Dvořák
The pity of it—Erbarmen: Blumenthal
Più non pensar—Oh, heart of mine: Astorga
Place this hand upon my bosom—Soura il sen (La sonnambula): Bellini
Placido è il mar (Idomeneo)—Calm is the glassy ocean: Mozart
The plain and simple ways of life—På det jaevne: Nielsen
La plainte du vent—The cry of the wind: Rhené-Baton

Plaisir d'amour—Love's wavering joy/Fugitive love/The joys of love/
    Fleeting love/Love's raptured song/Joy of love: Martini
Plamya Parizha—The flames of Paris: Asafyev
Planctus Mariae—The lament of Mary: Anon
The plane tree—Ombra mai fù (Serse): Handel
The players—I pagliacci: Leoncavallo
Plead softly my song—Kling' leise, mein Lied: Liszt
Pleasant scenery—Freundliche Landschaft (Waldscenen): Schumann
The pleasant summer's come—Der Sommer ist so schön: R Franz
The pleasing colour—Der liebe Farbe (Die schöne Müllerin): Schubert
Pleasing landscape—Freundliche Landschaft (Waldscenen): Schumann
The pleasure of melancholy—Wonne der Wehmut: Beethoven
Pleasures of home—Ich wand're nicht: Schumann
The pledge—Die Bürgschaft: Weill
The pledge of love—Slavíkovský polečko malý (Moravské Dvojzpěvy):
    Dvořák
Il pleure dans mon coeur—Tears falling in my heart: Schmitt
Il pleut des pétales de fleurs—The petals drop noiselessly down: Rhené-
    Baton
Il pleuvait—The rain fell: Massenet
Pli selon pli—Fold within fold: Boulez
The ploughboy—Le petit vailet: Gerhard
Pluck the strings in Cythara—Zwingt die Saiten in Cythara (Schwingt
    freudig euch empor): Bach
La plus belle—The fairest one: Godard
Plus grand dans son obscurité (La reine de Saba)—Far greater in his lowly
    state: Gounod
Plus nulz regretz—Grieve ye no more: Josquin
Ply chimney sweep thine office—Ramonez bien la cheminée: Hesdin
The poacher—Der Wildschütz: Lortzing
Pod jabloni—Under the apple tree: Suk
Pod Moskvoy/V ogne—Near Moscow/In the fire: Kabalevsky
Podnyataya tselina—Virgin soil upturned: Dzerzhinsky
Poem ekstaza—Poem of ecstasy: Skriabin
Poem of a day—Poème d'un jour: Fauré
Poem of ecstasy—Poem ekstaza: Skriabin
The poem of struggle—Pesna bor'by: Kabalevsky
Poème d'un jour—Poem of a day: Fauré
Poems of Mary, Queen of Scots—Gedichte der Königin Maria Stuarda:
    Schumann
Poesien—Poesy: Grieg
Poesy—Poesien: Grieg
Poet and peasant—Dichter und Bauer: Suppé
Un poète disait que (Tristesses)—Now a poet once said: Milhaud

Poetic and religious harmonies—Harmonies poétiques et religieuses: Liszt
A poet's consolation—Sängers Trost: Schumann
The poet's eventide walk—Dichters Abendgang: R Strauss
The poet's heart—Digterhjertet: Grieg
The poet's last lay—En Digters sidste: Grieg
A poet's love—Dichterliebe: Schumann
Poet's mind—Digtervise: Grieg
The poet's recovery—Dichters Genesung: Schumann
Pohádka—Fairy tale: Smetana
Pohrební písen—Dirge: Bartók
Poissons d'or—Goldfish: Debussy
Polednice—The noon witch: Dvořák
Polish diary 1958—Diario polacca 1958: Nono
The Polish Jew—Le Juif polonaise: Erlanger
Il pomo d'oro—The golden apple: Cesti
Pompe vane di morte (Rodelinda)—Vain the pomp of funeral splendour/
    Empty pageant of mourning: Handel
Le pont—The bridge: Poulenc
Poor Hans—Der arme Thoms: Zelter
Poor Henry—Der arme Heinrich: Rheinberger
Poor little violets—Poveri fiori (Adriana Lecouvreur): Cileà
Poor Peter—Der arme Peter: Schumann
The poor sailor—Le pauvre matelot: Milhaud
Popule meus—O my people/Tell me, my people: Victoria
Poor wretched man, a slave of sin—Ich armer Mensch, ich Sudenknecht:
    Bach
Popatřiž na mne (Biblické Písně)—Turn Thee to me: Dvořák
Poppies—Mohnblumen: R Strauss
Por los campos verdes—Thrice the emerald meadows: Guastavino
Porgi amor (Le nozze di Figaro)—God of love/Soothing spells/Hear, O love
    my bitter sighing: Mozart
The portrait—Vachissima sembianza: Donaudy
The portrait—Ihr Bild: Schubert
Portrait of a maiden—Schilderung eines Mädchens: Beethoven
Portrait of death—Bilder des Tods: Bresgen
Ports of call—Escales: Ibert
Poruchik Kizhe—Lieutenant Kije: Prokofiev
Poseĺ—The messenger: Chopin
Die Post (Die Winterreise)—The post: Schubert
Die Post—The postman's horn: Schubert-Heller
The post—Die Post (Die Winterreise): Schubert
Posthumous fame—Nachruf: Wolf
The postilion—Der Postillion: Reger
Der Postillion—The postilion: Reger

Le postillion de Longjumeau—The coachman of Longjumeau: Adam
Postillion Kronos—An schwager Kronos: Schubert
The postman's horn—Die Post: Schubert-Heller
Posuerunt morticinia—The dead bodies of Thy faithful and true servants:
  Byrd
Poterti dir vorrei (Partenope)—I'd fain to thee express: Handel
La poule [symphony]—The hen: Haydn
Pour ce que Plaisance est morte (Deux rondels)—Because Plaisance is
  dead: Debussy
Poveri fiori (Adriana Lecouvreur)—Poor little violets: Cileà
Povest o nastoyashchem cheloveke—The story of a real man: Prokofiev
The power of destiny—La forza del destino: Verdi
The power of evil—Vrazh'ya sila: Serov
The power of song—Die Macht des Gesanges: Brahms
The power of the enemy—Vrazh'ya sila: Serov
Powers eternal—Ciel pietoso, ciel clemente (Zelmira): Rossini
Pozdvihuji očí svých (Biblické Písně)—I will lift mine eyes: Dvořák
Praise be unto the Father—Gloria Patri: Tallis
Praise God in all his splendour—Lobet Gott in seinen Reichen: Bach
Praise God! the year is nearly ended—Gottlob! nun geht das Jahr zu
  Ende: Bach
Praise Him the highest—Lobe den Herren: Bach
Praise Him, the Lord, the Almighty—Lobe den Herren, den mächtigen
  König der Ehren: Bach
The praise of God—Die Eh're Gottes aus der Natur: Beethoven
Praise of indolence—Lob der Faulheit: Haydn
The praise of music—Der glorreiche Augenblick: Beethoven
Praise of spring—Lob des Frühlings: Mendelssohn
Praise Jehovah all ye heathen—Laudate Dominum: Mozart
Praise of the Virgin—Maria's Lob (Marienlieder): Brahms
Praise our God who reigns in Heaven—Lobet Gott in seinen Reichen: Bach
Praise the Creator—Sia benedetto: Wolf-Ferrari
Praise the Lord among His holy ones—Laudibus in Sanctis: Byrd
Praise the Lord, O my soul—Lobe den Herrn, meine Seele: Bach
Praise the Lord, ye servants—Laudate pueri Dominus: Byrd
Praise thou the Lord, Jerusalem—Preise, Jerusalem, den Herrn: Bach
Priase to God in every land—Jauchzet Gott in allen Landen: Bach
Praise to the Father—Gloria Patri: Byrd
Praise to God the Father be given—Lob sei Gott, dem Vater, g'tan
  (Nun komm, der Heiden Heiland) (Schwingt freudig euch empor): Bach
Praise to the Lord! the almighty, the king of creation—Lobe den Herrn,
  den mächtigen König der Ehren: Bach
Praised be Thou, O Jesus Christ—Gelobet seist du, Jesu Christ: Bach
Pray for peace—Priez pour paix: Poulenc

Prayer—Bitte: Beethoven
The prayer—Das Gebet (Das Examen): P Burkhard
Prayer—Gebet: Henschel
A prayer—Gebet: Hiller
A prayer—Gweddi: A Hughes
Prayer—Gebet: Liszt
Prayer—La prière (Petites légendes): Milhaud
A prayer—Fromm: Reger
Prayer—Gebet: Schumann
Prayer—Gebet: Wolf
Prayer during the battle—Gebet während der Schlacht: Schubert
The prayer of the bullfighter—La oración del torero: Turina
The prayer of the outcast—Dank des Paria: Wolf
A prayer to Mary—Ruf zu Maria (Marienlieder): Brahms
Le pré-aux-clercs—The scholars' meadow: Hérold
Precz z moich iczu!—Go leave my sight: Chopin
Preda son d'un fido amore—I'm the slave of love's devotion: S Palma
La prédication aux oiseaux—The sermon to the birds: Liszt
Preise, Jerusalem, den Herrn—Praise thou the Lord, O Jerusalem: Bach
Prelude—Vorspiel (Spanisches Liebeslieder): Schumann
Prelude à l'après-midi d'un faune—Prelude to "The afternoon of a
    faun": Debussy
Prelude to "The afternoon of a faun"—Prelude à l'apres-midi d'un
    faune: Debussy
Première—The first: Aubert
Premonition—Vorgefühl: Schoenberg
Prepare the way—Bereitet die Wege: Bach
Presence—Gegenwart: R Franz
Presence of the loved one—Dass sie hier gewesen: Schubert
Le présent—The offering: Poulenc
The pretended gardener—La finta semplice: Mozart
The pretended simpleton—La finta semplice: Mozart
Pretty swallow—Liebe Schwalbe, kleine Schwalbe: Brahms
The pretty warbler—La fauvette avec ses petits (Zemir et Azor): Grétry
Preussisches Märchen—Prussian fairy tales: Blacher
A prey to my passion—Eprise se d'un (Anacreon chez Polycrate): Grétry
Preziosas Sprüchlein gegen Kopfweh—Little forehead, no more aching:
    Cornelius
Při řekách Babylonských (Biblické Písně)—By the waters of Babylon:
    Dvořák
Při vyšíváni—Over her embroidery: Dvořák
The price—Das Lösegold: Reichardt
Pride of my heart—Du meines Herzens Krönelein: R Strauss
La prière (Petites légendes)—The prayer: Milhaud

Priez pour paix—Pray for peace: Poulenc
Prigioniera ho l'alma in pena (Rodelinda)—Captive tho' my soul is pining:
    Handel
Il prigioniero—The prisoner: Dallapiccola
Prihody lisky hystrousky—The cunning little vixen: Janáček
Přyd' království Tvé—Thy kingdom come: Hába
Priletel pták—The message: Bartók
Die Primel—The primrose: Mendelssohn
Primeval light—Urlicht [2nd symphony]: Mahler
The primrose—Die Primel: Mendelssohn
(The) primroses—Die Schlüsselblumen: Liszt
Prince Eugene—Prinz Eugen: Loewe
Prince Igor—Knyaz' Igor: Borodin
The prince with the lilies—Liliomos herceg: E Ábrányi
The princes of Sheba hither came—Puer natus in Bethlehem (Orgelbüchlein): Bach
Princess Caprice—Die liebe Caprice: Fall
The princess of the inn—La princesse d'auberge: Blockx
La princesse d'auberge—The princess of the inn: Blockx
Il principe felice—The happy prince: Bossi
Printemps—Springtime: Hindemith
Prinz Eugen—Prince Eugene: Loewe
Prinzesschen—Little princess: Manén
La prise de Troie—The capture of Troy: Berlioz
Prison songs—Canti di prigionia: Dallapiccola
The 'prisoned nightingale—Die gefangene Nachigall: Henschel
The prisoner—Il prigioniero: Dallapiccola
Prisoners' dance—Fangernes dans (Aladdin): Nielsen
Privetstvennaya uvertyura—Overture of welcome: Miakovsky
Prizrak—The vision: Prokofiev
Proclaim to every son of France—Partant pour la Syrie: Queen Hortense
Prodaná Nevěsta—The bartered bride: Smetana
The prodigal son—Il figliuol prodigo: Ponchielli
A prole do bêbê—Baby's family: Villa Lobos
Le promenoir des deux amants—The walk of the two lovers: Debussy
Proměny (Moravské dvojzpěvy)—Destined: Dvořák
Promise, love—Júrame: Grever
Promises made and broken—Hat gesagt—bleibt's nicht dabei: R Strauss
The prophet—Le prophète: Meyerbeer
Prophet bird—Vogel als Prophet (Waldscenen): Schumann
Le prophète—The prophet: Meyerbeer
Propitius esto Domine—Help us, O Lord, deliver us: M Haydn
Proriv—The break-through: Pototsky
Prosba—The request: Martinů
Proses lyriques—Lyrical prose: Debussy

Proud and peerless—Per la gloria d'adorarvi (Griselda): G B Bononcini
Provençal song—Chant provençal: Massenet
Provençal song—Provenzalisches Lied: Schumann
Provenzalisches Lied—Provençal song: Schumann
Der Prozess—The trial: Einem
Prsten (Maravské Dvojzpěvy)—The ring: Dvořák
The prude—Die Spröde: Brahms
Die Prufung des Kussens—The test of kissing: Beethoven
Prussian fairy tales—Preussisches Märchen: Blacher
Psallite Domino—Come ye with psalmody: Byrd
Psaulme de l'église à Genève—From the church at Geneva: Liszt
Pskovityanka—Ivan the terrible: Rimsky-Korsakov
Les p'tites Michu—The little Michus: Messager
Ptolemy—Tolomeo: Handel
Puck—Smatrold: Grieg
Puer natus in Bethlehem (Orgelbüchlein)—A child is born in Bethlehem/
    The princes of Sheba hither came: Bach
Puer nobis nascitur—To all men a child is come: Praetorius
Puis qu'elle a pris ma vie—Since she my life has taken: Massenet
Puis qu'on ne peut fléchir/Aubade (Le roi d'Ys)—In olden Spain: Lalo
Puisque l'aube grandit (La bonne chanson)—Since dawn is breaking: Fauré
Puisque tout passe—Since all is passing: Hindemith
Punch-bowl song—Zum Punsche: Schubert
Pupille neve—Love leads to battle: G B Bononcini
Pupillette/Vezzosette e care—Oh! sweet eyes so ardently: Falconieri
Puppenwiegenlied—Doll's slumber song: Schumann
Pur dicesti o bocca bella—Now in the meadows/Thou hast whispered/
    Speak, I pray thee/Lips of roses/Mouth so charmful: Lotti
Pur ti miro, pur ti stringo (L'incoronazione di Poppea)—I behold thee,
    I enfold thee: Monteverdi
A pure and tender blossom—Du bist wie eine Blume: A Rubinstein
The pure light of the lamp—Mir tat die Helligkeit der Lampe weh
    (Chinesische Liebeslieder): Liebermann
I Puritani—The Puritans: Bellini
The Puritans—I Puritani: Bellini
Pussy willows—Maienkatzchen: Brahms
The Pyrenees—Els Pirineus: Pedrell

Q

Quaestio temporis—A question of time: Křenek
The quail—Der Wachtelschlag: Beethoven
The quail—Der Wachtelschlag: Schubert
Qual farfalletta (Partenope)—Light is my heart: Handel
Qual farfalletta amante—Like any foolish moth/As a butterfly that
    blindly: D Scarlatti
Qual nave smarrita (Radamisto)—E'en like a ship/The vessel storm driven:
    Handel
Quand, à tes genoux—When love at thy side: Aubert
Quand'ero paggio (Falstaff)—When I was a page: Verdi
Quand' io era giovinetto—When I was a merry stripling: G Gabrieli
Quand je te vois souffrir—In sickness and health: I Albeniz
Quand je vous ayme ardentement—Love's burning passion: Arcadelt
Quand tu dors—When you slept: Kjerulf
Quando col mio s'incontra—Dearest, where'er I view thee: Clari
Quando emblada—Haunted: Guarnieri
Quando la gemma di questo anallo—The day this jewel upon my finger:
    Braga
Quando mai spietata (Radamisto)—Let my pray'rs/When my eyes: Handel
Quando men vo (La bohème)—As through the street: Puccini
Quando ti vi pela primeira vez—When I first saw you: Guarnieri
Quando ti vidi—When thy fair beauty: Wolf-Ferrari
Quando uma flôr desabrocha—Flowers are gay when they open: Mignone
Quant j'ai ony la tabourin (Chansons de Charles d'Orléans)—Whene'er the
    tambourine I hear: Debussy
Quanto godrà (Admeto)—What rapturous joy: Handel
Quanto mai felice siete (Ezio)—Happy is the lowly maiden: Handel
Quare fremuerunt—Why fumeth in sight in Gentiles spite: Tallis
Quarrel—Perpatuar: Bartók
I quattro rusteghi—The four ruffians/School for fathers: Wolf-Ferrari
Que l'heure est donc brève—How short does the hour seem: Massenet
Quebra o coco, menino—Break the coconut: Guarnieri
The queen—La reine [symphony]: Haydn
Queen of heaven(s)—Regina coeli: Brahms
Queen of my heart—Caro mio ben: Giordani
Queen of my soul—Wie bist du, meine Königen: Brahms
The queen of Sheba—La reine de Saba: Gounod
The queen of spades—Pikovaya dama: Tchaikovsky
Queen of the seagulls—Reine des monettes: Poulenc
The queen's lace handkerchief—Das Spitzentuch der Königin: J Strauss II
Quejas ó la maja y el ruiseñor—The maiden and the nightingale: Granados
Quel bel core—That gentle heart: Magni

255

Quel d'amore è un certo male (Amalasunta)—Love's fond fever: Chelleri
Quel funesti appareil (Jepthé)—How appalling a sight: Montéclair
Quel galant!—What gallant!/Which gallant can compare: Ravel
Quel language accablant (Iphigénie en Tauride)—How crushing are such words: Gluck
Quel rescelletto—The brooklet: Paradisi
Quella barbara catena—This hard bondage: F Ciampi
Quella che tutta fé (Serse)—Friendship and love/She that for me did pine: Handel
Quella fiamma che m'accende—Fervent passion, fiercely burning/In my heart the flames: Marcello
Quem vidistis pastores—Say O shepherds, whom ye saw: Dering
Questadunque è l'iniqua mercede (I due Foscari)—So my valour and my victories: Verdi
Queste ad un lido fatal (Nerone)—Far from the scene: Boito
Question—Liebliches Kind, kannst du mir sagen: Brahms
Question—Frage: Mendelssohn
The question—Der Neugierige (Die schöne Müllerin): Schubert
A question—Frage: Schumann
Question and answer—Demande et réponse: Coleridge-Taylor
Question and answer—Frage und Antwort: J Marx
Question and answer—Frage und Antwort: Wolf
A question of time—Quaestio temporis: Křenek
Questioning—Starvicino: Rosa
Questionings—Fragen: Brahms
Questions—Fragen: Brahms
Questions and answers—Comment, disaient-ils: Liszt
Questo e il cielo (Alcino)—Beauty lately: Handel
Queues de boeuf (La bonne cuisine): Ox tails: Bernstein
Qui donc vous a donné vos yeux—Who gave you your sweet eyes: Godard
Qui la voce (I Puritani)—Yes, 'tis here: Bellini
Quick march—Geschwindmarsch (Bunte Blätter): Schumann
Quick silver—Leichtes Blut: J Strauss II
Quid igitur faciam—What course shall I then pursue: Byrd
Quiescat Domine—O let thine anger cease from us: Byrd
The quiet Don—Tirhy Don: Dzerzhinsky
Quiet evening—Stiller Nacht: R Franz
Quiet night—Nacht und Träume: Schubert
Quiet of the woods—Waldeinsamkeit: Reger
The quiet waterlily—Die stille Wasserrose: R Franz
The quiet wood—O kühler Wald: Brahms
Quietly, my heart—Still, mein Herz (Das Examen): P Burkhard
Quis dabit capiti meo aquam—Lament on the death of Lorenzo de' Medici: Isaac

Quis est homo—What man is he: Byrd
Quis te comprehendat—Who can comprehend Thee: Mozart
Quite happy—Glückes genug (Kinderscenen): Schumann
Quixote keeping vigil by his arms—Don Quijote velando las armas: Esplà

R

Rabbit at top speed—Civet à toute vitesse (La bonne cuisine): Bernstein
Der Rabe—The raven: Bălan
Der Rabe—The raven: Kranich
Radiant at eve—Abendlich strahlt der Sonne (Das Rheingold): Wagner
Radost—Joy: Smetana
The rails—Relsi: Deshevov
Rain and tears—Regen: J Marx
The rain fell—Il pleuvait: Massenet
Rain in sunshine—Sonnenregen: Reger
Rain of tears—Tränenregen (Die schöne Müllerin): Schubert
Raindrops—Regentropfen: M Mayer
Raindrops—Regentropfen: E Palm
Rainsong—Regenlied: Brahms
Raise high the door—Macht hoch die Tür: Bauernfeld
Rakastava—The lover: Sibelius
Ramonez bien la cheminée—Ply chimney-sweep thine office: Hesdin
Rappresentazione di anima e di corpo—The spectacle of the soul and the
    body: Cavalieri
A rare thing—Una cosa rara: Soler
Rast (Die Winterreise)—Rest: Schubert
Raste Krieger/Ellen's Gesang—Rest thee soldier/Soldier, rest: Schubert
Der Rastelbinder—The tinker: Lehár
Rastlose Liebe—Restless love: R Franz
Rastlose Liebe—Restless love: Schoeck
Rat einer Alten—The old woman's advice: Wolf
The rat catcher—Der Rattenfänger: Wolf
Rätsel (Myrthen)—A riddle on the letter H/The enigma: Schumann
Der Rattenfänger—The pied-piper/The rat catcher: Wolf
Rattlin', roarin' Willie—Bänkelsänger Willie: Schumann
Die Rauberbrüder—The robber brothers: Cornelius
Der Rauch—Smoke: J Marx
The raven—Der Rabe: Bălan
The raven—Der Rabe: Kranich
Re del abisso (Un ballo in maschera)—Lord of the depths: Verdi
Il re pastore—The shepherd king: Mozart
Reading the stars—Volta la terrea fronte alle stelle (Un ballo in
    maschera): Verdi
Ready be, my soul, alway—Mache dich, mein Geist bereit: Bach
The reaper—Erntelied: Mendelssohn
Reaper John, come take thy sickle—Jean, p'tit Jean: Bax
The reaper's song—Schnitterliedchen (Album für die Jugend): Schumann
The reason why—Juch he!: Brahms

Receive thou my first—Si voli il primo (Lucrezia Borgia): Donizetti
Die Rechte Stimmung—In men and women no true harmony: Telemann
The recluse—Der Einsame: Schubert
Recognition—Danksagung an den Bach (Die Winterreise): Schubert
Recollections—Erinnerung (Album für die Jugend): Schumann
Recollections of the theatre—Nachklänge aus dem Theater (Album für
    die Jugend): Schumann
Recondita armonia (Tosca)—Strange harmony of contrasts: Puccini
La rencontre imprévue—The unexpected meeting: Gluck
Recordare Domini—Call to Thy remembrance, Lord: Byrd
Recordati, oh bella (Teseo)—O fair as a flower: Handel
Recueillement—Contemplation/Meditation: Debussy
Recueillement—Devotion: Liszt
Red and white roses—Rote Rosenknospen (Zigeunerlieder): Brahms
Red haired Jane—Die rote Hanne: Schumann
The red poppy—Krasny mak: Gière
Red, red, red—Piros, piros, piros: Erkel
Red rose—Heidenröslein: Schubert
Red the parting sun—Sonne taucht in Meeres: Henschel
Rede, Mädchen (Liebeslieder Walzer)—Oh, give an answer: Brahms
Die Redlichkeit ist eine von den Gottesgaben (Ein ungefärbt Gemüte)—
    Sincerity, a gift it is: Bach
Reflections—Berherzigung: Wolf
The reformed drunkard—L'ivrogne corrigé: Gluck
Le réfuge—The retreat: I Albeniz
Rég megmondtam bús gerlice—Long ago I told you: Bartók
La regata Veneziana—The Venetian regatta: Rossini
Regen—Rain and tears: J Marx
Regenlied—Rainsong: Brahms
Regentropfen—Raindrops: M Mayer
Regentropfen—Raindrops: E Palm
Régi jó idök—Good old times: K Ábrányi
Regina coeli—Queen of heaven(s): Brahms
Regnava nel silenzio (Lucia di Lammermoor)—Silent the sombre wings:
    Donizetti
Regret—Velet' vtáčku (Moravské Dvojzpěvy): Dvořák
Regt sich's dir warm in Herzen—Spare not one smile: Børresen
Reife—Ripeness: Manén
Reign here a queen—Wie bist du, meine Königin: Brahms
La reine [symphony]--The queen: Haydn
La reine de Saba—The queen of Sheba/Irene: Gounod
Reine des mouettes—Queen of the seagulls: Poulenc
Reiselied—The traveller' song: Mendelssohn
Reisenbuch aus den österreichischen Alpen—Travel book from the
    Austrian Alps: Křenek

Der Reiter—A merry soldier: Brahms
Reiterlied—Song of the trooper: Reger
Reitsestück (Album für die Jugend)—The horseman: Schumann
Rejoice! the old year is now ended—Gottlob! nun geht das Jahr zu
  Ende: Bach
Rejoice ye hearts—Erfreut euch, ihr Herzen: Bach
Rejoice, ye heavens—Laetentus coeli: Byrd
Rejoice that you this light behold—Wohl euch! die ihr dies Licht gesehn
  (Weihnachtsoratorium): Bach
Rejoice ye souls, elect and holy—Wohl euch, ihr auserwählten Seelen
  (O ewiges Feuer): Bach
Réjouissez vous bourgeoises—Dainty damsels: Anon
Der Rekrut—Cock up your beaver: Schumann
Rekviyem pam'yati Lysenka—Requiem in memory of Lysenko: Verykivsky
A release—Erlösung: Blumenthal
Release—Befreit: R Strauss
The relief—Die Ablosung: Hollaender
Relsi—The rails: Deshevov
Remember now, O Virgin Mary—Souvenez-vous, Vierge Marie: Massenet
Remember us with loving kindness—Gedenk' an uns mit deiner Liebe
  (Wir danken dir, Gott, wir danken dir): Bach
Remembrance—Andenken: Beethoven
Remembrance—Erinnerung: Brahms
Remembrance—Angedenken: Cornelius
Remembrance—Andenken: Mendelssohn
Remembrance—Nachklang: Schoeck
Remembrance of a lullaby—Dolçe recort: Longás
Remembrance of the House of Usher—Vechera u Dome Usher:
  G Karnovitch
Remembrances—Efterklang: Grieg
Reminiscence—Reminiszenz: Cornelius
Reminiscences of mountain and fiord—Fra Fjeld og Fjord: Grieg
Reminiscences of the pantomine—Nachklänge aus dem Theater (Album
  für die Jugend): Schumann
Reminiszenz—Reminiscence: Cornelius
Renard—The fox: Stravinsky
Rencontre (Poème d'un jour)—Meeting: Fauré
La rencontre imprévue/Les pèlerins de la Mecque—The pilgrims of (to)
  Mecca/The unexpected meeting: Gluck
Rend' il sereno al ciglio (Sosarme)—To thy sad brow let joy return/
  Mother, O hide me/No more in sorrow languish: Handel
Rendete a gli occhi miei (Sonnets of Michaelangelo)—Give back to my
  eyes: Britten
Renewal—Genesung: R Franz
Le renvoy—Return, my faithless heart!: Compère

Reply of a virtuous wife—Réponse d'une épouse sage: Roussel

Réponse d'une épouse sage—Reply of a virtuous wife: Roussel

Request—Bitte: R Franz

The request—Prosba: Martinů

Requiem in memory of Lysenko—Rekviyem pam' yati Lysenka: Verykivskyi

Reserve—Verborgenheit: R Franz

Resignation—Kein Wort: Blumenthal

Resignation—Ergebung: Fielitz

Resignation—Entsagung: Mendelssohn

Resignation—Ergebung: Schoeck

Resolution—Vorsatz: Lassen

Resonet in laudibus—Joyful hearts to heaven raise: Handel

Respice Domine—Behold, O Lord: Byrd

Rest—Ombra mai fù (Serse): Handel

Rest—Du bist die Ruh': Schubert

Rest—Rast (Die Winterreise): Schubert

Rest in peace—Come è bello (Lucrezia Borgia): Donizetti

Rest, my soul—Ruhe, meine Seele: R Strauss

Rest of the weary—Laschia ch'io pianga: Handel

Rest on me thou eye of darkness—Bitte: R Franz

Rest thee, my darling—Ruhe, Süssliebchen: Brahms

Rest thee, my lady—Ruhe, Süssliebchen: Brahms

Rest thee, my spirit—Ruhe, meine Seele: R Strauss

Rest thee soldier—Raste Krieger: Schubert

Rest, thou art my peace—Du bist die Ruh': Schubert

Rest ye here, wearied spirits—Ruhet hie, matte Sinne (O angenehme
   Melodei): Bach

Resta di darmi noia—Cease then to give me sorrow: Gesualdo

Resta, Oh cara! —Dearest we part now: Mozart

Reste! —Stay!: Chaminade

Resteknek nótája—Loafer: Bartók

Resting place—Aufenthalt (Schwanengesang): Schubert

Restless love—Rastlose Liebe: R Franz

Restless love—Rastlose Liebe: Schoeck

Restraint—Hemmung: Schoenberg

Resurrection—Risurrezione: Alfano

Resurrection—Seliger Tod: Blumenthal

Resurrection—Gestorben war ich vor Liebeswonne: Liszt

Resveillez moi—Wake me from sleep: Garnier

El retablo de Maese Pedro—Master Peter's puppet show: Falla

Le retour des promis—Come out, my dearest: Dessauer

Le retour du printemps—Spring's return: Godard

The retreat—Le refuge: I Albeniz

Retrospect—Rückblick (Die Winterreise): Schubert

Retrospect—Rückleben: R Strauss
Return (home)—Heimkehr: Brahms
Return again, O Lord—Sed veni, Domine: Byrd
Return from the banquet—Heimkehr vom Feste: Blech
Return my faithless heart!—Le renvoy: Compère
Return now, you wild rushing storm winds—Zurücke geflügelten Winde (Zerreist, zersprenget, Zertrümmer der Gruft): Bach
The return of spring—Der Frühling kommt!: Goetz
The return of the sun—Vozvrashcheniye solntsa: Golub'yov
The return of Tobias—Il retorno di Tobia: Haydn
Return, oh my beloved—Ritorna, o caro e dolce (Rodelinda): Handel
Reunion—Le revoir: Rhené-Baton
Le rêve—The dream: Bruneau
Le rêve/En fermant les yeux (Manon)—The dream: Massenet
Le rêve—A dream: Rollinat
Un rêve—A dream: Séverac
Rêve d'un soir—Dream of an hour: Chaminade
Reveil de la mariée—The awakening of the bride: Ravel
Reveille—Revelge: Mahler
Le reveille de la mariée/Chanson de la mariée—Wake up, my dear: Ravel
Revelge—The dead drummer/Reveille: Mahler
Revenez, amours, revenez (Thésée)—Oh, return: Lully
Rêverie—Dreamland: Rhené-Baton
Der Revisor—The government inspector: Orff
Le revoir—Reunion: Rhené-Baton
The revolt—Myatezh: Khodzha-Eynatov
The reward of love—Der liebe Lohn (Brautlieder): Cornelius
Das Rheingold—The Rhinegold: Wagner
Rheinische Lieder—Songs of the Rhine: Cornelius
Rheinlegendchen (Des Knaben Wunderhorn)—Rhine legend/Legend of the Rhine: Mahler
Rhine legend—Rheinlegendchen (Des Knaben Wunderhorn): Mahler
The Rhinegold—Das Rheingold: Wagner
The Rhine's green waters—Im Rhein im schönen Strome: Liszt
Ribbons and flowers I cannot wear—Wie kann ich froh und lustig sein?: Mendelssohn
Ricetti gramezza e pavento (Non sa che sia dolore)—Away now with lessons: Bach
The rich sweetheart—Bohatá milá: Martinů
Richard Coeur de Lion—Richard the Lion-hearted: Grétry
Richard the Lion-hearted—Richard Coeur de Lion: Grétry
Riche, j'ai semé les richesses (Don César de Bazan)—With a heart bounding lightly: Massenet
A riddle on the letter H—Rätsel (Myrthen): Schumann

The ride of the Valkyries—Der Ritt der Walküren (Die Walküre): Wagner
The ride on the knee—Beim Ritt auf dem Knie: Brahms
The ride to Nantes—La tour à Nantes: Meister
Ride-a-cock-horse—Ritter vom Steckenpferd (Kinderscenen): Schumann
Ridente la calma—Peace and content/How calm is my spirit/In blessed
    contentment: Mozart
Ridente speme vola nell'alma—Hope, smile upon me: Rispoli
Riding full tilt—A toutes brides (Tel jour telle nuit): Poulenc
Riding past—Vorbeimarsch: Reger
Righteous art thou—Pietà, Signore: Stradella
Righteous heaven—Se pietà de me non senti (Giulio Cesare): Handel
The righteous living forever—Periti autem: Mendelssohn
Rikadla—Children's rhymes: Janáček
Rimes tendres—Love songs: Aubert
The ring—Pierścien: Chopin
The ring—Prsten (Moravské Dvojzpěvy): Dvořák
Der Ring (Frauenliebe und -leben)—Thou ring upon my finger/Ring on my
    finger/The ring: Schumann
The ring—Du Ring an meinem Finger (Frauenliebe und -leben): Schumann
Der Ring des Nibelungen—The ring of the Nibelungs: Wagner
The ring of the Nibelungs—Der Ring des Nibelungen: Wagner
Ring on my finger—Du Ring an meinem Finger/Der Ring (Frauenliebe und
    -leben): Schumann
Ringeltanz—Merry-go-round: Gade
Ripeness—Reife: Manén
Ripportai gloriosa (Atlanta)—I have won: Handel
The rise and fall of the city (town) of Mahagonny—Aufstieg und Fall der
    Stadt Mahagonny: Weill
Rise, o soul this happy morning—Schmücke dich, o liebe Seele: Bach
The rising of the mists—Tågen letter (Moderen): Nielsen
Rising passion—Vznikající vášeň: Smetana
Risurrezione—Resurrection: Alfano
The rite(s) of spring—Vesna svya shchennaya: Stravinsky
Ritorna, o caro e dolce (Rodelinda)—Come back again, my dear/Return oh
    my beloved: Handel
Ritorna vincitor (Aida)—May laurels crown thy brow: Verdi
Ritornerai fra poco—Tell me, ah, where art speeding/Soon thou wilt be
    returning: Hasse
Il ritorno di Tobia—The return of Tobias/Tobias: Haydn
Der Ritt der Walküren/Walküren-ritt (Die Walküre)—The ride of the
    Valkyries: Wagner
Ritter Blaubart—Knight Bluebeard: Reznicek
Ritter Kurts Brautfahrt—The knight's wedding-ride: Wolf

Ritter vom Steckenpferd (Kinderscenen)—Knight of the rocking-horse/ Knight of the hobby-horse/On the rocking horse/Ride-a-cock-horse: Schumann

Ritual fire dance—Danza del fin del día (El amor brujo): Falla

Ritual fire dance—Danza ritual del fuego (El amor brujo): Falla

The river king—Der Wassermann: Schumann

Rivolgete a lui lo sguardo—Turn your eyes towards him: Mozart

R'kod Hat'laim (Shire' Chalutzim)—Our flock will dance: Binder

The road to my love—Gang zur Liebsten: Brahms

Roam as I may—Vado ben spesso: Rosa

The robber brothers—Die Rauberbrüder: Cornelius

Robert le diable—Rovert the devil: Meyerbeer

Robert the devil—Robert le diable: Meyerbeer

Robert, toi que j'aime (Robert le diable)—Mercy for me/Oh, Robert, oh my beloved: Meyerbeer

Robin and Marion—Le jeu de Robin et Marion: La Halle

Rocio—Dew drops: Guastavino

Rock-a-by—Meciendo: Guastavino

Rococo Ständchen—An old-world serenade: Meyer-Helmund

Rodina Velikaya—The great motherland/Great fatherland: Kabalevsky

The rogue—Der Schalk: R Franz

Rogues like you—Solche hergelauf'ne Laffen (Die Entführung aus dem Serail): Mozart

Roguish song—Canción picaresca: Palomino

Le roi Carotte—King Carotte: Offenbach

Le roi de Lahore—The king of Lahore: Massenet

Le roi du Thule (La damnation de Faust)—The king of Thule: Berlioz

Le roi d'Ys—The king of Ys: Lalo

Le roi d'Yvetot—The king of Yvetot: Adam

Le roi l'a dit—The king said so: Lalo

Le roi malgré lui—King in spite of himself: Chabrier

Roman carnival—Carnaval romain: Berlioz

Roman festivals—Feste romane: Respighi

Román népi táncok—Romanian folk dances: Bartók

The romance of spring—Jarní romance: Fibich

Romanesque song—Chanson romanesque (Don Quichotte à Dulcinée): Ravel

Romanian folk dances—Román népi táncok: Bartók

Romantic song—Air romantique: Poulenc

Romanze von den drei Schneidern—Ballad of the three tailors: Himmel

Romeo and Juliet—I Capuletti ed I Montecchi: Bellini

Romeo and Juliet—Romeo i Dzhul'yetta: Prokofiev

Romeo i Dzhul'yetta—Romeo and Juliet: Prokofiev

Rompo i lacci (Flavio)—Thus I break the ties that bound me: Handel
La ronde—The dancing ring: Caplet
Ronde—Roundelay: Godard
La ronde autour du monde—Dancing round the world: Pierné
La rondine—The swallow: Puccini
Rorate coeli—Drop dew ye heavens: Tye
Rosa d'amor—Sweet rose of love: Dering
La rosa y el sauce—The rose and the willow: Guastavino
Röschen biss den Apfel an—Rosy, o the careless girl: Pfitzner
Rose among the heather—Heidenröslein: Schubert
Rose and huntsman—Knabe und Rose: Henschel
The rose and the cross—Roza i krest: Krein
The rose and the lily—Die Rose, die Lilie: R Franz
The rose and the lily—Die Rose, die Lilie (Dichterliebe): Schumann
The rose and the willow—La rosa y el sauce: Guastavino
The rose bearer—Der Rosenkavalier: R Strauss
A rose breaks into bloom—Es ist ein' Ros' entsprungen: Brahms
Die Rose, die Lilie—The rose and the lily: R Franz
Die Rose, die Lilie (Dichterliebe)—The rose and the lily: Schumann
Rose, lovely flower—Caro mio ben: Giordani
Der Rose Pilgerfahrt—The pilgrimage of the rose: Schumann
The rosebud—Rosenknoppen: Grieg
Rose-bud—Heidenröslein: Schubert
Rosebud red—Röslein, Röslein: Schumann
Rosebuds—Se savan rose: Arditi
The rose-bush—Der Rosenstock: Himmel
The rose-chain—Das Rosenband: R Strauss
Rose-garland—Das Rosenband: Schubert
Rose-leaves are falling—Vedrai carmo, se sei buonino (Don Giovanni):
    Mozart
Rose-lipt maid—Mein Mädel hat einen Rosenmund: Brahms
Rosemary—Rosmarin: Brahms
Rosemary—Rozmarýna: Dvořák
Rosemary—Rosmarin: R Franz
Rosemary—Rozmarýn: Martinů
Rosen aus dem Süden—Southern roses/Roses from the south/Roses of
    the south/Fair May is past/Roses in June: J Strauss II
Rosen stackt (Neue Liebeslieder)—Roses red: Brahms
Das Rosenband—Rose-garland/The band of roses: Schubert
Das Rosenband—The rose-chain: R Strauss
Rosenbaum—Rose-tree: Manén
Der Rosenkavalier—The cavalier of the rose/The knight of the rose/
    The rose bearer: R Strauss
Rosenknoppen—The rosebud: Grieg

Rosenlied—The song of the roses: Sibelius
Röslein, Röslein—Rosebud red: Schumann
Der Rosenstock—The rose-bush: Himmel
Rosenzweige—Roses: Fielitz
Roses—Rosenzweige: Fielitz
Les roses de l'autre année—The roses of yesteryear: Schmitt
Les roses d'Ispahan—The roses of Ispahan: Fauré
Roses from the south—Rosen aus dem Süden: J Strauss II
Roses in June—Roses aus dem Süden: J Strauss II
Roses in the field—V tej bystrickej bráne: Bartók
The roses of Ispahan—Les roses d'Ispahan: Fauré
Roses of the south—Rosen aus dem Süden: J Strauss II
Roses of yesterday—Hoesternae rosae: Rummel
The roses of yesteryear—Les roses de l'autre année: Schmitt
The roses on my breast—Deine Rosen an der Brust (Lieder der Liebe):
    Kilpinen
Roses red—Rosen stackt (Neue Liebeslieder): Brahms
Roses three—Röslein dreie in der Reihe (Zigeunerlieder): Brahms
Rose-tree—Rosenbaum: Manén
Rosička—Dew: Martinů
Röslein drei in der Reihe (Zigeunerlieder)—Roses three: Brahms
Röslein, Röslein—Little rose: Schumann
Rosmarin—Rosemary: Brahms
Rosmarin—Rosemary: R Franz
Le rossignol—The nightingale: Delibes
Rossignols amoureux (Hippolyte et Aricie)—Oh! ye sweet nightingales/
    Nightingales in the wood: Rameau
Rosy, o the careless girl—Röschen biss den Apfel an: Pfitzner
Die rote Hanne—Red-haired Jane: Schumann
Der rote Tod—The masque of the red death: F Schreker
Rote Äugelein—Couldst thou only see me now: R Franz
Rote Rosenknospen (Zigeunerlieder)—Blushing rose buds/Red and
    white roses: Brahms
Rotkäppchen—Little Red Ridinghood: Abt
Le rouet d'Omphale—Omphale's spinning wheel: Saint-Saëns
Rough weather—Schlechtes Wetter: R Strauss
Une roulotte couverte en tuiles (Tel jour telle nuit)—A gypsy wagon
    roofed with tiles: Poulenc
A round—Rundgesang (Album für die Jugend): Schumann
Round dance—Piiritanssi (Ungdom): Palmgren
Roundelay—Ronde: Godard
Roundelay—Rundgesang (Album für die Jugend): Schumann
Rounds—Cirandas: Villa-Lobos
Roverborgen—The brigands' castle: Kuhlau

Row gently here—Leis' rudern hier: Schumann
The royal children—Die Königskinder: Humperdinck
Roza i krest—The rose and the cross: Krein
Rozlovčení (Moravské Dvojzpěvy)—The parting: Dvořák
Rozmarýn—Rosemary: Martinů
Ruckblick (Die Winterreise)—Looking backward/The days that were/
    A backward glance/Retrospect: Schubert
Ruckkehr—A home-coming: Wolf
Rückleben—Retrospect: R Strauss
Rozmarýna—Rosemary: Dvořák
Ruf vom Berge—Call from the mountain/A voice from the hills:
    Beethoven
Ruf zu Maria (Marienlieder)—A prayer to Mary/A cry to Mary: Brahms
Ruft und fleht den Himmel an (Christen, ätzet diesen Tag)—Call and
    implore the heavens: Bach
Ruhe im Walde—Afar in the wood: Kjerulf
Ruhe, meine Seele—Rest thee, my spirit/Rest, my soul: R Strauss
Ruhe, Süssliebchen—Rest thee, my lady/Sleep my darling/Sweet
    darling, rest in the shade/Rest thee, my darling/Slumber song: Brahms
Ruhet hie, matte Sinne (O angenehme Melodie)—Rest ye here, wearied
    spirits: Bach
Ruhetal—The vale of rest: Mendelssohn
A ruin an empty shell—Une ruine coquille vide (Tel jour telle nuit):
    Poulenc
Une ruine coquille vide (Tel jour telle nuit)—A ruin an empty shell:
    Poulenc
Die Ruinen von Athen—The ruins of Athens: Beethoven
The ruins—Huszt: Kodály
The ruins of Athens—Die Ruinen von Athen: Beethoven
Ruisseau, dont le bruit charmant (Cassandre)—Thy music, oh! gentle
    stream: Bouvard/Bertin
The ruler of the spirits—Der Beherrschen der Geister: Weber
Rundgesang (Album für die Jugend)—A round/Roundelay: Schumann
The runic rock—Es ragt in's Meer: R Franz
Rusalka's song to the moon—Písen Rusalky omésička (Rusalka): Dvořák
Russian Easter (Festival) overture—La grande pâque russe: Rimsky-
    Korsakov
Rustic chivalry—Cavalleria rusticana: Mascagni
Rustic song—Ländliches Lied (Album für die Jugend): Schumann
The rustic wedding—Die landliche Hochzeit [symphony]: Goldmark
Rustle of spring—Frühlingsrauschen: Sinding
Rustling tree top—Lindes rauschen: Brahms

S

Så bittert var mit hjerte (Moderen)—So bitter was my heart: Nielsen
Saa du Knøssen, som strøg farbi—Have you seen the brave peasant lad/
    See the fellow that passed just now: Grieg
Saarella palaa—Fire on the island: Sibelius
La sabotée de Saint-Loup—Dance of Saint-Loup: Blanchard
Sacerdotes domini—In the temple of the priests: Byrd
Sacred song—Geistliche Lied: Mendelssohn
Sacrificial chant—Opferlied: Beethoven
Sacrificial hymn—Opferlied: Beethoven
Sad bride—Die Braut: Henschel
Der sad en fisker så tankefuld—A fisherman sat thoughtfully: Nielsen
Sad heart—Hoffnungslos: Reger
Sad heart—Der Leidende: Schubert
Sad is my weary soul—Tutta raccolta ancor nel palpitante (Scipione):
    Handel
Sad of heart—Voda a plàc (Moravské Dvojzpěvy): Dvořák
Sad river—Smutna rzeka: Chopin
The sad shepherdess—Die Bekehrte: Wolf
Sadly I languish—Laschia ch'io piango (Rinaldo): Handel
Sadness—Wehmut: Schubert
Sadness—Wehmut: Schumann
Der Saëmann (Lieder um dem Tod)—The sower: Kilpinen
Saenk kun dit hoved—Lower thy head: Nielsen
Saeterjentens Söntag—Chalet girl's Sunday: Bull
Ein safek—No doubt: Miron
The saffron—Die Zeitlose: R Strauss
Sag' an, o lieber Vogel mein—Tell me, my dear bird: Schumann
Sag' es nicht—Never tell: Reger
Sag' mir—Tell me: R Franz
Saga-Drøm—Gunnar's dream/The dream of Saga: Nielsen
The sages of Sheba—Sie werden aus Saba Alle kommen: Bach
The sage—L'oracolo: Leoni
Sagt mir, o schönste Schäf'rin mein—Tell me, o beauteous shepherdess:
    Brahms
Sagt, wo sind die Veilchen hin?—Say, where are the violets: Schulz
Sagt's ihr—Oh! tell me love: Kotchubei
Sahst du nach dem Gewitterregen—After the summer rain: Berg
The sailor's farewell—Seemans Scheid'elied: Mendelssohn
The sailor's farewell—Seemans Abschied: Wolf
Sailor's song—Matrosernes Opsang: Grieg
St Anthony and the fishes—Des Antonius von Padua Fischpredigt (Des
    Knaben Wunderhorn): Mahler

St Anthony's sermon to the fishes—Des Antonius von Padua Fischpredigt (Des Knaben Wunderhorn): Mahler

St Cecelia mass—Missa St Cecelia: Haydn

St Francis of Paola walking on the water—St François de Paule marchant sur les flots: Liszt

St François de Paule marchant sur les flots—St Francis of Paola walking on the water: Liszt

A saint in her halo—Une sainte en son auréole (La bonne chanson): Fauré

St John baptized in Jordan's tide—Am Jordan Sanct Johannes stand (Die Meistersinger von Nürnberg): Wagner

St John passion—Johannespassion: Bach

St Joseph's song—Der heilige Josef singt: Wolf

Saint Ludmila—Svatá Ludmila: Dvořák

St Luke passion—Lukaspassion: Bach

Saint Mary once did wander—Maria ging aus wandern: Brahms

St Matthew passion—Matthäuspassion: Bach

St Nepomuks Vorabend—The eve of St Nepomuk: Wolf

St Paul—Paulus: Mendelssohn

Une sainte en son auréole (La bonne chanson)—A saint in her halo: Fauré

Salamander—There sat a salamander: Brahms

Salitana—Love's greeting: Favra

Les saltimbanques—The acrobats: Ganne

Salvation—Erlösung: Webern

Salvation now is come to earth—Es ist das Heil uns kommen her (Orgelbüchlein): Bach

Salvator mundi—Most loving Saviour: Tallis

Salve Regina—Hail, thou most holy: Byrd

The sandman—Der Sandmann: Blech

The sandman—Sandmännchen (Volkskinderlieder): Brahms

The sandman—Le marchand de sable qui passe: Roussel

The sandman—Der Sandmann: Schumann

Der Sandmann—The sandman: Blech

Der Sandmann—The dustman: M Mayer

Der Sandmann—The sandman: Schumann

Sandmännchen (Volkskinderlieder)—The sandman/The little dustman/The little sandman/Folding time: Brahms

Sang til Juletraeet—Christmas song: Grieg

Der Sänger—The bard: Schubert

Der Sänger—The singer: Schumann

Der Sänger—The minstrel: Wolf

Der Sängers Habe—Minstrel's treasure: Schubert

Sängers Trost—A poet's consolation: Schumann

Sanglots—Sobs: Poulenc

Saper vorreste (Un ballo in maschera)—If you are asking/You'd fain be hearing: Verdi

Sapphic ode—Sapphische Ode: Brahms
Sapphische Ode—Sapphic ode: Brahms
Sarcasms—Sarkazmy: Prokofiev
Den Sårede—The wounded heart: Grieg
Sari—Der Zigeunerprimas: Kálmán
Sarkazmy—Sarcasms: Prokofiev
Satu (Ungdom)—Fairy tale: Palmgren
The saucepan song—Sospan fach: T V Davies
Sanfte soll mein Todeskummer (Osteroratorium)—Peaceful shall be my departure: Bach
Le sauterelle (Le bestiare)—The grasshopper: Poulenc
Saved—Le navire est à l'eau: Blumenthal
Saviour make me all Thine own—Ich will dir mein Herz schenken: Bach
Saviour of my heart—Herzlieber Jesu: Brahms
Saviour of the nations, come—Nun komm, der Heiden Heiland (Orgelbüchlein): Bach
Saviour, with our sins we've paid Thee—Heiland, uns're Missetaten (Drei Volkstexte): Webern
Say gentle ladies—Voi che sapete (Nozze di Figaro): Mozart
Say O shepherds, whom ye saw—Quem vidistis pastores: Dering
Say to Irene—Dì ad Irene (Atalanta): Handel
Say, where are the violets—Sagt, wo sind die Veilchen hin?: Schulz
Say, wherefore vainly—Wozu noch Mädchen: R Strauss
Say ye who borrow—Voi che sapete (Le nozze di Figaro): Mozart
Say you will not forget—Vergiss mein nicht: E de Curtis
Saying is not doing—Hat gesagt—bleibt's nicht dabei: R Strauss
The scale of D flat—Ich bitt' dich: Beethoven
Scanty grass—Une herbe pauvre (Tel jour telle nuit): Poulenc
Scarce a gleam of sun—Dans un bois solitaire: Mozart
Scarce in full blossom—In seiner Blüte bleichen (Rienzi): Wagner
Scarf dance—Pas des écharpes: Chaminade
The scarlet feather—La petite mariée: Lecocq-Monckton
Scatterbrained and shallow people   Leichtgesinnte Flattergeister: Bach
Scenes of childhood—Kinderscenen: Schumann
The scent of elders flow'ring—Was duft doch der Flieder (Die Meistersinger von Nürnberg): Wagner
The scent of roses—Toujours ou jamais: Waldteufel
Schafe können sicher weiden (Was mir behagt)—Sheep may safely graze/Flocks in pastures green abiding/Happy flock/Like a shepherd/Calm and tranquil lie the sheepfolds/In peace thy sheep may graze/Green and peaceful are the pastures: Bach
Der Schäfer—The shepherd: Wolf
Schäfer und Schäferin—Shepherd and shepherdess: Graun
Schäfers Nachtlied—Shepherd's night song: Cornelius

Schaffe in mir Gott ein rein Herz—Make me, O Lord God, pure in heart: Brahms

Schaff's mit mir, Gott, nach deinem Willen—Deal with me Father: Bach

Die Schale der Vergessenheit—The cup of oblivion: Brahms

Der Schalk—The rogue: R Franz

Die schankle Wasserlilie—The lovely waterlily: R Franz

Schastye—Happiness: Khachaturian

Schatten—In the shadow: Blumenthal

Das Schattengewässer—The shadowy waters: Kalomiris

Schatzerl klein—Little sweetheart: Webern

Der Schatzgräber—The treasure-digger: Schreker

Der Schatzgräber—The treasure-seeker: Schumann

Schätzlein und Kätzlein—My pretty and my kitty: Meyer-Helmund

Schatz-walzer—Treasure waltz/Sweethearts: J Strauss II

Schau her, das ist ein Taler (Tiefland)—Look here, this is a dollar: d'Albert

Schau, lieber Gott—Behold dear God: Bach

Schauet doch und sehet—Behold and see: Bach

Die schäumenden Wellen von Belials Bächen (Jesus schläft, was soll ich hoffen)—The white-foaming billows of Belial's torrents: Bach

Der Schauspieldirektor—The impresario/An operatic squabble: Mozart

Schaut hin! dort liegt im finstern Stall (Weihnachts-Oratorium)—Beside Thy cradle here I stand: Bach

Scheiden und Meiden—Parting/At parting/Separation: Brahms

Scheidenlied—Parting: Mendelssohn

Schein uns, du liebe Sonne—Shine down on us, dear sun: Schoenberg

Schelmenliedchen—Kissing-time: Reger

Schelomo—Solomon: Bloch

Schenk mir deinen goldenen Kamm—Give me thy golden comb: Schoenberg

Schicksalslied—Song of destiny: Brahms

Schein mir's, als ich sah die Sonne—When I saw the sun: Webern

Der Schiffer—The skipper/On the lake: Schubert

Das Schifflein—The ferry-boat: Mendelssohn

Schilderung eines Mädchens—A maiden's portraiture/Portrait of a maiden: Beethoven

Der schildwache Nachtlied (Des Knaben Wunderhorn)—The sentinel's night song: Mahler

Schilflied—Song among the reeds: Berg

Schimmernder, flimmernder Schmetterling—Glittering, fluttering butterfly: Manén

Schlachtgesang—Battle song: R Strauss

Schlaf, Kindlein, schlaf/Weihnachten—Sleep, baby, sleep/Cradle song: Brahms

Schlafe, mein Liebster (Weihnachtsoratorium)—Slumber my lov'd one: Bach

271

Schlafe wohl (Martha)—May gentle sleep attend thee: Flotow
Schlafendes Jesuskind—The Christchild asleep: Wolf
Schläfert aller Sorgen Kummer (Gott ist unsere Zuversicht)—Fall asleep,
    ye cares and troubles: Bach
Schlaflied—The forest calls: Schubert-Heller
Schlaflos—Sleepless: Liszt
Schlafloser Augen leuchte—Sun of the sleepless: Mendelssohn
Schlage doch, gewünschte Stunde—Strike at last thou hour desired/
    Strike thou hour, so long expected/Chimes ring out the moment
    longed for: Bach
Schlagende Herzen—Longing hearts: R Strauss
Das Schlaraffenland—Fool's paradise: Brahms
Schlect' Wetter—Bad weather: Reger
Schlechtes Wetter—Bad weather/Rough weather: R Strauss
Schliesse, mein Kind/Wiegenlied—Sleep now, my child: Reger
Schliesse mir die Augen beide—Close both my eyes/Close, o close my
    eyes at parting: Berg
Schliesse mir die Augen beide—The gentle touch: Goetz
Schlimm für die Männer—Awkward for the men: Henschel
Das Schloss am Meere—The castle by the sea: R Strauss
Schlosser auf (Liebeslieder Walzer)—Locksmith, ho: Brahms
Schlummerlied—Slumber-song: R Franz
Schlummerlied—Slumber song: Reger
Schlummerlied—Slumber lay/Slumber song/The greenwood calls/Call of
    the woods: Schubert
Schlummerlied (Albumblätter)—Lullaby/Slumber song: Schumann
Schlummert ein, ihr matten Augen (Ich habe genug)—Slumber now, ye
    weary eyelids/Close, tired eyes/Fall asleep ye weary eyes: Bach
Die Schlüsselblumen—(The) primroses: Liszt
Schlusslied des Narren—Clown's song/When that I was/Feste's closing
    song from Twelfth Night: Schumann
Schmeichelkätzchen—A coaxing kitten: Reger
Schmerz der Liebe—Grief of love: Nicolai
Dem Schmerz sein Recht—Let anguish have its due: Berg
Schmerzen (Wesendonck Lieder)—Grief/Agonies: Wagner
Schmetterling—The butterfly: Cornelius
Der Schmetterling—The butterfly: Schubert
Der Schmetterling—Butterflies: Schulz
Schmetterling—Butterfly: Schumann
Der Schmetterling auf einem Vergissmeinnicht—The butterfly on a
    forget-me-not: F X Mozart
Der Schmetterling ist in die Rose verliebt—The butterfly's fallen in
    love: R Franz
Der Schmidt—The smith: Schumann

Der Schmied—The forge/The blacksmith/The smith: Brahms
Schmücke dich, o liebe Seele—O my soul, prepare to meet Him/Rise, o
    soul, this happy morning: Bach
Schmücke dich, o liebe Seele—Deck thyself, (o) my soul, with gladness:
    Bach
Schmücke dich, O liebe Seele—Deck thyself out, o my soul: Brahms
Schnee—Snow: Hildach
Der Schnee ist zergangen—The snow is all melted: R Franz
Der Schnee zerrinnt—Now melts the snow: Schubert
Schneeglöckchen—Snowdrop: Schumann
Schneewittchen—Little snowdrop: Reinecke
Schnitter Tod—Death, the reaper: Brahms
Schnitterliedchen (Album für die Jugend)—The reaper's song: Schumann
Die Schnur die Perl' an Perle—The pearly shining necklace: Brahms
Der Scholar—The itinerant scholar: Wolf
The scholars meadow—Le pré-aux-clercs: Hérold
Schön Blümelein—The charming flower/Fairest flower: Schumann
Schön Hedwig—Fair Hedwig: Schumann
Schön ist das Fest—Springtime is gliding: Schumann
Schön ist die Welt—So fair is the world: Lehár
Schön lacht der holde Frühling—Already spring is smiling: Mozart
Schön Rhotraut—What is the good King Rangang's daughter's name:
    Dieren
Schön Rothraut—Gay madcap: Schumann
Schön sind, doch kalt—Glorious, but cold: R Strauss
Schön sind Rosen—Fair are roses: Kirnberger
Schöne Fremde—A lovely foreign land/A lovely land far away/Far-off
    land/Solitude: Schumann
Die schöne Galathe—Beautiful Galathea: Suppé
Die schöne Magelone—The fair Magelone: Brahms
Die schöne Müllerin—The fair maid of the mill/Maid of the mill: Schubert
Schöne Wiege—Beauteous cradle/Lovely cradle of my grieving/Lovely
    cradle of my sorrow: Schumann
Schöner Augen, schöne Strahlen—Lovely eyes with loving power: Brahms
Ein schöner Stern—New hope: Blumenthal
Schönster Schatz, mein Engel—Dearest heart, my angel: Brahms
School for fathers—I quattro rusteghi: Wolf-Ferrari
The school for lovers—Cosi fan tutte: Mozart
The schoolmaster—Der Schulmeister [symphony]: Haydn
Die Schöpfung—The creation: Fortner
Die Schöpfung—The creation: Haydn
Schöpfungsmesse—Creation mass: Haydn
Der Schreckenberger—Captain Dreadnaught/The adventurer: Wolf
Schubert to his piano—An mein Clavier: Schubert

Die Schuldigkeit des ersten und fürnehmsten Gebotes—The obligation of the first and greatest Commandment/The first Commandment: Mozart

Der Schulmeister [symphony]—The schoolmaster: Haydn

Dem Schutzengel—The guardian angel: Brahms

Die Schwalbe—Dame swallow: Humperdinck

Die Schwalben—The swallows: Schumann

Schwanda the bagpiper—Svanda Dudak: Weinberger

Der Schwanderer [concerto]—The organ grinder: Hindemith

Schwanengesang—The swan song/Swan songs: Schubert

Die schwartze Spinne—The black spider: Burkhard

Schwartzer Wald (Neue Liebeslieder)—Darksome wood: Brahms

Das Schwartzwaldmädel—The girl from the black forest: Jessel

Der schwartze Amsel—The blackbird: Meyer-Helmund

Schwebe, schwebe, blaues Auge—Eyes of beauty, blue as azure: Liszt

Schweig', aufgetürmtes Meer! (Jesus schläft, was soll ich hoffen?)—Peace thou unruly sea: Bach

Schweig einmal still (Italianische Liederbuch)—Just you be quiet/Silence I say: Wolf

Das Schweigen—A silence: Blumenthal

Die schweigsame Frau—The silent woman: R Strauss

Schweigt, stille, plauderte nicht—Coffee cantata: Bach

Schweizerlied—Swiss song: R Franz

Der schwere Abend—A valediction: Blumenthal

Der schwere Abend—The sultry evening: Schumann

Schwergewicht—Dead weight: Křenek

Schwermut—Despair: Brahms

Schwesterlein—Sister, dear sister/Sister fair: Brahms

Die Schwestern—The sisters: Brahms

Schwingt freudig euch empor—Soar joyfully on high: Bach

Schwung—Frenzy: R Strauss

Der Schwur—The oath: Meyer-Helmund

Der Schwur—The vow: Reger

Scintille diamant (Les contes d'Hoffman)—Mirror song: Offenbach

Sciolgo le labbra a un cantico—Joy bells are pealing: Magaldi

Scipio—Scipione: Handel

Scipione—Scipio: Handel

Scipio's dream—Il sogno di Scipione: Mozart

Scythian suite—Skifskaya syuita: Prokofiev

Se dig for—Beware: Grieg

Se dig ud en sommerdag—Go wandering on a summer's day: Nielsen

Se dolce m'era gia (Floridante)—When thou wert by my side: Handel

Se fedel vuoi ch'io ti creda (Orlando)—If you would of love assure me: Handel

Se Florindo è fedele (La donna ancora è fedele)—If Florindo be faithful/
  Should Florindo be faithful: A Scarlatti
Se il ciel mi divide (Alessandro nell' indie)—If heaven doth divide me:
  Piccinni
Se il padre perdei (Idomeneo)—Though I have lost my father: Mozart
Se il rigor (La Juive)—Though faithless men: Halévy
Se la giurata fede (Tosca)—No, if my plighted fealty: Puccini
Se meritar potessi—If only by deserving: Bruni
Se mi portate affetto—If you have ever borne me: V Ciampi
Se non fossero—Were not the pains: Pergolesi
Se non mi vuolamar (Tamerlano)—The land of dreams: Handel
Se pensi amor tu solo (Deidamia)—It is not wealth or grandeur: Handel
Se peri l'amato bene (Riccardo Primo)—Must he die, for whom I
  languish: Handel
Se pietà di me non senti (Giulio Cesare)—Righteous heaven/If you do not
  take pity on me: Handel
Se Savan rose—Rosebuds: Arditi
Se tu m'ami—If thou lov'st me: Fesch
Se tu m'ami—If thou lov'st me/The cocquette/Gentle shepherd: Pergolesi
Se tu m'ami—If you, sighing: Rousseau
S'e tuo piacer ch'io mora (Atalanta)—If but my death may ease thee:
  Handel
Se un bell' ardire (Ezio)—If manly valour: Handel
Se vedrà l'amena sponda (Partenza)—If she see: Handel
Se vuol ballare (Le nozze di Figaro)—If you would dance: Mozart
The sea—Die Meere: Brahms
The sea—La mer: Debussy
The sea—Das Meer erstraht: R Franz
Sea calm—Meeres Stille: Schubert
The sea hath pearls—Das Meere hat seine Perlen: R Franz
The sea is infinite—La mer est infinie (L'horizon chimérique): Fauré
Sea symphony—Sinfonia del mare: Nystroem
Sea voyage—Meerfahrt: Hauptman
The sea was moaning furiously—More yarostno stonalo: Davidenko
The sea waters roar—So tönet denn, schaumende Wellen: Brahms
The sea-fairy—Die Meerfee: Schumann
Sealed (in)—Verseigelt: Blech
The search—Ich fuhr über Meer: Kjerulf
The sea's music—Havetš visa: Nyström
The season hath cast its cloak—Le temps a laissé son manteau (Deux
  rondels . . .): Debussy
Sea-song—Havet (Barnlige Sanger): Grieg
The seasons—Die Jahreszeiten: Haydn
The seasons—Die Jahreszeiten: Křenek

Seat thyself—Nein, Geliebter (Neue Liebeslieder): Brahms
Seawake—Sillage: F Schmitt
Sebben, crudele—Although, cruel one/Tho' not deserving: Caldara
Seclusion—Verborgenheit: Wolf
The secret—Das Geheimnis: Beethoven
The secret—Geheimnis: Brahms
The secret: Geheimnis: Goetz
Secret—Hemmelighed: Grieg
A secret—Verborgene Liebe: Kjerulf
Secret—Geheimes (Schwanengesang): Schubert
The secret—Die Stille: Schumann
The secret—Tajemstvi: Smetana
The secret—Das Geheimnis: R Strauss
Secret departure—Heimliches Verschwinden: Schumann
Secret greetings—Heimliche Grüsse: Fielitz
The secret kingdom—Das geheime Königreich: Křenek
Secret love—Tajná láska: Martinů
The secret marriage—Il matrimonio segreto: Cimarosa
Secret nook—Weiche Gräser (Neue Liebeslieder): Brahms
Secret sorrows—In die Ferne: Kalliwoda
The security—Die Bürgschaft: Weill
Sed tu, Domine—But Thou, O my God: Byrd
Sed veni, Domine—Return again, O Lord: Byrd
Sedmdesát tisíc—Seventy thousand: Janáček
Seduction—Verfuhrung: R Strauss
See how the darkness—Vedi! le fosche (Il trovatore): Verdi
See my song—De mon coeur (Mignon): Thomas
See now we must go up to Jerusalem—Sehet, wir geh'n hinauf gen
    Jerusalem: Bach
See now what love (great affection)—Sehet, welch eine Liebe: Bach
See the fellow that passed just now—Saa du knøssen, som strøg forbi:
    Grieg
See the gipsy—Túrót eszik a cigány: Kodály
See the merry wine—Viva il vino (Cavalleria rusticana): Mascagni
See what His love will do!—Seht was die Liebe tut! (Ich bin ein
    gutes Hirt): Bach
Die Seejungfer—The mermaid's song/Now the dancing sunbeams: Haydn
Die Seele des Weines (Der Wein)—The wine's soul: Berg
Die Seele ruht in Jesu Händen (Herr Jesu Christ, wahr'r Mensch und Gott)—
    The soul in Jesu's hands reposes: Bach
Seele vergiss sie nicht—Soul, O forget them not: Cornelius
Seele, wie bist du schöner—Soul, you are more beautiful: Berg
Seelen Bräutigam, Jesu, Gottes Lamm!—Jesu sacred name: Bach

276

Seemans Abschied—The sailor's farewell: Wolf
Seemans Scheidelied—The sailor's farewell: Mendelssohn
Il segreto di Susanna—Susanna's secret—Wolf-Ferrari
Il segreto per esser felici (Lucrezia Borgia)—If you wish for true happiness:
    Donizetti
Sehet, welch eine Liebe—See now what love (great affection): Bach
Sehet, wir geh'n hinauf gen Jerusalem—See now we must go up to
    Jerusalem/Come let us go up to Jerusalem: Bach
Sehnsucht—Longing/Yearning: Beethoven
Sehnsucht [op 14]—Longing/Yearning/Parted: Brahms
Sehnsucht [op 49]—Wishes/Yearning: Brahms
Sehnsucht—Last night/Longing: Kjerulf
Sehnsucht—The dying sound/Yearing/Distance: F Mendelssohn
Sehnsucht—Longing: Schoenberg
Sehnsucht [D 636]—Ideal hope/Wonder/Longing: Schubert
Sehnsucht/Die Lerche wolkennahe Lieder—Lark's sweet cloud-approaching
    music/Longing/Yearning: Schubert
Sehnsucht—Longing: Schumann
Sehnsucht—Longing: Sibelius
Sehnsucht—Longing: R Strauss
Sehnsucht nach dem Frühling—Desire for spring/Children's desire for
    spring/Longing for spring: Mozart
Sehnsucht nach der Waldgegend—Longing for the forest lands: Schumann
Seht was die Liebe tut! (Ich bin ein guter Hirt)—See what His love will
    do!: Bach
Sei gegrüsset, Jesu gütig—Thee I greet, Thy love I treasure: Bach
Sei Lob und Ehr' dem Höchsten Gut—Sing praises to God who dwells on
    high: Bach
Sei Lob und Preis mit Ehren—All honour, praise and blessing: Bach
Sei mein! (An Bertha)—Be mine: Cornelius
Sei mir gegrüsst—Oh! love long lost/Thee would I greet/Angel of beauty:
    Schubert
Sei still—Be still: Liszt
Sei still mein Herz—Be still my heart: Spohr
Seit ich ihn gesehen (Frauenliebe und -leben)—Since mine eyes have
    seen him/Since I first saw him/Since mine eyes beheld him/Since first
    I beheld him: Schumann
Seitdem dein Aug'—E'er since thine eye: R Strauss
Se'l pensier che mi strugge—All the thought which torments me: Marenzio
Selbstgeständnis—A personal confession: Wolf
Selig alle—Blessed are they: Mozart
Selig ist der Mann—Blessed is the man: Bach
Selig sind, die aus Erbarmen (Brich dem Hungrigen dein Brot)—Blest are
    they who feel compassion: Bach

Selig sind, die Verfolgung leiden (Der Evangelimann)—Blest are they who are persecuted: Kienzl

Selig, wer an Jesum denkt—Blest is he who thinks on Him: Bach

Selige Nacht!—O happy eve!: R Franz

Selige Nacht—Blissful night: J Marx

Selige Welt—Happy world: Schubert

Seliger Eingang—At heaven's gate: Henschel

Seliger Tod—Resurrection: Blumenthal

Seliger Tod/Gestorben war ich vor Liebeswonne—Death stricken was I/Resurrection: Liszt

Seligkeit—Bliss/Earthly paradise: Schubert

Die Seligpreisungen—The beatitudes: Schein

Seligster Erquickungs-Tag (Wachet, betet, seid bereit)—Thou most blest, all quickening day/Blessed resurrection day: Bach

Šelma sedlák—The cunning peasant: Dvořák

La selva incantada—The enchanted forest: Righini

Selve amiche—Friendly forest: Caldara

Semero ikh—Seven they are seven: Prokofiev

Semmit ne bánkodjál—Cease your bitter weeping: Kodály

Semplicetto! a donna credi (Alcina)—Trust a woman? How simple-minded Handel

Sempre libera (La traviata)—Let me ever as I wander/Free as air/Shall I always: Verdi

Semya—The family: Khodzha-Eynatov

Semya Tarasa—Tara's family: Kabalevsky

Sen panny Marie—The dream of the Virgin Mary: Martinů

Die Sendung—The message: Himmel

Senex puerum portabat—Simeon took the infant/Simeon carried the young child: Byrd

Das Sennen Abschied—The Alpine herdsman's farewell: Schumann

Die Sennin—The cowgirl: Schumann

Sensazione lunare—A moonlight idyll: Sibella

Senseless the man—Folle è colui (Ezio): Handel

Le sentier perdu—The lost path: Massenet

Sentimental colloquy—Colloque sentimental (Fêtes galantes): Debussy

The sentinel's night song—Der Schildwache Nachtlied: Mahler

Sento che un giusto sdegno (Faramondo)—Wrath in my bosom nesting: Handel

Sento un certo non so che (L'incoronazione di Poppea)—Something strange I know not what: Monteverdi

Separated lovers—Amoureux séparés: Roussel

The separation—Als die Geliebte sich trennen wolte: Beethoven

Separation—La partenza: Beethoven

Separation—Scheiden und Meiden: Brahms

Separation—Trennung: Brahms

Separation—Nach dem Abschiede: Wolf

Separation—and reunion—Das Lied der Trennung: Mozart
September morning—Septembermorgen: J Marx
September serenade—Automne: Chaminade
Septembermorgen—September morning: J Marx
The seraglio—Die Entführung aus dem Serail: Mozart
Serdtse gor—The heart of the mountains: Balanchivadze
Serena i vaghi rai (Semiramide)—Aside dark sorrow laying: Rossini
Sérénade (La jolie fille de Perth)—The shades of night: Bizet
Serenade—Serenata: Bossi
Serenade—La serenata: Braga
Serenade—Leise, um dich nicht zu wecken: Brahms
Serenade—Ständchen: Brahms
Serenade—Ständchen: R Franz
Sérénade/C'est une fleur sauvage—Wildflower: Pierné
Serenade—Ständchen (Schwanengesang): Schubert
Serenade—Ständchen: Schumann
Serenade—Ständchen: R Strauss
The serenade—Das Ständchen: Wolf
Sérénade d'Arlequin/A Columbine—To Columbine: Massenet
Sérénade florentine—Florentine serenade: Duparc
Serenade in the night—Violino Tzigano: Bizio
Serenade italienne—Italian serenade: Chausson
Serenata—Serenade: Bossi
La serenata—Serenade/Angel's serenade: Braga
The serf ballerina—Krepostnaya balerina: Korchmarev
The sermon to the birds—La prédication aux oiseaux: Liszt
The serpent woman—La donna serpente: Casella
Serse—Xerxes: Handel
La serva padrona—The maid mistress/The maid as mistress/Servant-
    mistress: Pergolesi
Servant-mistress—La serva padrona: Pergolesi
Set me free, O Lord my God—Libera me Domine: Byrd
Ein Seufzer—A sigh: B Klein
Seufzer—A heartfelt sigh: Wolf
Seufzer eines Ungeliebten und Gegenliebe—Desponding and responsive
    love/The sigh of one unloved and mutual love: Beethoven
Seufzer, Tränen, Kummer, Not (Ich hatte viel Bekümmernis)—Sighing,
    weeping, trouble, want: Bach
Sevastopolstï—The defenders of Sevastopol: Koval
The seven boon companions—Von den sieben Zechbrüdern: R Strauss
Seven last songs—Canciones amatorias: Granados
The seven last words—Die sieben Worte des Erlöser: Haydn
The seven last words—Die sieben Worte unseres lieben Erlöser und
    Seligmachers Jesu Christ: Schütz

The seven seals—Die sieben Siegel: R Strauss
Seven sketches—Vázlatok: Bartók
Seven they are seven—Semero ikh: Prokofiev
The seventh ring—Der siebente Ring: Webern
Seventy thousand—Sedmdesát tisíc: Janáček
Severny veter—North wind: Knipper
Sevillanas—At Seville: Laparra
Shade departed—Ombra cara (Radamisto): Handel
Shade like unto thine—Ombra mai fù (Serse): Handel
The shade of Don Juan—L'ombra di Don Giovanni: Alfano
The shades of evening—Le soir: Gounod
The shades of night—Sérénade (La jolie fille de Perth)/A la voix d'un
    amant fidèle: Bizet
Shadow gloom—Finstere Schatten (Neue Liebeslieder): Brahms
The shadow of the trees—L'ombre des arbres (Ariettes oubliées):
    Debussy
Shadow song—Ombre légère (Dinorah): Meyerbeer
Shadows, cypress, urns funereal—Ombre, piante, urne funeste (Rodelinda)
    Handel
Shadows of death—Todessehnen: Brahms
Shadows so sweet—Ombra mai fù (Serse): Handel
The shadowy waters—Das Schattengewässer: Kalomiris
The shake-down song—Las agachadas: Copland
Shall I always—Sempre libera (La traviata): Verdi
Shall I endure this anguish?—Vivere per penare (Floridante): Handel
Sharp poisoned arrow—Nagen am Herzen (Neue Liebeslieder): Brahms
Shchedryk—A Christmas song: Leontovych
She dances—Hun danser: Grieg
She had gone to the edge—Elle était descendue (Tristesses): Milhaud
She is gravely gay—Elle est gravement gaie (Tristesses): Milhaud
She is thine—Frühlingsnacht: Schumann
She is too small—Kicsi a lány: Erkel
She shall see me—A suoi piedi padre esangue (Tamerlano): Handel
She that for me did pine—Quella che tutta fé (Serse): Handel
She was carrying bunches of lilac—Elle avait emporté (Tristesses):
    Milhaud
She was so fair—Hun er saa hvid: Grieg
Sheep may safely graze—Schafe können sicher weiden (Was mir behagt):
    Bach
The sheep's polka—Lampaan polska: Kuula
The shell—Therese: Brahms
The shelter—L'abri: Bloch
Shema Yisroel—Hear ye, Israel: Milhaud
The shepherd—Der Hirt: Liszt

The shepherd—Der Schäfer: Wolf
Shepherd and shepherdess—Schäfer und Schäferin: Graun
Shepherd boy—Gjaetergut: Grieg
The shepherd king—Il re pastore: Mozart
Shepherd on the rock—Der Hirt auf dem Felsen: Schubert
The shepherd sings—Il pastore canta: Recli
Shepherdess—Pastýřka: Smetana
Shepherdess I love—La pastoreta: Alió
The shepherds—Die Hirten (Weihnachtslieder): Cornelius
Shepherds cantata—Entfliehet, verschwindet, entweichet, ihr Sorgen:
    Bach
Shepherd's chorus—Hirtenchor (Rosamonde): Schubert
Shepherd's farewell—Les adieux du berger: Godard
Shepherd's night song—Schäfers Nachtlied: Cornelius
Shepherds quaked when the angels told them—Angelus ad pastores ait:
    H L Hassler
The shepherd's reproach—Im Volkston: Meyer-Helmund
Shepherd's song—Chanson du berger: Godard
The shepherd's song—Hirtenlied: Mendelssohn
Shepherd's song at the manger—Hirtengesang an der Krippe (Christus):
    Liszt
Shew Thy mercy on me—Miserer mei: Byrd
Shine down on us, dear sun—Schein uns, du liebe Sonne: Schoenberg
Shine out in this fair place—Brillez dans ces beaux lieux (Les éléments):
    Destouches
The ship—Le beau navire (Petites légendes): Milhaud
The ship—La nave: Montemezzi
Ships, we have loved you—Vaisseaux, nous vous aurons aimés (L'horizon
    chimérique): Fauré
Shir Haemek—Song of the Emek: Lavry
Shir Nahal—Song of the port: Binder
Shire' Chalutzim—Pioneer songs of Palestine: Binder
Shiroka strana moya rodnaya—Broad is my native land: Dunayevski
Should Florinda be faithful—Se Florindo è fedele (La donna ancora è
    fedele): A Scarlatti
Show Thy reckoning! word of doom—Tue Rechnung! Donnerwort: Bach
Shrove Tuesday carnival—Venus im grünen: Straus
Shut—The buffoon: Prokofiev
The shy lover—Der bescheidene Schäfer: J Marx
Si ambulem in medio—Yea, though I tread the valley: Tye
Si come nella penna e nell' inchiostro (Sonnets of Michelangelo)—Just
    as there is a high, a low . . . : Britten
Si de mon premier rêve—My dreams since our first meeting: Aubert
Si dessus voz levres de roses—Thy lips like roses: Le Jeune
Si di rama en rama (Acis y Galatea)—Trusting little linnet: Literes

Si diversi sembianti (Siroe)—Yes, my brow oft is clouded: Handel
Si, figlia, io moro, addio (Tamerlano)—Yes, daughter, I die: Handel
Si j'ai perdu mon amant—If indeed I've lost my lover: Delusse
Si j'étais jardinier—Love's garden: Chaminade
Si le bonheur (Faust)—When all was young/If thou but smile: Gounod
Si les filles d'Arles—Maids may boast: Gounod
Si mes vers avaient des ailes—If my songs were only winged: Hahn
Si mi chiamano Mimi (La bohème)—They call me Mimi: Puccini
Si puo rimirar—My heart only sighs: Gaffi
Si, scherza sempre amor (Partenope)—Yes jesting love ever sports: Handel
Si tout ceci (Tristesses)—If all this is but a fleeting dream: Milhaud
Si tra i ceppi (Berenice)—'Tween the branches and the blossoms/Love
     that's true/Yea, 'mid chains: Handel
Si tu veux, Mignon—If you will beloved: Massenet
Si voli il primo (Lucrezia Borgia)—Receive thou my first: Donizetti
Sia benedeto—Praise the creator: Wolf-Ferrari
Sia pur sonno dì morte—Music softly streaming: A Scarlatti
Sichers Glück—Lasting happiness: Bocquet
The Sicilian vespers—Les vêpres siciliennes: Verdi
Sicut audivimus—Like as we oft have heard: Byrd
Sicut cervus desiderat—Like as the hart: Palestrina
Sicut Moses serpentum—Thus as Moses: Schütz
Siderum rector—Lord God almighty: Byrd
Sie ist dahin—Death of the nightingale: Mozart
Sie liebten sich beide—They worshipped each other: R Franz
Sie werden aus Saba alle kommen—The sages of Sheba/They all from
     Sheba shall come: Bach
Sie werden euch in den Bann tun—Ye shall from God's house be cast
     forth: Bach
Sie wissens nicht—Maiden and nightingale: R Strauss
Die sieben Siegel—The seven seals: R Strauss
Die sieben Worte unseres lieben Erlöser und Seligmachers Jesu Christ—
     The seven last words: Schütz
Die siebente Ring—The seventh ring: Webern
Siechentrost—Solace in affliction: Bach
Der Sieg—The victory: Schubert
Siegfried's funeral march—Trauermarsch (Gotterdämmerung): Wagner
Sieh' da ein herrlich Frauenbild (Der Zigeunerbaron)—O see a vision
     greets my sight: J Strauss II
Sieh' das ist es—Wouldst thou keep undimmed: Henschel
Sieh' wie ist die Welle (Liebeslieder Walzer)—Bright thy sheen: Brahms
Siehe, ich komme (Himmelskönig, sei wilkommen)—Lo, I come: Bach
A sigh—Soupir: Bemberg
Sigh—Soupir: Duparc
A sigh—Ein Seufzer: B Klein

A sigh goes stirring—Es geht ein Wehen: Bach
The sigh of one unloved and mutual love—Seufzer eines Ungeliebten und Gegenliebe: Beethoven
Sighing, weeping, trouble, want—Seufzer, Tränen, Kummer, Not (Ich hatte viel Bekümmernis): Bach
Sighs—Suk: Grieg
Signor, lo credi a me (Admeto)—My lord, only believe: Handel
Signore, ascolta (Turandot)—Lo, I entreat thee, Sire!: Puccini
The signpost—Der Wegweiser (Die Winterreise): Schubert
S'il est un charmant gazon—O where is there a sward so green/If there be a charming lawn: Liszt
A silence—Das Schweigen: Blumenthal
Silence—Molchanie: Miaskowsky
Silence—Die Stille: Schumann
Silence I say—Schweig einmal still (Italienisches Liederbuch): Wolf
Silence prevailed in heaven—Factum est silentium: Dering
Silent and lone—A les je tichý (Cigánské melodie): Dvořák
Silent and speechless—Tace il labro: Sarri
Silent longing—Leise Lied: R Strauss
Silent love—Stille Liebe: R Franz
Silent love—Du fragst mich, du mein blondes Lieb: Kjerulf
Silent love—Stille Liebe: Schumann
Silent love—Verschweigene Liebe: Wolf
Silent night, holy night—Stille Nacht, heilige Nacht: Grüber
Silent reproach—Stiller Vorwurf: Schumann
Silent safety—Stille Sicherheit: R Franz
Silent tears—Stille Tränen: Schumann
Silent the sombre wings—Regnava nel silenzio (Lucia di Lammermoor): Donizetti
The silent town—Die stille Stadt: Sibelius
The silent water-lily—Die stille Wasserrose: Liszt
Silent woe—Stille Lied: Fielitz
The silent woman—Die schweigsame Frau: R Strauss
Silent worship—Non lo diro col labbro (Tolomeo): Handel
The silken band—Chudoba (Moravské dvojzpévy): Dvořák
Sillage—Seawake: F Schmitt
The silver ring—L'anneau d'argent: Chaminade
Simeon carried the young child—Senex puerum portabat: Byrd
Simeon took the infant—Senex puerum portabat: Byrd
A simile—Albumblatt: Kjerulf
Similitudine—Echo: Bossi
Sin solntsa—Son of the sun: Vasilenko
Since all is passing—Puisque tout passe: Hindemith

Since beauty that is boundless—S'infinita bellezza: Arcadelt
Since dawn is breaking—Puisque l'aube grandit (La bonne chanson):
  Fauré
Since first I saw thy face—Als ich dich kaum geseh'n: M Mayer
Since I first beheld him—Seit ich ihn gesehen (Frauenliebe und -leben):
  Schumann
Since I first saw him—Seit ich ihn gesehen (Frauenliebe und -leben):
  Schumann
Since I have suffered much—Par ce que j'ai souffert (Tristesses): Milhaud
Since mine eyes beheld him—Seit ich ihn gesehen (Frauenliebe und
  -leben): Schumann
Since mine eyes have seen him—Seit ich ihn gesehen (Frauenliebe und
  -leben): Schumann
Since she my life has taken—Puisqu'elle a pris ma vie: Massenet
Since we parted—Col partir: Handel
Sincerity, a gift it is—Die Redlichkeit ist eine von den Gottesgaben
  (Ein ungefärbt Gemüte): Bach
Sind es Schmerzen, sind es Freuden—Are they sorrows, are they
  pleasure/What emotions o'er me stealing?/Are they pains?/Is it pain?/
  Is it joy?/Is it bliss or is it sorrow?: Brahms
S'infinita bellezza—Since beauty is boundless: Arcadelt
Sinfonia del mare—Sea symphony: Nystroem
Sing aloud with gladness—Exultate Deo: S Wesley
Sing, beloved Christians sing!—Singt ihr lieben Christen all!: Praetorius
Sing on—Venez, venez (Titon et l'Aurore): Mondonville
Sing praises—Erschallet, ihr Lieder: Bach
Sing praises to God who dwells on high—Sei Lob und Ehr' dem Höchsten
  Gut: Bach
Sing, sing—Syng, syng: Kjerulf
Sing, sons of the free—Freiwillige her!: Brahms
Sing we the birth—Das neugebor'ne Kindelein: Bach
Sing with joy and gladness—Exultate Deo: Palestrina
Sing ye a joyful song—Zpivejte Hospodinu (Biblické Písně): Dvořák
Sing ye the praises to the highest—Adoramus te: Brahms
Sing ye to the Lord—Singet den Herrn: Bach
S'inganna chi crede—He's wrong who imagines: Sarti
The singer—Der Sänger: Schumann
Singet den Herrn—Sing ye to the Lord: Bach
Singing—Gesungen: Schumann
Singing dervishes—Éneklö Dervisek: E Ábrányi
Singlehearted—Treue: Blumenthal
Sings my love—Singt mein Schatz: Wolf
Singt ihr lieben Christen alle!—Sing, beloved Christians sing!: Praetorius
Singt mein Schatz wie ein Fink—When my love sings like a robin: Pfitzner

Singt mein Schatz—And my love were the lark/Sings my love: Wolf
Sinks the night—Triolett: Schumann
Sinners come—Kommet her, ihr frechten Sünde: Mozart
S'io ti vedess' una sol—Ah could my eyes behold thee: Lassus
Šípek (Moravské Dvojpěvy)—The wild rose: Dvořák
Sir Olaf—Herr Oluf: Loewe
Sir spring—Herr Lenz: R Strauss
Siralmas nékem—Exile: Kodály
Široké rukávy a široké gatě (Cigánské melodie)—In his wide and ample,
　　airy linen vesture: Dvořák
Sirotek—The orphan: Dvořák
Sirs your toast—Votre toast, je peux vous la rendre (Carmen): Bizet
Sister Angelica—Suor Angelica: Puccini
Sister dear sister: Schwesterlein: Brahms
Sister fair—Schwesterlein: Brahms
The sisters—Die Schwestern: Brahms
The skaters—Les patineurs: Waldteufel
The skaters' waltz—Les patineurs: Waldteufel
Skaz o kamennom tsvetke—The stone flower: Prokofiev
Skaz o partisane—Tale of a partisan: Koval'
Skazanie o bitve za Russkuyu zemlyn—Story of the fight for the Russian
　　land: Shaporin
Skazanie o nevidimom grade Kitezhe i deve Ferronii—The legend of the
　　invisible city of Kitezh and the maiden Fevronia: Rimsky-Korsakov
Skazka—Fairy tale: Prokofiev
Skazka o Tsare Saltane—The tale of the Tsar Saltan: Rimsky-Korsakov
Skazki gipsovovo bozhka—Tales of a plaster idol/The tales of a plaster
　　Buddha: Knipper
Skies are blue—Cielo azul: Longás
The skies are getting brighter—Aufbruch: R Franz
Skifskaya syuita—Scythian suite: Prokofiev
The skipper—Der Schiffer: Schubert
Sklicenost—Anxiety: Smetana
Skolie—A stirrup cup: Wolf
Skovstilhed—Peace of the woods: Grieg
Der Skreg en fugl—A bird's cry: Sinding
Skromna (Moravské Dvojzpěvy)—The modest maid/Like a violet: Dvořák
Skřýše má a pavéza (Biblické Písně)—Lord, Thou art my refuge: Dvořák
Skupoy Ritsar—The miserly knight: Rachmaninov
The skylark's song—Lerchengesang: Brahms
Skymning (Ljus och skugga)—Twilight: Palmgren
Slav song—Chanson slave: Chaminade
Slavískovský polečko malȳ (Moravské Drojzpěvy)—The pledge of love:
　　Dvořák

Sleep and black shadow—Un grand sommeil noir: Stravinsky
Sleep, baby, sleep—Schlaf, Kindlein, schlaf: Brahms
Sleep, dearest, sleep—Dors, enfant, dors: Randegger
Sleep my darling—Ruhe, Sussliebchen: Brahms
Sleep now, my child—Schliesse, mein Kind: Reger
The sleeper—Nachtwandler: Brahms
The sleeper—La dormeuse (Petites légendes): Milhaud
Sleepers, wake!—Wachet auf, ruft uns die Stimme: Bach
Sleeping flowers—Le sommeil des fleurs: Saint-Saens
The sleeping beauty in the wood—Dornröschen (Volkskinder Lieder):
   Brahms
Sleeping beauty—Pavane de la belle au bois dormant (Ma mère l'oye):
   Ravel
The sleeping princess—Spyashchaya knyazhna: Borodin
Sleepless—Schlaflos: Liszt
The sleepwalker—La sonnambula: Bellini
The sleepwalker—Nachtwandler: Brahms
Slepicka—The little hen: Smetana
Sliczny chłopiec—The bonnie lad: Chopin
A slight mistake—Eine kleines Versehen: Meyer-Helmund
The slighted heart—Dyby byla kosa nabrósená (Moravské Dvojzpěvy):
   Dvořák
Slovak peasants' dance—Tóth legények tánca (Tiz könnyű): Bartók
Slumber dear maid—Ombra mai fù (Serse): Handel
Slumber lay—Schlummerlied: Schubert
Slumber my lov'd one—Schlafe, mein Liebster (Weihnachtsoratorium):
   Bach
Slumber, my pretty one—Hajej, muj andilku (Hubička): Smetana
Slumber now ye weary eyelids—Schlummert ein, ihr matten Augen
   (Ich habe genug): Bach
Slumber song—Wiegenlied: d'Albert
Slumber song—Ruhe, Sussliebchen: Brahms
Slumber song—Wiegenlied: Cornelius
Slumber song—Bei der Wiege: Mendelssohn
Slumber song—Schlummerlied: Reger
Slumber song—Schlummerlied: Schubert
Slumber song—Schlummerlied (Albumblätter): Schumann
Slumbering deep—Die Meere: Brahms
Slumber-song—Schlummerlied: R Franz
Slyš ó Bože (Biblické Písně)—Hear my prayer, O God: Dvořák
Smart John and his Marg'ret—Arme Peter (1): Schumann
Smatrold—Puck: Grieg
Smile and I'll teach thee—Vedrai carino, se sei buonino (Don Giovanni):
   Mozart
Smile not o'er my grieving—Per pièta, non ricercate: Mozart

Smiles about thy lips are straying—Bitteres zu sagen denkst du: Brahms

Smiling Bacchus—Del mio caro Bacco (Serse): Handel

Smiling the dawn approacheth—Ecco ridente in cielo (Il barbiere di Siviglia): Rossini

Smír Tantalův—Tantalus's atonement: Fibich

The smith—Der Schmied: Brahms

The smith—Der Schmidt: Schumann

Smoke—Der Rauch: J Marx

Smrt Hippodamia—Hippodamia's death: Fibich

The smuggler—Der Kontrabandiste: Schumann

Smutna rzeka—Sad river: Chopin

Smutný milý—The unhappy lover: Martinů

Snail—Snegl: Grieg

The snail—Älvan och snigeln: Sibelius

The snares of death—Circumdederunt me: Byrd

Snegl—Snail: Grieg

Snegurochka—The snow maiden: Rimsky Korsakov

Snow—Schnee: Hildach

The snow is all melted—Der Schnee ist zergangen: R Franz

The snow maiden—Snegurochka: Rimsky-Korsakov

Snow-drift—Chasse-neige: Liszt

Snowdrop—Schneeglöckchen: Schumann

Snow-fall—Temps de neige: Séverac

Snurretoppen (Humoreske)—The top/The spinning top: Nielsen

So ben mi ch'a bon tempo—Let ev'ry heart be merry: Vecelii

So bitter was my heart—Så bittert var mit hjerte (Moderen): Nielsen

So clear thine eyes—Dein blaues Auge: Brahms

So gehst du nun, mein Jesu, hin—Thou goest now my Saviour forth: Bach

So do they all—Così fan tutte: Mozart

So du mit deinem Munde—If thou shalt confess with thy mouth: Bach

So fair is the world—Schön ist die Welt: Lehár

So glaube nun! (Alles nur nach Gottes Willen)—Have faith in God: Bach

So I returned—Ich wandte mich und sahe: Brahms

So ist es denn des Himmels Will—Is it then holy heaven's will: H Albert

So, it will be on a clear summer day—Donc, ce sera par un clair jour d'été (La bonne chanson): Fauré

So lass uns wandern—Thus we will wander: Brahms

So lasst mich scheinen/Mignon [D 727]—O let me seem now/Illusion's magic spell/So let me dream till I awaken: Schubert

So lasst mich scheinen/Mignon [D 877]—Oh, let me dream/So whilst I am not/So let me dream: Schubert

So lasst mich scheinen—So let me seem to be: Wolf

So let me dream—So lasst mich scheinen: Schubert

So let me seem to be—So lasst mich scheinen: Wolf
So let me sing God's praises—Herr, gib, dass ich dein' Ehre (Was willst
du dich betrüben): Bach
So like a flower—Du bist wie eine Blume: Liszt
So my valour and my victories—Questa dunque è l'iniqua mercede (I due
Foscari): Verdi
So oder so—No matter which/This or that: Beethoven
So secretly—Gang zur Liebsten: Brahms
So sei nun, Seele, deine (Meine Seufzer, meine Tränen)—To Him my
spirit yield Thee: Bach
So shall my weeping—Laschia ch'io pianga (Rinaldo): Handel
So shall one day's disaster—E pur cosi in un giorno (Giulio Cesare):
Handel
So silly doth the moon hide—Verstohlen geht der Mond auf: Brahms
So sind wir nun Botschafter (Paulus)—Now we are ambassadors:
Mendelssohn
So, sir page—Non più andrai (Le nozze di Figaro): Mozart
So soon were our hearts united—Gar lieblich hat sich gestellet: Brahms
So stehen wir—No more we twain go forth a-Maying/'Tis ended/Thus
stand we/My love and I agree: Brahms
So strongly does her memory—Son souvenir emplit (Tristesses): Milhaud
So tönet denn, schäumende Wellen—The sea waters roar/Ye waves: Brahms
So truly God his world did bless—Also hat Gott die Welt geliebt: Bach
So wahr die Sonne scheinet—Fidelity: Schumann
So whilst I am not—So lasst mich scheinen [D 877]: Schubert
So white is she—Hun er saa hvid: Grieg
So will ich frisch und frohlich sein—I'll ever gay and merry be: Brahms
So willst du—Wilt deign to be near me/In pity then/And may I believe
it?/O wilt thou/O say you believe me/At last/In how kind a fashion:
Brahms
So wird denn Herz und Mund (Es ist dir gesagt, Mensch, was gut ist)—
It is my heart: Bach
So wünsch' ich ihr ein gute Nacht—I wished her thus: Brahms
So wünsch' ich mir zu guter letzt—I fain would know/When I shall meet
my life's last day: Bach
So your gay life of pleasure is over—Non più andrai (Le nozze di
Figaro): Mozart
Soar joyfully on high—Schwingt freudig euch empor: Bach
Soaring—Flucht: Schubert
Soaring—Aufschwung (Fantasiestücke): Schumann
Sobald Damoetas Chloen sieht/Die Verschweigung—When first young
Damon/Damon and Chloe: Mozart
Sobre las olas—Over the waves: Rosas
Sobs—Sanglots: Poulenc

Socrate immaginario—The man who thought he was Socrates: Paisiello
Soffri in pace (Atalanta)—Know what pangs: Handel
Soft amid the bed of roses—Leise, umdich nich zu wecken: Brahms
Soft as the zephyr—Bist du!: Liszt
Soft dews from heaven falling—Kein Hälmlein wächst auf Erden:
    W F Bach (attrib)
Softly as a sweet harmonica—Frêle comme un harmonico: Rhené-Baton
Softly awakes my heart—Mon coeur s'ouvre à ta voix (Samson et Dalila):
    Saint-Saëns
Softly murmuring stream—Der Jüngling an der Quelle: Schubert
Softly sighs the voice of evening—Leise, leise, fromme Weise (Die
    Freischütz): Weber
Softly through my heart—Leise zieht durch: R Franz
Il sogno di Scipione—Scipio's dream: Mozart
Soir—Evening: Fauré
Le soir—The shades of evening/The moonbeam/Evensong: Gounod
Un soir dans les montagnes—An evening in the mountains: Liszt
Soir d'hiver—Winter's night: Rhené-Baton
Soirée en mer—Evening at sea: Saint-Saens
Solace in affliction—Siechentrost: Bruch
Solace in sorrow—Trost im Unglück (Des Knaben Wunderhorn): Mahler
Solace in tears—Trost in Tränen: Brahms
Solace of tears—Trost in Tränen: Schubert
Solche hergelauf'ne Laffen (Die Entführung aus dem Serail)—Rogues like
    you: Mozart
Der Soldat—The soldier: Schumann
Der Soldat—The soldier: Wolf
Die Soldatenbraut—The soldier's bride/The soldier's sweetheart:
    Schumann
Soldatenlied—Soldier's song: Schumann
Soldatenmarsch (Album für die Jugend)—A soldier's march: Schumann
The soldier—Der Soldat: Schumann
The soldier—Válečník: Smetana
The soldier—Der Soldat: Wolf
The soldier of fortune—Der Glücksritter: Wolf
Soldier, rest—Raste Krieger: Schubert
The soldier's bride—Die Soldatenbraut: Schumann
The soldier's death—Geleit: Brahms
The soldier's farewell—Des Kriegers Abschied: Beethoven
A soldier's march—Soldatenmarsch (Album für die Jugend): Schumann
Soldier's song—Katonadal: Kodály
Soldier's song—Soldatenlied: Schumann
The soldier's sweetheart—Die Soldatenbraut: Schumann
A (The) soldier's tale—Histoire du soldat: Stravinsky

Solen er sa rød, mor—The sun is so red, oh mother dear: Nielsen
Solenne in quest' ora (La forza del destino)—In this solemn hour: Verdi
The solitary—Der Einsame: Schubert
The solitary in autumn—Der Einsame im Herbst (Das Lied von der Erde): Mahler
The solitary one—Der Einsame: R Strauss
Solitary traveller—Ensom Vandrer: Grieg
Solitude—Einsamkeit: R Kahn
Solitude—Einsamkeit: Medtner
Solitude—An die Einsamkeit: Mozart
Solitude—Einsamkeit: Schumann
Solitude—Schöne Fremde: Schumann
Solitude, ah, how welcome—Solitudine avvenne: A Scarlatti
Solitude in summer fields—Feldeinsamkeit: Brahms
Solitude in the fields—Feldeinsamkeit: Brahms
Solitudine avvenne—Solitude, ah, how welcome: A Scarlatti
Soll dann der Pales (Was mir behagt)—Then shall this past'ral: Bach
Soll sich der Mond nicht heller scheinen—And when the moon: Brahms
Solnedgang—Sunset: Grieg
Solomon—Schelomo: Bloch
Solovey—The nightingale: Stravinsky
Soluppgång—Sunrise: Sibelius
Solveig's cradle song—Solveig's vuggevise: Grieg
Solveigs Sang—Solveig's song: Grieg
Solveig's song—Solveigs Sang: Grieg
Solveigs vuggevise—Solveig's cradle song: Grieg
Som en rejselysten flåde (Moderen)—Like a fleet eager to set sail: Nielsen
Sombre grove—Bois épais (Amadis de Gaule): Lully
Sombre woods—Bois épais (Amadis de Gaule): Lully
El sombrero de tres picos—The three-cornered hat: Falla
Somebody—Jemand: Schumann
Something strange I know not what—Sento un certo non sò che (L'incoronazione di Poppea): Monteverdi
Sometimes I am sad—Parfois, je suis triste (Tristesses): Milhaud
Le sommeil des fleurs—Sleeping flowers: Saint-Saëns
Der Sommer ist so schön—The pleasant summer's come: R Franz
Sommerabend—Summer evening: Brahms
Sommerfugl—Butterfly: Grieg
Sommermüd—Weary of summer: Schoenberg
Die Sommernacht—Oh, summer night: Henschel
Ein Sommernachtstraum—A midsummer night's dream: Mendelssohn
Sommertage—Summer days: Berg
Sommi Dei! (Radamisto)—Ye high powers: Handel
Son—A dream: Stetsenko

Son and stranger—Die Heimkehr aus der Fremde: Mendelssohn
Son confusa pastorella (Poro)—'Tis confusing for a shepherdess: Handel
Son contenta di morire (Radamisto)—Am I fated thus to perish: Handel
Son of the muses—Der Musensohn: Schubert
Son vergin vezzosa (I puritani)—Ah! with joy my heart is pounding:
    Bellini
A son of the muses—Der Musensohn: Schubert
Son of the sun—Sün solntsa: Vasilenko
Son of the wolf—Ulvens søn: Nielsen
Son Pereda, son ricco d'onore (La forza del destino)—I, Pereda, for
    honour am fated: Verdi
Son souvenir emplit (Tristesses)—So strongly does her memory: Milhaud
Soñando—Breathless: Cobian
Song—Lied: Chabrier
A song—Chanson: Poulenc
Song album for the young—Liederalbum für die Jugend: Schumann
Song among the reeds—Schilflied: Berg
Song for the new year—Neujahrslied: Schumann
(A) Song from afar—Lied aus der Ferne: Beethoven
Song from 'Ivan'—Lied aus dem Gedichte 'Ivan': Brahms
Song from Ossian's 'Fingal'—Gesang aus Fingal: Brahms
Song for Jeanne—Chanson pour Jeanne: Chabrier
Song from the tomb—Śpiew grobowy: Chopin
The song o' green fields—La chanson des prés: Godard
Song of a maid—Mädchenlied: Brahms
Song of April—Chanson d'avril: Bizet
A song of autumn—Melodieux automne: Ladmirault
A song of beauty—Von der Schönheit (Das Lied von der Erde): Mahler
Song of Chiemsee—Eliland: Fielitz
Song of destiny—Schicksalslied: Brahms
Song of faith—A Magyarokhoz: Kodály
Song of freedom—Lied der Freiheit: Mozart
A song of friendship—Lied der Freundschaft: R Strauss
Song of grief—Air grave: Poulenc
Song of hope—Hatikvah (Shire' Chalutzim): Binder
Song of Lynceus the lynx-eyed, keeper of the watch-tower—Lied
    Lynceus des Türmers: Schumann
A song of May—Mailied: Beethoven
A song of May—Maienlied: Mendelssohn
Song of Mignon—Mignons Lied: Liszt
The song of my country—Pesnya o rodine: Dunayevski
Song of my heart—Sydämeni laulu: Sibelius
Song of Orkenise—Chanson d'Orkenise: Poulenc
Song of Pan—Zu Tanze, zu Sprunge (Geschwinde, geschwinde, ihr
    wirbelnden Winde): Bach

Song of praise to a wife—Cantique à l'épouse: Chausson
The song of Provence—Clocko: Lehár
Song of repentance—Busslied: Cornelius
A song of rest—Pax Dei: E W Naylor
Song of St Mary—Marienlied: J Marx
Song of solace—Chanson triste: Duparc
Song of spring—Frühlingsgesang (Album für die Jugend): Schumann
A song of spring—Lenzgesang: Sibelius
A song of spring—Frühlingslied: Mendelssohn
Song of springtime—Chanson de printemps: Gounod
Song of the clever gypsy girl—Canción de la gitana habilidosa: Castel
The song of the earth—Das Lied von der Erde: Mahler
Song of the Emek—Shir Haemek: Lavry
Song of the elves—Elfenliedchen: Medtner
Song of the endless night—Chanson de la nuit durable: Séverac
Song of the fates—Gesang der Parzen: Brahms
Song of the fisherman—Chanson du pêcheur: Fauré
Song of the flea—Es war einmal ein König: Beethoven
Song of the forests—Pesn o lesakh: Shostakovich
Song of the lentisk gatherers—Chanson des cueilleuses de lentisques:
    Ravel
Song of the little bay horse—Chanson pour le petit cheval: Séverac
Song of the mountain lad—Des Knaben Berglied: Schumann
Song of the mountains—De Norske Fjelde (Barnlige Sanger): Grieg
Song of the night—Nachtlied: R Franz
Song of the night—Wanderers Nachtlied: Loewe
Song of the night—Lied an die Nacht: Reichardt
Song of the night—Nachtlied: Schumann
Song of the nightingale—Wehmut: Schumann
Song of the port—Shir Nahal: Binder
Song of the prisoner in the tower—Lied des Verfolgten im Turm (Des
    Knaben Wunderhorn): Mahler
Song of the Rhine wine—Gesang über das Rheinweinlied (Fest-
    ouverture): Schumann
The song of the roses—Rosenlied: Sibelius
Song of the Savoyard—Pagenlied: Mendelssohn
A song of the sea—Lied maritime: Indy
Song of the sirens—Il vostro maggio (Rinaldo): Handel
Song of the skylark—Lerchengesang: Brahms
Song of the spirits over the waters—Gesang der Geister über den Wassern:
    Schubert
The song of the storm—Sturmhymnus: Weingartner
Song of the trooper—Reiterlied: Reger
Song of the wind—Lied vom Winde: Wolf

Song of the water-gnome—Celý svět nedá ti (Rusalka): Dvořák
Song of the will-o-the-wisp—Canción del fuego fatuo (El amor brujo):
   Falla
Song of the youths—Gesang der Junglinge: Stockhausen
Song of travel—Wanderlied: Schumann
Song of triumph—Triumphlied: Brahms
Song of triumph—Pesnya likovaniya: Veprik
A song of Venice—Chant vénitien: Bemberg
A song of youth—Von der Jugend (Das Lied von der Erde): Mahler
Song without end—Chanson perpetuelle: Chausson
Songe—Dream: Caplet
Songs from Karad—Karádi Nóták: Kodály
Songs my mother taught me—Když mne stará matka (Cigánské melodie):
   Dvořák
Songs of a bride—Brautlieder: Cornelius
Songs of a bride-to-be—Lieder der Braut (Myrthen): Schumann
Songs of a wayfarer—Lieder eines fahrenden Gesellen: Mahler
Songs of a young wayfarer—Lieder eines fahrenden Gesellen: Mahler
Songs of Bilitis—Chansons de Bilitis: Debussy
Songs of childhood—Canciones de niños: Revueltas
Songs of death—Lieder um den Tod: Kilpinen
The songs of Hukvaldy—Ukvalské pisně: Janáček
Songs of love—Lieder der Liebe: Kilpinen
Songs of the harper—Harfenspieler Lieder: Wolf
Songs of the Rhine—Rheinische Lieder: Cornelius
Songs on the death of children (infants)—Kindertotenlieder: Mahler
Songs without words—Lieder ohne Worte: Mendelssohn
Songster, whither away?—Vöglein wohin so schnell?: Lassen
The songstress—La canterina: Haydn
Die Sonn' ist hin—The sun's last ray: R Franz
La sonnambula—The sleepwalker: Bellini
Die Sonne scheint nicht mehr—The golden morning light: Brahms
Sonne taucht in Meeres—Red the parting sun: Henschel
Sonnenregen—Rain in sunshine: Reger
Sonnenuntergang—Sunset: Cornelius
Sonnenuntergang—Sunset lights the west: R Franz
Sönner af Norge—Minstrel, awaken: Blom
Sonnet paye—A heathen sonnet: Massenet
Sonntag—Sunday: Brahms
Sonntag—Sunday: R Franz
Sonntag—Sunday: Schumann
Sonntags am Rhein—Sunday on the Rhine/Holiday on the Rhine/
   Sunday by the Rhine: Schumann
Sonntagslied—The festival/Alone: Mendelssohn

Sonntagsmorgen—Sunday morn: Mendelssohn
Sono amate—One I love: D Scarlatti
Soon as summer—Treibt der Sommer: R Franz
Soon thou wilt be returning—Retornerai fra poco: Hasse
Soothing—Beruhigung: Goetz
Soothing spells—Porgi amor (Le nozze di Figaro): Mozart
The sorcerer's apprentice—L'apprenti sorcier: Dukas
Sorge infausta (Orlando)—Clouds may rise/Omninous a storm upsurging:
    Handel
Sorrow—Tristesse: Liszt
Sorrow—Tre giorno son che Nina: Pergolesi
Sorrow I fear not—Wehe, so willst du: Brahms
Sorrow ne'er ending—Leid ohne Ende (Albumblätter): Schumann
Sorrow of heart—Tristitia et anxietas: Byrd
Sorrow whose phantoms—Wehe, so willst du: Brahms
Sorrow with song come drown—Nichts labt mich mehr: Mozart
The sorrowful maiden—Die traurige Mädchen: R Franz
Sorrowful song—Chanson triste: Duparc
Sorrow's tears—Nicht die Träue kann es sagen: Cornelius
Sortilège (Petites légendes)—Magic: Milhaud
Sortunut—The broken voice: Sibelius
Sospan fach—The saucepan song: T V Davies
Souhait—A wish: Massenet
The soul in Jesu's hands reposes—Die Seele ruht in Jesu Handen (Herr
    Jesu Christ, wahr'r Mensch und Gott): Bach
Soul, O forget them not—Seele vergiss sie nicht: Cornelius
The soul of solitude—Die Einsame: Pfitzner
The soul of the iris—L'âme des iris: Rhené-Baton
Soul so subtle—L'âme evaporée: Daia
A soul that loves God purely—Ein ungefärbt Gemüte: Bach
The souls of the righteous—Justorum animee: Byrd
A sound of oars—Un bruit de rames: Rhené-Baton
The sound of rejoicing is heard—Man singet mit Freuden: Bach
Sounds of autumn—Az oszi lárma: Bartók
Soupir—A sigh: Bemberg
Soupir—Sigh: Duparc
Sous l'effort d'un bras invisible (Semiramis)—All at once: Catel
Sous les branches—Under the trees: Bossi
Sous les branches—'Neath the branches: Massenet
Sous les toits de Paris—Under the roofs of Paris: Moretti
Sousedká—The neighbours: Smetana
Southern maid so fair—Dolores waltz: Waldteufel
Southern roses—Rosen aus dem Süden: J Strauss II
Souvenez-vous, Vierge Marie—Remember now, Oh Virgin Mary: Massenet

Souvenir—Errinerung (Album für die Jugend): Schumann
Souvent de nos biens—How often our happiness flows: Aubert
The Soviet East—Sovietskii vostok: Vasilenko
Sovietskii vostok—The Soviet East: Vasilenko
Sovra il sen (La sonnambula)—Place this hand upon my bosom/While this heart: Bellini
The sower—Der Säemann (Lieder um dem Tod): Kilpinen
Soyons unis—Join we our souls: Rhené-Baton
Spanisches Lied—Spanish song: Brahms
Spanisches Liederbuch—Spanish songbook: Wolf
The Spanish hour—L'heure espagnole: Ravel
Spanish love-song—Chanson espagnole: Chaminade
Spanish song—Spanisches Lied: Brahms
Spanish songbook—Spanisches Liederbuch: Wolf
Spanish tales—Cuentos de España: Turina
Spare not one smile—Regt sich's dir warm in Herzen: Børresen
Spargi d'amaro pianto (Lucia de Lammermoor)—Sorrowful here and lonely (Mad scene): Donizetti
Sparkleth the forge near roadside pound—Brennessel steht an Weges Rand (Zigeunerlieder): Brahms
Spartacus—Spartak: Khachaturian
Spartak—Spartacus: Khachaturian
Spätherbst—Late autumn: Brahms
Spätherbstnebel—Autumn fogs: Wolf
Speak—Parla!: Arditi
Speak, I pray thee—Pur dicesti o bocca bella: Lotti
Speak, my tongue—Pange lingua: W S G Williams
Speak to me of love—Parlez-moi d'amour: Lenoir
The spectacle of the soul and the body—Rappresentazione di anima e di corpo: Cavalieri
The spectral self—Der Doppelgänger: Schubert
Le spectre de la rose (Les nuits d'été)—The spirit of the rose/The spectre of the rose: Berlioz
The spectre of the rose—Le spectre de la rose (Les nuits d'été): Berlioz
Spectre-dance—Der Geistertanz: Schubert
The spectre's bride—Svatební košile: Dvořák
The spectre's dance—Der Geistertanz: Schubert
Speed thee, birdie—Dyby byla (Moravské dvojzpěvy): Dvořák
Speed thee, birdie—Velet' vtáčku (Moravské dvojzpěvy): Dvořák
The spell—Le charme (Petites légendes): Milhaud
The spell of springtide—Värtagen: Sibelius
Spell of the fields—Feldeinsamkeit: Brahms
The spendthrift spring—Wir bringen dir die Kette (Die Bürgschaft): Schubert

Spera si, mio caro bene (Admeto)—Do not doubt my true affection:
Handel

La speranza e giunta (Ottone)—Spring: Handel

Sphärenklange—Music from heaven: Josef Strauss

Spiagge amate (Paride ed Elena)—Fondly complaining/Lovely meadows:
Shick

The spider's feast—Le festin d'araignée: Roussel

Der Spielmann—The minstrel: Hildach

Der Spielmann—The musician: Schumann

Spietati! lo vi giura! (Rodelinda)—Ye gracious powers: Handel

Śpiew grobowy—Song from the tomb: Chopin

Spillemaend—The minstrel's song: Grieg

Spillevoerket (Humoreske)—The musical box: Nielsen

Die Spinnerin—At the spinning wheel: Schumann

Die Spinnerin—Spinning song: Wolf

Spinnerlied—Bee's wedding: Mendelssohn

Spinnerliedchen—Spinning song: Erk

The spinning girl—Die kleine Spinnerin: Mozart

Spinning Jenny—Die kleine Spinnerin: Mozart

The spinning room—Székely fonó: Kodály

Spinning song—Spinnerliedchen: Erk

Spinning song—Die Spinnerin: Wolf

The spinning top—Snurretoppen: Nielsen

The spirit also helpeth us—Der Geist hilft unserer Schwachheit auf: Bach

The spirit bard—Der Bardenges Bardengeist: Beethoven

The spirit of the rose—Le spectre de la rose (Les nuits d'été): Berlioz

Spirito amato (Poro)—Blessed spirit: Handel

Spirito ben nato (Sonnets of Michelangelo)—Noble soul: Britten

Das Spitzentuch der Königin—The queen's lace handkerchief: J Strauss II

Splendente te Deus—O God when Thou appearest: Mozart

Sposa Euridice (Orfeo ed Euridice)—Loved one, Euridice/I have lost
my Euridice/Have I lost thee?: Gluck

Sposalizio (Années de pèlerinage)—The marriage: Liszt

Lo sposo deluso—The deluded spouse: Mozart

Spottlied aus 'Wilhelm Meister'—Lampoon from 'Wilhelm Meister': Wolf

Sprache der Liebe—Language of love: Schubert

Spraellmanden—The jumping-jack: Nielsen

Spring—Tavasz: Bartók

Spring—Der Frühling: Brahms

Spring—Wiosna: Chopin

Spring—Frühling: R Franz

Spring—Au printemps: Gounod

Spring—Våren: Grieg

Spring—La speranza e giunta (Ottone): Handel

Spring—Lenz: Hildach
Spring—Frühlingslied: Meyer-Helmund
Spring—Frühling (Vier letzte Lieder): R Strauss
Spring all the year—Frühling übers Jahr: Wolf
Spring and love—Frühling und Liebe: R Franz
Spring bells—Frühlingsglocken: Blech
Spring chorus—Frühlings-chor (Manuel Venegas): Wolf
Spring comes laughing—Ach es schmeckt doch gar zu gut (Mehr han en
    neue Oberkeet): Bach
Spring delights—Frühlingsspiel: Blech
Spring flowers—Frühlingsblumen: Reinecke
Spring in summer—Frühling im Sommer: Cornelius
Spring in the Mosel valley—Frühling im Moseltal (Siechentrost): Bruch
Spring is come again—Frühlings Wiederkehr: Goetz
Spring is flying—Våren flyktar hastigt: Sibelius
Spring is here!—Er ist's: Schumann
Spring is here—Er ist's: Wolf
Spring is the year's pleasant king—Hört doch! der sanfen Flöten
    (Schleicht, spielende Wellen): Bach
Spring journey—Frühlingsfahrt: Schubert
A spring journey—Frühlingsfahrt: Schumann
Spring longings—Frühlingssehnsucht (Schwanengesang): Schubert
A spring morning—Frühlingslied: Mendelssohn
Spring morning in the wood—Vaarmorgen i skogen: A Backer-Grøndahl
Spring night—Frühlingsnacht: Schumann
The spring of love—Liebesfrühling: R Franz
Spring showers—Forårsregn: Grieg
Spring song—Frühlings Lied: Kjerulf
Spring song—Es brechen im schallenden Reigen/Frühlingslied: Mendelssohn
Spring song—Der Frühling naht mit Brausen/Frühlingslied: Mendelssohn
Spring song—Frühlingslied/In dem Walde: Mendelssohn
Spring song—Die blauen Frühlingsaugen: A Rubinstein
Spring song—Leise zieht: A Rubinstein
Spring song—Frühlingsgesang (Album für die Jugend): Schumann
Spring song—Frühlingslied: Schumann
Spring time—Frühling: Lehár
Spring-chimes—Frühlingsglocken: Wolf
The springmaid—Die Sprudelfee: Reinhardt
Spring's approach—Frühlings Ankunft: R Franz
Spring's arrival—Frühlings Ankunft: Schumann
Spring's delights—Frühlingswonne: R Franz
Spring's harbinger—Frühlingsbotschaft: Schumann
Spring's profusion—Frühlingsgedränge: R Franz
Spring's return—Le retour du printemps: Godard

Spring's return—Wein, Weib und Gesang: J Strauss II
Spring-tide—Faro: Dvořák
Springtide—Våren: Grieg
Springtide wandering—Frühlingsfahrt: Schumann
Springtime—Vesnyanky: Barvins'kyi
Springtime—Der Frühling: Brahms
Springtime—Våren: Grieg
Springtime—Printemps: Hindemith
Springtime—Vesnyanky: Verykivskyi
Springtime ditty—Lenz-Tageweis: Manén
Spring-time in Funen—Fynsk forår: Nielsen
Springtime is gliding—Schön ist das Fest: Schumann
Spring-time is solemn—Ernst ist der Frühling: Wolf
Die Spröde—The prude: Brahms
Die Spröde—The coy shepherdess: Wolf
Sprona il tamburo e incora (La fille du regiment)—Hark, how the drums
    are rolling: Donizetti
Die Sprudelfee—The springmaid: Reinhardt
Der Sprung über den Schatten—The leap over the shadow: Křenek
Spyashchaya knyazhna—The sleeping princess: Borodin
Srši jiskry—In the forge: Dvořák
Die Stadt (Schwanengesang)—The town: Schubert
Stabat Mater—At the foot of the cross: Dvořák
Stal—Steel: Mosolov
Stal'noi skok—The age of steel: Prokofiev
Stances—Stanzas: Massenet
Stand still—Stehe still!: Wagner
Ständchen—Serenade: Brahms
Ständchen—Serenade: R Franz
Ständchen (Schwanengesang)—Serenade/Evening breezes softly sighing/
    Gentle the night winds: Schubert
Ständchen—Evening breezes: Schubert-Heller
Ständchen—Serenade: Schumann
Ständchen—Serenade: R Strauss
Das Ständchen—The aged minstrel/The serenade: Wolf
Stanzas—Stances: Massenet
Star of love—Estrellita: Ponce
Star of my soul—Caro mio ben: Giordani
The star of the north—L'étoile du nord: Meyerbeer
Star vicino—To be near thee/To be near my beloved/Questioning/Might
    I linger near thee/When I dwell near/To be near to the lov'd one:
    Rosa
Staren—The starling: Sinding
Starkes lieben (Himmelskönig, sei willkommen)—Great Thy love, Lord:
    Bach

The starling—Staren: Sinding
Starry summer night—Nuit d'étoiles: Debussy
The stars—Die Sterne: Schubert
Stars—Sterne: Webern
The stars have gone to their rest—Die Sterne gingen zur Ruh (Tiefland):
    d'Albert
La statue de bronze—The bronze statue: Satie
Stay!—Reste!: Chaminade
Stay, my beloved—Bist du bei mir: Bach
Stay, sweet bird—Várj meg madaram: Kodály
Stay with me for ever—Du bist meine Sonne (Giuditta): Lehár
Stay with us—Bleib' bei uns, denn es will Abend werden: Bach
Steel—Stal: Mosolov
Steersman's song—Mit Gewitter und Sturm (Der fliegende Holländer):
    Wagner
Steh' ich bei meinem Gott—I trust in God's good will: Bach
Stehe still (Wesendonck Lieder)—Be still/Stand still!: Wagner
Steig auf, Geliebter—Arise, beloved spirit/Arise, beloved vision: Brahms
Stein, der über alle Schätze (Tritt auf die Glaubensbahn)—Stone
    beyond all jewels shining/Stone, which is above all treasures: Bach
Stelle, perfida stelle (Partenza)—O stars, treacherous stars: Handel
Die Sterne—The stars: Schubert
Sterne—Stars: Webern
Die Sterne gingen zur Ruh (Tiefland)—The stars have gone to their rest:
    d'Albert
Die Sterne schau'n in stiller Nacht—The angel: Mendelssohn
The stigmatized ones—Die Gezeichneten: Schreker
Still as the night—Stille wie die Nacht: C Böhm
Still as the night—Stille wie die Nacht: Goetz
Still is the night—Erinnerung: Abt
Still, mein Herz (Das Examen)—Quietly, my heart: P Burkhardt
Die Stille—Stillness/Silence/The secret: Schumann
Stille Liebe—Silent love: R Franz
Stille Liebe—Silent love: Schumann
Stille Nacht, heilige Nacht—Silent night, holy night: Grüber
Stille Sicherheit—Silent safety/Love's sanctuary/In seclusion: R Franz
Die stille Stadt—The silent town: Sibelius
Stille Tränen—Hidden tears/Silent tears: Schumann
Die stille Wasserrose/Die Lotosblume—The quiet waterlily/Lotus flower:
    R Franz
Die stille Wasserrose—The silent water-lily: Liszt
Stille wie die Nacht—Still as the night: C Böhm
Stille wie die Nacht—Still as the night: Goetz
Stiller Abend—Quiet evening: R Franz
Stiller Gang—Night-fall: R Strauss

Stiller Vorwulf—Silent reproach: Schumann

Stilles Leid (Eliland)—Silent woe: Fielitz

Stillness—Die Stille: Schumann

Stillung Maria mit dem Auferstandenen (Das Marienleben)—Consolation of Mary with the risen Christ: Hindemith

Stimme der Liebe—Voice of love: Schubert

Stimmungsbilder—Moods and fancies: R Strauss

Stirb, Lieb' und Freud'—Die, love and joy: Schumann

A stirrup cup—Skolie: Wolf

Stolen happiness—Ukradennoye schast' ye: Dan'kevych

Stone beyond all jewels shining—Stein, der über alle Schätze (Tritt auf die Glaubensbahn): Bach

The stone breaker—Lied des Steinklopfers: R Strauss

The stone flower—Kamennïy tsvetok: Molchanov

The stone flower—Skaz o kamennom tsvetke: Prokofiev

The stone guest—Kamennyi gost': Dargomyzhsky

The stonecutter—Jens vejmand: Nielsen

Stonemasons—Kamenyari: Lyudkevych

Stood a maiden—Das Mädchen: Brahms

Storchenbotschaft—The stork's message: Wolf

Stories from the Vienna woods—Geschichten aus dem Wienerwald: J Strauss II

The stork's message—Storchenbotschaft: Wolf

The storm—Der Sturm: Humperdinck

The storm—Groza: Trambitsky

The storm—Der Sturm: Weingartner

A storm has brewed—Il s'en va tard: Jannequin

The storm winds are roaring—Es rausche die Winde: Liszt

Stormy morning—Der stürmische Morgen (Die Winterreise): Schubert

The stormy night—Gewitternacht: R Franz

The story of a real man—Povest o nastoyashchem cheloveke: Prokofiev

The story of Babar—L'histoire de Babar: Poulenc

Story of the birth of Christ—Historia con der Geburt Jesu Christi: Schütz

Story of the fight for the Russian land—Skazanie o bitve za Russkuyu zemlyn: Shaporin

Stout hearted—Beherzigung: Brahms

Strahlt zuweilen auch ein mildes Licht—Ever and anon: Brahms

A strange event—Curiose Begebenheit: Meyer-Helmund

Strange harmony of contrasts—Recondita armonia (Tosca): Puccini

Strange land—Fremde Erde: Rathaus

A strange story—Curiose Geschichte (Kinderscenen): Schumann

Strange the joy that overwhelms me—Lass mich ihm am Busen hangen: Schumann

Strange world—Fremde Erde: Rathaus

The stranger—La straniera: Bellini
The stranger—Pierrot et Pierrette: Holbrooke
The stranger—Fremder Mann (Album für die Jugend): Schumann
La straniera—The stranger: Bellini
Straszny Dwór—The haunted mansion: Moniuszko
The straw Guy—Jámbor Gál János háza: Kodály
A straying son—Ein irrender Sohn: Nilsson
The stream—Wohin: Schubert-Rachmaninov
The stream that past me flowed—Der Strom, der neben mir verrauschte:
   Brahms
The streamlet flows onwards—Es rauschet das Wasser: Brahms
The street is on fire—Ucca, ucca, ég az ucca: Bartók
The street-organ—Un organetta suona per la via: Sibella
Streite, siege, starker Held (Nun komm, der Heiden Heiland)—Marvel
   O men, at this great mystery: Bach
Strews the ground with leaves each flower—Blätter lässt die Blume
   fallen: R Franz
Strike at last thou hour desired—Schlage doch, gewünschte Stunde: Bach
Strike, O strike—Batti, batti, O bel Masetto (Don Giovanni): Mozart
Strike thou hour, so long expected—Schlage doch, gewünschte Stunde:
   Bach
Der Strom, der neben mir verrauschte—O where?/The stream that past
   me flowed/The flood that spent in torrent roaring: Brahms
Der Strom floss, der Mond vergass (Chinesische Liebeslieder)—On
   waters the silver moon was spilling: Liebermann
A stronghold sure—Ein' feste Burg ist unser Gott: Bach
Struna nala děna (Cígánské melodie)—Tune thy strings: Dvořák
The stubborn lovers—Tvrdé palice: Dvořák
Studenti! Udite! (Germania)—Ye students and comrades: Franchetti
Ein Stundlein wohl vor Tag—One hour before the day/Just before
   daybreak: R Franz
Ein Stundlein wohl vor Tag—Just before dawn: Wolf
Der Sturm—The storm: Humperdinck
Der Sturm—The tempest: F Martin
Der Sturm—The storm: Weingartner
Der Sturm auf der Mühle—The attack on the mill: Weis
Sturmhymnus—The song of the storm: Weingartner
Der stürmische Morgen (Die Winterreise)—Stormy morning: Schubert
Sù, ferisci—Cruel archer: Steffani
Submission—Ergebung: Wolf
The subscribers—Die Abonnenten: E Strauss
Such a day such a night—Tel jour telle nuit: Poulenc
Suicidio! (La gioconda)—Ah! suicide: Ponchielli
Suite dos cântigos sertanejos—Folk-song suite: Villa-Lobos

Suk—Sighs: Grieg
Sul fil d'un soffio etesio (Falstaff)—From secret caves and bowers: Verdi
Suleika's song—Lied der Suleika (Myrthen): Schumann
The sultry evening—Der schwere Abend: Schumann
Summer—Nyár: Bartók
Summer—An leuchtenden Sommermorgen: Schumann
Summer—Blauer Sommer: R Strauss
Summer day on the mountain—Jour d'été à la montagne: D'Indy
Summer days—Sommertage: Berg
Summer days are coming—Leise zieht durch mein Gemut: Mendelssohn
Summer evening—Sommerabend: Brahms
Summer evening—Nyári este: Kodály
Summer holidays—Les belles vacances: Jacques-Dalcroze
A summer lullaby—Wiegenlied im Sommer: Wolf
Summer night—Lys Nat: Grieg
Summer nights—Les nuits d'été: Berlioz
Summertime—Im Sommer: R Franz
Summer waves—In des Sees Wogenspiele: Schubert
(A) Summer's night—Mondnacht: Schumann
S'un casto amor (Sonnets of Michelangelo)—If love be chaste: Britten
The sun is so red, oh mother dear—Solen er så rød, mor: Nielsen
Sun of my soul—Ave vera Virginitas: Josquin
Sun of the sleepless—Schlafloser Augen leuchte: Mendelssohn
Sun of the sleepless—An den Mond: Schumann
The sun on the Ganges—Già il sole dal Gange: A Scarlatti
Sunbeams down streaming—Die gold'ne Sonne, voll Freud' und Wonne:
    Bach
Sunday—Sonntag: Brahms
Sunday—Sonntag: R Franz
Sunday—Sonntag: Schumann
Sunday by the Rhine—Sonntags am Rhein: Schumann
Sunday morn—Sonntagsmorgen: Mendelssohn
Sunday on the Rhine—Sonntags am Rhein: Schumann
The sunken bell—La campana sommersa: Respighi
Sunrise—Soluppgång: Sibelius
A sunrise on a sick-bed—L'alba del malato: Rocca
Sunrise to sunset—Alba e tramonto: Gilbaro
The sun's last ray—Die Sonn' ist hin: R Franz
Sunset—Sonnenuntergang: Cornelius
Sunset—Solnedgang: Grieg
The sunset—Il tramonto: Respighi
Sunset glow—Im Abendrot: Schubert
Sunset lights the west—Sonnenuntergang: R Franz
Sunt lacrymae rerum (Années de pèlerinage)—There are tears in the
    affairs of life: Liszt

Suor Angelica—Sister Angelica: Puccini
Sur le pavé—Pavements of Paris: Auric
Sur les bords de la Seine—Along the banks of the Seine: Blanchard
Sur les lagunes (Nuits d'été)—On the lagoons: Berlioz
Sur l'herbe—The abbé said 'How now': Ravel
Sure and certain hope—Unverlierbare Gewähr (Lieder um dem Tod):
   Kilpinen
Surge illuminare—Arise, shine forth in splendour: Byrd
Surrexit Pastor bonus—O Lord, Thou hast searched me out: Mendelssohn
Sursum corda (Années de pèlerinage)—Let us lift up our hearts: Liszt
Sus, egayons nous au Seigneur—Come let us sing: Le Jeune
Susanna's secret—Il segreto di Susanna: Wolf-Ferrari
Susceptimus Deus—We wait for Thy loving kindness, O God: Byrd
Súsedova stajňa—The neighbour's stable: Martinů
Das süsse Mädel—The sweet girl: Rheinhardt
Süsser Freund (Frauenliebe und -leben)—Sweet my friend/Dear friend/
   Sweetest friend: Schumann
Süsser Trost, mein Jesus kommt—Comfort sweet, (Lord) my Jesus
   comes/Blessed morn, when Jesus was born/Sweet comfort, my Jesus
   comes: Bach
Suur' olet, herra—Great is the Lord: Sibelius
Svanda Dudak—Schwanda the bagpiper: Weinberger
En Svane—A swan: Grieg
Svarta rosor—Black roses: Sibelius
Svatá Ludmila—Saint Ludmila: Dvořák
Svatební košile—The spectre's bride: Dvořák
Svegliatevi nel core (Giulio Cesare)—Arouse thyself to anger: Handel
Svetly ruchey—Clear streams: Shostakovich
Svuj chéb kdo jídal—Who never ate his bread with tears: Vycpalek
Svunde Dage—Vanished days: Grieg
The swallow—Volkslied: Brahms
The swallow—La rondine: Puccini
Swallow from over the seas—Das Mädchen spricht: Brahms
Swallow, where flies thou?—Vöglein, wohin so schnell?: Kjerulf
The swallows—Die Schwalben: Schumann
The swallow's flying west: Volkslied: Brahms
The swallow's wooing—Gólya, gólya, gilice: Kodály
A swan—En Svane: Grieg
A swan—Un cygne: Hindemith
The swan—Joutsen (Ungdom): Palmgren
The swan—Le cygne (Histoires naturelles): Ravel
The swan—Le cygne (Le carnaval des animaux): Saint-Saëns
The swan song—Schwanengesang: Schubert
Swan songs—Schwanengesang: Schubert
Sway'd by the pride of youth—Habt ihr sie schon geseh'n: R Franz

Sweet bargain—Anmutiger Vertag (Lieder der Liebe): Kilpinen
The sweet blue eyes of spring—Die blauen Frühlingsaugen: A Rubinstein
Sweet child, if I were king—Enfant, si j'étais roi: Liszt
Sweet comfort, my Jesus comes—Süsser Trost, mein Jesus kommt: Bach
Sweet darling, rest in the shade—Ruhe, Süssliebchen: Brahms
Sweet forgetting—Nel dolce dell' oblio: Handel
The sweet girl—Das süsse Mädel: Rheinhardt
Sweet greeting—Aus den östrichen Rosen: Schumann
Sweet image—Thou—Du bist die Ruh': Schubert-Heller
Sweet love, now I must leave thee—Ach Lieb, ich muss nun scheiden:
    R Strauss
Sweet love, what can hinder thy coming so long?—Geliebter, wo
    zaudert dein irrender Fuss?: Brahms
Sweet lovely May—O süsser Mai: R Strauss
Sweet melodies—Wie Melodien ziegt es mir: Brahms
Sweet my friend—Süsser Freund (Frauenliebe und -leben): Schumann
Sweet pretty maiden—Mia piccirella (Salvator Rosa): Gomes
Sweet rose of love—Rosa d'amor: Dering
Sweet violets—Märzveilchen: Schumann
Sweet woman oft in silence prays—Die Frauen sind oft fromm: R Strauss
Sweetest friend—Süsser Freund (Frauenliebe und -leben): Schumann
Sweetest infant all endearing—Dormi, dormi, bel bambino: F Ricci
Sweetheart dearest—Herziges Schätzle du!: R Franz
Sweetheart gentle and pretty—Douce dame jolie: Machaut
Sweetheart is there—Liebchen ist da!: R Franz
Sweethearts—Schatz-walzer: J Strauss II
Swift as a bird—Toi que l'oiseau (Guillaume Tell): Rossini
Swiftly fly the birds—Jägerlied: Schumann
The Swiss magistrate—Le magistrat suisse: Françaix
Swiss song—Schweizerlied: R Franz
Sydämeni laulu—Song of my heart: Sibelius
Sylvester-lied (Album für die Jugend)—New Year's song/New Year's eve:
    Schumann
The symbol—Wie die Wolke nach der Sonne: Brahms
Symphonie cévenole sur un chant montagnard français—Symphony on a
    French mountain air: D'Indy
Symphonie fantastique—Fantastic symphony: Berlioz
Symphony on a French mountain air—Symphonie cévanole sur un chant
    montagnard français: D'Indy
Eit Syn—A fair vision/A vision: Grieg
Det Syng (Haugtussa)—Allurement: Grieg
Syng, syng—Sing, sing/Nightingale, sing: Kjerulf
Szabadban—Out of doors: Bartók
Szant a babím—My sweetheart is ploughing: Bartók

Száraz ágtól messze virít a rozsa—From the withered branch no rose
  blooms: Bartók
Székely fonó—The spinning room/The Székely spinning room: Kodály
Székely keserves—Transylvanian lament: Kodály
The Székely spinning room—Székely fonó: Kodály
Szines álomban—In vivid dreams: Bartók

T

Il tabarro—The cloak: Puccini

Le tableau parlant—The talking table: Grétry

Tableaux d'une exposition—Pictures at an exhibition: Mussorgsky

Tace il labro—Silent and speechless: Sarri

Tacea la notte (Il trovatore)—The night was calm and peaceful/'Twas
    night and all around was still: Verdi

Der Tag der ist so freudenreich—O Hail this brightest day of days: Bach

Der Tag, der ist so freudenreich (Orgelbüchlein)—This day, so rich in
    joy and love: Bach

Der Tag ist hin—Gone is the day: Bach

Der Tag ist vergangen—Day is past: Webern

Der Tag mit seinem Lichte—Now daylight's youthful glory: Bach

Tagen letter (Moderen)—The rising of the mists: Nielsen

Tajemstvi—The secret: Smetana

Tajná láska—Secret love: Martinů

Tak for dit Rad—Thy warning is good/Friend, thou art staunch/Thanks
    for thy counsel: Grieg

Takálják ki—Let them find out: Erkel

Take away thy lip—Loin de moi ta levre qui ment: Massenet

Take me to Thee for Thine own—Nimm mich dir zu eigen hin (Sie werden
    aus Saba alle kommen): Bach

Take my counsel, dear Climène—Crois mon conseil, chère Climène (Le
    promenoir des deux amants): Debussy

Take one bright ray of sunshine—Nimm einen Strahl der Sonne: Beethoven

Take the tribute—Nimm sie hin denn (An die ferne Geliebte): Beethoven

Taksigelse—Thanks: Grieg

Tale of a partisan—Skaz o partisane: Koval'

Tale of a peasant—Lenda do caboclo: Villa-Lobos

The tale of Balaton—Balatoni rege: E Ábrányi

The tale of the Tsar Saltan—Skazha o Tsara Saltana: Rimsky-Korsakov

Tales from the Vienna Woods—Geschichten aus der Wiener Wald:
    J Strauss II

Tales of a grandmother—Babushkiny skazki: Prokofiev

Tales of a plaster idol—Skazki gipsovovo bozhka: Knipper

The tales of Hoffmann—Les contes d'Hoffmann: Offenbach

Tales of the plaster Buddha—Skazki gipsovovo Buddi: Knipper

Talismane (Myrthen)—Talismans: Schumann

Talismans—Talismane (Myrthen): Schumann

Talitha Kumi—The daughter of Jairus: Wolf-Ferrari

The talking table—Le tableau parlant: Grétry

A Tamás templon karnagya—The cantor of St. Thomas Church: E Ábrányi

Der Tambour—The drummer-boy: Wolf

Der Tamboursg'sell—The drummer boy: Mahler
The taming of the shrew—La bisbetica domata: Castelnuovo-Tedesco
The taming of the shrew—Der widerspenstigen Zähmung: Goetz
The taming of the shrew—Ukroshchenie stroptivoy: Shebalin
Tamperretsscene (Maskarade)—Divorce court scene: Nielsen
Tánc suite—Dance suite: Bartók
Tant que mes yeux—A memory: Berkeley
Tanta coisa a dizer te—There is so much to tell you: Guarnieri
Tantalus's atonement—Smír Tantalův: Fibich
Tanto de meu estado me acho incerto—All of my life: J Berger
Der Tanz ins Glück—Whirled into happiness: Stolz
Ein Tanzchen—A dance: Reger
Tanzlied—Call to the dance: Schumann
Tanzlied des Pierrot (Die tote Stadt)—Pierrot's dance song: Korngold
Tanzlied im Mai—Dance-song in May: R Franz
Tape and double—Doppelt beflugeltes Band: Křenek
Der tapfere Soldat—The chocolate soldier: Straus
Tara's family—Semya Tarasa: Kabalevsky
Tártájárás—Autumn manoeuvres: Kálmán
Tarvet i Ispahan (Aladdin)—Market place at Ispahan: Nielsen
Tasso, lamento e trionfo—Tasso's lament and triumph: Liszt
Tasso's lament and triumph—Tasso, lamento e trionfo: Liszt
Die Taubenpost (Schwanengesang)—The carrier pigeon/The carrier-dove:
    Schubert
Täuschung (Die Winterreise)—Delusion/Deception/Illusion/The false
    dream: Schubert
Die tausend Grüsse—Greeting: Schumann
Tausend und eine Nacht—A thousand and one nights: J Strauss II
Tavasz—Spring: Bartók
Tavern song—Bordal: Kodály
Tcherevichky—The little shoes/Oxana's caprices: Tchaikovsky
Te deprecor—We humbly beseech Thee: Byrd
Te mane laudum—With songs of praise: Byrd
Te souviens-tu?—Do you remember?: Godard
The tear—An die Geliebte: Beethoven
A tear—Die Träne: Blumenthal
A tear: Une larme: Mussorgsky
Teardrops—Tränenregen (Die schöne Müllerin): Schubert
A tearful dream—Ich hab' im Traum: Hüe
Tears—Nachtlang: Brahms
Tears—Tränen: R Franz
Tears—Das Weinen: Schubert
Tears falling in my heart—Il pleure dans mon coeur: Schmitt

Tears fall in my heart—Il pleur dans mon coeur (Ariettes oubliées): Debussy

Tears of joy—Wenn ich in deine Augen seh' (Dichterliebe): Schumann

Tears of price—Der Himmel hat eine Träne geweint: Reger

Teasing song—Legénycsúfoló: Bartok

Tel jour telle nuit—Such a day such a night: Poulenc

Tell fair Irene—Dì ad Irene (Atalanta): Handel

Tell me—Sag' mir: R Franz

Tell me—Der Jüngling: Kjerulf

Tell me—O ihr Herren: Schumann

Tell me, ah, where art speeding—Ritornerai fra poco: Hasse

Tell me fair ladies—Voi che sapete: Mozart

Tell me, my dear bird—Sag' an, o lieber Vogel mein: Schumann

Tell me, my people—Popule meus: Victoria

Tell me not—Non mi dir (Don Giovanni): Mozart

Tell me, O beauteous shepherdess—Sagt mir, o schönste Schäf'rin mein: Brahms

Tell me, thou cruel love—Dimmi, crudele amore (Muzio Scovola): Handel

Tell thy lover—No non chiudar (Germania): Franchetti

The tempest—An den Sturmwind: Cornelius

The tempest—Bouře: Fibich

The tempest—Der Sturm: F Martin

The tempest of my heart—Il balen (Il trovatore): Verdi

The templar and the Jewess—Der Templar und die Jüdin: Marschner

Der Templar und die Jüdin—The templar and the Jewess/The knight and the Jewess: Marschner

Le temps des roses—The time of roses: Gounod

Il tempo vola e se ne fuggon gli anni—Time as he flies: Palestrina

Le temps a laissé son manteau (Deux rondels . . .)—The season has cast its cloak: Debussy

Temps de neige—Snow-fall: Séverac

Les temps des lilas—The time of lilac: Chausson

Tempt me not—Locke nur: Telemann

Temptation—Navozhdenuje: Prokofiev

Temptation—Lockung: Schoenberg

Ten easy pieces—Tiz könnyü zongoradarab: Bartók

Tender and pure—Von adler Art: Brahms

Tender lay—Air tendre: Engel

Tenebras factae sunt—Darkness made dim the world: M Haydn

Teresa—Therese: Brahms

Terra adorata (Don Sebastiano)—Home of my fathers: Donizetti

Terra tremuit—Lo, the earth did quake: Byrd

La terrasse des audiences au clair de lune—People on a terrace in moonlight: Debussy

La terre les eaux va buvant—Earth, of the rain drinks to her mind: Lassus

Terve kuu—Hail moon: Sibelius
Tes yeux—Your eyes: Rabey
Tesoro mio—Waltzing the hours away: Becucci
The test of kissing—Die Prufung des Küssens: Beethoven
La testament de la tante Caroline—Aunt Caroline's will: Roussel
Das Thal—The valley: R Strauss
Thamos, King of Egypt—König Thamos: Mozart
Thank God! now all is well!—Gottlob, es geht uns wohl (Wir danken
    dir, Gott, wir danken dir): Bach
Thank you, my friends—Nehmt meinen Dank: Mozart
Thanks—Taksigelse: Grieg
Thanks—Dank: Schoenberg
Thanks for thy counsel—Tak for ait Rad: Grieg
Thanks to the brook—Danksagung an den Bach (Die Winterreise): Schubert
Thanks unto thee—Voce de donna (La gioconda): Ponchielli
Thanksgiving—Liebesfeier: R Franz
Thanksgiving—Kling: R Strauss
That gentle heart—Quel bel core: Magni
That I might die—Morir vogl'io: Astorga
That I no more would see thee—Nicht mehr zu dir zu gehen: Brahms
That love's a naughty little god—L'amour est enfant trompeur: Meister
That night in May—Die Mainacht: Brahms
That she has been here—Dass sie hier gewesen: Schubert
That your mother should take you—Che tua madre (Madama Butterfly):
    Puccini
That's the tune—C'est bien l'air (L'étoile du nord): Meyerbeer
The thaw—L'odolom: Leontovych
Thee I greet, Thy love I treasure—Sei gegrüsst, Jesu gütig: Bach
Thee would I greet—Sei mir gegrüsst: Schubert
Then learn, haughty beauty—Impara ingrata (Atalanta): Handel
Then shall this past'ral—Soll dann der Pales (Was mir behagt): Bach
Then the same day at evening—Am Abend aber desselbigen Sabbats: Bach
There and back—Hin und zurück: Hindemith
There are tears in the affairs of life—Sunt lacrymae rerum (Années de
    pèlerinage): Liszt
There be none of beauty's daughters—Keine von der Erde schönen:
    Mendelssohn
There comes a ship full laden—Es kommt ein Schiff geladen: Beck
There is a charm that bids me hie—Mich zieht es nach dem Dörfchen
    hin: Schumann
There is a glowing dagger—Ich hab' ein glühend Messer (Lieder eines
    fahrenden Gesellen): Mahler
There is a land—Es gibt ein Reich (Ariadne auf Naxos): R Strauss
There is a voice within my heart—Una voce poco fà (Il barbiere di
    Siviglia): Rossini

There is no mount so high—Es ist kein Berg so hoch: Hildach
There is no star—Nincsen annyi tenger csillag: Erkel
There is nought of soundness in all my body—Es ist nichts Gesundes
    an meinem Liebe: Bach
There is much to tell you—Tanta coisa a dizer te: Guarnieri
There is someone I love—J'ai quelqu'un dans le coeur (Tristesses): Milhaud
There lived an aged king—Es war ein alter König: A Rubinstein
There lived an old fiddler—Es wohnet ein Fiedler: Brahms
There lived once a handsome Jewess—Es war eine schöne Jüdin: Brahms
There lived once a carpenter—Es war einmal ein Zimmergesell: Brahms
There 'mong the willows—Dort in den Weiden: Brahms
There reigned a monarch in Thule—Es war ein König in Thule: Liszt
There sat a salamander—Salamander: Brahms
There sat a snow-white birdie—Es sass ein schneeweiss Vögelein: Brahms
There sounds in the air—Es klingt in der Luft: R Franz
There walked a pretty maiden—Es ging ein Maidlein zarte: Brahms
There was a king in Thule—Es war ein König in Thule: Liszt
There was a margrave—Es war ein Markgraf überm Rhein: Brahms
There was an aged monarch—Es war ein alter König: Meyer-Helmund
There was an aged monarch—Es war ein alter König: A Rubinstein
There was an ancient king—Es war ein alter König: Henschel
Therefore be ye not anxious—Darum sollt ihr nicht sorgen (Es wartet
    alles auf dich): Bach
Therefore is light given—Warum ist das Licht gegeben: Brahms
Therese—Teresa/The shell: Brahms
There's no more you can say—Parle-moi d'autre chose: Delage
There's nought, O heart—Verzicht, O Herz (Neue Liebeslieder): Brahms
There's nought upon this earth—Nel mondo e nell' abisso (Riccardo
    Primo): Handel
These are hours of joy's creating—L'ora, o Tirsi (Manon Lescault): Puccini
These are the holy ten commandments—Dies sind die heil'gen zehn
    Gebot (Orgelbüchlein): Bach
These broken sighs—Non sospirar: Handel
They call me Mimi—Si mi chiamano Mimi (La bohème): Puccini
They mowed the pasture already—Lekászalták már a rétet: Bartók
They peep in each nest—Die himmlische Vorsicht der ewigen Güte
    (Schleicht, spielende Wellen): Bach
They worshipped each other—Sie liebten sich beide: R Franz
The thieving magpie—La gazza ladra: Rossini
The thievish magpie—La gazza ladra: Rossini
Thine are the heavens—Tui sunt coeli: Byrd
Thine eyes—Dein Auge: Reger
Thine eyes—Ihre Augen: R Strauss
Thine eyes are black—Fekete szem éjezakája: Erkel

Thine image—Dein Bildnis: Cornelius
Thine image pure—Dein Bildnis wunderselig: Schumann
Thine is my heart—Ungeduld (Der schöne Müllerin): Schubert
Thine only—Dein!: C Böhm
Things visible and invisible—Les choses visibles et invisibles (Messe de la
  Pentecôte): Messiaen
Think on this, my soul—Denk' es, o Seele: Wolf
The third day he rose again—Kommt wieder aus der finstern Gruft: Bach
The third foot-print: Det tredje Fottrin: F Backer-Grøndahl
This day is born Emmanuel—En natus est Emanuel: Praetorius
This day, so rich in joy and love—Der Tag, der ist so freudenreich
  (Orgelbüchlein): Bach
This fair rose may tell—Della rosa il bel vermiglio (Bianca e Falliero):
  Rossini
This glad day—Haec dies: Byrd
This happy morn—Nobis est natus: Praetorius
This hard bondage—Quella barbara catena: F Ciampi
This is my land—Zot admati: Lavry
This is the day—Haec dies: Byrd
This is the day—Haec dies: Palestrina
This lowly tomb—In questa tomba oscura: Beethoven
This or that—So oder so: Beethoven
Tho' his voice was breathed afar—Una voce poco fà (Il barbiere di
  Siviglia): Rossini
Tho' not deserving—Sebben, crudele: Caldara
Thomas the rhymer—Tom der Reimer: Loewe
Those dark green leaves—Das Mach das unkelgrüne Laub: Meyer-Helmund
Those eyes at least now open—Aprite un pò quegl'occhi (Le nozze di
  Figaro): Mozart
Those were the days—Wohl waren es Tage: R Franz
Thou all my bliss—Caro mio ben: Giordani
Thou art—Bist du!: Liszt
Thou art a priest for ever—Tu es sacerdos in aeternum: S Wesley
Thou art all fair—Du bist aller Dinge schön: M Franck
Thou art like a flower—Du bist wie eine Blume: Liszt
Thou art like a lovely flower—Du bist wie eine Blume: Schumann
Thou art like a tender flow'ret—Du bist wie eine Blume: Liszt
Thou art my heart's own idol—Idolo del cor mio (L'incoronazione di
  Poppea): Monteverdi
Thou art my queen—Wie bist du, meine Königin: Brahms
Thou art my rest—Du bist die Ruh': Schubert
Thou art repose—Du bist die Ruh': Schubert
Thou art the queen of all heaven—Ave regina coelorum: Lasso
Thou bee so tiny—Du kleine Biene: Cornelius

Thou blessed Virgin—Allmacht'ge Jungfrau (Tannhäuser): Wagner
Thou canst, o death, no further now affright me—Du mächst, O Tod,
	wir nun nicht ferne bange (Ach, lieben Christen, seid getrost): Bach
Thou charming bird—Charmant oiseau (La perle du Brésil): F David
Thou forest green—Du gröne Rast: R Franz
Thou gentle gazer—Du liebes Auge: R Franz
Thou gentle girl—Dein Herzlein mild: Brahms
Thou goest now my Saviour forth—So gehst du nun, mein Jesu, hin:
	Bach
Thou guide of Israel—Du Hirte Israel, höre: Bach
Thou hast whispered—Pur dicesi o bocca bella: Lotti
Thou knowest fairest maiden—Tu sai, madonna mia: Lassus
Thou know'st, beloved—Tu sa' ch'io so (Sonnets of Michelangelo):
	Britten
Thou know'st the land—Kennst du das Land: Liszt
Thou Lord alone, dost crown—Du Herr, du krönst allein (Es wartet
	alles auf dich): Bach
Thou lov'st me not—Du liebst mich nicht: Schubert
Thou most blest, all-quickening day—Seligster Erquickungs-Tag (Wachet,
	betet, seid bereit): Bach
Thou my only light—Du mein einzig Licht: Brahms
Thou only, dear one—O duše draha (Pisné milostné): Dvořák
Thou poor vain world—Ach arme Welt: Brahms
Thou queen of all the world—Cedan l'antiche: Marenzio
Thou ring upon my finger—Du Ring an meinem Finger/Der Ring
	(Frauenliebe und -leben): Schumann
Thou shalt die—Morrai si (Rodelinda): Handel
Thou shalt love the Lord thy God—Diliges Dominum: Byrd
Thou shalt not, thou must—Du sollst nicht, du musst: Schoenberg
Thou shepherd of Israel hear—Du Hirte Israel, höre: Bach
Thou standest like a flower—Du bist wie eine Blume: A Rubinstein
Thou tender trailing ivy—Die grüne Hopfenkranke (Liebeslieder Walzer):
	Brahms
Thou that art equal to the Father—Der du bist dem Vater gleich (Schwingt
	freudig euch empor): Bach
Thou that born of heaven art—Der du von dem Himmel bist: J Marx
Thou traitor, who dost seek the Lord to kill—Du Falscher, suche
	nur den Herrn zu fallen (Weihnachtsoratorium): Bach
Thou very good and David's son—Du wahrer Gott und Davids Sohn: Bach
Thou who down from heaven—Der du von dem Himmel bist: Wolf
Thou who from heaven art sent—Der du von dem Himmel bist: Liszt
Thou who from Thy heavenly home—Der du von dem Himmel bist: Loewe
Thou who with ice are girdled—Tu che di gel sel cinta (Turandot):
	Puccini

Thou whose praises never end—Hochgelobter Gottessohn (Bleib' bei uns, denn es will Abend werden): Bach
Though deep has been my falling—Aus meiner Sünden tiefe: Lassus
Though divided—Ombra cara (Radamisto): Handel
Though faithless men—Se il rigor (La Juive): Halévy
Though faithless men—Se il rigor (La Juive): Halévy
Though I have lost my father—Se il padre perdei (Idomeneo): Mozart
    dell'armi (Partenope): Handel
Though I speak—Wenn ich mit Menschen: Brahms
Though my day be dark—Ogni pena più spietata: Pergolesi
Though now she slight me—Ben che mi sprezzi (Tamerlano): Handel
A thought like music—Wie Melodien zieht es mir: Brahms
Thoughts—Pensiero: Leoncavallo
Thoughts at eventide—Abendempfindung: Mozart
Thoughts of darkness—Ihr Gedanken: Erlanger
Thoughts of home—Das Heimweh: F Mendelssohn
Thoughts of the Black Sea—Duma Chornomorska: Yanovskyi
Thoughts of thee—Denk' ich dein! : R Franz
A thousand and one nights—Tausend und eine Nacht: J Strauss II
The threat—Vynruzka: Janáček
The threat—La menace: Roussel
Three angels were singing—Es sungen drei Engel (3rd symphony): Mahler
Three autumn tears—Haróm öszi könnycsepp: Bartók
Three Botticelli pictures—Trittico Botticelliano: Respighi
The three comrades—Drei Wandrer: Hermann
Three days and nights—Tre giorno son che Nina: Pergolesi
Three days have passed—Tre giorno son che Nina: Pergolesi
The three gipsies—Die drei Zigeuner: Liszt
The three gipsies—Die drei Zigeuner: Schoeck
Three goblets—Tri kubka: Aleksandrov
The three graces—Libellentanz: Lehár
The three holy kings—Die heiligen drei Könige: R Strauss
Three kings—Die Könige: Cornelius
Three lovely birds—Trois beaux oiseaux: Ravel
Three riders rode out of the city gate—Es ritten drei Reiter zum Tore
    hinaus: Kämpf
Three roses were growing—Es stunden drei Rosen: Brahms
Three traditional rhymes—Drei Volkstexte: Webern
Three voices—Weg der Liebe: Brahms
Three waltzes—Drei Walzer: Straus
The three wise kings: Epiphanias: Wolf
The three-cornered hat—El sombrero de tres picos: Falla

The threepenny opera—Die Dreigroschenoper: Weill
Threnody for the victims of Hiroshima—Tren-Ofiarum Hiroszimy: Penderecki
The thresher—D'un vanneur de blé aux vents: Berkeley
Thrice happy is he who stands—Beato in ver chi puo: Handel
Thro' my frame—Gelido, in ogni vena (Siroe): Handel
Thro' the pinewood—Im Haine: Schubert
Thro' valley, thro' woodland—Per valli, per boschi: Blangini
A throbbing of gladness—Un moto di gioja: Mozart
Thron der Liebe, Stern der Güte (Liebe)—Throne of mercy, star of goodness: Cornelius
Throne of mercy, star of goodness—Thron der Liebe, Stern der Güte: (Liebe): Cornelius
Through alley and lane—Ich geh' durch: Wolf
Through the field—Ging heut' Morgen übers Feld (Lieder eines fahrenden Gesellen): Mahler
Through the valley now 'tis light—Will über Nacht wohl durch das Tal: R Franz
Through the woods—Durch den Wald: R Franz
Through the woods as oft I wander—Auf gehemem Waldespfade: R Franz
Throughout the long days—Cunctis diebus: Byrd
Thru the emerald meadows—Por los campos verdes: Guastavino
The thrush sings loud today—Zur Drossel sprach der Fink: d'Albert
Thus as Moses—Siant Moses serpentum: Schütz
Thus betrayed—Mi tradi (Don Giovanni): Mozart
Thus by one sole disaster—È pur così in un giorno (Giulio Cesare): Handel
Thus I break the ties that bound me—Rompo i lacci (Flavio): Handel
Thus I call my beloved—Chiamo il mio ben così (Orfeo ed Euridice): Gluck
Thus saith the Lord—Haec dicit Dominus: Byrd
Thus spake Zarathustra—Also sprach Zarathustra: R Strauss
Thus stand we—So stehen wir: Brahms
Thy blue eyes—Dein blaues Auge: Brahms
Thy blue eyes—Mit deinen blauen Augen: Lassen
Thy cherry-red lips—O amoureusich mondeken Root: Beethoven
Thy dear fingers—Deine weissen Lilienfinger: R Franz
Thy deep blue eyes—Mit deinen blauen Augen: Lassen
Thy farewell—Tú partida: A Brandt
Thy father's heart—Il lacerato spirito (Simon Boccanegra): Verdi
Thy kingdom come—Zu uns komme dein Reich: Cornelius
Thy kingdom come—Přijd' království Tvé: Hába
Thy lips like roses—Si dessus voz levres de roses: Le Jeune
Thy love rapture—Geliebter, wo zaudert dein irrender Fuss: Brahms

Thy lovely eyes—Krásne oi' Tve: Janáček
Thy music, oh! gentle stream—Ruisseau, dont le bruit charmant
    (Cassandre): Bouvard/Bertin
Thy name I whisper—Ich flüstre deinen Namen: Kücken
Thy sentence is useless—Invan mi danni! (Nerone): Boito
Thy warning is good—Tak for dit Rad: Grieg
Ti rivaggo, Fanny (Il castello di Kenilworth)—Be thou welcome, dear
    friend: Donizetti
The tide—Die Flut: Blacher
Tief im Herzen (Spanische Liebeslieder)—Grief within my heart: Schumann
Tiefes Lied—The weary heart: Schubert
Tiefland—The lowland: d'Albert
Tikhy Don—The quiet Don: Dzerzhinsky
Til Foraret—To the spring: Grieg
Til min Dreng—To my son: Grieg
Til mit hjertes Dronning—To the queen of my heart: A Backer-Grøndahl
Til Norge—To the Motherland: Grieg
Till Eulenspiegels lustige Streiche—Till Eulenspiegel's merry pranks:
    R Strauss
Till Eulenspiegel's merry pranks—Till Eulenspiegels lustige Streiche:
    R Strauss
Till havs—At sea: Sibelius
Time as he flies—Il tempo vola e se ne fuggon gli anni: Palestrina
The time of lilac—Les temps des lilas: Chausson
The time of roses—Le temps des roses: Gounod
Time the charioteer—An Schwager Kronos: Schubert
Timor et hebitudo—Trembling and fearfulness: Byrd
The tinker—Der Rastelbinder: Lehár
Tintenheinz und Platscherlottchen—Inky Jimmy and dripping Polly: Blech
Tiranni miei pensieri (Tolomeo)—The moon: Handel
Tirhy Don—The quiet Don: Dzerzhinsky
'Tis a dream—Ist ein Traum (Der Rosenkavalier): R Strauss
'Tis a faithful lover's greeting—Partout des cris de joie (La jolie fille de
    Perth): Bizet
'Tis a lady wise and noble—Une dame noble et sage (Les Huguenots):
    Meyerbeer
'Tis confusing for a shepherdess—Son confusa pastorella (Poro): Handel
'Tis ended—So stehen wir: Brahms
'Tis hope that sustains us—Non sò se sia la speme (Serse): Handel
'Tis in vain that I seek—O mes soeurs (Mary Magdalaine): Massenet
'Tis life's unkindest lesson—Das ist im Leben: Meyer-Helmund
'Tis now three days—Tre giorno son che Nina: Pergolesi
'Tis poverty—O Armut, der kein Reichtum gleicht (Die Elenden
    sollen essen): Bach

'Tis snowing—Il neige: Bemberg
'Tis spring—Er ist's: Reger
'Tis that day I so long awaited—Per me giunto è il dì supremo (Don Carlos): Verdi
'Tis the day—Mattinata: Leoncavallo
'Tis the day of Christ our Lord—Hodie Christus natus est: Byrd
'Tis this that gives the silv'ry shade—Das macht das dunkelgrüne Laub: R Franz
'Tis thou to whom—Aus dem Dankliede zu Gott: Haydn
'Tis whispered—L'ultima canzone: Tosti
'Tis worth observing—Finche lo strale (Floridante): Handel
Tit er jeg glad—Oft am I happy: Nielsen
Titania am I—Je suis Titantia (Mignon): Thomas
Titus—La clemenza di Tito: Mozart
Tiz könnyű zongoradarab—Ten easy pieces: Bartók
Tizennégy zongoradarab—Fourteen bagatelles: Bartók
To—An: Wolf
To a brook—An eine Quelle: Schubert
To a brooklet—An eine Quelle: Schubert
To a child—Auf ein Kind: Schoeck
To a Christmas rose—Auf eine Christblume: Wolf
To a portrait—An ihr Bild: Kjerulf
To a violet—An ein Veilchen: Brahms
To a young gentleman—A un jeune gentilhomme: Roussel
To all men a child is come—Puer natus nascitur: Praetorius
To an Aeolian harp—An eine Aeolsharfe: Brahms
To an Aeolian harp—An eine Aeolsharfe: Wolf
To an autumn forest—An einen Herbstlied: J Marx
To an infant—An einen Säugling: Beethoven
To Anne, at the spinet—D'Anne jouant de l'espinette: Ravel
To be near my beloved—Star vicino: Rosa
To be near thee—Star vicino: Rosa
To be near to the lov'd one—Star vicino: Rosa
To be sung on the water—Auf dem Wasser zu singen: Schubert
To be sung to mother—Der Mutter vorzusingen: Blech
To Bertha—An Bertha: Cornelius
To brune Öjne—Two brown eyes/Two hazel eyes: Grieg
To Chloe—An Chloë: Mozart
To Columbine—A Columbine: Massenet
To coy beauties—An spröde Schönen: F X Mozart
To death—An den Tod: Schubert
To despoil this your treasure—Perrapir quel tesoro (Serse): Handel
To evening—Illalle: Sibelius
To far-off climes—Ferne: Mendelssohn

To get along with girls—Mit Madeln sich vertragen: Beethoven
To God we render thanks and praise—Lob sei dem allmächtigen Gott
(Orgelbüchlein): Bach
To heaven pain and sorrow—Dem Himmel will ich klagen: Brahms
To her—An Sie: R Strauss
To her beloved—Die Liebende schreibt: Brahms
To her I go—Je vais revoir ma charmante maîtresse (Le devin du village):
Rousseau
To her I shall be faithful—Mein Herz in steten Treuen: Schoenberg
To Him my spirit yield Thee—So sei nun, Seele deine (Meine Seufzer,
meine Tränen): Bach
To hope—An die Hoffnung: Beethoven
To hope—An die Hoffnung: Mozart
To hope, on recovering from illness—Der Genesene an die Hoffnung:
Wolf
To Jordan's stream came Christ our Lord—Christ, unser Herr, zum Jordan
kam: Bach
To joy let us drain—Libiamo ne' lieti calici (La traviata): Verdi
To many a maid—Ich kose süss (Neue Liebeslieder): Brahms
To me, in joy returning—Wie sehr lieblich und schöne: Schütz
To me thy heart awarding—Willst du dein Herz mir schenken: Bach (?)
To music—An die Musik: Schubert
To my baby—Meinem Kinde: R Strauss
To my betrothed—Widmung: Schumann
To my fair one—A Mignonne: Massenet
To my friends—An die Freunde: Schubert
To my native home I'm near—Di piacer mi balza il cor (La gazza ladra):
Rossini
To my son—Til min Dreng: Grieg
To my son—Lied an meinen Sohn: R Strauss
To Nerina—A Nerina: Bossi
To none will I my love—Ich trage meine Minne: R Strauss
To one in paradise—Au paradis!: Luzzatti
To one unknown—Auf eine Unbekannte: Cornelius
To our fair Provence—Di Provenza il mar (La traviata): Verdi
To our girls—Našim děvám: Smetana
To Queen Elizabeth—An die Königin Elisabeth: Schumann
To rest, to rest—Zur Ruh', zur Ruh': Wolf
To save thy life—Per salvarti idolo mio (Lotario): Handel
To sleep—An den Schlaf: Wolf
To solitude—An die Einsamkeit: Mozart
To solitude himself who gives—Wer sich der Einsamkeit ergibt: Schubert
To spring—Au printemps: Gounod
To springtime my song I utter—Jeg giver mit digt til Våren: Grieg

To the beautiful lady—Der vielschönen Fraue: R Franz
To the beloved—An die Geliebte: Wolf
To the beloved—An die Geliebte: Beethoven
To the beloved one—Die Liebende schreibt: Brahms
To the beloved one—Nähe des Geliebten: Schubert
To the country where they are at war—Au pays où se fait la guerre: Duparc
To the departed—A la trépassée: Massenet
To the departed one—Traumbild: R Franz
To the distant beloved—An die ferne Geliebte: Beethoven
To the eternal—Dem Unendlichen: Schubert
To the evening star—Mädchenlied: Raff
To the evening star—An den Abendstern: Schumann
To the evening star—Der Abendstern: Schumann
To the faithless one—Als die Geliebte sich trennen wolte: Beethoven
To the hero: Dem Helden: Schumann
To the home that she left—Donde lieta (La bohème): Puccini
To the lute—An die Laute: Schubert
To the lyre—An die Leier: Schubert
To the moon—An den Mond: Bocquet
To the moon—An den Mond: Brahms
To the moon—An den Mond (Schwanengesang): Schubert
To the moon—An den Mond/Füllest wieder Busch und Tal: Schubert
To the moon—Gruss, lieber Mond: Schubert
To the moon—An den Mond: Schumann
To the motherland—Til Norge: Grieg
To the night—An die Nacht: C Böhm
To the (a) nightingale—An die Nachtigall: Brahms
To the nightingale—Au rossignol: Gounod
To the nightingale—An die Nachtigall: Henschel
To the nightingale—Er liegt und schäft: Schubert
To the nightingale—An die Nachtigall: Schumann
To the proud one—An die Stolze: Brahms
To the queen of my heart—Til mit hjertes Donning: A Backer-Grøndahl
To the Rhine—Warnung vor dem Rhein: Mendelssohn
To the Rhine—Auf dem Rhein: Schumann
To the river—A la rivière: Huybrechts
To the setting sun—An die untergehende Sonne: Schubert
To the songs of art—An die Künstler: Mendelssohn
To the spring—Til Foraret: Grieg
To the spring rain—An den Frühlingsregen: Reger
To the stream—Am Strome: Schubert
To the sunshine—An den Sonnenschein: Schumann
To the wind—An den Wind: R Franz

To the wine glass of a dead friend—Auf das Trinkglas eines verstorbenen
    Freundes: Schumann
To thee I kneel—O toi l'objet (Iphigénie en Aulide): Gluck
To thee, in a dream—Ach, Liebster, in Gedanken: Reger
To Thee, Jehovah—Dir, dir, Jehovah: Bach
To Thee, Lord Jesus, thanks we give—Wir danken dir, Herr Jesu
    Christ (Orgelbüchlein): Bach
To thee, mighty Neptune—Nettuno s'onori (Idomeneo): Mozart
To thee will I sing, fair springtime—Jeg Giver mit digt til Våren: Grieg
To thy sad brow let joy return—Rend' il sereno al ciglio (Sosarme):
    Handel
To us a child is born—Die Kön'ge aus Saba kamen dar (Sie werden aus
    Saba alle kommen): Bach
To us a child is born—Uns ist ein Kind geboren: Bach
To us a little child is born—Parvalus nobis nascitur: Praetorius
To us is born Emanuel—En natus est Emanuel: Praetorius
To win thy love—Um deine Liebe: Dohnányi
To your toast—Votre toast, je peux vous la rendre (Carmen): Bizet
Toast to Stalin—Zdravitsa: Prokofiev
Tobias—Il ritorno di Tobia: Haydn
Die Tochter Jeptha's—Jeptha's daughter/The daughter of Jeptha:
    Schumann
Der Tod, das ist die kühle Nacht—O death, it is the cold: Allitsen
Der Tod, das ist die kühle Nacht—Death is the cooling night/Oh,
    death is like the cooling night/Death is the cool night: Brahms
Der Tod, das ist die kühle Nacht—O death thou art the tranquil night:
    Cornelius
Der Tod und das Mädchen—Death and the girl (maiden):
    Schubert
Der Tod und der einsame Trinker (Lieder um den Tod)—Death and
    the lonely drinker: Kilpinen
Tod und Verklärung—Death and transfiguration: R Strauss
Today God's only-gotten Son—Heut triumphieret Gottes Sohn
    (Orgelbüchlein): Bach
Todeslied des Bojaren—Death-song of the Boyard: Mendelssohn
Todessehnen—Shadows of death: Brahms
Todessehnsucht (see also: Komm, süsser Tod, komm, sel'ge Ruh')—
    Longing for death: Bach
Tödliche Krankheit—Deadly sickness: Henschel
Todtengräbers Heimweh—The grave digger: Schubert
Todtengräberslied—Gravedigger's song: Schubert
Together—Lehn deine Wang an meine Wang: Jensen
Toi que l'oiseau (Guillaume Tell): Swift as a bird: Rossini
The token—Das Zeichen: Himmel

Tolomeo—Ptolemy: Handel
The tom cat—Der Kater: J N David
Tom der Reimer—Thomas the rhymer/Tom the rhymer: Loewe
Tom the rhymer—Tom der Reimer: Loewe
Tom Thumb—Petit Poucet (Ma mère l'oye): Ravel
The tomb—Au cimetière (Les nuits d'été): Berlioz
The tomb of Anacreon—Anakreons Grab: Wolf
The tomb of the Naiads—Le tombeau des Naïades (Chansons de Bilitis):
    Debussy
Le tombeau des Naïades (Chansons de Bilitis)—The tomb of the
    Naiads: Debussy
Tomorrow—Morgen: R Strauss
Tomorrow you will love—Vous aimerez demain: Massenet
Tom-tit—Le capinera: Benedict
Ein Ton—A tone/The voice/Haunted: Cornelius
Der Ton—A tone: J Marx
Ton menton pose dans ta main—Your sweet small chin: Rhené-Baton
A tone—Ein Ton: Cornelius
A tone—Der Ton: J Marx
The tongues of fire—Les langues de feu (Messe de la Pentecôte): Messiaen
Too cruel is the bitter pain—È pena troppo barbara: Galuppi
Too fair shone hope—Mir ist's zu wohl ergangen: Henschel
Too late—Zu spät: Blumenthal
Too late—Aleik mindig elkesnek: Kodály
The top—Snurretoppen (Humoreske): Nielsen
The toper in spring—Der Trinker im Frühling: Patáky
Topolini—Mickey Mouse: Castelnuovo-Tedesco
Torches that burn—Tristes apprets (Castor et Pollux): Rameau
The toreador's song—Votre toast, je peux vous la rendre: Bizet
Torna a Surriento—Come back to Sorrento: E de Curtis
Torrent—Wasserflut (Die Winterreise): Schubert
Tortoises—Tortues (Carnaval des animaux): Saint-Saëns
Tortues (Carnaval des animaux)—Tortoises: Saint-Saëns
Tortured and torn—Il lacerato spirito (Simon Boccanegra): Verdi
Tot—Dead: Schoenberg
Die tote Nachtigall—The dead nightingale: Liszt
Die tote Stadt—The dead city: Korngold
Toteninsel—Isle of the dead: Rachmaninov
Die Toteninsel—The isle of the dead: Reger
Der Totenkranz—Mother's grave: Manén
Totentanz—Dance of death: Bresgen
Tóth legények tánca (Tíz könnyű zongoradarab)—Slovak peasants'
    dance: Bartók
Touches blanches—White keys: Milhaud

Touches noires—Black keys: Milhaud
Touha—Longing: Martinů
Touha—Longing: Smetana
Toujours—Always: Blumenthal
Toujours (Poème d'un jour)—For ever: Fauré
Toujours ou jamais—The scent of roses: Waldteufel
The toupee artist—Tupeyny khudozhnik: Shishov
Le tour à Nantes—The ride to Nantes: Meister
Tournament of song—Freudig begrüssen (Tannhäuser): Wagner
Tout gai!—All gay!/Be gay: Ravel
The town—Die Stadt (Schwanengesang): Schubert
The toy wheel—Brinquedo de roda: Villa Lobos
A tragedy—Trägodie: Schumann
Tragic hour—Hora grave: Elgelbrecht
Trägodie—A tragedy: Schumann
Trailing rose-tree—Vaga rosa: Kreutzer
Trällerliedchen (Album für die Jugend)—Humming song: Schumann
Il tramonto—The sunset: Respighi
Die Träne—A tear: Blumenthal
Tränen—Tears: R Franz
Tränenregen (Die schöne Müllerin)—Rain of tears/Teardrops/Doubt:
    Schubert
Transfigured night—Verklärte Nacht: Schoenberg
Transformation—Wandlung: Blumenthal
Transylvanian dances—Erdélyi táncok: Bartók
Transylvanian lament—Szekely keserves: Kodály
Trauer—Grief: Cornelius
Trauermarsch (Die Gotterdämmerung)—Siegfried's funeral music:
    Wagner
Die Trauernde—The mourner/The forlorn/Alone/My mother loves me
    not: Brahms
Die Trauernde—The mourner: R Franz
Der Traum—The dream: Blech
Ein Traum—A dream: Grieg
Traum durch die Dämmerung—Dream in the twilight: Reger
Traum durch die Dämmerung—Dream in the twilight/Dreaming in the
    twilight: R Strauss
Traum eines Kinds—A child's dream: Schumann
Traumbild—To the departed one: R Franz
Das Traumbild—A sleep one day/The vision: Mozart
Träume—Dreams: R Franz
Träume (Wesendonck Lieder)—Dreams: Wagner
Träume auf dem Ozean—Dreams on the ocean: Gung'l
Der träumende See—The peaceful lake: Schumann
Traumerei (Kinderscenen)—Dreaming: Schumann

Traumes Wirren (Fantasiestücke)—Dreams: Schumann
Traumgekrönt—A crown of dreams: Berg
Traumleben—Dream-life: Schoenberg
Traumnacht—The house of dreams: Weingartner
Traun! Bogen und Pfeil sind gut für den Feind—Ho! broadsword and
    spear/With sword and bow/Ay! cross-bow and dart/One shaft from
    thy bow: Brahms
Das traurige Mädchen—The sorrowful maiden: R Franz
Traurnaya oda—Funeral ode: Krein
Travel book from the Austrian Alps—Reisenbuch aus den Österreichischen
    Alpen: Křenek
The traveller—Le voyageur: Godard
The traveller's song—Reiselied: Mendelssohn
A traveller's song—Wanderlied: Schumann
La traviata—The lost one/The frail one: Verdi
Tre giorno son che Nina—'Tis now three days/For three long days/
    Three days and nights/My Nina still lies dreaming/Three days have
    passed/Sorrow: Pergolesi (?)
Treacherous world, I trust thee not—Falsche Welt, dir trau' ich nicht:
    Bach
Treachery—Verrath: Brahms
Treasure waltz—Schatz-walzer: J Strauss II
The treasure-digger—Der Schatzgräber: Schreker
The treasure-seeker—Der Schatzgräber: Schumann
Det tredje Fottrin—The third foot-print: F Backer-Grøndahl
The tree—Jag är ett träd: Sibelius
The tree and the gardener—Ich bin dein Baum, O Gartner: Schumann
The trees by the river—Am Wildbach die Waiden: Brahms
Trees that sway—Lindes rauschen: Brahms
Treibt der Sommer—Soon as summer: R Franz
Trembling and fearfulness—Timor et hebitudo: Byrd
Tren-Ofiarum Hirozimy—Threnody for the victims of Hiroshima:
    Penderecki
Trennung—Parting/Separation: Brahms
Trenning—Parting: Henschel
Tresbelle, bonne jeune et gente—My gentle ladye young and fair: Meister
The tresses of hair—La chevelure (Chansons de Bilitis): Debussy
Tretet ein, hoher Krieger—Enter in, Lordly warrior: Pfitzner
Tretet ein, hoher Krieger—Now advance, haughty warrior/Enter in,
    noble warrior: Wolf
Treu Röschen—Fair red-rose: Loewe
Treue—Single hearted: Blumenthal
Treue—Faithfulness: Cornelius
Treue—Fidelity: Haydn

Treue Liebe—True love/Faithful love: Brahms

Treue Liebe dauert lange—Love long tried hath long endured/Love, if true, must last for ever: Brahms

Treulich geführt ziehet dahin (Lohengrin)—Faithful and true/Bridal chorus: Wagner

Tri kubka—Three goblets: Aleksandrov

Tri stikhotvoreniya iz yaponsky liriki—Japanese lyric poems: Stravinsky

The trial—Der Prozess: Einem

The trial of Harmony and Invention—Il cimento dell' Armonia e dell' Inventione: Vivaldi

The trial of Lucullus—Der Verhör des Lukullus: Dessau

Tribue Domine—Grant, I beseech Thee: Byrd

Tribulatio proxima est—Tribulation cometh nigh us: Byrd

Tribulation cometh nigh us—Tribulatio proxima est: Byrd

Tribulations civitatum—We have heard the grievous tribulations: Byrd

Il tricerbero (Rinaldo)—Dreadful Cerberus: Handel

Der Trinker im Frühling—The toper in spring: Petáky

Das Trinklied vom Jammer der Erde (Das Lied von der Erde)—Drinking song of the earth's misery (sorrow): Mahler

Triolett—Sinks the night: Schumann

Trionfo di Afrodite—The triumph of Aphrodite: Orff

Trip, blithe streamlet—Và godendo vezzoso e bello: Handel

Trip to Paris—Voyage à Paris: Poulenc

The triptych—Il trittico: Puccini

Tristes apprets (Castor et Pollux)—Torches that burn: Rameau

Tristesse—Sorrow: Liszt

Tristitia et anxietas—Sorrow of heart: Byrd

Tritt auf die Glaubensbahn—The path of faith now run/Walk in the way of faith: Bach

Il trittico—The triptych: Puccini

Trittico Botticelliano—Three Botticelli pictures: Respighi

The triumph of Aphrodite—Trionfo di Afrodite: Orff

Triumphal hymn—Triumphlied: Brahms

Triumphlied—Song of triumph/Triumphal hymn: Brahms

Tro og håb spiller (Moderen)—Faith and hope play: Nielsen

Trockne Blumen (Die schöne Müllerin)—Dry flowers/Faded flowers: Schubert

Trois beaux oiseaux—Three lovely birds: Ravel

The Trojans—Les Troyens: Berlioz

The Trojans at Carthage—Les Troyens à Carthage: Berlioz

Troldtog—March of the dwarfs: Grieg

Die Trömmel gerühret (Egmont)—The drums loud are beating/The drums they are beating: Beethoven

Trommel-Ständchen—Drum serenade: Loewe

Troopers' drinking song—Landsknechtstrinklied: Hindemith
Trost—Consolation: Cornelius
Trost im Gesang—Comfort in song: Schumann
Trost im Unglücke (Des Knaben Wunderhorn)—Consolation in sorrow/
    Solace in sorrow/Comfort in sorrow: Mahler
Trost in Tränen—Comfort in tears/Solace in tears: Brahms
Trost in Tränen—Trust in tears/Solace of tears/Comfort in tears:
    Schubert
Tröste mir, Jesu, mein Gemüte (Ach, Herr, mich armen Sünder)—
    Comfort me, Jesu, in my sadness: Bach
Trostlos schluchzet Philomele (Zaïde)—The caged nightingale: Mozart
The troubadour—Il trovatore: Verdi
The trouble of spring—En våruisa: Palmgren
The trout—Die Forelle: Schubert
Il trovatore—The troubadour: Verdi
Les Troyens—The Trojans: Berlioz
Les Troyens à Carthage—The Trojans at Carthage: Berlioz
Trübe wird's, die Wolken jagen—Dark the sky, the clouds are flying:
    R Franz
Trudom—Faith: Grieg
True believers and baptized shall be saved—Wer da glaubet und getauft
    wird: Bach
True constancy—La vera constanza: Haydn
True love—Liebestreu: Brahms
True love—Treue Liebe: Brahms
True love—Wahre Liebe: Hindemith
True lover's heart—Aus der Erde quellen: Brahms
True love's bliss—Glückes genug: R Strauss
Truly, truly, I say unto you—Wahrlich, wahrlich, ich sage euch: Bach
Der Trunkene im Frühling (Das Lied von der Erde)—The drunken man
    in spring/Wine in spring/The drunkard in spring: Mahler
Trust a woman? How simple-minded—Semplicetto! a donna credi
    (Alcina): Handel
Trust in spring—Frühlingsglaub: Mendelssohn
Trust in tears—Trost in Tränen: Schubert
Trusting little linnet—Si di rama en rama (Acis y Galatea): Literes
Truth—Parole: Brahms
The tryst—Møte (Haugtussa): Grieg
The trysting place—Der Gang zum Liebchen: Brahms
Tsar's bride—Tsarskaya Nevesta: Rimsky-Korsakov
Tsarskaya Nevesta—Tsar's bride: Rimsky-Korsakov
Tu che di gel sel cinta (Turandot)—Thou who with ice are girdled: Puccini
Tu es sacerdoes in aeternum—Thou art a priest for ever: S Wesley
Tu lo sai—Faithless as fair: A Scarlatti

Tu lo sai—Ask thy heart: Torelli
Tu me dirais—I would believe: Chaminade
Tú partida—Thy farewell: A Brandt
Tu sa' ch'io so (Sonnets of Michelangelo)—Thou know'st beloved: Britten
Tu sai, madonna mia—Thou knowest fairest maiden: Lassus
Tu veux avoir la préférence—You think of Strephon: Rameau
Tu vois le feu du soir (Tel jour telle nuit)—You see the fire of evening: Poulenc
Tua mi speranza (Amadigi di Gaula)—My hope-star royal!: Handel
Tue Rechnung! Donnerwort—Show thy reckoning! Word of doom: Bach
Tui sunt coeli—Thine are the heavens: Byrd
Tulerunt Dominum meum—Lo, from his tomb: Mendelssohn
Tune thy strings—Struna nala děna (Cigánske melodie): Dvořák
Tungsind—Melancholy: Grieg
Tuo mi chiami—Yours you call me: D Scarlatti
Tupeyny khudozhnik—The toupee artist: Shisov
Turkisches Schenkenlied—Turkish drinking song: Mendelssohn
Turkish drinking song—Turkisches Schenkenlied: Mendelssohn
Turn once again—Caro mio ben: Giordani
Turn Thee to me—Popatřiž na mne (Biblické Písně): Dvořák
Turn, turn, away thy face—Ach, wende diesen Blick: Brahms
Turn your eyes towards him—Rivolgete a lui los guardo: Mozart
Túrót eszik a cigány—See the gipsy: Kodály
Tuscan landscapes—Paesaggi toscani: Tommasini
The tutor in trouble—L'ajo nell imbarazzo: Donizetti
Tutto è disposto (Le nozze di Figaro)—All is prepared now: Mozart
Tutta raccolta ancor nel palpitante (Scipione)—Sad is my weary soul: Handel
Tutta rea la vita umana (Scipione)—Base and worthless: Handel
Tvrdé palice—The stubborn lovers: Dvořák
'Twas for thee—War es dir: Brahms
'Twas in the beauteous month of May—Im wunderschönen Monat Mai: R Franz
'Twas in the cool of eventide—Am Adend da es kühle war (Matthäuspassion): Bach
'Twas in the lovely month of May—Im wunderschönen Monat Mai (Dichterliebe): Schumann
'Twas night and all around was still—Tacea la notte (Il trovatore): Verdi
'Tween the branches and the blossoms—Si tra i ceppi (Berenice): Handel
The twelve—Dvenadtsat: Salmanov
Twice a thousand years—Dreimal tausend Jahre: Schoenberg
Twilight—Abenddämmerung: Brahms
Twilight—Crépuscule: Gounod

Twilight—Crépuscule: Massenet
Twilight—Skymning (Ljus och skugga): Palmgren
Twilight—Crépuscule: Rhené-Baton
Twilight—Zwielicht: Schumann
Twilight dropping down—Dämmerung senkt: Brahms
Twilight falls to earth—Dämmerung senkt: Brahms
Twilight from above—Dämmerung senkte sich von oben: Schoeck
The twilight hour—Abenddämmerung: Brahms
The twilight of the gods—Gotterdämmerung: Wagner
Two brown eyes—To brune Öjne: Grieg
Two captives—Die Gefangenen: Blumenthal
Two columbines together—Deux ancolies se balançaient (Tristesses): Milhaud
Two comely maidens—Es gingen zwei Gespielen gut: Schoenberg
The two comrades—Frühlingsfahrt: Schumann
The two days—Les deux journées: Cherubini
The two deeps—Die Meere: Brahms
Two elegies—Két elégia: Bartók
Two faded roses—Zwei welke Rosen: R Franz
The two Foscari—I due Foscari: Verdi
The two grenadiers—Die beiden Grenadiere: Schumann
Two hazel eyes—To brune Öjne: Grieg
Two hearts in three-quarter time—Zwei Herzen im Dreivierteltakt: Stolz
The two marksmen—Die beiden Schützen: Lortzing
The two pathways—Die zwei Tugenswege: Schubert
Two pictures—Két kép: Bartók
Two pork cutlets—Zwei Schweinekarbonaden: Seiber
Two portraits—Két portré [orchestral]: Bartók
Two portraits—Két arckép: Bartók
Two Romanian dances—Két Román tánc: Bartók
Two rondels of Charles d'Orléans—Deux rondels de Charles d'Orléans: Debussy
The two shy people—I due timidi: Rossini
Twofold end—Dwojaki koniec: Chopin
Ty ukvalsky kostelicku—Yon little church: Janáček
Tyteberet—The berry/Wild berries: Grieg

U

U maměnky—At home: Martinů
U potoka—At the brook: Dvořák
Über allen Gipfeln ist Ruh'/Wanderers Nachtlied—All around is silence
   and rest/Over hill and vale/Wanderer's night song: Liszt
Über allen Gipfeln ist Ruh'/Wanderers Nachtlied—Everywhere the
   moorland is still/Song of the night: Loewe
Über allen Gipfeln ist Ruh'/Wanderers Nachtlied—O'er the forest branches/
   Lull'd are all the breezes/Night has cast her shadow/Night descends
   in peace: Schubert
Über den Wellen—O'er the billows: Franckenstein
Über der dunklen Heide—Far o'er the moorland reaches: Henschel
Über die Grenzen des All . . .—Over the brink of beyond: Berg
Über die Heide—Over the moor: Brahms
Über die tausend Berge (Lieder der Liebe)—Over the thousand mountains:
   Kilpinen
L'ubriaco—The drunkard: Malipero
Ucca, ucca, 'eg az ucca—The street is on fire: Bartók
Gli ucelli—The birds: Respighi
Ud går du nu på livets vej—Now you start out on the road of life:
   Nielsen
Udfarten—Outward bound: Grieg
Die Uhr—The clock: Loewe
Ujigyakorlat (Tiz könnyű zongoradarab)—Finger exercise: Bartók
Ukradennoye schast'ye—Stolen happiness: Dan'kevych
Ukroshchenie stroptivoy—The taming of the shrew: Shebalin
Ukvalské pisně—The songs of Hukvaldy: Janáček
Die Ulme zu Hirsau—The elm of Hirsau: R Strauss
L'ultima canzone—'Tis whispered: Tosti
Ultima rosa—Lingering, lonely rose: Sibella
Ulvens søn—Son of the wolf: Nielsen
Um deine Liebe—To win thy love: Dohnányi
Um Mitternacht—At midnight: Bruch
Um Mitternacht—In stilly night/The approach of night: R Franz
Um Mitternacht—At midnight hour/At midnight: Mahler
Um Mitternacht—At midnight the blushing roses: Reger
Um Mitternacht—At midnight: Wolf
Um schlimme Kinder artig zu machen—How to make naughty children
   good: Mahler
Umsonst—In vain: R Franz
Un bel di (Madama Butterfly)—One fine day: Puccini
Un di, ero piccina (Iris)—Once in my childhood: Mascagni
Un di la bella clori—One day with Cupid playing: Cesarini

Das Unaufhörliche—The perpetual/The incessant: Hindemith
Unbegehrt—Forsaken: Reger
Unbewegte lave Luft—Not a breath in heaven stirs: Brahms
Und die Rosen, die prangen—And the roses, they flourish: R Franz
Und gehst du über den Kirchhof—If through the church yard/O should'st
thou pass: Brahms
Und hab' so grosse—Love-longings: Reger
Und gestern hat er mir Rosen gebracht—Last eve he brought me/Yesterday
roses he brought me: J Marx
Und ob die Wolke (Die Freischütz)—What though the clouds: Weber
Und schäfst du, mein Mädchen—Day-break: Schumann
Und sprich—And say: Liszt
Und unser lieben Frauen—And in a dream: Bauernfeind
Und wüssten's die Blumen (Dichterliebe)—If even the flow'rets/The
broken heart/Grief: Schumann
Under the apple-tree—Pod jabloni: Suk
Under the lilacs—Flieder: Reger
Under the lime-tree—Bei der Linde: R Franz
Under the roofs of Paris—Sous les toits de Paris: Moretti
Under the trees—Sous les branches: Bossi
Underlige Aftenlufte—Wondrous fragrance in the evening: Nielsen
The undiscovered country—L'ile inconnue (Les nuits d'été): Berlioz
Unendliche Freude—The heart here wells over: Schubert
Unentrinnbar—Inescapable: Schoenberg
Unerhört—Unheard: Cornelius
The unexpected meeting—La rencontre imprévue: Gluck
Unfall—A mishap: Wolf
Unfold thou frozen Christ—Blüh auf, gefrorner Christ: Wellesz
Ungarische Tänze—Hungarian dances: Brahms
Ungbirken—The young birch (tree)/The birch tree: Grieg
Ungeduld (Die schöne Müllerin)—Impatience/Thine is my heart: Schubert
Ungeduld—I'd carve it on the bark: Schubert-Heller
Ein ungefärbt Gemüte—A soul that loves God purely: Bach
Unglückliche Liebe/Als Luis die Briefe—Unrequited love/Love-letters:
Mozart
The unhappy lover—Smutný milý: Martinů
Unheard—Unerhört: Cornelius
Uninhibited—Frech und froh: Wolf
United are we—Freiwillige her!: Brahms
Universi populi—Voice your joy together now: Praetorius
The unknown land—L'ile inconnue (Les nuits d'été): Berlioz
The unlucky fisherman—Wie ulfru Fischt: Schubert
The unquenchable—Det Uudslukkelige: Nielsen
Unrequited love—Unglückliche Liebe: Mozart

Uns ist ein Kind geboren—To us a child is born: Bach

Uns ist ein Kindlein heut' gebor'n—Now cheer our hearts this eventide:
  Bach

Unser Leben ist ein Schatten—Our days are as a shadow: J Bach

Unser Mund sei voll Lachens—Let our hearts e'er be joyful/Let our
  mouth be full of laughter: Bach

Unser taglich Brot gib uns heute—Give us this day our daily bread:
  Cornelius

Unspoken love—Verschweigene Liebe: Wolf

Unspoken words—Musica proibita: Gastaldon

Unter deinen Schirmen (Jesu meine Freude)—In Thine arm I rest me:
  Bach

Unter dem Mandelbaum—Beneath the almond tree: Henschel

Unter'm Fenster—Beneath the window: Schumann

Die Unterscheidung: Difference: Schubert

Unto Christ the victim—Victimae paschali: Byrd

Unto sin oppose resistance—Widerstehe doch der Sünde: Bach

Unto us this day is born—Natus est nobis: Vittoria

Untreu—Faithless: Cornelius

Unvergessen—A memory: Reger

Unverlierbare Gewähr (Lieder um dem Tod)—Sure and certain hope:
  Kilpinen

Up! Lords of Erebus—O voi dell' Erebo (La resurrezione): Handel

Up there on the hill—Wer hat dies Liedlein erdacht? (Des Knaben
  Wunderhorn): Mahler

Up, up my heart with gladness—Auf, auf! mein Herz, mit Freuden: Bach

Up, up, with trumpet tone—Auf, auf, mit hellem Schall (Auf Christi
  Himmelfahrt allein): Bach

Up with the glossy holly—Nichts labt mich mehr als Wein: Mozart

Uphold us, Lord, with Thy word—Erhalt uns, Herr, bei deinem Wort:
  Bach

Upon the tufted branches—An wollen Buschelzweigen: R Kahn

L'uragano—The hurricane: Rocca

Urlicht—Pimeval light: Mahler

Urna fatale del mio destino (La forza del destino)—Ill-omen'd coffer:
  Verdi

O ursozinho de algodâo (A prolé do bêbê)—The little cotton bear:
  Villa Lobos

Usez mieux, O beautés fières—Hark to me, oh ye fair maidens: Lully

Ut eruas nos a malis—Deliver us from all evil: Byrd

Ute i Skären—The outermost isles: Myström

Det Uudslukkelige [song]—The unquenchable: Nielsen

Det Uudslukkelige [symphony]—The inextinguishable: Nielsen

V

V buryu—In the storm: Khrennokov

V dobrým sme se sešil (Moravské Dvojzpěvy)—Parting without sorrow: Dvořák

V lese—In the woods: Smetana

V ogne/Pod Moskvoy—In the fire/Near Moscow: Kabalevsky

V přírodě—In nature's realm: Dvořák

V tej bystrickej bráne—Roses in the field: Bartók

V zoufalství—Desolation: Smetana

Và godendo vezzoso e bello (Serse)—Trip, blithe streamlet: Handel

Va, Speme infida, pur—Go thou false and fickle hope: Handel

Vaarmorgen i skogen—Spring morning in the wood: A Backer-Grøndahl

Vachissima sembianza—The portrait: Donaudy

Vado a morir (Arminio)—I go to death: Handel

Vado ben spesso—Roam as I may/The guiding light: Rosa

Vado, ma dove?—Whither I'm going, I know not: Mozart

V'adoro, pupille (Giulio Cesare)—Ye dear eyes/I adore you arrows of love: Handel

Vaegtersang—Watchman's song: Grieg

Vaerhilset, Damer—Your servant, fair ladies/Be greeted, you ladies: Grieg

Vaga Rosa—Trailing rose-tree: Kreutzer

The vagabond—La vagabonde: Bloch

The vagabond and the princess—Der Vagabond und die Prinzessin: Poldini

Der Vagabond und die Prinzessin—The vagabond and the princess: Poldini

La vagabonde—The vagabond: Bloch

Vaghe pupille, no non piangete (Orlando)—Eyes, cease from weeping: Handel

La vague et la cloche—The wave and the bell: Duparc

A vágyak éjjele—Night of desire: Bartók

Vai, azulão—My bluebird: Guarnieri

Vain his pleading—Vergebliches Ständchen: Brahms

Vain is all lamentation—Vani soni i lamenti (Giulio Cesare): Handel

Vain is the power—Wehe, so willst du: Brahms

Vain serenade—Vergebliches Ständchen: Brahms

The vain suit—Vergebliches Ständchen: Brahms

Vain the pomp of fun'ral splendour—Pompe vane di morte (Rodelinda): Handel

Vainement Pharaon (Joseph)—Vainly Pharaoh: Méhul

Vainly first I sought to bear it—Anfangs wollt' ich fast verzagen: Liszt

Vainly Pharaoh—Vainement Pharaon (Joseph): Méhul

Vaisseaux, nous vous aurons aimés (L'horizon chimérique)—Ships, we have loved you: Fauré

Valdstejn—Wallenstein: Weinberger

The vale of rest—Ruhetal: Mendelssohn
Válečnik: The soldier: Smetana
A valediction—Der schwere Abend: Blumenthal
A valediction—Abschied: Wolf
Valet will ich dir geben—Farewell I gladly bid Thee: Bach
Valiant—Mutiges Lied: Blech
The Valkyrie—Die Walküre: Wagner
The valley—Le vallon: Gounod
The valley—Das Tal: R Strauss
Le vallon—The valley: Gounod
La valse—The waltz: Ravel
Vandring i Skoven—Wandering in the wood/Wood wandering/Woodland
    wandering: Grieg
Vani sono i lamenti (Giulio Cesare)—Vain is all lamentation: Handel
Vanished days—Svundne Dage: Grieg
Vanne, segu' il mio desio (Floridante)—O, what pleasure: Handel
Vänskapens blomma—Friendship: Sibelius
Var et en dröm—Was it a dream?: Sibelius
Våren—Springtide/Spring/Springtime: Grieg
Våren flyktar hastigt—Spring is flying: Sibelius
Várj meg madaram—Stay, sweet bird: Kodály
Varjojen saari—Island of shadows: Palmgren
Vårtagen—The spell of springtide: Sibelius
En Varvisa—The trouble of spring: Palmgren
Der Vater hat ihm ja ein ewig (Gott fähret auf mit Jauchzet)—The
    Father hath appointed him: Bach
Vater unser, der du bist im Himmel—Our Father, who art in heaven:
    Cornelius
Vater unser im Himmelreich—Our Father in heaven: Bach
Vater unser im Himmelreich (Orgelbüchlein)—Our Father, Thou in
    heav'n above: Bach
Die Vätergruft—The last of his clan: Liszt
Vázlatok—Seven sketches: Bartók
Věc Makropulos—The Makropulos affair: Janáček
Večerní písně—Evening songs: Smetana
Vechera u Dome Usher—Remembrance of the House of Usher:
    G Karnovitch
Ved en ung hustrus Båre—At the bier of a young woman: Grieg
Ved en ung kunstners båre—At the bier of a young artist: Nielsen
Ved Gjaetle-bekken (Haugtussa)—Mountain brook: Grieg
Ved moders Grav—At mother's grave: Grieg
Ved Rundarne—On the way home/The wanderer's return/Memories
    of childhood: Grieg
Vedi! le fosche (Trovatore)—See how the darkness/Gipsy chorus/Anvil
    chorus: Verdi

Vedrai carino, se sei buonino (Don Giovanni)—Come let me prove thee/
Rose-leaves are falling/If you will promise me/Smile and I'll teach
thee: Mozart

Veggio co' bei vostri occhi un dolce lume (Sonnets of Michelangelo)—
With your lovely eyes: Britten

Végigmentem a Tárkányi—I walked to the end of the great street in
Tárkány: Bartók

Veil your lightnings—M'allontano sdegnose pupille (Atalanta): Handel

Veilchen—The violet/Violets: Cornelius

Das Veilchen—The violet: Liszt

Das Veilchen—The violet: Mozart

Velet' vtáčku (Moravské Dvojzpěvy)—Speed thee, birdie/Regret: Dvořák

Velikaya druzhba—The great friendship: Muradeli

Veljeni vierailla mailla—Brotherhood: Sibelius

Venematka—Boat journey: Sibelius

Venetian air—Venezianisches Lied (Myrthen): Schumann

The Venetian regatta—La regata Veneziana: Rossini

Venetianisches Gondollied—When through the piazzetta/Row gently here:
Mendelssohn

Venez, ma bien aimée (Tristesses)—O come, dear loved one: Milhaud

Venez sous la tonelle (Tristesses)—O come into the arbour: Milhaud

Venez, venez (Titon et l'Aurore)—Sing on: Mondonville

Venezianisches Lied (Myrthen)—Venetian air: Schumann

Vengeance, vengeance—Parto, parto, ma tu ben mio (La clemenza di Tito):
Mozart

Veni Domine—O come quickly Lord: Byrd

Veni, Domine—Hear my prayer, O Lord: Mendelssohn

Venite comedite—O come ye: Byrd

Le vent de l'Esprit (Messe de la Pentecôte)—The wind of the Holy Spirit:
Messiaen

Venus im Grünen—Shrove Tuesday carnival: Straus

Les vepres siciliennes—The Sicilian vespers: Verdi

Ver aeternum—Eternal spring: Goltermann

La vera constanza—True constancy: Haydn

Verachtest du den Reichtum seiner Gnade? (Herr, deine Augen sehen nach
dem Glauben)—Despisest thou the riches of His goodness?: Bach

Verachtet mir die Meister nicht (Die Meistersinger von Nürnberg)—Despise t
not: Wagner

Verborgene Liebe—A secret: Kjerulf

Verborgenheit—Reserve: R Franz

Verborgenheit—Withdrawal/Seclusion: Wolf

Verbum supernum prodiens—The word descending from above: Tallis

Verbundenheit—Obligation: Schoenberg

Verdankt sei es dem Glanz/Mich locket nicht—Dear placid vale/I seek
not glory: Mozart

Verdant meadows—Verdi prati (Alcina): Handel
Verdant pastures—Verdi prati (Alcina): Handel
Un verde practicello—The fairest mead: Wolf-Ferrari
Verdi prati (Alcina)—Verdant meadows/Verdant pastures: Handel
Verfehlte Liebe—Misplaced affection: R Franz
Verführung—Seduction: R Strauss
Vergangen ist mir Glück und Heil—Of ev'ry joy I am bereft/No more
    can earthly joy be mine: Brahms
Vergebliches Ständchen—The vain suit/The disappointed serenader/
    Vain serenade/Vain his pleading: Brahms
Verger—Orchard: Hindemith
Vergessen—Forebodings: R Franz
Vergib uns uns're Schuld—Forgive us our trespasses: Cornelius
Vergiftet sind meine Lieder—My songs are poisoned: Liszt
Vergintutt' amor—Virgin, fount of love: Durante
Vergine chiara—Virgin whose glory: Palestrina
La verginella come la rosa—Love for the first time: Bertoni
Vergiss es ferner nicht (Wir danken dir, Gott, wir danken dir)—Forget
    us not, O Lord: Bach
Vergiss mein nicht—Forget-me-not/Say you will not forget: E de Curtis
Vergiss mein nicht—Forget me not: R Franz
Vergiss mein nicht—Forget me not: Mozart
Vergiss mein nicht, mein allerliebster Gott—Forget me not/Forsake me
    not: Bach
Das Verhör des Lukullus—The trial of Lucullus: Dessau
Verily I say unto you—Wahrlich, wahrlich, ich sage euch: Bach
Verklärte Nacht—Transfigured night: Schoenberg
Verlass' mich nicht—Forsake me not: R Franz
Verlassen—Forsaken: Liszt
Verlassen—Forsaken: Schoenberg
Das verlassene Mägdlein—The forsaken maiden: Goetz
Das verlassene Mägdlein—The deserted servant-girl/The girl left lonely/
    The deserted maiden: Schumann
Das verlassene Mägdlein—The girl left lonely: Wolf
Der verliebte Jäger—The lovesick hunter: Reger
Der verlorene Haufen—The lost battalion: Schoenberg
Verlorene Jugend—Lost youth: Brahms
Die verlorene Tochter—The lost daughter: Loewe
Verlorne Müh (Des Knaben Wunderhorn)—Wasted effort/Labour lost:
    Mahler
Verlust—Loss: Cornelius
Verlust—Forsaken/Bereavement/The broken heart: F Mendelssohn
Vernügt Ruh'—O blessed rest: Bach
Ein verrathenes Geheimnis—The betrayed secret: Blumenthal
Verratene Liebe—Love betrayed: Schumann

Verrath—Treachery: Brahms
Verrath—The betrayal: Meyer-Helmund
Verrufene Stelle (Waldscenen)—Haunted spot/Haunted place: Schumann
Versatility—Vielseitigkeit: Schoenberg
Verschling der Mogrund (Italienisches Liederbuch)—Let an abyss/May chasms engulf: Wolf
Die Verschweigung/Sobald Damoetas Chloen sieht—When first young Damon/Damon and Chloe: Mozart
Verschwiegene Liebe—Silent love/Love that keeps its council/Unspoken love: Wolf
Die Verschwiegenen—The flowers' secret: R Strauss
Die verschwiegene Nachtigall—The nightingale: Grieg
Die Verschworenen—The conspirators/The household war: Schubert
Versiegelt—Sealed (in): Blech
Verstolen geht der Mond auf—So silly doth the moon hide: Brahms
Verstumme Höllenheer (Wo soll ich fliehen hin)—Be silent, Host of Hell: Bach
Versunken—Engulfed: Brahms
Versunken—Enraptured: Schubert
Vértanuk Sirjánál—At the martyr's grave: Kodály
Vert-vert—The green parrot: Offenbach
Verwechslung—An error: Meyer-Helmund
Very bread—Bone pastor: Palestrina
Verzagen—Lament: Brahms
Verzicht, O Herz (Neue Liebeslieder)—There's nought, O heart: Brahms
Der verzweifelte Liebhaber—The despairing lover: Wolf
Verzweiflung—Despair: Brahms
Die Verzweiflung—Despair: Haydn
Veselá dievča—The gay girl: Martinů
Veslemøy (Haugtussa)—The mountain maid: Grieg
Vesna svyashchennaya—The rite(s) of spring: Stravinsky
Vesnon'ko, vesno—In springtime: Stetsenko
Vesnyanky—Springtime: Barvins'kyi
Vesnyanky—Springtime: Verykivskyi
Vespers—Vespro della beata Vergine: Monteverdi
Vespro della beata Vergine—Vespers: Monteverdi
The vessel storm driven—Qual nave smarrita (Radamisto): Handel
Vesti la giubba (Pagliacci)—On with the motley: Leoncavallo
Vetrate di chiesa—Church windows: Respighi
Der Vetter aus Dingsda—The cousin from nowhere: Künneke
La veuve—The widow: P Cannon
Vex no more, sad melancholy—Weichet nur, betrübte Schatten: Bach
La vezzosa pastorella—In the cool and dewy morning: Bruni
Vezzosette e care/Pupillette—Oh! sweet eyes so ardently: Falconieri

334

Vi sletternes sønner (Tove)—We sons of the plains: Nielsen
Victimae paschali—Unto Christ the victim: Byrd
Victorious my heart is—Vittoria, mio core: Carissimi
Victorious, victorious—Vittoria! vittoria!: Carissimi
The victor's return—Deutschland: Mendelssohn
The victory—Der Sieg: Schubert
The victory's won—Vittoria, mio core: Carissimi
La vida breve—Life is short: Falla
Vide Domine afflictionem—Behold, O Lord God: Byrd
La vie—Life: Pierné
La vie antérieure—The former life: Duparc
La vie parisienne—Parisian life: Offenbach
Der vielschönen Fraue—To the beautiful lady: R Franz
Vielseitigkeit—Versatility: Schoenberg
Vieni, deh vien, la notte è placide—Come with me: Catalani
Vieni, mi disse un giorno—Hither to thee once spoke: Magaldi
Vieni o figlio (Ottone)—Come to me, soothing sleep: Handel
Vieni·omai, deh vieni—Come, O death: Cesti
Vieni, torna, idolo mio (Teseo)—Come now, turn now: Handel
Vienna, city of my dreams—Wien, du Stadt meiner Träume: Sieczÿnski
Vienna girls—Weaner Mad'ln: Ziehrer
Vienna maidens—Weaner Mad'ln: Ziehrer
Viens—Come: Godard
Viens!—Come: Saint-Saëns
Viens aurore—Come sweet morning: A L(ehmann)
Viens, les gazons sont vert—Come, the lawns are green: Gounod
Viens, mon bien-aimé—Come, my love, to me: Chaminade
Vier ernste Gesänge—Four serious songs: Brahms
Vier Husarenlieder—Four hussar songs: Schumann
Vier letzte Lieder—Four last songs: R Strauss
La Vièrge à la crèche—Mary at the cradle: Franck
Der vierjährige Posten—The four years' sentry: Schubert
Vieux chant à danser—In the hay: Borjan
Vigil—Kinderwacht: Schumann
Vigilate—Watch ye alway/Be ye watchful: Byrd
The village—Das Dorf: Reger
The village band—Die Dorfmusik: Fryberg
Village dance—A falu tánca (Két kép): Bartók
Village gossip—Mer hahn en neue Oberkeet: Bach
Village scenes—Dedinské Scény: Bartók
The village songstress—Die Dorfsängerinnen: Fioravanti
Village scenes—Falun: Bartók
The village soothsayer—Le devin du village: Rousseau
The village without a bell—Das Dorf ohne Glocke: Künneke

Villager's song—Ländliches Lied (Album für die Jugend): Schumann
Villanelle (Les nuits d'été)—Love in May: Berlioz
Villanelle—Landliches Lied: Schumann
Villanelle des petits canards—Villanelle of the little ducks: Chabrier
Villanelle of the little ducks—Villanelle des petits canards: Chabrier
Ville chérie, o ma patrie (Les cloches de Corneville)—With joy in my heart: Planquette
Le villi—The witch: Puccini
Vilse—Astray: Sibelius
Le vinherbe—The magic potion: Martin
Vinets—From the depth of the ocean: Brahms
Vintage song—Weinlesezeit (Album für die Jugend): Schumann
Vintage time—Weinlesezeit (Album für die Jugend): Schumann
Vintovochka—The little rifle: Davidenko
The violet—Veilchen: Cornelius
The violet—Das Veilchen: Mozart
Violets—Veilchen: Cornelius
The violets—Le violette: A Scarlatti
Le violette—Dewy violets/The violets: A Scarlatti
Violin—Violon (Fiancailles pour rire): Poulenc
Violino Tzigano—Serenade in the night: Bixio
Violon (Fiancailles pour rire)—Violin: Poulenc
Virágzás (Két kép)—In full flower: Bartók
Virgin, fount of love—Vergin tutt' amor: Durante
Virgin soil upturned—Podnystaya tselina: Dzerzhinsky
Virgin whose glory—Vergine chiara: Palestrina
The Virgin's slumber-song—Maria Wiegenlied: Reger
The Virgin's threads—Fils de la Vièrge: Schmitt
Viri Galilei—Ye men of Galilee: Byrd
A vision—Eit Syn: Grieg
The vision—Das Traumbild: Mozart
The vision—Prizrak: Prokofiev
Vision—Allnächtlich im Traume (Dichterliebe): Schumann
Vision entrancing—Dolce pensiero (Semiramide): Rossini
A vision of glory—In goldener Fülle: R Strauss
The vision of Isaiah—Des Gesicht Jesajas: Burkhard
Vision of the night—Bild der Nacht: Curschmann
The visit to the tomb—Visitatio sepulchri: Anon
Visitatio sepulchri—The visit to the tomb: Anon
The visitation—Die Heimschung: Schuller
Vissi d'arte, vissi d'amore (Tosca)—Love and music: Puccini
Visslaren och hans hund—The whistler and his dog: Pryor
Vittoria, mio core/Vittoria! vittoria!—The victory's won/I triumph!
    I triumph/Victorious my heart is/Victorious, victorious: Carissimi

Vittoria! vittoria!/Vittoria, mio core—The victory's won/I triumph!
     I triumph/Victorious my heart is/Victorious, victorious: Carissimi
Viva il vino (Cavalleria rusticana)—See the merry wine: Mascagni
Vivere per penare (Floridante)—Shall I endure this anguish?: Handel
Vivete in pace (Nerone)—Abide in peace: Boito
Vizkereszt—Epiphany: Kodály
Vltava—The Moldau: Smetana
Vo far guerra (Rinaldo)—I'll wage war: Handel
Voce di donna (La gioconda)—Thanks unto thee: Ponchielli
Una voce poco fa (Il barbiere di Siviglia)—There is a voice within my
     heart/Tho' his voice was breath'd afar: Rossini
Voda a plác (Moravské Dvojzpěvy)—Sad of heart: Dvořák
Vodník—The water goblin: Dvořák
Die Vögel—The birds: Schubert
Vögel als Prophet (Waldscenen)—Prophet bird: Schumann
Der Vögelhändler—The bird-seller: Zeller
Das Vöglein—The little bird: Wolf
Vöglein durchrauscht (Liebeslieder Walzer)—Bird in the air: Brahms
Die Vöglein im Walde—Birdie in the wood: Kreutzer
Vöglein Schwermut (Lieder um den Tod)—The little bird despair: Kilpinen
Vöglein, wohin so schnell?—Bird, say whither thy flight?: R Franz
Vöglein, wohin so schnell?—Swallow, where flies thou?: Kjerulf
Vöglein, wohin so schnell?—Birdling, whither away?/Songster, whither
     away?: Lassen
Voglio chinar la fronte—Fain would I bow: Magaldi
Voglio provar (Amore traditore)—Now shalt be known: Bach (?)
Voi, amanti, che vedete—All you lovers: Giardini
Voi avete un cor fedele—You've a heart benign and loyal: Mozart
Voi che sapete (Le nozze di Figaro)—Say gentle ladies/Ladies pray tell me/
     Say ye who borrow/Tell me fair ladies/How can love?/You who have
     knowledge/Ye who have duly learnt/Ye who of loving: Mozart
The voice—Ein Ton: Cornelius
A voice from the hills—Ruf vom Berge: Beethoven
The voice of Jesus—Jelenti magát Jézus: Kodály
Voice of love—Stimme der Liebe: Schubert
The voice of one saying—Vox dicentis clama: E W Naylor
The voice of the tempest—Mädchens Klage: Schubert-Heller
Voice of the woods—Waldesgespräch: Schumann
Voice your joy together now—Universi populi: Praetorius
Voices of spring—Frühlingsstimmen: J Strauss II
Voices of spring—Frühlingsgedränge: R Strauss
Voices of the summer night—Nachtgeflüster: Reger
Voina i mir/Voyna i mir—War and peace: Prokofiev
Volkskinderlieder—Children's folk-songs: Brahms

Volkslied—National song/The swallow/The swallow's flying west: Brahms
Volkslied—For what, for what may prove: R Franz
Volkslied/Es ist bestimmt—Mourn not: Mendelssohn
Volksliedchen—Little folk song/My William/Green hat/When at early
dawn/Love-thoughts/Folk song: Schumann
Voll jener Süsse—Filled with that sweetness: Schoenberg
Vollendet ist das grosse Werk (Die Schöpfung)—Achieved is the glorious
work: Haydn
Volo di notte—Night flight: Dallapiccola
Volta la terrea fronte alle stelle (Un ballo in maschera)—Reading the
stars: Verdi
Vom Auge zum Herzen—From the eye to the heart: R Franz
Eine vom Ballet—The dancing Viennese: Straus
Vom Berge—On the mountain: R Franz
Vom Fischer un syner Fru—The fisherman and his wife: Schoeck
Vom Gebirge (Neue Liebeslieder)—From yon hills: Brahms
Vom Hausregiment—Of household rule: Hindemith
Vom Heideknaben—The heather boy: Schumann
Vom Himmel sank—From heaven sank: R Kahn
Vom Küssen—From kissing: Reger
Vom Schlaraffenland—Cloud cuckoo land: Schubert
Vom Tode—Death: Beethoven
Vom verwundetung Knaben—The wounded lover/The wounded youth:
Brahms
Von alten Liebesliedern—Before my fair one's window: Brahms
Von dem Landleben—Country-life: Keiser
Von den sieben Zechbrüdern—The seven boon-companions: R Strauss
Von der Jugend (Das Lied von der Erde)—A song of youth/Youth/
About youth: Mahler
Von der Liebe—Love: Reger
Von der Schönheit (Das Lied von der Erde)—A song of beauty/Beauty/
About beauty: Mahler
Von dunklem Schleier—Night gloom and shadows: R Strauss
Von edler Art—Tender and pure: Brahms
Von ewiger Liebe—Love is for ever/Eternal love/Love eternal/Love
triumphant: Brahms
Von fremden Ländern (Kinderscenen)—From foreign lands and people/
From foreign parts/Of strange countries: Schumann
Von Gott kommt mir ein Freudenschein (Erschallet, ihr Lieder)—A
heavenly light falls from the sky: Bach
Von Gott will ich nicht lassen—From God shall nought divide me: Bach
Von Heute auf Morgen—From today till tomorrow: Schoenberg
Von Himmelhoch—From heaven above to earth I come: Schein
Von Himmel hoch da komm ich her (Orgelbüchlein)—From Heaven
above to earth I come: Bach

Von Waldberkkränzter höhe—From where the upland towers: Brahms

Vonò Dag (Haugtussa)—An evil day: Grieg

Vor deinen Thron tret' ich hermit—Before Thy throne, my God, I
 stand: Bach

Vor dem Fenster—By the window/At the window/Her window: Brahms

Vor der Tür—At the door/The coquette and her lover: Brahms

Vor meiner Wiege—The cradle: Schubert

Vorabend (Brautlieder)—Evening: Cornelius

Vorbeimarsch—Riding past: Reger

Vergefühl—Premonition: Schoenberg

Vorrei—Could I: Tosti

Vorrei morire! —Oh! let me die: Tosti

Vorrei spiegarvi, oh Dio—If I, oh heaven, could tell you: Mozart

Vorresti si vorresti—Thy hope would hear me: D Scarlatti

Vorsatz—Resolution: Lassen

Vorspiel (Spanische Liebeslieder)—Prelude: Schumann

Vorüber—Long ago: Brahms

Vorüber die stuhnende Klage—Forgotten, forgotten: Schubert

Il vostro maggio (Rinaldo)—Lose not the hours/Song of the sirens:
 Handel

Votre toast, je peux vous la rendre (Carmen)—To your toast/Sirs,
 your toast/The toreador's song: Bizet

Vou-me embora—Farewell: Guarnieri

Vous aimerez demain—Tomorrow you will love: Massenet

Vous m'avez regardé (Tristesses)—In your eyes: Milhaud

Vous tous qui la terre—Make ye a joyful sounding noyse: Le Jeune

The vow—Der Schwur: Reger

The vow of faith—Zajata (Moravské Dvojzpévy): Dvořák

Vox dicentis clama—The voice of one saying: E W Naylor

The voyage—L'invitation au voyage: Duparc

Voyage à Paris—Trip to Paris: Poulenc

Voyage to Hades—Fahrt zum Hades: Schubert

Le voyageur—The traveller: Godard

Voyez le tort d'amour—The harm of love: Sandrin

Voyne i mir/Voina i mir—War and peace: Prokofiev

Vozvrashcheniye solntsa—The return of the sun: Golub'yov

Vrazh'ya sila—The power of evil/Hostile force/The power of the
 enemy: Serov

Vsevydy ashcheye Oko—The all-seeing eye: Radziyevs'kyi

Vstavaite lyndi russkiye! (Aleksandr Nevsky)—Arise ye Russian people:
 Prokofiev

Vtak mnohém s roci mrtvo jest (Pisné milostné)—Death reigns in many
 a human breast: Dvořák

Vté sladké moci (Pisné milostné)—When thy sweet glances: Dvořák

Vug, o Vove—Waft, oh waters: Grieg

Vuggesang—Cradle song/Father's cradle-song: Grieg

Vuggesang i mørketiden—Cradle song in the northern winter: F Backer-Grøndahl

Vulcan's song—Au bruit des lourds (Philémon et Baucis): Gounod

Vuře Šuhaj, vuře (Moravské dvojzpěvy)—The last wish: Dvořák

Vybukh—Explosion: Yanovskyi

Výlety páně Broučkovy—Mr Broucek's excursion to the moon: Janáček

Vynruzka—The threat: Janáček

Vysoká veža—The high steeple: Martinů

Vždy odolal jsem čarozraku (Dalibor)—I ever have withstood a woman's charms: Smetana

Vznikající vášeň—Rising passion: Smetana

W

Wach auf mein Herzensschöne—Awake, my pretty maiden/Awake, my love, my sweeting: Brahms

Wach auf, mein Hort—Awake, sweet joy: Brahms

Wachet auf, ruft uns die Stimme—Now let every tongue above Thee/Glory now to Thee be given/Sleepers, wake!: Bach

Wachet auf, ruft uns die Stimme—Wake, awake, for night is flying: Bach

Wachet auf, ruft uns die Stimme—Wake, awake for night is flying: Buxtehude

Wachet, betet, seid bereit allezeit—Watch ye, pray ye: Bach

Wacht auf, ihr Adern und ihr Glieden (Unser Mund sei voll Lachens)—Awake, my powers and all within me: Bach

Wacht auf, wacht auf, verlorne Schafe (O Ewigkeit du Donnerwort)—Awake, awake, ye sheep that wander: Bach

Der Wachtelschlag—The quail: Beethoven

Der Wachtelschlag—The quail: Schubert

Wachterlied auf der Wartburg—Watchman's song of the tower: Wolf

Der Waffenschmied von Worms—The armourer: Lortzing

Waft, oh waters—Vug, o Vove: Grieg

Wahn! Wahn! (Die Meistersinger von Nürnberg)—Mad! Mad!: Wagner

Wahre Liebe—True love: Hindemith

Wahre, wahre deinen Sohn (Neue Liebeslieder)—Guard thy son: Brahms

Während des Regens—While the rain falls: Brahms

Wahrlich, wahrlich, ich sage euch—Truly, truly, I say unto you/Verily, verily, I say unto you: Bach

Wailing, crying, mourning, sighing—Weinen, Klagen, Sorgen, Zagen: Bach

Die Waise—The orphan: Grieg

Die Waise—The orphan girl: Schumann

Waiting—Erwartung: Wolf

Waiting—Wartend: Mendelssohn

Waiting—Erwartung: Wolf

The waiting one—L'attente: Saint-Saëns

Waiting on Thee—Oculi omnium: Byrd

Wake, awake, for night is flying—Wachet auf, ruft uns die Stimme: Bach

Wake, awake, for night is flying—Wachet auf, ruft uns die Stimme: Buxtehude

Wake me from sleep—Resveillez moi: Garnier

Wake, the welcome day appeareth—Jesus unser Trost und Leben: Bach

Wake up, my dear—Chanson de la mariée: Ravel

Waken lords and ladies gay—Jagdlied: Mendelssohn

Der Wald—The forest: Smyth

Waldeinsamkeit—Quiet of the woods: Reger

Waldesgespräch—Forest legend/Loreley/Dialogue in the woods/Overheard in the woods/Voice of the woods: Schumann

Waldesgrüss—The forest's greeting: Reinecke
Waldesnacht—Gloom of the woods: Brahms
Waldesrauschen—In the woods/Forest murmers: Liszt
Waldfahrt—The woods; R Franz
Waldmädchen—The wood fay: Schumann
Waldmädchen—The forest fairy: Wolf
Das Waldschloss—The enchanted castle/The forest castle: Mendelssohn
Waldseligkeit—Alone in the forest: R Strauss
Waldsonne—Woodland sunshine: Schoenberg
Waldszenen—Forest scenes: Schumann
Waldweben—Forest murmers (Siegfried): Wagner
Die Waldvögelein—The wood minstrels: Mendelssohn
Das Waldvöglein—The cushat dove: Anon
Waldvöglein—Fly forth, fly forth, my pretty dove: Ditforth
Waldvöglein's Bitte—The falcon: Gerle
Walk in the way of faith—Tritt auf die Glaubensbahn: Bach
The walk of the two lovers—Le promenoir des deux amants: Debussy
Die Walküre—The Valkyrie: Wagner
Walküren-ritt/Der Ritt der Walküren (Die Walküre)—Ride of the Valkyries:
    Wagner
Wallenstein—Valdsteyn: Weinberger
Der Wallensteiner Landknecht beim Trunk—Soldier's drinking song:
    Schubert
Die Wallfahrt nach Kevlaar—The pilgrimage to Kevlaar: Humperdinck
Walloon uplands—Fagnes de Wallonie: Poulenc
The walnut tree—Der Nussbaum (Myrthen): Schumann
Walpurgis night—Walpurgisnacht: Brahms
Walpurgisnacht—Walpurgis night: Brahms
The waltz—La valse: Ravel
A waltz dream—Ein Walzertraum: Straus
Waltz song—Ah! je veux vivre (Romeo et Juliette): Gounod
Waltzing the hours away—Tesoro mio: Becucci
Ein Walzertraum—A waltz dream: Straus
Die wandelnde Glocke—The bell that walked: Schumann
Ein Wanderer—A wanderer: Brahms
The wanderer—In der Fremde: R Franz
Der Wanderer—The wanderer: Schoenberg
The wanderer—Der Wanderer: Schoenberg
Wanderers Nachtlied—The wanderer's night song: Goetz
Wanderers Nachtlied/Über allen Gipfeln ist Ruh'—All around is silence
    and rest/Over hill and dale/Wanderer's night song: Liszt
Wanderers Nachtlied/Der du von dem Himmel bist—Song of the night/Thou
    who from Thy heavenly home: Loewe

Wanderers Nachtlied/Über allen Gipfeln ist Ruh'—Song of the night/
  Everywhere the moorland is still: Loewe
Wanderers Nachtlied/Der du von dem Himmel bist—Wanderer's night
  song/Thou that born of heaven art: J Marx
Wanderers Nachtlied/Über allen Gipfeln ist Ruh' (Schwanengesang)—
  O'er the forest branches/Lull'd are all the breezes/Night has cast
  her shadow/Night descends in peace/Wanderer's night-song: Schubert
Wanderers Nachtlied—Wanderer's song in the night: Wolf
The wanderer's night song—Wanderers Nachtlied: Goetz
Wanderer's night song—Wanderers Nachtlied: Liszt
Wanderer's night song—Wanderers Nachtlied: J Marx
The wanderer's night song—Wanderers Nachtlied (Schwanengesang):
  Schubert
The wanderer's return—Ved Rundarne: Grieg
Wanderer's song—Wanderlied: Schumann
Wanderer's song in the night—Wanderers Nachtlied: Wolf
Wanderer's song to the storm—Wanderers Sturmlied: R Strauss
Wanderers Sturmlied—The wanderer's song to the storm: R Strauss
Wandering—Das Wandern (Die schöne Müllerin): Schubert
Wandering—Wanderung: Schumann
Wandering in the wood—Vandring i Skoven: Grieg
Wandering miller—Das Wandern (Die schöne Müllerin): Schubert
The wandering minstrel—Der wanderne Musikant: Mendelssohn
Wandering minstrel—Der Musensohn: Schubert
The wandering minstrel—Der Musikant: Wolf
Das Wandern (Die schöne Müllerin)—Wandering/Wandering miller/A-roving:
  Schubert
Wanderlied—Wanderer's song/The farewell/A traveller's song/Song of
  travel: Schumann
Der wanderne Musikant—The wandering minstrel: Mendelssohn
Wanderträume—Dreams: Fielitz
Wanderung—Wandering: Schumann
Wandervöglein—The passage-bird: Goetz
Wandl' ich in dem Morgentau—Wand'ring in the morning: Wolf
Wandl' ich in dem Wald—When I in the dusky forest/When I walk in
  dreamy woodlands: R Franz
Wandlung—Transformation: Blumenthal
WANDRER . . . see WANDERER
Wand'rer by the tempest—Ein Obdach gegen Sturm: R Strauss
Wand'ring in the morning—Wandl' ich in dem Morgentau: Wolf
The waning—Le déclin: Bloch
Das Wappenschild—The coat-of-arms: Schoenberg
War and peace—Voyna i mir: Prokofiev
War es dir—'Twas for thee/O my love: Brahms

War Gott nicht mit uns diese Zeit—Were God not with us in this time: Bach

Wär ich der Regen—Wishes: Blumenthal

War march of the priests—Kriegsmarsch der Priester (Athalia): Mendelssohn

War song—Kriegslied (Album für die Jugend): Schumann

The warbling lark—En kviddrende Laerke: A Backer-Grøndahl

The warning—Die Warnung: Haydn

Warning—Warnung: Meyer-Helmund

Warning—Warnung: Mozart

Warning—Warnung: Reger

Warning—Warnung: Schoenberg

Warning—Warnung: Schumann

Warning against the Rhine—Warnung vor dem Rhein: Mendelssohn

Die Warnung—The warning: Haydn

Warnung—Warning: Meyer-Helmund

Warnung/Männer suchen stets zu Naschen—Warning/Gentle maid in life's sweet morning: Mozart

Warnung—Warning: Reger

Warnung—Warning: Schoenberg

Warnung—Warning: Schumann

Warnung vor dem Rhein—Warning against the Rhine/Beware of the Rhine/To the Rhine: Mendelssohn

The warrior—Wojak: Chopin

The warrior's farewell—Des Kriegers Abschied: Beethoven

The warrior's foreboding—Kriegers Ahnung (Schwanengesang): Schubert

Warrior's song—Kriegslied: Berlioz

Warrior's song—Kriegslied (Album für die Jugend): Schumann

Warte nur—Only wait: Reger

Wartend—Waiting: Mendelssohn

Warum?—Why?: Brahms

Warum? (Fantasiestücke)—Why?: Schumann

Warum betrübst du dich—Ah why such distress: Bach

Warum bin ich vergänglich—Wherefore am I: R Kahn

Warum ist das Licht gegeben—Wherefore now hath light/Wherefore hath the light/Therefore is light given: Brahms

Warum sind denn die Rosen—O why are all the roses so pale: Cornelius

Warum sollt ich mich denn grämen—Wherefore soul of mine, art grieving/All my heart today rejoices: Bach

Warum wollt ihr erschrecken? (Weihnachtsoratorium)—With fear why are ye taken?: Bach

Was betrübst du dich, mein Herze—Why cast down, my heart within me: Ba

Was betrübst du dich, meine Seele—Why so troubled?: Schütz

Was den Höchsten Glanz erfüllt (Höchsterwunschtes Freudenfest)—What God's splendour doth reveal: Bach

Was duftet doch der Flieder (Die Meistersinger von Nürnberg)—How
  sweet the elder smells/The scent of elders flow'ring: Wagner
Was fang' ich am'—What shall I do?: Blech
Was frag' ich nach der Welt (Sehet, welch eine Liebe hat uns der Vater
  erzeiget)—Let all with gladsome voices: Bach
Was fürchtst du, Feind Herodes, sehr?—Herod, why dreadest thou a foe?:
  Bach
Was Gott dem Abraham verheissen (Weihnachtsoratorium)—What God
  to Abraham revealed: Bach
Was Gott tut, das ist wohl getan—What God does, that is rightly done/
  What God does, only that is right: Bach
Was hab' ich arme dirn' getan?—Ah me, poor maid: C Böhm
Was ich hab'—What I have: C Böhm
Was ihr wollt—As you like it: Humperdinck
Was it a dream?—Var et en dröm?: Sibelius
Was Liebe sei?—Oh, what is love?: Liszt
Was mein Gott will, das g'scheh allzeit—What my God wills, that happens
  always: Bach
Was meinst du—What think you: Hindemith
Was mir behagt/Jagdkantate—My one delight/Hunting cantate/Birthday
  cantata: Bach
Was once a pretty tiny birdie flew—Ein kleiner hübscher Vogel (Liebeslieder
  Walzer): Brahms
Was pocht mein Herz so sehr?—Why beats my heart so loud?: R Franz
Was soll der Zorn (Italienisches Liederbuch)—What is this rage/Why all
  this wrath: Wolf
Was soll ich sagen?—What shall I say?: Grieg
Was soll ich sagen?—What can I say?: Schumann
Was this the man—Ah, fors' è lui (La traviata): Verdi
Was will die einsame Träne—Why tarries this lonely teardrop: R Franz
Was will die einsame Träne—What will this tear/Lonely tear: Schumann
Was zögerst du?—Haunted: Blumenthal
Wasserfahrt—On the lake/Waterparty: R Franz
An Wasserflüssen Babylon—Beside the streams of Babylon: Bach
Wasserflut (Die Winterreise)—Flood/Torrent: Schubert
Der Wassermann—The river king: Schumann
Wasserose—Water lily: R Strauss
Wasted effort—Verlorne Müh (Des Knaben Wunderhorn): Mahler
Watch ye alway—Vigiláte: Byrd
Watch ye, pray ye—Wachet, betet, seid bereit allzeit: Bach
The watchful lover—Der Gang zum Liebchen: Brahms
Watchman's song—Vaegtersang: Grieg
Watchman's song of the tower—Wachterlied auf der Wartburg: Wolf

The water carrier—Les deux journées: Cherubini
The water goblin—Vodník: Dvořák
Water lily—Wasserose: R Strauss
Water party—Wasserfahrt: R Franz
The water-sprite—Der Nöck: Loewe
Wave—Onda: Ponce
The wave and the bell—La vague et la cloche: Duparc
The way of the world—Lauf der Welt: Grieg
The way to paradise—Cesta k ráji: Martinů
The wayside cross—Boží mulka: Martinů
Wayside inn—Herberge (Waldscenen): Schumann
We adore Thee—Adoramus te: Brahms
We adore Thee, O Lord Christ—Adoramus te Christe: Viadana
We all believe in one true God—Wir glauben all' an einen Gott: Bach
We all must bear much sorrow—Wir müssen durch viel Trübsal: Bach
We are building a town—Wir bauen eine Stadt: Hindemith
We became thus an open shame—Facti sumus opprobrium: Byrd
We build a town—Wir bauen eine Stadt: Hindemith
We Christians may—Wir Christenleut (Orgelbüchlein): Bach
We have heard the grievous tribulations—Tribulations civitatum: Byrd
We have made night—Nous avons fait la nuit (Tel jour telle nuit):
    Poulenc
We humbly beseech Thee—Te deprecor: Byrd
We know thou often times—Man weiss oft: Hindemith
We praise Thee, O God—Wir danken dir, Gott: Bach
We shall be so in love—Nous nous aimerons (Tristesses): Milhaud
We sons of the plains—Vi sletternes sønner (Tove): Nielsen
We venerate Thy cross—Crucem tuam adoramus: Goodman
We wait for Thy loving kindness, O God—Suscepimus Deus: Byrd
We wandered far through foreign lands—My cizinou jsme bloudili
    (Jakobin): Dvořák
We wandered (once)—Wir wandelten: Brahms
Weaner Mad'ln—Vienna girls/Vienna maidens: Ziehrer
The weary heart—Tiefes Leid: Schubert
Weary of summer—Sommermüd: Schoenberg
The weary one's evensong—Des Müden Abendlied: R Franz
Weary, with sword in hand—Biterolf: Wolf
The weathercock—Die Wetterfahne (Die Winterreise): Schubert
The weather-vane—Die wetterfahne (Die Winterreise): Schubert
The weaver—Mein Liebster ist ein Weber: Hildach
Wechsellied zum Tanze—Come with me, fairest: Brahms
Wedding—Lakodalom (Dedinské Scény): Bartók

The wedding—Zhenit' ba: Mussorgsky
The wedding—Les noces: Stravinsky
Wedding day at Troldhaugen—Bryllupsdag pa Troldhaugen: Grieg
Wedding in carnival—Farsangi ladoalom: Poldini
Wedding march—Hochzeitmarsch (Ein Sommernachtstraum): Mendelssohn
The wedding of Thetis and Peleus—Le nozze de Teti e Peleo: Cavalli
Wedding song—Hochzeitslied: Schoenberg
Wedding songs—Hochzeitlieder: E Strauss
The weeping—Das Weinen: Schubert
Weeping, crying, sorrow, sighing—Weinen, Klagen, Sorgen, Zagen: Bach
Weeping for ever—Laschia ch' io pianga (Rinaldo): Handel
Weg der Liebe—Love will find out the way/The path of love/Love's way/
    Three voices: Brahms
Weg mit allen Schätzen (Jesu meine Freude)—Hence with earthly treasure:
    Bach
Der Wegweiser (Die Winterreise)—The signpost: Schubert
Weh, wie zornig ist das Mädchen (Spanische Liebeslieder)—O how cruel:
    Schumann
Wehe, so willst du—Vain is the power/Why do you thus try to hold me?/
    Sorrow I fear not/Sorrow whose phantoms/Dost thou yet seek: Brahms
Wehmut [D 404]—My sad heart: Schubert
Wehmut [D 772]—Sadness: Schubert
Wehmut—Sadness/Song of the nightingale: Schumann
Der Weiberorden—The woman's order: Telemann
Weiche Gräser (Neue Liebeslieder)—Secret nook: Brahms
Weichet nur, betrübte Schatten—Vex no more, sad melancholy: Bach
Weicht all', ihr Übeltäter (Ach Herr, mich armen Sünder)—Hence, all ye
    evil-doers: Bach
Die Weihe des Hauses—Consecration of the house: Beethoven
Weihnachten/Schlaf, Kindlein, schlaf—Cradle song/Sleep, baby, sleep:
    Brahms
Weihnachtsbaum—Christmas tree: Liszt
Weihnachtslied—Christmas carol: Schumann
Weihnachtsoratorium—Christmas oratorio: Bach
Der Wein—Wine: Berg
Der Wein der Liebenden (Der Wein)—The lover's wine: Berg
Der Wein des Einsamen (Der Wein)—The lonely man's wine: Berg
Wein, Weib, und Gesang—Wine, women and song: J Strauss II
Das Weinen—The weeping/Tears/Fount of tears: Schubert
Weinen, Klagen, Sorgen, Zagen—Wailing, crying, mourning, sighing/
    Weeping, crying, sorrow, sighing: Bach
Weinlesezeit (Album für die Jugend)—Merry vintage time/Vintage song/
    Vintage time: Schumann
Weise im Park—Lawn in the park: Webern

Weisser Jasmin—White jasmine: R Strauss

Weisst du noch?—Dost thou mind?/Dost thou know?: R Franz

Weit, weit (Myrthen)—How can I be blithe/The bonnie lad that's far away: Schumann

Welch' Übermass der Güte schenkst du mir (Wir Dank opfert, der preiset mich)—What overflow of goodness: Bach

Welcome and farewell—Willkommen und Abschied: Schubert

Welcome, precious treasure—Willkommen, werter Schatz (Schwingt freudig euch empor): Bach

Welcome, thou longed for day—Come sereno è il di (Bianca e Falliero): Rossini

Welcome to May—Mai, lieber Mai (Album für die Jugend): Schubert

Welcome to spring—O, douce joie: Gounod

Welcome to spring—Im Grünen: Mendelssohn

Welcome! ye soft whisp'ring zephyrs—Aure soavi e liete ombre: Handel

A welcome vision—Freundliche Vision: R Strauss

Well-beloved and happy time—Cara e lieta goiventu (Il ritorno d'Ulisse): Monteverdi

Die Welt sucht Ehr' und Ruhm (Was frag' ich nach der Welt)—The world seeks praise and fame: Bach

Wenn—If thou wert my love: R Strauss

Wenn alle Welt—If all the world: Reger

Wenn dein Mütterlein (Kindertotenlieder)—When thy mother dear: Mahler

Wenn den langen Weg/Gesellenreise—The journey of life: Mozart

Wenn der Frühling auf die Berge steigt—When the spring blooms: R Franz

Wenn die kleinen Veilchen blühen—Wild violets: Stolz

Wenn die Lieb' aus deinen blauen Augen/An Chloe—To Chloe/With a swanlike beauty gliding: Mozart

Wenn die Linde blüht—When the linden blooms: Reger

Wenn drüben die Glocken klingen—When yonder the bells are ringing: R Franz

Wenn du, mein Liebster (Italienisches Liederbuch)—When you go up to heaven/When thou my love: Wolf

Wenn du nur zuweilen lächelst—Grant me but one single smile: Brahms

Wenn ein müder Lieb begraben—True love's plaint: Brahms

Wenn einer in den Spiegel siehet—If someone looks into the mirror: Henze

Wenn Gott es hätt' gewollt—If God had willed it so: Reger

Wenn ich an deinem Munde hingesunken (Chinesische Liebeslieder)—When resting on your bosom: Liebermann

Wenn ich ein Vöglein wär'—Were I a bird: Schumann

Wenn ich früh—When at early dawn: Schumann

Wenn ich in deine Augen seh'—When gazing in thine eyes: Bleichmann

Wenn ich in deine Augen (Dichterliebe)—Whene'er thine eyes/Tears of joy: Schumann

Wenn ich mit Menschen—Thou I speak: Brahms
Wenn ich's nur wüsste—Would 'twere a token: R Franz
Wenn Liebe erwacht—Love's awakening: Künneke
Wenn mein Schatz fröhliche Hochzeit macht (Lieder eines fahrenden
    Gesellen)—When my sweetheart marries/On my love's wedding day:
    Mahler
Wenn mein Stündlein vorhanden ist—When my last hour: Bach
Wenn sich die Menschen (Lulu)—Although for my sake/Lulu's song:
    Berg
Wenn sich zwei Herzen scheiden—When two young hearts do sever:
    R Franz
Wenn sich zwei Herzen scheiden—Whene'er two hearts: Mendelssohn
Wenn so lind (Liebeslieder Walzer)—When thy glance is fond: Brahms
Wenn Vöglein klagen—When little birds complain: Schoenberg
Wenn wir in höchsten Nöten sein—When we in deep distress and grief:
    Brahms
Wenn wir in höchsten Nöten sein (Orgelbüchlein)—When in the hour of
    utmost need: Bach
Wer bist du? (Bereitet die Wege)—Who art Thou?: Bach
Wer da glaubet und getauft wird—I will lift up mine eyes unto the hills/
    True believers and baptized shall be saved: Bach
Wer Dank opfert, der preiset mich—Whoso doth offer thanks: Bach
Wer ein Liebchen hat gefunden (Die Entführung aus dem Serail)—
    When a maiden takes your fancy: Mozart
Wer fasst, wie gross du, Schöpfer bist (Lob und Ehre und Weisheit
    und Dank)—What tongue can tell: Bach (Attrib)
Wer hat dies Liedlein erdacht? (Des Knaben Wunderhorn)—Who thought
    up this song?/Who made up this song?/Up there on the hill/Far over
    the hill: Mahler
Wer Lieben will, muss leiden—Love and sorrow: R Strauss
Wer machte dich so krank—Who made you so ill: Schumann
Wer mich liebet—He who loves me: Bach
Wer nie sein Brot/Harfenspieler—Who never ate with tears/Who ne'er
    his bread: Schubert
Wer nie sein Brot—Who ne'er his bread/Who never ate with tears his
    bread: Liszt
Wer nur den lieben Gott lässt walten (Orgelbüchlein)—If thou but
    suffer(est) God to guide thee/If thou wilt suffer God to guide thee/
    He who trusts in God to guide him: Bach
Wer sich der Einsamkeit ergibt/Harfenspielder—Who gives to loneliness/
    To solitude himself who gives/Whoe'er for loneliness: Schubert
Wer uns getraut (Zigeunerbaron)—Who wedded us: J Strauss II
Wer weiss, wie nahe mir mein Ende?—O teach me, Lord, my days to
    number/Who knows when my death approaches: Bach

Wer weiss, woher das Brünnlein quillt (Siechentrost)—Who knoweth
  whence the brooklet flows: Bruch
Were God not with us in this time—War Gott nicht mit uns diese Zeit:
  Bach
Were I a bird—Wenn ich ein Vöglein wär': Schumann
Were not the pains—Se non fossero: Pergolesi
Die Wetterfahne (Die Winterreise)—The weather-vane/The weathercock:
  Schubert
Weyla's song—Gesang Weylas: Wolf
The whales—Les baleines: Pierné
What can I say?—Was soll ich sagen?: Schumann
What course shall I then pursue—Quid igitur faciam: Byrd
What delight you give—Wie bist du, meine Königin: Brahms
What emotions o'er me stealing?—Sind es Schmerzen, sind es Freuden:
  Brahms
What gallant!—Quel galant!: Ravel
What God does, only that is right—Was Gott tut, das ist wohl getan:
  Bach
What God does, that is rightly done—Was Gott tut, das ist wohl getan:
  Bach
What God to Abraham revealed—Wass Gott dem Abraham verheissen
  (Weihnachtsoratorium): Bach
What God's splendour doth reveal—Was des Höchsten Glanz erfüllt
  (Hochsterwunschtes Freudenfest): Bach
What great delight—Wie bin ich froh: Webern
What I am, what I do—Non so più cosa son (Le nozze di Figaro): Mozart
What I have—Was ich hab': C Böhm
What is life to me—Che farò (Orfeo ed Euridice): Gluck
What I love—Ce que j'aime: Rhené-Baton
What is the good King Rangang's daughter's name—Schön Rhotraut:
  Dieren
What is this rage—Was soll der Zorn (Italienisches Liederbuch): Wolf
What joyous airs—Ces airs joyeux (L'enfant prodigue): Debussy
What man is he—Quis est homo: Byrd
What my God wills, that happens always—Was mein Gott will, das g'scheh
  allzeit: Bach
What overflow of goodness—Welch' Übermass der Güte schenkst du mir
  (Wer Dank opfert, der preiset mich): Bach
What pure sky—Che puro ciel (Orfeo ed Euridice): Gluck
What rapturous joy—Quanto godrà (Admeto): Handel
What said I?—Che dissi? (Otello): Rossini
What shall I, a sinner do?—Ach, was soll ich Sünder machen?: Bach
What shall I do?—Was fang' ich an?: Blech
What shall I do without Eurydice—Che farò senza Euridice (Orfeo ed
  Euridice): Gluck

What shall I say?—Was soll ich sagen?: Grieg
What she likes—Gdzie lubi: Chopin
What the west wind said—Ce qu'a vu le vent d'ouest: Debussy
What you think—Was meinst du: Hindemith
What though the clouds—Und ob die Wolke (Die Freischütz): Weber
What tongue can tell—Wer fasst, wie gross du, Schöpfer bist (Lob und Ehre
    und Weisheit und Dank): Bach (attrib)
What will this tear—Was will die einsame Träne: Schumann
When a gallant youth—Kommt ein schlanker Bursch gegangen (Der
    Freischütz): Weber
When a maiden takes your fancy—Wer ein Liebchen hat gefunden (Die
    Entführung aus dem Serail): Mozart
When Adam fell, the human race—Durch Adams Fall ist ganz verdebt
    (Orgelbüchlein): Bach
When all was love—Erinnerung: J Marx
When all was young—Si le bonheur (Faust): Gounod
When angels visit us—Lasst uns das Angesicht (Es erub sich ein Streit):
    Bach
When at early dawn—Wenn ich früh: Schumann
When at early dawn—Volksliedchen: Schumann
When bright and glorious—Allor che sorge (Rodrigo): Handel
When by earthly joys surrounded—In des Lebens Frühlingstagen (Fidelio):
    Beethoven
When by storms—Da tempeste (Giulio Cesare): Handel
When called by Thee—Komm, Jesu, komm: Bach
When daily living sinfully—Peccantem me quotidiae: Byrd
When Eve from out of paradise—Als Eva aus dem Paradies (Die Meister-
    singer von Nürnberg): Wagner
When first I saw thee—Als ich dich kaum gesehen: Lassen
When first young Damon—Sobald Damoetas Chloen sieht: Mozart
When for the palm in song—Als du in kühnem Sange (Tannhäuser): Wagner
When furious winds—Del minaccia del vento (Ottone): Handel
When gazing in thine eyes—Wenn ich in deine Augen seh': Bleichmann
When I behold—Blick' ich umher (Tannhäuser): Wagner
When I dream—Nar jag drömmer: Sibelius
When I dwell near—Star vicino: Rosa
When I first saw you—Quando te vi pela primeira vez: Guarnieri
When I in the dusky forest—Wandl' ich in dem Wald: R Franz
When I rise each morn I wonder—Morgen steh' ich auf und frage: Liszt
When I saw the sun—Schein mir's, als ich sah die Sonne: Webern
When I walk in dreamy woodlands—Wandl' ich in dem Wald: R Franz
When I shall meet my life's last day—So wünsch' ich mir zu guter letzt:
    Bach
When I was a merry stripling—Quand' io ero giovinetto: G Gabrieli
When I was a page—Quand' ero paggio (Falstaff): Verdi

When in danger—Ogni vento (Agrippina): Handel
When in dewy fields at morn—Wandl' ich in dem Morgentau: Pfitzner
When in the hour of utmost need—Wenn mir in höchsten Nöten sein
  (Orgelbüchlein): Bach
When Israel came out of Egypt—In exitu Israel: S Wesley
When little birds complain—Wenn Vöglein klagen: Schoenberg
When love at thy side—Quand, a tes genoux: Aubert
When love has gone—Es ist vorbei: C Franz
When May displays her flowers—Ce moys de May, ma verte cotte:
  Jannequin
When me fair dreams awaken—Par che mi dica ancora (Il castello di
  Kenilworth): Donizetti
When midnight dreams—Allnachtlich im Traume: R Franz
When midnight fears assail him—Di notte il pellegrino (Riccardo Primo):
  Handel
When mute and sad—Ich schleich umher: Brahms
When my eyes—Quando mai spietata sorte (Radamisto): Handel
When my last hour—Wenn mein Stundlein vorhanden ist: Bach
When my love sings like a robin—Singt mein Schatz wie ein Fink: Pfitzner
When my sweetheart marries—Wenn mein Schatz fröhliche Hochzeit macht
  (Lieder eines fahrenden Gesellen): Mahler
When night has fallen—A notte cupa (Nerone): Boito
When on the cross the Saviour hung—Da Jesus an dem Kreuze stund
  (Orgelbüchlein): Bach
When roses bloom—Hoffnung: J Reichardt
When the linden blooms—Wenn die Linde blüht: Reger
When the spring blooms—Wenn der Frühling auf die Berge steigt: R Franz
When that I was—Schusslied des Narren: Schumann
When thou my love—Wenn du, mein Liebster (Italienisches Liederbuch):
  Wolf
When thou wert by my side—Se dolce m'era già (Floridante): Handel
When through the piazzetta—Venetianisches Gondollied: Mendelssohn
When thy blue eyes—Mit deinen blauen Augen: Lassen
When thy fair beauty—Quando ti vidi: Wolf-Ferrari
When thy glance is fond—Wenn so lind (Liebeslieder Walzer): Brahms
When thy mother dear—Wenn dein Mutterlein (Kindertotenlieder):
  Mahler
When thy sweet glances—Vté sladké moci (Pisné milostné): Dvořák
When to that song I listen—Hörer jeg Sangen klinge: Grieg
When two fond hearts—Due bell' alme (Deidamia): Handel
When two young hearts do sever—Wenn sich zwei Herzen scheiden: R Franz
When we in deep distress and grief—Wenn wir in höchsten Nöten sein:
  Brahms
When will God recall my spirit?—Liebster Gott, wann werd' ich sterben:
  Bach

When winds are fiercely raving—Del minaccia del vento (Ottone): Handel
When with thine eyes of azure—Mit deinen blauen Augen: R Strauss
When yonder the bells are ringing—Wenn drüben die Glocken klingen:
    R Franz
When you go up to heaven—Wenn du, mein Liebster (Italienisches
    Liederbuch): Wolf
When you peer into my heart—Cantiga ingenua: Coelho
When you slept—Quand tu dors: Kjerulf
Whene'er poor Peter—Arme Peter (3): Schumann
Whene'er the sounding harp is heard—Es tönt ein voller Harfenklang:
    Brahms
Whene'er the tambourine I hear—Quand j'ai ouy la tambourin (Chansons
    de Charles d'Orléans): Debussy
Whene'er thine eyes—Wenn ich in deine Augen (Dichterliebe): Schumann
Whene'er two hearts—Wenn sich zwei Herzen scheiden: Mendelssohn
Where am I?—Où suis-je (Sapho): Gounod
Where art thou?—Dove sei amato bene (Rodelinda): Handel
Where art thou hasting?—Wo geh'st du hin, du Stolze?: Brahms
Where beauty and mirth—Libiamo, ne' lieti calici (La traviata): Verdi
Where can eyes like mine—Onde porei meus olhos: J Berger
Where fall my burning teardrops—Aus meinen Tränen: Schumann
Where goest Thou?—Wo gehest du hin?: Bach
Where hast thou gone my master—Lo mestre: Alió
Where have they fled—Wo sind sie hin?: Grieg
Where is he—Wo weilt er?: Liszt
Where is my dwelling place—Wo ist mein Aufenthalt: Wellesz
Where is the Lamb that willed to leave me—Wo ist mein Schäflein,
    das ich liebe: Bach
Where, my thoughts, where do you flutter?—Dove voli ò mio pensiero:
    A Scarlatti
Where now art thou?—Dove sei amato bene (Rodelinda): Handel
Where shall I find salvation?—Wo find' ich Trost?: Wolf
Where sorrows touch me nearest—Aus meinen grossen Schmerzen: R Franz
Where the fine trumpets sound—Wo die schönen Trompeten blasen
    (Des Knaben Wunderhorn): Mahler
Where the lark sings—Wo die Lerche singt: Léhar
Where the mountains rise—Wo die Berge (An die ferne Geliebte):
    Beethoven
Where the shining trumpets are blowing (blow)—Wo die schönen Trompeten
    blasen (Des Knaben Wunderhorn): Mahler
Where the splendid trumpets blow—Wo die schönen Trompeten blasen
    (Des Knaben Wunderhorn): Mahler
Where to?—Wohin? (Die schöne Müllerin): Schubert
Where will you drive me, Love—Dove mi spingi, Amor: L Rossi
Where'er I go—All' meine Herzgedanken: Brahms

Wherefore am I—Warum bin ich vergänglich: R Kahn
Wherefore has appeared the Son of God—Dazu ist erschienen der Sohn
    Gottes: Bach
Wherefore hath the light—Warum ist das Licht gegeben: Brahms
Wherefore the Lord Jesus—Liebster Herr Jesu: Bach
Wherefore now hath light—Warum ist das Licht gegeben: Brahms
Wherefore, O Saviour—Liebster Herr Jesu! Wo bleibst du so lange: Bach
Wherefore soul of mine, art grieving—Warum sollt ich mich denn grämen:
    Bach
Wherefore was I not intended—Non vi piacque (Siroe): Handel
Which gallant can compare—Quel galant!: Ravel
While from the wine cup—Finch' han dal vino (Don Giovanni): Mozart
While her parents were a-praying—Une petite fille: Bax
While the rain falls—Während des Regens: Brahms
While the world is dreaming—Così piange pierrot: Bixio
While this heart—Sovra il sen (La sonnambula): Bellini
Whims—Grillen (Fantasiestücke): Schumann
Whimsical betrothal—Fiancailles pour rire: Poulenc
Whirled into happiness—Der Tanz ins Glück: Stolz
Whisp'ring songs—Leise Lieder: R Strauss
Whisp'rings of the Vienna woods—Geschichten aus der Wiener Wald:
    J Strauss II
The whistler and his dog—Visslaren och hans Hund: Pryor
White Horse Inn—Im Weissen Rossl: Benatzky (et al)
White jasmine—Weisser Jasmin: R Strauss
White keys—Touches blanches: Milhaud
The white lady—La dame blanche: Boildieu
The white moon—La lune blanche (La bonne chanson): Fauré
The white pig—Du bist wie eine Blume: Berners
The white rose—La bianca rosa: Handel
The white seal—Maktah: Delage
The white snowflakes—Hó hull a Sárba: Antalffy
The white-foaming billows of Belial's torrents—Die schäumende Wellen
    von Belials Bächen (Jesus schläft, was soll ich hoffen?): Bach
Whither—Wohin: Schubert
Whither I'm going I know not—Vado, ma dove?: Mozart
Whither shall I fly—Wo soll ich fliehen hin?: Bach
Whither wouldst thou repair—Où voulez-vous aller?: Gounod
Whitsun mass—Messe de la Pentecôte: Messiaen
Who art thou—Wer bist du? (Bereitet der Wege): Bach
Who called you here?—Wer reif dich denn? (Italienisches Liederbuch): Wolf
Who can comprehend Thee—Quis te comprehendat: Mozart
Who gave you your sweet eyes—Qui donc vous a donné vos yeux: Godard
Who gives to loneliness—Wer sich der Einsamkeit ergibt: Schubert
Who has banished from your heart—Di Provenza il mar (La traviata): Verdi

Who is Sylvia?—An Sylvia: Schubert
Who knoweth whence the brooklet flows—Wer weiss, woher das Brünnlein
    quillt (Siechentrost): Bruch
Who knows my swain's affliction—Chi sà, chi sà, qual sia: Mozart
Who knows when my death approaches—Wer weiss, wie nahe mir mein
    Ende?: Bach
Who made up this song?—Wer hat dies Liedlein erdacht? (Des Knaben
    Wunderhorn): Mahler
Who made you so ill—Wer macht dich so krank: Schumann
Who ne'er his bread—Wer nie sein Brot: Liszt
Who ne'er his bread—Wer nie sein Brot: Schubert
Who never ate his bread with tears—Svuj chéb kdo jídal: Vycpalek
Who never ate with tears—Wer nie sein Brot: Schubert
Who never ate with tears his bread—Wer nie sein Brot: Liszt
Who plays among the roses—Chi scherza colla rose (Imeneo): Handel
Who thought to see thee languish—Ah! non credea mirarte (La sonnambula):
    Bellini
Who thought up this song?—Wer hat dies Liedlein erdacht? (Des Knaben
    Wunderhorn): Mahler
Who treads the path of duty—In diesen heil'gen Hallen (Die Zauberflöte):
    Mozart
Who wants the gipsy-maiden—Chi vuol la zingarella (I zingari in Fiera):
    Paisiello
Who wedded us—Wer uns getraut (Zigeunerbaron): J Strauss II
Whoe'er for loneliness—Wer sich der Einsamkeit ergibt: Schubert
Who'll buy my roses—Gehn wir im Prater: Mozart
Whoso doth offer thanks—Wer Dank opfert, der preiset mich: Bach
Why?—Warum?: Brahms
Why?—Warum? (Fantasiestücke): Schumann
Why beats my heart so loud?—Was pocht mein Herz so sehr?: R Franz
Why blame thee now—Ich grolle nicht (Dichterliebe): Schumann
Why cast down, my heart within me—Was betrübst du dich, mein Herze: Bach
Why do you thus try to hold me?—Wehe, so willst du: Brahms
Why feels my heart so dormant?—Nel cor più non mi sento (La molinara):
    Paisiello
Why fumeth in sight in gentile's spite: Quare fremuerunt: Tallis
Why gaze you upon me—Du milchjunger Knabe: Pfitzner
Why go barefoot—Feinsliebchen, du sollst mir nicht: Brahms
Why is my mood so happy?—Wie trag ich doch im Sinne: Cornelius
Why must I go on venting my ardent desire in tears—A che più debb' io
    mai l'intensa voglia (Sonnets of Michelangelo): Britten
Why should we seek—Wie sollten wir geheim: R Strauss
Why so troubled?—Was betrübst du dich, meine Seele: Schütz
Why tarries this lonely teardrop—Was will die einsame Träne: R Franz

Wichtige Begebenheit (Kinderscenen)—Great event/An important event: Schumann

Der widerspenstigen Zähmung—The taming of the shrew: Goetz

Widerstehe doch der Sünde—Unto sin oppose resistance/Christian, never let sin o'er power thee: Bach

Widmung—Dedication: R Franz

Widmung—To my betrothed/Devotion/Dedication/Heart's desire: Schumann

The widow—La veuve: P Cannon

Wie Bäche reisst das Ende von etwas mich dahin (chamber music)—Like brook the end of something sweeps one away: Henze

Wie bin ich froh—What great delight: Webern

Wie bist du, meine Königin—Thou art my queen/Queen of my soul/Mine art thou/How art thou, O my queen/Ah! sweet my love, thou charmest me/Fair as the morn/What delight you give/My queen/Gracious and kind Reign here a queen: Brahms

Wie der Quell so lieblich/Minnelied—Love song: Mendelssohn

Wie des Abends (Liebeslieder Walzer)—Like the sunset's crimson splendour: Brahms

Wie des Mondes Abbild—As the moon's reflections: R Franz

Wie die Wolke nach der Sonne—Longings/Like the driven cloud/Enchantment/The symbol: Brahms

Wie einst—Long ago: J Marx

Wie froh und frisch—How free and fresh/How light and gay: Brahms

Wie Georg von Frundsberg von sich selber sang—How George von Frundsberg sang about himself: Schoenberg

Wie glänzt der helle Mond—How coldly shines the moon: Pfitzner

Wie hast du dich, mein Gott (Ich hatte viel Bekümmerniss)—How hast Thou then my God: Bach

Wie glänzt der helle Mond—Bright shines the silver moon/Now shines the silver moon: Wolf

Wie ist die Erde so schön—How lovely is the earth: Blech

Wie kann ich froh und lustig sein?—How can I blithe and cheerful be?/Ribbons and flowers I cannot wear: Mendelssohn

Wie kannst du ruhig schlafen?—How canst thou sleep: Blumenthal

Wie komm ich denn zur Tür herein?—How may I open your chamber door: Brahms

Wie Lieb ich dich hab' (An Bertha)—How fondly I love: Cornelius

Wie lieblich klingt es in den Ohren (Ich freue mich in dir)—How sweetly echo in my hearing: Bach

Wie lieblich sind deine Wohnungen (Ein Deutsches Requiem)—How lovely is Thy dwelling place: Brahms

Wie Melodien zieht es mir—Like melodies it floweth/A thought like music/Sweet melodies/Like strains of sweetest music/Melodious strains: Brahms

Wie möchte je wohler sein (Siechentrost)—How could I greater bliss: Bruch

Wie oft in Meeres tiefsten Schlund (Der fliegende Holländer)—Engulfed in ocean's deepest wave: Wagner

Wie rafft ich mich auf in der Nacht—In the night/I woke and arose in the night/I roused me from sleep: Brahms

Wie schnell verschwindet—As fame and power fast fade away/As flowers that waken: Brahms

Wie schön leuchtet der Morgenstern [chorale; cantata]—How brightly beams the morning star/How brightly shines yon star of morn: Bach

Wie schön leuchtet der Morgenstern [chorale prelude]—O morning star! how fair and bright/How brightly shines the morning star: Bach

Wie sehr lieblich und schöne—To me, in joy returning: Schütz

Wie sich ein Vat'r erbarmet (Wer Dank opfert, der preiset mich)—For as a loving Father: Bach

Wie singt die Lerche schön—How sweet the skylark's song/How sweetly sings the lark: Liszt

Wie soll ich fröhlich sein (Italienisches Liederbuch)—How can I be happy/How can I e'er rejoice: Wolf

Wie sollten wir geheim—Why should we seek: R Strauss

Wie stolz und stattlich—How proud and stately: Henschel

Wie trag ich doch im Sinne/Musje morgenrots Lied—Why is my mood so happy: Cornelius

Wie ulfru Fischt—The unlucky fisherman: Schubert

Wie will ich lustig lachen (Zerreißt, zersprenget, zertrummert die Gruft)—How jovial is my laughter: Bach

Wie wohl is mir—O friend of souls what joy to waken: Bach

Wieder mocht' ich dir begegnen—Could I once again caress thee/Once again I fain would meet thee: Liszt

Wiegenlied—Slumber song: d'Albert

Wiegenlied—Lullaby/Cradle song: Blech

Wiegenlied—Lullaby/Cradle song: Brahms

The wild dove—Holoubek: Dvořák

The wild horseman—Wilder Reiter (Album für die Jugend): Schumann

Wild horses—Hémiones (Carnaval des animaux): Saint-Saëns

Wild rose—Heidenröslein: Brahms

The wild rose—Šípek (Moravské Dvojzpévy): Dvořák

(The) wild rose—Heidenröslein: Schubert

Wild rosebud—Heidenröslein: Schubert

Wild violets—Wenn die kleinen Veilchen blühen: Stolz

Die wilden Schwäne—The enchanted swans: Reinecke

Wilder Reiter (Album für die Jugend)—The little rough rider/The wild horseman: Schumann

Wildflower—C'est une fleur sauvage: Pierné

The wildflower—En blomma stod vid vägen: Sibelius
Der Wildschütz—The poacher: Lortzing
Wilkommen, werter Schatz (Schwingt freudig euch empor)—Welcome,
   precious treasure: Bach
Will he come today?—Kommt feins Liebchen heut'?: R Franz
Will über Nacht wohl durch das Tal—Through the valley now 'tis night:
   R Franz
William Ratcliff—Gugliemo Ratcliff: Mascagni
William Tell—Guillaume Tell: Rossini
Willkommen, lieber schöner Mai—All hail thou lovely laughing May:
   Schubert
Willkommen, mein Wald!—Now, welcome my wood: R Franz
Willkommen und Abschied—Welcome and farewell: Schubert
Will-o'-the-wisp—Feux follets: Liszt
Will-o'-the-wisp—Irrlicht (Die Winterreise): Schubert
Will-oo-not sleep?—Die Wittewoll schlafen?: Blech
Willow song—Assisa a piè d'un salice (Otello): Rossini
The willow tree—Am Dorfsee: Reger
Willow, willow—Lacrimoso son io: Mozart
The willow song—Canzone del salice (Otello): Rossini
Willst du dein Herz mir schenken—Give me that heart of thine/
   Give me thy heart/The heart I ask from thee/The heart that thou
   hast given/If thou thy heart will give me/To me thy heart awarding/
   Wilt thou not give/Wilt thou to me: Bach (?)
Willst du glanz gewinnen—Go where glory waits thee: Kjerulf
Wilt deign to be near me—So willst du: Brahms
Wilt thou my child—Mögst du, mein Kind (Der fliegende Holländer):
   Wagner
Wilt thou not give—Willst du dein Herz mir schenken: Bach (?)
Wilt thou to me—Willst du dein Herz mir schenken: Bach (?)
The wind of the Holy Spirit—Le vent de l'Esprit (Messe de la
   Pentecôte): Messiaen
Wind of the waters—Am Bodensee: Schumann
Windmills—Windräder: J Marx
The window pane—Die Fensterscheibe: Schumann
Windräder—Windmills: J Marx
Wine—Der Wein: Berg
Wine in spring—Der Trunkene im Frühling (Das Lied von der Erde):
   Mahler
Wine, women and song—Wein, Weib und Gesang: J Strauss II
The wine's soul—Die Seele des Weines (Der Wein): Berg
Winter bonfire—Zimniy koster: Prokofiev
A winter dedication—Winterweihe: R Strauss
A winter evening—Ein Winterabend: Webern

Winter is ended—L'hiver a cessé (La bonne chanson): Fauré
Winter journey—Die Winterreise: Schubert
Winter love—Winterliebe: R Strauss
A winter lullaby—Wiegenlied im Winter: Wolf
Winter night—Winternacht (Lieder um dem Tod): Kilpinen
Winter song—Winterlied: Mendelssohn
Winter time—Winterzeit (Album für die Jugend): Schumann
Ein Winterabend—A winter evening: Webern
Winterliebe—Winter love: R Strauss
Winterlied—Winter song: Mendelssohn
Das Wintermärchen—A winter's tale: Humperdinck
Winternacht—Winter-night: R Franz
Winternacht (Lieder um dem Tod)—Winter night: Kilpinen
Winternacht—Winternight: R Strauss
Winter-night—Winternacht: R Franz
Winternight—Winternacht: R Strauss
Die Winterreise—Journey in winter/Winter journey: Schubert
Winter's night—Soir d'hiver: Rhené-Baton
A winter's tale—Das Wintermärchen: Humperdinck
Winterweihe—A winter dedication: R Strauss
Winterzeit (Album für die Jugend)—Winter time: Schumann
Wiosna—Spring: Chopin
Wir bauen eine Stadt—We build a town/We are building a town:
    Hindemith
Wir bringen dir die Kette (Die Bürgschaft)—The spendthrift spring:
    Schubert
Wir Christenleut' (Orgelbüchlein)—We Christians may: Bach
Wir danken dir Gott—We praise Thee, O God: Bach
Wir danken dir, Herr Jesu Christ (Orgelbüchlein)—To Thee, Lord
    Jesus, thanks we give: Bach
Wir gehn nun wo der Tudelsack (Mer hahn en neue Oberkeet)—Come
    let us to the bagpipe's sound: Bach
Wir geniessen die Himmlischen (4th symphony)—In the pleasure of
    heaven we're joyous: Mahler
Wir glauben all an einen Gott—We all believe in one true God: Bach
Wir müssen durch viel Trübsel—We must all bear much sorrow/We must
    through much tribulation: Bach
Wir müssen uns trennen—The hour of our parting/Dear lute: Brahms
Wir wandelten—We wandered (once): Brahms
Wird er wohl noch meiner gedenken?—Now, will not he sometimes in
    thinking?: R Franz
Wirf, mein Herze, wirf dich noch (Mein Gott, wie lang', ach lange?)—
    Cast, oh cast thyself, my heart: Bach
Das Wirthaus (Die Winterreise)—The inn: Schubert

Der Wirtin Töchterlein—The maid of the inn: Loewe
The wise and the foolish virgins—De favitska jungfrurna: Atterberg
The wise one—Die Kluge: Orff
The wish—Deseo: Guastavino
A wish—Souhait: Massenet
Wish—Wunsch: Reger
Wishes—Wär' ich der Regen: Blumenthal
Wishes—Sehnsucht: Brahms
The witch—Le villi: Puccini
Witches' song of May—And'res Maienlied: Mendelssohn
With a painted ribbon—Mit einem gemalten Band: Beethoven
With a painted ribbon—Mit einem gemalten Band: Schoeck
With a primrose—Med en primula veris: Grieg
With a swanlike beauty gliding—Wenn die Lieb' aus deinen blauen
     Augen: Mozart
With a water-lily—Med en Vandlilje: Grieg
With all one's heart—Ot vsevo serdtsa: Zhukovskyi
With black sails—Mit schwarzen Segeln: Wolf
With cunning conniving—Che fiera costume: Legrenzi
With desiring—Mit Verlangen (Geschwinde, geschwinde, ihr wirbelnden
     Winde): Bach
With dusky sails—Mit schwarzen Segeln: R Franz
With fear why are ye taken?—Warum sollt ihr erschrecken? (Weihnachts-
     oratorium): Bach
With heart and hand—Le coeur et la main: Lecocq
With Jesus will I go—Ich folge Christo nach (Weinen, Klagen, Sorgen, Zegen):
     Bach
With joy in my heart—Ville cherie, O ma patrie (Les cloches de
     Corneville): Planquette
With loving caresses—Lusinghe piỳ care (Alessandro): Handel
With mournful sounds of weeping—Con rauco mormorio (Rodelinda):
     Handel
With murmer hoarsely swelling—Con rauco mormorio (Rodelinda):
     Handel
With myrtle and roses—Mit Myrthen und Rosen: Schumann
With other tongues—Loquebantur variis: Palestrina
With peace and joy I journey thither—Mit Fried und Freud ich fahr
     dahin: Bach
With songs of praise—Te mane laudum: Byrd
With sword and bow—Traun! Bogen und Pfeil sind gut für den Feind:
     Brahms
With the green ribbon—Mit dem grünen Lautenbande (Die schöne
     Müllerin): Schubert
With thee—Bei dir sind meine Gedanken: Brahms

With thy roses on my breast—Deine Rosen an der Brust: Kilpinen
With thy rosy lips, my maiden—Mädchen mit dem roten Mündchen:
    R Franz
With voice of melody—Cantate Domino: Byrd
With your lovely eyes—Veggio co' bei vostri occhi in dolce lume
    (Sonnets of Michelangelo): Britten
Withdrawal—Verborgenheit: Wolf
Within a garden—In einem Rosengärtelein: Reger
Within a garden rosery—In einem Rosengärtelein: Hildach
Within my breast—Arme Peter (2): Schumann
Within my heart—Im tiefsten Herzen: Cornelius
Within, out of diversity, a serious mind is formed—Innen aus Verschiedenem
    entsteht (Chamber music): Henze
Within the tomb forgotten—In questa tomba oscura: Beethoven
Within these sacred bowers (portals)—In diesen heil'gen Hallen (Die
    Zauberflöte): Mozart
Within these temple walls—In diesen heil'gen Hallen (Die Zauberflöte):
    Mozart
Within this palace—In questa reggia (Turandot): Puccini
Without thee!—Ce que je suis sans toi: Gounod
Die Wittewoll schlafen?—Will-oo-not sleep?: Blech
Wizardry—Zauber: d'Arba
Wo die Berge (An die ferne Geliebte)—Where the mountains rise:
    Beethoven
Wo die Lerche singt—Where the lark sings: Lehár
Wo die schönen Trompeten blasen (Des Knaben Wunderhorn)—Where
    the splendid trumpets blow/Where the fine trumpets sound/Where the
    shining trumpets are blowing (blow): Mahler
Wo find' ich Trost—Where shall I find salvation?: Wolf
Wo gehst du hin, du Stolze?—Where are thou hasting?/Where goest thou?:
    Brahms
Wo Gott der Herr nicht bei uns hält—Had not the Lord been on our side:
    Bach
Wo ist mein Schäflein, das ich liebe—Where is the Lamb that willed to
    leave me?: Bach
Wo sind sie hin?—Where have they fled?: Grieg
Wo soll ich die Freude—O joy out of measure/O how throbs my heart/
    How can I sustain?/Oh can there be given?: Brahms
Wo soll ich fliehen hin—O whither shall I flee/Whither shall I fly:
    Bach
Wo treff' ich meinen Jesum (Mein liebster Jesus ist verloren)—Alas!
    where shall I Jesus seek: Bach
Wo weilt er?—Where is he?: Liszt
Woe, grief, despair—Parfons regretz: Josquin

Woe is me—Meghalok, meghalok: Kodály

Woe is you, Rusalka—Běda, běda, ubohá, Rusalko bledá: Dvořák

Woe! quite alone!—Allein! weh, ganz allein (Elektra): R Strauss

Woe's me the parting hour—Ach Gott, wie weh tut Scheiden: Brahms

Wohin? (Die schöne Müllerin)—Where to?/Whither?: Schubert

Wohin—Whither: Schubert

Wohin—The stream: Schubert-Rachmaninov

Wohin ich geh'/Grüss—Greeting: Mendelssohn

Wohl euch, ihr auserwählten Seelen (O ewiges Feuer)—O well for you,
    ye souls elected/Rejoice ye souls, elect and holy/O taste and see:
    Bach

Wohl euch! die ihr dies Licht gesehen (Weihnachtsoratorium)—Rejoice
    that you this light behold: Bach

Wohl mir, dass ich Jesum habe (Herz und Mund und Tat und Leben)—
    Jesu, joy of man's desiring: Bach

Wohl schau' ich nach Nord—Out over the Forth: M Mayer

Wohl schön bewandt (Liebeslieder Walzer)—How sweet: Brahms

Wohl waren es Tage—Those were the days: R Franz

Wohlzutun und mitzuteilen (Brich dem Hungrigen dein Brot)—Do thine
    alms: Bach

Wojak—The warrior: Chopin

Das Wölklein—The cloudlet: Reger

Die Wollust in den Maien—The merry time of Maying: Brahms

The woman without a kiss—Die Frau ohne Küss: Kollo

The woman without a shadow—Die Frau ohne Schatten: R Strauss

The woman-hater—Enemie de les dones: Gerhard

Woman's a fickle jade—La donna è mobile (Rigoletto): Verdi

A woman's life and love—Frauenliebe und -leben: Schumann

Woman's love and woman's life—Frauenliebe und -leben: Schumann

The woman's order—Der Weiberorden: Telemann

Women may swear they'll never desert you—Ogni momento dicon le
    donne (L'oca del Cairo): Mozart

Women of Magdala—Les femmes de Magdala: Massenet

Wonder—Sehnsucht [D 636]: Schubert

The wonderful fleet—Dyvnyi flot: Kozyts'kyi

Wondrous fragrance in the evening—Underlige Aftenlufte: Nielsen

Wonne der Wehmut—The pleasure of melancholy/Delight in melancholy/
    Ecstasy of woe: Beethoven

Wonne der Wehmut—Delight of melancholy: R Franz

The wood is green and gay—Liebes Frühlings: R Franz

The wood minstrels—Die Waldvöglein: Mendelssohn

Wood wandering—Vandring i Skoven: Grieg

The wood-demon—Der Erlkönig: Loewe

The wooden prince—A fából faragott Királyfi: Bartók

The woodfay—Waldmädchen: Schumann
Woodland sunshine—Waldsonne: Schoenberg
Woodland wandering—Vandring i Skoven: Grieg
The woods—Im Grünen: Mendelssohn
Woodman's song—Metsamiehen: Sibelius
The woods—Waldfahrt: R Franz
Wooing—Gang zur Liebsten: Brahms
The wooing of a girl—Leánykérö: Bartók
The wooing of Pelops—Namluvy Pelopvy: Fibich
The wooing of the rose—Le mariage des roses: Franck
The word descending from above—Verbum supernum prodiens: Tallis
The workman—Der Arbeitsmann: R Strauss
The world lies dark—Nun liegt die Welt: Henschel
The word of God my treasure is—Mein Seelenschatz ist Gottes Wort (Gleich
   wie der Regen und Schnee): Bach
A word of love—Ein Wort der Liebe: Cornelius
The world on the moon—Il mondo della lune: Haydn
The world seeks praise and fame—Die Welt sucht Ehr' und Ruhm (Was
   frag' ich nach der Welt): Bach
Ein Wort der Liebe—A word of love: Cornelius
Wotans Abschied von Brünnhilde (Die Walküre)—Wotan's farewell to
   Brunnhilde: Wagner
Wotan's farewell to Brunnhilde—Wotans Abschied von Brünnhilde (Die
   Walküre): Wagner
Would God that I at home—Gott woll' dass ich daheime war (Siechen-
   trost): Bruch
Would I could hide—Ove celare (Don Sebastiano): Donizetti
Would I could pass hence—Ich möchte hingehn: Liszt
Would I like to be a cornet—Möcht ich ein Kornet sein? (Chamber
   music): Henze
Would she were here—Dass sie hier gewesen: Schubert
Would 'twere a token—Wenn ich's nur wüsste: R Franz
The would-be musician—Il musico ignorante: Clari
Wouldst thou keep undimmed—Sieh das ist es: Henschel
The wounded heart—Den Sårede: Grieg
Wozu noch Mädchen—Say, wherefore vainly: R Strauss
Wrath in my bosom nesting—Sento che un giusto sdegno (Faramondo):
   Handel
The wrathful Diana—Der zurrende(n) Diana: Schubert
The wren—La capinera: Benedict
Wretched sinner you—Armer Sunder, du (Drei Volkstexte): Webern
The wounded lover—Vom verwundetung Knaben: Brahms
The wounded youth—Vom verwundetung Knaben: Brahms
The wreath—Der Kranz: Brahms

Das Wunder—The miracle: Humperdinck
Wunsch—Wish: Reger
Der Wunsch des Liebhabers—The lover's wish: Schoenberg
Wüsstest du den Weg—My pretty bird: Kjerulf

X

Xerxes—Serse: Handel

Y

Ye bells of old Marling—Ihr Glocken von Marling: Liszt
Ye Christians in the nation!—Helft mir Gott's Güte preisen (Orgelbüch-
lein): Bach
Ye dear eyes—V'adoro, pupille (Giulio Cesare): Handel
Ye eyes of darkness—Ihr schwarzen Augen (Neue Liebeslieder): Brahms
Ye gods of endless night—Divinités du Styx (Alceste): Gluck
Ye gods watching over me—L'insana parola (Aida): Verdi
Ye gracious powers—Spietati! Io vi giura! (Rodelinda): Handel
Ye halls beloved—Dich teure Halle (Tannhäuser): Wagner
Ye happy flock—Beglückte Heerde (Du Hirte Israel, höre): Bach
Ye high powers—Somme Dei! (Radamisto): Handel
Ye men of Galilee—Viri Galilei: Byrd
Ye must close to the day—Fermez vous pour jamais: Lully
Ye pangs of anxious thought—Affani del pensier (Ottone): Handel
Ye powers that dwell below—Divinités du Styx (Alceste): Gluck
Ye servants of the Lord of might—Or sus, serviteurs du Seigneur: Le Jeune
Ye shall from God's house be cast forth—Sie werden euch in den Bann
tun: Bach
Ye shall weep and lament—Ihr werdet weinen und heulen: Bach
Ye students and comrades—Studenti! Udite! (Germania): Franchetti
Ye waves—So tönet denn, schaumende Wellen: Brahms
Ye who acknowledge a universal creator—Die, ihr des unermesslichen
Weltalls/Deutsches Kantate: Mozart
Ye who have duly learnt—Voi che sapete (Le nozze di Figaro): Mozart
Ye who have yearned alone—Nur wer die Sehnsucht kennt: Schubert
Ye who of loving—Voi che sapete (Le nozze di Figaro): Mozart
Ye who the great creator—Die ihr des unermesslichen Weltalls/
Deutsches Kantate: Mozart
Ye, who the sons of God dare call ye—Ihr, die ihr euch von Christo
nemet: Bach
Yea and Nay—Ni jamais, ni toujours: A L(ehmann)
Yea, 'mid chains—Si tra ceppi (Berenice): Handel
Yea, their blood most wantonly did they shed—Effuderunt sanguinem:
Byrd
Yea, though I tread the valley—Si ambulem in media: Tye
Yea though our sins be ne'er so great—Aus tiefer Not schrei ich zu dir:
Bach
A year ago tomorrow—Demain fera un an qu'à Audaux (Tristesses):
Milhaud
The year of spring—Oiseaux, si tous les ans: Mozart
Yearning—Sehnsucht: Beethoven
Yearning—Sehnsucht: Brahms

Yearning—Sehnsucht: F Mendelssohn
Yearning—Sehnsucht/Die Lerche wolkennahe Lieder: Schubert
Years of travel—Années de pèlerinage: Liszt
The years roll by—L'année en vain chasse l'année (L'enfant prodigue):
    Debussy
Yellow fever—Fièvre jaune: Honegger
The yellow jacket—Die gelbe Jacke: Lehár
Yeomen—Landsknechte: Schoenberg
Yes, daughter, I die—Si, figlia, io moro, addio (Tamerlano): Handel
Yes, for thee time's power—Ah! non credea mirarti (La sonnambula):
    Bellini
Yes I must live and suffer—Ah! non son' io che parto: Mozart
Yes, jesting love ever sports—Si, scherza sempre amor (Partenope): Handel
Yes my brow oft is clouded—Si diversi sembianti (Siroe): Handel
Yes, thou art wretched—Ja, du bist elend: R Franz
Yes, 'tis here—Qui la voce (I Puritani): Bellini
Yes, yes, thy foes I soon will conquor—Ja, ja, ich kann die Feinde
    schlagen (Selig ist der Mann): Bach
Yesh le gan (Shire' Chalutzim)—I've a garden: Binder
Yesterday roses he brought me—Und gestern hat er mir Rosen gebracht:
    J Marx
Les yeux—Lovely eyes: Aubert
Yks' voima—One power: Sibelius
Yö meren rannalla—Night on the sea: Kaski
Yo tinc un burro—I have a burro: J Rodrigo
Yonder, near the church—Là-bas, vers l'église: Ravel
Yonder now the sun is sinking—Drüben geht die Sonne scheiden:
    R Franz
Yonder see the dawn appear—Llanfair: W S G Williams
Yosif prekrasnyi—The handsome Joseph: Vaslenko
You are arrogant—Hoffärtig seid ihr (Italienisches Liederbuch): Wolf
You are like a flower—Du bist wie eine Blume (Myrthen): Schumann
You are my heart's delight—Dein ist mein ganzes Herz! (Die gelbe Jacke/
    Das Land des Lächelns): Lehár
You are rest and peace—Du bist die Ruh': Schubert
You know the waves' eternal motion—Du fatter ej Bølgernes evige
    bryst: Grieg
You little church—Ty ukvalsky kostelicku: Janáček
You may try to vex or flout me—Bitteres zu sagen denket du: Brahms
You say I was deceived—Du sprichst, dass ich mich täuschte: Brahms
You say my heart deceived me—Du sprichst, dass ich mich täuschte: Brahms
You say you did not love me—Du sprichst, dass ich mich täuschte: Brahms
You see the fire of evening—Tu vois le feu du soir (Tel jour telle nuit):
    Poulenc

You that saved me—M'hai salvato (La wally): Catalani
You think of Strephon—Tu veux avoir la préférence: Rameau
You who are powerful—Ihr Mächtigen (Zaide): Mozart
You who have knowledge—Voi che sapete (Le nozze di Figaro): Mozart
You'd fain be hearing—Saper vorreste (Un ballo in maschera): Verdi
The young birch (tree)—Ungbirken: Grieg
The young exile—Der Jüngling in der Fremde: Beethoven
The young farm servant—Die junge Magd: Hindemith
Young Hans and Margot—Arme Peter (1): Schumann
The young nun—Die junge Nonne: Schubert
A young poet—Ein junger Dichter: J Marx
Young Venevil—Klein Venevil: Kjerulf
Your eyes—Tes yeux: Rabey
Your servants, fair ladies—Vaer hilset, i Damer: Grieg
Your sweet eyes are of blue—Die zwei blauen Augen (Lieder eines
    fahrenden Gesellen): Mahler
Yours you call me—Tuo mi chiami: D Scarlatti
The youth—Duten: Grieg
Youth—Mládi: Janáček
Youth—Von der Jugend (Das Lied von der Erde): Mahler
Youth by the brook—Der Jüngling am Bache: Schubert
The youth enchanted—Der bezauberte Knabe: Henschel
The youth to his mother—Der Knabe an die Mutter: Henschel
The youth upon the hill—Der Jüngling auf dem Hügel: Schubert
The youthful day awakes—Der junge Tag erwacht: R Franz
A youthful heart—Un jeune coeur (Les aveux indiscrets): Monsigny
Youthful lovers—Les ingénus (Fêtes galantes): Debussy
Youth's magic horn—Des Knaben Wunderhohn: Mahler
You've a heart benign and loyal—Voi avete un cor fedele: Mozart
Yubileinaya kantata—Jubilee cantata: Vasilenko
Yuletide cradle song—Julens Vuggesang: Grieg
Yver, vous n'estes qu'un villain (Chansons de Charles d'Orléans)—
    Cold winter, villain that thou art: Debussy

Z

Z Českých luhů a hájů—From Bohemia's woods and fields: Smetana

Z mrtveno domu—The house of the dead: Janáček

Za krasny Petrograd—For red Petrograd: Triodin

Zahnweh—Ode to the toothache: Schumann

Zajata (Moravské Dvojzpěvy)—The maid imprisoned/The vow of faith: Dvořák

Zalo dievča, zalo travu—The mower: Dvořák

Zapisnik zmizeleho—Diary of a young man/Diary of one who vanished (disappeared)/Diary of the man who vanished: Janáček

Zaporozhets za Dunayem—The Dnieper Cossack on the Danube: Hulak-Artemovs'kyi

Zar und Zimmermann—Czar and carpenter/Peter the shipwright: Lortzing

Der Zarewitsch—The Czarevich: Lehár

Zarya—The dawn: Molchanov

Zauber—Wizardry: d'Arba

Der Zauberer—The conjurer: Mozart

Die Zauberflöte—The magic flute: Mozart

Das Zauberlied—The magic of thy voice: Meyer-Helmund

Zavod—The foundry: Moslov

Zde vlese u potoka (Pisné milostné)—In deepest forest glade: Dvořák

Zdravitsa—Toast to Stalin: Prokofiev

Ze šumavy—From the Bohemian forest: Dvořák

Zeffiretti lusinghieri (Idomeneo)—Gentle zephyrs: Mozart

Zeffiretto—Little zephyrs: Handel

Das Zeichen—The token: Himmel

Der Zeisig—The finch: Schumann

Die Zeitlose—The saffron: R Strauss

Zeitmasse—Measures of time: Stockhausen

Zelenaj se, zelenaj (Moravské Dvojzpěvy)—Omens: Dvořák

Zhenitba—The marriage: Mussorgsky

Zhar-ptitsa—Firebird: Stravinsky

Zhenit'ba—The wedding: Mussorgsky

Das Ziel—The goal: Schoeck

Zigeuner—Gipsies: J Marx

Der Zigeunerbaron—The gypsy baron: J Strauss II

Die Zigeunerin—The gipsy girl/The gipsy maid: Wolf

Zigeunerliebe—Gipsy love: Léhar

Zigeunerliedchen—Gipsy ditties: Schumann

Zigeunerlieder—Gipsy songs: Brahms

Zigeunermelodien—Gipsy songs: Dvořák

Der Zigeunerprimas—Sari/The gipsy primate: Kálmán

Zimniy koster—Winter bonfire: Prokofiev

La zingara—Gipsy maid: Donizetti
Die Zirkusprinzessin—The circus princess: Kálmán
Zitronenfalter im April—Lemon butterfly in April: Wolf
Zitti, zitti moviarmo a vendetta (Rigoletto)—Hush, in silence fulfil we
　　our errand: Verdi
Zlatý kolovrat—The golden spinning wheel: Dvořák
Zlonické Zvony—The bells of Zlonice: Dvořák
Zold leveles diófa—Green leaved walnut tree: Erkel
Zolotyi obruch—The golden hoop: Lyatoshyna'kyi
Zolotoy Petushok—The golden cockerel: Rimsky-Korsakov
Zolushka—Cinderella: Prokofiev
Zot admati—This is my land: Lavry
Zpívejte hospodinu (Biblické Písné)—Sing ye a joyful song: Dvořák
Zrinyi szózata—Hymn of Zrinyi: Kodály
Zu deinen Füssen—Here at thy feet: Meyer-Helmund
Zu dir Jehovah ... see: Dir, dir Jehovah
Zu meiner Laute—Beneath her window: Zelter
Zu spät—Too late: Blumenthal
Zu Tanze, zu Sprunge (Geschwinde, geschwinde, ihr wirbelnden Winde)—
　　O'er mountain and valley/Song of Pan: Bach
Zu uns komme dein Reich—Thy kingdom come: Cornelius
Zueignung—Devotion: R Strauss
Der zufrieden gestellte Äolus—The appeasement of Aeolus: Bach
Die Zufriedenen—In paradise: Blumenthal
Die Zufriedenheit—Contentment: Mozart
Das Zügenglöcklein—The passing bell: Schubert
Zum neuen Jahr-Kirchengesang—A hymn for the new year: Wolf
Zum Punsche—Punch-bowl song: Schubert
Zum Schlafen—The golden bird: Reger
Zum Schluss (Neue Liebeslieder)—Conclusion: Brahms
Zum Schluss (Myrthen)—The end/In conclusion: Schumann
Zur Drossel sprach der Fink—The thrush sings loud today: d'Albert
Zur Ruh', zur Ruh'—To rest, to rest: Wolf
Zur Warnung—By way of warning: Wolf
Der zürende Barde—The angry bard: Schubert
Der zurenden Diana—The angry Diana/The wrathful Diana: Schubert
Zurücke geflügelten Winde (Zerreist, zersprenget, Zertrümmer der
　　Gruft)—Return now, you wild rushing storm: Bach
Zvědavá dievča—The inquisitive girl: Martinů
Zvolenovcí chlapci—The lads of Zvolyn: Martinů
Die zwei blauen Augen (Lieder eines fahrenden Gesellen)—Your sweet
　　eyes of blue: Mahler
Zwei Herzen im Dreivierteltakt—Two hearts in three-quarter time: Stolz
Zwei Schweinekarbonaden—Two pork cutlets: Seiber